Spillner

World Guide to Abbreviations
Part 2, I-R

Paul Spillner

World Guide
to Abbreviations

Internationales Wörterbuch
der Abkürzungen von Organisationen

2nd Edition - A List of more than
50,000 Abbreviations with an
International Bibliography of
Dictionaries of Abbreviations

Part 2, I-R

R. R. BOWKER COMPANY, NEW YORK
VERLAG DOKUMENTATION, MÜNCHEN-PULLACH 1971

126467

R
421.8
S 756
v. 2

Das vorliegende Wörterbuch enthält Abkürzungen von:

Ämtern
Agenturen
Anstalten
Ausschüssen
Ausstellungen
Banken
Behörden
Bünden
Büros
Firmen
Föderationen
Gemeinschaften
Genossenschaften
Gesellschaften
Hochschulen
Instituten
Institutionen
Klubs
Körperschaften
Konferenzen
Kongregationen
Kongressen
Logen
Luftverkehrsunternehmen
Messen
Militärischen Dienststellen, Verbänden
    und Einheiten
Nachrichtenagenturen
Orden
Organisationen
Parteien
Schulen
Stiftungen
Tagungen
Unionen
Universitäten
Verbänden
Vereinen
Vereinigungen
usw.

This dictionary contains abbreviations of:

Agencies
Associations
Authorities
Banks
Boards
Bureaus
Clubs
Colleges
Committees
Communities
Companies
Confederations
Congregations
Congresses
Corporations
Establishments
Exhibitions
Fairs
Federations
Firms
Foundations
Guilds
Institutes
Institutions
Lodges
Military Organizations
News Agencies
Offices
Orders
Organizations
Political Parties
Schools
Societies
Trusts
Unions
Universities
etc.

Copyright © 1971
by Verlag Dokumentation Saur KG, München-Pullach und Berlin
ISBN 3-7940-1198-8
Printed and bound in West-Germany
Distributed in USA and Canada by R. R. Bowker Company
1180 Avenue of the Americas, New York, N. Y. 10036

Vorwort zum Teil 2

Abkürzungen in ihren mannigfaltigen Erscheinungsformen begegnen uns heute überall. Sie treten in allen Bereichen der Dokumentation, Information und Kommunikation auf und sind oft die entscheidenden Informationsträger. Wer einen Text verstehen, wer mitreden will, muß ihre Bedeutung kennen. Leider bereitet aber gerade das Herausfinden der Bedeutung nur zu häufig Schwierigkeiten, weil die verfügbaren Hilfsmittel nicht ausreichen.

Infolge der ständigen Zunahme der Abkürzungen in der ganzen Welt kann gegenwärtig niemand auf diesem Gebiet zu irgendeinem Zeitpunkt auf dem laufenden sein und alle Fragen zutreffend beantworten. Man wird sich vorerst damit begnügen müssen, wenigstens auf Teilgebieten zu versuchen, möglichst viele Antworten zu bringen. Dieses Buch ist ein solcher Versuch.

Die erste 1968 erschienene Ausgabe hat im In- und Ausland reges Interesse gefunden. Die anhaltende Nachfrage veranlaßte den Verlag, schon jetzt die zweite Ausgabe folgen zu lassen. Sie ist im Vergleich zur ersten neu gestaltet und wesentlich erweitert worden.

Ich habe die Arbeit übernommen, weil diese Veröffentlichung meinen langjährigen Bestrebungen entgegenkommt. Es geht mir u.a. darum, die in der „lateinisch" schreibenden Welt verwendeten Abkürzungen mit ihren Bedeutungen und weiteren zweckdienlichen Informationen zu sammeln und diese Dokumentation der Allgemeinheit nutzbar zu machen.

Im vorliegenden Buch werden die Abkürzungen so gebracht, wie sie in der Praxis vorkommen. Es wurden also nicht nur die offiziellen Versionen verzeichnet. Auch Abkürzungen, die der Vergangenheit angehören, wurden aufgeführt. Bei Abkürzungen, die mit oder ohne Punkt(e) auftreten, folgte ich im allgemeinen dem jeweils überwiegenden Brauch. Einzelheiten über die Anlage des Buchs bringen die „Hinweise für den Benutzer".

Wegen der erheblichen Inhalterweiterung, die sich nach der Auslieferung des ersten Bandes im Herbst 1970 ergab, wird das Werk statt in 2 Bänden nun in drei Bänden erscheinen; dennoch war es dem Verlag möglich, den angekündigten Preis für das Gesamtwerk unverändert zu belassen. Band 3, der im Frühjahr 1972 vorliegen wird, enthält auch eine umfassende internationale Bibliographie und eine Abhandlung über Abkürzungen.

Möge das Buch vielen Ratsuchenden helfen, auch wenn es nur in einem begrenzten Umfang Auskunft geben kann. Ich bitte die Benutzer um Hinweise, die der Verbesserung des Buchs dienen.

Vielleicht regt die hier gebrachte verwirrende Vielfalt der national und international gebrauchten Abkürzungen aber auch dazu an, sie durch Normung zu einem wirklich guten Kommunikationsmittel zu machen. Das würde uns allen die Arbeit gewiß vereinfachen.

Mannheim, im Oktober 1971   Paul Spillner

Preface to Part 2

Today, we constantly come across abbreviations of various types. They are used in all fields of documentation, information and communication, and are often in fact the decisive carriers of information. Anybody wanting to understand a text and to participate in a discussion must know the meaning of these abbreviations. Unfortunately, however, it is finding the meaning that often proves very difficult, as available reference material is inadequate.

Owing to the continuous increase of abbreviations all over the world, no one, at present, can be up to date in this field and be able to provide the proper answers. For the time being, efforts should be limited to giving as many answers as possible at least in some sectors. This book is an attempt to do so.

The first edition published in 1968 has been received with considerable interest in Germany and abroad. The continuing demand for this book caused the publisher to arrange for the second edition already at this early date. As compared with the first edition the present one has a new layout and has been enlarged substantially.

I undertook this work because such a publication meets the efforts I have made over a great number of years. It is one of my goals to compile abbreviations (together with their meanings and other pertinent information) found in those parts of the world that use Roman characters, and to make this documentation available to the public.

The abbreviations are presented in this book in the same way as they are used in practice. Thus, not only official versions but also abbreviations used in the past have been included. As to abbreviations found with or without period(s), I have normally given the most common usage. Details of the layout are provided in the "Guide for the User".

Because of significant changes in its contents which became apparent after distribution of Volume 1 in the fall of 1970, the work will now appear in three volumes instead of in two; however, it has been possible for the publisher to leave the announced price unaltered. Volume 3, which will be available in the spring of 1972, will also include a comprehensive international bibliography and an essay on abbreviations.

I hope this book will prove helpful to many people looking for advice even though it can provide information only within a limited scope. Any suggestions by users that may contribute to improving the book will be appreciated.

The perplexing variety of nationally and internationally used abbreviations contained herein might even suggest standardization, thereby making abbreviations an effective means of communication. This would certainly make things easier for all of us.

Mannheim, October 1971   Paul Spillner

Hinweise für den Benutzer

1. Die Abkürzungen werden in der alphabetischen Reihenfolge a . . . z gebracht. Ä, æ, ç, ö, ő, ø, ü werden wie ae, c, oe, ue eingereiht. Zeichen wie . − ( ) ´ ` ˆ ¨ ~ ° ˇ & + sind für die alphabetische Reihung ohne Bedeutung.

1.1. Alphanumerische Folgen stehen an der von dem (den) Buchstaben bestimmten alphabetischen Stelle.

1.2. Römische Zahlzeichen werden wie arabische Ziffern eingereiht.

2. Die Schriftarten werden wie folgt verwendet:

2.1. Halbfett für die Abkürzung

2.2. Grundschrift für den übrigen Text

3. Innerhalb einer (mit einer links herausgerückten Abkürzung beginnenden) Wortstelle sind die Bedeutungen ebenfalls in ihrer alphabetischen Reihenfolge aufgeführt (vgl 1.).

3.1. Der Abkürzung folgt die Angabe des Bedeutungsbereichs (Land, Organisation, international, militärisch usw.) und/oder die Angabe der Sprache (vgl 3.3.).

3.2. Folgen einer Abkürzung mehrere Bedeutungen, werden diese durch Semikolon (;) voneinander getrennt (vgl aber 4.). Das Semikolon trennt auch Abkürzungen verschiedener Buchstabenfolgen jedoch gleicher Bedeutung.

3.3. Der Doppelpunkt (:) trennt im allgemeinen abgekürzte erläuternde Hinweise voneinander und vom übrigen Text.

3.4. Sonstige Erläuterungen stehen in eckigen Klammern [ ].

3.5. Runde Klammern ( ) schließen Bestandteile von Abkürzungen und von Bedeutungen ein. Bei den Bedeutungen werden diese Klammern mitunter auch dazu benutzt, ein Wort zu kennzeichnen, das an die Stelle des vorangehenden gesetzt werden kann, bzw. Wortteile zu markieren, die, läßt man sie weg, eine andere Bedeutung oder eine andere Schreibung ergeben.

3.6. Abgesehen von der Verwendung in Wörtern, die mit Bindestrich geschrieben werden, wird dieser Strich am Schluß der Zeile bei Worttrennung gesetzt. Der Bindestrich steht allerdings am Anfang der Zeile, wenn er zugleich als Trennungsstrich dient, das Wort jedoch stets mit Bindestrich zu schreiben ist.

4. Gilt eine Abkürzung für gleiche Bedeutungen in mehreren Sprachen, werden diese verschiedensprachigen Bedeutungen nicht durch das Semikolon (vgl 3.2.) getrennt, sondern durch das Sprachenzeichen, dem ein Doppelpunkt folgt (vgl 3.3.).

5. Die nachfolgende alphabetische Zusammenstellung führt alle zur Erläuterung usw. in den Teilen 1 und 2 (A...R) dieses Buchs verwendeten Abkürzungen auf, und zwar einschließlich solcher Abkürzungen, die wegen ihrer alphabetischen Folge erst im Teil 3 (S...Z) gebracht werden können.

Guide for the User

1. The abbreviations are presented in alphabetical order from a to z. Ä, ae, ç, ö, ő, φ, ü are arranged as ae, c, oe, ue. Symbols and (diacritic) signs such as . − ( ) ` ` ~ ° ˘ & + are of no importance as regards alphabetical order.

1.1. Alphanumeric sequences are listed in the alphabetical place of the respective letter(s).

1.2. Roman numerals are arranged like Arabic numerals.

2. Styles of type are used as follows:

2.1. boldface for the abbreviation

2.2. plain for the remaining text

3. Within each entry (beginning with the abbreviation protruding to the left), the meanings are likewise listed in alphabetical order (cf. 1.).

3.1. Each abbreviation is followed by an explanatory remark (label) indicating the area or sphere in which the abbreviation is used (country, organization, international, military etc.) and/or the pertinent language (cf. 3.3.).

3.2. If several meanings are listed after an abbreviation, these meanings are separated by a semicolon (;) (however, cf. 4.). A semicolon is also used to separate abbreviations different in spelling but having the same meaning.

3.3. The colon (:) normally separates explanatory remarks (usually abbreviated) from each other as well as from the remaining text (cf. 3.1.).

3.4. Any additional explanations are put in brackets [ ]

3.5. Parentheses ( ) are components of abbreviations as well as of meanings. However, parentheses are also used for marking a word that can be substituted for the preceding word, and for marking that part of a word, which, if omitted, will result in a different meaning or spelling.

3.6. With the exception of its use in hyphenated words, the hyphen (-) is put at the end of a line to indicate the division of a word. However, if the division of a hyphenated word coincides with the position of the hyphen at the end of a line, the hyphen is placed at the beginning of the following line to indicate that the word must always be hyphenated.

4. If an abbreviation stands for identical meanings in different languages, these meanings are not separated by a semicolon (cf. 3.2.) but by the language symbol followed by a colon (cf. 3.1., 3.3.).

5. The following alphabetical list shows all the abbreviations used for explanatory purposes etc. in parts 1 and 2 (A to R) of this publication, including those abbreviations that can only be provided in Part 3 (S to Z) owing to the alphabetical arrangement.

	Verzeichnis erläuternder und sonstiger Abkürzungen, Wörter und Zeichen	List of abbreviations, words and symbols used for explanatory or other purposes
. . .	bis [z.B. 1950 . . . 65; A . . .I]	till [e.g. 1950 . . . 65], to [e.g. A . . . I]
&	und	and
=	ist gleich, gleich	same as
A	Österreich	Austria
AB	sv: Aktiebolag [Aktiengesellschaft]	[stock company]
ABC	atomar, biologisch, chemisch	atomic, biological, chemical
ADN	Aden	Aden
af	Afrikaans	Afrikaans
AFGH	Afghanistan	Afghanistan
AG	Aktiengesellschaft	[stock company]
a.G.; aG	auf Gegenseitigkeit	
AL	Albanien	Albania
Ala.		Alabama [US]
Apr	April	April
auch:		[also]
Aug	August	August
AUS	Australien	Australia
B	Belgien	Belgium
Bahn	Eisenbahn(wesen)	[railroad, railway]
BDS	Barbados	Barbados
BG	Bulgarien	Bulgaria
bg	bulgarische Sprache	Bulgarian language
BH	Britisch-Honduras	British Honduras
bis		[till]
BL	Basutoland [jetzt: Lesotho = LS]	Basutoland [now: Lesotho =LS]
Bln	Berlin	Berlin
BlnO	Berlin (Ostsektor)	Berlin (Eastern sector)
BlnW	Berlin (Westsektoren)	Berlin (Western sectors)
BR	Brasilien	Brazil
BRD	Bundesrepublik Deutschland [bedeutet auch den Zeitabschnitt ab etwa 1949 im Bereich der BRD]	[Federal Republic of Germany, refers also to period from about 1949 in the FRG]
BUR	Birma	Burma
C	Cuba	Cuba
Cal(if).		California [US]
CDN	Kanada	Canada
CEE	f: Communauté Economique Européenne [Europäische Wirtschaftsgemeinschaft = EWG]	[European Economic Community = EEC]
CGO	Kongo (Leopoldville) (Kinshasa)	Congo (Leopoldville) (Kinshasa)
CH	Schweiz	Switzerland
CI	,Elfenbeinküste	Ivory Coast
Cie.	Compa(g)nie f: Compagnie	[company]
CL	Ceylon	Ceylon
CO	Kolumbien	Colombia

Co.	Compa(g)nie	company
Colo.		Colorado [US]
Conn.		Connecticut [US]
Corp.		Corporation
CR	Costa Rica	Costa Rica
cs	tschechische Sprache	Czech language
CS	Tschechoslowakei	Czechoslovakia
CY	Zypern	Cyprus
d	deutsche Sprache	German language
D	Deutsches Reich [bedeutet auch den Zeitabschnitt bis etwa 1945 im Bereich des Deutschen Reichs]	[German Reich, refers also to period until about 1945 in the German Reich]
da	dänische Sprache	Danish language
DA	Danzig	Danzig
dann:		[later on, afterwards]
D.C.		District of Columbia [US]
DDR	Deutsche Demokratische Republik	[German Democratic Republic = GDR]
Dez	Dezember	[December]
D.F.	s: Distrito Federal [Mexico]	
DIN	den Deutschen Normenausschuß (DNA), 1 Berlin 30, Burggrafenstraße 4-7 betreffend	[concerning the German Committee on Standardization]
DK	Dänemark	Denmark
DOM	Dominikanische Republik	Dominican Republic
DRV	Demokratische Republik Vietnam	[Democratic Republic Vietnam]
DY	Dahome	Dahomey
DZ	Algerien; Demokratische Volks-staatliche Republik Algerien	[Algeria]
e	englische Sprache	English language
E	Spanien	Spain
EAK	Kenia	Kenya
EAT	Tanganjika; Tansania	Tanganyika; Tansania
EAU	Uganda	Uganda
EC	Ecuador	Ecuador
e.G.	eingetragene Genossenschaft	[registered cooperative society]
egGmbH	eingetragene Genossenschaft mit beschränkter Haftpflicht	[registered cooperative society with limited liability]
eo	Esperanto	Esperanto
ET	Ägypten; Vereinigte Arabische Republik	Egypt; United Arab Republic
ETH	Äthiopien	Ethiopia
eV	=e.V.= eingetragener Verein	[registered association, society, etc]
EW	Estland	Est(h)onia
F	Frankreich	France
f	französische Sprache	French language
Feb	Februar	February
Ffm	Frankfurt (Main) [BRD]	
fi	finnische Sprache	Finnish language
FL	Liechtenstein	Liechtenstein
Fla.		Florida [US]

FNRJ	sh: Federativna Narodna Republika Jugoslavija [Föderative Volksrepublik Jugoslawien = FVRJ]	[Federal People's Republic of Yugoslavia]
früher		[formerly]
GB	Vereinigtes Königreich von Großbritannien und Nordirland	United Kingdom of Great Britain and Northern Ireland
GCA	Guatemala	Guatemala
gegen		[against, versus]
gegr	gegründet	founded, established
GH	Ghana	Ghana
GmbH	Gesellschaft mit beschränkter Haftung	[corporation with limited liability]
GR	Griechenland	Greece
H	Ungarn	Hungary
Herts		Hertfordshire [GB]
HK	Hongkong	Hong Kong
hu	ungarische Sprache	Hungarian language
I	Italien	Italy
i	italienische Sprache	Italian language
IL	Israel	Israel
Ill.		Illinois [US]
Inc.		Incorporated
IND	Indien	India
INT	internationale Organisation	international organization
i.O.	in Oldenburg [BRD]	
i.Pr.	in Preußen [D]	[in Prussia]
IR	Iran	Iran
IRQ	Irak	Iraq
IS	Island	Iceland
J	Japan	Japan
JA	Jamaika	Jamaica
Jan	Januar	January
jetzt:		[now]
JOR	Jordanien	Jordan
Jul	Juli	July
Jun	Juni	June
K	Kambodscha	Cambodia, Cambodge
KG	Kommanditgesellschaft	
KGaA	Kommanditgesellschaft auf Aktien	
Ky.		Kentucky [US]
KZ	Konzentrationslager	[concentration camp]
l	lateinische Sprache	Latin language
L	Luxemburg	Luxemb(o)urg
LAO	Laos	Laos
LR	Lettland	Latvia
LRS	sn: Ljudska republika Slovenija [Volksrepublik Slowenien]	[People's Republic Slovenia]
	sn: Ljudska republika Srbija [Volksrepublik Serbien]	[People's Republic Serbia]
LS	Lesotho [vgl: BL]	Lesotho [see: BL]
LT	Litauen	Lithuania
Ltd.		Limited

M	Malta	Malta
MA	Marokko	Morocco
Mai		[May]
mal	malaiische Sprache	Malay language
Mar	März	March
Mass.		Massachusetts [US]
mbH	mit beschränkter Haftung	[with limited liability]
MC	Monaco	Monaco
Md.		Maryland [US]
med	medizinisch	medical
MEX	Mexiko	Mexico
Mich.		Michigan [US]
mil	militärisch, Militärwesen [im weitesten Sinne einschließlich z.B. Kriegervereine usw.]	military [in the broadest sense including e.g. veterans organizations, etc.]
Mo.		Missouri [US]
MOC	Moçambique	Mozambique
MS	Mauritius	Mauritius
MT	Tanger	Tangier
MW	Malawi	Malawi
N	Norwegen	Norway
nach WK1	Zeitabschnitt unmittelbar nach dem ersten Weltkrieg [D]	period immediately following World War I [D]
nach WK2	Zeitabschnitt etwa von 1945 . . . 49 [D]	period from about 1945 . . . 49 [D]
N.H.		New Hampshire [US]
NIC	Nicaragua	Nicaragua
NIG	Niger	Niger
N.J.		New Jersey [US]
nl	niederländische Sprache [einschließlich Flämisch]	Dutch language [including Flemish]
NL	Niederlande	Netherlands
N.M.		New Mexico [US]
no	norwegische Sprache	Norwegian language
NOTAM	[Nachrichten für Luftfahrer]	Notice to Airmen
Nov	November	November
NRW	Nordrhein-Westfalen [BRD]	North Rhine-Westfalia [BRD]
NS	nationalsozialistisch [bedeutet auch den Zeitabschnitt von 1933 . . . 45 im Deutschen Reich]	National Socialist [refers also to period from 1933 . . . 45 in the German Reich]
N.S.W.		New South Wales [AUS]
N.V.	nl: Naamlooze Vennotschap [Aktiengesellschaft]	[stock company]
N.Y.		(State of) New York [US]
NZ	Neuseeland	New Zealand
oHG	offene Handelsgesellschaft	
Okt	Oktober	[October]
Oldb	Oldenburg [BRD]	
O/Y	fi: osakeyhtiö [Aktiengesellschaft]	[stock company]
P	Portugal	Portugal
PA	Panama	Panama
Pa.		Pennsylvania [US]

PAK	Pakistan	Pakistan
PAN	Angola	Angola
PE	Peru	Peru
Penn.		Pennsylvania [US]
PI	Philippinen	Philippines
PL	Polen	Poland
pl	polnische Sprache	Polish language
POL	[Kraft- und Schmierstoffe]	petrol, oil, and lubricants
Post	Post(wesen)	post [mail]
PQ		Province of Quebec [CDN]
Pr.	Preußen [D]	[Prussia]
pt	portugiesische Sprache	Portuguese language
PTM	Malaysia	Malaysia
P.T.T.	f: postes, télégraphes, téléphone [Post-, Telegrafen- und Telefon- verwaltung]	[post, telegraph and telephone administration]
Pty.	[Gründergesellschaft]	Proprietary
PY	Paraguay	Paraguay
R	Rumänien	Rumania, Romania
RA	Argentinien	Argentina
RC	Volksrepublik China	People's Republic of China
RCA	f: République Centrafricaine [Zentralafrikanische Republik]	Central African Republic
RCB	Kongo (Brazzaville)	Congo (Brazzaville)
RCH	Chile	Chile
rGmbH	registrierte Genossenschaft mit beschränkter Haftung	[registered cooperative society with limited liability]
RI	Indonesien	Indonesia
RL	Libanon	Lebanon
RM	Madagaskar	Madagascar
RMM	Mali	Mali
ro	rumänische Sprache	Rumanian (Romanian) language
R.P.R.	ro: Republica Populara Româna [Volksrepublik Rumänien]	[People's Republic of Rumania (Romania)]
RSR	Südrhodesien	Southern Rhodesia
RWA	Ruanda	Ruanda
S	Schweden	Sweden
s	spanische Sprache	Spanish language
s/	f: sur [am, an der]	[on]
S.A.	f: Société Anonyme i: Società Anonima pl: Spółka Akcyjna pt: Sociedade Anônima s: Sociedad Anónima [Aktiengesellschaft]	[stock company]
SAAB	S: sv: [Svenska Aeroplan AB]	
S.A.F.	f: Société Anonyme Française [französische Aktiengesellschaft]	[French stock company]
SATCOM		U.S.Army Satellite Communications Agency, Fort Monmouth, N.J.
SAV	sk: Slovenská Akadémia Vied a Umení, Bratislava	
S.C.		South Carolina [US]

SEATO	[Südostasienvertragsorganisation]	South-East Asia Treaty Organization
SDS	Sozialistischer Deutscher Studentenbund	
SED	DDR: Sozialistische Deutsche Einheitspartei	
seit		[since]
SEMA	f: Société d'Economie et de Mathématiques Appliquées	
Sep	September	September
S. et O.	f: Seine-et-Oise	
SEV	CH: Schweizerischer Elektrotechnischer Verein	
SF	Finnland	Finland
SGP	Singapur	Singapore
sh	serbokroatische Sprache	Serbocroatian language
SHAEF		Supreme Headquarters Allied Expeditionary Forces
SHAPE		Supreme Headquarters Allied Powers Europe
sk	slowakische Sprache	Slovakian language
SMHI	S: sv: Sveriges Meteorologiska och Hydrologiska Institut	
sn	slowenische Sprache	Slovenic language
SN	Senegal	Senegal
SNCF	f: Société Nationale des Chemins de Fer Français	[National French Railway]
SP	Somalia	Somalia
S.p.A.	i: Società per Azioni	
später		[later on]
SPD	Sozialdemokratische Partei Deutschlands	
SPER	f: Syndicat des industries de matériel professionnel électrotechnique et radioélectrique, Paris	
SS	Schutzstaffel [der NSDAP]	
St.	Sankt f: Saint	Saint
StEG	Staatliche Erfassungsgesellschaft für öffentliches Gut mbH	
STRATCOM		U.S. Army Strategic Communications Command
stud	studentisch [D, BRD]	
SU	Union der Sozialistischen Sowjetrepubliken	Union of Socialist Soviet Republics
sv	schwedische Sprache	Swedish language
S.W.		South West
SYR	Arabische Republik Syrien	Arab Republic Syria
T	Thailand	Thailand
(TA)		GB: Territorial Army
TAGO		The Adjutant General's Office, Washington, D.C.
TASCOM		Theater Army Support Command
Tenn.		Tennessee [US]

TG	Togo	Togo
TH	Technische Hochschule	[technical university]
(Thür)	Thüringen	Thuringia
TN	Tunesien	Tunisia
TR	Türkei	Turkey
tr	türkische Sprache	Turkish language
TRA	Telegraphentechnisches Reichsamt [seit 1920]	
TU	Technische Universität	[technical university]
TV	Fernsehen, Television	television
U	Uruguay	Uruguay
UAMCE	f: Union Africaine et Malgache de Coopération Economique [gegr 1964]	
UdSSR	Union der Sozialistischen Sowjetrepubliken	[Union of Socialist Soviet Republics]
UIC	f: Union Internationale des Chemins de Fer	
UIPN	f: Union Internationale pour la Protection de la Nature	
um		[about]
UN	Vereinte Nationen	United Nations
UNESCO	UN: Organisation der Vereinten Nationen für Erziehung, Wissenschaft und Kultur	United Nations Educational, Scientific, and Cultural Organization
UNICEF	UN: Welt-Kinderhilfswerk der Vereinten Nationen	United Nations (International) Children's (Emergency) Fund
u.p.a.	sv: utan personligt ansvar	
UPU	f: Union Postale Universelle [Weltpostverein]	Universal Postal Union
URSI	f: Union radio-scientifique internationale, Bruxelles [B]	
US	Vereinigte Staaten von Amerika	United States of America
U.S.		United States
USAEC		United States Atomic Energy Commission
USAEPG		United States Army Electronic Proving Ground
USAF		United States Air Force
USAREUR		United States Army, Europe
USASI		United States of America Standards Institute
USCG		United States Coast Guard
USMC		United States Marine Corps
usw.		[etc.]
V	Vatikanstadt	Vatican City
Va.		Virginia [US]
VAB	Versicherungsanstalt Berlin	
V.a.G.	Verein auf Gegenseitigkeit	
VDE	Verband Deutscher Elektrotechniker eV, 6 Ffm	
VDEh	Verein Deutscher Eisenhüttenleute, 4 Düsseldorf	

VDI	Verein Deutscher Ingenieure, 4 Düsseldorf	
VDMA	Verein Deutscher Maschinen-bauanstalten eV, 6 Ffm	
VdNE	Verband deutscher nichtbundes-eigener Eisenbahnen	
VdRBw	Verband der Reservisten der Bundes-wehr	
VdTÜV	Vereinigung der Technischen Über-wachungsvereine eV, 43 Essen	
VEB	DDR: volkseigener Betrieb	
VEB(K)	DDR: volkseigener Betrieb (kommunal geleitet)	
Verband		[organization]
vgl	vergleiche [l: confer(atur) =cf.]	[see also]
VN	Vietnam	Vietnam
VÖV	Verband öffentlicher Verkehrs-betriebe, 5 Köln	
vorher		[formerly]
vorm.	vormals	[formerly]
VSE	CH: Verband Schweizerischer Elektrizitätswerke	
VVB	DDR: Vereinigung volkseigener Betriebe	
WAG	Gambia	Gambia
WAL	Sierra Leone	Sierra Leone
WAN	Nigeria	Nigeria
W.C.		West Central
WGB	Weltgewerkschaftsbund	
WHO	Weltgesundheitsorganisation	World Health Organization
WK1	während des ersten Weltkriegs	during World War I
WK2	während des zweiten Weltkriegs	during World War II
WMO	[Weltorganisation für Meteorologie]	World Meteorological Organization
WOEC		World Organization for Early Child-hood Education
WTAO		World Touring and Automobile Organization
(Württ)	Württemberg [BRD]	
Y.M.C.A.	[CVJM]	Young Men's Christian Association
YU	Jugoslawien	Yugoslavia
YV	Venezuela	Venezuela
Z	Sambia	Zambia
ZA	Südafrika	South Africa
z.B.	zum Beispiel	[for example]
ZfL	DDR: Zentrale für Landtechnik	
ZfS	DDR: Zentralstelle für Standardi-sierung	
ZIF	DDR: Zentralinstitut für Fertigungs-technik des Maschinenbaues, Karl-Marx-Stadt	
ZVEI	Zentralverband der Elektrotech-nischen Industrie eV, 6 Ffm	

I. d: Ingenieurschule; Innung; d: mil:
Inspektion; d: Institut; e: Institute;
F: f: Institut de France; e: Institution
I.A. GB: e: Imperial Airways; GB: e:
mil: Indian Army; F: f: mil: Inspec-
tion de l'Artillerie
IA GB: e: mil: Inspector of armourers
I.A. F: f: Institut Agricole (Agrono-
mique); GB: e: Institute of Actuaries
IA P: pt: Instituto de Angola, Luanda
I.A. I: i: mil: Intendenza d'armata
IA CDN: US: e: International Alliance
of Theatrical Stage Employees and
Motion Picture Machine Operators of
the United States and Canada; S: sv:
Internationell aktion, Stockholm [gegr
1954]
I.A. F: f: mil: Inter-Armes [école spé-
ciale militaire] ; IL: e: Israel Airlines
IA IL: e: Israel Atomic [d: Kernfor-
schungszentrum Nahal Soreq]
IAA d: Ibero-Amerikanisches Archiv
I.A.A. GB: e: Incorporated Accountants
and Auditors; Incorporated Association of Architects and Surveyors
IAA US: e: Independent Airlines Association; Indian Association of America
I.A.A. DZ: f: Institut Agricole d'Algérie; GB: e: Institute of Automobile
Assessors
IAA US: e: Insurance Accountants Association; e: International Academy of
Astronautics [gegr 1960] ; CDN: US:
e: International Acetylene Association; INT: e: International Advertising Association, London; International Aerosol Association, Zürich
[CH] ; e: International Amateur Association; US: e: International Apple
Association; INT: e: International
Association of Allergology [gegr
1945] ; INT: d: Internationale Arbei-
terassoziation [1. Internationale
1864] ; Internationale Automobil-
ausstellung, Ffm; Internationales

Arbeitsamt, Genf [CH]
IAAA GB: e: Institute of Air Age Activ-
ities
I.A.A.A. e: Irish Amateur Athletic
Association;
IAAAA US: e: Intercollegiate Associa-
tion of Amateur Athletes of America
IAAB INT: e: Inter-American Associa-
tion of Broadcasters, Santiago [RCH,
gegr 1946]
IAABO INT: e: International Associa-
tion of Approved Basketball Officials
IAAC e: International African-American
Corporation; INT: e: International
Agricultural Aviation Centre, Den
Haag [NL] ; International Antarctic
Analysis Centre; International Asso-
ciation for Analogue Computation,
Bruxelles [B]
IAACC INT: e: Inter-Allied Aeronautical
Commission of Control
IAACR RA: s: Instituto Agrario Argen-
tino de Cultura Rural
IAADF INT: e: Inter-American Associa-
tion for Democracy and Freedom
IAAE AUS: NZ: e: Institution of Auto-
motive and Aeronautical Engineers,
Melbourne; INT: e: International
Association of Agricultural Econo-
mists, Chicago, Ill. [US]
IAAEE INT: e: International Associa-
tion for the Advancement of Ethnol-
ogy and Eugenics
IAAF INT: e: International Amateur
Athletic Federation, London [gegr
1912]
IAAHU e: International Association of
Accident and Health Underwriters
IAAI e: International Association of
Arson Investigators
IAAJ INT: e: International Association
of Agricultural Journalists
IAALD INT: e: International Associa-
tion of Agricultural Librarians and
Documentalists, Harpenden,Herts'[GB]

I.A.A.M. GB: e: Incorporated Association of Assistant Masters

IAAM INT: e: International Association of Aircraft Manufacturers, Paris

I.A.A.M.S.S. GB: e: Incorporated Association of Assistant Masters in Secondary Schools

IAAO e: International Association of Assessing Officers

IAAP US: e: Illinois Association for Applied Psychology; INT: e: International Association of Applied Psychology, Paris [gegr 1920]

IAARC INT: e: International Administrative Aeronautical Radio Conference

I.A.A.S. GB: e: Incorporated Association of Architects and Surveyors, London

IAAS INT: e: International Association of Agricultural Students

IAATI e: International Association of Auto Theft Investigators

I.A.B. GB: e: Imperial Agricultural Bureau; Industrial Advisory Board; F: f: Institut Agricole de Beauvais

IAB BRD: d: Interministerieller Ausschuß Bauwirtschaft [Bundesregierung] ; INT: nl: Internationaal Arbeidsbureau; INT: e: International Council of Scientific Unions Abstracting Board; d: Internationales Ausstellungsbüro; INT: sv: Internationella arbetsbyrån

IABA INT: e: Inter-American Bar Association; International Aircraft Brokers' Association, Paris [gegr 1951] ; International Amateur Boxing Association; e: Irish Amateur Boxing Association

IABC e: International Association of Bookstall Contractors

IABE INT: e: The Ibero-American Bureau of Education, Madrid

IABG BRD: d: Industrieanlagen-Betriebsgesellschaft mbH, 8 München 33

IABLA INT: e: Inter-American Bibliographical and Library Association, Gainesville, Fla. [US, gegr 1930]

IABPAI US: e: International Association of Blue Print and Allied Industries

IABPBD CDN: US: e: International Alliance of Bill Posters, Billers and Distributors of the United States and Canada

I.-A.B.P.C. e: Inter-Allied Bureau of Press Control

IABSE INT: e: International Association for Bridge and Structural Engineering, CH-8006 Zürich [gegr 1929]

IABSOIW US: e: International Association of Bridge, Structural and Ornamental Iron Workers

IABV INT: d: Internationaler Arbeitskreis für betriebswirtschaftliche Vergleiche in der Elektroindustrie, Genf [CH]

IABW BlnW: d: Industrieausschuß Berlin-West

IAC D: e: nach WK2: Import Advisory Committee, Ffm [JEIA] ; IND: e: Indian Airlines Corporation, New Delhi 1; US: e: mil: Information Analysis Center [Department of Defense]

I.A.C. F: f: Institut d'Agronomie Coloniale; GB: e: Institute of Amateur Cinematographers; CGO: [d: Institut für Zivilluftfahrt, Kinshasa]

IAC BR: pt: Instituto Agronómico de Campinas; P: pt: Instituto de Alta Cultura, Lisboa

I.A.C. GB: e: Insurance Acts Committee

IAC US: e: Insurance Advertising Conference; INT: e: Inter-American Conference [Organization of American States, gegr 1948] ; UN: e: International Advisory Committee on Research in the Natural Sciences Programme of UNESCO, Paris; INT: e: International Aerological Commission

IA&C D: e: nach WK2: Internal Affairs and Communications [division of OMGUS]

IAC INT: nl: Internationaal Agrarisch Centrum, Wageningen e: International Agricultural Centre; US: e: International Arms Corporation; IR: e: Iranian Airways Company, Teheran; I: i: Istituto d'Alta Cultura

IACA US: e: Independent Air Carriers Association; e: Inter-American Cultural Association

IACAC e: Inter-American Commercial Arbitration Commission

I.A.C.A.C.S. GB: e: mil: Interdenominational Advisory Committee on Army Chaplaincy Services

IACAHP INT: e: Inter-African Advisory Committee for Animal Health and Production

IACB e: Inter-American Coffee Board; INT: e: International Advisory Committee on Bibliography

IACBC INT: e: International Advisory Committee on Biological Control

IACBDT INT: e: International Advisory Committee on Bibliography, Documentation and Terminology

IACC INT: e: International Agricultural Coordination Commission; International Association of Color Consultants, Paris; International Association of Congress Centres

IACCP INT: e: Inter-American Council of Commerce and Production, Montevideo [gegr 1941]

IACD INT: e: International Association of Clothing Designers, Philadelphia, Pa. [US]

IACDOCTERPAS; IACDT INT: e: International Advisory Committee on Documentation, Terminology in Pure and Applied Science

IACED INT: e: Inter-African Advisory Committee on Epizootic Diseases, Muguga

IACFEC INT: e: Inter-American Consultative Financial and Economic Committee

IACH US: e: Interassociation Committee on Health

IACI e: Inter-American Children's Institute; INT: e: International Association of Conference Interpreters

IACL INT: e: International Association of Criminal Law; International Academy of Comparative Law, Den Haag [NL, gegr 1924]

IACME INT: e: International Association of Crafts and Small and Medium-Sized Enterprises, 1211 Genève [CH, gegr 1947]

IACO INT: e: Inter-African Coffee Organization

IACOD UN: e: International Advisory Committee on Documentation, Libraries and Archives [UNESCO]

IACOMS INT: e: International Advisory Committee on Marine Sciences

IACP CDN: US: e: International Association of Chiefs of Police; INT: e: International Association for Child Psychiatry and Allied Professions

IACP&AP INT: e: = IACP

I.A.C.S. IND: e: Indian Association for the Cultivation of Science, Calcutta [gegr 1876]; e: International Academy of Christian Sociologists

IACSAC INT: e: Inter-American Catholic Social Action Confederation

IACSS INT: e: Inter-American Conference on Social Security

IACW INT: e: Inter-American Congress of Women

IACWC INT: e: International Advisory Committee on Wireless Communications [gegr 1927]

IAD B: nl: Inlichtings- en actiedienst; US: e: Institute for American Democracy; INT: e: International Astro-

physical Decade [1965 ... 75] ; BlnW:
d: Internationaler Austauschdienst eV,
1 Berlin 12 [Touristik]

IADB INT: e: mil: Inter-American Defence Board, Washington, D.C.; US:
e: Inter-American Development Bank,
New York

IADC INT: e: mil: Inter-American Defense College, Fort McNair, Washington, D.C. [gegr 1962] ; INT: e: Inter-American Development Commission

IADF INT: e: Inter-American Association for Democracy and Freedom, New York [gegr 1950]

IADI f: Institut Américain de Droit International

IADL INT: e: International Association of Democratic Lawyers, Bruxelles 5

IADPC US: e: Inter-Agency Data Processing Committee

IADR INT: e: International Association for Dental Research

I.A.D.S. GB: e: Imperial Alliance for the Defence of Sunday

IADS INT: e: International Association of Dental Students; International Association of Department Stores, Paris 8 [gegr 1928]

IAE F: f: Institut d'Administration des Entreprises; US: e: Institute of Aeronautical Engineers

I.A.E. e: Institute of Agricultural Engineering; Institute of Automobile Engineers; GB: e: Institution of Aeronautical Engineers; Institution of Agricultural Engineers; AUS: GB: e: Institution of Automobile Engineers; e: Institution of Automotive Engineers; s: Instituto Asistencia Estadual; INT: f: Internationale des Artistes Expérimentaux

IAEA IND: e: Indian Adult Education Association; US: e: Institute of Automotive Engineers of America; UN: e: International Atomic Energy Agency,

Wien 1 [A]

I.A.E.C. e: International Adult Education Circle

IAECOSOC INT: e: Inter-American Economic and Social Council

I.Ae.E. GB: e: Institution of Aeronautical Engineers

IAEF INT: eo: Internacia Asocio de la Esperantistaj Fervojistoj

IAEI US: e: International Association of Electrical Inspectors

IAEL US: e: International Association of Electrical Leagues

IAEO UN: d: Internationale Atomenergie-Organisation, Wien e: International Atomic Energy Organization

IAEP INT: e: International Atomic Energy Pool

I.A.E.P.C. e: Incorporated Association of Electric Power Companies

IAeS US: e: Institute of the Aeronautical Sciences

IAES US: e: International Association of Electrotypers and Stereotypers

IAESC INT: e: Inter-American Economic and Social Council

IAESP BR: pt: Instituto Agronómico de Estado de São Paulo

IAESTE INT: e: International Association for the Exchange of Students for Technical Experience, 53 Bonn-Bad Godesberg [BRD]

IAEVI INT: e: International Association for Educational and Vocational Information

I.A.F. GB: e: mil: Indian Air Force; Indian Armoured Formation; US: e: Industrial Areas Foundation

IAF INT: e: mil: Inter-American Force; INT: e: International Abolitionist Federation, Genève [CH, gegr 1875] ; International Aeronautical Federation; INT: d: Internationale Astronautische Föderation, Paris [gegr 1950-51] e: International Astronautical Federation; INT: e: International Automobile Federation, Paris; INT: nl: Internationale Athletiek Federatie; e: mil: Italian Air Force

IAFAC INT: e: Inter-American Federation of Automobile Clubs

IAFC CDN: US: e: International Association of Fire Chiefs

IAFD INT: e: International Association of Food Distribution, Bern [CH]

IAFE YV: s: Instituto Autónomo de Ferrocarriles de Estado; e: International Association of Fairs and Expositions

IAFF INT: e: International Art Film Federation; e: International Association of Fire Fighters

IAFH BRD: d: Institut für Aeromechanik und Flugtechnik der Technischen Hochschule Hannover

IAFP RA: s: Instituto de Anatomía y Fisiología Patológicas

IAFRI INT: [d: Internationaler Verband der forstlichen Forschungsanstalten]

IAFWNO INT: e: Inter-American Federation of Working Newspapermen's Organizations

IAG US: e: Institute of American Genealogy; GB: e: Institute of Animal Genetics; INT: e: International Association of Geodesy, Paris [gegr 1896] ; International Association of Gerontology [gegr 1950] ; INT: d: Internationale Arbeitsgemeinschaft für den Unterrichtsfilm, Paris 5 [gegr 1950]

IAGA INT: e: International Association of Geomagnetism and Aeronomy [gegr 1919]

IAGFCC US: e: International Association of Game, Fish and Conservation Commissioners

IAGLO CDN: US: e: International Association of Governmental Labor Officials, Washington, D.C.

IAGLP CDN: US: e: International Association of Great Lakes Ports

IAGM US: e: International Association of Garment Manufacturers

I.Agr. f: Institut Agronomique

IAGS INT: e: Inter-American Geodetic Survey, Fort Clayton, Canal Zone

IAH INT: e: International Association of Hydrology; INT: d: Internationale Arbeiterhilfe [gegr 1921] sv: Internationella arbetarhjälpen

IAHA INT: e: Inter-American Hospital Association; Inter-American Hotel Association [gegr 1941] ; International Animal Husbandry Association; International Arabian Horse Association

IAHF INT: d: Internationale Amateur-Handball- Föderation e: International Amateur Handball Federation [gegr 1928]

I.A.H.M. GB: e: Incorporated Association of Headmasters

IAHP US: e: Institute for the Achievement of Human Potential, Philadelphia; INT: e: International Association of Horticultural Producers, Den Haag [NL, gegr 1948]

IAHR INT: e: International Association for the (Study of) History of Religions, Amsterdam [NL] ; International Association for Hydraulic Research, Delft [NL, gegr 1935]

IAHS INT: e: International Academy of the History of Science

I.-A.-I. D: d: Ibero-amerikanisches Institut, Bonn, Hamburg

IAI GB: e: Institute of Arbitrators, Incorporated; INT: s: Instituto Africano Internacional e: International African Institute, London [gegr 1926] d: Internationales Afrika-Institut; INT: e: International Anthropological Institute, Paris; International Association of Identification; International Automotive Institute, Monaco

I.A.I. e: Institute for Atomic Information

for the Lay Man; I: i: Istituto per
l'Addestramento nell'Industria
IAIAA INT: e: International Association for Iranian Art and Archaeology
IAIABC INT: e: International Association of Industrial Accident Boards and Commissions
IAIAS INT: e: Inter-American Institute of Agricultural Sciences [gegr 1944]
IAIC US: e: International Association of Insurance Counsel
IAICM US: e: International Association of Ice Cream Manufacturers
IAIU e: Insurance Agents International Union
IAJAM US: e: Industrial Association of Juvenile Apparel Manufacturers
IAJC INT: e: Inter-American Juridical Committee
IAJE INT: eo: Internacia Asocio de Juristoj-Esperantistoj [gegr 1957]
IAJH INT: d: Internationale Arbeitsgemeinschaft für Jugendherbergen
IAK N: no: Institutt for Atomenergi Kjeller; INT: d: Internationale Arbeitskonferenz; Internationales Auschwitz-Komitee
IAKS INT: d: Internationaler Arbeitskreis Sportstättenbau
IAL IS: e: Icelandic Airlines Loftleidir
I.A.L. GB: e: Imperial Airways Limited; Imperial Arts League; B: f: Institut Africain, Louvain
IAL GB: e: International Aeradio Ltd.; INT: e: International Arbitration League; International Association of Theoretical and Applied Limnology [gegr 1922]; INT: nl: Internationale Artiesten-Loge d: Internationale Artisten-Loge
I.A.L. e: Irish Academy of Letters
IALA INT: e: International African Law Association, London WC 2; International Association of Lighthouse Authorities, Paris 16 [gegr

1957]; International Auxiliary Language Association, New York [gegr 1934]
I.A.L.D.C. GB: e: Incorporated Association of London Dyers and Cleaners
I.A.L.L. INT: e: International Association for Labor Legislation
IALL INT: e: International Association of Law Libraries, Los Angeles, Cal.
IALP INT: e: International Association of Logopedics and Phoniatrics [1924]
IALS INT: e: International Association of Legal Science [gegr 1950]
IALSSA e: International Air Line Stewards and Stewardesses Association
I.A.Ltd. GB: e: Imperial Airways Ltd.
IAM US: e: Institute of Appliance Manufacturers; CDN: e: mil: Institute of Aviation Medicine [RCAF]; US: e: International Association of Machinists [AFL-CIO]; INT: e: International Association of Meteorology (and Atmospheric Physics); INT: d: Internationale Arbeitsgemeinschaft für Müllforschung, Zürich [CH]; BRD: d: Internationaler Arbeitskreis für Musik, 35 Kassel
IAMA INT: e: International Abstaining Motorists' Association [gegr 1956]; D: d: Internationale Automobil- und Motorrad-Ausstellung, Berlin 1934
I.A.M.A. e: Irish Association of Municipal Authorities
IAMAL US: e: Insects Affecting Man and Animals Laboratory, Gainesville, Fla
IAMAM INT: e: mil: International Association of Museums of Arms and Military History
IAMAP INT: e: International Association of Meteorology and Atmospheric Physics, Ontario [CDN, gegr 1919]
IAMB INT: nl: Internationaal Anti-Militaristisch Bureau, Heemstede [NL, gegr 1921] e: International Anti-Militarist Bureau against War and Reaction

I.A.M.B. INT: e: International Association of Microbiologists

I.A.M.C. GB: e: mil: Indian Army Medical Corps

IAMC US: e: Institute for the Advancement of Medical Communication

IAMCA US: e: International Association of Milk Control Agencies

IAMCR INT: e: International Association for Mass Communication Research [gegr 1957]

IAME RA: s: Industria Aeronáutica y Mecánica Estado, Córdoba

IAMFE INT: e: International Association of Mechanization of Field Experiments [agriculture]

IAMFS e: International Association of Milk and Food Sanitarians

IAMKK D: d: nach WK1: Interalliierte Militärkontrollkommission

IAML INT: e: International Association of Music Libraries, 35 Kassel [BRD, gegr 1951]

IAMLT INT: e: International Association of Medical Laboratory Technologists, CH-8006 Zürich

IAMM e: International Association of Medical Museums

IAMM&D US: e: mil: Institute for Advanced Materials, Mechanics and Design, Watertown, Mass.

IAMO INT: d: Interafrikanisch-Madegassische Organisation; INT: e: Inter-American Municipal Organization

IAMPTH US: e: International Association of Master-Penmen and Teachers of Handwriting

IAMRI INT: e: International Association for Maritime Radio Interests, Croydon [GB]

IAMS INT: e: International Association of Microbiological Societies [gegr 1930]

IAMT INT: e: mil: Inter-Allied Military Tribunal

I.A.M.V. INT: nl: Internationale Anti-Militaristische Vereniging

IAMWF INT: e: Inter-American Mine Workers Federation

IAMY INT: e: International Assembly of Muslim Youth

IAN BR: pt: Instituto Agronómico do Norte; INT: f: Internationale des Amis de la Nature

IANA Rhodesien: e: Inter-African News Agency

IANC INT: e: International Airline Navigators Council, Kastrup [DK]; International Anatomical Nomenclature Committee, Manchester [GB]

IANEÇ INT: e: Inter-American Nuclear Energy Commission, Washington, D.C.

IANF NATO: e: Interallied Nuclear Force [proposed]

I.A.N.Z. NZ: e: Institute of Actuaries of New Zealand

IAO US: e: Independent Aviation Operators; INT: nl: Internationale Arbeidsorganisation d: Internationale Arbeitsorganisation, Genf [CH] sv: Internationella arbetsorganisation

I.A.O.C. GB: e: mil: Indian Army Ordnance Corps

IAOL INT: e: International Association of Oriental Libraries

I.A.O.S. IRL: e: Irish Agricultural Organization Society, Dublin [gegr 1894]

I.A.P. GB: e: Institute of Agricultural Parasitology; Institute of Animal Physiology

IAP US: e: International Academy of Pathology, Washington, D.C. [gegr 1906]; e: International Academy of Proctology; INT: e: International Association of Psychotechnics

IAPA INT: e: Interamerican Press Association, New York 21, N.Y. [gegr 1942]; International Association of Plastic Arts

IAPB INT: e: International Association

for the Prevention of Blindness, Paris [gegr 1929]

IAPCW INT: e: International Association for the Promotion of Child Welfare [gegr 1921]

IAPES US: e: International Association of Personnel in Employment Security

IAPESGW e: International Association for Physical Education and Sports for Girls and Women

IAPF INT: e: mil: Inter-American Peace Force

I.A.P.G.W.B. GB: e: Incorporated Association for Promoting the General Welfare of the Blind

IAPH INT: e: International Association of Ports and Harbo(u)rs, Tokyo

IAPHC CDN: US: e: International Association of Printing House Craftsmen

I.A.Phys. GB: e: Institute of Animal Physiology

IAPI US: e: Institute of American Poultry Industries; RA: s: Instituto Argentino para la Promoción del Intercambio

IAPIP INT: e: International Association for the Protection of Industrial Property, CH-8008 Zürich [gegr 1897]

I.A.P.K. INT: eo: Internacia Asocio de Poŝtmarkkolektantoj

I.A.P.L. RA: [d: Argentinisches Institut zur Förderung des Handels]

IAPL INT: e: International Association for Penal Law

IAPN INT: e: International Association of Professional Numismatics, Paris 9 [gegr 1951]

IAPO INT: e: International Association of Physical Oceanography, Göteborg [S, gegr 1919]

IAPOI INT: e: International Association of Public Opinion Institutes

IAPP IND: e: Indian Association for Plant Physiology; INT: e: International Association for Plant Physiology

IAPPW US: e: International Association of Pupil Personnel Workers

I.A.P.S. GB: e: Incorporated Association of Preparatory Schools

IAPS e: International Academy of Political Science

IAPSC INT: e: Inter-African Phytosanitary Commission, London

IAPT INT: e: International Association for Plant Taxonomy, Utrecht [NL, gegr 1950]

IA-PVO SU: mil: [d: Luftabwehr-Jagdfliegerkräfte]

IAPW US: e: International Association of Personnel Women

IA-PWO = IA-PVO

IAQ INT: e: International Association for Quality

IAQR INT: e: International Association of Quarternary Research

IAR US: e: mil: Inactive Air Reserve; US: e: Institute for Atomic Research; BRD: d: Institut für angewandte Reaktorphysik, 75 Karlsruhe; D: e: nach WK2: International Authority for the Ruhr

IARA INT: e: Inter-Allied Reparations Agency, Bruxelles d: Interalliiertes Reparationsamt [gegr 1946]

IARAC INT: e: International Association of Recognized Automobile Clubs

I.Arb. GB: e: Institute of Arbitrators

IArbA INT: d: Internationales Arbeitsamt, Genf [CH]

IARC IND: e: Indian Agricultural Research Council; e: International Amateur Radio Club; INT: e: International Amateur Recording Contest

I.A.R.D. e: Incorporated Association of Retail Distributors

IARD US: e: Information Analysis and Retrieval Division, American Institute of Physics, New York

I.A.R.D.P. GB: e: Incorporated Association for the Relief of Distressed Prot-

estants
IARE B: f: Institut Archéologique Reine Elisabeth; US: e: International Association of Railway Employees
IARF INT: e: International Association for Liberal Christianity and Religious Freedom, Den Haag [NL, gegr 1900]
IARI IND: e: Indian Agricultural Research Institute, New Delhi; US: e: Industrial Advertising Research Institute, Princetown, N.J.
IARIW INT: e: International Association for Research in Income and Wealth, New Haven, Conn. [US, gegr 1947]
I.A.R.L. INT: e: International Association for Liberal Christianity and Religious Liberty, Utrecht [NL, gegr 1900]
IARM RA: s: Instituto Argentino de Racionalización de Materiales
I.A.R.O. GB: e: mil: Indian Army Reserve of Officers
IARS INT: e: International Anesthesia Research Society
IARU INT: e: International Amateur Radio Union [gegr 1925]
I.A.R.V.O. e: Incorporated Association of Rating and Valuation Officers
I.A.S. e: Incorporated Association of Surveyors
IAS US: e: Indiana Academy of Science; IND: e: Indian Academy of Sciences
I.A.S. IND: e: Indian Administrative Service; Indian Agricultural Service; Indian Astronautical Society; US: e: Institute for Advanced Studies
IAS US: e: Institute of Aeronautical (Aerospace) Sciences, New York; INT: e: International Association of Seismology (and Physics of the Earth's Interior); International Association of Siderographers; INT: d: Internationaler Arbeitskreis Sicherheit beim Skilauf [gegr 1967]; US: e: Iowa

Academy of Science
I.A.S. e: Irish Archæological Society; Irish Art Society
IASA BR: pt: Indústrias químicas e metalurgicas S.A., São Paulo; AUS: e: Institute of Accountants, South Australia; US: e: Insurance Accounting and Statistical Association; INT: e: International Air Safety Association
IASAP US: e: Intercollege Association for Study of the Alcohol Problem
IASB INT: e: International Aircraft Standard Bureau
IASC INT: e: Interamerican Safety Council; International Association of Seed Crushers, London E.C.4 [gegr 1910]; International Association of Skal Clubs
IASF F: f: Industrie Aéronautique et Spatiale Française
IASH INT: e: International Association of Scientific Hydrology, Louvain [B, gegr 1924]
IASHR INT: e: International Association for the Study of History of Religions
IASI INT: e: Inter-American Statistical Institute, Washington, D.C. [gegr 1940]
IASL INT: [d: Internationale Gesellschaft für die Erforschung der Leber]
IASLIC IND: e: Indian Association of Special Libraries and Information Centres [gegr 1955]
IASM US: e: Independent Association of Stocking Manufacturers; I: i: Istituto per l'Assistenza allo Sviluppo del Mezzogiorno
IASP INT: e: International Association for Social Progress [gegr 1924]
IASPEI INT: e: International Association of Seismology and Physics of the Earth's Interior
IASS e: Inter-American Schools Service; INT: e: International Association for Shell Structures, Madrid [E]; International Association of Soil Science

IASSW INT: e: International Association of Schools of Social Work, New York [gegr 1929]

IASV INT: d: Internationale Arbeitsgemeinschaft von Sortimentsbuchhändler-Vereinigungen, Delft 2 [NL]

IATA INT: e: International Air Traffic Association [1919 . . . 39]; International Air Transport Association, Montreal 3 PQ [CDN, gegr 1945]; International Amateur Theatre Association, Brussels [B, gegr 1952]

I.A.T.C. INT: e: International Advisory Telephone Committee; International Air Transport Commission (Conference) (Convention)

IATC US: e: International Association of Tool Craftsmen; International Association of Torch Clubs

IATCB US: e: Interdepartmental Air Traffic Control Board

IATE INT: e: International Association for Temperance Education [gegr 1954]

IATL US: e: International Academy of Trial Lawyers; INT: e: International Association of Theological Libraries

IATM INT: e: International Association for Testing Materials

IATME INT: e: International Association of Terrestrial Magnetism and Electricity, Washington, D.C.

IATSE CDN: US: e: International Alliance of Theatrical Stage Employees and Moving Picture Machine Operators of the United States and Canada

IATTC INT: e: Inter-American Tropical Tuna Commission, La Jolla, Calif.

IATU INT: e: Inter-American Telecommunications Union

IATUC INT: [d: Internationaler Arabischer Gewerkschaftsverband]

IATUL INT: e: International Association of Technological University Libraries, Bethlehem, Pa. [US, gegr 1955]

I.A.U. e: International Academic Union

IAU INT: e: International Association of Universities, Paris 16 [gegr 1950]; International Astronomical Union, Hailsham, Sussex [GB, gegr 1919]; INT: d: Internationale Armbrust-Union; US: e: Italian Actors Union

IAUF d: Institut für Automation und Unternehmensforschung

IAUPE INT: e: International Association of University Professors of English

IAUPL INT: e: International Association of University Professors and Lecturers [gegr 1945]

IAUYMF INT: e: International Association of Users of Yarn of Man-made Fibres

IAV INT: e: International Association of Vulcanology [Neapel, gegr 1919]

IAVA US: e: Industrial Audio-Visual Association

IAVFH INT: e: International Association of Veterinary Food Hygienists [gegr 1955]

IAVG INT: e: International Association for Vocational Guidance, Brussels [B, gegr 1953]

I.A.W. D: d: mil: Inspekteur des Ausbildungswesens

IAW INT: e: International Alliance of Women "Equal Rights – Equal Responsibilities" [gegr 1904]

IAWA INT: e: International Association of Wood Anatomists, Zürich 6 [CH, gegr 1931]

I.A.W.E.C. e: International Alliance of Women for Equal Citizenship

IAWF INT: e: International Amateur Wrestling Federation

IAWM GB: e: Industrial Association of Wales and Monmouthshire

IAWMC INT: e: International Association of Workers for Maladjusted Children, Paris [gegr 1951]

IAWP e: International Association of Women Police

IAWPR INT: e: International Association on Water Pollution Research
IAWR INT: d: Internationale Arbeitsgemeinschaft der Wasserwerke im Rheineinzugsgebiet [gegr 1970] ; US: e: mil: Institute for Air Weapons Research [University of Chicago]
IAWRT INT: e: International Association of Women in Radio and Television, 5 Köln [BRD]
IAWS US: e: Intercollegiate Association of Women Students
I.A.W.S. e: Irish Agricultural Wholesale Society, Ltd. [gegr 1898]
IB E: s: Iberia, Líneas Aéreas Internacionales de España S.A., Madrid 6
I.B. e: Immigration Branch; Index Bureau
IB CH: d: Inlandbank AG, Zürich [CH, gegr 1933]
I.B. e: Inquiry Branch
IB A: d: Österreichisches Institut für Bauforschung
I.B. f: Institut de Beauté; Institut de Biologie; GB: e: Institute of Bankers
IB NL: nl: Instituut voor Bodemvruchtbaarheid; PL: pl: Instytut Bibliograficzny
I.B. e: Intelligence Branch; International Bureau; d: Internationales Büro
IBA US: e: Independent Bankers Association
I.B.A. GB: e: Industrial Bankers' Association, London E.C. 2
IBA BRD: d: Industrie-Betreuungs-Agentur GmbH, 8 München 27; US: e: Institute for Bioenergetic Analysis
I.B.A. GB: e: Institute of British Architects
IBA INT: e: International Bar Association, New York 17 [gegr 1947] ; International Bookstall Contractors Association; International Bowling Association [gegr 1926] ; US: e: International Briquetting Association
IBA; iba INT: d: Internationale Bäckerei-Fachausstellung [BRD, 1961 in Ffm,

Mai 1951 in BlnW] ; Internationale Baufachausstellung; Internationale Buchkunst-Ausstellung; Internationale Büroausstellung, Berlin 1934
IBA US: e: Investing Builders Association; Investment Bankers Association of America, Chicago
I.B.A. e: Irish Bleachers Association
IBAA US: e: Investment Bankers Association of America, Chicago
IBAB B: f: Institut Belge pour l'Amélioration de la Betterave
I.B.A.E. GB: e: Institution of British Agricultural Engineers
Ibag D: d: Industriebedarfs-AG, Berlin; CH: d: Industrie-Beteiligungs-AG, Zürich
IBAG BRD: d: Internationale Baumaschinen AG, Neustadt (Weinstr)
IBAH INT: e: Inter-African Bureau for Animal Health, Muguga
IBAHP INT: e: Inter-African Bureau for Animal Health and Protection, Muguga
IBAM BR: pt: Instituto Brasileiro de Administração Municipal
IBAN B: f: Institut Belge pour l'Alimentation et la Nutrition
I.B.A.P.T. GB: e: Incorporated British Association of Physical Training
IBAS BRD: d: Interessengemeinschaft der Bediensteten der alliierten Stationierungsstreitkräfte
I.B.A.U. e: Institute of British-American Understanding
IBB S: sv: Industribyggnadsbyrån, Göteborg; BRD: d: Ingenieurbüro Bölkow [gegr 1948] ; Interessenverband derzeitiger und ehemaliger Beschäftigter bei den Besatzungsmächten eV, München [gegr 1954] ; US: e: International Brotherhood of Bookbinders; INT: d: Internationales Behälterbüro, Paris
IBBA US: e: Inland Bird Banding Association
IBBD BR: pt: Instituto Brasileiro de Bibliografia e Documentação, Rio de

Janeiro

IBBDFH US: e: International Brother-hood of Blacksmiths, Drop Forgers and Helpers

IBBH INT: d: Internationaler Bund der Bau- und Holzarbeiter, Kopenhagen [DK, gegr 1891]

IBBY e: International Board on Books for Young People [gegr 1951]

IBC US: e: mil: Iceland Base Command; RCH: s: Instituto Bacteriólogico de Chile; NL: nl: Instituut TNO voor Bouwmaterialen en -constructies, Delft; MEX: US: e: International Boundary and Water Commission; CDN: US: International Boundary Commission United States – Canada – Alaska; INT: e: International Boxing Club; International Broadcasting Convention, London [7 . . . 11.9.1970]

I.B.C. e: International Broadcasting Corporation

IBC BR: [e: Brazilian Coffee Institute]

IBCA US: e: Industrial Bag and Covers Association; e: International Bureau for Cultural Activities

IBCAG INT: d: Internationaler Bund Christlicher Angestellten-Gewerkschaften [vorher: IBCAV]

IBCATHAR INT: d: Internationaler Bund Christlicher Angestellten-, Techniker-, Höherer Angestellten- und Reisendenverbände, Paris

IBCAV INT: d: Internationaler Bund Christlicher Angestelltenverbände [später: IBCAG]

IBCC INT: e: International Building Classification Committee

IBCG INT: d: Internationaler Bund Christlicher Gewerkschaften, Brüssel [B, gegr 1920]

IBCGTB INT: d: Internationaler Bund der Christlichen Gewerkschaften im Textil- und Bekleidungsgewerbe, Gent [B, gegr 1901]

IBCHBV INT: d: Internationaler Bund Christlicher Holz- und Bauarbeiterverbände, Utrecht [NL, gegr 1937]

IBCIN NL: nl: Internationaal Biologisch Contact- en Informatiebureau voor Nederland

IBCLV INT: d: Internationaler Bund Christlicher Landarbeiterverbände, Brüssel [B, gegr 1901]

IBCS e: International Bureau of Commercial Statistics

I.B.D. GB: e: mil: Infantry Base Depot; GB: e: Institute of British Decorators (and Interior Designers)

IBD PL: pl: Instytut Budowy Dróg; UN: e: International Bureau for Declaration of Death, Geneva [CH, gegr 1952]

IBDC B: f: Institut Belge de Droit Comparé

IBDF BR: pt: Instituto Brasileiro de Direito Financeiro

IBE B: f: Institut Belge de l'Emballage, Bruxelles

I.B.E. GB: e: Institute of British Engineers; INT: e: International Bureau of Education, 1211 Genève [CH, gegr 1925] d: Internationales Büro (Amt) für Erziehungsfragen; INT: e: International Exhibition Bureau

IBEC US: e: International Basic Economy Corporation; PAK: e: International Book Exchange Centre, Karachi

IBECC BR: pt: Instituto Brasileiro de Educação, Ciência e Cultura

IBED INT: e: Interafrican Bureau for Epizootic Diseases, Muguga [gegr 1951]

IBEG BRD: d: Industrieentwicklungs- und Beteiligungsgesellschaft mbH, Bonn; INT: d: Internationaler Bund der Erziehungsgemeinschaften, Paris [gegr 1948]

IBELCO B: f: Institut Belge de Coopération Technique

IBER B: nl: Instituut der Bedrijfsrevisoren
IBERIA E: s: Líneas Aéreas Internacionales de España S.A., Madrid 6
IBERLANT NATO: e: Iberian Atlantic Area
IBERSOM B: f: Institut Belge pour l'Encouragement de la Recherche Scientifique Outre-Mer, Bruxelles
I.B.E.W. US: e: International Brotherhood of Electrical Workers, Washington, D.C. [gegr 1891]
IBEWA US: e: International Brotherhood of Electrical Workers of America [= I.B.E.W.]
IBF BRD: d: Institut für Begabten-Förderung, 8 München 80; Institut für Betriebsführung GmbH & Co, 4 Düsseldorf
I.B.F. GB: e: Institute of British Foundrymen
IBF BRD: d: Interessengemeinschaft der Bekleidungsgroßhändler und Fabriklager; INT: e: International Badminton Federation [gegr 1934]
IBFD INT: e: International Bureau of Fiscal Documentation, Amsterdam [NL]
IBFG INT: d: Internationaler Bund Freier Gewerkschaften, Brüssel [B, gegr 1949]
IBFMP INT: e: International Bureau of the Federations of Master Printers, London N 1 [gegr 1923]
IBFO US: e: International Brotherhood of Firemen and Oilers
I.B.G. GB: e: Incorporated Brewers' Guild
IBG D: d: WK2: Ingenieurbüro Glückauf, Blankenburg (Harz) [Ubootbau; gegr 1943] ; GB: e: Institute of British Geographers; e: International Boxing Guild
IBGE BR: pt: Instituto Brasileiro de Geografia e Estatística
I.B.H.P. B: f: Institut Belge des Hautes Pressions
IBI I: i: Istituto Biochimico Italiano; US: e: Insulation Board Institute; d:

Internationales Bibliographisches Institut; INT: d: Internationales Burgenforschungsinstitut, Rapperswil [CH, gegr 1949]
I.B.I.A. GB: e: Institute of British Industrial Art.
IBIT BR: pt: Instituto Brasileiro para Investigação da Tuberculose
IBK BRD: d: Institut für das Bauen mit Kunststoffen, 61 Darmstadt; DDR: d: Institut für Bekleidungskultur
I.B.K. GB: e: Institute of Bookkeepers
IBK INT: d: Internationale Beleuchtungskommission [gegr 1900]
IBKG i C. Pl: pl: Instytut Badania Koniunktur Gospodarczych i Cen
IBKh SU: [e: Bakh Institute of Biological Chemistry]
IBKO INT: nl: Internationaal Bureau van het Katholiek Onderwijs
IBKS INT: d: stud: Internationale Bewegung Katholischer Studenten "Pax Romana", Fribourg [CH]
I.B.L. GB: e: Institute of British Launderers
IBL PL: pl: Instytut Badań Literackich; Instytut Badawczy Leśnictwa; US: e: International Brotherhood of Longshoremen
IBLA TN: f: Institut des Belles-Lettres Arabes; INT: e: Inter-American Bibliographical and Library Association
I.B.L.C. B: L: f: Institut Belgo-Luxembourgeois du Change
IB Leś PL: pl: Instytut Badawczy Leśnictwa
IBM MEX: s: Instituto de Biología, Universidad de México; US: e: International Business Machines Corporation, New York
IBMA e: International Bar Managers Association
IBME RA: s: Instituto de Biología y Medicina Experimental
IBMG INT: d: Internationales Büro für

Maße und Gewichte [e: IBWM]
IBMR INT: e: International Bureau for Mechanical Reproduction, Paris 9 [f: BIEM]
IBMV 1: Institutum Beatae Mariae Virginis
IBN B: f: Institut Belge de Normalisation, B-1040 Bruxelles 4
IBNA INT: d: Internationaler Bund neutraler Angestelltengewerkschaften, Straßburg
IBO NL: nl: Instituut voor Bosbouwkundig Onderzoek; INT: e: International Broadcasting Organization [Prag, gegr 1946]; BRD: d: Internationale Bodenseemesse, Friedrichshafen a.B.; INT: d: Internationaler Bauorden nl: Internationale Bouworde
IBOP US: e: International Brotherhood of Operative Potters
ibp BRD: d: Industrie + Büro-Personal Leasing GmbH, 68 Mannheim
IBP I: i: Industrie Buitoni Perugina
I.B.P. F: f: Institut de Calcule Blaise Pascal
IBP US: e: Institute for Better Packaging
I.B.P. GB: e: Institute of British Photographers; Institute for Business Planning
IBP INT: e: International Biological Program(me) d: Internationales Biologisches Programm [ICSU]; INT: d: Internationaler Bund der Privatangestellten [gegr 1920]
I.B.P.C. f: Institut Biologique Physico-Chimique
I.B.P.C.S. INT: e: International Bureau for Physico-Chemical Standards
IBPT P: pt: Instituto de Biologia e Pesquisas Tecnológicas
IBR US: e: Institute of Boiler and Radiator Manufacturers, New York
I.B.R. B: nl: Instituut der Bedrijfsrevisoren
IBRA B: f: Institut Belge de Régulation et d'Automatisme

IBRAD INT: e: = IBRD
IBRAPE BR: pt: Indústria Brasileira de Produtos Electronicos e Eléctricos
IBRC e: International Business Relations Council
IBRD UN: e: International Bank for Reconstruction and Development, Washington, D.C.
IBRI INT: e: International Building Research Institute
IBRO INT: e: International Brain Research Organization
IBS D: d: Industriebeamten-Sparbank eGmbH, Berlin; BR: pt: Instituto Brasileiro de Siderurgia; NL: nl: Instituut voor Biologisch en Scheikundig Onderzoek van Landbouwgewassen; e: Interafrican Bureau of Soils; US: e: Intercollegiate Broadcasting System; Int: e: International Broadcasters Society; International Bureau of Scouting; INT: d: Internationale Berufssekretariate
IBSA US: e: International Barber Schools Association
I.B.S.A. e: Inanimate Bird Shooting Association; International Bible Students' Association
IBSAC GB: e: Industrialized Building Systems and Components Exhibition, London [1964 etc.]
IBSAF INT: e: International Bureau for Standardization of Artificial Fibres
IBSB INT: d: Internationaler Blinden-Schachbund
IBSC INT: d: Internationaler Brauerei-souvenir-Sammler-Club
IBSL INT: d: Internationaler Bund der Schuh- und Lederarbeiter [gegr 1907]; Internationales Berufssekretariat der Lehrer, Brüssel [B, gegr 1951]
I.B.S.S. GB: e: Imperial Bureau of Soil Science
I.B.S.T. GB: e: Institute of British Surgical Technicians
IBT; IBTCWH US: e: International

Brotherhood of Teamsters, Chauffeurs, Warehousemen, and Helpers of America

IBTE ETH: e: Imperial Board of Telecommunications of Ethiopia; INT: e: International Bureau of Technical Education

I.B.T.N. INT: f: Exposition Internationale Blanchisserie, Teinture, Nettoyage, Paris [1952]

IBTO CS: [d: Forsehungsinstitut für Nachrichtenwesen, Prag]

I.B.T.O. INT: e: International Broadcasting and Television Organization

IBTT INT: e: International Bureau of Technical Training, Paris [gegr 1931]

IBTU INT: da: Internationale Bygnings- og Träindustriarbejder-Union, København [gegr 1934]

IBU INT: e: International Boxing Union d: Internationale Box-Union [gegr 1911] ; International Broadcasting Union, Genève [CH, gegr 1925]; INT: d: Internationale Binnenschiffahrts -Union [gegr 1952] ; INT: nl: Internationale Boksunie; INT: d: Internationale Bürgermeisterunion für deutsch -französische Verständigung (und europäische Zusammenarbeit)

IBUPL INT: e: International Bureau for the Unification of Penal Law

I.B.U.P.U. INT: e: International Bureau of the Universal Postal Union

IBUSz; IBUSZ H: hu: Idegenforgalmi, Beszerzési, Utazási és Szállitási Rt.,Budapest [gegr 1902, d: Fremdenverkehrs-, Einkaufs-, Reise- und Transport-AG, Budapest]

IBUZ YU: l: Institutum Botanicum Universitatis Zagrabiensis

IBV INT: d: Internationaler Bergarbeiter -Verband, London [gegr 1880] ; Internationale Bierdeckelsammler-Vereinigung (Internationale Interessengemeinschaft der Bierdeckelsammler); Inter-

nationaler Bodensee-Verkehrsverein; Internationaler Bohrtechniker-Verband

IBVL NL: nl: Instituut voor Bewaring en Verwerking van Landbouwproducten

IBVT NL: nl: Instituut voor Bewaring en Verwerking van Tuinbouw-producten

IBWC MEX: US: e: International Boundary and Water Commission

IBWM INT: e: International Bureau of Weights and Measures, Sèvres [gegr 1875]

IBWS INT: e: International Bureau of Whaling Statistics

IBWW INT: e: International Federation of Building and Woodworkers [gegr 1934]

IBWZ INT: d: Internationale Bank für wirtschaftliche Zusammenarbeit, Moskau

IBZ CH: d: Inlandbank AG, Zürich

IC US: e: Illinois Central Railroad Company

I.C. GB: e: Imperial Conference; Industrial Court; F: f: mil: Infanterie Coloniale

IC S: sv: Bilägarnas inköpscentral, Stockholm

I.C. F: f: mil: Inspection de la Cavalerie; F: f: Institut Catholique; e: Institute of Charity; GB: e: Institute of Chemistry of Great Britain and Ireland; f: Institut de Chimie; e: mil: Intelligence Corps; f: Intendance Coloniale; Rhodesien: e: Intensive Conservation Area Committee; e: Intergovernment Committee; Interim Commission (for the International Trade Organization) [Geneva, CH] ; International Conference; International Corps; d: Internationaler Club; INT: i: Internazionale Communista; e: Internment Camp; INT: e: Islamic Congress; I: i: Ispettorato Compartimentale (Agrario)

I.C.A. e: Ice Cream Alliance, Ltd.; GB: e: Imperial College of Agriculture

[West Indies] ; E: s: Industria y Comercio de Alimentación; GB: e: Industrial Copartnership Association; F: f: Ingénieurs Civils de l'Aéronautique; Institut de Chimie Appliquée; GB: e: Institute of Chartered Accountants; Institute of Company Accountants; Institute of Contemporary Arts, London

ICA P: pt: Instituto do Café de Angola, Luanda; e: Intercontinental Airways; INT: s: Federación Internacional Cristiana de los Trabajadores de las Industrias Alimenticias, del Tabaco y de la Hostelería, Bruxelles [B]; INT: e: International Cartographic Association; US: e: International Chefs Association; INT: e: International Chiropractors Association, Davenport, Iowa [US, gegr 1926] ; US: e: International Claim Association; e: International Colonization Association; International Commission on Acoustics; INT: e: International Confederation of Agriculture, Paris [gegr 1889] ; International Confederation of Associations, London [gegr 1885] ; INT: e: International Congress on Acoustics; International Congress of Archivists; International Control Agency; International Cooperation Administration, Washington, D.C. [gegr 1955] ; International Co-operative Alliance, London W 1 [gegr 1895] ; International Council on Archives, Paris 7 [gegr 1948] ; INT: f: Fédération Internationale chrétienne des travailleurs de l'alimentation, du tabac et de l'hôtellerie, Bruxelles [B] ; INT: nl: Internationale Cooperatieve Alliantie

I.C.A. e: Irish Cyclists' Association

ICA IL: e: Israel Consumers' Association; US: e: Italian Charities of America

ICAA INT: e: International Confederation of Artists' Associations [gegr 1935] ; International Committee on Aerospace Activities

I.C.A.A. e: Invalid Children's Aid Association

ICAA US: e: Investment Counsel Association of America

ICAAAA US: e: Intercollegiate Association of Amateur Athletes of America

I.C.A.B. F: f: mil: Inspection de la Cavalerie et de l'Armée Blindée

ICAB GB: e: International Cargo Advisory Bureau, London SW 7 [British European Airways]

I.C.A.C. GB: e: Imperial Communications Advisory Committee

ICAC INT: e: International Civil Aviation Committee; International Committee of Anti-Militarist Clergymen [gegr 1926] International Confederation for Agricultural Credit; International Cotton Advisory Committee, Washington 25, D.C. [gegr 1939]

ICACE NATO: e: Intelligence Center Allied Command Europe

ICAD INT: e: International Committee for Automobile Documentation; International Council of Amateur Dancers

ICAE INT: e: International Commission of Agricultural Engineering [gegr 1930] ; International Conference of Agricultural Economists [gegr 1929]

ICAED INT: e: Interafrican Advisory Committee on Epizootic Diseases

ICAES INT: e: International Congress of Anthropological and Ethnological Sciences

I.C.A.E.W. GB: e: Institute of Chartered Accountants in England and Wales

ICAF US: e: mil: Industrial College of the Armed Forces, Fort McNair, Washington, D.C.; INT: e: International Committee of Aeronautical Fatigue

ICAI E: s: Instituto Católico de Artes e Industrias, Madrid [gegr 1909] ; INT: e: International Commission for Agricultural Industries, Paris 7 [gegr 1934] ;

International Committee for Aid to
Intellectuals
ICAITI INT: s: Instituto Centroameri-
cano de Investigación y Tecnología
Industrial [gegr 1956]
ICALU INT: e: International Confed-
eration of Arab Labour Unions
I.C.A.M. F: f: Institut Catholique d'Arts
-et-Métiers, Lille; GB:.e: Institute of
Corn and Agricultural Merchants
ICAMR US: e: Interdepartmental Com-
mittee for Applied Meteorological Re-
search
ICAN CO: s: Instituto Columbiano de
Asuntos Núcleares, Bogotá; INT: e:
International Commission for Air Na-
vigation [gegr 1919]
ICANA RA: US: s: Instituto Cultural
Argentino-Norte-Americano, Buenos
Aires [gegr 1927]
ICAO INT: e: International Civil Avia-
tion Organization, Montreal 3 [CDN,
gegr 1947]
ICAOPA INT: e: International Council
of Aircraft Owners and Pilot Associa-
tions
ICAR IND: e: Indian Council of Agri-
cultural Research; R: ro: Institutul
de Cercetări Agronomice al Rominiei,
Bucureşti
ICARE RCH: [e: Chilean Institute for
Rational Administration]
ICARES INT: f: Institut International
Catholique des Recherches Sociales,
Genève [CH, gegr 1936]
I.C.A.R.T. F: f: Institut Supérieur des
Carrières Artistiques, Paris 6
ICAS US: e: mil: Institute of Combined
Arms and Support, Fort Leavenworth;
US: e: Interdepartmental Committee
for Atmospheric Sciences, Washington,
D.C.; INT: e: International Council
of Aeronautical (Aerospace) Sciences
I.C.A.S. I: i: Istituto Cattolico Attività
Sociali, Roma

ICATU INT: e: International Confeder-
ation of Arab Trade Unions
ICB IND: e: Indian Coffee Board; D: e:
nach WK2: Information Control
Branch [ACA]; INT: nl: Internation-
aal Centrum van de Bosbouw; INT: e:
International Container Bureau, Paris 8
[gegr 1933]; e: International Coop-
erative Bank
ICBA INT: e: International Community
of Booksellers Associations, Delft [NL]
ICBBA US: e: International Cornish Ban-
tam Breeders' Association
ICBC INT: e: International Colorado
Beetle Committee
ICBD INT: e: International Council of
Ballroom Dancing, London [gegr 1950]
ICBO e: International Conference of
Building Officials
ICBP INT: e: International Committee
(Council) for Bird Preservation, Lon-
don SW 7 [gegr 1922]; International
Conference of Benzol(e) Producers
I.C.B.S. GB: e: Incorporated Church Build-
ing Society
I.C.B.U. e: Irish Catholic Benevolent
Union
ICC GB: e: Imperial Communication
Committee; US: e: Indian Claims
Commission; Institute of Chinese Cul-
ture; BRD: d: stud: Intercorporativer
Convent; INT: e: International Asso-
ciation for Cereal Chemistry; Interna-
tional Chamber of Commerce, F-75
Paris 8 [gegr 1920]; International
Children's Centre, Paris 16 [gegr 1950];
UN: e: International Climatological
Commission [World Meteorological
Organization]; INT: e: International
standing committee for the study of
corrosion and protection of under-
ground pipelines; International Communications Conference; UN: e: International Computation Centre, Rome
[UNESCO]; INT: e: International

Congregational Council, London [gegr 1891] ; International Consultative Committee; International Control Commission

I.C.C. d:e: Internationaler Country-Club

ICC US: e: Interstate Commerce Commission, Washington, D.C. [gegr 1887] ; US: e: mil: Inventory Control Center

ICCA RCA: f: Industrie Cotonnière Centrafricaine; US: e: Infants' and Children's Coat Association; INT: s: Instituto Centroamericano de Ciencias Agrícolas; INT: e: International Committee on Coordination for Agriculture; International Corrugated Case Association, Paris 9

ICCAM INT: e: International Committee of Children's and Adolescents' Movements

ICCASP e: Independent Citizens' Committee of the Arts, Sciences and Professions

ICCB CO: GB: s: Instituto Cultural Colombo-Británico; INT: e: International Catholic Child Bureau, Paris [gegr 1948]

ICCBC INT: e: International Committee for Colorado Beetle Control

ICCC IND: e: Indian Central Coconut Committee; UN: e: Inter-Council Coordinating Committee [UNESCO] ; INT: e: International Conference of Catholic Charities, Rome; International Council of Christian Churches [gegr 1948]

ICCE INT: e: International Council of Commerce Employers, Paris [gegr 1948]

ICCF INT: e: International Committee on Canned Food; International Correspondence Chess Federation

ICCH e: International Commodity Clearing House

ICCIA UN: e: Interim Coordinating Committee for International Commodity Arrangements, New York [ECOSOC, gegr 1947]

ICCJ INT: e: International Committee for Cooperation of Journalists

ICCL INT: e: International Committee of Comparative Law

ICCLA e: International Centre for the Coordination of Legal Assistance

ICCLA/CLC INT: e: International Committee on Christian Literature for Africa and Christian Literature Council

ICCP R: ro: Institutul de Cercetări pentru Cultura Porumbului; e: Interdepartmental Committee on Commercial Policy; INT: e: International Conference on Cataloguing Principles [IFLA] ; International Council for Children's Play

ICCS INT: e: International Centre of Criminological Studies

ICCTA UN: e: International Committee for the Coordination of Terminological Activities [UNESCO] ; INT: e: International Consultative Council of Travel Agents, London [gegr 1952]

ICCTE INT: e: International Federation of Commercial, Clerical and Technical Employees, Amsterdam [NL, gegr 1921]

ICCTU INT: e: International Confederation of Christian Trade Unions, Utrecht [NL, gegr 1920]

ICCY US: e: International Cultural Center for Youth, New York

ICD e: Information Control Division [OMGUS] ; ZA: e: International Centre for Development

I.C.D. e: International College of Dentists

ICD INT: e: International Committee of Dermatology; International Congress of Druggists; INT: f: Internationale des Coiffeurs de Dames

ICDC e: International Cable Development Corporation

ICDO INT: e: International Civil Defence Organization, Geneva [CH,gegr

1931]

ICDP INT: e: International Confederation for Disarmament and Peace, London N 3; I: i: Istituto di Credito di Diritto Pubblico

I.C.D.S. e: Industrial Civil Defence Service

ICE US: e: Institute of Ceramic Engineers; GB: e: Institute of Chemical Engineers, London

I.C.E. e: Institute of Christian Education; GB: e: Institute of Civil Engineers, London; Institution of Chemical Engineers; Institution of Civil Engineers, London

ICE INT: e: International Cultural Exchange, London W 1 [gegr 1956] ; I: i: Istituto Cattolico Educazione; Istituto Nazionale per il Commercio con l'Estero

I.C.E.B.W. BRD: d: Internationaler Club elektrostatisch beschichteter Werkstücke [Werbegag der Firma AEG, 1970]

ICEBY INT: e: International Conference for the Education of Blind Youth

ICEC INT: e: International Council for Exceptional Children

ICEC3 INT: e: Third International Cryogenic Engineering Conference and Exhibition [BlnW 1970]

ICECHIM R: ro: Institutul de Cercetări Chimice, București

ICEDS US: e: Insurance Company Education Directors Society

ICEF R: ro: Institutul de Cercetări Forestiere, București; UN: e: International Children's Emergency Fund, New York [gegr 1946] ; INT: e: International Committee for Ethnographic Films; International Council for Educational Films, Paris 5 [gegr 1950]

I.C.E.I. e: Institution of Civil Engineers of Ireland

ICEI US: e: Internal Combustion Engine Institute

ICEIL R: ro: Institutul de Cercetări și Experimentări pentru Industria Lemnului, București

I.C.E.L. GB: e: Institute of Civil Engineers in London

ICEM INT: nl: Intergouvernementele Commissie voor Europese Migratie e: Intergovernmental Committee for European Migration, 532 Bad Godesberg [BRD, gegr 1951]

ICEMEA R: ro: Institutul de Cercetări pentru Mecanizarea și Electrificarea Agriculturii, București

ICENTTO NL: nl: Interprovinciale Commissie voor Eenmaking van de Nederlandse Terminologie in het Technisch Onderwijs

ICEPROM R: ro: Institutul de Cercetări și Proiectări Metalurgice, București

ICER INT: e: Information Center of the European Railways; US: e: Institute for Central European Research; INT: e: International Conference on Electromagnetic Relays

ICES CGO: f: Institut Congolais d'Enseignement Social, Léopoldville; R: ro: Institutul de Cercetări și Experimențe Silvice, București; INT: e: International Council for the Exploration of the Sea, Charlottenlund [DK, gegr 1902]

ICESA US: e: Interstate Conference of Employment Security Agencies

ICET R: ro: Institutul de Cercetări Electrotehnice, București; INT: e: International Council on Education for Teaching

ICETEX CO: s: Instituto Colombiano de Especialización Técnica en el Exterior

ICETK INT: e: International Committee on Electrochemical Thermodynamics and Kinetics

ICETT GB: e: Industrial Council for Educational and Training Technology

ICEWG US: e: Interim Communications -Electronics Working Group

I.C.F. e: Industrial Christian Fellowship; F: f: Société des Ingénieurs Civils de France; Institut Cinématographique de France; R: ro: Institutul de Cercetări Forestiere, Bucureşti

ICF R: ro: Institutul de Cercetări Chimico-Farmaceutice, Bucureşti; INT: e: International Canoe Federation, Stockholm 7 [S, gegr 1924] ; International Federation of Chemical and General Workers' Unions, Geneva [CH, gegr 1907] ; US: e: Italian Catholic Federation

ICFA US: e: Independent College Funds of America

Icfag D: d: Internationale Continental -Film-AG, Berlin

ICFB INT: e: International Catholic Film Bureau, Brussels [B, gegr 1928]

ICFC GB: e: Industrial and Commercial Finance Corporation Ltd., London [gegr 1945]; INT: e: International Centre of Films for Children, Brussels [gegr 1957]

ICFG INT; e: International Cold Forging Group, Paris

ICFO INT: e: International Catholic Film Office

ICFPW INT: e: International Confederation of Former Prisoners of War, Paris 16 [gegr 1949]

ICFTA INT: e: International Committee of Foundry Technical Associations, Zürich 23 [CH]

ICFTU INT: e: International Confederation of Free Trade Unions, Brussels [B, gegr 1949]

ICFTU-ARO INT: e: ICFTU - Asian Regional Organization, New Delhi [IND]

ICFW INT: e: International Christian Federation of Food, Drink, Tobacco and Hotelworkers

I.C.G. GB: e: Indian Conciliation Group; Institute of Certified Grocers; Institute for Child Guidance; F: f: Institut prévisionnelle et de contrôle de gestion

ICG INT: e: International Commission on Glass, 75 Karlsruhe-Durlach [BRD, gegr 1953] ; International Congress of Genetics

I.C.G. INT: e: International Consultative Group for Peace and Disarmament, Geneva [CH, gegr 1932]

ICGA INT: e: International Classic Guitar Association

I.C.G.B.I. GB: e: Institute of Chemistry of Great Britain and Ireland

ICGEL GB: e: International Crushing and Grinding Equipment Ltd.

ICGS INT: e: International Catholic Girls Society, Fribourg [CH, gegr 1897]

I.Ch. f: Institut de Chimie

I.C.H. s: Instituto de Cultura Hispánica

I.Ch. 1: Institutum Charitatis

ICHC INT: e: International Committee for Horticultural Congresses, Den Haag [NL, gegr 1923]

ICHCA INT: e: International Cargo Handling Coordination Association, London [gegr 1952]

ICHEC B: f: Institut Catholique des Hautes Etudes Commerciales

I.Chem. E. GB: e: Institution of Chemical Engineers

IChO PL: pl: Instytut Chemii Ogólnej

ICHPER INT: e: International Council on Health, Physical Education and Recreation

ICHS INT: e: International Committee on Historical Sciences, Lausanne [CH, gegr 1926]

ICHV R: ró: Institutul de Cercetări Horti-Viticole

I.C.I. US: e: Illinois Central Industries

ICI GB: e: Imperial Chemical Industries Ltd., London

I.C.I. F: f: Inspecteur des Contributions Indirectes; GB: e: mil: Inspector of Catering in India; F: f: Institut de Coopération Intellectuelle; CO: s: Instituto de Colonización e Immigración

ICI INT: e: International Castle Research Institute [d: IBI] ; e: International Colonial Institute; INT: e: International Commission on Illumination; US: e: Investment Casting Institute, Chicago 3, Ill.; I: i: Istituto Coloniale Italiano; Istituto Cotoniero Italiano; Istituto per la Contabilità Industriale

ICIA INT: e: International Credit Insurance Association, CH-8001 Zürich US: e: International Crop Improvement Association

I.C.I.A.N.Z. AUS: e: Imperial Chemical Industries of Australia and New Zealand Ltd., Melbourne

ICIB IND: e: Indian Commercial Information Bureau

I.C.I.C. IND: e: Industrial Credit and Investment Corporation [= ICICI]

ICIC INT: e: International Commission on Irrigation and Canals

ICICI IND: e: Industrial Credit and Investment Corporation of India Ltd., Bombay [gegr 1955]

ICID INT: e: International Commission on Irrigation and Drainage, New Delhi 1 [IND, gegr 1950]

ICIDCA C: s: Instituto Cubano de Investigaciónes de los Derivados de la Caña de Azúcar, Habana

ICIE e: International Council of Industrial Editors

ICIM INT: f: Internationale des Cadres des Industries Métallurgiques, Paris

ICIMC R: ro: Institutul de Cercetări și Încercări a Materialelor de Construcții, București

ICIP INT: e: International Confederation of Intellectual Professions; International Conference on Information Processing [Paris 1959, IFIP]

ICIPU I: i: Istituto di Credito per le Imprese di Pubblica Utilità

ICIREPAT INT: e: International Cooperation in Information Retrieval between Examining Patent Officers

ICIT C: s: Instituto Cubano de Investigaciónes Tecnológicas

ICITA INT: e: International Cooperative Investigations of the Tropical Atlantic

I.C.I.T.E. I: i: Instituto Centrale per l'Industrializzazione e la Tecnologia Edilizia, Milano

ICITO INT: e: Interim Commission for the International Trade Organization, Geneva [CH]

ICIW INT: e: International Confederation of (Professional and) Intellectual Workers, Paris [gegr 1923]

ICJ INT: e: International Commission of Jurists, Den Haag [NL, gegr 1952] ; International Court of Justice, Den Haag [NL, gegr 1899]

ICJW INT: e: International Council of Jewish Women, Montreal [CDN, gegr 1912]

I.C.K. INT: eo: Internacia Centra Komitato de la Esperanto-Movado

ICL INT: e: International Christian Leadership; GB: e: International Computers Ltd., London; INT: e: International Confederation of Labor [vorher: IFCTU] ; e: Irish Central Library for Students

ICLA INT: e: International Committee on Laboratory Animals [gegr 1956] ; International Comparative Literature Association [gegr 1954]

ICLE I: i: Istituto Nazionale di Credito per il Lavoro Italiano all'Estero

ICM TN: f: Industries Chimiques Maghrébines de Tunis; INT: e: International Confederation of Midwives, London W 1; International Council for Music; INT: d: Internationaler Congress für Metallbearbeitung, Hannover [BRD, 8...11.9.1970]

I.C.M. e: Irish Church Missions

I.C.M.A. GB: e: Independent Cable Makers' Association

ICMA US: e: International Circulation Managers Association; International City Managers Association, Chicago; INT: e: International Congress for Modern Architecture

ICMC INT: e: International Catholic Migration Commission, Geneva [CH,gegr 1951]; International Circulation Mangers Commission, Paris 8

ICMCI INT: [d: Internationaler Mikrowellenkongreß, Tokio [7...11.9.1964]

ICME INT: e: International Commission for Medical Equipment

ICMEA R: ro: Institutul de Cercetări pentru Mecanizarea şi Electrificarea Agriculturii, Bucureşti

ICMF INT: e: International Colloquium on Magnetic Films

ICMICA INT: e: International Catholic Movement for Intellectual and Cultural Affairs, Fribourg [CH, gegr 1947]

ICML R: ro: Institutul de Cercetări pentru Construcţii, Materiale, Lemn, Bucureşti

ICMLF INT: e: International Catholic Migrant Loan Fund

ICMLT INT: e: International Congress of Medical Laboratory Technologists

ICMMP INT: e: mil: International Committee of Military Medicine and Pharmacy, Liège [B, gegr 1921]

ICMR IND: e: Indian Council of Medical Research

ICMS US: e: Interdepartmental Committee for Meteorological Services

ICMSA e: Irish Creamery Milk Suppliers Association

ICN INT: e: International Council of Nurses, 1200 Genève [CH, gegr 1899]

ICNA US: e: Infants and Children's Novelties Association

ICNAF INT: e: International Commission for the Northwest Atlantic Fisheries [gegr 1950]

I.C.N.D.A.F. e: Ivory Cross National Dental Aid Fund

I.C.N.E. e: Institute for Christian-National Education

ICNND US: e: mil: Interdepartmental Committee on Nutrition for National Defense

ICNT INT: e: International Committee for Natural Therapeutics

I.C.O. GB: e: Institute of Chemists-Opticians; CY: e: Insurgents' Corrective Organization

ICO US: e: Interagency Committee on Oceanography; e: Intergovernmental Committee on Oceanography; INT: e: International Chemistry Office, Paris; International Coffee Organization; International Commission on Oceanography; International Commission for Optics, Rochester, N.Y. [gegr 1948]; International Congress of Otolaryngology, Paris

ICOB NL: [f: coopérative d'achat de livres]

ICOC IND: e: Indian Central Oilseeds Committee

ICOFUND L: e: f: International Commodity Share Fund, Société Anonyme

ICOGRADA INT: e: International Council of Graphic Design Associations, Amsterdam C [NL]

I.C.O.I. GB: e: Information Council of the Optical Industry

IColaD INT: e: International Commission on Irrigation and Drainage, New Delhi

ICOLD INT: e: International Commission on Large Dams, Paris 8 [World Power Conference]

ICOM B: nl: Interdiocesane Commissie der Opiniemachten; INT: e: International Council of Museums, Paris 16 [gegr 1946]

ICOMI BR: pt: Indústria e Comércio de Minérios

ICON WAN: e: Investment Company of Nigeria Ltd.

ICONTEC CO: s: Instituto Colombiano de Normas Técnicas, Bogotá, D.E.

ICOP CO: s: Instituto Colombiano de Opinión Pública

ICOR INT: e: Intergovernmental Conference on Oceanic Research

ICOS INT: e: International Committee of Onomastic Sciences, Louvain [B, gegr 1949]

ICOTAF f: Industrie Cotonnière Africaine

ICP e: Indochinese Communist Party

I.C.P. F: f: Institut Catholique de Paris; Institut de Chimie de Paris

ICP INT: e: International Club for the Use of Plastics in Building and Construction, Liège [B] ; International Congress of Plastics; International Council of Psychologists

ICPA IND: e: Indian Commercial Pilots' Association

I.C.P.A. e: Industrial Co-Partnership Association

ICPA INT: e: International Commission for the Prevention of Alcoholism, Washington, D.C. [gegr 1953] ; International Cooperative Petroleum Association, New York [gegr 1946]

ICPB INT: [d: Internationales Komitee für Vogelschutz, London SW 7]

I.C.P.C. INT: e: International Cable Protection Committee

ICPC INT: e: International Criminal Police Commission [gegr 1923] ; US: e: mil: Inter-Range Communications Planning Committee

I.C.P.E. R: ro: Institutul de Cercetări şi proiectare pentru industria electrotechnică, Bucureşti

ICPHS INT: e: International Council for Philosophy and Humanistic Studies, Paris [gegr 1949]

ICPIGP INT: f: Internationale chrétienne professionnelle pour les industries graphiques et papétières, Amsterdam [NL, gegr 1925]

I.C.P.I.S. INT: e: International Christian Press and Information Service

ICPM INT: e: International Commission for Plant Raw Materials

ICPO INT: e: International Criminal Police Organization, 92 St.Cloud [F, gegr 1923]

ICPRB US: e: Interstate Commission on Potomac River Basin

ICPS INT: e: International Conference on the Properties of Steam, New York

ICPSH R: ro: Institutul de Cercetări şi Proiectări pentru Industria Hîrtiei, Celulozei şi Stufului, Bucureşti

ICPU INT: e: International Catholic Press Union, Paris [gegr 1936]

I.C.R. US: e: Illinois Central Railroad Company

ICR US: e: Institute for Creative Research; INT: e: International Congress of Radiology, London; International Council for Reprography

I.C.R.B. INT: e: International Centre of Rural Broadcasting, Rome [I, gegr 1936]

ICRC IND: e: Indian Cancer Research Centre; INT: e: International Committee of the Red Cross, Geneva [CH, gegr 1863]

ICRCP e: International Centre for Relief to Civilian Population

ICRDA US: e: Independent Cash Register Dealers Association

ICRE e: International Council of Religious Education

I.C.R.F. GB: e: Imperial Cancer Research Fund

ICRH INT: e: International Congress on Religious History

ICRI INT: e: International Institute for Interdisciplinary Cycle Research, Oegstgeest [NL]

ICRICE INT: e: International Centre of Research and Information on Collective Economy, Liège [B, gegr 1947]

I.C.R.K. INT: nl: Internationaal Comité van het Rode Kruis

ICRO INT: e: International Cell Research Organization

ICRP INT: e: International Commission on Radiological Protection

I.C.R.R. US: e: Illinois Central Railroad Company

ICRS INT: e: International Commission on Radium Standards

ICRSC INT: e: International Council for Research in the Sociology of Cooperation

ICRU INT: e: International Commission on Radiological Units and Measurements, Washington, D.C.

I.C.S. GB: e: Imperial College of Science, London; IND: e: Indian Ceramic Society; Indian Chemical Society; GB: e: Indian Civil Service; Institute of Chartered Shipbrokers

ICS INT: e: International Chamber of Shipping, London EC 3 [gegr 1921]; International College of Surgeons

I.C.S. e: International Confederation of Students; International Correspondence Schools; I: i: Istituto Centrale di Statistica

I.C.S.A. e: Intercollegiate Community Service Association; International Christian Social Association

ICSA e: International Civil Service Agency; INT: e: International Council for Scientific Agriculture, Rome [I, gegr 1925]

ICSAB e: International Civil Service Advisory Board

ICSB D: e: nach WK2: Intelligence Control Staff, Berlin (British): e: International Centre of School Building

ICSBC US: e: Interstate Council of State Boards of Cosmetology

ICSC IND: e: Indian Central Sugarcane Committee; R: ro: Institutul de Cercetări Științifice pentru Construcții, București; US: e: Interim Communications Satellite Committee, Washington, D.C.; INT: e: International Committee of Silent Chess; US: e: International Council of Shopping Centers

ICSCHM INT: e: International Commission for a History of the Scientific and Cultural Development of Mankind

ICSEM INT: e: International Commission for the Scientific Exploration of the Mediterranean

ICSH INT: e: International Committee on Standardization in Hematology, 78 Freiburg [BRD]

ICSHB INT: e: International Committee for Standardization in Human Biology

ICSI INT: e: International Conference (Congress) on Scientific Information

ICSID INT: e: International Council of Societies of Industrial Design, Bruxelles [B, gegr 1957]

ICSL GB: e: International Computing Services Limited

ICSM INT: e: International Committee of Scientific Management

ICSMFE INT: e: International Conference on Soil Mechanics and Foundation Engineering

ICSOR R: ro: Institutul Central pentru Proiectarea și Sistematizarea Orașelor și Regiunilor, București

ICSPE INT: e: International Council of Sports and Physical Education

ICSPRO INT: e: International Calcium Products Research Organization [gegr 1963]

ICSRD US: e: Interdepartmental Committee on Scientific Research and Development

ICSS US: e: Interuniversity Committee on the Superior Student

ICSSD INT: e: International Committee

for Social Sciences Documentation, Paris 7 [gegr 1950]

ICSSW INT: e: International Committee of Schools for Social Work

I.C.S.T. GB: e: Imperial College of Science and Technology

ICSTO GB: e: International Civil Service Training Organization

ICSU INT: e: International Christian Social Union; International Council of Scientific Unions

ICSU-AB INT: e: International Council of Scientific Unions-Abstracting Board

I.C.S.V. INT: nl: Internationaal Christelijk Sociaal Verbond d: Internationale Christlich-Soziale Vereinigung

ICSW INT: e: International Conference of Social Work, New York 17 [gegr 1928]

I.C.T. GB: e: Imperial College of Technology

ICT BRD: d: Institut für Chemie der Treib- und Explosivstoffe, 7501 Berghausen-Hummelberg

I.C.T. F: f: Institut de Chimie de Toulouse; GB: e: Institute of Clay Technology; International Computers and Tabulators Ltd., London [gegr 1960]

ICT INT: e: International Council of Tanners, London SE 1 [gegr 1926]; CH: e: Investors Capital Trust, 1200 Genève

I.C.T.A. GB: e: Imperial College of Tropical Agriculture [West Indies]

ICTA US: e: International Center for the Typographic Arts, New York [gegr 1961]; INT: e: International Confederation of Technical Agriculturists; International Cooperative Trading Agency; International Council of Travel Agents, London W 1

ICTAA GB: e: Imperial College of Tropical Agriculture Association

ICTBA US: e: Infants', Children's and Teens' Wear Buyers Association

I.C.T.C. GB: e: mil: Infantry Clerks' Training Centre, Cichester

ICTF INT: e: International Cocoa Trades Federation, London EC 3

ICTMM INT: e: International Congress on Tropical Medicine and Malaria [gegr 1913]

ICTO f: Industrie Cotonnière de l'Oubangui et du Tchad

I.C.T.R.F. e: Ice Cream and Temperance Refreshment Federation

ICTT INT: s: Internacional del Personal de los Servicios de Correos, Telégrafos y Teléfonos [Bern, CH, gegr 1920]

I.C.T.U. e: Irish Congress of Trade Unions [gegr 1959]

I.C.U. ZA: e: Industrial and Commercial Workers' Union, Kapstadt

ICU INT: e: International Chemistry Union, Paris; J: e: International Christian University d: Internationale Christliche Universität

ICUAE INT: e: International Congress of University Adult Education

ICUFON INT: e: Intercontinental Ufo [unidentified flying objects] Research Analytic Network

ICUMSA INT: e: International Commission for Uniform Methods of Sugar Analysis

I.C.U.R. F: f: Institut de Chimie de l'Université de Rennes

I.C.V. F: f: Institut Coopératif du Vin; INT: nl: Internationaal Christelijk Vakverbond

ICV INT: e: International Commission of Viticulture

ICVA e: International Council of Voluntary Agencies

I.C.W. GB: e: Institute of Clayworkers

ICW NL: nl: Instituut voor Cultuurtechniek en Waterhuishouding; INT: e: Inter-American Commission of Women, Washington, D.C.; US: e: International Chemical Workers; INT: e:

International Council of Women [gegr 1888]

ICWA IND: e: Indian Council of World Affairs, New Delhi [gegr 1943]

I.C.W.A. e: Institute of Cost and Works Accountants

ICWA US: e: Institute of Current World Affairs

ICWG INT: e: International Cooperative Women's Guild. London E 1 [gegr 1921]

ICWM INT: e: International Committee on Weights and Measures

ICWP INT: e: International Council of Women Psychologists, Washington, D.C. [gegr 1946]

I.C.W.S. INT: e: International Cooperative Wholesale Society, Ltd., Manchester [GB, gegr 1924]

ICWSG US: e: Infants' and Children's Wear Salesmen's Guild

ICWU CDN: US: International Chemical Workers' Union

I.C.Y.F. e: Inter-County Youth Federation

ICYF INT: e: International Catholic Youth Federation, Rome [I, gegr 1948]

ICZ R: ro: Institutul de Cercetări Zootehnice al Romaniei, București; INT: e: International Congress of Zoology

ICZN INT: e: International Commission for Zoological Nomenclature, London [gegr 1895]

I.D. US: e: Immigration Department; D: d: mil: Infanterie-Division

ID DDR: d: mil: Infanterie-Division; US: e: mil: Infantry Division; S: sv: mil: ingenjorsdepartementet

I.D. GB: e: mil: Inniskilling Dragoons; GB: e: Institute of Directors

ID US: e: Institute of Distribution

I.D. e: mil: Intelligence Department (Detachment) (Division)

ID N: no: Internasjonal Dugnad; e: International Department; INT: sv:

Internationella domstolen, Den Haag; e: Investigation Department

IDA IRL: e: Industrial Development Authority, Dublin 2: US: e: Industrial Diamond Association of America

I.d.A. D: d: mil: Inspekteur der Artillerie

IDA US: e: mil: Institute for Defense Analyses; INT: e: Interamerican Development Association; US: e: Intercollegiate Dramatic Association; INT: e: International Development Association, Washington, D.C. 20433 [gegr 1959] ; International Diplomatic Academy; IRL: e: Irish Dental Association; Irish Drug Association

IDAB US: e: International Development Advisory Board

I.D.A.C. GB: e: Import Duties Advisory Committee

IDACE INT: f: Association des industries des aliments diététiques de la CEE, Paris 2

IDAD BRD: d: Interessengemeinschaft der angesiedelten Deutschen

IDAF S: sv: Institutet för distributionsekonomisk och administrativ forskning, Göteborg

idaflieg BRD: d: stud: Interessengemeinschaft Deutsche Akademische Fliegergruppen eV, Braunschweig

I.D.A.M.F. e: Interdenominational African Ministers Federation

IDB CDN: e: Industrial Development Bank; INT: e: Interamerican Development Bank, Washington, D.C. 20577

IDBP PAK: e: Industrial Development Bank of Pakistan

I.D.C. GB: e: mil: Imperial Defence College; Imperial Defence Committee

IDC BUR: e: Industrial Development Corporation, Rangoon; ZA: e: Industrial Development Corporation of South Africa, Limited; INT: e: International Dairy Congress; International Danube Commission, Vienna [A, gegr 1920] ; INT: d: Internationale Dokumentations-Gesellschaft Chemie mbH, 6 Ffm [gegr 1967]

IDCA AUS: e: Industrial Design Council of Australia

I.D.C.C. J: e: Industrial Development and Consulting Company, Tokyo

I.D.C.D. e: Interdepartmental Committee of Dentistry

IDCNA US: e: Insulation Distributor Contractors National Association

IDCSP US: e: mil: Initial Defense Communications Satellite Program (Project)

I.D.D.A. GB: e: Inspectors under Dangerous Drugs Act

IDDRG INT: e: International Deep Drawing Research Group, London WC 2

I.d.E. D: d: mil: WK1: Inspektion des Eisenbahnwesens

IDE DK: f: Institut Danois des Echanges Internationaux de Publications Scientifiques et Littéraires; US: e: Institute for Democratic Education

IDEA US: e: Institute for Development of Educational Activities; s: Instituto de Estudios Africanos; US: e: International Downtown Executives Association

IDEEA US: e: mil: Information Data Exchange Experimental Activity, Frankford Arsenal, Philadelphia, Pa.

Idegahei D: d: mil: WK1: Inspektion des Gasschutzdienstes für das Heimatgebiet

Ideis D: d: mil: WK1: Inspektion des Eisenbahnwesens

IDEO DOM: [f: Institut Dominicain d'Etudes Orientales]

IDEP US: e: mil: Interservice Data Exchange Program

IDERSOM B: f: Institut Belge pour l'Encouragement de la Recherche Scientifique Outre-Mer, Bruxelles

IDERT f: Institut d'Enseignement et de Recherches Tropicales

I.d.F. D: d: mil: WK1: Inspektion der Fliegertruppen

IDF INT: e: International Dairy Federation, Brussels [B, gegr 1903] ; International Democratic Fellowship, London [gegr 1955] ; International Dental Federation, Brussels [B, gegr 1900] ; International Diabetes Federation, Den Haag [NL, gegr 1949] ; INT: d: Internationale Düsseldorfer Fachmessen [BRD] ; e: mil: Israeli Defense Force

IDFA BRD: d: Interessengemeinschaft Deutscher Fachmessen und Ausstellungsstädte, 7 Stuttgart 1

I.D.F.A. IRL: e: Irish Dryers and Finishers Association

IDFF INT: d: Internationale Demokratische Frauenföderation, 108 Berlin [DDR, gegr 1945]

IDFM BRD: d: Internationale Deutsche Fotoamateur-Meisterschaft

IdG NL: nl: mil: Inspectie der Genie

I.d.G. D: d: mil: Inspektor der Garnisonverwaltung

IDH e: Infectious Diseases Hospital; DDR: d: Gesellschaft für Innerdeutschen Handel; Innerdeutscher Handel; BRD: d: Interessenvereinigung Deutscher Homophiler eV

I.D.H.E.C. F: f: Institut des Hautes Etudes Cinématographiques, Paris

IDI US: e: Industrial Designers Institute [gegr 1938] ; F: f: Institut de développement industriel; INT: f: Institut de Droit International, Genève [CH, gegr 1873] s: Instituto de Derecho Internacional

I.D.I. e: Insurance Department and Inspectorate

IDI INT: e: International Development and Investment Company; I: i: Istituto del Dramma Italiano; Istituto Dinamometrico Italiano

IDIB GB: e: Industrial Diamond Information Bureau

IDICT C: s: Instituto de Documentación Científica y Técnica [gegr 1962]

IDIEM RCH: s: Instituto de investigaciónes y ensayes de materiales, Santiago

IDIL NL: nl: Informationsdienst inzake lectuur

IdInt NL: nl: mil: Inspectie der Intendance

IDIS e: International Dairy Industry Society

IDJE BRD: d: Internationaler Diakonischer Jugendeinsatz, 2 Hamburg 22

I.d.K. D: d: Inspekteur der Kavallerie

IDK d: Interessengemeinschaft (Interessenverband) Deutscher Komponisten

IdK INT: d: Internationale der Kriegsdienstgegner, Enfield [GB, gegr 1921]

IDK H: hu: Irodalomtörténeti Dokumentációs Központ, Budapest

IDL US: e: Instrument Development Laboratories, Inc., Attleboro, Mass.; BRD: d: Interessengemeinschaft der Lohnsteuerzahler

I.D.L.F. e: Irish Distressed Ladies' Fund

IDLIS INT: e: International Desert Locust Information Service

IDMA INT: e: International Dancing Masters Association

I.D.N. F. f: Institut Industriel du Nord de la France

I.D.N.B. B: nl: Informatiedienst voor Nederlands België, Gent

IDI CDN: e: Industrial Development Office

I.d.O. D: d: Inspekteur der Ordnungspolizei

IDO INT: e: International Dental Organization; International Disarmament Organization [planned]; INT: d: Internationale Detektiv-Organisation, 4407 Emsdetten

IDOC; **Idoc** Internationales Kirchliches Dokumentationszentrum, Rom

IDOE INT: e: International Decade of Ocean Exploration

IDORT BR: pt: Instituto de Organização Racional do Trabalho, São Paulo

I.D.P. F: f: Institut Dentaire de Paris

IDR A: d: Interessenverband der Radiohörer, Wien 1; e: International Dental Relief

IDRB US: e: Industrial Design Registration Bureau

IDRES US: e: Institute for the Development of Riverine and Estuarine Systems

IDS BRD: d: stud: Initiativausschuß Deutscher Studentenschaften [gegr 1969]

I.D.S. F: f: Inspection Départementale de la Santé

IdS. D: d: WK2: Inspekteur der Sicherheitspolizei

IDS D: d: Interessengemeinschaft der Sperrholzfabriken; INT: d: International Dendrology Society, London WC 2; e: International Development Services; US: e: Investory Diversified Services, Inc.,Minneapolis 2, Minn.

IDSA IND: e: Indian Dairy Science Association; US: e: Information and Data Systems Agency; International Development Service of America

IDSCS US: e: mil: Initial Defense Satellite Communications System

I.d.Sipo u.d.SD D: d: WK2: Inspekteur der Sicherheitspolizei und des Sicherheitsdienstes

IDSO INT: d: Internationale Diamanten-Sicherheits-Organisation

IDT R: ro: Institutul de Documentare Tehnică, București

I.D.T.M.O. F: f: mil: Inspection Divisionnaire du Travail et de la Main-d'Œuvre

IDTW CDN: US: e: International Union of Doll and Toy Workers of the United States and Canada

I.D.U. F: f: Inspecteur Départemental

de l'Urbanisme
IDU BRD: d: Interessengemeinschaft der Urheber, Berlin [gegr 1968] ; INT: e: International Dendrology Union; INT: nl: Internationale Demokratische Unie
IDV; idv DDR: d: Institut für Datenverarbeitung, Dresden
IdW d: Institut der Wirtschaftsprüfer
IDW BRD: d: Institut für Dokumentationswesen, 6 Ffm-Niederrad
IDZ BlnW: d: Internationales Design -Zentrum Berlin eV [gegr 1969]
I.E. GB: e: Institute of Electronics; Institute of Export; f: Institut Egyptien; Institut Electrotechnique
IE³ US: e: Institute of Electrical and Electronic Engineers [=IEEE]
I.E.A. IND: e: Indian Economic Association
IEA GB: e: Institute of Economic Affairs, London SW 1; AUS: e: Australian Institution of Engineers; BR: pt: Instituto de Energia Atómica, São Paulo; s: Instituto de Estudios Africanos; RA: s: Instituto de Experimentaciones Agropecuarias; GB: e: Instruments, Electronics, Automation [international exhibition, London] ; INT: e: International Economic Association, Paris 8 [gegr 1949] ; e: International Electrical Association; INT: d: Internationale Elektrotechnische Ausstellung; INT: e: International Entomological Association; International Ergonomics Association; US: e: International Executives Association
IEAF e: mil: Imperial Ethiopian Air Force
IEAG EC: s: Instituto Ecuatoriano de Antropología y Geografía
I.E.Aust. AUS: e: Australian Institution of Engineers
IEAV INT: d: Internationaler Eisenbahn -Alkoholgegner-Verband
IEAZ RA: s: Instituto Experimental de Agricultura Zootécnica

IEB US: e: Industry Evaluation Board
I.E.B. F: f: Institut d'Etude des Biocatalysateurs, Paris; BR: pt: Instituto de Estudos Brasileiros
IEB INT: d: Interamerikanische Entwicklungsbank, Washington, D.C.; e: International Education Board; I: i: Istituto di Entomologia, Bologna
I.E.C. GB: e: Imperial Economic Committee; RCB: f: Institut d'Etudes Centrafricaines, Brazzaville
IEC INT: e: International Economic Conference; International Egg Commission; International Electrotechnical Commission, Genève [CH, gegr 1906]
I.E.C. e: International Emergency Committee
IEC US: e: International Equipment Company; e: International Exchange Committee; US: e: Interstate Electronics Corporation, Anaheim, Calif.
IECAMA ETH: e: Imperial Ethiopian College of Agriculture and Mechanical Arts
IED GB: e: Institution of Engineering Designers; INT: e: International Electronic Devices Conference
IEDA DZ: f: Institut d'Etudes du Développement Africain, Alger
IEDD GB: e: Institution of Engineering Draughtsmen and Designers
IEDP E: s: Instituto Español de Derecho Procesal
IEE BRD: d: e: Installation Efficiency Engineering Betriebsberatung GmbH, 4 Düsseldorf
I.E.E. f: Institut d'Economie Européenne; GB: e: Institute of Economic Engineering
IEE US: e: Institute of Electrical Engineers, New York; Institute of Environmental Engineers; GB: e: Institution of Electrical Engineers, London WC 2: INT: e: International

Employment Exchange [gegr 1950]

IEEE US: e: Institute of Electrical and Electronic Engineers, New York; E: s: Instituto Español del Envase y Embalaje

IEEF INT: [d: Internationaler Eisenbahner-Esperantisten-Verband]

IEES US: e: International Educational Exchange Service [Department of State]

I.E.E.T.A. F: f: mil: Inspection des Etudes et des Expériences Techniques de l'Artillerie

I.E.F. e: mil: Indian Expeditionary Force; F: f: Inspection des Eaux-et-Forêts

IEF INT: e: International Equestrian Federation

I.E.F. I: eo: Itala Esperanto-Federacio; e: mil: Italian Expeditionary Force; TR: tr: Izmir Enternasyonal Fuari

IEFC UN: e: International Emergency Food Committee (Council), Washington, D.C.

IEG GB: e: Information Exchange Group

I.E.G. F.: f: Institut Electrotechnique de Grenoble

IEG BRD: d: Intererdgas GmbH

IEGSP F: f: Union Intercommunale pour l'Etude et la Gestion des Services Publics à Caractère Industrial et Communal

IEH s: Instituto de Estudios Hispánicos

IEI GB: e: Institute of Engineering Inspection, London

I.E.I. F: f: Institut d'Estétique Industrielle

IEI INT: e: International Enamellers Institute; INT: d: Internationales Esperanto-Institut   e: International Esperanto Institute; I: i: Istituto di Economia Internazionale

IEIA INT: e: International Export-Import Association

IEIC GB: e: Institution of Engineers-in-Charge

I.E.I.I. e: Institution of Engineering Inspection Incorporated

IEK INT: d: Internationales Exekutiv-Komitee

IEKV INT: d: Internationale Eisenbahn-Kongreß-Vereinigung, Brüssel [B, gegr 1884]

IEL GB: e: Industrial Exhibitions Limited, London W 1; YU: sn: Institut za Elektrozveze, Ljubljana

I.E.L. INT: eo: Internacia Esperanto-Ligo

IELA INT: e: International English Language Association, London W 1

IEMA IND: e: Indian Electrical Manufacturers' Association

IEMAC ET: IL: e: mil: Israeli-Egyptian Mixed Armistice Commission

IEMC US: e: Industrial Equipment Manufacturers Council

I.E.M.E. GB: e: mil: Inspectorate of Electrical and Mechanical Equipment

IEME E: s: Instituto Español de Moneda Extranjera

IEMEMC GB: e: mil: Instrument, Electrical and Miscellaneous Equipment Modification Committee

I.E.M.L. F: f: Institut Electromécanique de Lille

IEMVT F: f: Institut d'Elevage et de Médecine Vétérinaire Tropicaux

I.E.M.W. A: eo: Internacia Esperanto-Museo en Wien

I.E.N. F: f: Institut Electrotechnique de Nancy; I: i: Istituto per l'Energia Nucleare

IENA INT: d: Internationale Erfinder- und Neuheiten-Ausstellung, Nürnberg [BRD]

IENGF I: i: Istituto Elettrotecnico Nazionale "Galileo Ferraris", Torino

I.E.N.S. e: Indian and Eastern Newspapers Society

I.E.O. F: f: Institut d'Etudes Occitanes, Toulouse

IEO INT: e: Union of International Engineering Organizations, Paris

IEOS SU: [e: Institute of Elemental -Organic Compounds]

I.E.P. F: f: Institut d'Etudes Politiques [Université de Paris] ; INT: f: Institut Européen pour la Promotion des Entreprises, Paris

IEPA US: e: International Economic Policy Association

IER US: e: Institute of Engineering Research; US: e: mil: Institute for. Exploratory Research, Fort Monmouth, N.J.

I.E.R. F: f: Institut des Etudes Rhodaniennes [Université de Lyon]

I.E.R.A.C. EC: s: Instituto Ecuatoriano de Reforma Agraria y Colonización

IERC US: e: International Electronic Research Corporation, Burbank, Calif.

IERE GB: e: Institution of Electronic and Radio Engineers, London WC 1

IEREGEM RCB: f: Institut Equatorial de Recherches et d'Etudes Géologiques et Minières, Brazzaville

IERGM f: Institut Equatorial de Recherches Géologiques et Minières

IERI US: e: Illuminating Engineering Research Institute, New York

I.E.R.N. f: Institut Européen pour la Recherche Nucléaire

IES AUS: e: Illuminating Engineering Societies of Australia, Melbourne; GB: e: Illuminating Engineering Society, London; US: e: Illuminating Engineering Society, New York

I.E.S. GB: e: Indian Educational Service

IES US: e: Institute of Environmental Sciences; S: sv: Institutet för engelsktalande studerande, Stockholm; GB: e: Institution of Engineers and Shipbuilders in Scotland; e: International Employment Service; US: e: Iowa Engineering Society

IESA US: e: Insurance Economics Society of America

IESC US: e: International Executive Service Corps [gegr 1964]

IESE E: s: Instituto de Estudios Superiores de la Empresa, Barcelona

I.E.S.N.E.C. GB: e: Institution of Engineers and Shipbuilders of the North -East Coast

I.E.S.S. GB: e: Institution of Engineers and Shipbuilders in Scotland

IESSA P: pt: Instituto de Educação e Serviço Social de Angola

IESSM P: pt: Instituto de Educação e Serviço Social de Moçambique

IEST 68 INT: d: Internationale Essener Song-Tage [25...29.9.1968]

I.E.S.T.O. F: f: Institut d'Etudes Supérieures de Techniques d'Organisation, Paris 3

IESUA DZ: f: Institut de l'Energie Solaire de l'Université d'Alger

I.E.T. F: f: Institut Electrotechnique de Toulouse

IETI INT: d: Intereuropäische Triennale der Jugendbuch-Illustratoren

IETK INT: d: Internationales Eisenbahn -Transportkomitee

IEV BR: pt: Instituto Experimental de Veterinária; INT: d: Internationale Eisenbahnkongreßvereinigung, Brüssel [B, gegr 1885] ; Internationale Eislauf-Vereinigung, Stockholm; Internationaler Eisenbahnverband, Paris [gegr 1922] ; Internationaler Eisschießverband

IEW INT: e: International Federation of Evangelical Workers' Associations, Utrecht [NL]

IEY1970 UN: e: International Education Year [UNESCO]

IF S: sv: idrottsförening

I.F. GB: e: mil: Imperial Forces; Indian Forces

iF BRD: d: Sonderschau "Die gute Industrieform" [Hannovermesse]

I.F. GB: e: mil: The Royal Inniskilling Fusiliers; GB: e: Institute of Fuel; F: f: Institut de France

IF R: ro: Institutul de Fiziologie, Bucureşti; INT: d: Internationaler Fliegerbund [gegr 1926]

I.F. e: International Fellowship; Iran Foundation; d: Italienischer Fußballverband

I.F.A. GB: e: Incorporated Faculty of Arts; IND: e: Indian Football Association

IFA US: e: Industrial Forestry Association; DDR: d: Industrieverwaltung Fahrzeugbau [jetzt:] Volkseigene Betriebe für Fahrzeugbau

I.F.A. GB: e: Institute of Foreign Affairs; F: f: Institut Français de l'Alcool

IFA DDR: d: Institut für Ausbautechnik im Hochbau, Dresden

IfA BRD: d: Institut für Automation der deutschen Sparkassen- und Girozentralen, 6 Ffm

IFA BRD: d: Institut für Automation IFA Beratungsgesellschaft für Automation mbH, 4 Düsseldorf; CO: s: Instituto de Fomento Algodonero; N: no: Institutt for Atomenergi, Kjeller [gegr 1948]; R: ro: Institutul de Fizică Atomică, Măgurele-Bucureşti; US: e: Intercollegiate Fencing Association; BRD: d: Interessengemeinschaft freier Aktionäre eV; D: d: Interessengemeinschaft für Arbeiterkultur, Berlin; BRD: d: Interessengemeinschaft für Handwerksarbeit, 2 Hamburg; Internationale Fachring-Handels-GmbH, Osnabrück [gegr 1960]

Ifa D: d: Internationale Film-AG, Berlin

IFA d: Internationale Film-Allianz; BRD: d: Internationale Fotoausstellung, München

I.F.A. INT: d: Internationaler Fachausschuß für Arbeiterhandball

IFA INT: e: International Federation of Actors, Paris 16; International Fertility Association, Buenos Aires [RA, gegr 1951]; International Finn Association; International Fiscal Association, Amsterdam C [NL, gegr 1938]; International Food Association; International Friendship Association [gegr 1926]; IRL: e: Irish Features Agency [d: Nachrichtenagentur]

IfaA BRD: d: Institut für angewandte Arbeitswissenschaft (IfaA) eV, 5038 Rodenkirchen

IfaB D: d: Institut für angewandte Botanik, Hamburg

IfA-BAU BRD: d: Institut für Arbeits- und Baubetriebswissenschaft, 7 Stuttgart 1

IFABO A: d: Internationale Fachausstellung für Büroorganisation, Wien

I.F.A.B.S.M. e: Incorporated Federated Association of Boot and Shoe Manufacturers

I.F.A.C. F: f: Institut Français d'Action Coopérative; Institut des Fruits et Agrumes Coloniaux [später:] Institut Français de Recherches Fruitières Outre-Mer, Paris

IFAC INT: e: International Federation of Advertising Clubs; International Federation of Automatic Control, 4 Düsseldorf 10 [BRD, gegr 1957]

I.F.A.C. e: International Fellowship in Arts and Crafts

IFACP F: RA: [d: französisch-argentinisches Institut für Berufsausbildung, Buenos Aires]

IFADA BRD: d: Internationale Fachausstellung der Damenhutindustrie, 5 Köln

IFAFP INT: e: International Federation of Associations of Film Producers

IfAG BRD: d: Institut für Angewandte Geodäsie, 6 Ffm

Ifage BRD: d: Ifage-Filmproduktion, Internationale Fernseh-Agentur GmbH, 62 Wiesbaden

Ifago D: d: Industriefinanzierungs-AG Ost, Berlin

IFAK BRD: d: Institut für Absatzforschung Andreas Ketels, 62 Wiesbaden

IFAK-HANSA BRD: d: Institut für Absatzforschung Andreas Ketels, 2 Hamburg 22

IFAL f: Institut Français d'Amérique Latine

IFALPA INT: e: International Federation of Air Line Pilots Associations, London W 2 [gegr 1948]

IFALS INT: e: International Federation of Arts, Letters and Sciences

IFAM BRD: d: Internationale Fotoamateur-Meisterschaft [Zeitschrift hobby, 7 Stuttgart 1]

IFAN F: f: Institut Français d'Afrique Noire

I.F.A.O. f: Institut Français d'Archéologie Orientale du Caire

I.F.A.O.M. F: f: mil: Inspection des Forces Aériennes d'Outre-Mer

IFAP INT: nl: Internationale Federatie der Agrarische Producenten, Washington, D.C. [gegr 1946] e: International Federation of Agricultural Producers

IFAS BRD: d: Institut für Angewandte Sozialwissenschaft, 53 Bonn-Bad Godesberg; L: e: International Financial Advisory Service, Luxembourg

IFAT F: f: Institut Français d'Amérique Tropicale, Cayenne; BRD: d: Internationale Fachmesse für Abwassertechnik, München

IFATCA INT: e: International Federation of Air Traffic Controllers Associations, 505 Porz-Wahn [BRD, gegr 1961]

IFATCC INT: e: International Federation of Associations of Textile Chemists and Colourists, 4000 Basel 7 [CH]

IFATU INT: e: International Federation of Arab Trade Unions

IFAWPCA INT: e: International Federation of Asian and Western Pacific Contractors Associations

IfB DDR: d: Institut für Bedarfsforschung; BRD: d: Institut für Betriebsgestaltung GmbH, 7323 Boll

ifb CH: d: Institut für Betriebswissenschaft, 9000 St.Gallen

IFB s: Instituto Filosófico Balmesiano; BlnW: d: Internationale Filmfestspiele Berlin; e: International Film Bureau

Ifbeg D: d: Industriegesellschaft für bedruckte Gewebe mbH, Berlin

I.F.B.O.A. INT: e: International Federation of Bank Officials' Associations

IFBPW INT: e: International Federation of Business and Professional Women [gegr 1930]

IFBWW INT: e: International Federation of Building and Woodworkers [gegr 1891]

I.F.C. F: f: Institut Français du Caoutchouc, Paris; da: International Faglig Central

IFC INT: e: International Fashion Council; International Finance Corporation, Washington, D.C. 20433 [gegr 1956]; International Fisheries Commission

I.F.C. INT: e: International Food Conference

IFC e: International Formulation Committee; International Freighting Corporation

IFCA e: International Federation of Catholic Alumnae

IFCATI INT: e: International Federation of Cotton and Allied Textile Industries, Zürich [CH]

IFCC F: f: Institut Français du Café, du Cacao et autres plantes stimulantes; INT: e: International Federation of Camping and Caravanning, Brussels;

International Federation of Children's Communities, Paris [gegr 1948]; International Federation of Culture Collections of Microorganisms

IFCCA INT: e: International Federation of Community Centre Associations

IFCCTE INT: e: International Federation of Commercial, Clerical and Technical Employees, Genève [CH, gegr 1921]

I.F.C.E. F: f: Institut Français des Combustibles et de l'Energie, Paris

IFCE INT: e: International Federation of Consulting Engineers

IFCJ INT: e: International Federation of Catholic Journalists, Paris 2 [gegr 1926]

I.F.C.L. e: International Fixed Calendar League

IFCM INT: e: International Federation of Christian Metalworkers Unions, Luxembourg [gegr 1920]

IFCMU INT: e: International Federation of Christian Miners' Unions, Luxembourg [gegr 1901]

IFCO US: e: Interreligious Foundation for Community Organization

IFCP INT: e: International Federation of Catholic Pharmacists

I.F.C.S. B: f: Institut de Formation Coloniale et Sociale

I.F.C.T. F: f: Institut Français de Coopération Technique

IFCTIO US: e: International Federation of Commercial Travelers Insurance Organizations

IFCTU INT: e: International Federation of Christian Trade Unions, Brussels [B, gegr 1920]

IFCTUBWW INT: e: International Federation of Christian Trade Unions of Building and Wood Workers [gegr 1937]

IFCTUGPI INT: e: International Federation of Christian Trade Unions of Tex-

Graphical and Paper Industries, Amsterdam [NL, gegr 1925]

IFCTUSETMSCT INT: e: International Federation of Christian Trade Unions of Salaried Employees, Technicians, Managerial Staff and Commercial Travellers

IFCTUTCW INT: e: International Federation of Christian Trade Unions of Textile and Clothing Workers

IFCTUTGW INT: e: International Federation of Christian Trade Unions of Textile and Garment Workers [gegr 1901]

IFCUAW INT: e: International Federation of Christian Unions of Agricultural Workers, Brussels [B]

IFCWU INT: e: International Federation of Catholic Workers Unions

IFCY INT: e: International Federation of Catholic Youth

IfD BRD: d: Institut für Demoskopie, Gesellschaft zum Studium der öffentlichen Meinung, 7753 Allensbach

IFD DDR: d: Institut für Dokumentation, Berlin; INT: d: Internationale Föderation des Dachdeckerhandwerks,Wien 1; INT: e: International Federation for Documentation

IFDA US: e: Institutional Food Distributors of America

I.F. & D.B.D. GB: e: mil: Inspector of Fortifications and Director of Bomb Disposal

IFDU BRD: d: Institut für den Unterrichtsfilm, 8 München

IfE DDR: d: Institut für Energetik, Leipzig

I.F.E. GB: e: Institution of Fire Engineers; PA: s: Instituto do Fomento Econômico

IFE BRD: d: Interessenverband der Freiwilligeneinheiten, Mainz; INT: nl: Internationale Federatie van Esperantisten; US: e Italian Films Export

[gegr 1951]

I.F.E.C. F: f: Institut Français de l'Emballage et du Conditionnement; Institut des Frères des Ecoles Chrétiennes

IFEC INT: e: International Food Emergency Committee

IFEES INT: e: International Federation of Electro-Encephalographical Societies

I.F.E.F. INT: eo: Internacia Federacio Esperantista Fervojista

I.F.E.I. I: i: Istituto Finanziario Edilizio Italiano

IFEMA US: e: Industrial Finishing Equipment Manufacturers Association; e: International Fund for Equipment and Mutual Aid

IFEMS INT: e: International Federation of Electron Microscope Societies, Cambridge [GB, gegr 1951]

IFEO INT: e: International Federation of Eugenic Organizations

IFES INT: e: International Federation of Evangelical Students

IFET INT: e: International Federation of Employers and Technicians, Amsterdam [NL, gegr 1921]

IFEWA INT: e: International Federation of Evangelical Workers' Associations

IFF DDR: d: Institut für Förderungstechnik, Leipzig; BRD: d: Institut für Führungsberatung, 61 Darmstadt; INT: d: Internationale Frauen-Föderation; Internationale Industriefilm -Festspiele; INT: e: International Fencing Federation, Paris [gegr 1913]; e: International Film Foundation; INT: sv: Internationella försoningsförbundet

I.F.F.A. F: f: Institut Française de la Fièvre Aphteuse

Iffa; IFFA BRD: d: Institut für forstliche Arbeitswissenschaft, 2057 Reinbek

IFFA INT: d: Internationale Fleischer(ei)

-Fachausstellung, 8 München [BRD];
INT: e: International Federation of Film Archives [gegr 1938]

I.F.F.E.T. F: f: Institut Français du Film Educatif et Technique

IFFF INT: d: Internationale Frauenliga für Frieden und Freiheit, Genf [CH]

I.F.F.I. F: f: Institut Français du Froid Industriel

IFFJ INT: e: International Federation of Free Journalists of Central Europe and Eastern Europe and Baltic and Balkan Countries, New York [gegr 1948]

IFFJP INT: e: International Federation of Fruit Juice Producers, Paris

IFFPA INT: e: International Federation of Film Producers' Associations

IFFS INT: e: International Federation of Film Societies

IFFTU INT: e: International Federation of Free Teachers' Unions, Bruxelles [B, gegr 1951]

IfG CS: d: Institut für Gewerbeförderung, Reichenberg; A: d: Institut für Gewerbeforschung, Wien 19

IFG RA: s: Instituto de Fisiografia y Geologia; BRD: d: Interregional Fluggesellschaft mbH, 4 Düsseldorf

IFGA INT: e: International Federation of Grocers' Associations, Bern [CH, gegr 1927]

IFGO INT: e: International Federation of Gynaecology and Obstetrics, Geneva [CH, gegr 1954]

IFGVP INT: e: International Federation of Gastronomical and Vinicultural Press, Paris 7

IFH INT: d: Internationale Föderation des Handwerks

IFHE INT: e: International Federation of Home Economics, Paris 11 [gegr 1908]

IFHP; IFHTP INT: e: International Federation for Housing and Town Planning, Den Haag [NL]

I.F.I. GB: e: Imperial Forestry Institute

IFI US: e: Industrial Fasteners Institute, Cleveland, Ohio; Information for Industry Ltd.; BRD: d: Interessengemeinschaft für Indianerkunde; INT: d: Internationale Föderation der Innenarchitekten, Schaffhausen [CH, gegr 1963] e: International Federation of Interior Designers; CH: d: Internationales Fernlehr-Institut, Baden; I: i: Istituto Finanziario Industriale, S.p.A., Torino; Istituto Farmacoterapico Italiano

IFIA INT: e: International Federation of Ironmongers and Iron-Merchants Associations, Zürich 1 [CH]

IFIDA US: e: Independent Film Importers and Distributors of America

I.F.I.E. s: Instituto Forestal de Investigaciónes y Experiencias

IFIE INT: e: International Federation of Industrial Employers

IFIF INT: d: Internationale Föderation von Industriegewerkschaften und Fabrikarbeiterverbänden, Amsterdam [NL, gegr 1907]

I.F.I.F. US: e: International Federation for Internal Freedom

IFIG INT: d: Internationale Forschungs- und Informationsstelle für Gemeinwirtschaft, Lüttich [B]

Ifil I: i: Istituto Finanziario Italiano Laniero S.p.A., Milano [gegr 1919]

IFIP INT: e: International Association for Information Processing

IFIP/ICC INT: e: IFIP/International Computation Center

IFIPS INT: e: International Federation of Information Processing Societies

I.Fire E. GB: e: Institution of Fire Engineers

IFIS INT: e: International Food Information Service [gegr 1969]

IFIWA INT: e: International Federation

of Importers and Wholesale Grocers Associations, Brussels 7 [B]

IFJ INT: e: International Federation of Journalists, Brussels [B, gegr 1952]

IFJAFC INT: e: International Federation of Journalists of Allied or Free Countries [gegr 1941]

IFJU = IFFJP

IFK BRD: d: Industrieverband Füllhalter und Kugelschreiber eV; INT: d: Installationsfragen-Kommission [gegr 1926]

IfK DDR: d: Institut für Körpererziehung; D: d: Deutsches Institut für Konjunkturforschung, Berlin [gegr 1925, ab Ende 1941: Deutsches Institut für Wirtschaftsforschung]

IFKAB INT: nl: Internationale Federatie van Katholieke Arbeiders Bewegingen, Brussel [gegr 1950]

IFKh SU: [e: Institute of Physical Chemistry]

IFKM INT: e: Internationale Föderation für Kurzschrift und Maschinenschreiben [gegr 1954, e: IFST, = INTERSTENO]

I.F.L. IND: e: Indian Federation of Labour

I.f.L. D: d: Institut für Leibesübungen, Berlin

IFL GB: e: Institute of Fluorescent Lighting; BRD: d: Institut für Führungslehre der Technischen Akademie eV, 56 Wuppertal

IfL BRD: d: Institut für Landeskunde, 53 Bonn-Bad Godesberg; DDR: d: Institut für Lehrerbildung; Institut für Leichtbau und ökonomische Verwendung von Werkstoffen, Dresden

IFL INT: d: Internationale Frauenliga; INT: e: International Fellowship League d: Internationale Freundschaftsliga, London W 3 [gegr 1931]; INT: e: International Federation of Lithographers, Process Workers and Kindred Trades; International Friendship League [=International Fellowship League]

IFLA INT: e: International Federation of Landscape Architects, London WC 1 [gegr 1948] ; International Federation of Library Associations, London WC 1

Iflakheim D: d: mil: WK1: Inspektion der Flugzeugabwehr (kanonen) in der Heimat

Iflakop D: d: mil: WK1: Inspektion der Flugzeugabwehr(kanonen) im Operationsgebiet

IFLFF INT: d; Internationale Frauenliga für Frieden und Freiheit, Genf [CH, gegr 1915]

IFLS INT: e: International Federation of Law Students, Louvain [B]

IF&LW; IFLWU CDN: US: e: International Fur and Leather Workers' Union

IFM F: MEX: f: Institut Franco-Mexicain de Formation Professionnelle; INT: d: Internationale Fördermittelmesse , Basel [CH] ; INT: e: International Falcon Movement [gegr 1947] ; International Federation of Musicians

IFMA US: e: Institutional Food Manufacturers Association; INT: d: In - ternationale Fahrrad- und Motorrad -Ausstellung [BRD]

IfMB BRD: d: Informationskurs für Moderne Betriebswirtschaft der Arbeitsgemeinschaft Wirtschaft, 6 Ffm

IFMC INT: e: International Folk Music Council, London W 2 [gegr 1947]

IFME INT: e: International Federation for Medical Electronics

IFMP INT: e: International Federation for Medical Psychotherapy

IFMSA INT: e: International Federation of Medical Student Associations [gegr 1950]

IFNSA INT: e: International Federation of the National Standardizing Associations

I.F.O. F: f: Institut Français d'Océanie, Nouméa

Ifo BRD: d: Ifo – Institut für Wirtschaftsforschung, 8 München 27; D: d: Interessengemeinschaft für Oberschlesien

IFO INT: d: Internationale Filmorganisation; Internationale Flüchtlingsorganisation [UN] ; e: International Farmers Organization

IFOCAP F: f: Institut de Formation pour des Cadres Paysans

IFOFSAG INT: e: International Fellowship of Former Scouts and Guides

IFOG INT: e: International Federation of Olive Growers, Rome [I]

IFOP F: f: Institut Français de l'Opinion Publique; e: International Federation of Oriental Press

IFOR INT: e: International Fellowship of Reconciliation, London

IFORS INT: e: International Federation of Operational Research Societies, Paris 16 [gegr 1958]

IFOSA INT: e: International Federation of Stationers' Associations

IFOSCE INT: e: International Federation of Organizations for School Correspondence and Exchange

I.f.o.W. D: d: Institut für ostdeutsche Wirtschaft, Königsberg i.Pr.

I.F.P. F: f: Institut Français du Pétrole, des Carburants et Lubrifiants, Paris [gegr 1944] ; Institut Français de Photographie, Paris 16

IFP BRD: d: Institut für Plasmaphysik GmbH, 8 München

IFPA US: e: Industry Film Producers Association

IFPAAW INT: e: International Federation of Plantation, Agricultural and Allied Workers

IFPCS INT: e: International Federation of Unions of Employees in Public and Civil Service, London [gegr 1935]

IFPCW INT: e: International Federation

of Petroleum and Chemical Workers, Denver 2, Colo. [US]

IFPE US: e: Institute of Fiscal and Political Education

IFPEC US: e: Independent Film Producers Export Corporation

IFPI INT: e: International Federation of the Phonographic Industry, London

IFPLVB INT: d:Internationale Föderation der Plantagen- und Landarbeiter und verwandter Berufsgruppen

IFPM INT: e: International Federation of Physical Medicine, London [gegr 1950]

IFPRA INT: e: Inter-American Federation of Public Relations Associations

IFPW INT: e: International Federation of Petroleum Workers, Denver, Colo.

I.F.R. GB: e: Indian Famine Relief

IFR BRD: d: Institut Dr. Förster, Reutlingen

IfR DDR: d: Institut für Regelungstechnik; BRD: d: Institut für Rundfunktechnik GmbH, München, Hamburg

IFR INT: d: Internationaler Frauenrat, Paris 9 [gegr 1888] ; INT: e: International Federation of Radio Officers, London

IFRA CH: d: Institut für Rationelle Arbeitstechnik AG, CH-8125 Zollikerberg/Zürich

IFRABA BRD: d: Internationale Frankfurter Briefmarkenausstellung [1953]

IFRB INT: e: International Frequency Registration Board, Geneva [CH, gegr 1947]

IFRF INT: e: International Flame Research Foundation, Ijmuiden [NL]

World index of social science institutions
(Internationales Verzeichnis der sozialwissenschaftlichen Institutionen)

1970. Unesco, Paris. Ca. 1000 Karteikarten in Leinenordner 26,5 x 19,5 DM 52,–

Dieses Verzeichnis enthält auf über 1000 Karteikarten detaillierte Angaben zu all den sozialwissenschaftlichen Forschungs-, Ausbildungs- und Dokumentationsinstitutionen, für die dem sozialwissenschaftlichen Dokumentationszentrum der Unesco bis Juni 1970 Informationen zur Verfügung standen.

Alle Angaben basieren auf dem Material, das die jeweiligen Institutionen selbst zur Verfügung stellten. Es wurden auch alle noch tätigen Körperschaften, die vor der Erstellung des vorliegenden Index in den Berichten des „International Social Science Journal" beschrieben wurden (mit Quellenangabe) aufgenommen.

Das Karteikartensystem erlaubt eine laufende Erneuerung, Erweiterung und Aktualisierung des gebotenen Materials. Das Verzeichnis ist zweisprachig, englisch/französisch.

Verlag Dokumentation
8023 München-Pullach, Jaiserstraße 13
1000 Berlin 12, Schlüterstraße 49
Schweiz: Karger Libri AG, Arnold-Böcklin-Straße 25, CH-4000 Basel 11

IFRI US: e: International Fund Raising Institute

IFRM INT: e: International Federation for the Rights of Man, Paris [gegr 1922, 1948]

I.F.R.U. F: GB: f: Institut Français du Royaume Uni

I.F.S. IND: e: Indian Forest Service

IFS BRD: d: Institut zur Förderung des Schriftsteller-Nachwuchses H. Ulbrich KG, 2 Hamburg 1

IfS DDR: d: Institut für Schienenfahrzeuge, 1 Berlin-Adlershof; BRD: d: Institut für Schiffbau, 2 Hamburg; Institut für Segelflugforschung, 78 Freiburg; Institut für Sozialforschung, 6 Ffm

IFS S: sv: Institutet för Samhällsfrågor

I.F.S. GB: e: mil: Instrument Flying School; e: International Faculty of Sciences

IFS INT: e: International Federation of Settlements and Neighbourhood Centres; International Federation of Ski; International Federation of Surveyors [gegr 1926]; International Flower Service

IFSB INT: d: Internationaler Fernschachverband

IFSCC INT: e: International Federation of Societies of Cosmetic Chemists, London

IFSDA INT: e: International Federation of Stamp Dealers' Associations [1950]

IFSDP INT: d: Internationale Föderation der Sozialistischen und Demokratischen Presse e: International Federation of the Socialist and Democratic Press, Amsterdam [NL]

IFSEM INT: e: International Federation of Societies for Electron Microscopy, Delft [NL]

I.F.S.M.U. IRL: e: Irish Free State Medical Union

IFSNC INT: e: International Federation of Settlements and Neighbourhood Centres

IFSO US: e: International Federation of Sanitarians Organizations

IFSP INT: e: International Federation of Philosophy [gegr 1948]

IFSPO INT: e: International Federation of Senior Police Officers, Paris 9

IfSS BRD: d: Institut für Selbsthilfe und Sozialforschung, 5 Köln

I.F.S.S.O. IRL: e: Irish Free State Stationery Office

I.F.S.T. GB: e: Institute of Food Science and Technology

IFST INT: e: International Federation of Shorthand and Typewriting [=IFKM]

IFSTA INT: e: International Federation of Secondary Teachers' Associations

IFSW INT: e: International Federation of Social Workers, Paris [gegr 1932]

IFT e: Institute of Food Technologists

IfT DDR: d: Institut für Typung, Berlin

IFT INT: e: International Federation of Translators

I.F.T.A. F: f: Institut Français de Transport Aérien

IFTA INT: e: International Federation of Teachers' Associations, Lausanne [CH, gegr 1926]; International Fine Technics Association [gegr 1961]

IFTC INT: e: International Federation of Thermalism and Climatism; International Film and Television Council, Rome [gegr 1958]

I.F.T.I.M. F: f: Institut de Formation aux Techniques d'Implantation et de Manutention, Sèvres

IFTR INT: e: International Federation for Theatre Research

IFTU INT: e: International Federation of Trade Unions [gegr 1901,1919]

IFTW INT: e: International Federation of Tobacco Workers, Brussels [gegr 1876]

IFTWA INT: e: International Federation

of Textile Workers' Associations, London [gegr 1893]

IFU S: sv: Institutet för försäkringsutbildning; BRD: d: Institut für Unternehmerforschung, Bad Reichenhall; Internationale Film-Union, 548 Remagen; INT: d: Internationale Fruchtsaft-Union, Paris 9

IFUC CDN: e: Interprovincial Farm Union Council

IFUEPCS INT: e: International Federation of Unions of Employees in Public and Civil Services

IFUMA BRD: d: Institut für Marktforschung und Absatzförderung, 5 Köln

IFUS INT: e: International Federation of University Sport

IFUW INT: e: International Federation of University Women, London SW 3 [gegr 1919]

IfV DDR: d: Institut für Verkehrsforschung

IFV BRD: d: Institut für Verkehrswissenschaften, 5 Köln; INT: d: Internationaler Faustball-Verband

IFVA INT: [d: Internationale Vereinigung der Variete Artisten, Wien 9]

IFVME GB: e: mil: Inspectorate of Fighting Vehicles and Mechanical Equipment

IFW BRD: d: Institut für Warenprüfung, 7012 Fellbach

IfW DDR: d: Institut für Wasserwirtschaft; BRD: d: Institut für Werkzeugforschung, 563 Remscheid; Institut für Wirtschaftsforschung

IFWA INT: e: International Federation for Weeks of Art, Brussels [gegr 1936]

IFWEA INT: e: International Federation of Workers' Educational Associations, London W 1 [gegr 1947]

IFWHA INT: e: International Federation of Women's Hockey Associations

I.F.W.J. INT: e: International Federation of Working Journalists

IFWL INT: e: International Federation of Women Lawyers [gegr 1944]

IFWTA INT: e: International Federation of Workers' Travel Associations, London SW 1

I.f.W.u.S. D: d: Institut für Weltwirtschaft und Seeverkehr, Kiel

IFWVO e: International Federation of War Veterans Organizations

IfWW BRD: d: Institut für Welt-Wirtschaft, 5 Köln

IFYC INT: e: International Federation of Young Co-operators [gegr 1951]

IFYE INT: e: International Farm Youth Exchange

IFYHA INT: e: International Federation of Youth Hostels Associations

IfZF BRD: d: Institut für Zeitforschung

I.G. F: f: Indépendants de Gauche

IG BRD: d: Industriegewerkschaft; e: mil: Inspector General

I.G. F: f: Institut de Géographie

IG PL: pl: Instytut Geografii

I.G. e: mil: Intendant-General; f: mil: Intendant Général; I: i: Intendenza generale; d: Interessengemeinschaft; CH: d: Interessengemeinschaft für den Handel mit optischen Waren in der Schweiz; A: d: Interessengemeinschaft österreichischer Annoncen-Expeditionen GmbH, Wien 1; INT: d: Internationaler Gerichtshof

IG GB: e: mil: Irish Guards

IGA d: Industriegasanstalt; Industrie-Gewerbe-Ausstellung

I.G.A. F: f: Inspecteurs Généraux de l'Administration; Inspection Générale de l'Agriculture

IGA BRD: d: Interessengemeinschaft der Arbeitslosen; INT: eo: Internacia Geografa Asocio, Tailfingen (Württ) [gegr 1955] e: International Geographical Association

IGA; iga BRD: DDR: d: Internationale Gartenbau-Ausstellung [Hamburg,

Erfurt]
IGA INT: e: International Geneva Association; International Go Association; International Golf Association, New York, N.Y.; e: Irish Gas Association
IGAA US: e: Independent Grocers'Alliance of America
I.G.A.A. F: f: mil: Inspection Générale de l'Armée de l'Air
I.G.A.C. F: f: Inspection Générale de l'Aéronautique Civile
I.G.A.C.C. F: f: Inspection Générale de l'Aviation Civile et Commerciale
IGAEA US: e: International Graphic Arts Education Association
IGAFA INT: d: Internationale Schau für Gastronomie und Fremdenverkehr [später:] Internationale Fremdenverkehrsausstellung verbunden mit der... Bundesfachschau für das Hotel- und Gaststättengewerbe, München
IGAME F: f: Inspecteur générale de l'administration en mission extraordinaire
IGAP INT: d: Internationale Gesellschaft für ärztliche Psychotherapie
IGAS e: International Graphic Arts Society
I.Gas E. GB: e: Institution of Gas Engineers
IGAWA BRD: d: Informationszentrum Gas/Wasser, 43 Essen
IGB BRD: d: Industriegewerkschaft Bergbau; INT: d: Internationaler Genossenschaftsbund, London W 1 [gegr 1895]; Internationaler Gewerkschaftsbund [gegr 1901]; Internationales Gewerkschaftsbüro
IGBE BRD: d: Industriegewerkschaft Bergbau und Energie
IGC e: Intergovernmental Committee; INT: e: Intergovernmental Copyright Committee, Paris 7 [gegr 1952]; US: e: International Garden Club; INT: e: International Geological Congress; International Geophysical Committee, London NW 1; International Geophysical Cooperation; e: International Gift Corporation; INT: e: International Grassland Congress
IGCB B: f: Institut Géographique du Congo Belge, Léopoldville
IGCC INT: e: Intergovernmental Copyright Committee, Paris 7 [gegr 1952]
I.G.C.M. GB: e: Imperial Guild of Church Musicians
IGCP P: pt: Instituto Geográfico e Cadastral Portugal
IGCR INT: e: Inter-Governmental Committee on Refugees
I.G.C.S. F: f: Inspection Générale des Carrières de la Seine
IGD US: e: mil: Inspector General's Department
IGDC INT: d: Internationale Gesellschaft der Damen-Coiffeure
IGDL NL: nl: mil: Indische Geneeskundige Dienst Landmacht
IGds; I.Gds. GB: e: mil: Irish Guards
I.G.D.T. F: f: mil: Inspecteur Général de la Défense du Territoire
I.G.E. GB: e: Institution of Gas Engineers, London; I: i: mil: Intendenza Generale dell'Esercito; US: e: International General Electric Company, New York
IGEC US: e: International General Electric Company, New York
Igedo BRD: d: Interessengesellschaft für Damenoberbekleidung, 4 Düsseldorf; Internationale Verkaufs- und Modewoche, 4 Düsseldorf
Igefa D: d: = IG Farben
IGEHO INT: d: Internationale Fachmesse der Gemeinschaftsverpflegung und Hotellerie, Basel [CH]
IGEJA INT: nl: Internationaal Geofysisch Jaar
IGEPHO BRD: d: Interessengemeinschaft von Photo-Spezialhändlern eV, Stuttgart [gegr 1954]

I.G.E.R. F: f: Institut National de Gestion et d'Economie Rurale

IGESUCO NATO: e: International Ground Environmental Subcommittee

I.G.F. F: f: Inspection Générale des Finances; GB: e: mil: Inspector General of Fortifications; F: f: Institut Géographique de France

IGF D: d: = IG Farben; INT: d: Internationale Graphische Föderation e: International Graphical Federation, Bern [CH, gegr 1949] ; INT: e: International Gymnastic Federation, Geneva [CH, gegr 1881]

IGFA BRD: d: Interessengemeinschaft der Film-Amateure an der Saar, Saarbrücken; INT: d: Internationale Gesellschaft zur Förderung des Automobilsports, 5 Köln; Internationale Gesellschaft für Automatik; e: International Game Fish Association

Igfag D: d: = IG Farben

IG Farben; I.G. Farben D: d: Interessengemeinschaft Farbenindustrie AG, Ffm

IGfNM = IGNM

IGG BR: pt: Instituto Geográfico e Geológico, São Paulo

I.G.H. GB: e: Incorporated Guild of Hairdressers; F: f: mil: Inspection Générale de l'Habillement; e: mil: Inspector General of Hospitals

IGH INT: d: Internationaler Gerichtshof, Den Haag [NL]

IGHAT US: e: "I'm Gonna Holler About Taxes" [club at Chicago; gegr 1952]

IGI INT: f: Groupement international des fabricants de papier-peints e: International Wallpaper Manufacturers Association d: Internationaler Verein der Tapetenfabrikanten, Brüssel [B] ; BRD: d: Interessengemeinschaft Ionosphäre

I.G.I.P. F: f: Inspection Générale de l'Instruction Publique

IGJ INT: d: Internationales Geophysikalisches Jahr 1957/58

I.G.K. INT: d: Internationaler Genetik-Kongreß; Internationale Gesellschaft für neue katholische Kirchenmusik

I.G.L.F. e: Irish Grand Lodge of Freemasons

IGLR BRD: d: Interessengemeinschaft Luft- und Raumfahrt, 8 München

IGM BRD: d: Industriegewerkschaft Metall; B: f: mil: Institut Géographique Militaire, Bruxelles; A: d: Institut für Geschichte der Medizin; RA: s: mil: Instituto Geográfico Militar; INT: d: Internationale Gebrauchtflugzeugmesse [BRD] ; Internationale Gesellschaft für Moorforschung, Vaduz [FL] ; I: i: mil: Istituto Geografico Militare

I.G.M. I: i: mil: Istituto Guerra Marittima

IGMB B: f: mil: Institut Géographique Militaire, Belgique; NL: nl: Instituut voor Graan, Meel en Brood

IGMER INT: nl: Internationaal Genootschap voor Medische Endoscopie en Röntgenkinematografie

IG Metall BRD: d: Industriegewerkschaft Metall

IGMI I: i: mil: Istituto Geografico Militare Italiano

I.G.M.P. F: f: mil: Ingénieurs Militaires des Poudres

IGMW INT: d: Internationale Gesellschaft für Musikwissenschaft

I.G.N. F: f: Inspection Générale de la Navigation; Institut Géographique National

IGN A: d: Interessengemeinschaft für Normungsarbeiten

I-GN US: e: International Great Northern Railroad

IGNF F: f: Institut Géographique National de France

IGNF.CL F: L: f: Institut Géographique

National de France - Cadastre du Luxembourg

IGNM INT: f: Internationale Gesellschaft für Neue Musik [gegr 1922]

I.G.N.R.R. US: e: International Great Northern Railroad

IGO e: mil: Inspector General's Office; BRD: d: Interessengemeinschaft Odenwald, 612 Michelstadt

I.G.O. D: d: Interessengemeinschaft Deutscher Ölmühlen; IRL: e: Irish Genealogical Office

IGOA US: e: Independent Garage Owners of America

IGOSS UN: e: Integrated Global Ocean Station System [UNESCO]

Igoz D: d: Internationale Gemeinschaft oberschlesischer Zuckerfabriken

IGPAI P: pt: Inspecção General dos Productos Agricolas e Industriais, Repartição de Normalização, Lisboa

IG PAN PL: pl: Instytut Geografii Polskiej Akademii Nauk

IGPCE INT: e: International Great Plains Conference of Entomologists

IGPF BRD: d: Industriegewerkschaft Post und Fernmeldewesen

I.G.P.M. F: f: Inspection Générale des Poids et Mesures

IGR IND: e: Indian Government Railways; f: mil: Inspection Générale du Ravitaillement; BRD: d: Interessengemeinschaft der Rückerstattungspflichtigen eV, Nürnberg; Interessengemeinschaft für Rundfunkschutzrechte eV, Düsseldorf

I.G.R. INT: d: Internationale Gesellschaft für Radiobiologie [gegr 1933]

I.G.R.A.F. GB: e: mil: Inspector-General of the Royal Air Force

IGROF INT: [d: Internationale Rorschach-Gesellschaft, gegr 1952]

IGS GB: e: mil: Imperial General Staff; IND: e: Indian Geographical Society; US: e: International Geranium Socie-

ty; e: International Graduate School

IGSP INT: d: Internationale Gesellschaft der Schriftpsychologie

IGSS GCA: s: Instituto Guatemalteco de Seguridad Social

IGT WAN: e: Igala Tribal Union

I.G.T. GB: e: mil: Inspector-General to the Forces for Training; Inspector - General of Transportation

IGT YV: s: Inspectoría General de Tránsito; US: e: Institute of Gas Technology, Chicago,Ill.; NL: nl: Stichting Instituut voor Grafische Techniek, Amsterdam

IGTM NL: nl: Internationale Gas-Transport-Maatschappij, Den Haag

IGU PL: pl: Instytut Geograficzny Uniwersytetu Łódzkiego; INT: d: Internationale Gas-Union, Brüssel 4 [B] ; Internationale Geographische Union, New York 36 [gegr 1922] ; Internationale Gesellschaft zur Bekämpfung unheilbarer Krankheiten einschließlich Siechtum und vorzeitigen Tod, Berlin [BlnW] ; Internationale Gewerbeunion, Genf [gegr 1947] ; INT: e: International Gas Union, Brussels 4 [B] ; International Geographical Union, New York 36 [gegr 1922]

IGUW PL: pl: Instytut Geografii Uniwersytetu Warszawskiego

IGV d: Institut für Getreideverarbeitung; INT: d: Internationaler Gemeindeverband, Den Haag [NL, gegr 1913] ; Internationaler Genfer Verband [Fachverband der Kellner]

IGVK A: d: Interessengemeinschaft der Versuchsanstalten und des Kurswesens an technischen und gewerblichen Lehranstalten Österreichs, Wien 9

I.G.W. GB: e: mil: Inspector-General of Waterguard; BRD: d: Interessengemeinschaft ehemaliger Gefolgschaftsmitglieder der Wehrmacht, Göttingen

IGWF INT: e: International Garment

Workers' Federation, London [gegr 1893]

IGWUA US: e: International Glove Workers' Union of America

IGY INT: e: International Geophysical Year [1957...58]

IGZ BRD: d: Interessengemeinschaft der Zigarettenhersteller

IH D: d: Ingenieur-Hilfe [VDI]

I.H. F: f: mil: Inspection de l'Habillement; e: Institute of Hygiene

IH P: pt: Instituto hidrográfico, Lisboa; US: e: International Harvester Company

I.H.A. GB: e: Institute of Hospital Almoners

IHA US: e: International Hahnemannian Association; e: International Horse Association; INT: e: International Hospitals Association; International Hotel Alliance [gegr 1921]; International Hotel Association, Paris 8 [gegr 1946]

I.H.A. INT: e: International Hotelmen's Association [gegr 1869]

IHA US: e: International House Association, Inc., New York [gegr 1947]; INT: d: Internationale Werkzeugmaschinen-Ausstellung, 3 Hannover [BRD]

Ihagee D: d: Ihagee-Kamerawerk Steenbergen & Co., Dresden

IHATIS INT: e: International Hide and Allied Trades Improvement Society, Brussels 6 [B]

IHB DDR: d: Industrie- und Handelsbank; INT: d: Internationaler Handballbund; US: e: International Health Board [Rockefeller Foundation]; INT: e: International Hockey Board; INT: d: Internationales Hydrographisches Büro e: International Hydrographic Bureau, Monte Carlo [MC, gegr 1921]; BRD: d: Investitions- und Handels-Bank AG, Darmstadt

IHC NL: nl: Industrieele Handelscombinatie

I.H.C. F: f: Institut d'Hydrologie et de Climatologie

IHC US: e: Intercontinental Hotels Corporation, New York 17 [gegr 1946]; International Harvester Company; INT: e: International Health Conference; GB: e: International Help for Children, London [gegr 1947]; INT: e: International Hunting Council, Paris [gegr 1930]

I.H.C. e: Irish Herald's College

IHCA INT: e: International Hebrew - Christian Alliance, London [gegr 1925]

IHD UN: d: Internationales Hydrologisches Dezennium [ab 1. Jan 1965] e: International Hydrological Decade [UNESCO]

IHE US: e: Institut of Home Economics; GB: e: Institution of Highway Engineers

IHEA US: e: Industrial Heating Equipment Association

I.H.E.A. F: f: Institut des Hautes Etudes Agraires

I.H.E.A.L. F: f: Institut des Hautes Etudes de l'Amérique Latin

IHEB e: International Heat Economy Bureau

I.H.E.C. F: f: Institut des Hautes Etudes Cinématographiques

I.H.E.D.N. F: f: mil: Institut des Hautes Etudes de la Défense Nationale

I.H.E.D.R. F: f: Institut des Hautes Etudes de Droit Rurale

I.H.E.I. F: f: Institut des Hautes Etudes Internationales, Paris

I.H.E.I.U.P. F: f: Institut des Hautes Etudes Internationales de l'Université de Paris

I.H.E.O.M. F: f: Institut des Hautes Etudes d'Outre-Mer, Paris

I.H.E.P. F: f: Institut des Hautes Etudes Politiques

IHES US: e: Illinois Horticultural Experiment Station

IHEU INT: d: Internationale Humanistische und Ethische Union   e: International Humanist and Ethical Union, Utrecht [NL, gegr 1952]

IHF US: e: Industrial Hygiene Foundation of America; INT: d: Internationale Handball-Föderation; INT: e: International Lawn Hockey Federation, Brussels 5 [B, gegr 1924] ; International Hospital Federation, London [gegr 1947]

IHFA US: e: Industrial Hygiene Foundation of America

IHFBC INT: e: International High Frequency Broadcasting Conference, Mexico City

IHFM US: e: Institute of High Fidelity Manufacturers, New York 10

IHFPA RCH: s: Instituto de Higiene y Fomento de la Producción Animal

IHGB BR: pt: Instituto Histórico e Geográfico Brasileiro

I.H.I. F: f: Institut d'Hygiène Industrielle et de Médecine du Travail

IHI d: Internationales Handelsinstitut; INT: d: Internationales Hilfskomitee für Intellektuelle, Genf [CH, gegr 1933] ; J: e: Ishikawajima-Harima Heavy Industries Ltd., Tokyo

IHK d: Industrie- und Handelskammer; INT: d: Internationale Handelskammer, Paris [gegr 1919]   sv: Internationella handelskammaren

IHKM PL: pl: Instytut Historii Kultury Materialnej

IHKn d: Industrie- und Handelskammern

IHL INT: e: International Homoeopathic League, London [gegr 1925]

IHLADI E: s: Instituto Hispano-Luso -Americano de Derecho Internacional, Madrid

IHLC INT: e: International Humanitarian Law Commission

IHM INT: d: Internationale Handwerksmesse, 8 München [BRD]

IHO INT: e: International Health Organization

I.H.P. F: f: Institut Henri-Poincaré

I.H.R. e: Institute of Historical Research; Institute of Human Relations

IHR S: sv: Institutet för högre reklamutbildning

I.H.R.B. GB: e: Industrial Health Research Board

IHS US: e: Indiana Horticultural Society;   e: International Haemophilia Society; US: e: Italian Historical Society of America

IHSA US: e: Italian Historical Society of America

IHT BRD: d: Institut für Härtetechnik, 2800 Bremen; DDR: d: Institut für Halbleitertechnik, Teltow; BRD: d: Institut für Hochtemperaturforschung, 7 Stuttgart

IHTU GB: e: mil: Interservice Hovercraft Trials Unit

IHV INT: d: Internationaler Handballverband;   Internationaler Hotelbesitzerverein;   Internationaler Hotelverband;   Internationaler Hotelverein

I.H.V.E. GB: e: Institution of Heating and Ventilating Engineers, London

II e: Ikebana International

I.I. GB: e: Imperial Institute; D: d: mil: Inspektion der Marine-Infanterie; NL: nl: Koninklijk Instituut van Ingenieurs

IIA US: e: Incinerator Institute of America, New York 17;   Information Industry Association

I.I.A. GB: e: Inspector under the Inebriates Act;   Institute of Industrial Administration; INT: f: Institut International d'Agriculture; F: f: Institut International d'Anthropologie, Paris

IIA INT: s: Instituto Internacional del Ahorro, Amsterdam [NL, gegr 1924]; US: e: Insurance Institute of America; International Information Administration, Washington, D.C. [gegr 1952]

I.I.A. INT: e: International Institute of Agriculture; International Institute of Anthropology

IIA IRL: e: Irish International Airlines

IIAA e: Institute of Inter-American Affairs

IIAC INT: f: Institut International d'Archéocivilisation e: International Institute of Archaeocivilization

IIAF e: mil: Imperial Iranian Air Force

IIAI P: pt: Instituto de Investigação Agronómica de Angola, Nova Lisboa

IIAL e: International Institute of Arts and Letters

I.I.A.L.C. e: International Institute of African Languages and Culture

IIAP INT: e: International Institute of Artists and Photographers

IIAS INT: e: Inter-American Institute of Agricultural Sciences; International Institute of Administrative Sciences, Brussels 4 [B, gegr 1930]

IIASH e: International Institute for the Advancement of the Science of Hypnology

IIAZ e: International Institute of the Arid Zone

IIB INT: f: Institut International de Bibliographie, Bruxelles [B, gegr 1895]; Institut International des Brevets, Den Haag [NL, gegr 1947]

I.I.B.D. GB: e: Incorporated Institute of British Decorators

IIBDID GB: e: Incorporated Institute of British Decorators and Interior Designers, London

IIBEM IND: e: Indian Institute of Biochemistry and Experimental Medicine

IIC BRD: d: Institut für industrielle Cinematographie, 6 Ffm [gegr 1966]; INT: f: Institut International du Commerce; Institut International pour la Conservation des Objets de Musées; RCH: s: Instituto de Ingenieros de Chile; US: e: International Information Committee, Washington, D.C.; INT: e: International Institute of Commerce; International Institute for the Conservation of Historic and Artistic Works; Internationale Institute for the Conservation of Museum Objects, London [gegr 1950]; International Interchange Committee

IICA INT: s: Instituto Interamericano de Ciencias Agrícolas, San José [CR]; Instituto Internacional de las Cajas de Ahorro; Instituto Internacional de Ciencias Administrativas [Bruxelles 4, B]; P: pt: Instituto de Investigação Científica de Angola, Junta de Investigaçãoes do Ultramar, Luanda

IICAF e: Institute for International Collaboration in Agriculture and Forestry

IICC INT: f: Institut international d'étude et de documentation en matière de concurrence commerciale e: International Institute for Study and Research in the Field of Commercial Competition, Brussels 3 [B, gegr 1937]

IICE INT: f: Institut International des Caisses d'Epargne, Amsterdam [NL, gegr 1924]

I.I.C.I. INT: f: Institut international de coopération intellectuelle, Paris

I.I.C.M. INT: f: Institut International des Classes Moyennes

IICM P: pt: Instituto de Investigação Científica de Moçambique, Juanta de Investigações do Ultramar, Lourenço Marques

IICS INT: f: Institut International de

Chimie Solvay
IICT RA: s: Instituto de Investigaciones Científicas y Tecnológicas
IID INT: f: Institut International de Documentation, Bruxelles [B]   d: Internationales Institut für Dokumentation   e: International Institute of Documentation
I.I.D.C. US: e: International Industrial Development Conference, San Francisco, Calif. [1957]
I.I.D.P. F: f: Institut International du Droit Publique
I.I.E. GB: e: Imperial Institute of Entomology; US: e: Institute of International Education, New York
IIE INT: f: Institut International d'Embryologie;   Institut International de l'Epargne, Amsterdam [NL, gegr 1924]; s: Instituto de ingeniera eléctrica; INT: e: International Institute of Embryology   d: Internationales Institut für Embryologie
IIEB INT: f: Institut International d'Etudes Bancaires
IIEC E: s: Instituto de Investigaciones y Experiencias Cinematogáficas, Madrid;   i: Istituto Internazionale di Educazione Cinematografica
I.I.E.I.C. e: International Institute Examinations Inquiry Committee
IIEL INT: f: Institut International d'Etudes Ligures, Bordighera [gegr 1947]
IIEO INT: e: International Islamic Economic Organization
IIEP INT: e: International Institute for Educational Planning, Paris 16
IIF US: e: Institute of International Finance, New York; INT: f: Institut International du Froid, Paris 17 [gegr 1920]
IIFA INT: f: Institut International du Film d'Art   e: International Institute of Films on Art

IIFP INT: f: Institut International des Finances Publiques
IIHA UN: e: International Institute of the Hylean Amazon, Manaus [BR]
IIHF INT: e: International Ice Hockey Federation
IIHS US: e: Insurance Institute for Highway Safety
III INT: f: Institut indianiste interaméricain   f: Institut Interaméricain d'Affaires Indigènes   s: Instituto Indigenista Interamericano, México 7, D.F.   e: Inter-American Indian Institute   d: Interamerikanisches Indianisches Institut [gegr 1940]; INT: f: Institut isostatique international   e: International Isostatic Institute, Helsinki [SF, gegr 1936]
I.I.I. B: f: Intergroupe des intérêts intellectuels
III US: e: International Institute of Interpreters, New York
I.I.I. I: i: Istituto Investigativo Italiano
IIIC INT: e: International Institute for Intellectual Cooperation
IIJP RA: s: Instituto de Investigaciones Jurídico-Políticas
IIK INT: eo: Internacia Instruista Kunlaborado
IIL US: e: Institute of Industrial Launderers; INT: e: Institute of International Law, Geneva [CH, gegr 1873]
IILC NL: nl: Internationaal Instituut voor Landaanwinning en Cultuurtechniek, Wageningen
IILI INT: s: Instituto Internacional de Literatura Iberoamericana, Albuquerque, N.M. [US, gegr 1938]
IILS INT: e: International Institute for Labour Studies [CH-1211 Genève]
I.I.M. IND: e: Indian Institute of Metals; GB: e: Institute of Industrial Managers
IIM BRD: d: Institut für Instrumentelle Mathematik, 53 Bonn; RA: s: In-

stituto de Investigaciones Microquí-
micas

I.I.M. I: i: mil: Istituto Idrografico
della Marina

IIMA P: pt: Instituto de Investigação
Médica de Angola, Nova Lisboa

IIMC e: International Institute of the
Middle Classes

IIMEBE INT: e: International Institute
for Medical Electronics and Biological Engineering

IIMM P: pt: Instituto de Investigação
Médica de Moçambique, Lourenço
Marques

IIMP RCH: s: Instituto de Investigaciones de Materias Primas

IIMQ I: i: Istituto Italiano del Marchio
di Qualitá, Roma, Milano

I.I.M.R.D. GB: e: Imperial Institute
Mineral Resources Department

IIMT e: International Institute of Mil-
ling Technology

IIMUA s: Instituto de Investigaciones
Médicas de la Universidad de Los An-
des

IIN GCA: s: Instituto Indigenista Nacional; INT: s: Instituto Interamericano del Niño, Montevideo [U, gegr
1919]; I: i: Istituto d'Interesse Nazionale

IINS e: Interuniversity Institute of
Nuclear Sciences

IIO US: e: Institute for International
Order

IIOE INT: d: Internationale Indische
-Ozean-Expedition [1964...65] e: International Indian Ocean Expedition

IIOP I: i: Istituto Italiano per l'Opi-
nione Pubblica

IIOST INT: f: Institut International
d'Organisation Scientifique du Travail [gegr 1927]

IIP IND: e: Indian Institute of Petroleum; INT: f: Institut International
de Philosophie, Paris [gegr 1937];

Institut International de la Presse,
Zürich 1 [gegr 1951] s: Instituto
Internacional de la Prensa; INT: [f:
Groupement International de l'Indu-
strie Pharmaceutique]; INT: e: Inter-
national Institute of Philosophy, Paris
[gegr 1937]; I: i: Istituto Italiano di
Pubblicismo

IIPA IND: e: Indian Institute of Public Administration; GB: e: Institute
of Incorporated Practitioners in Advertising; P: pt: Instituto das Indústrias de Pesca em Angola, Luanda

IIPD I: i: Istituto Italiano di Psicologia
della Direzione

IIPE INT: f: Institut international de
planification de l'éducation, Paris 16;
GB: e: Institution of Incorporated
Plant Engineers

IIPER e: International Institution of
Production Engineering Research

IIPF INT: e: International Institute for
Public Finance

IIPP f: Institut International de Philosophie Politique

IIPR I: i: Istituto Italiano per le Pubbliche Relazioni

IIPS INT: f: Institut International de
Physique Solvay

IIR US: e: Institute for Industrial Re-
lations; BRD: d: Institut für Interne
Revision eV, 6 Ffm; INT: e: Inter-
national Institute of Refrigeration,
Paris 17 [gegr 1920]; International
Institute of Reprography; INT: i:
Istituto Internazionale del Risparmio

I.I.R.A. INT: e: International Industrial Relations Association

IIRB INT: f: Institut International de
Recherches Betteravières, Tirlemont
[B, gegr 1931]

I.I.R.G. INT: f: Institut International
de Recherches Graphologiques

IIRI INT: e: International Industrial
Relations Institute

IIRS IRL: e: Institute for Industrial Research and Standards, Dublin 9

IIRSA INT: f: Institut International de Recherche Scientifique d'Adiopodoumé, Abidjan

IIRST INT: f: Institut International de Recherches Scientifiques sur le Tourisme

IIS IND: e: Indian Information Service, New Delhi [d: Nachrichtenagentur] ; Indian Institute of Science; US: e: Institute for Intercultural Studies; INT: f: Institut international de la soudure   d: Internationales Institut für Schweißtechnik, London SW 7 [gegr 1948] ; INT: f: Institut International de Statistique, Den Haag [NL, gegr 1885]   d: Internationales Institut für Statistik; INT: s: Instituto Internacional de Sociología;   Instituto Internacional de la Soldadura, London [gegr 1948] ; INT: nl: Internationaal Instituut voor het Spaarwezen   d: Internationales Institut des Sparwesens (der Sparkassen), Amsterdam C [NL, gegr 1924] ; INT: e: International Institute of Sociology

IISA INT: f: Institut international des sciences administratives, Bruxelles 4 [B, gegr 1930]

IISBR INT: e: International Institute of Sugar Beet Research, Tirlemont [B, gegr 1931]

IISCO IND: e: Indian Iron and Steel Company

IISI INT: e: International Iron and Steel Institute, Brussels [B]

IISL INT: e: International Institute of Space Law, Dallas, Texas [US] ; INT: i: Istituto Internazionale di Studi Liguri, Bordighera [gegr 1947]

IISM BRD: d: Internationales Institut Schloß Mainau

IISN B: f: Institut interuniversitaire des sciences nucléaires, Bruxelles

[gegr 1951]

I.I.S.O. e: Institution of Industrial Safety Officers

IISPS INT: e: International Institute of Social and Political Sciences

IISR IND: e: Indian Institute of Sugarcane Research

IISRP INT: e: International Institute of Synthetic Rubber Producers

IISSP INT: f: Institut International des Sciences Sociales et Politiques

IIST INT: f: Institut International des Sciences Théoriques

IISTR INT: e: International Institute of Scientific Travel Resarch

IIT US: e: Illinois Institute of Technology; IND: e: Indian Institute of Technology: e: Institute of Industrial Technicians; RCB: f: Institut Interafricain du Travail, Brazzaville [gegr 1953] ; INT: f: Institut International du Théâtre, Paris [gegr 1948] ; RA: s: Instituto de Investigaciones Técnicas; CO: s: Instituto de Investigaciones Tecnológicas, Bogotá

IITB BRD: d: Institut für Informationsverarbeitung in Technik und Biologie, 75 Karlsruhe

I.I.T.E. GB: e: mil: Inspector of Infantry Training Establishments

IITRI US: e: Illinois Institute of Technology, Research Institute

IITS INT: e: International Institute of Theoretical Sciences

IIUDP INT: f: Institut International pour l'Unification du Droit Privé; Institut International pour l'Unification du Droit Public

IIUPL INT: e: International Institute for the Unification of Public Law

IIV; IIVw INT: d: Internationales Institut für Verwaltungswissenschaften, Brüssel [B, gegr 1930]

IIW INT: e: International Institute of Welding, London SW 7 [gegr 1948]

IIY UN: e: International Institute of Youth [UNESCO]

I.J. GB: e: Institute of Journalists

IJ NL: nl: Nederlandse Vereniging voor Internationaal Jeugdverkeer

IJAB BRD: d: Internationaler Jugendaustausch und Besucherdienst der BRD

IJABC US: e: mil: Iwo Jima Air Base Command

IJB UN: d: Internationale Jugendbücherei, München [BRD, gegr 1949]

IJC CDN: US: e: International Joint Commission

IJF INT: d: Internationale Journalisten-Föderation, Brüssel [B, gegr 1952]; INT: d: Internationale Judo-Föderation e: International Judo Federation

IJGD INT: d: Internationale Jugend-Gemeinschaftsdienste

IJI INT: f: Institut Juridique International

IJK INT: d: Internationale Juristen-Kommission, Genf [CH, gegr 1952]

IJM INT: sv: Internationella Järnvägsmissionen

IJMA IND: e: Indian Jute Mills Association; US: e: Infant and Juvenile Manufacturers Association

IJN J: e: mil: Imperial Japanese Navy

IJO INT: d: Internationale Journalistenorganisation, Prag

ijpd BRD: d: Internationaler Jugendpressedienst

IJRS INT: d: Internationales Jahr (Internationale Jahre) der ruhigen Sonne [e: = IQSY]

IJS US: e: Institute of Jazz Studies

IJV INT: d: Internationale Journalisten-Vereinigung

IJWU US: e: International Jewelry Workers Union

I.K. da: idrætsklub; sv: idrottsklubb(en)

IK S: sv: Statens industrikommission

[1914...20, 1939...50];D: d: Innungs(kranken)kasse; SU: [e: Institute of Crystallography]; YU: sh: Izvršni Komitet

IKA GR: [d: Sozialversicherung]; RA: s: Industrias Kaiser Argentina, Cordoba; DDR: d: Volkseigene Betriebe für Installation, Kabel und Apparate; INT: d: Internationale Kochkunstausstellung, Ffm; Internationaler Künstleragentenverband; INT: sv: Internationella Kooperativa Alliansen

IKAB INT: d: Internationale Katholische Arbeiterbewegung

IKAe INT: d: Internationales Institut für experimentelle Kunst und Ästhetik, Wien, Ffm, Prag

IKA-EUHOGA INT: BRD: d: Internationale Kochkunstausstellung – Bundesfachschau für das Hotel- und Gaststättengewerbe

Ikafa D: d: Interessengemeinschaft Freier Kabel- und Leitungsdrahtfabrikanten

IKAMA INT: d: Internationaler Kongreß mit Ausstellung für Meßtechnik und Automatik, Düsseldorf [BRD]

IKB BRD: d: Industriekreditbank AG; Industrieverband Kunststoff-Böden und Wandbeläge eV, 6 Ffm

IKBAG BRD: d: Industriekreditbank AG

IKBK INT: d: Internationales Katholisches Büro für das Kind

I.K.E.S. INT: eo: Internacia Komisiono Esperanto kaj Sociologio

IKF INT: d: Internationale Kommission der Feuerwehren; INT: sv: Internationella Kvinnoförbundet [gegr 1888]

IKFF INT: sv: Internationella kvinnoförbundet för fred och frihet [Genève, CH, gegr 1915]

IKG BRD: d: Interessengemeinschaft ehemaliger Kriegsgefangener, Hamburg;

INT: d: Internationale Kommission für Glas, 75 Karlsruhe-Durlach [gegr 1953] ; d: Israelitische Kultusgemeinde

IKGS US: e: Indiana-Kentucky Geological Society

IKH CH: d: Interkantonale Kontrollstelle für Heilmittel

IKhF SU: [e: Institute of Chemical Physics]

IKHH INT: d: Internationale Konferenz für (eine) gemeinsame Hilfssprache des Handels und Verkehrs

IKhPM SU: [e: Institute of the Chemistry of Polymers and Monomers]

IKhTI SU: [e: Ivanovo Institute of Chemical Technology]

IKI INT: d: Internationales Kali-Institut, Bern [CH]

IKIA INT: d: Internationaler Kongreß für Ingenieur-Ausbildung

IKJ INT: d: Internationales Kuratorium für das Jugendbuch

I.K.K. J: Iino Kaiun Kaisha Ltd.,Tokyo [Reederei, gegr 1899]

IKK d: Innungskrankenkasse; INT: nl: Internationale Kamer van Koophandel; INT: d: Internationale Kriminalpolizeiliche Kommission, Wien [=IKPK]

I.K.L. INT: d: Internationale Katholische Liga

IKL CH: d: Interverbandskommission für Leichtathletik; SF: fi: Isänmaallinen Kansanliike [e: national patriotic moevement]

IKMB INT: d: Internationale Katholische Mittelstandsbewegung, Brüssel 4

IKN INT: d: Internationale Kommission für Numismatik, Den Haag [NL, gegr 1936]

Iko D: d: mil: WK1: Ingenieurkomitee

IKO NL: nl: Instituut voor Kernphysisch Onderzoek

IKOFA INT: d: Internationale Kolonialwaren- und Feinkostausstellung, 8 Mün-

chen[jetzt:] Internationale Lebensmittel- und Feinkostausstellung

Ikofest D: d: mil: WK1: Festungsabteilung des Ingenieurkomitees

Ikopi D: d: mil: WK1: Pionierabteilung des Ingenieurkomitees

IKOR NL: nl: Interkerkelijk Overleg inzake Radioaangelegenheden

IKP nl: Indische Katholieke Partij; INT: d: Internationaler Kongreß für Pädiatrie; Internationaler Kongreß der Fachpresse

IKPK INT: d: Internationale Kriminalpolizeiliche Kommission, Wien

IKPO INT: d: Internationale Kriminalpolizeiliche Organisation, Paris 16 [= Interpol]

I.K.R. D: d: mil: Infanterie-Kraftwagen-Regiment

IKR INT: d: Internationales Katholisches Rundfunkbüro [gegr 1928]

Ikraft D: d: mil: Inspektion des Kraftfahrwesens

IKrK; IKrk. d: Innungskrankenkasse

IKRK INT: d: Internationales Komitee vom Roten Kreuz, Genf [CH]

IKS CH: d: Interkantonale Kontrollstelle für Arzneimittelprüfungen, Bern

IKSJ INT: d: stud: Internationale Katholische Studierende Jugend

IKSt CH: d: Interkantonale Kommission für den Straßenverkehr

I.K.U.E. INT: eo: Internacia Katolika Unuiĝo Esperantista, Liège [B]

IKV BRD: d: Institut für Kunststoffverarbeitung in Industrie und Handwerk, 51 Aachen [gegr 1950] ; INT: d: Internationale Kartographische Vereinigung; Internationale Kriminalistische Vereinigung [gegr 1889] ; **Internationaler Konditormeister-Verband**; Internationaler Krankenhausverband, London [gegr 1947]

IKVSA INT: d: Internationale Katholi-

sche Vereinigung für Soziale Arbeit,
Brüssel [gegr 1925]
IKW BRD: d: Interessengemeinschaft
kriegsgeschädigte Wirtschaft eV, 53
Bonn; INT: d: Internationale Konfe-
renz für Wärmeübertragung
IL US: e: Independence League; GB: e:
Institute of Linguists; BRD: d: In-
stitut für Lackprüfung, 63 Gießen;
PL: pl: Instytut Łączności; e: In-
ternational Baseball League; INT: f:
Internationale Libérale "Union Libé-
rale Mondiale", London
I.L. e: Isolation League; I: i: Ispettorato
del Lavoro
ILA US: e: Illinois Library Association;
Indiana Library Association; IND: e:
Indian Library Association [gegr 1919] ;
GB: e: Institute of Landscape Archi-
tects, London; INT: d: Internationale
Luftfahrt-Ausstellung; 1. Internatio-
nale Luftschiffahrt-Ausstellung, Ffm
[1909] ; ILA–Internationales Ar-
beiterhilfswerk, Zürich 31 [CH] ; INT:
e: International Laundry Association,
London W 2 [gegr 1950] ; International Law Association, London EC 4
[gegr 1873] ; International Leprosy
Association, London [gegr 1913] ;
CDN: US: e: International Longshore-
men's Association
ILAA INT: e: International Legal Aid
Association, London WC 2; e: International Literary and Artistic Asso-
ciation
ILAB INT: nl: Internationale Liga van
Antikwaar Boekhandels e: Interna-
tional League of Antiquarian Book-
sellers, Brussels [gegr 1947]
ILAFA INT: s: Instituto Latinoameri-
cano del Ferro y Acero, Santiago
[RCH]
Ilag D: d: WK2: Interniertenlager
ILAR US: e: Institute of Laboratory
Animals Resources

ILB NL: nl: Instituut voor Landbouw-
bedrijfsgebouwen; INT: e: Interna-
tional Labo(u)r Board; International
Liaison Bureau
ILC GB: e: Industrial Liaison Centre;
US: e: mil: Institute of Land Combat,
Alexandria, Va. [gegr 1967]
I.L.C. F: f: Institut Linguistique et
Commercial, Paris 8
ILC INT: e: International Labeling Cen-
ter
I.L.C. GB: e: International Labour Club,
Manchester
ILC INT: e: International Labo(u)r Con-
ference; UN: e: International Law
Commission
ILCE MEX: s: Instituto Latinoamerica-
no de Cinematografía Educativa, Mé-
xico 18, D.F.
ILCMP INT: e: International Liaison
Committee on Medical Physics
ILCOP INT: e: International Liaison
Committee of Organizations for Peace
[gegr 1949]
I.L.D. e: Import Licensing Department
I.L.E. GB: e: Institution of Locomo-
tive Engineers
ILE INT: e: International (Industrial)
Lubrication Exhibition, London
ILEA GB: e: Inner London Education
Authority
ILEC F: f: Institut de Liaison et
d'Etudes des Industries de Consomma-
tion
I.L.E.I. INT: eo: Internacia Ligo de
Esperantistaj Instruistoj
ILEPTO INT: eo: Internacia Ligo de
Esperantista Poŝt-kaj Telegraf-Ofi-
cistaro
ILF INT: d: Internationale Landarbei-
terföderation e: International Land-
workers' Federation, Utrecht [NL,
gegr 1920] sv: Internationella Lant-
arbetarfederationen
ILFI INT: e: International Labour Film

Institute, Brussels [B]

ILG US: e: Irish Linen Guild

ILGA e: Institute of Local Government Administration

ILGWU US: e: International Ladies Garment Workers Union, New York [gegr 1910]

ILI US: e: Indiana Limestone Institute; Institute of Life Insurance; INT: e: Interafrican Labour Institute, Brazzaville [RCB, gegr 1953]

ILID DDR: d: Institut für Landwirtschaftliche Information und Dokumentation [gegr 1962]

ILIR US: e: Institute of Labor and Industrial Relations [Illinois University]

ILIS INT: sv: Internationella Luftfartsutställningen i Stockholm [1936]

ILITA B: nl: Internationaal Literair-en Toneelagentschap, Gent

ilk S: internasioni lingklub, Stockholm

ILK INT: d: Internationale Luftfahrtkommission; d: Internationales Lagerkomitee [im KZ]

ILLRI US: e: Industrial Lift and Loading Ramp Institute

I.L.M. e: Institute of Labour Management; B: f: Institut de Langues Modernes, 1060 Bruxelles

ILM INT: d: Internationale Liga für Menschenrechte, New York

ILMA US: e: Incandescent Lamp Manufacturers Association; s: Instituto Latinoamericano de Mercadeo Agrícola

I.L.M.A. e: Irish Linen Merchants' Association

ILMAC INT: d: Internationale Fachmesse für Laboratoriumstechnik, Meßtechnik und Automatik in der Chemie, Basel [CH] e: International Exhibition of Laboratory, Measurement and Automation Techniques in Chemistry f: Salon international de la technique de laboratoire, de la technique de mesure et de l'automatique en chimie;

e: mil: Israel-Lebanon Mixed Armistice Commission

ILMO INT: e: International Legal Metrology Organization, Paris

ILMT INT: d: Internationale Leichtmetalltagung, Leoben [A]

ILMTWU US: e: International Longshoremen's and Marine Transport Workers' Union

I.L.N.A. IND: e: Indian Languages Newspapers' Association

ILO NL: nl: Instituut voor Landbouwhuishoudkundig Onderzoek; INT: e: International Labo(u)r Office (Organization), CH-1211 Genf 22 [gegr 1919]

I Loco E GB: e: Institution of Locomotive Engineers

ILOWB INT: US: e: International Labor Office, Washington Branch

ILP GB: e: Independent Labour Party

I.L.P.A. US: e: International Labor Press Association

ILPNR INT: e: International League for the Protection of Native Races

I.L.R. D: d: mil: Infanterie-Lehrregiment; Infanterie-Leibregiment

ILR NL: nl: Instituut voor Landbouwtechniek en Rationalisatie

I.L.R. e: International League of Reform

ILRI IND: e: Indian Lac Research Institute

ILRM INT: e: International League for the Rights of Man, New York

I.L.S. e: Incorporated Law Society

ILS F: e: Institute for Learning Systems, Paris; INT: e: International Latitude Service [gegr 1895]; International Lunar Society [gegr 1956]

I.L.S. IRL: e: Irish Literary Society

ILSA s: Industrias Lácteas Sociedad Anónima; F: f: Inspection des Lois Sociales en Agriculture; CDN: US: e: International Longshoremen's Association

I.L.S.T.M. GB: e: Incorporated Liverpool School of Tropical Medicine

ILTA US: e: Indiana Library Trustee Association

ILTF INT: e: International Lawn Tennis Federation, London [gegr 1912]

ILTUB BlnW: d: Institut für Luftfahrzeugbau der Technischen Universität Berlin

ILU GB: e: Institute of London Underwriters; e: International Legal Union

Iluft D: d: mil: WK1: Inspektion der Luftschiffertruppen

ILUG INT: sv: Internationella luftfartsutställningen i Göteborg

Iluk D: d: mil: WK1: Inspektion des Militär-Luft- und Kraftfahrwesens

ILUS US: e: Inventors' League of the United States

ILV BRD: d: Institut für Lebensmitteltechnologie und Verpackung, München

ILWU US: e: International Longshoremen's and Warehousemen's Union

ILZ DDR: d: Institut für Leihverkehr und Zentralkataloge, Berlin [seit 1 Sep 1970]

ILZRO INT: e: International Lead and Zinc Research Organization, London, New York

I.M. RM: f: Indépendants de Madagascar; d: Innenminister(ium); D: d: Innere Mission; f: Institut Musulman

IM S: d: Ausstellung Instrumente und Meßtechnik, Stockholm; PL: pl: Instytut Metalurgii

I.M. f: mil: Intendance Maritime; Intendant Militaire

IM INT: d: Internationale Instrumenten- und Meßtechnische Konferenz

I.M. F: f: mil: corps des interprètes militaires

I.M.A. IND: e: Indian Medical Association; GB: e: mil: Indian Medical Academy

IMA US: e: Industrial Marketing Associates; Industrial Medical Associa-

tion; BRD: d: Informationsgemeinschaft für Meinungspflege und Aufklärung, 3 Hannover

I.M.A. e: Institute for Mediterranean Affairs; GB: e: Institutional Management Association, Cambridge

IMA BRD: d: Institut für Management -Ausbildung', 35 Kassel; Institut für Marktpsychologie und Absatzforschung 2 Hamburg; CH: d: Schweizerisches Institut für Landmaschinenwesen und Landarbeitstechnik; RA: s: Instituto de Matemática Aplicada; BRD: d: Interministerieller Ausschuß; US: e: International Management Association; INT: e: International Mineralogical Association, Madrid [gegr 1958]

I.M.A. GB: e: International Music Association, London; US: e: Iowa Manufacturers Association; IRL: e: Irish Medical Association; I: i: Istituto di Medicina Aeronautica

IMABA INT: d: Internationale Markenausstellung [Basel 1948, Luxemburg 1952]

IMAC F: f: Institut de Mécanographie Appliqué, Paris 12

IMACE INT: f: Association des industries margarinières des pays de la CEE, Bruxelles 4 [B]

IMAG BRD: d: Internationaler Messe- und Ausstellungsdienst GmbH, 8 München 2

IMAJ J: e: International Management Association of Japan, Tokyo

IMAKA CH: d: Institut für Management- und Kaderausbildung, Zürich

IMALSO B: nl: Intercommunale Maatschappij van de Linkerscheldeover, Antwerpen

I.M.A.M. I: i: Industrie Meccaniche e Aeronautiche Meridionali, Napoli

I Mar E e: Institute (Institution) of Marine Engineers

IMARO BRD: d: Interministerieller Ausschuß für Raumordnung, 53 Bonn

IMAS SN: f: Industrie d'Extraction, d'Exploitations et d'Exportation de Marbre et d'Agglomérés Sénégalaise

I.M.A.S.A. INT: e: International Medico-Athletic and Scientific Association

IMASLA MA: e: International Muslim Academy of Sciences, Letters and Arts

IMAT I: i: Istituto di Microbiologia Agrarie e Tecnica

IMAU INT: e: International Movement for Atlantic Union, Washington 9, D.C. [und] Neuilly s/Seine [F]

I.M.B. e: Institute of Microbiology

IMB INT: d: Internationaler Metallarbeiterbund, Genf [CH, gegr 1893]

IMBA BlnW: d: Internationales Musiker-Brief-Archiv

IMBT US: e: Iron Masters Board of Trade

IMC GB: e: Institute of Measurement and Control, London; US: e: Institute of Medicine of Chicago

I.M.C. F: f: Institut Maritime et Colonial; 1: Institutum Missionum a Consolata

IMC US: e: Intercontinental Monetary Corporation, New York; International Mailbag Club; INT: e: International Maritime Committee, Antwerpen [B], Hamburg 36 [BRD, gegr 1897]; US: e: International Match Corporation; INT: e: International Materials Conference, Washington, D.C. [1951... 53]; International Meteorological Committee; CDN: e: International Minerals and Chemicals Corporation; INT: e: International Missionary Council, New York [gegr 1920]; International Monetary Conference; International Music Council, Paris 16 [gegr 1949]

IMCA US: e: International Motor Contest Association

IMCB INT: e: International Mine Clearance Board, London

IMCC US: e: mil: Integrated Mission Control Center

I.M.C.E. GB: e: Institution of Municipal and County Engineers

IMCE INT: e: International Meeting of Cataloguing Experts [København, DK, Aug 1969]

IMCI CI: f: Industries Métallurgiques de la Côte d'Ivoire

IMCO UN: e: Intergovernmental Maritime Consultative Organization, London W 1 [gegr 1948]

IMCOS INT: e: International Meteorological Consultant Service

IMCS INT: 1: e: "Pax Romana", International Movement of Catholic Students, Fribourg [CH, gegr 1921]

I.M.D. GB: e: Indian Medical Department; Indian Meteorological Department

IMD US: e: Institute of Metals Division, New York [AIME]; Institute for Muscle Disease; Rhodesien: e: Iron and Minerals Development

IMDBI IR: e: Industrial and Mining Development Bank of Iran, Teheran

IME I: i: Industria Macchine Elettroniche IME S.p.A., oo153 Roma; US: e: Institute of Makers of Explosives; GB: e: Institute (Institution) of Mechanical Engineers, London; Institute (Institution) of Mining Engineers; Institution of Municipal Engineers

I.M.E.A. GB: e: Incorporated Municipal Electrical Association

IMEA US: e: Indiana (Iowa) Music Educators Association

IMechE GB: e: Institute (Institution) of Mechanical Engineers, London

IMECO INT: e: International Measurement Confederation, Budapest [H]

IMEDE; Imede CH: f: Institut pour l'Etude des Méthodes de Direction de l'Entreprise, Lausanne

IMEG GB: e: International Management and Engineering Group

I.M.E.I. e: Institute of Marine Engineers Incorporated

IMEI H: hu: Ipari Minöség-ellenörző Intézet, Budapest

IMEKO INT: d: Internationale Meßtechnische Konferenz (Konföderation), Budapest 5 [H] [vgl: IMECO]

IMEL SU: d: Institut Marx-Engels-Lenin

IMEM US: e: International Mass Education Movement

IMet GB: e: Institute of Metals.

I.Meth. e: Independent Methodists

IMETRA B: f: Institut de Médecine Tropicale Reine Astrid, Léopoldville

I.M.F. GB: e: Institute of Metal Finishing, London; R: ro: Institutul Medico-Farmaceutic

IMF INT: d: Internationale Musikfestwochen, Luzern [CH]; INT: e: International Marketing Federation, Chicago, Ill.; International Metalworkers' Federation, Geneva [CH, gegr 1893]; International Monetary Fund, Washington 25, D.C.; International Motorcycle Federation, Geneva [CH, gegr 1904]; UN: e: International Music Fund [UNESCO]

IMFM F: f: Institut de mécanique des fluides de Marseille

IMFW; IMFWUNA US: e: International Molders and Foundry Workers' Union of North America

IMG INT: d: Internationale Modulargruppe [gegr 1960]; Internationale Moselgesellschaft, 55 Trier; Internationale Musik-Gesellschaft [1899... 1914]; D: d: mil: nach WK2: Internationaler Militärgerichtshof, Nürnberg

IMGD NL: nl: mil: Inspectie Militaire Geneeskundige Dienst

I.M.H. e: Inspectorate of the Ministry of Health

IMH PL: pl: Instytut Ministerstwa Hutnictwa

IMHV BRD: d: Interessengemeinschaft musikwissenschaftlicher Herausgeber und Verleger [gegr 1966 in Kassel]

IMI US: e: Ignition Manufacturers Institute; GB: e: Imperial Mycological Institute; Institute of the Motor Industry; d: Internationales Metaphysisches Institut; US: e: International Marketing Institute, Cambridge, Mass.; e: International Metaphysical Institute; IL: e: mil: Israel Military Industries, Tel Aviv; IL: e: Israel Music Institute [publisher]; I: i: Istituto Mobiliare Italiano, Roma

IMIB US: e: Inland Marine Insurance Bureau

IMIMI US: e: Industrial Mineral Insulation Manufacturers Institute

I Min E GB: e: Institution of Mining Engineers

IMIS S: sv: Internationella motorcykelsalongen i Stockholm; INT: [d: Internationale Ausstellung für Meßtechnik und Gerätebau, Warschau [PL, 3 ... 11.Juli 1967]

IMIT MEX: s: Instituto Mexicano de Investigaciónes Tecnológicas

I.M.I.U. INT: e: International Marine Insurance Union

IMK BRD: d: Innenministerkonferenz

I.M.K.K. D: d: nach WK1: Interalliierte Militär-Kontroll-Kommission

IML DDR: d: Institut für Marxismus-Leninismus [beim ZK der SED]

I.M.L. F: f: Institut Médico-Légal

IML US: e: Irradiated Materials Laboratory

IMLB INT: d: Internationale Musikleihbibliothek

IMLO NL: nl: Internationale Maatschappij voor Landbouwkundige Ontwikkeling

IMLT GB: e: Institute of Medical Laboratory Technology

IMM GB: e: Institution of Mining and Metallurgy, London [gegr 1892] ; INT: d: Internationale Markenmeisterschaft [Autorennen]

IMMA I: i: Industrie Meridionali Munizioni Affini

I.M.M.Co. e: International Mercantile Marine Company

IMMO e: Intermediate Main Meteorological Office

IMMOA INT: e: International Mercantile Marine Officers Association, London

IMMRAN INT: e: International Meeting of Marine Radio Aids to Navigation

IMMSW US: e: International Union of Mine, Mill and Smelter Workers, Denver, Colo.

IMNOS BRD: d: Interministerieller Ausschuß für Notstands- und Sanierungsfragen [gegr 1950, später:] Interministerieller Ausschuß für regionale Wirtschaftspolitik

I.M.N.S. GB: e: Imperial Military Nursing Service; Indian Military Nursing Service

IMO B: f: Institut maritime d'Ostende; INT: e: Inter-American Municipal Organization [gegr 1938] ; INT: d: Internationale Meteorologische Organisation e: International Meteorological Organization [jetzt: WMO]

IMP GB: e: Ideas Marketing Pool Ltd.

I.M.P. e: Independence for Malaya Party; F: f: Ingénieurs Militaires des Poudres; e: Institute of Medical Psychology; Institute of Mental Physics

IMP BRD: d: Institut für Marktpflege GmbH & Co. KG, 65 Mainz

I.M.P. F: f: Institut Médico- Pédagogique; Institut Moderne Polytechnique, Boulogne s/Seine

IMP PL: pl: Instytut Mechaniki Precyzyjnej; Instytut Medycyny Pracy; CH: d: Interkantonale Mobile Polizei; PL: [d: Internationale Messe in Posen] ;

IL: e: Israeli Music Publications [Verlag, seit 1949]

IMPA RA: s: Compañía Industria Metalúrgica & Plástica S.A., Buenos Aires; INT: e: International Movement for Peace Action, Brussels [B]

IMPBA US: e: International Model Power Boat Association

IMPDAA US: e: Independent Motion Picture Distributors Association of America

Impes I: i: Industrie Meccaniche Precisione e Stampaggi S.p.A., Collegno

IMPEX F: f: Service des Importations et des Exportations

IMPHQA INT: f: Institut mondial pour la protection de la haute qualité alimentaire

IMPI e: International Microwave Power Institute

IMPO CH: d: Schweizerische Import-Messe Zürich

IMPPA US: e: Independent Motion Picture Producers Association

IMPRINTA '70 BRD: d: IMPRINTA '70 – vom Original zur Druckform – Kongreß mit technischen Demonstrationen, Düsseldorf [erstmals 28. Sep ... 4. Okt 1970]

IMQ I: i: Istituto Italiano del Marchio di Qualità, Roma

IMR PTM: e: Institute of Medical Research, Kuala Lumpur; US: e: Institute of Motivational Research; CH: d: Institut für Messe- und Raumplanung AG, Zürich; INT: d: Internationaler Missionsrat [gegr 1921] ; Internationaler Musikrat

IMRAMN INT: e: International Meeting on Radio Aids to Marine Navigation [London 1946]

IMRC INT: e: International Marine Radio Committee

IMRNR MEX: s: Instituto Mexicano de

Recursos Naturales Renovables

IMRO BG: [d: Innere Makedonische Revolutionäre Organisation, gegr 1893 in Saloniki] [e: Internal Macedonian Revolutionary Organization]

I.M.S. IND: e: Indian Mathematical Society; GB: e: Indian Medical Service

IMS US: e: Industrial Management Society; Industrial Mathematics Society

I.M.S. e: Industrial Medical Service; S: sv: Informationsbyrån för mellanfolkligt samarbete för fred, Stockholm; B: f: Inspection médicale scolaire; e: Inspector of Medical Services

IMS e: Institute of Management Sciences; US: e: Institute of Mathematical Statistics

I.M.S. GB: e: Institute of Mine Surveyors

IMS BRD: d: Institut für Medizinische Statistik GmbH, 6 Ffm

I.M.S. DK: e: International Male Studio, Copenhagen V; INT: e: International Migration Service, Geneva [CH, gegr 1921]

IMS NATO: e: International Military Staff d: Internationaler Militärstab; INT: e: International Musicological Society [Basel, CH, gegr 1927]; I: i: Istituto di Medicine Sociale

IMSA US: e: International Municipal Signal Association, Inc.,New York

IMSC US: e: Industry Missile and Space Conference

IMSF BRD: d: Institut für Marxistische Studien und Forschungen, 6 Ffm [gegr 1968]

I.M.S.G. GB: e: Imperial Merchant Service Guild

I.M.T. F: f: Inspection Médicale du Travail; GB: e: mil: Inspector of Mechanized Troops; e: Institute of the Motor Trade; B: f: Institut de Médecine Tropicale Prince Léopold

IMT P: pt: Instituto de Medicina Tro-

pical, Lisboa; D: e: mil: nach WK2: International Military Tribunal [Nürnberg]

I.M.T.A. e: Imported Meat Trade Association; GB: e: Institute of Municipal Treasurers and Accountants

I.M.T.D. GB: e: mil: Inspector of the Military Training Directorate

I.M.T.E. INT: e: International Machine Tool Exhibition, London

IMTFE INT: e: mil: International Tribunal for the Far East

IMTNE INT: e: International Meteorological Teleprinter Network in Europe

IMTP US: e: mil: Industrial Mobilization Training Program

IMTPA B: f: Institut de Médecine Tropicale Princesse Astrid, Léopoldville

IMU S: sv: Institutet för marknadsundersökningar AB, Stockholm

imu INT: d: Internationale Möbel-Union, Paris

IMU US: e: International Mailers Union; INT: e: International Mathematical Union

IMUA US: e: Inland Marine Underwriters' Association; US: e: mil: Interservice Material Utilization Agency

IMUJ PL: pl: Instytut Matematyczny Uniwersytetu Jagiellońskiego

IMUK INT: d: Internationale Mathematische Unterrichtskommission

I Mun E GB: e: Institution of Municipal Engineers

IMUZ PL: pl: Instytut Meioracji Użytków Zielonych

IMV INT: d: Internationaler Metzgermeisterverband, Brüssel 4 [B]; Internationaler Milchwirtschaftsverband, Brüssel 4 [B]

IMVS AUS: e: Institute of Medical and Veterinary Science

IMWA INT: e: International Working Men's Association [gegr 1923]

IMWI BRD: d: Institut für Markt- und

Werbe-Information, 4 Düsseldorf

IMYCW INT: e: International Movement of Young Christian Workers

IMZ BRD: d: Internationales Musikzentrum

I.N. F: f: Imprimerie Nationale; e: mil: Indian Navy

In d: mil: Inspektion

IN US: e: Institute of Navigation

I.N. I: i: mil: Istituto Nautico

IN e: mil: Italian Navy

In 1 D: d: mil: Inspektion der Waffenschulen; Heeres-Inspektion des Erziehungs- und Bildungswesens [Reichswehrministerium]

In 2 D: d: mil: Inspektion der Infanterie

In 3 D: d: mil: Inspektion der Kavallerie

In 4 D: d: mil: Inspektion der Artillerie

In 5 D: d: mil: Inspektion der Pioniere; Inspektion der Pioniere und Festungen [Reichswehrministerium]

In 6 D: d: mil: Inspektion für Heeresmotorisierung

In 6 F D: d: mil: Inspektion der Verkehrstruppen (Fahrtruppen)

In 6 K D: d: mil: Inspektion der Verkehrstruppen (Kraftfahrtruppen) [Reichswehrministerium]

In 7 D: d: mil: Inspektion der Nachrichtentruppen

IN 8 D: d: mil: Nachschubabteilung

INA IND: e: Indian National Airways, New Delhi; IND: e: mil: Indian National Army

Ina D: d: mil: WK1: Infanterie-Nachrichten-Abteilung

I.N.A. F: f: mil: Infanterie Nord-Africaine; GB: e: mil: Institute (Institution) of Naval Architects, London; F: f: Institut National Agronomique, Paris [gegr 1876]

INA CO: s: Instituto Nacional de Abastecimientos; US: e: Insurance Company of North America [gegr 1792]; BRD: d: Internationale Nachrichten-Agentur, Ffm; INT: e: International Newsreel Association, Paris 18; IRQ: e: Iraqui News Agency; IRL: e: Irish News Agency, Dublin [1949...57]; IL: e: Israeli News Agency; I: i: Istituto Nazionale di Abitazioni; Istituto Nazionale Apicultura; Istituto Nazionale delle Assicurazioni, Roma

I.N.A.C. F: f: Institut National d'Agronomie Coloniale; Institut National de la Conserve; I: i: Istituto Nazionale per le Applicazioni del Calcolo, Roma

INACAP RCH: [d: Nationales Institut für Berufsfortbildung]

Inach D: d: mil: WK1: Inspektion der Nachrichtentruppen

Inachera D: d: mil: WK1: Inspektion der Nachrichten-Ersatzabteilungen

INACO RA: s: Instituto Nacional de Comercio [gegr 1953]

INACOL B: f: Institut National pour l'Amélioration des Conserves de Légumes

INADES f: Institut Africain pour le Développement Economique et Social

INAEICM F: f: Institut National Agricole d'Etudes et d'Initiatives Coopératives et Mutualistes

InAF e: mil: Indian Air Force

INAH MEX: s: Instituto Nacional de Antropología e Historia

INAIL I: i: Istituto Nazionale per l'Assicurazione contro gli Infortuni sul Lavoro

INALA B: f: Institut National du Logement et de l'Habitation

Inalwa INT: e: International Airlift West Africa [d: Biafra-Luftbrücke 1968... 69 des IKRK]

INAM I: i: Istituto Nazionale per l'Assicurazione contro le Malattie

INANTIC PE: s: Instituto Nacional de Normas Técnicas y Certificación, Lima

I.N.A.O. F: f: Institut National des Appellations d'Origine des Vins et Eaux -de-Vie

I.N.A.P.L.I. I: i: Istituto Nazionale per l'Addestramento ed il Perfezionamento dei Lavoratori dell'Industria

INARC f: Institut Nord-Africain de Recherches Cottonières; I: i: [d: Architekturinstitut]

INB PL: pl: Inspekcja Nadzoru Budowlanego

I.N.B. F: f: Institut National du Bois

INBEFO BRD: d: Institut für berufsbegleitende Fortbildung GmbH, 68 Mannheim

INBEL B: [e: Belgian Institute of Information and Documentation]

INBH B: f: Institut National Belge du Houblon

INBK PL: pl: Instytut Naukowo-Badawczy Kolejnictwa

INBPW PL: pl: Instytut Naukowo-Badawczy Przemysłu Weglowego

INBR B: f: Institut National Belge de Radiodiffusion

INBRACON BR: pt: Indústrias Brasileiras Concordias

INBTP CGO: [d: Nationales Institut für Bauten und öffentliche Arbeiten, Kinshasa]

INC RA: [d: Nationales Fleischinstitut, seit 1955]; IND: e: Indian National Congress [d: Partei]

I.N.C. F: f: Inspection de la Navigation Commerciale; s: Instituto Nacional de Colonización

INC CDN: e: International Nickel Company of Canada; INT: e: International Numismatic Commission, Paris [gegr 1936]

I.N.C.A. B: f: Institut National de Crédit Agricole

INCA US: e: mil: Integrated Communication Agency; INT: e: International Newspaper Color Association; I: i: Istituto Nazionale Confederale di Assistenza

INCAP INT: s: Instituto de Nutrición de Centro América y Panamá, Guatemala [gegr 1946]

INCC US: e: International Newspaper Collectors Club

INCE I: i: Istituto Nazionale per i Cambi con l'Estero

INCEI NIC: s: Instituto Nacional de Comercio Exterior e Interior

INCF I: i: Istituto Nazionale di Cultura Fascita

INCFO US: e: Institute of Newspaper Controllers and Finance Officers

INCHEBA CS: [d: Internationale Chemische Messe, Bratislava]

INChHUK SU: [d: Institut für künstlerische Kultur, Petersburg, gegr 1922]

INCIDI INT: f: Institut International de Civilisations Différentes, Bruxelles [gegr 1894]

I.N.C.I.S. I: i: Istituto Nazionale per le Case degli Impiegati dello Stato

I.N.C.M. F: f: Institut National des Classes Moyennes

INCO CDN: e: International Nickel Company of Canada Ltd.; US: e: Internatial Nickel Company, Inc.

IN. CO. ME. I: i: Industriale Cotonicola Meridionale

INCOMEX CO: s: Instituto Colombiano de Comercio Exterior

INCOMI BR: pt: Indústria e Comércio de Minérios S.A.

INCONOR; INCONTEC CO: s: Instituto Colombiano de Normas, Bucaramagna

INCORACO MT: e: International Commercial Radio Corporation

INCP BR: pt: Instituto Nacional de Ciências Políticas

INCRA INT: e: International Copper Research Association

INCREF GB: e: International Children's Rescue Fund

INDA BRD: d: Schulungs-Institut für Text- und Datenverarbeitung, 5 Köln;

I: i: Istituto Nazionale del Dramma Antico

INDAG WAN: e: Industrial and Agricultural Company

Indag D: d: Industrielle Diskonto AG, Berlin; Industrie-Unternehmungen AG, Hannover

Indatom F: [d: Industriegruppe für Kerntechnik, Paris, gegr 1955]

INDC INT: e: International Nuclear Data Committee, Vienna [A, IAEO]

Ind.C.C.F. CDN: e: Independent Cooperative Commonwealth Federation

INDE GCA: s: Instituto Nacional de Electrificacion

INDEC GB: e: Independent Nuclear Disarmament Election Committee

INDECAM Kamerun: f: Indépendants Camerounais

INDECO Z: e: Industrial Development Company

INDER C: s: Instituto Nacional de Deportes, Educación Física y Recreación

INDETA BRD: d: Interessengemeinschaft Deutscher Tanzmusikverbraucher

INDICI INT: e: International Institute of Different Civilization, Brussels [B]

Indisk D: d: Industrielle Diskonto AG, Berlin

INDITECNOR RCH: s: Instituto Nacional de Investigaciones Tecnológicas y Normalización, Santiago

INDOC BRD: d: INDOC Industrie- und Fernsehfilm GmbH, 8 München-Obermenzing; Internationale Dokumentationsgesellschaft für Chemie mbH, 6 Ffm

INDROFA INT: d: Internationale Drogisten-Fachausstellung [BRD]

INDUBAN E: s: Banco de Financiación Industrial S.A., Madrid [gegr 1964]

Indufag D: d: AG für Industrie-und Handelsfinanzierungen, Berlin

Indufina BRD: d: Industriebeteiligungs- und Finanzierungsgesellschaft mbH, München

INDUGAS BRD: d: INDUGAS Gesellschaft für industrielle Gasverwendung mbH, Essen

I.N.E. GB: e: Institution of Naval Engineers; F: f: Institut National de l'Embouteillage

INE P: pt: Instituto Nacional de Estatística, Lisboa; E: s: Instituto Nacional de Estadística; I: i: Istituto Nazionale Esportazione

INEA INT: d: Internationaler Elektronik-Arbeitskreis, 6 Ffm e: International Electronics Association; I: i: Istituto Nazionale di Economia Agraria

INEAC CGO: f: Institut National pour l'Etude Agronomique du Congo, Kinshasa [gegr 1933: ... Agronomique au Congo belge]

In.E.B. D: d: mil: Inspektion des Erziehungs- und Bildungswesens

InEBH BRD: d: mil: Inspektion des Erziehungs- und Bildungswesens im Heer

INECEL EC: s: Instituto Ecuatoriano de Electrificación, Quito

I.N.E.D. F: f: Institut national d'études démographiques

INEFCO GB: e: Insurance Export Finance Company [gegr 1962]

INEI I: i: Istituto Nazionale per l'Esame delle Invenzioni

INEJ E: s: Instituto Nacional de Estudios Jurídicos

INEL INT: d: Internationale Fachmesse für industrielle Elektronik, Basel [CH]

INEP Kongo: f: Institut National d'Etudes Politiques

INEPS B: [d: Institut für Körpererziehung und Sport]

INERM F: f: Institut Nationale d'Etudes Rurales Montagnards

INET RA: s: Instituto Nacional de Estudios del Teatro

I.N.E.T.O.P. F: f: Institut National d'Etudes du Travail et de l'Orientation Professionnelle

Inex DDR: d: VEB Industrieanlagen-Export; D: d: AG für Industrie und Export, Berlin

INF BR: pt: Instituto Nacional de Farmacologia; INT: d: Internationale Naturisten-Föderation, Wien [gegr 1953] e: International Naturist Federation

INFA F: f: Institut pour l'Etude du Fascisme [gegr 1934]; INT: e: International Fiscal Association; I: i: Istituto Nazionale Fisioterapico per l'Adolescenza

I.N.F.B.T.A. e: Incorporated National Federation of Boot Trades Associations

INFCO ISO: e: Committee on Scientific and Technical Information on Standardization

In.Fest. D: d: mil: Inspektion der Festungen

I.N.F.H. e: Incorporated National Federation of Hairdressers

Infi BlnW: d: Internationales Forschungsinstitut [des SDS]

Infima INT: d: Internationale Filmwoche Mannheim [BRD]

INFIND B: f: Bureau de l'Information pour Indigènes, Léopoldville

INFIR I: i: Istituto Nazionale per il Finanziamento della Ricostruzione

InfKAS S: sv: mil: Infanteriets kadett-och aspirantskola, Holmstad [gegr 1926]

InfKS S: sv: mil: Infanteriets kadettskola, Solna

In.Flak/LS. D: d: mil: Inspektion der Flak und des Luftschutzes

INFN I: i: Istituto Nazionale di Fisica Nucleare, Roma [gegr 1951]

INFONAC NIC: s: Instituto de Fomento Nacional

INFOP GCA: s: Instituto de Fomento de la Producción

Infoplan BRD: d: Infoplan Gesellschaft für Öffentlichkeitsarbeit mbH, 6 Ffm

INFORCONGO B: f: Office d'information et des relations publiques du Congo belge et du Ruanda-Urundi, Bruxelles

INFORFILM e: International Informatic Film Service

Inform DDR: d: Informationsbüro der Kommunistischen und Arbeiterpartei "Für dauerhaften Frieden, für Volksdemokratie" [1947...56]

Informa BRD: d: Informa Industriefilm GmbH, Düsseldorf [gegr 1961]; Veranstaltungen der Arbeitsgemeinschaft "D moderne Küche" in Düsseldorf

Informex MEX: [d: Nachrichtenagentur]

INFORMOTOR S: sv: Bilismens och motororganisationernas informationsverksamhet, Stockholm

INFPS I: i: Istituto Nazionale Fascista della Previdenza Sociale

INFRA; Infra INT: e: International Freedom Academy

Infratest BRD: d: Infratest Marktforschung, Wirtschaftsforschung, Motivforschung, Sozialforschung GmbH & Co., 8 München

InfS BRD: d: mil: Infanterieschule

Inf. Sch. D: d: mil: Infanterieschule

Inf Sch e: mil: Infantry School

InfSS S: sv: mil: Infanteriskjutskolan

InFüLw BRD: d: mil: Inspektion Führungsdienste der Luftwaffe

InFüSBw BRD: d: mil: Schule der Bundeswehr für Innere Führung

InFüTr BRD: d: mil: Inspektion der Führungstruppen

ING I: i: Istituto Nazionale Geodetico

INGA CH: d: Internationale Nahrungs- und Genußmittel-Aktiengesellschaft, Zürich [seit 1965: Interfranck Holding AG]

INGAA US: e: Independent Natural Gas Association of America

INGE RA: s: Instituto Nacional de Grano y Elevadores

INGF I: i: Istituto elettrotecnico nazionale Galileo Ferraris, Torino

INGIC I: i: Istituto Nazionale Gestione

Imposte di Consumo [gegr 1966]
IngKS S: sv: mil: Ingenjörtruppernas kadettskola, Solna
IngOS S: sv: mil: Ingenjörofficersskolan, Stockholm
Ingosstrach SU: [d: staatliche Auslandsversicherung]
IngS d: Ingenieurschule; DK: da: Ingeniør-Sammenslutningen; S: sv: mil: Ingenjörtruppskolan, Solna
Ing.u.DOS; Ing.u.DO.Sch. D: d; mil: Ingenieur- und Deckoffizierschule
INGy H: hu: Ideiglenes Nemzetgyűlés
I.N.H. F: f: Institut National d'Hygiène
InHFlaTr BRD: d: mil: Inspektion der Heeresflugabwehrtruppe
INHSA GCA: s: Industria Harinera Guatemalteca S.A.
I.N.I. RI: Ikatan Nasional Indonesia; F: f: Institution Nationale des Invalides; MEX: s: Instituto Nacional Indigenista
INI E: s: Instituto Nacional de Industria, Madrid; I: i: Istituto Nazionale Infortuni
INIA E: s: Instituto Nacional de Investigaciones Agronómicas
I.N.I.A.S.A. I: i: Istituto Nazionale per l'Istruzione e l'Addestramento Professionale nel Settore Artigiano
INIC BR: pt: Instituto Nacional de Imigração e Colonização
INICHAR B: f: Institut National de l'Industrie Charbonnière, Liège
INII P: pt: Instituto Nacional de Investigação Industrial, Lisboa
INIRO RI: nl: Indonesisch Instituut voor Rubber Onderzoek
INIS INT: d: Internationales Nuklearinformationssystem e: International Nuclear Information System [IAEO]
I.N.J.A. F: f: Institut National des Jeunes Aveugles
INK H: hu: Ideiglenes Nemzeti Kormány;

INT: d: Internationaler Nomenklaturkongreß, Genf [CH]
InKpfTr BRD: d: mil: Inspektion der Kampftruppen
I.N.L. B: f: Institut National du Logement, Bruxelles; BR: pt: Instituto Nacional do Livro
INLACA E: s: Industria Lactea de Carabobo, S.A.
INLE E: s: Instituto Nacional del Libro Español, Madrid
INLEGMASCH INT: [d: Internationale Fachausstellung "Moderne Ausrüstungen und neue technologische Vorgänge in der Leichtindustrie", Moskau, SU]
INM US: e: mil: Inspector of Naval Material
INMA BRD; d: Institut für Marktforschung GmbH, 7 Stuttgart; F: f: Institut National de Médicine Agricole
InMFü BRD: d: mil: Inspektion der Marineführungsdienste
InMRüst BRD: d: mil: Inspektion für Angelegenheiten der Marinerüstung
InMSan BRD: d: mil: Inspektion des Marine-Sanitätsdienstes
InMVers BRD: d: mil: Inspektion der Marineversorgung
InMWa BRD: d: mil: Inspektion der Marinewaffen
InN e: mil: Indian Navy
INN RA: s: Instituto Nacional de la Nutrición
Innis GB: e: mil: Royal Inniskilling Fusiliers
Innis DG GB: e: mil: Royal Inniskilling Dragoon Guards
Innisks = Innis
InnM. A: d: Innenministerium
INNS OF COURT GB: e: mil: The Inns of Court Regiment (Territorial Army)
INO INT: e: International NOTAM Office
INOE INT: eo: Internacia Naturista Organizo Esperantista, Yerres (S.et O). [F]

INOF I: i: Istituto Nazionale di Ortofrutticoltura

INO i K PL: pl: Instytut Naukowy Organizacji i Kierownictwa

INOMARCOS BRD: d: INOMARCOS AG Institut für Operational Research Marketing und Computersysteme, 4 Düsseldorf

I.N.O.P. F: f: Institut National d'Orientation Professionnelle

INORCOL CO: s: Instituto de Normas Colombiana, Bucaramagna

INOS YV: s: Instituto Nacional de Obras Sanitarias, Caracas

INOSP YV: s: Instituto Nacional de Orientación y Selección Professional

In.Ost. D: d: mil: Inspektor der Landesbefestigung Ost

Inotorg SU: D: [d: Handelszentrale der Handelsvertretung der UdSSR in Berlin]

In. P. D: d: mil: Inspektor des Personalprüfungswesens des Heeres

INP ET: e: Institute of National Planning; B: f: Institut National de la Publicité; E: s: Instituto Nacional de Previsión; BR: pt: Instituto Neo-Pitagórico, Curitiba [gegr 1909] ; US: e: International News Photos, New York

INPABO P: pt: Instituto Paranaense de Botânica

I.N.P.A.R. F: f: Institut National de Promotion Agricole de Rennes

I.N.P.C.B. B: f: Institut National des Parcs au Congo Belge

INPET I: i: Istituto Nazionale Petrolio

INPFC INT: e: International North Pacific Fisheries Commission, Vancouver 8, B.C. [CDN]

I.N.P.H. B: f: Institut National pour la Promotion de l'Habitation

I.N.P.I. F: f: Institut National de la Propriété Industrielle, 75 Paris 8

INPI PE: s: Instituto Nacional para el Progreso Industrial

InPiTr BRD: d: mil: Inspektion der Pioniertruppen

INPM BR: pt: Instituto Nacional de Pesos e Medias

INPOLYGRAPHMASCH SU: [d: Fachausstellung "Moderne graphische Technik", Moskau]

INPPSS E: s: Instituto Nacional para le Producción de Semillas Selectas

INPRESSA NL: e: Indonesian Press Agency, Den Haag

INPRO BRD: d: Institut für Investitions- und Produktionsgüter-Marktforschung, 62 Wiesbaden

INPRODMASCH INT: [d: Internationale Ausstellung "Neuzeitliche mechanisierte und automatisierte Einrichtungen, Verpackungsmaschinen und Fördermittel für die Nahrungsmittelindustrie", Moskau, SU]

I.N.P.S. f: Institut National de la Prévoyance Sociale; I: i: Istituto Nazionale della Previdenza Sociale

INQF INT: d: Internationale Vereinigung für Quartärforschung

INQUA INT: e: International Association on Quaternary Research

INR B: f: Institut National Belge de Radiodiffusion; GR: f: Institut National de Radiodiffusion; BRD: d: Institut für Neutronenphysik und Reaktortechnik, 75 Karlsruhe

I.N.R.A. F: f: Institut National de la Recherche Agronomique, Paris 7

INRA C: s: Instituto Nacional de Reforma Agraria; BG: [f: Comité Supérieure de Normalisation de la République Populaire de Bulgarie]

INRAB B: f: Institut National de Recherches Antiarcticaux de Belgique

INRAT TN: f: Institut National de la Recherche Agronomique de Tunisie

INRDG Guinea: f: Institut de Recherche et de Documentation de Guinée

INRE C: s: Instituto Nacional de Reforma Agronómica

INRESCOR CH: d: Internationale Forschungsgesellschaft der Firmen Cluett, Peabody International AG, Zug & Heberlein, Zürich

INRF US: e: International Nutrition Research Foundation

INRO RI: nl: Indonesisch Instituut voor Rubberonderzoek

INRT E: s: Instituto Nacional de Racionalización del Trabajo [=IRATRA]

INRWF IND: e: Indian National Railway Workers' Federation

Inrybprom INT: [d: internationale Fischereiausstellung, Leningrad, SU]

INS US: e: Immigration and Nationalization Service; IND: e: Indian News Service [d: Nachrichtenagentur]

In.S. D: d: mil: Inspektion für Flugsicherheit und Gerät

INS GB: e: Institute of Nuclear Studies

I.N.S. f: Institut National de Sécurité; F: f: Institut National des Sports; Institut National de la Statistique; B: f: Institut National de la Statistique

INS PL: pl: Instytut Nauk Społecznych; US: e: International News Service, New York [d: Nachrichtenagentur, gegr 1909]

INSA E: s: Industria y Navegación S.A.

I.N.S.A. F: f: Institut National des Sciences Appliquées, Lyon

INSAFI Salvador: s: Instituto Salvadoreño de Fomento Industrial

INSAFOP Salvador: s: Instituto Salvadoreño de Fomento de la Producción

INSAI CH: i: Istituto Nazionale Svizzero di Assicurazione contro gli Infortuni

InSan BRD: d: mil: Inspektion des Sanitäts- und Gesundheitswesens [BMVtdg]

InSanTr BRD: d: mil: Inspektion der Sanitätstruppe

INSBA B: f: Institut National Supérieur des Beaux-Arts

I.N.S.C. F: f: Institut Normal des Sciences Commerciales, Boulogne s/Seine

INSCAIRS US: e: Instrumentation Calibration Incident Repair Service

InSchT BRD: d: mil: Inspektion der Schiffstechnik

INSDOC IND: e: Indian National Scientific Documentation Centre, New Delhi [gegr 1952]

INSEA INT: e: International Society for Education through Art

INSEAD F: f: Institut européen d'administration d'affaires, Fontainebleau [gegr 1958]

I.N.S.E.E. F: f: Institut National de Statistique et d'Etudes Economiques, Paris

INSERM F: f: Institut National de la Santé et de la Recherche Médicale

INSJ J: e: Institute of Nuclear Study, Japan

I.N.S.M. F: f: Institut National des Sourds-Muets

INSOC B: f: Institut universitaire d'information sociale et économique, Bruxelles

INSORD US: e: mil: Inspector of Naval Ordnance

I.N.S.P. CI: f: Institut national de santé publique, Abidjan

Insp.d.Fl. D: d: mil: WK1: Inspektion der Fliegertruppen

Insp.f.s. CS: cs: Inspektorát finanční stráže

InspizFJg BRD: d: mil: Inspizient der Feldjäger

I.N.S.P.T. F: f: Institut National de Sécurité et de Prévention Technique

INSRE f: Institut National de la Statistique et de la Recherche Economique

INSTA INT: sv: Internordiska standardiseringskommissionen [DK, N, S, SF]

Inst. Bks. GB: e: The Institute of Bankers

Inst. C.E. GB: e: The Institution of Civil Engineers

Inst. Ch. e: Institute of Charity

Inst. E.E. GB: e: The Institution of Electrical Engineers

Inst. F. GB: e: The Institute of Fuel
Inst. Gas E. GB: e: The Institution of Gas Engineers
Inst. M.E. e: Institute of Marine Engineers; GB: e: The Institution of Mechanical Engineers
Inst. M.M. GB: e: The Institution of Mining and Metallurgy
I.N.S.T.N. F: f: Institut National des Sciences et Techniques Nucléaires, 91 Gif-sur-Yvette [gegr 1956]
Inst. N.A. e: Institution of Naval Architects
Inst. P. GB: e: The Institute of Physics
InstRE US: e: Institute of Radio Engineers
InstRgt BRD: d: mil: Instandsetzungsregiment
Inst.R.N.V.R. GB: e: mil: Instructor of Royal Naval Volunteer Reserve
Inst. T. GB: e: Institute of Transport
Inst. W.E. GB: e: The Institution of Water Engineers
INSURV US: e: mil: Board of Inspection and Survey [Navy]
INT BRD: d: Industriegesellschaft für neue Technologien mbH, 899 Lindau; DDR: d: Institut für Nachrichtentechnik, Berlin-Oberschöneweide; BR: pt: Instituto Nacional de Tecnologia, Rio de Janeiro; US: e: Department of the Interior
int. I: i: interni [d: Innenministerium]
INT I: i: Istituto Nazionale della Tecnica
INTA E: s: Instituto Nacional de Técnica Aeronáutica (Aerospacial), Madrid; RA: s: Instituto Nacional de Tecnología Agropecuaria; US: e: International Newspaper and Trade Advertising, New York, N.Y. 10036; e: International New Thought Alliance
INTAKO; Intako INT: d: Internationaler Tanzlehrer-Kongreß [1970 in Hannover, BRD]
INTAL RA: s: Instituto para la Integra-

ción de América-Latina, Buenos Aires
INTAMEL INT: e: International Association of Metropolitan City Libraries
Int. AOB BRD: d: Internationale Arbeitsgemeinschaft für organische Betriebsgestaltung, 638 Bad Homburg
INTAPUC INT: e: International Association of Public Cleansing
INTASGRO e: mil: Interallied Tactical Study Group
INTAVA INT: e: International Aviation Association
INTC e: Intelligence Committee
Int Cor; INT CORPS e: mil: Intelligence Corps
I.N.T.D. F: f: Institut National des Techniques de la Documentation, Paris
INTECNOR PY: s: Instituto Nacional de Tecnología y Normalización, Asunción
INTEKA INT: d: Internationale Ausstellung "Technik in Wärmekraftanlagen", Essen [BRD, erstmals 1...7.Jun 1970]
INTELCENPAC US: e: mil: Intelligence Center Pacific Ocean Areas
INTELSAT INT: d: Internationales Konsortium für Nachrichtensatelliten e: International Telecommunications Satellite Consortium f: Organisation internationale des télécommunications par satellite
INTEM INT: [e: Inter-American Institute of Music Education]
INTERAL INT: [d: Internationale Biennale der Nahrungsmittel und Ausrüstungsgüter, Paris, 9...15. Nov. 1970]
INTERALPEN A: d: Studiengesellschaft für Alpenwasserkräfte in Österreich
INTERASMA INT: e: International Association of Asthmology f: Association Internationale d'Asthmologie, Milan [I
Interatom BRD: d: Interatom Internationale Atomreaktorbau GmbH, 506 Bensberg
INTERBAKE INT: [d: Internationale

Bäckerei- und Konditorei-Messe, London]

Interbank INT: e: International Bank for Reconstruction and Development

INTERBAU 1956 BlnW: d: Internationale Bauausstellung Berlin 1956

INTERBIMALL INT: [d: Internationale Zweijahresmesse für Maschinen zur Bearbeitung von Holz, Möbeln, Tür- und Fenstereinfassungen, Platten usw., Milano, I]

Interblitz BRD: d: Internationales Schach-Blitzturnier für Vierermannschaften, Köln

Interboot INT: d: Internationale Boot-Ausstellung am Bodensee, 799 Friedrichshafen

INTERBRAU 1971 INT: d: Internationale Fachausstellung der Maschinen- und anderer Ausrüstungsindustrien für die Brau- und Getränkewirtschaft, München [13...19. Sep 1971]

INTERBYTMASCH INT: [d: Internationale Ausstellung für Kommunal- und Haushaltsausrüstung, Moskau, SU]

Interchemie INT: [d: internationale Chemieorganisation, Sitz Halle (Saale), DDR]

INTERCHIC INT: d: Internationale Bekleidungsmesse, BlnW

Interchoc BRD: d: Interchoc-Süßwaren-Vertriebsgesellschaft mbH & Co. KG, 415 Krefeld

INTERCONTAINER INT: d: Internationale Gesellschaft für den Transcontainer-Verkehr "INTERCONTAINER"

INTERCONTEX INT: [d: internationale Damenkonfektions- und Textil-Fachmesse, Amsterdam, NL]

INTERCOOP e: International Agricultural Cooperative Society

intercop BRD: e: d: International Copying Machines & Co mbH, 2 Hamburg

INTERCOP '68 BRD: d: Wanderausstellung über die Zusammenarbeit der BRD mit den Entwicklungsländern Afrikas, Asiens und Lateinamerikas [am 19. März 1968 in Köln eröffnet]

INTERDATA INT: [d: IFIP- Ausstellung von Datenverarbeitungsmaschinen]

Interdrama 68 INT: [d: internationales Festival der Jugendamateurtheater, BlnW, 5...11.Mai 1968]

Interdropa INT: d: Internationale Fachmesse für Drogerie und Parfumerie, Zürich [CH]

INTEREXPO INT: f: Comité des organisateurs de participations collectives nationales aux manifestations économiques internationales, Wien 1 [A]

INTERFEREX INT: d: Internationale Fachmesse für Eisenwaren, Werkzeuge und Haushaltartikel, Basel [CH]

Interfilm INT: d: Internationales Evangelisches Filmzentrum

Interfinish INT: d: Internationale Tagung für Oberflächentechnik der Metalle, Hannover [BRD]

Interflora GB: [d: Blumenhändlerdienst]

Interflug DDR: [d: Luftverkehrsunternehmen, Berlin]

INTERFRIGO INT: d: Internationale Gesellschaft der Eisenbahnen für Kühltransporte, Basel 20 [CH]   f: Société ferroviaire internationale de transports frigorifiques

Interfund INT: e: International Monetary Fund

Interfunk BRD: d: Einkaufsgenossenschaft europäischer Radio-, TV und Elektrofachhändler eGmbH, 7 Stuttgart

intergalva 1970 INT: [d: Konferenz von Experten für Oberflächenbehandlung, Düsseldorf, BRD]

Intergas 70 INT: [d: internationale Gasindustrie-Ausstellung Moskau, SU]

INTERGASTRA INT: d: Internationale Fachausstellung für das Hotel- und Gaststättengewerbe, 7 Stuttgart

Intergu INT: d: Internationale Gesellschaft für Urheberrecht, 8 München f: Société internationale pour le droit d'auteur

INTERHOSPITAL INT: d: Internationale Krankenhausausstellung mit 6. Deutschem Krankenhaustag [11...14.Mai 1971 in Stuttgart, BRD]

INTERHOTEL DDR: d: Vereinigung INTERHOTEL [gegr 1964...65]

INTERHYBRID INT: e: Intercontinental Association for Hybrid Maize f: Association intercontinentale du maïs hybride, Paris [gegr 1951]

INTERKAMA INT: d: Internationaler Kongreß mit Ausstellung für Meßtechnik und Automatik, Düsseldorf [BRD]

INTERLAINE INT: f: Comité des industries lainières de la CEE, Bruxelles [B] d: Ausschuß der Wollindustrie der EWG

INTERLAIT F: f: Société Interprofessionnelle du Lait

INTERMAG INT: e: International Magnetics Conference

INTERMARKET BRD: d: Gesellschaft für internationale Markt- und Meinungsforschung mbH, 4 Düsseldorf

INTERMEDES INT: e: mil: International Medical Defence Symposia [3...6.Jun 1967 in Uppsala, S]

INTERNEMO 70 INT: d: Internationale Erfinder- und Neuheiten-Ausstellung, Oberhausen [BRD, 5... 13.Sep 1970]

INTER/NEPCON INT: e: International Electronic Production Conference [Brighton, GB]

INTERNET INT: e: International Congress on Project Planning by Network Analysis

InternorGa INT: d: Internationale Fachmesse für die nordeuropäische Gastronomie, Hamburg [BRD, jetzt:] Internationale Fachausstellung für die Gastronomie, für Bäckereien und Konditoreien

INTEROCEAN INT: d: Internationaler Kongreß mit Ausstellung für Meeresforschung und Meeresnutzung [10...

15.Nov 1970 in Düsseldorf, BRD] e: international congress for oceanic research and exploitation

inter-oil INT: d: Internationale Ausstellung zum 6.Welt-Erdöl-Kongreß [19...26. Juni 1963 in Ffm, BRD]

INTERPACK INT: d: Internationale Messe für Verpackungsmaschinen, Verpackungsmittel und Süßwarenmaschinen, Düsseldorf [BRD]

Interpatent D: d: Interessenverband Deutscher Patentinhaber und Erfinder eV, Berlin

INTERPHOTO INT: d: Internationaler Photo- und Kinohändler-Bund, 2 Hamburg [BRD]

Interplas INT: e: International Plastics Exhibition in Europe, London

Interpol INT: = ICPO

Interposta BRD: d: Internationale Postwertzeichen-Ausstellung, Hamburg 1959

Interpublic US: e: The Interpublic Group of Companies, Inc.,New York

Interschutz INT: d; Internationale Ausstellung für Brand-, Strahlen- und Katastrophenschutz (Der Rote Hahn) [1961 in Köln, BRD]

INTERSHOE INT: d: Internationaler Fachverband des unabhängigen Schuheinzelhandels f: Fédération internationale du commerce indépendant de la chaussure

INTERSTENO INT: f: Fédération internationale de sténographie et de dactylographie; d: Internationale Föderation für Kurzschrift und Maschinenschreiben, Les Hirondelles, Payerne [CH, = IFKM]

Interstoff BRD: d: Fachmesse für Bekleidungstextilien, Ffm

Inter-SU F: f: Bureau de liaison des sanatoriums universitaires et de protection anti-tuberculeuse des étudiants Paris [gegr 1953]

Intersuc F: [d: Messe für Schokoladen, Biskuits und sonstige Confiserieartikel]

INTERSUGAR INT: e: International Sugar Council, London

INTERTANKO INT: e: International Tanker Owners' Association

INTERTOOL INT: [d: Internationale Messe für Werkzeug und Werkzeugmaschinen, Kopenhagen, DK]

Interverband CH: d: Interverband für Skilauf = IVS

Intervision INT: [d: Vereinbarung für Programmaustausch und gemeinsame Fernsehübertragungen der OIRT]

INTERVITIS BRD: [d: Weinbauausstellung 1969 in Offenburg (Baden)]

INTERWIRT BRD: d: Institut für Unternehmensberatung GmbH, 785 Lörrach

INTERZUM INT: d: Internationale Messe der Zulieferer für Möbel, Polstermöbel und Holzverarbeitung, Köln [BRD, heute:] Internationale Zubehör- und Werkstoff-Messe für Holzverarbeitung, Möbel, Polstermöbel und Matratzen, für den Ausbau von Häusern, Schiffen und Fahrzeugen sowie für den Leichtbau

INTHERM INT: d: Internationale Fachmesse Ölfeuerung und Gasfeuerung, Stuttgart [BRD, jetzt:] ... für Haushalt und Industrie

INTI RA: s: Instituto Nacional de Tecnología Industrial, Buenos Aires

Intima 70 BRD: [d: "Sexmesse",20... 24. Aug 1970 in Offenbach (Main)]

Int.Mil. F: f: mil: Intendance Militaire

INTN PY: s: Instituto Nacional de Tecnología y Normalización

Intog D: d: Internationale Tonfilm-GmbH

Intomar NL: [d: Institut für angewandte Marktforschung]

Intourist SU: [d: Allunionsgesellschaft für internationalen Tourismus in der SU, Moskau, Prospekt Marxa 16]

INTP RM: f: Institut National des Télé-

communications et Postes

InTra BRD: d: InTra - 1.Fachübersetzergenossenschaft eGmbH, 7 Stuttgart M

Intra RL: e: [International Traders] Bank, Beirut

Intrag CH: d: Intrag AG, Verwaltung von Investmenttrusts, Zürich, Lausanne; D: d: Industrie-Treuhand-AG, Berlin

INTRATA EAT: e: International Trading and Credit Company of Tanganyika Ltd.

IntS S: sv: mil: Intendenturförvaltningsskolan, Stockholm [gegr 1942]

INTSHU TG: f: Institut Togolais des Sciences Humaines

InTTr BRD: d: mil: Inspektion der Technischen Truppe

INTUC IND: e: Indian National Trade Union Congress

Int.Verw. D: d: mil: Intendantur-Verwaltung

INU YU: sh: Institut za Narodnu Umjetnost, Zagreb; I: i: Istituto Nazionale di Urbanistica

INUTOM B: f: Institut Universitaire des Territoires d'Outre-Mer, Anvers

I.N.V. B: f: Institut National du Verre, Charleroi

InvA A: d: Invalidenamt

InvEK A: d: Invalidenentschädigungskommission

INVESTBANCO BR: pt: Banco de Investimento e Desenvolvimento Industrial S.A., São Paulo

INVNÜ BRD: d: Institut für Nachrichtenverarbeitung und Nachrichtenübertragung, 75 Karlsruhe [Universität]

INVU CR: s: Instituto Nacional de Vivienda y Urbanismo

INVUFLEC F: f: Institut National de Vulgarisation des Fruits, Légumes et Champignons

IO S: sv: Idrotts-Orden, Göteborg; CDN: e: Imperial Oil

I.O. GB: e: India Office; Institute of

Ophthalmic Opticians; F: f: Institut Océanographique, Paris [gegr 1906] ; Institut d'Optique; INT: f: Internationale Ouvrière

IO YU: sh: Izvršni Odbor

I.O.A. IND: e: Indian Overseas Airlines, Ltd., Bombay; GB: e: Institute of Actuaries; Institute of Arbitrators, Inc.

I.O.A.E. e: Institution of Automobile Engineers

IOAT INT: e: International Organization Against Trachoma [gegr 1924]

IOB e: Imperial Ottoman Bank; DDR: d: Informations- und Organisations-Büro

I.O.B. GB: e: Institute of Bankers; Institute of Brewing; Institute of Builders

IOB BRD: d: Interessengemeinschaft der in der Ostzone enteigneten Betriebe eV, 53 Bonn; DDR: d: Internationales Organisationsbüro

I.O.B.B. e: Independent Order of B'nai B'rith

IOBC e: Indian Ocean Biological Centre, Cochin

I.O.B.I. e: Institute of Bankers of Ireland

I.O.B.K. GB: e: Institute of Book-Keepers

I.O.B.S. GB: e: Institute of Bankers in Scotland

I.O.C. GB: e: Imperial Opera Company; Institute of Chemistry

IOC BR: pt: Instituto Oswaldo Cruz; UN: e: Intergovernmental Oceanographic Commission, Paris 7 [UNESCO] ; INT: d: Internationales'Olympisches Comité (Komitee) e: International Olympic Committee, Lausanne [CH] ; INT: e: International Opium Commission; International Ornithological Congress; CDN: e: Iron Ore Company of Canada

IOCA US: e: Independent Oil Compounders Association

IOCC US: e: Interstate Oil Compact Commission

IOCO YU: sh: Izvršni Odbor Centralnog Odbora

IOCU INT: e: International Organization of Consumers Unions, Den Haag [NL]

IOCV INT: e: International Organization of Citrus Virologists, Campinas

IOCY INT: e: International Office of Catholic Youth

IODBE GB: e: Imperial Order Daughters of the British Empire

IOD&D GB: e: Institution of Designers and Draughtsmen

I.O.D.E. GB: e: Imperial Order Daughters of the Empire

IOD(G) S: sv: Institutet för Ortnamnsog Dialektforskning, Göteborg

I.O.E. GB: e: mil: Inspectorate of Explosives; e: Institute (Institution) of Electronics; F: f: Institut d'Observation Economique

IOE INT: e: International Office of Epizootics, Paris 17 [gegr 1924] ; International Organization of Employers [gegr 1919]

IÖD INT: d: Internationale der Öffentlichen Dienste, London EC 1

IÖGF A: d: Institut für österreichische Geschichtsforschung [gegr 1854]

I.O.F. US: e: Independent Order of Foresters; GB: e: Institute of Fuel

IOF INT: d: Internationale Orientierungslauf-Föderation

I. of E. e: Institute of Export

I.O.F.F. S: sv: Internationella orden frihetens folk

I. of W.R. GB: e: Isle of Wight Railway

I.O.G.T. INT: e: International Order of Good Templars [gegr 1851 in US]

IOI s: Interayuda Obrera Internacional

IOIE INT: e: International Organization of Industrial Employers

I.O.J. e: Institute of Journalists

IOJ INT: d: Internationale Organisation der Journalisten, Prag [CS] e: International Organization of Journalists

IOK INT: d: Internationales Olympi-

sches Komitee sv: Internationella
Olympiska Kommittén

IOKh SU: [e: Institute of Organic Chemistry, Academy of Sciences]

IOKSz H: [e: Union of Handicrafts Cooperatives]

I.O.L. GB: e: India Office Library

IOLO YU: sn: Izvršni Odbor Ljudskega Odbora

IOM F: f: Indépendants d'Outre-Mer; GB: e: Institute of Office Management, London; US: e: Institute of Metals; INT: e: International Organization for Migration [später:] ICEM

IOMA US: e: Independent Oxygen Manufacturers Association

I.O.M.C.S.A. GB: e: Isle of Man Civil Service Association

I.O.M.E. GB: e: Institute of Marine Engineers

I.O.M.E.F. GB: e: Isle of Man Employment Federation

IOMP INT: e: International Organization for Medical Physics

I.O.M.R. GB: e: Isle of Man Railway

I.O.M.S.P. GB: e: Isle of Man Steam Packet

IOMTR INT: e: International Office for Motor Traders and Repairs, Den Haag [NL, gegr 1947]

ION US: e: Institute of Navigation; INT: d: Arbeitsgruppe Ionosphäre und Aurora-Phänomene [ESRO]

IONKh SU: [e: Kurnakov Institute of General and Inorganic Chemistry]

IONKhAN SU: [e: Institute of General and Inorganic Chemistry, Academy of Sciences]

IONO YU: sh: Izvršni Odbor Narodnog Odbora

I.O.O.F. US: e: Independent Order of Odd Fellows [gegr 1714]

IOOF YU: sn: Izvršni Odbor Osvobodilne Fonte

IOOTS INT: e: International Organization of Old Testament Scholars

I.O.P. GB: e: Institute of Packaging; Institute of Painters in Oil Colours; Institute of Patentees, Inc.; Institute of Petroleum; Institute of Physics (and the Physical Society); Institute of Plumbing; Institute of Printing

IOP INT: e: International Organization of Palaeobotany

IOPAB INT: e: International Organization for Pure and Applied Biophysics, Boston 15 [US]

IOPH e: International Office of Public Health (Hygiene)

IOPM PL: pl: Instytut Organizacji Przemysłu Maszynowego

I.O.Q. GB: e: Institute of Quarrying

I.O.R. e: Independent Order of Rechabites

IOR PL: pl: Instytut Ochrony Roślin

IO RLO YU: sn: Izvršni Odbor, Rajonski Ljudski Odbor

I.O.R.M. US: e: Improved Order of Red Men

IORS e: International Orders Research Society

IOS S: sv: mil: Infanteriofficersskolan, Stockholm

I.O.S. e: Institute of Sociology

IOS PL: [d: Institut für spanabhebende Formung, Krakau]

I.O.S. e: Insurance Officials Society; INT: d: Internationale Organisation für Sukkulentenforschung

IOS CH: e: Investors Overseas Services, Geneva; IRQ: e: Iraqui Organization for Standardization, Baghdad

IOSA US: e: International Oil Scouts Association

I.O.S.M. GB: e: Independent Order of the Sons of Malta

IOSOT INT: e: International Organization for the Study of the Old Testament

IOST INT: f: Institut international d'organisation scientifique du travail

[d: Völkerbund]

I.O.S.T.A. F: f: Institut d'Organisation Scientifique du Travail en Agriculture, Paris 9

I.O.T. e: Institute of Taxation; GB: e: Institute of Transport

IOTA f: Institut d'Ophtalmologie Tropical de l'AOF, Bamako

I.O.T.A. f: Institut d'Optique Théorique et Appliquée

IOV RCH: s: Instituto Oceanográfico de Valparaiso

IOVPT INT: d: Internationale Organisation für Vakuum-Physik und -Technik, Brüssel [B]

IOVST INT: e: International Organization for Vacuum Science and Technology, Brussels [B]

I.O.W. GB: e: Institute of Welding

IOZV INT: d: Internationale Organisation für Zivilverteidigung, Genf 6 [CH, gegr 1931]

IP US: e: mil: Industrial Police [in BRD: Industrie-Polizei, ehemalige deutsche Wacheinheiten bei der US-Besatzungsmacht]; DIN: d: Innere Normenprüfstelle; e: Institute of Packaging; GB: e: Institute of Petroleum, London; Institute of Physics (and the Physical Society)

I.P. F: f: Institut Pasteur; Institut du Pétrole

IP INT: e: mil: International Patrol [d: der Militärpolizei der vier Besatzungsmächte in Wien, A, nach WK2]

IPA US: e: Illinois Pharmaceutical Association; Indiana Pharmaceutical Association; IND: e: India Press Agency; IL: e: Information Processing Association of Israel, Jerusalem

I.P.A. f: mil: Inspection des Parcs d'Automobiles; GB: e: Institute of Practitioners in Advertising; e: Institute of Public Administration; AUS: e: Institute of Public Affairs

IPA BR: pt: Instituto de Pesquisas Agronómicas; f: Institut Pédagogique Africain; Institut de Préparation aux Affaires; R: ro: Institutul de Proiectări pentru Amelioratii, Bucureşti; INT: d: Internationale Pelzfachausstellung; e: International Pediatric Association; INT: e: International Phonetic Association, London [gegr 1886]; International Police Association, Geneva [CH]; ETH: e: International Press Agency [d: Nachrichtenagentur]; INT: e: International Psychoanalytical Association, London; International Publishers Association, Zürich [CH, gegr 1896]; BRD: d: Interparlamentarische Arbeitsgemeinschaft; US: e: Iowa Pharmaceutical Association; I: i: Ispettorati Provinciali dell'Agricoltura

IPAA US: e: Independent Petroleum Association of America; Industrial Photographers Association of America; e: International Prisoners Aid Association; INT: e: International Psychoanalytical Association

IPAC US: e: Illinois Public Aid Commission; 1: Institutum Pontificale Archeologiae Christianae; e: Iran Pan-American Oil Company

IPACK-IMA INT: [d: Internationale Ausstellung für Verpackungswesen, industrielle Förder- und Transportmittel sowie Nahrungsmittelindustriemaschinen, Mailand, I]

IPANY US: e: Individual Psychology Association of New York

IPAPI I: i: Istituto Provinciale Assistenza Prima Infanzia

IPAR US: e: Institute of Personality Assessment and Research

IPARA INT: e: International Publishers Advertising Representatives Association

IPARC INT: e: International Permanent Association of Road Congresses

I.P.A.S. F: f: Indépendants et Paysans d'Action Sociale [d: Partei, gegr 1956]
IPASE BR: pt: Instituto de Previdência e Assistência aos Servidores do Estado
IPB RCB: f: Institut Pasteur de Brazzaville; d: Internationales Patentbüro
IPBAM; IPBM INT: e: International Permanent Bureau of Automobile Manufacturers, Paris [f: BPICA]
IPBMM INT: e: International Permanent Bureau of Motor Manufacturers [= IPBAM]
IPC NATO: e: Industrial Planning Committee; e: Industrial Property Committee; US: e: Institute of Paper Chemistry; Institute of Printed Circuits, Chicago 3, Ill.; f: Institute Politique Congolais; R: ro: Institutul de Proiectăre a Construcțiilor, Bucureşti; INT: e: Inter-African Phytosanitary Commission, London [gegr 1954]; International Peace Campaign [gegr 1936]; e: International People's College; PE: e: International Petroleum Company; INT: e: International Police Conference; International Poliomyelitis Congress; International Poplar Commission [UN]; International Prison Commission; International Psychological Congress; International Publishers' Congress; GB: e: International Publishing Corporation, London; US: e: Investors Planning Corporation of America; IRQ: e: Iraq Petroleum Company
IPCA GB: e: Industrial Pest Control Association
I.P.C.A. BE: f: Institut Provincial de Coopération Agricole; R: ro: Institutul de Proiectăre de Construcții Agrozootehnice, Bucureşti
IPCA e: International Petroleum Cooperative Alliance
IPCCIOS INT: f: Conseil Régional Indo-Pacifique du Comité International de l'Organisation Scientifique (CIOS), Hongkong
IPCEA US: e: Insulated Power Cable Engineers Association, Montclair, N.J.
IPCH US: e: Institute of Paper Chemistry
I.P.C.H. R: ro: Institutul de Proiectăre a Construcțiilor Hidrotehnice, Bucureşti
I.P.C.I. R: ro: Institutul de Proiectăre a Construcțiilor Industriale, Bucureşti
I.P.C.L. F: f: Institut du Pétrole, des Carburants et Lubrifiants
I.P.CO. US: e: International Paper Company, Georgetown, S.C.
IPCOG e: WK2: Informal Policy Committee on Germany
IPCR J: e: Institute of Physical and Chemical Research
IPCRSIAA F: f: Institut Professionnel de Contrôle et de Recherches Scientifiques des Industries de l'Alimentation Animale
I.P.C.S. GB: e: Institute (Institution) of Professional Civil Servants
I.P.D. e: Impounded Parcels Department; Industrial Property Department
IPD i Rz PL: pl: Instytut Przemysłu Drobnego i Rzemiosła
I.P.E. GB: e: Incorporated Plant Engineers; E: s: Industria Papelera Española, Madrid; GB: e: Institution of Production Engineers, London; I: i: Istituto de Politica Estera
IPEA US: e: Independent Poster Exchanges of America
IPEAA US: e: Industrial Packaging Engineers Association of America
IPEAL BR: pt: Instituto de Pesquisas e Experimentação Agropecuárias de Leste
I.P.E.L. B: f: Institut Provincial de l'Education et des Loisirs
I.P.E.O. I: i: Istituto per l'Europa Orientale
IPEP e: International Permanent Exhibition of Publications
I.P.E.S. f: Institut de préparation aux

enseignements du second degré

IPEU US: e: International Photo-Engravers Union of North America

IPEX INT: e: International Printing Machinery and Allied Trades Exhibition, London [1955]

IPF DDR: d: Institut für Post-und Fernmeldewesen, Berlin; INT: d: Internationale Proletarische Freidenker

I.P.F. e: International Peace Force

IPF INT: e: International Pharmaceutical Federation; International Police Federation

I.P.F.A. f: mil: Inspection permanente des fabrications d'artillerie

IPFC UN: e: Indo-Pacific Fisheries Council, Bangkok [gegr 1948]

I.P.G. F: f: Institut Polytechnique de Grenoble

IPG INT: d: mil: Internationale Planungsgruppe [Luftverteidigung, B, BRD,NL] e: International Planning Group

I.P.H. F: f: Inspection Principale des Halles; Institut de Paléontologie Humaine

IPHARMEX INT: d: Internationale Apotheker-Fachmesse, Basel [CH]

IPHC INT: e: International Pacific Halibut Commission

IPHF US: e: Illinois Poultry and Hatchery Federation; INT: e: International Professional Horticultural Federation

IPHO INT: e: International Public Health Office

IPHV INT: d: Internationaler Postwertzeichen-Händlerverein, Berlin

IPI GB: e: Institute of Patentees and Inventors; C: s: Instituto de Política Internacional

I.P.I. R: ro: Institutul de Proiectări Industriale, Bucureşti

IPI US: e: Interchemical (Printing Inks) Corporation, New York 36; INT: d: Internationales Presse-Institut, Zürich [CH, gegr 1951] e: International Press

Institute; e: International Potash Institute

I.P.I.A. R: ro: Institutul de Patalogie şi Igienă Animala, Bucureşti

IPIMIGEO s: Instituto Panamericano de Ingeniera de Minas y Geologia

IPK BRD: d: Institut für Phonetik und Kommunikationsforschung, 53 Bonn; Institut für politische Planungen und Kybernetik, 532 Bad Godesberg; CH: d: Schweizerische Interessengemeinschaft für Pharmazeutische und Kosmetische Produkte; INT: d: Internationale Pappelkommission; Internationale Petroleum -Kommission [gegr 1907]

IPKI RI: Ikatan Pendukung Kemerdekaan Indonesia [d: Freiheitskämpfer]

IPKO INT: e: International Information Centre on Peace-Keeping Operations, Paris 16 [gegr 1966]

IPL I: i: Ispettorato Provinciale del Lavoro

I.P.L.M.A. e: Irish Power Loom Manufacturers' Association

IPM GB: e: Institute of Personnel Management; DDR: d: Institut für Polygraphische Maschinen, Leipzig; BRD: d: Institut für Praktische Mathematik, 61 Darmstadt

Ip.M. H: hu: Iparügyi Miniszter(ium), Budapest

IPMANA e: Interstate Postgraduate Medical Association of North America

IPMI; IPMPI US: e: International Photographers of the Motion Picture Industries

IPMS INT: e: International Polar Motion Service

I.P.N. F: f: Institut de Physique Nucléaire Institut Pédagogique National, Paris

IPNA s: Instituto Cultural Peruano -Norteamericano

IPNC f: Institut des Parcs Nationaux du Congo

IPNCB B: f: Institut des Parcs Nationaux

du Congo Belge, Bruxelles

I.P.N.C.B. B: f: Institut pour la Protection de la Nature au Congo Belge

IPNRK CGO: f: Institut des Parcs Nationaux et des Réserves Naturelles de Katanga

I.P.O. F: f: Institut Polytechnique de l'Ouest

IPO NL: nl: Instituut voor Plantenziektenkundig Onderzoek, Wageningen; IL: e: Israel Philharmonic Orchestra; I: i: Istituto per l'Oriente

I.P.O.E.E. GB: e: Institution of the Post Office Electrical Engineers

IPOR US: e: International Public Opinion Research Inc., New York

IPOSTA D: d: Internationale Postwertzeichen-Ausstellung, Berlin [1930]

IPP WAL: e: Independence People's Party; US: e: Independent Progressive Party; BRD: d: Institut für Plasmaphysik GmbH der Max-Planck-Gesellschaft zur Förderung der Wissenschaften eV, 8046 Garching; Institut für praktische Psychologie, Stuttgart

IPPAI I: i: Istituto Provinciale Protezione ed Assistenza Infanzia

IPPAU e: International Printing Pressmen and Assistants' Union of North America

IPPC INT: e: International Penal and Penitentiary Commission for the Prevention of Crime and the Treatment of Delinquents

IPPF INT: e: International Penal and Penitentiary Foundation, Brussels [B]; International Planned Parenthood Federation, London [gegr 1948]

IPPJ J: e: Institute of Plasma Physics of Japan, Nagoya University

IPPS GB: e: Institute of Physics and the Physical Society, London

IPPT INT: d: Internationale des Personals der Post-, Telegraphen-und Telephon-Betriebe [gegr 1911]

IPR US: e: Institute of Pacific Relations,

New York [gegr 1925]; Institute of Public Relations

IPRA INT: e: International Public Relations Association

IPRB e: Inter-Allied Post-War Requirements Bureau

IPRE GB: e: Incorporated Practitioners in Radio and Electronics [vorher:] Institute of Practical Radio Engineers

IPR i S PL: pl: Instytut Przemysłu Rolnego i Spożywczego

IPRO BRD: d: IPRO Gesellschaft für Öffentlichkeitsarbeit, 6 Ffm

IPROCHIM R: ro: Institutul de Proiectări de Fabrici și Produse Chimice, București

I.Prod.E. GB: e: Institute (Institution) of Production Engineers, London

IPROIL R: ro: Institutul pentru Proiectarea Industriel Lemnului, București

IPROMET R: ro: Institutul de Proiectări de Uzine și Instalații Metalurgice, București

IPROMIN R: ro: Institutul de Proiectări Miniere, București

IPROUP R: ro: Institutul de Cercetări și Proiectări de Utilaj Petrolifer, București

IPS GB: e: Incorporated Phonographic Society

I.P.S. e: Incorporated Poetry Society; GB: e: Indian Police Service; Indian Political Service; e: Industrial Promotion Services; PY: s: Instituto de Previsión Social; e: International Peace Society

IPS US: e: International Planning Staff; INT: e: International Confederation for Plastic Surgery; S: sv: Internationella pedagogiska seminariet, Lillsved; INT: sv: Internationella permanenta skiljedomstolen, Den Haag [NL]; e: Ionospheric Prediction Service

IPSA CH: f: Information et Publicité, S.A. Genève; MEX: s: Ingeniera y

Puertos S.A., México; INT: e: International Political Science Association, Paris 7 [gegr 1947]

IPSF INT: e: International Pharmaceutical Students' Federation [gegr 1949]

IPSI e: International Political Science Institute

IPSIC PL: pl: Instytut Przemysłu Szkła e Ceramiki

IPSMF R: ro: Institutul pentru Perfectionarea și Specializarea Medicilor și Farmaciștilor, București

IPSOA I: i: Istituto Post-Universitario per lo Studio dell'Organizzazione Aziendale, Torino [gegr 1952]

IPSRA INT: e: International Professional Ski Racers Association [gegr 1962]

IPSSB US: e: Information Processing Systems Standards Board [USASI]

IPSSG US: e: International Printers Supply Salesmen's Guild

IPST IL: e: Israel Programme for Scientific Translations, Jerusalem

IPT e: Institute of Petroleum Technologists (Technology); BR: pt: Instituto de Pesquisas Tecnológicas, São Paulo; NATO: e: International Planning Team

IPTA e: International Piano Teachers Association

IPTC CH: e: Industrial Products Trading Corporation, Zürich

IPTI RI: Ikatan Penderita Tjatjat Indonesia

IPTPA INT: e: International Professional Tennis Players Association

IPTT INT: f: Internationale du personnel des postes, télégraphes et téléphones [gegr 1911]

IPU WAN: e: Ibadan Progressive Union; INT: e: International Paleontological Union; International Peasant Union, New York, N.Y. 10019; e: International Population Union; INT: d: Interparlamentarische Union, Genf [CH, gegr 1889] e: Inter-Parliamentary Union

I.P.U.C. R: ro: Institutul Proiectări de Utilaje de Construcții, București

I.P.U.S.A. U: s: Industria Papelera Uruguaya S.A.

IPV BRD: d: Industrie-Pensions-Verein, 293 Varel [gegr 1925]

I.P.V. F: f: Institut de Paléontologie Végétale

I.P.W.D. GB: e: India Public Works Department

I.P.W.R. US: e: Institute of Post-War Reconstruction, New York

IPY INT: e: International Polar Year

IPZ BRD: d: mil: Informations- und Pressezentrum [BMVtdg]

I.P.Z.V. BRD: d: Island-Pferde-Züchter- und Besitzervereinigung, 5 Köln

I.Q. US: e: I Quit [antismoking organization]

IQA BR: pt: Instituto de Químico Agrícola

IqAF e: mil: Iraqi Air Force

IQB BR: pt: Instituto Químico Biológico

IQC INT: e: International Quality Centre

IQS GB: e: Institute of Quality Surveyors London

IQSY INT: e: International Quiet Sun Year(s) [1964...65, d: IJRS]

I.R. F: f: Indépendants de la Résistance; IND: e: Indian Railways

IR DK: da: Industriraadet; D: d: mil: Infanterie-Regiment; SF: sv: mil: Infanteriregemente; e: mil: Infantry Regiment; GB: e: Institute of Refrigeration, London

I.R. f: Institut du Radium; Institut J.J. Rousseau; F: f: Internés Résistants

IR IL: e: Israel Railways

IRA e: Indian Rights Association; US: e: Industrial Recreation Association; BRD: d: Industriegemeinschaft zur Förderung des Radfahrwesens und Radsports

I.R.A. GB: e: mil: Inspector of the Royal Artillery; GB: e: Institute of Registere

Architects, London

IRA S: sv: Institutet för rationell arkivering; CH: d: Institut für Rationalisierung und Automation GmbH, Zürich 1; US: e: Intercollegiate Rowing Association; BRD: d: Interessengemeinschaft der Radfahrer, München; Interministerieller Referentenausschuß; INT: eo: Internacia Radio-Asocio; INT: d: Internationale Rauchwaren-Auktion [DDR]; US: e: International Reading Association; e: International Recreation Association; US: e: International Research Associates; D: e: International Ruhr Authority; IRL: e: Irish Republican Army

I.R.A. IND: e: Islamic Research Association, Bombay [gegr 1933]

IRAA US: e: Independent Refiners Association of America

IRABOIS F: f: Institut de Recherches Appliquées au Bois

IRAC US: e: Industrial Research Advisory Council; CDN: f: Institut royal d'architecture du Canada; US: e: Interdepartmental Radio Advisory Committee; Interfraternity Research and Advisory Council; e: International Records Administration Conference

I.R.A.-C.A. e: Inebriates Reformation and After-Care Association

IrAF e: mil: Iraqui Air Force

IRAM RA: s: Instituto Argentino de Racionalización de Materiales, Buenos Aires; INT: e: International Rail Markers Association [gegr 1926]

IRAMD f: Institut des Recherches et d'Applications des Méthodes de Développement

IRAMM f: Institut de Recherche et d'Action contre la Misère Mondiale

Iran Air IR: e: Iran Air - Iran National Airlines Corporation, Teheran

IRANDOC IR: e: Iranian Documentation Centre, Teheran

IRAS N: no: Industriforbundets Rasjonaliseringskontor

IRASA INT: e: International Radio Air Safety Association, Paris

IRAT f: Institut de Recherches Agronomiques Tropicales et des Cultures Vivrières; INT: d:Internationales Rationalisierungs-Institut, Genf [CH]

IRATE; IRATRA E: s: Instituto Nacional de Racionalización del Trabajo, Madrid 6

IRB US: e: Industrial Relations Board; J: e: Institute of Radiation Breeding; BR: pt: Instituto de Resseguros do Brasil; e: Internal Revenue Bureau

I.R.B. IRL: e: Irish Republican Brotherhood [gegr 1850]

I.R.C. e: Indian Relief Committee

IRC IND: e: Indian Roads Congress; RI: Indonesia Raja Congres; US: e: Industrial Relations Center; Industrial Relations Counsellors Inc.; GB: e: Industrial Reorganization Corporation, London [gegr 1966] ; INT: e: International Rainwear Council, Genoa [I]; US: e: International Rectifier Corp.; INT: e: International Red Cross, Geneva [CH]; US: e: International Rescue Committee [gegr 1935] ; INT: e: International Research Council [gegr 1919] ; US: e: International Resistance Co., Philadelphia 8, Pa.; INT: e: International Rice Commission, Bangkok; e: Italian Red Cross

I.R.C.A. f: Institution de Retraites Complémentaires Agricoles

IRCA F: f: Institut de Recherches sur le Caoutchouc en Afrique, Paris; INT: e: International Railway Congress Association [gegr 1885]

I.R.C.A. e: International Railways of Central America

I.R.C.A.M. f: Institut de Recherches Scientifiques du Cameroun, Yaoundé

IRCB B: f: Institut Royal Colonial Belge, Bruxelles

IRCC INT: e: International Radio Con-

sultative Committee [gegr 1927];
International Red Cross Committee,
Geneva [CH]

IRCE I: i: Istituto Nazionale per le
Relazioni Culturali con l'Estero

I.R.C.H.A. F: f: Institut National de
Recherche Chimique Appliquée

IRCI f: Institut de Recherches sur le
Caoutchouc en Indochine, Laikhé;
I: i: Istituto per le Relazioni Commer-
ciali Internazionali

IRCN F: f: Institut de Recherches de la
Construction Navale

IRCOSA Tanger: e: f: International Radio
Corporation Société Anonyme

IRCOTEX RCB: f: Institut de Recherche
du Coton et des Textiles Exotiques,
Bamako

IRCT F: f: Institut de Recherches Colo-
niales Tropicales; = IRCOTEX; US: e:
International Research on Communist
Techniques

IRCV f: Institut des Recherches sur le
Caoutchouc au Vietnam

IRD US: e: Industrial Relations Depart-
ment, Washington, D.C. [EIA];
Instruments and Regulators Division,
ASME, New York

I.R.D. e: Internal Revenue Department

IRD GB: e: International Research and
Development Company, Ltd.

IRDA GB: e: Industrial Research and
Development Authority

IRDC INT: e: International Rubber Development Committee, London EC 3

IRE US: e: Institute of Radio Engineers
[gegr 1913]; AUS: e: Institute of Refrigerating Engineers

I.R.E. e: Institution of Radio Engineers;
R: ro: Institut Romîn de Electricitate,
Bucureşti; Institutul National Român
pentru Studiul Amenajăii şi Folosiri Is-
voarelor de Energie, Bucureşti; I: i:
Istituto Ricerche Economiche

IREA SU: [e: Institute of Chemical Re-

agents]

I.R.E.A. AUS: e: Institution of Radio
Engineers, Australia; F: f: Institut de
Recherches de l'Economie Alimentaire

IREC AUS: e: Irrigation Research and
Extension Advisory Committee

IREE; IREEA AUS: e: Institution of
Radio and Electronics Engineers of
Australia, Sydney

IREF e: International Real Estate Federation

IREG; Ireg D: BlnW: d: Internationale
Rohstahl-Export-Gemeinschaft [jetzt:]
Montan-Union GmbH, 1 Berlin 15

IREM US: e: Institute of Real Estate
Managers

I.R.E.M.E. GB: e: mil: Inspector of Royal
Electrical and Mechanical Engineers

IREP F: f: Institut de Recherches et
d'Etudes Publicitaires, Paris

I.R.E.S. Mex:s: Instituto Revolucionario
de Estudios Sociales; CGO: f: Institut
de Recherches Economiques et Sociales
Kinshasa

IRESA DZ: f: Institut des Recherches
Economiques et Sociales

IRESE CH: f: Institut de Recherches et
d'Etudes Sociologiques et Economiques
Genève

IRESP B: f: Institut de Recherches Economiques, Sociales et Politiques

IRET f: Institut de Recherches et d'Enseignements Tropicaux, Abidjan; CH: e
Intercontinental Real Estate Trust, Geneva

IRF US: e: mil: Immediate Ready Force;
INT: e: International Religious Fellow-
ship; International Road Federation,
Washington 6, D.C. 20005, CH-1200
Geneva [gegr 1948]; International
Rowing Federation, Montreux [CH,
gegr 1892]

IRFAA CDN: US: e: International Rescue and First Aid Association

IRFE I: i: Ispettorato per i Rapporti

Finanziari con l'Estero

IRFED F: f: Institut International de Recherche et de Formation en vue du Développement Harmonisé, Paris

IRFIS I: i: Instituto Regionale per il Finanziamento alle Industrie in Sicilia

IRFV INT: d: Internationaler Regenmantelfabrikantenverband, Genua-Sturla [I]

IRG CH: d: Innerschweizerische Radio- und Fernsehgesellschaft, Luzern; B: f: Institut de Réescompte et de Garantie; INT: s: Internacional de Refractarios a la Guerra   f: Internationale des Résistants à la Guerre, Enfield, Middlesex [GB, gegr 1921]

I.R.G. D: d: Internationale Rohstahl-Gemeinschaft, Düsseldorf

IRGMA GB: e: Information Retrieval Group of the Museums Association

I.R.G.S. e: Industrial Research Geological Survey

irha US: e: Independent Retail Hardwaremen of America

IRHO F: f: Institut de Recherches pour les Huiles de Palme et Oléagineux

IRHT F: f: Institut de Recherche et d'Histoire des Textes [C.N.R.S.]

IRI US: e: IBEC Research Institute, New York;   Industrial Research Institute; I: i: Industria Radiotecnica Italiana; DK: da: Ingeniør-Sammenslutningen's Rådgivende Ingeniører; GB: e: Institution of the Rubber Industry, London SW 1; B: f: Institut des Relations Internationales;   Institut des Reviseurs d'Industrie; I: i: Istituto per la Ricostruzione Industriale [gegr 1933]

IRIA US: e: Infrared Information Analysis Center, Ann Arbor, Mich.; F: f: Institut de Recherche d'Informatique et d'Automatique, F-78 Le Chesnay [gegr 1967]

IRIC F: f: Institut de Recherches pour les Industries du Cuir; US: e: Inter-Regional Insurance Conference

IRIG US: e: Inter-Range Instrumentation Group

IRIS GB: e: Industrial Research and Information Services

IRK INT: d: Internationale Repräsentantenschaft des Kanusports;   Internationales Rotes Kreuz, Genf [CH] ;   d: International-Revolutionäre Kommunisten

IRKK INT: d: Internationale Rotes-Kreuz-Komitee [=IKRK]

IRL INT: d: Internationaler Ring für Landarbeit [f= CIOSTA] ; I: i: Ispettorato Regionale del Lavoro

IRLA US: e: International Religious Liberty Association

IRLCS INT: e: International Red Locust Control Service, Abercorn [gegr 1949]

IRLDA US: e: Independent Retail Lumber Dealers Association

IRLS INT: e: Interrogation Recording and Location System [by satellites]

IRM CH: f: Institut Suisse de Recherches Ménagères

I.R.M. B: f: Institut Royal Météorologique de Belgique, Bruxelles [gegr 1913]

I.R.M.A. e: Indian Rubber Manufacturers' Association

IRMA INT: e: European Industrial Research Management Association

I.R.M.B. B: f: = I.R.M.

IRMC INT: e: International Radio-Maritime Committee; GB: e: mil: Inter-Services Radio Measurements Committee

IRMCO IR: e: Iranian Rolling Mills Company

I.R.M.E.A. GB: e: Inland Revenue Minor Establishment Association

IRMIE I: i: Istituto per le Ricerche di Mercato ed Indagini Economiche

IRMS f: Institut de Recherches Métallurgiques de la Sarre

IRMU B: f: Institut Royal Météorologique à Uccle

IRO GB: e: Inland Revenue Office;
DDR: d: Institut für Rationalisierung
und Organisation; INT: nl: Internationale Radio-Organisatie d: Internationale Rundfunkorganisation [e= IBU] ;
UN: e: International Refugee Organization

IRO/KfS DDR: d: Institut für Rationalisierung und Organisation – Koordinierungsstelle für Standardisierung,
Dresden

IROM R: ro: Institutul Românesc de
Organizare Ştienţificǎ a Muncii, Bucureşti [gegr 1927]

IRP INT: f: Institut des Relations Paci-
fiques, New York [gegr 1925]

I.R.P. F: f: Institut des Relations Publiques, Paris 6

IRPA INT: e: International Radiation
Protection Association; PI: e: Irrigation Pump Administration

IRPL US: e: Interservice Radio Propagation Laboratory

I.R.P.P. e: Institute for Research in Plant
Physiology

IRR IRQ: [d: Irakische Eisenbahnen]

IRRA US: e: Industrial Relations Research Association; INT: e: International Routing and Reporting Authority

Irr.A. d: Irrenanstalt

IRRB INT: e: International Rubber Research Board, London EC 3 [gegr 1936]

IRRC US: e: International Relief and
Rescue Committee; INT: e: International Rubber Regulation Committee

Ir RC CDN: e: mil: Irish Regiment of
Canada

I.R.R.C.S. R: ro: Institutul Romîn pentru
Relaţiile Culturale cu Strǎinǎtatea

IRRDB INT: e: International Rubber
Research and Development Board,
London WC 2

Irred. I: i: Irredenta ["unerlöstes" Ita-
lien, politischer Bund vor 1918]

IRRI INT: e: International Rice Research
Institute, Los Banos [PI]

IRS IRL: e: Institute for Industrial Research and Standards, Dublin; DZ: f:
Institut de Recherches Sahariennes;
BRD: d: Institut für Reaktorsicherheit
der Technischen Überwachungsvereine
eV [gegr 1965] ; NL: nl: Instituut voor
Rationele Suikerproductie; US: e: Internal Revenue Service [Department of
the Treasury] ; INT: e: International
Rorschach Society, Biel [CH, gegr
1952] ; NZ: e: Irrigation Research Station

IRSAC CGO: f: Institut pour la Recherche Scientifique en Afrique Centrale,
Bukavu [gegr 1947]

IRSC RCB: f: Institut de Recherches
Scientifiques au Congo, Brazzaville

I.R.S.C. f: Institut de Recherches Scientifiques sur le Cancer

IRSC INT: e: International Radium Stand
ard Commission

I.R.S.D.A. GB: e: Inland Revenue Stamping Department Association

I.R.S.E. GB: e: Institute of Refrigerating
Service Engineers; Institution of Railway Signal Engineers

I.R.S.F. GB: e: Inland Revenue Staff
Federation; INT: e: International Roller Skating Federation [gegr 1924]

IRSFC INT: e: International Rayon and
Synthetic Fibres Committee, Paris 8
[gegr 1950]

IRSG INT: e: International Rubber Study
Group, London WC 2 [gegr 1944]

IRSIA B: f: Institut pour l'Encouragement de la Recherche Scientifique dans
l'Industrie et l'Agriculture, Bruxelles
[gegr 1944]

IRSID F: f: Institut des Recherches de
la Sidérurgie, Saint-Germain-en-Laye
[gegr 1946]

I.R.S.M. US: e: Institute of Radio Service
Men; RM: f: Institut de Recherche
Scientifique de Madagascar, Tananarive

IRSNB B: f: Institut Royal des Sciences Naturelles de Belgique
IRSO = JRSO
IRSS US: e: Instrumentation Range Safety Program
IRSTG INT: e: = IRSG
IRSU INT: e: = ISRU
IRT GB: e: Institution of Rubber Technologists, London; BRD: d: Institut für Rundfunktechnik GmbH, 2 Hamburg
IRTC US: e: mil: Infantry Replacement Training Center; L: e: f: International Radio and Television Corporation S.A., Luxembourg; INT: e: International Railway Transport Committee; International Road Tar Conference; International Road Transport Committee
IRTDA IND: e: Indian Roads and Transport Development Association
IRTE GB: e: Institute of Road Transport Engineers
I.R.T.O. TG: f: Institut de recherches scientifiques du Togo, Lomé
IRTO GB: e: International Radio and Television Organization
IRTPA WAN: e: Ijebu-Remo Taxpayers Association
IRTS US: e: International Radio and Television Society, New York
IRTU INT: e: International Railway Temperance Union, Bern [CH, gegr 1907]; International Road Transport Union
IRTWG US: e: Inter-Range Telemetry Working Group
IRU BRD: d: Initiative Republikanische Union [gegr 1968]
I.R.U. F: f: Institut de recherches pour l'urbanisme
IRU INT: e: International Railway Union, Paris [gegr 1922]; International Relief Union, Geneva [CH, gegr 1927]; International Road Transport Union, Geneva [CH, gegr 1947]

IRV INT: d: Internationale Rundfunkvereinigung, Prag [CS, gegr 1946]
IRWC INT: e: International Registry of World Citizens, Paris 5 [gegr 1949]
IRZ INT: d: Internationaler Rassehunde-Zuchtverband
IS S: sv: idrottssällskap; US: e: Independent Shoemen of America
I.S. e: India Society; D: d: mil: Infanterieschule
IS BRD: d: Ingenieurschule
I.S. f: Institut de Sérothérapie; Institut de la Soudure; GB: e: mil: Intelligence Service; e: International Society of Sculptors, Painters and Gravers; e: Irish Society (of Arts and Commerce)
IS YU: sn: Izvršni Svet
I.S.A. GB: e: mil: Indian School of Artillery; E: s: Industrias Subsidiarias de Aviación, S.A., Sevilla
ISA I: i: Industrie Siderurgiche Associate, Milano; US: e: mil: Institute of Systems Analysis [Army]; US: e: Instrument Society of America, Pittsburgh, Pa.15219; INT: d: Internationale Sozialistischer Alkoholgegner [gegr 1923]; BRD: d: Internationale Stewardessen-Ausbildung, München-Riem [gegr 1961]; INT: e: International Schools Association, Geneva [CH, gegr 1951]; US: e: mil: Office of the Assistant to the Secretary of Defense for International Security Affairs; US: e: International Service Agencies [association of health and social service agencies]; INT: e: International Settlement Authority; International Silk Association, Geneva [CH, gegr 1949]; International Skating Association; International Sociological Association, Geneva 24 [CH, gegr 1949]; International Federation of National Standardizing Associations [gegr 1926, ab 1946: ISO]
ISAA US: e: Insurance Service Association of America
I.S.A.B. e: Institute for the Study of

Animal Behaviour

ISAB S: sv: Internationella Speditioner AB, Göteborg

ISABU CGO: f: Institut des Sciences Agronomiques au Burundi, Burundi

ISAC INT: e: International Scientific Agricultural Council; US: e: mil: International Security Affairs Committee

ISAE IND: e: Indian Society of Agricultural Economics; INT: eo: Internacia Scienca Asocio Esperantista, Nis [YU, gegr 1906]

IsAF e: mil: Israeli Air Force

ISAGL US: e: International Shipmasters Association of the Great Lakes

I.S.A.L. IND: e: India Society of Art and Literature

I.S.A.L.P.A. GB: e: Incorporated Society of Auctioneers and Landed Property Agents

ISAP U: s: Instituto Sudamericano del Petróleo, Montevideo [gegr 1941]

I.S.A.P.C. GB: e: Incorporated Society of Authors, Playwrights and Composers

ISAR CGO: f: Institut des Sciences Agronomiques au Rwanda, Rwanda

ISAS J: e: Institute of Space and Aeronautical Science, Tokyo

I.S.A.S. e: International Screen Advertising Service

ISATATU INT: e: International Society of Air Travellers and Air Transport Users, London [gegr 1957]

ISAV GB: e: Institute of Sound and Vibration Research, Southampton

ISAW B: nl: Instituut voor Sociale Arbeidswetenschappen; INT: e: International Society of Aviation Writers, Ottawa [CDN, gegr 1956]

ISB Bolivien: s: Instituto de Sociología Boliviana; BRD: d: Institut für Selbstbedienung, Köln [gegr 1957]; INT: e: International Society of Biometeorology; INT: d: Internationaler Studentenbund, Prag [gegr 1946]; Internatio-

nales Sozialistisches Büro der Zweiten Internationale; INT: e: International Sanitary Bureau, Mexico City [gegr 1902]

I.S.B.A. GB: e: mil: Imperial Services Boxing Association; GB: e: Incorporaed Society of British Advertisers

ISBA INT: e: International Safety Belt Association

ISBB INT: e: International Society of Bioclimatology and Biometeorology

ISBE e: International Society for Business Education

ISBGA e: Irish Sugar Beet Growers Association

I.S.B.I. BRD: d: Internationales Schulbuch-Institut, Braunschweig

ISBI INT: e: International Savings Banks Institute, Amsterdam [NL, gegr 1924]

ISBIC US: e: mil: Interservice Balkan Intelligence Committee

ISBO Bolivien: s: Instituto de Sociología Boliviana, Sucre [gegr 1941]

ISBT e: International Society of Blood Transfusion

I.S.C. e: Icelandic Steamship Company; GB: e: Imperial Service College, Windsor; Imperial Shipping Committee; Incorporated Society of Chiropodists; GB: e: mil: Indian Staff Corps

ISC US: e: Indoor Sports Club; GB: e: mil: Information Services Centre, Germany; Inspectorate of Stores and Cloing; MA: f: Institut Scientifique Chérifien; INT: e: Interamerican Society of Cardiology [gegr 1946]; D: d: Internationaler Studentenclub, München [gegr 1926]; INT: [d: Internationale Schiffahrtskonferenz]; INT: f: Internationale des Syndicats Chrétiens; INT: e: International Sericultural Commission [f: CSI]; Internatioal Society of Cardiology, Geneva [CH, gegr 1950]; International Standards Conference; GB: e: International Student Council, London; INT: e: International Student Conference, Leyden [NL] ; International Sugar Council, London SW 1 [gegr 1953] ; US: e: Iowa State College of Agriculture and Mechanic Arts; ZA: e: Iron and Steel Corporation of South Africa

ISCA e: International Stamp Collectors Association; International Stewards and Caterers Association; INT: e: International Standards Steering Committee for Consumer Affairs [ISO/IEC]

ISCAN INT: e: International Sanitary Convention for Air Navigation

ISCAY INT: e: International Solidarity Committee with Algerian Youth

ISCB e: mil: Interallied Staff Communications Board; INT: e: International Society for Cell Biology

ISCBA US: e: Insulating Siding Core Board Association

ISCC e: International Society for Crippled Children; e: Inter-Service Components Technical Committee; US: e: Intersociety Color Council, Rochester 4, N.Y. [gegr 1930] ; Intersociety Cytology Council

ISCD INT: [d: Internationaler Verband der Industrie-Designer]

ISCE US: e: International Society of Christian Endeavor, Columbus, Ohio [gegr 1881]

I.S.C.E.A. B: f: Institut Supérieur de Commerce de l'Etat à Anvers [gegr 1852]

ISCEH US: e: International Society for Clinical and Experimental Hypnosis, Portland

ISCERG INT: e: International Society for Clinical Electroretinography

ISCM INT: e: International Society for Contemporary Music [gegr 1922]

ISCO e: International Scientific Council; I: i: Istituto Nazionale per lo Studio della Congiuntura

ISCOMAZORES NATO: e: Island Commander Azores

ISCOMBERMUDA NATO: e: Island Commander Bermuda

ISCOMFAROES NATO: e: Island Commander Faroes

ISCOMGREENLAND NATO: e: Island Commander Greenland

ISCOMICELAND NATO: e: Island Commander Iceland

ISCOMMADEIRA NATO: e: Island Commander Madeira

ISCON IND: e: Indian Steelworks Construction Company

ISCOR ZA: e: South African Iron and Steel Industrial Corporation Ltd., Pretoria

ISCP INT: e: International Society for Clinical Pathology, Detroit [gegr 1947]

ISCrim. INT: e: International Society of Criminology

ISCS e: mil: WK2: Information Services Control Section [SHAEF] ; e: International Cooperative Service

ISCSPU P: pt: Instituto Superior de Ciências Sociais e Política Ultramarina, Lisboa

ISCTC GB: e: mil: Inter-Service Components Technical Committee

ISCTP INT: e: International Study Commission for Traffic Police, Paris

ISCTR INT: e: International Scientific Committee for Trypanosomiasis Research, London

ISCUS IND: SU: e: Indian-Soviet Cultural Unity Society

ISCYRA e: International Star Class Yacht Racing Association

I.S.D. GB: e: Industrial Supplies Department [Board of Trade]

ISD D: e: nach WK2: Information Services Division [OMGUS] ; US: e: Institute of Surplus Dealers; INT: d: Internationaler Sozialdienst, Genf [CH] ; Internationaler Suchdienst, Arolsen

[BRD, gegr 1945]

ISDP nl: Indische Sociaal Democratische Partij

ISE US: e: Idaho Society of Engineers

I.S.E. GB: e: Indian Service of Engineers; India Society of Engineers

ISE US: e: Institute of Social Engineering; GB: e: Institution of Sanitary Engineers; Institution of Structural Engineers, London

I.S.E. f: Institut des Sciences de l'Education

ISE US: e: International Standard Electric Corporation, New York [gegr 1918]; I: i: Istituto per gli Studi di Economia; Istituto Sperimentale di Edilizia

ISEA US: e: Industrial Safety Equipment Association

I.S.E.A. F: f: Institut de science économique appliquée, Paris

ISEAN I: i: Istituto Studi Esperienze Architettura Navale

ISEB US: e: Independent Schools Education Board

ISEC US: e: International Standard Electric Corporation, New York [=ISE]; e: International Statistics Educational Centre

I.S.E.F. F: f: Institut de Statistiques et d'Etudes Economiques et Financières

ISEN F: f: Institut Supérieur d'Electronique du Nord, Lille

I.S.E.P. F: f: Institut Supérieur d'Electronique de Paris, Paris 6; R: ro: Institutul de Ştiinte Economice şi Planificare "V.I. Lenin", Bucureşti

ISER F: f: Institut Supérieur d'Economie Rurale

ISESE B: f: Institut supérieur d'études sociales de l'état

ISEU P: pt: Instituto Superior de Estudos Ultramarinos, Lisboa; US: e: International Stereotypers – Electrotypers Union of North America

ISEUL B: f: Institut des Sciences Economiques de l'Université de Louvain

ISEUNA US: e: = ISEU

ISF d: Internationaler Studentenbund für Föderation; e: International Schools Foundation; US: e: International Science Fair (Foundation); INT: e: International Shipping Federation Ltd., London EC 3 [gegr 1909]; International Society for Fat Research; International Spiritualist Federation [gegr 1923]; INT: sv: Internationella skridskoförbundet; Internationella skräddarförbundet

ISFA US: e: Intercoastal Steamship Freight Association; INT: e: International Scientific Film Association [gegr 1947]

I.S.F.A. e: International Society of Friends of Albania

I.S.F.C. f: Institut Scientifique Franco-Canadien

ISFC INT: e: International Scholarship Fund Committee

I.S.FF.SS. I: i: Istituto Sperimentale delle Ferrovie dello Stato

I.S.F.M. F: f: Institut Social Familial Ménager

I.S.G. e: Industrial Savings Groups

ISG DDR: d: Industriesportgemeinschaft; NL: nl: Internationaal Significh Genooschap; INT: [d: Internationale Schlafwagen- und Große Europäische Expreßzüge-Gesellschaft, Brüssel [B]] f: Compagnie Internationale des Wagons-Lits et des Grands Express Européens, Bruxelles [gegr 1876; vgl: ISTG]; BRD: d Isotopen-Studiengesellschaft, Karlsruhe [bis 1966]

ISGE INT: e: International Society of Gastroenterology [gegr 1935]

I.S.G.G. I: i: Istituto Sperimentale di Gerontologia e Geriatria

ISGS e: International Society for General Semantics

ISH DDR: d: Institut des Seeverkehrs und der Hafenwirtschaft; INT: d:

Internationaler Verband der Seeleute und Hafenarbeiter   e: International Seamen and Harbour Workers

ish INT: d: Internationale Sanitär- und Heizungsausstellung, 6 Ffm [BRD]

ISH INT: e: International Society of Haematology [gegr 1946]

I.S.H.A. F: f: Institut Scientifique d'Hygiène Alimentaire

ISHAM INT: e: International Society for Human and Animal Mycology [gegr 1954]

ISHRA GB: e: Iron and Steel Holding and Realization Agency

ISHS INT: e: International Society for Horticultural Science, Den Haag

I.S.H.U. e: International Student Hitch-Hiking Union

ISI IND: e: Indian Standards Institution, New Delhi 1;   Indian Statistical Institute; NL: nl: Informatie- en Studiecentrum voor de Europese Integratie van de Werksverbonden in Nederland; US: e: Institute for Scientific Information, Philadelphia, Pa. 19106

Isi D: d: Internationale Schallplattenindustrie GmbH, Leipzig

ISI US: e: International Safety Institute; International Services of Information Foundation, Inc.; INT: d: Internationales Statistisches Institut, Den Haag [NL, gegr 1885]   e: International Statistical Institute; GB: e: The Iron and Steel Institute, London S.W.1; I: i: Istituto Stomatologico Italiano; IS: Ithrótasamband Islands

ISIC Salvador: s: Instituto Salvadoreno de Investigaciónes de Café; INT: e: International Solvay Institute of Chemistry

ISIDAS I: i: Istituto Storico Italiano dell'Arte Sanitaria

ISIG GH: e: Industrial Standards Institute of Ghana, Accra [jetzt:] National Standards Board

ISIM INT: e: International Society of Internal Medicine [gegr 1948] ; I: i: Istituto Sperimentale Italiano del Metodo

ISIP YU: Internacianalna stalna izlosbo publikacija [d: internationale ständige Ausstellung von Publikationen, Zagreb]

ISIRI IR: e: Institute of Standards and Industrial Research of Iran, Teheran

ISIS US: e: Institute of Scrap Iron and Steel;   e: Integrated Scientific Information Service; GB: e: International Shipping Information Service, London; US: e: International Student Information Service; INT: e: International Symposium on Isotope Separation

ISIUA f: Institut Supérieur et International d'Urbanisme Appliqué

I.S.I.W.M. GB: e: Incorporated Society of Inspectors of Weights and Measures

ISK BRD: d: Industrieverband Schaumkunststoffe, 6 Ffm; N: no: Instituttet for sammenlignende kulturforskning, Oslo; INT: d: Internationaler sozialistischer Kampfbund [gegr 1930] ; Internationale Seidenbau-Kommission, Alès [F, gegr 1948]

I.S.K. INT: d: Internationale Ski-Kommission, Oslo [N]

ISKA INT: no: Internasjonalen for Stats- og Kommunalansatte, London EC 1

ISL US: e: Illinois State Library; BRD: F: f: Institut Franco-Allemand de Recherches de Saint-Louis; CH: d: Institut für Schnee- und Lawinenforschung, Weissfluhjoch / Davos

ISL Pl: pl: Instytut Śląski

I.S.L. US: e: International Soccer League; I: i: Istituto di Studi sul Lavoro

ISLA US: e: Idaho State Library Association

I.S.L.F.D. GB: e: Incorporated Society of London Fashion Designers

Islic IL: e: Israel Society of Special

Libraries and Information Centres

ISLO INT: e: d: International Solidary Labor Organization — Verein für internationale Solidarität ISLO eV, München

IS LRS YU: sn: Izvršni Svet, Ljudska Republika Slovenija

ISLTC INT: e: International Society of Leather Trades Chemists

ISLWF INT: e: International Shoe and Leather Workers' Federation, Earls Barton, Northampton [GB, gegr 1907]

I.S.M. GB: e: Incorporated Society of Musicians, London

ISM US: e: Institute of Sanitation Management; e: Institute of Statistical Mathematics; RM: f: Institut Scientifique de Madagascar, Tsinbazaza; INT: d: Internationale Saarmesse, Saarbrücken [BRD]

I.S.M.A. GB: e: Incorporated Sales Managers' Association

ISMA US: e: Indiana School Music Association; Indiana State Medical Association; d: Institut für staatliche Markt- und Meinungsforschung; e: International Superphosphate and Compound Manufacturers' Association Ltd.

ISMAC e: mil: Israeli-Syrian Mixed Armistice Commission

ISMDA US: e: Independent Sewing Machine Dealers of America

I.S.M.D.T.S. e: Iron, Steel and Metal Dressers Trade Society

ISME GB: e: Institute of Sheet Metal Engineering, London; INT: e: International Society for Music Education

ISMEO I: i: Istituto Italiano per il Medio ed Estremo Oriente, Roma

ISMES I: i: Istituto Sperimentale Modelli e Strutture

ISMH US: e: Illinois Society for Mental Hygiene; INT: e: International Society of Medical Hydrology

ISMIRAN SU: [d: Institut für Erdmagnetismus, Ionosphäre und Ausbreitung von Radiowellen, Krasnaja Pachra bei Moskau]

ISMIU BG: [d: Bulgarisches Institut für Normung, Meßtechnik und Meßgeräte, Sofia]

ISML I: i: Istituto Sperimentale dei Metalli Leggeri, Milano

ISMRC GB: e: mil: Inter-Services Metallurgical Research Council

ISMS US: e: Illinois State Medical Society; Iowa State Medical Society

ISMUN INT: e: International Students' Movement for the United Nations [gegr 1948, Genf, CH]

I.S.N. I: i: mil: Istituto Superiore di Navigazione

ISNB B: f: Institut Royal des Sciences Naturelles de Belgique, Bruxelles

ISNP INT: e: International Society of Naturopathic Physicians [gegr 1938]

I.S.O. I: i: Industria Scientifica Ottica, Milano; NL: nl: Inspectie Schriftelijk Onderwijs

ISO INT: e: International Organization for Standardization, CH-1211 Genf 20; International Self-Service Organization [gegr 1960]; International Shopfitting Organization; International Stevedore Organization; I: i: Istituto Storico Olandese

ISO/COPCO = COPCO

ISO/DATCO = DATCO

ISO/DEVCO = DEVCO

ISO/DEVCONF INT: e: ISO Conference for the Development of Standardization in the Developing Countries

ISO/DICO = DICO

ISO/EXCO INT: e: ISO Executive Committee

ISO/FINCO = FINCO

ISOL INT: f: Groupement des producteurs d'isolateurs et de pièces isolantes minérales à usage électro-technique de la CEE

I.S.O.L.A. I: i: Istituto Sardo Organizzazione Lavoro Artigiano

ISONEVO NL: nl: Instituut voor Sociaal Onderzoek van het Nederlandse Volk

ISO/ORCO INT: e: ISO Organization Committee

ISOP CH: [d: schweizerisches Institut für öffentliche Meinungsforschung =ISOPUBLIC]

ISO/PATCO INT: e: ISO Patent Committee

ISO/PLACO INT: e: ISO Planning Committee

ISOPUBLIC CH: d: ISOPUBLIC Markt- und Meinungsforschung, CH-8008 Zürich

Isorel F: f: Société pour la fabrication d'isolants et de revêtements ligneux "Isorel"

ISO/STACO INT: e: ISO Standing Committee for the Study of Scientific Principles of Standardization

ISO/SUPCO INT: e: ISO Supervisory Committee

I.S.O.T. B: f: Institut Supérieur d'Occupational Therapy

ISO/TC INT: e: ISO Technical Committee

ISP I: i: Igiene e Sanità Pubblica, Alto Commissariato

I.S.P. Malaya: e: Incorporated Society of Planters; GB: e: Institute of Sewage Purification; R: ro: Institutul de Studii şi Prospecţiuni, Bucureşti

ISP US: e: Inter-American Society of Psychology; INT: s: Internacional de Servidores Públicos f: Internationale des Services Publics, London EC 1; INT: e: International Society for Photogrammetry; US: e: International Swappers Paradise, Hartford 12, Conn.; I: i: Istituto di Studi Parlamentari

ISPA US: e: Idaho State Pharmaceutical Association; R: ro: Institutul de Studii şi Proiectări Agricole; INT: e: International Screen Publicity Association, London [gegr 1955] ; e: International

Small Printers Association; INT: e: International Sporting Press Association [gegr 1924]

ISPAS e: International Society of Professional Ambulance Services

ISPE US: e: Illinois Society of Professional Engineers; R: ro: Institutul de Studii şi Proiectări Energetice, Bucureşti

ISPI I: i: Istituto per gli Studi di Politica Internazionale

I.S.P.I.M.C. R: ro: Institutul de Studii şi Proiectări pentru Industria Materialelor de Construcţii, Bucureşti

ISPO INT: d: Internationale Sportartikelmesse, München [März 1970]

ISPROR R: ro: Institutul de Studii şi Proiectări a Construcţiilor Orăşneşti, Bucureşti

ISPS R: ro: Institutul de Studii şi Proiectări Silvice; INT: e: International Society of Plastic Surgeons [gegr 1955]

ISPT I: i: Istituto Speciale por Produtto Technico, Roma

ISPW INT: e: International Society for the Psychology of Writing

ISQC IND: e: Indian Society for Quality Control

I.S.R. IND: e: Indian State Railways; e: Institute of Seaweed Research

ISR INT: e: International Society of Radiobiology; International Society of Radiology; e: The International Synthetic Rubber Co. (Europe) Ltd., Bruxelles 5 [B] ; S: sv: Internationella studenthjälpens rikskommitté, Stockholm [gegr 1943] ; IR: [d: Iranische Eisenbahnen]

I.S.R.B. GB: e: mil: Inter-Services Research Bureau

ISRCSC GB: e: mil: Inter-Services Radio Components Standardization Committee

ISRD INT: e: International Society for Rehabilitation of the Disabled

I.S.R.E.S. F: f: Institut Scientifique de Recherches Economiques et Sociales

ISRO IND: e: Indian Space Research Organization

ISROP L: e: ISROP, The Israel European Company, Luxemburg [gegr 1963]

ISRR INT: e: International Society for Rorschach Research

ISRRA e: International Standard Rex Rabbit Association

ISRSM INT: e: International Symposium on Rocket and Satellite Meteorology [first meeting at Washington, D.C., April 1962]

ISRU INT: e: International Scientific Radio Union, Bruxelles 18 [B]

ISS GB: e: Institute of Strategic Studies, London; CH: d: Internationaler Sozialdienst der Schweiz; INT: e: International Social Service, Geneva [CH, gegr 1921]; e: International Society of Surgery; INT: e: International Student Service, Geneva [CH, gegr 1920]; I: i: Istituto Sperimentale della Strada

ISSA INT: e: International Social Security Association, Geneva [CH, gegr 1927]

I.S.S.&A.H.S. GB: e: mil: Incorporated Soldiers', Sailors' and Airmen's Help Society

I.S.S.B. GB: e: mil: Inter-Service Security Board

ISSC UN: e: International Social Science Council, Paris 16 [gegr 1952, UNESCO]

I.S.S.C. e: mil: Inter-Services Staff College

ISSCB INT: e: International Society for Sandwich Construction and Bonding [gegr 1957]

ISSCT INT: e: International Society of Sugar Cane Technologists, Réduit, Mauritius

ISSF BRD: d: stud: Internationaler Studentenbund − Studentenbewegung für übernationale Föderation eV, 53 Bonn; INT: e: International Service of the Society of Friends [Quakers]

I.S.S.I. I: i: Istituto Scientifico Sperimentale Industriale

ISSM INT: sv: Internationella sällskapet för samtida musik [gegr 1922]

ISSMFE INT: e: International Society of Soil Mechanics and Foundation Engineering, London SW 1

ISSO US: e: Institute of Strategic and Stability Operations

ISSP J: e: Institute for Solid State Physics, Tokyo

ISSS INT: e: International Society for Socialist Studies, London [gegr 1957] International Society of Soil Science, Amsterdam [NL, gegr 1924]

I.S.S.T. B: f: Institut pour les sciences sociales du travail; I: i: Istituto Scientifico Sperimentale per i Tabacchi

ISSTA IL: e: Israel Student Touring Association, Tel Aviv

IST B: f: Institut Supérieur du Travail; e: International Standard Trading Corporation

ISTA IND: e: Indian Scientific Translators Association; INT: e: International Seed Testing Association, Wageningen [NL, gegr 1924]

ISTAB BRD: d: Informationsstelle Absatz und Beschaffung, 7 Stuttgart [Technische Hochschule, seit 1962]

ISTAF BlnW: d: Internationales Stadionfest

ISTAT I: i: Istituto Centrale (Nazionale) di Statistica

IStB INT: d: Internationaler Studentenbund

I.S.T.C. e: Iron and Steel Trades Confederation

ISTCAMBI I: i: Istituto Nazionale per i Cambi con l'Estero

ISTD GB: e: Imperial Society of Teachers of Dancing Incorporated, London W 1 [gegr 1904]; Institute for the Study and Treatment of Delinquency;

INT: e: International Society of Tropical Dermatology

ISTDA US: e: Institutional and Service Textile Distributors Association

I.S.T.E.A. GB: e: Iron and Steel Trades Employers' Association

ISTESU e: International Secretariat for Teaching Educational Sciences in Universities

ISTG INT: d: Internationale Schlafwagen- und Touristik-Gesellschaft, 6 Ffm [BRD, vorher: ISG, gegr 1876]

IStG BRD: d: Internationale Studiengesellschaft für wirtschaftliche, wissenschaftliche und kulturelle Zusammenarbeit eV, 62 Wiesbaden

ISTIC e: Institute of Scientific and Technical Information of China

ISTITECNICA I: i: Istituto Nazionale della Tecnica

I.S.T.M. GB: e: Incorporated Society of Trained Masseurs

ISTM INT: e: International Society for Testing Materials

ISTPM F: f: Institut scientifique et technique des pêches maritimes

ISTRAK INT: d: Internationale Straßenteer-Konferenz

I Struct E GB: e: Institution of Structural Engineers

Ist.St.Rom. I: i: Istituto di Studi Romani

Istus INT: d: Internationale Studienkommission für den motorlosen Flug

ISTVC GB: e: mil: Inter-Service Technical Valve Committee, London SW 1

ISTVS INT: e: International Society for Terrain Vehicle Systems

I.S.U. INT: eo: Internacia Somera Universitato; INT: nl: Internationaal Salon der Uitvinders

ISU US: e: International Seamen's Union; INT: e: International Shooting Union, Stockholm [S, gegr 1907]; International Skating Union, Davos [CH, gegr 1892]; US: e: State University of Iowa [Iowa State University], Ames, Iowa

ISUSE INT: e: International Secretariat for the University Study of Education

I.S.V. CH: f: Communauté Interprofessionnelle de l'Importation Suisse de Vins; CH: d: Innerschweizer Schriftsteller-Verein; INT: d: Internationaler Schlittensportverband, Reichenberg (Böhmen); Internationaler Seidenbau-Verband; Internationaler Skiverband

ISVEIMER I: i: Istituto per lo Sviluppo Economico dell'Italia Meridionale

ISVR GB: e: Institute of Sound and Vibration Research, Southampton

ISVS INT: e: International Secretariat for Volunteer Service

ISVSK INT: d: Internationaler Ständiger Verband für Schiffahrtskongresse, Brüssel 4 [B, gegr 1900]

ISW CH: d: Interessengemeinschaft für den Schweizerischen Weinimport

ISWA BlnW: d: Institut für Sozial- und Wirtschaftspolitische Ausbildung eV, Berlin; INT: e: International Solid Wastes and Public Cleansing Association [d: ab 1 Jan 1970 Zusammenschluß von IAM und INTAPUC]

ISWC GB: e: International Short Wave Club, London; INT: e: International Society for the Welfare of Cripples, New York [gegr 1922, jetzt: ISRD]

ISWO e: International Sponsorship of War Orphans

ISY INT: [d: Internationales statistisches Jahr für Forschung und Entwicklung]

ISZ I: i: Istituto Sperimentale di Zootecnica

IT US: e: Institute of Technology

I.T. f: Institut Technique

IT PL: pl: Instytut Torfowy; YU: sh: Inženjeri i tehničari

ITA GB: e: Independent Television Authority and Television Companies Association Ltd., London; e: Indian Tea Association;

Association; US: e: Industrial Truck Association, Washington 4, D.C.

I.T.A. F: f: Institut Technique Agricole; Institut du Transport Aérien, Paris 7 [gegr 1924]

ITA INT: d: Internationales Tierseuchenamt, Paris [gegr 1924]; Internationale Tapetenausstellung [München, BRD, 1960]; US: e:International Telegraph Association; e: International Temperance Association; INT: e: International Touring Alliance [vorher: Association, gegr 1898]

I.T.A. e: Irish Temperance Alliance; Irish Tourist Association

I.T.A.C. GB: e: Imperial Three Arts Club

ITAC US: e: Independent Technical Advisory Committee; GB: US: Industrial Training Atlantic Convention

I.T.Aé. F: f: mil: Inspection Technique de l'Aéronautique

ITAG US: e: mil: Intelligence Threat Analysis Group, Office of the Assistant Chief of Staff for Intelligence, Alexandria, Va.; BRD: d: Internationale Tiefbohr-Kommanditgesellschaft (ITAG), Celle [gegr 1912]

ITAKO INT: d: Internationaler Tanzlehrerkongreß 1969, Stuttgart [BRD]

ITAL NL: nl: Instituut voor Toepassing van Atoomenergie in de Landbouw, Wageningen [gegr 1957]

ITALIA I: i: Agencia d'Italia, Roma [d: Nachrichtenagentur]

ITALJUG I: YU: sh: Italijansko-jugoslavenska Komora u Rimu

Italnavi I: i: Italnavi — Società di Navigazione per Azioni, Genoa [gegr 1924]

Italsider I: [d: Stahlkonzern, gegr 1961]

I.T.A.P. F: f: Institut Technique des Administrations Publiques

ITAT MEX: s: Instituto Técnico Administrative del Trabajo

ITAVI I: i: Servizio Telecommunicazione e Meteorologico dell' Aeronautica

ITB F: f: Institut technique de la betterave industrielle; CH: d: Institut für Touristik Basel; INT: d: Internationaler Turnerbund [gegr 1881]; Internationale Tourismus-Börse [BlnW]; INT: e: International Time Bureau, Paris

ITBB INT: f: Fédération Internationale des Travailleurs du Bâtiment et du Bo

ITBON NL: nl: Instituut voor Toegepast Biologisch Onderzoek in de Natu

ITBTP F: f: Institut des travaux du bâtiment et des travaux publics, Paris

I.T.C. GB: e: Imperial Tobacco Co.; Industrial Training Council; GB: e: mil: Infantry Training Centre; Initial Training Centre

ITC UN: e: Inland Transport Committee [ECE]; INT: e: International Tea Committee, London [gegr 1933]; International Timber Committee [gegr 1932]; International Tin Council, London; US: e: mil: Intern Training Center, Texarkana, Texas; INT: e: International Training Centre for Aeri Survey, Delft [NL]; International Tuberculosis Campaign; I: i: Istituto Tecnico Commerciale

ITCA GB: e: Independent Television Companies Association; US: e: International Typographical Composition Association

I.T.C.A.A. F: f: Institut Technique Coopératif des Aliments pour les Animaux

I.T.C.C. s: Instituto Técnico de la Construcción y del Cemento

ITCC INT: e: International Telephone Consultative Committee

ITCDA e: International Telephone Cable Development Association

I.T.C.F. F: f: Institut technique des céréales et des fourrages

I.T.C.L. GB: e: Indian Trade Commissioner in London

I.T.C.M.E. R: ro: Institutul de Studii, Cercetări şi Proiectări Tehnologice pentru Industria Constructoare de Maşini, Utilaje şi Industria Electro-tehnica, Bucureşti

ITCPN INT: e: International Technical Conference on Protection of Nature

ITD NL: nl: mil: Inspectie Technische Dienst; PL: pl: Instytut Technologii Drewna

ITDC e: International Trade Development Committee

ITDZ NL: nl: mil: Inspecteur Tandheel-kundige Dienst Zeemacht

ITE US: e: Institute of Traffic Engineers, Washington D.C. 20006; INT: e: Insti-tute of Telecommunication Engineers; BRD: d: Institut zur Erforschung tech-nologischer Entwicklungslinien, 3 Han-nover [später:] 2 Hamburg [gegr 1970] ; INT: f: Fédération Internationale des Travailleurs Evangéliques; INT: e: International Tests for Enamels Com-mittee; International Townplanning Exhibition

ITEB F: f: Institut Technique d'Elevage Bovin

ITEM INT: d: Internationale Technische Messe, Kopenhagen [DK]

ITEO e: International Trade and Employ-ment Organization

I.T.E.R.G. F: f: Institut Technique d'Etudes et des Recherches des Corps Gras, Paris 7

Itev D: d: Internationaler Theater-Kultur-Verband, Berlin

ITexM BRD: d: Institut für Textil-Markt-forschung eV, 6 Ffm

ITF F: f: Institut Textil de France, Bou-logne-sur-Seine; INT: d: Internationale Tonjäger- Föderation [f: FICS] ; INT: d: Internationale Transportarbeiter-Födera-tion e: International Transport Work-ers' Federation, London SW 4 sv: In-ternationella transportarbetarfederatio-

nen; INT: da: International Tobaks-arbejder-Forbund [e: IFTW]

I.T.F.H. GB: e: Industrial and Trade Fairs Holding Ltd.

ITFO US: e: International Trade Fairs Office [Department of Commerce]

ITFS US: e: Instructional Television Fixed Service

ITG INT: d: Internationale Tabakwissen-schaftliche Gesellschaft; Internatio-nale Technogeographische Gesellschaft eV, 1 Bln 19 [BlnW]

ITGWF INT: e: International Textile and Garment Workers' Federation, London SW 1

I.T.G.W.U. e: Irish Transport and General Workers' Union

ITI IND: e: Indian Telephones Industries, Ltd.; Industrial Training Institute; e: Industries Technical Institute Inc.; INT: f: Institut Technique Internatio-nal de Mécaniciens Navigants de l'Avia-tion Civile, Thiais e: International Technical Institute of Flight Engineers; INT: d: Internationales Theater-Insti-tùt, Paris 8 [gegr 1948] e: Internatio-nal Theatre (Theater) Institute; INT: e: International Thrift Institute, Am-sterdam C [NL, gegr 1924] ; e: Irish Timber Industries Ltd.

Itim IL: [d: Nachrichtenagentur]

ITIPAT f: Institut pour le technologie et l'industrialisation des produits agri-coles tropicaux

ITK S: sv: Institutet för tekniska kurser; PL: pl: Instytut Technologii Krzemia-nów; INT: d: Internationaler Tier-ärztlicher Kongreß; Internationales Eisenbahn-Transportkomitee, Bern [CH] ; Internationale Tagung über Elektrische Kontakte, München [BRD, 4...8. Mai 1970]

ITL BRD: d: Ingenieur- und Techniker-Lehrgangsinstitut, 8999 Weiler; S: sv: Isotoptekniska Laboratoriet, Stockholm [gegr 1959]

I.T.M. f: mil: Inspection Technique de la Marine; Inspection Technique du Matériel

ITM US: e: Institute of Thread Machiners

ITMA US: e: Institute for Training in Municipal Administration; INT: d: Internationale Textilmaschinen-Ausstellung, Basel [CH]

ITMEB e: International Tea Market Expansion Board

I.T.M.O. F: f: Inspection du Travail et de la Main-d'OEuvre

ITMRC INT: e: International Travel Market Research Council

I.T.N. F: f: Institut Technique de Normandie; I: i: Istituto Tecnico Nautico

I.T.O. GB: e: Income Tax Office

ITO DDR: d: Institut für Technologie und Organisation des Maschinenbaues, Karl-Marx-Stadt [seit 1960: ZIF]; BlnW: d: Institut für Tontechnik; UN: e: International Trade Organization, Geneva [CH, gegr 1948]

ITOA I: i: Istituto di Tecnica ed Organizzazione Aziendale

I.T.O.S. e: International Theosophical Order of Service

ITP d: Institut für Technische Physik; BRD: d: Internationale Television Produktion GmbH

I.T.P.A. F: f: Institut Technique de Pratique Agricole; e: Irish Textile Printers' Association

ITPAS P: pt: Instituto de Trabalho Previdência e Acção Social, Angola, Guiné Portuguesa, Moçambique e S. Tomé e Príncipe

I.T.P.E.S. F: f: Institut Technique de Prévision Economique et Social, Paris

I.T.P.S. GB: e: Income Tax Payers' Society

I.T.P.T. F: f: Institut Technique de la Pomme de Terre

ITR US: e: mil: Infantry Training Regiment [Marines]; PL: pl: Instytut Tele i Radiotechniczny

ITRC SYR: e: Industrial Testing and Research Centre, Damascus; INT: e: International Tin Research Council

ITRI INT: e: International Travel Resear Institute [IUOTO]

ITRL US: e: International Telephone an Radio Laboratories

ITS GB: e: International Technogeograpk ical Society; INT: e: International Tracing Service, Arolsen [BRD, gegr 1945]; International Trade Secretariats (Liaison Office), Geneva [CH]

ITSA US: e: Institute for Telecommunication Sciences and Aeronomy

ITSG e: mil: Interallied Technical Study Group; INT: e: International Tin Stud Group, Den Haag [NL]

ITSM US: e: McCann - Institute for Technical and Scientific Marketing

ITT US: e: Institute of Textile Technology; NL: nl: Instituut voor Tuinbouwtechniek, Wageningen; US: e: International Telephone and Telegraph Corporation, 320 Park Avenue, New York, N.Y. 10022 [gegr 16 Jun 1920,= IT&T

I.T.T.A. f: mil: Inspection Technique des Télécommunications de l'Air

ITTB BRD: d: Institut für Informationsverarbeitung in Technik und Biologie, 75 Karlsruhe [vorher: Institut für Schwingungsforschung]

ITTC US: e: International Telephone and Telegraph Corporation [= ITT]; e: International Towing Tank Conference

ITTCC INT: e: International Telegraph and Telephone Consultative Committee [f: CCITT, Genève, CH]

ITTE US: e: Institute of Transportation and Traffic Engineering [University of California, Los Angeles]; US: e: International Telephone and Telegraph Corporation Europe [vgl: ITT]

ITTF INT: e: International Table Tennis Federation [gegr 1926]

ITTLS US: s: ITT Laboratorios de España, Madrid [E, vgl: ITT]

ITTTA INT: e: International Technical Tropical Timber Association, Nogent -sur-Marne [F, gegr 1951]

ITTV INT: d: Internationaler Tischtennis-Verband, London, Wien

ITTWORLDCOM US: e: International Telephone and Telegraph World Communications, Inc. [vgl: ITT]

ITU WAN: e: Igbirra Tribal Union; UN: e: International Telecommunication Union, Geneva [CH, gegr 1932] ; INT: e: International Temperance Union, Lausanne [CH, gegr 1907] ; US: e: International Typographical Union

ITUBAG CH: d: Ingenieur- und Tunnel -Bau AG, Zürich

ITUC e: Irish Trade Union Congress

I.T.U.M. e: International Trade Union Movement

ITUV S: sv: mil: Inspektör för torped- och ubåtsvapen

ITV GB: e: Independent Television [gegr 1954] ; US: e: Industrial Television; Instructional Television

I.T.V. F: f: Institut Technique du Vin

ITV INT: d: Internationaler Tabakarbeiter-Verband, Brüssel [B, gegr 1876]

ITVV INT: d: Internationaler Transport -Versicherungs-Verband, Zürich 1 [CH]

ITWF INT: e: International Transport Workers' Federation, London SW 4 [= ITF]

ITXT US: e: Institute of Textile Technology

ITZN INT: e: International Trust for Zoological Nomenclature

IU US: e: University of Idaho

I.U. US: e: Indianapolis Union Railway Company

IU S: sv: Industriens uppslysningstjänst

[1942...59] ; INT: Interlingue-Union, CH-1033 Cheseaux [gegr 1928] ; D: d: Internationale Union [Gewerblicher Rechtsschutz] ; Internationale Union [Jugendverband] ; INT: d: Interparlamentarische Union [=IPU] ; INT: sv: Internationella ungdomshjälpen

IUA. A: d: Staatsamt für Inneres und Unterricht

IUA PL: pl: Instytut urbanistyki i architektury, Warszawa; INT: e: International Union of Advertising, Paris 17 [gegr 1949] ; International Union of Architects, Paris [gegr 1948] ; International Union of Arts

I.U.A. e: Irish Unionist Alliance

IUaA INT: d: Internationale Union angestellter Apotheker

IUAA INT: e: International Union of Advertisers Associations, Brussels 1; International Union of Alpine Associations, Geneva [CH, gegr 1932: IUMA]

IUAC INT: e: International Union against Cancer

IUADM INT: e: International Union of Associations of Doctor-Motorists, Utrecht [NL]

IUAES INT: e: International Union of Anthropological and Ethnological Sciences

IUAI INT: e: International Union of Aviation Insurers, London EC 3 [gegr 1934]

IUAJ INT: e: International Union of Agricultural Journalists, Paris 8

IUAO INT: e: International Union of Applied Ornithology [gegr 1955]

IUAPPA INT: e: International Union of Air Pollution Prevention Associations, 4 Düsseldorf [BRD]

IUAS INT: e: International Union of Agricultural Sciences, Paris 7

IUAT INT: e: International Union against Tuberculosis, Paris [gegr 1920]

IUB NL: nl: Inrichting Uitgeven Boekwerken

I.U.B. e: Insurance Unemployment Board

IUB INT: e: International Union of Biochemistry, London [gegr 1955]; International Universities' Bureau, Paris [gegr 1950]; GB: e: International University Booksellers Ltd., London; US: e: Interstate Underwriters Board

IUBS INT: e: International Union of Biological Sciences [gegr 1919]

I.U.C. e: Insurance Unions' Congress

IUC INT: e: International Union of Chemistry; International Union of Colleges Working for World Understanding; International Union of Crystallography [=IUCr]; International University Contact for Management Education, Rotterdam [NL]; e: Inter-University Council for Higher Education Overseas

IUCAF INT: e: Inter-Union Committee on the Allocation of Frequencies

IUCN INT: e: International Union for Conservation of Nature and Natural Resources, CH-1110 Morges [vgl: UIPN]

IUCr INT: e: International Union of Crystallography, Groningen [NL, gegr 1947]

IUCRM e: Inter-Union Commission on Radio Meteorology

IUCSR INT: e: International Union for Co-operation in Solar Research

IUCSTR INT: e: Inter-Union Commission on Solar and Terrestrial Relationships

IUCW INT: e: International Union for Child Welfare, Geneva [CH, gegr 1946]

IUCWL INT: e: International Union of Catholic Women's Leagues [gegr 1910]

IUD US: e: Industrial Union Department [AFL-CIO]

IUDZG INT: e: International Union of Directors of Zoological Gardens, Philadelphia, Pa.

IUE US: e: International Union of Electrical Workers; International Union of Electrical, Radio and Machine Workers; INT: e: International Union for Electroheat, Paris

IUEC US: e: International Union of Elevator Constructors

IÜD BRD: d: Institut für Übersetzen und Dolmetschen, 66 Saarbrücken

IUEF e: International University Exchange Fund

I.U.E.W. e: Industrial Union of Engineering Workers

IUF CH: d: Interessengemeinschaft der Schweizerischen Uhren-Fabrikanten; INT: e: International Union of Food and Allied Workers Associations, Geneva [CH]

I.U.F. INT: e: International University Federation for the League of Nations, Lausanne [CH, gegr 1924]

IUFD INT: e: International Union of Food and Drink Workers' Associations Geneva [CH, gegr 1920]

IUFDT INT: e: International Union of Food, Drink and Tobacco Workers' Associations, Geneva [CH]

I.U.F.L.N. INT: e: = I.U.F.

IUFO INT: e: International Union of Family Organizations, Paris 9 [gegr 1947]

IUFRO INT: e: International Union of Forest Research Organizations, London [gegr 1890]

IUFTAV INT: d: Internationale Union für Forschung, Technik und Anwendung des Vakuums, Brüssel 4 [B]

IUGB INT: e: International Union of Game Biologists

IUGG INT: e: International Union of Geodesy and Geophysics, Paris 7 [gegr 1919]

IUGS INT: e: International Union of Geological Sciences, Antwerp [B]

I.U.H.E.I. CH: f: Institut Universitaire de Hautes Etudes Internationales, CH-1211 Genève 21

I.u.HK. d: Industrie- und Handelskammer

IUHPS INT: e: International Union of the History and Philosophy of Science, F-75 Paris 6 [gegr 1956]

IUHR INT: d: Internationale Union der Hotel-, Restaurant- und Café-Angestellten, Stockholm [gegr 1920] e: International Union of Hotel, Restaurant and Bar Workers sv: Internationella Unionen för Hotell-, Restaurang och Kaféanställda

IUHS INT: e: International Union of the History of Sciences, Paris 2 [1947... 56, dann: IUHPS]

IUI S: sv: Industriens utredningsinstitut; INT: e: International Union of Interpreters

IUJHUSC CDN: US: e: International Union of Journeymen Horseshoers of the United States and Canada

IUKP INT: d: Internationale Union der Katholischen Presse, Paris [gegr 1936]

IUL INT: d: Internationale Union der Lebens- und Genußmittelarbeiter-Gewerkschaften, Genf [CH, gegr 1920] da: Internationale Union af Levneds- og Nydelsesmiddelarbejder-Forbund; INT: da: International Ungdoms Liga

IULA INT: e: International Union of Local Authorities, Den Haag [NL,gegr 1913]

IULC WAN: e: Independent United Labour Congress

IULCS INT: e: International Union of Leather Chemists Societies [gegr 1948]

IULCW INT: e: International Union of Liberal Christian Women, Den Haag [gegr 1910]

IULEC e: Inter-University Labour Education Committee

IULIA US: e: International Union of Life Insurance Agents

I.U.L.V.T.F.T. e: International Union for Land Values Taxation and Free Trade

IUMA INT: e: International Union of Mountaineering Associations, Geneva [CH, gegr 1932, später: IUAA]

IUMAC INT: e: International Union of Medical Automobile Clubs, Paris [gegr 1933]

IUMI INT: e: International Union of Marine Insurance, Zürich 1 [CH, gegr 1874]

IUMMSW US: e: International Union of Mine, Mill and Smelter Workers

IUMSWA US: e: International Union of Marine and Shipbuilding Workers of America

I.U.N. F: f: Institut Universitaire Naval; I: i: Istituto Universitario Navale

IUNS INT: e: International Union of Nutritional Sciences, Paris 6 [gegr 1946]

IUOE US: e: International Union of Operating Engineers

IUOTO INT: e: International Union of Official Travel Organizations, Geneva [CH, gegr 1925, 1947]

IUOW CDN: US: e: International Union of Oil Workers

IUP INT: d: Internationale Union von Verbänden der Privatgüterwagenbesitzer, St. Gallen [CH]; INT: e: International Union of Physiology

IUPA INT: e: International Union of Practitioners in Advertising, Paris [gegr 1949]

IUPAB INT: e: International Union of Pure and Applied Biophysics

IUPAC INT: e: International Union of Pure and Applied Chemistry, Basel [CH]

IUPAP INT: e: International Union of Pure and Applied Physics, Paris 15

IUPEE vgl: UIPDEE

IUPIP INT: e: International Union for the Protection of Industrial Property, Geneva [CH]

623

IUPM INT: e: International Union for Protecting Public Morality, Paris [gegr 1951] ; d: Internationale Union Prosper Montagné, Paris

IUPN INT: e: International Union for the Protection of Nature [gegr 1948, ab 1957: IUCN, vgl: UIPN]

IUPS INT: e: International Union of Physiological Sciences, Minneapolis [US, gegr 1953]

IUPW US: e: Independent Union of Petroleum Workers

IUR INT: e: International Union of Railways, Paris [gegr 1922] ; e: International University of Radiophonics; INT: sv: Internationella ungdomsbokrådet

IURA INT: e: International Union of Radio Amateurs, West Hartford [US]

IURN SU: f: Institut unifié de recherches nucléaires, Kalinin

IUS INT: e: International Union of Students [d: ISB, Prag [CS] , gegr 1946]

IUSA e: International Underwater Spearfishing Association

IUSDT INT: e: International Union of Social Democratic Teachers [gegr 1952]

IUSF e: Industries of the United States Fund

IUSP INT: e: International Union of Scientific Psychology

IUSS INT: e: International Union for Social Studies

IUSSI INT: e: International Union for the Study of Social Insects, Paris [gegr 1952]

IUSSP INT: e: International Union for the Scientific Study of Population

IUSY INT: e: International Union of Socialist Youth, Vienna [A, gegr 1946]

I.U.T. F: f: Institut Universitaire de Technologie

IUTAM INT: e: International Union of Theoretical and Applied Mechanics, Bruxelles [B, gegr 1946]

IUTMCT INT: e: International Union for Thermal Medicine and Climatothalassotherapy

IUUW US: e: International Union of United Welders

IUVAA INT: nl: Internationale Unie var Verenigingen van Artsen-Automobilisten, Utrecht [NL, e: IUADM]

IUVDT INT: e: International Union against the Venereal Diseases and the Treponematoses, Paris

IUVSTA INT: e: International Union of Vacuum Science, Technique and Applications, Brussels 4 [B, d: IUFTAV]

IUVW L: d: Internationale Universität für vergleichende Wissenschaften, Luxemburg

IUWDS INT: e: International Ursigram and World Days Service, Boulder, Colo. 80302 [US]

IUYCD INT: e: International Union of Young Christian Democrats

IV d: Industrie-Verband; Invalidenversicherung; YU: Izvršno Veće

IVA US: e: Independent Voters' Association; S: sv: Ingeniörsvetenskapsakademien, Stockholm 5 [gegr 1919] ; Bolivien: s: Instituto de Vacuna Antivariolosa; INT: d: Internationale Vereinigung der Privatanschlußgleisebenutzer, St. Gallen [CH] ; Internationale Verkehrsausstellung [München, BRD, 1965]

IVAKV INT: d: Internationale Vereinigung Ärztlicher Kraftfahrer-Verbände, Utrecht [NL, e: IUADM]

IVAL B: nl: Instituut voor Verzekering tegen Arbeidsongevallen in de Landbouw

IVAN B: nl: Instituut voor Verzekering tegen Arbeidsongevallen in de Nijverheid

IVB DDR: d: Institut für Verwaltungsorganisation und Bürotechnik, Leipzig; BRD: d: Interzonen-Verkehrsbeobachtung [Dienststelle]

IVBA INT: e: International Volleyball Association, Paris [gegr 1947]

IVbdD NL: nl: mil: Inspectie Verbindingsdienst

IVBH INT: d: Internationale Vereinigung für Brückenbau und Hochbau, CH-8006 Zürich [gegr 1929]

IV BiH YU: sh: Izvršno Vijeće Bosne i Hercegovine

IVBV INT: d: Internationaler Verband der Bibliothekar-Vereine [e: IFLA]

IVC BRD: d: Industrievereinigung Chemiefaser eV, 6 Ffm, Arndtstr. 18; INT: e: Permanent Committee for the International Veterinary Congresses, Utrecht [NL, gegr 1906]

I.V.C.C. F: f: Institut des vins de consommation courante

I.V.C.F. e: International Varsity Christian Fellowship

IVCLG INT: d: Internationaler Verband Christlicher Landarbeitergewerkschaften, Brüssel [B, f: FISCOA]

IVDJ INT: d: Internationale Vereinigung Demokratischer Juristen, Brüssel [B, gegr 1946, f: AIJD]

IVE GB: e: Institute of Vitreous Enamellers; BRD: d: Institut für Verbrauchs- und Einkaufsforschung GmbH, 2 Hamburg 26; INT: e: Internationale Vereinigung der Eisenwaren- und Eisenhändlerverbände, CH-8001 Zürich [gegr 1909]

IVF CH: d: Internationale Verbandstoff -Fabrik, Schaffhausen; INT: sv: Internationella Vänskapsförbundet

IVfgR INT: d: Internationale Vereinigung für gewerblichen Rechtsschutz, CH-8008 Zürich [gegr 1897]

IVFZ INT: e: International Veterinary Federation of Zootechnics, Madrid [E, gegr 1951]

IVG BRD: d: Industrie-Verwaltungs-Gesellschaft, 53 Bonn; DDR: d: Institut für Getreideverarbeitung, Bergholz

-Rehbrücke

I.V.G. INT: d: Internationale Vereinigung für Germanische Sprach- und Literaturwissenschaft [gegr 1955]

IVG INT: d: Internationale Vereinigung der Gewerkschaften [im WGB]

IVGWP INT: d: Internationaler Verband der Gastronomie- und Weinbau-Presse, Paris 7 [f: FIPGV, e: IFGVP]

IvH NL: nl: Instituut voor Handelswetenschappen

IVH A: d: Interessengemeinschaft volksdeutscher Heimatvertriebener

I.V.H. INT: nl: Internationale Vrijwillige Hulpdienst

IVHA NL: nl: Instituut tot Voorlichting bij Huishoudelijke Arbeid

IVHF INT: d: Internationaler Verband für Hydraulische Forschung, Delft [NL, f: AIRH, e: IAHR, gegr 1935]

IVI US: e: Independent Voters of Illinois; S: sv: Industriens Verkskyddsinstitut AB

IVIC YV: s: Instituto Venezolano de Investigaciónes Cientfficas, Caracas

IVIO NL: nl: Instituut voor Individueel Onderwijs

IVJH INT: d: Internationale Vereinigung für Jugendhilfe, Genf [CH, gegr 1946, e: IUCW]

IVK S: sv: Institutet för Växtforskning och Kyllagring, Nynäshamn [gegr 1941] d: Institut für Verbrennungsmotoren und Kraftfahrwesen; INT: d: Internationales Vorbereitungskomitee [der IMEKO]; YU: sh: Invalidska Vrhovna Komisija

I.V.K.B.J. INT: nl: Internationaal Verbond van de Katholieke Boerenjeugdbewegingen

IVKM INT: d: Internationaler Verband der Katholischen Mädchenschutzvereine, Fribourg [CH, gegr 1897]

IVKO NL: nl: Individueel Voortgezet Kunstzinnig Onderwijs

IVKW BRD: d: Interessenvertretung der Kriegs- und Währungsgeschädigten

I.V.K.W.V. INT: nl: Internationaal Verbond van Katholieke Werkgeversverenigingen

IVL NL: nl: Instituut voor Veredeling van Landbouwgewassen; INT: d: Internationale Vereinigung der Lehrerverbände, Lausanne [CH, gegr 1926]; Internationale Vereinigung der Limnologen [gegr 1922, e: IAL]

IVLD INT: d: Internationale Vereinigung der Organisationen von Lebensmittel-Detaillisten, Bern [CH, gegr 1927]

I.V.L.I.C. INT: d: Internationaler Verein der Leder-Industrie-Chemiker

I.V.L.I.S. INT: nl: Internationale Vereeniging van Leder-Industrie-Scheikundigen

IVMB INT: d: Internationale Vereinigung der Musikbibliotheken [f: AIBM]

IVMP INT: d: Internationaler Verband für Materialprüfung

IVO NL: nl: Instituut voor Veeteeltkundig Onderzoek T.N.O.; Instituut voor Volksontwikkeling

IvP NL: nl: Instituut voor Plantenveredeling; Instituut voor Pluimveeteelt

IVP INT: d: Internationaler Verband der Petroleumarbeiter, Denver [US]

IVPI INT: d: Internationale Vereinigung der Phonographischen Industrie

IVR INT: d: Internationale Vereinigung des Rheinschiffsregisters, Rotterdam/NL

IVRO NL: nl: Instituut voor Rassenonderzoek van Landbouwgewassen

IVRS INT: d: Internationale Vereinigung der revolutionären Schriftsteller

IVRV INT: d: Internationale Vereinigung für vergleichende Rechtswissenschaft und Volkswirtschaftslehre

I.V.S. GB: e: Indian Veterinary Service

IVS INT: d: Internationaler Verband für Seezeichenwesen, Paris 16 [e: IALA]; Internationale Vereinigung für Schalen-

tragwerke, Madrid 7 [E]; INT: e: International Voluntary Service [d: IZD CH: d: Interverband für Skilauf

IVSF INT: d: Internationale Vereinigung für Sozialen Fortschritt [= IVSS]

I.V.S.P. INT: e: International Voluntary Service for Peace

IVSS INT: d: Internationale Vereinigung für Soziale Sicherheit, Genf [CH, gegr 1927]

I.V.St. D: d: mil: Industrieversuchsstelle der Kriegsmarine

IVST INT: d: Internationaler Verband für Sozialtourismus

IVSU INT: e: International Veterinary Students Union

IVT NL: nl: Instituut voor de Veredeling van Tuinbouwgewassen; INT: d: Internationale Vereinigung der Textileinkaufsverbände, 5 Köln [BRD]

IVTC B: e: International Audio-Visual Technical Centre, Anvers

IVTCDV INT: d: Internationaler Varieté-Theater- und Circus-Direktorenverband eV

IVU INT: d: Internationale Vegetarier-Union nl: Internationale Vegetarische Unie e: International Vegetarian Union, London [gegr 1908]; Internationale Verleger-Union, Zürich [CH, gegr 1896]

IVVC INT: nl: Internationaal Verbond voor Vrijzinnig Christendom en Geloofsvrijheid

I.V.V.V. INT: nl: Internationaal Verbond van Vrije Vakverenigingen, Brussel

IVW BRD: d: Informationsgemeinschaft zur Feststellung der Verbreitung von Werbeträgern, 53 Bonn-Bad Godesberg INT: d: Internationale Vereinigung der Werktätigen der öffentlichen Dienste; Internationale Vereinigung der Widerstandskämpfer und Opfer des Faschismus

I.V.W.A. e: Indian Village Welfare Association

IVWB INT: d: Internationaler Verband der Wand- und Bodenplattenfabrikanten

IVWCO INT: e: International Voluntary Work Camp Organization

IVWSR INT: d: Internationaler Verband für Wohnungswesen, Städtebau und Raumordnung, Den Haag [NL]

IVWV INT: d: Internationaler Verband für Wasserbauliches Versuchswesen, Delft [NL, f: AIRH, e: IAHR]

IVZ BRD: d: Industrieverband Verkehrszeichen

I.W. GB: e: Institute of Welding; Institution of Water Engineers

IW PL: pl: Instytut Włókiennictwa

IWA US: e: Independent Watchmen's Association

I.W.A. e: Indian Workers Association; e: Industrial Workers of Africa

Iwa A: d: Innsbrucker Wirtschaftsvereinigung der öffentlichen Angestellten rGmbH

IWA US: e: Institute of World Affairs; Insurance Workers of America; BRD: d: Interministerieller Wirtschaftsausschuß [BMWi]; BRD: d: Internationale Fachausstellung "Wirtschaft und Werbung" [Essen 1955]; INT: e: International Women's Auxiliary to the Veterinary Profession, Paris 7; CDN: US: e: International Woodworkers of America

I.W.A. e: International Working Men's Association; e: Ironfounding Workers' Association

I.W.A.C. e: mil: Indian Women's Auxiliary Corps

IWB BlnW: d: Industriewärmestelle Berlin; INT: e: International Waterpolo Board

IWC INT: d: Internationale Ausstellung Wäscherei – Chemischreinigung [Ffm, BRD, 1968]; CH: e: International Watch Co., Schaffhausen; INT: e:

International Whaling Commission, London SW 1 [gegr 1946]; International Wheat Council, London SW 1 [gegr 1949]

I.W.C. e: International Writers' Club

IWCA e: International World Calendar Association

IWCAC INT: e: International Wireless Communications Advisory Committee

IWCCA US: e: Inland Waterways Common Carriers Association

IWCI US: e: Industrial Wire Cloth Institute

I.W.D. e: International Women's Day

IWE BlnW: d: Informationsbüro West

I.W.E. GB: e: Institution of Water Engineers

IWF DDR: d: Institut für Wirtschaftswissenschaftliche Forschung [MfS]; BRD: d: Institut für den wissenschaftlichen Film; INT: d: Internationaler Währungsfonds, Washington 25,D.C.; INT: nl: Internationale Wegfederatie

IWG D: d: mil: Inspektion für Waffen und Gerät, Berlin-Spandau; e: Interim Working Group; A: d: Internationale Werbegesellschaft mbH, Wien 1; e: International Working Group

I.W.G.C. GB: e: mil: Imperial War Graves Commission

IWGYC INT: e: International Working Group Youth and Co-operation, London

IWH BRD: d: Interessengemeinschaft Westdeutscher Heimatzeitungen

IWHA INT: e: International Women's Hockey Association

IWHS GB: e: Institute of Works and Highways Superintendents

IWIU US: e: Insurance Workers International Union

I.W.J.F. INT: [d: Judo-, Jiu-Jitsu-, Karate-Weltföderation]

IWK BRD: d: Industrie-Werke Karlsruhe AG [jetzt: IWKA]

IWKA BRD: d: Industriewerke Karlsruhe Augsburg AG

IWL DDR: d: Industriewerke Ludwigs-
felde; BRD: d: Institut für gewerb-
liche Wasserwirtschaft und Luftrein-
haltung eV, 5 Köln [gegr 1956] ; US:
e: Italian Welfare League

IWLA US: e: Izaak Walton League of
America

I.W.M. GB: e: mil: Imperial War Museum,
South Kensington, London; GB: e: Institution of Work Managers

IWMA e: Institute of Weights and Measures Administration

I.W.M.A. INT: e: International Working
Men's Association

IWO INT: e: International Wine Office,
Paris 8 [gegr 1924] ; US: e: International Workers Order, New York

IWOCA B: nl: Instituut voor Wetenschappelijk Onderzoek in Centraal Afrika
[f: IRSAC]

IWONL B: nl: Instituut tot Aanmoediging
van het Wetenschappelijk Onderzoek in
Nijverheid en Landbouw

Iw.Opt. D: d: mil: Instandsetzungswerk-
statt für optisches Gerät beim Heeres
-Zeugamt

IWP PL: pl: Instytut Wzornictwa Przemysłowego; INT: e: International Working Party

IWR INT: d: Internationaler Weizenrat,
London SW 1 [gegr 1949]

I.W.R. GB: e: Isle of Wight Railway

IWRB INT: e: International Wildfowl
Research Bureau

IWRI INT: e: International Wildfowl
Research Institute

IWRMA US: e: Independent Wire Rope
Manufacturers Association

IWRPF e: International Waste Rubber
and Plastic Federation

IWRS INT: e: International Wood Research Society

I.W.S. e: Industrial Welfare Society

IWS BRD: d: Industriewerke Saar Gmb
6691 Schwarzerden; GB: e: Institute
of Water Study; INT: d: Internationales Wollsekretariat e: Internationa
Wool Secretariat, London SW 1

IWSA INT: e: International Water Supply Association, London W 1 [gegr
1949] ; International Workers Sport
Association, Beyne-Heusay [B, gegr
1913]

IWSc e: Institute of Wood Science

IWSG INT: e: International Wool Study
Group, London SW 1 [gegr 1947]

I.W.S.G.G.B. GB: e: International Wom-
en's Service Groups in Great Britain

I.W.St.K. D: d: mil: WK2: Italienische
Waffenstillstandskommission

IWT BRD: d: Industriewerke Transport-
systeme, 2 Hamburg 39; GB: e: Institute of Wireless Technology; INT:
d: Internationaler Wettbewerb der besten Tonaufnahme des Deutschen Tor
jäger-Verbandes (DTV)

IWTA PAK: e: Inland Water Transport
Authority

I.W.T.D. GB: e: Inland Water Transport
Department

I.W.T.D.S. GB: e: Inland Water Transport Department Section

IWT/MIL e: mil: Working Group on Inland Water Transport, Military Sub
-Group

IWTO INT: d: Internationale Woll-Tex-
til-Organisation e: International Woo
Textile Organization, Bradford, Yorkshire [GB, gegr 1929]

IWU BRD: d: Institut für Wirtschafts-
und Unternehmensberatung GmbH,
56 Wuppertal 1; INT: nl: Internationale Wielerunie

IW Univ US: e: Illinois Wesleyan University

IWV DDR: d: Institut für Werkzeuge und
Vorrichtungen, Karl-Marx-Stadt [frü-
her: Chemnitz] ; INT: d: Internatio-

nale Warenhaus-Vereinigung, Forschungsgesellschaft für Betriebsführung, Paris [F, f: AIGM, e: IADS]

IWVA CDN: US: e: mil: International
War Veterans' Alliance

IWW US: e: Industrial Workers of the
World [gegr 1905 in Chicago] ; CDN:
US: International Woodworkers of
America [= IWWA]

IWWA CDN: US: International Woodworkers of America

IWWK BRD: d: Institut für Weltwirtschaft
an der Universität Kiel

IWYF e: International World Youth
Friendship

IWZ BRD: d: Institut für Wirtschafts-
praktische Zweckforschung Dr.Bruno
Heinz Jonzeck, 7477 Onstmettingen

I.Y. GB: e: mil: Imperial Yeomanry

IYA US: e: Interlake Yachting Association

IYC INT: e: International Youth Congress

IYCS INT: e: International Young
Christian Students

IYF INT: e: International Youth Federation for the Conservation of Nature

IYHF INT: e: International Youth Hostel
Federation [f: FIAJ]

IYL UN: e: International Youth Library
[UNESCO, d: IJB, f: BIJ]

IYQS e: = IQSY

IYRU INT: e: International Yacht Racing Union, London SW 1 [gegr 1906]

IYTP TR: [d: Partei der Neuen Türkei]

IZ PL: pl: Instytut Zootechniki

IZA B: nl: Internationaal Zeemanshuis
Antwerpen

IZB YU: sh: Inspektorat za Zaštitu Bilja;
BRD: d: Institut zur Erforschung zu-
künftiger Bildungssysteme [1969 vor-
geschlagen]

IZC INT: e: International Zoological
Congress

IZD INT: d: Internationaler Zivildienst,
Zürich [CH, gegr 1920, e: IVS]

IZFS D: e: nach WK2: Interzonal Facilities [ACA]

IZL IL: Irgun Zwai Leumi [d: politische
Partei, gegr 1936]

IZO INT: d: Internationale Zivilluftfahrt
-Organisation [e: ICAO]

IZS INT: e: International Zoological
Station

IZSN INT: e: International Zoological
Station Naples [I]

IZV D: d: Interessengemeinschaft zugelassener Verkaufsstellen der Reichszeugmeisterei in Berlin [NSDAP]

J BRD: d: Münzstätte Hamburg
J. D: d: mil: Justiariat [Rechtsabteilung]
J.A. F: f: Jeunes Aveugles
JA US: e: Jewish Agency for Palestine,
New York [= JAFP] ; e: Joint Agen-
cy; US: e: mil: Judge Advocate;
d: Jugendamt; YU: sn: Jugoslovanska
Armada; YU: sh: Jugoslovenska Armi-
ja; CH: d: Justizabteilung
JAA US: e: Judge Advocates Association
JAAC US: e: mil: Joint airlift allocations
committee
JAACS US: e: John A. Andrew Clinical
Society
JAAF J: e: mil: Japanese Army Air Force
J.A.A.L. US: e: Junior Auxiliary of the
American Legion
JAAOC CDN: GB: US: e: mil: joint anti
-aircraft operations centre (center)
JAARS US: e: Jungle Aviation and Ra-
dio Service
JAAS US: e: Jewish Academy of Arts
and Science
JAB D: d: Joh. A. Benckiser GmbH,
Chemische Fabrik, Ludwigshafen
[gegr 1823] ; e: Joint Africa Board;
US: e: mil: Joint Amphibious Board;
e: Joint Audit Board; US: e: Juvenile
Aid Bureau, New York
JaboStff BRD: d: mil: Jagdbomberstaffel
JAC B: f: Jeunesse Agricole Catholique;
F: f: Jeunesse Agricole Chrétienne;
Jeunesse Anarchiste Communiste
J.A.C. e: Joint Advisory Committee
JAC US: e: mil: Joint Aircraft Committee
J.A.C. e: Juvenile Advisory Council
JACC NATO: e: Joint Area Collection
Centre; US: e: Joint Automatic Con-
trol Conference
JACCI US: e: Joint Allocation Commit-
tee Civil Intelligence
JACE US: e: mil: Joint Alternate Com-
mand Element
J.A.C.F. B: f: Jeunesse Agricole Catho-
lique Féminine; F: f: Jeunesse Agri-

cole Chrétienne Féminine
JACKPOT US: e: mil: Joint Airborne
Communications Center - Command
Post
JACL US: e: Japanese American Citi-
zens League
JACMAS AUS: e: Joint Approach Cen-
tral Meteorological Advisory Service
JAD U: s: Junta Americana de Defensa
de la Democracia
JADE J: e: mil: Japanese air defense
environment
JADF J: e: mil: Japan Air Defense Force
JAE B: nl: Jonge Antwerpse Esperan-
tisten
JÄ d: Jugendämter
Jäg.R.; Jäg.Rgt. D: d: mil: Jäger-Regimen
JAERI J: e: Japan Atomic Energy Re-
search Institute
JAF S: sv: Järnhandlarnas arbetsgivar-
förening; e: mil: Jordanian Air Force
J.A.F. GB: e: mil: Judge-Advocate of
the Fleet
JAFC J: e: Japanese Atomic Fuel Cor-
poration, Tokai-Mura
JÁFI H: hu: Jármüfejlesztési Intézet,
Budapest
JAFP US: e: Jewish Agency for Pales-
tine, New York [gegr 1897]
J.A.F.R.C. e: Joint Anti-Fascists Refu-
gee Committee
Jafü D: d: mil: Jagdführer
JAG e: mil: Judge Advocate General;
BRD: d: Jungingenieur-Arbeitsgemein-
schaft [VDE]
JAGC US: e: mil: Judge Advocate Gen-
eral's Corps
JAGD US: e: mil: Judge Advocate Gen-
eral's Department (Division)
Jageri D: d: mil: WK1: Jagdgeschwader
Richthofen
JAGN US: e: mil: Judge Advocate Gen-
eral of the Navy
JAGO US: e: mil: Judge Advocate Gen-
eral's Office

JAIEG US: e: Joint Atomic Information Exchange Group

JAIF J: e: Japan Atomic Industrial Forum, Inc.

J.A.K. DK: da: Jord, Arbejde, Kapitalrørelse [d: Partei]

JAK YU: Jugoslovenski Akademski Klub

JAL J: e: Japan Air Lines Co. Ltd., Tokyo [BRD: 6 Ffm, Kaiserstr. 79] ; BRD: d: "Journalfranz" Arnulf Liebing oHG, 87 Würzburg 2

JALB NATO: e: Joint Administration and Logistics Board

JALPG US: e: Joint Automatic Language Processing Group [ALPAC]

JAMA US: e: mil: Japan Air Materiel Area

JAMAG US: e: mil: Joint American Military Advisory Group

JAMCO J: US: e: Japan Aircraft Maintenance Company Ltd.[Boeing]

JAMMAT US: e: Joint American Military Mission for Aid to Turkey

JAMU CS: cs: Janákova Akademie Musických Umění

JANAF Panel US: e: mil: Joint Army-Navy-Air Force Panel

JANAIC US: e: mil: Joint Army-Navy-Air Force Intentions-of-the-Enemy Council [Korea]

JANAIR US: e: mil: Joint Army-Navy Instrumentation Research

JANBMC US: e: mil: Joint Army-Navy Ballistic Missile Committee

JANIC US: e: mil: Joint Army-Navy Information Center

J.A.N.M.B. US: e: mil: Joint Army-Navy Munition Board

JANTB e: mil: Joint Army-Navy Technical Board

JANWSA US: e: mil:Joint Army-Navy War Shipping Administration

J.A.P. B: f: Jeunes Alliances Paysannes de Belgique; US: e: Jewish Agency for Palestine, New York [gegr 1897]

JAPA US: e: Jane Addams Peace Association

JAPC J: e: Japan Atomic Power Company; US: e: mil: Joint Air Photo Center

J.A.P.G.W.C. e: Jewish Association for the Protection of Girls, Women and Children

JAPIB GB: e: mil: Joint air photographic intelligence board

JAPIC GB: e: mil: Joint air photographic intelligence centre; e: mil: Joint air photo interpretation center

JAPIU e: mil: Joint air photo interpretation unit

JAPO US: e: Joint Area Petroleum Office

JAR F: f: Jeunes Auteurs Réunis, Paris [d: Buchverlag]

JARE E: s: Junta de Auxilio a los Republicanos Españoles

JARI J: e: Japanese Association of Railway Industries

JARIB GB: e: mil: Joint Air Reconnaissance Intelligence Board

JARIV GB: e: mil: Joint Air Reconnaissance Intelligence Centre

JARO NL: nl: Jeugd-Amateur-Radio-Omroep

J.A.S. JA: e: Jamaica Agricultural Society

JAS JA: e: Jamaica Air Service [d: Luftverkehrsgesellschaft] ; US: e: Jewish Agricultural Society; GB: e: mil: Joint Anti-Submarine School; DK: da: Jydsk Arkaeologisk Selskab

J.A.S.A. J: e: Japan Amateur Sports Association [gegr 1911]

JASCO US: e: WK2: Joint American Study Commission (Office of Alien Property); US: e: mil: Joint assault signal company

JASDF J: e: mil: Japan Air Self-Defense Force

JASRAC J: e: Japanese Society of Rights of Authors and Composers

J.A.S.T. JA: e: Jamaican Association of Sugar Technologists

Jasta D: d: mil: WK1: Jagdstaffel

JAT YU: Jugoslovenski Aero-Transport [Belgrad, gegr 1947]

JATCRU GB: e: mil: Joint Air Traffic Control Radar Unit

JATP US: e: Jazz at the Philharmonic [d: Musikantengruppe]

JAW d: Japanische Akademie der Wissenschaften; Jugendaufbauwerk

JAWPB US: e: mil: Joint Atomic Weapons Publication Board

JAYF GB: e: Jersey Association of Youth and Friendship

J.A.Z.U. YU: sh: Jugoslovenska akademija znanosti i umjetnosti, Zagreb

J.B. e: Joint Board

JB S: sv: AB Jordbrukarbanken [gegr 1923]; d: Jugendbeirat; D: d: NS: Jugendbetriebszelle [der HJ]; d: Jugendbücherei; D: d: NS: Jungbann [HJ]; D: d: Jungbanner [Verband]; Jungdeutscher Bund; Jungreformatorische Bewegung

JBA US: e: Junior Bluejackets of America

JBC US: e: Joint Blood Council; D: d: Jüdischer Box-Club, Berlin

JBCPS GB: e: Journeymen Bakers' and Confectioners' Pension Society

JBD DDR: d: mil: Jagdbombenfliegerdivision

J.B.F. GB: e: Journeymen Butchers' Federation of Great Britain

JBG S: sv: Svenska järn- och balkgrossisters förening; DDR: d: mil: Jagdbombenfliegergergeschwader

J.B.G. e: Jewish Board of Guardians; e: mil: Jewish Brigade Group

JBH H: hu: Járási Begyütési Hivatal; d: Jugendbundheim

JBI J: [d: japanische Vereinigung für die technische Kontrolle von Lagern]

JBL GB: e: Junior Bird League

JBM D: d: Jugendbund der Bischöflichen Methodistenkirche

JBMA US: e: John Burroughs Memorial Association [American Museum of Natural History]

J.B.S.A. GB: e: Jerusalem British School of Archæology

JB St Univ US: e: John B. Stetson University [Florida]

JBT US: e: Jewellers Board of Trade

JBTB NL: nl: Jongeren Boeren- en Tuindersbond

JBU DK: da: Jydsk Boldspil-Union

JB Univ US: e: John Brown University [Arkansas]

JBUSDC BR: US: e: mil: Joint Brazil-United States Defense Commission

JBUSMC BR: US: e: mil: Joint Brazil-United States Military Commission

JBV D: d: Jüdische Buchvereinigung, Berlin

JC d: Jacht-Club

jc S: sv: mil: jaktcentral

J.C. GB: e: Jesus College [Oxford or Cambridge]; e: Jew's College; d: f: Jocke-Club; e: Jockey Club

JC US: e: Judicial Council; D: d: Jung-Concordia (Deutscher Rad- und Motorfahrverband)

J.C. e: Juvenile Court; 1: Juventas Catholica; P: pt: Juventude Católica

JCA J: e: Japan Consumers' Association, Tokyo; US: e: Jewelry Crafts Association

J.C.A. e: Jewish Colonization Association

JCA US: e: Joint Commission on Accreditation of Universities; US: e: mil: Joint Communication Activity; Joint Communications Agency; NATO: e: Joint Construction Agency Europe

JCAC US: e: Joint Civil Affairs Committee

JCAE US: e: Joint Committee on Atomic Energy [=JCCAE]

JCAEC US: e: Joint Congressional Atomic Energy Committee [=JCCAE]

JCAESSL US: e: Joint Council of the Associated Engineering Societies of St. Louis

JCAFB US: e: mil: James Connally Air Force Base [Texas]

JCAH US: e: Joint Commission on the Accreditation of Hospitals

JCAM e: Joint Commission on Atomic Masses

JCAR e: Joint Commission on Applied Radioactivity

JCB e: Joint Communications Board; Joint Coordinating Board

JCBC US: e: Joint Committee on Building Codes

JCBL US: e: John Carter Brown Library

JCC GB: e: Joint Codification Policy Committee; US: e: mil: Joint Communication(s) Center; US: e: Joint Computer Committee

J.C.C. e: Joint Conciliation Committee

JCC e: Joint Coordination Center

JCCAE US: e: Joint Congressional Committee on Atomic Energy [=JCAE,JCAEC]

J.C.C.E.A. GB: e: Joint Committee of Customs and Excise Associations

JCCRG US: e: mil: Joint Command and Control Requirements Group

J.C.E. ET: e: Jockey Club of Egypt, Alexandria

JCEA PE: s: Junta de Control de Energía Atómica, Lima

JCEC US: e: mil: Joint Communications-Electronics Committee

JCEE US: e: Joint Council on Economic Education

JCEG US: e: mil: Joint Communications-Electronics Group

JCEI GB: e: Joint Council of Engineering Institutions

JCET US: e: Joint Council on Educational Television

JCGOB NL: nl: Jongelieden Christelijke Geheelonthoudersbond

JCGRO e: mil: Joint Central Graves Registration Office

J.-Ch.-A. D: d: Japan-Chemie-Ausschuß

JCHARS e: Joint Commission of High Altitude Research Stations

JCHP UN: e: Joint Committee on Health Policy [Children's Fund]

JCI INT: f: Jeune Chambre Internationale e: Junior Chamber International, Miami Beach, Fla. [gegr 1944]

J.C.I.C. ZA: e: Johannesburg Consolidated Investment Company

JCII J: [d: japanisches Institut für die technische Kontrolle von Fotoapparaten, Film- und Fernsehkameras]

JCIS NATO: e: Joint Counterintelligence Section

JCIWG US: e: mil: Joint Cutover Integrated Working Group [Army]

JCL US: e: Junior Classical League

JCLE US: e: Joint Committee on Library Education

JCLWC US: e: Joint Committee on Library Work As A Career [gegr 1947]

JČMF CS: cs: Jednota Ceskoslovenských Matematiků i Fysiků

JCMIH US: e: Joint Commission on Mental Illness and Health

J.C.M.J.C. GB: e: Joint Committee of Master and Journeyman Cloggers [Oldham]

JCMS US: e: Jackson Country Medical Society

JCOC US: e: Joint Civilian Orientation Conference; US: e: mil: Joint Combat Operations Center [Army-Air Force]

JC of C US: e: Junior Chamber of Commerce

JCP J: e: Japanese Communist Party; US: e: Joint Committee on Printing of the Congress of the United States, Washington 25, D.C.; US: e: mil: Joint Committee on Printing Guidance [USAF]

J.C.P.C. GB: e: Judicial Committee of the Privy Council

JCPCUS US: e: Joint Committee on Printing of the Congress of the United States, Washington 25, D.C.

JCQD US: e: mil: Jersey City Quartermaster Depot

J.C.R. F: f: Jeunesse communiste révolutionnaire [gegr April 1966]

JCR US: e: Joint Council for Repatriation

JCRA US: e: Jewish Committee for Relief Abroad

JCRNFE US: e: Joint Committee on Reduction of Nonessential Federal Expenditures

JCRR China: US: e: Joint Commission on Rural Reconstruction

JCS GB: e: Jersey Cattle Society of the United Kingdom; US: e: mil: Joint Chiefs of Staff; INT: e: Joint Commission for Spectroscopy [ICSU, IAU, IUPAP]

J.C.S. e: Justices' Clerks' Society

J.C.S.A. e: Joint Committee for Soviet Aid

JČSP CS: cs: Jednota Československých Právníků

JCSRE NATO: e: Joint Chiefs of Staff Representatives Europe

JCSRG US: e: mil: Joint Chiefs of Staff Requirements Group

JCSTR e: mil: Joint Commission on Solar and Terrestrial Relationships

JCSUCR e: Joint Commission on Standards, Units and Constants of Radioactivity

JC Univ US: e: John Carroll University [Ohio]

JCW D: d: Jacht-Club Wannsee, Berlin

JD DDR: d: mil: Jagdfliegerdivision

J.D. F: f: Jeunesse Démocratique; s: Junta Directiva; S: sv: justitiedepartementet

JD CH: d: Justizdepartement; Justizdirektion

JDA J: e: Japan Domestic Airlines; J: e: mil: Japanese Defence Agency

JDB J: e: Japan Development Bank, Tokyo; D: d: Jugendbund der Deutschen Baptistengemeinden

J.D.C. e: Joint Distribution Committee

J. de G. s: Junta de Gobierno

J.D.F. L: f: Jeunesse Démocratique Féminine; B: nl: Jong Davidsfonds

JDFAA J: e: Japanese Defense Facilities Administration Agency

JDG D: d: Jugendbund der Deutschen Gewerkvereine

J.d.G. s: J. de G.

JDJ D: d: Jungdeutsche Jugend

JDK NL: nl: Joodsch-Democratische Kiespartij

JDL US: e: Jewish Defense League [um 1969]; GB: e: Junior Drama League

JDP YU: Jugoslovensko Profesorsko Drustvo

J.D.P.A.S. e: Jewish Discharged Prisoners' Aid Society

JDPC US: e: mil: Joint Defense Production Committee

JDREMC GB: e: Joint Departmental Radio and Electronics Measurements Committee

JDS US: e: John Dewey Society; YU: sn Jugoslovenska Demokratska Stranka

JDU CS: cs: Jednota Duchovních a Učitelů Náboženství Církve Československ

JDŽ YU: Jugoslovenske Državne Željeznice [=JŽ, d: Staatsbahn]

J(E) GB: e: mil: Jamaica Engineer Corps

JE e: joint enterprise

J.E. F: f: Jury d'Expropriation

JEA J: e: Japan Export Association; US: e: Jesuit Educational Association; e: Jewish Education Association; BRD: US: Joint Engineering Agency, Augsburg

JCE P: pt: Junta de Exportação do Algodão, Lisboa

JEAC P: pt: Junta de Exportação do Algodão Colonial, Lisboa 1

J.E.B. e: Japan Evangelical Board

JEB US: e: Joint Economy/Emergency Board

JEC J: e: Japanese Electrotechnical Committee

J.E.C. B: f: Jeunesse Estudiantine Catholique; F: f: Jeunesse Etudiante Chrétienne

JEC CDN: GB: US: e: Joint Economic Committee

J.E.C. e: Joint Emergency Committee

JEC P: pt: Junta de Exportação do Café, Lisboa; Junta de Exportação dos Cereais, Nova Lisboa, Angola

JECA J: e: Japan Electrical Contractors' Association, Tokyo

JECC J: e: Japan Electronic Computer Corp., Tokyo [gegr 1961]; GB: e: Joint Egyptian Cotton Committee, Manchester 2

J.E.C.E.J.A. e: Joint Emergency Committee for European Jewish Affairs

J.E.C.F. B: f: Jeunesse Etudiante Catholique Féminine; F: f: Jeunesse Etudiante Chrétienne Féminine

JECI INT: f: Jeunesse Etudiante Catholique Internationale

JEDEC US: e: Joint Electronic Devices Engineering Council, Washington, D.C.

JEEP F: f: Jeunes Equipes d'Education Populaire; N: NL: e: Joint Establishment Experimental Pile, Kjeller [N, gegr 1951]

JEF INT: f: Jeunesses européennes fédéralistes d: Junge Europäische Föderalisten, Paris [gegr 1950]

J.E.F. e: mil: Jewish expeditionary force; Joint Expeditionary Force; YU: eo: Jugoslavia Esperanto-Federacio

JEG D: d: Jugendbund der Evangelischen Gemeinschaft

J.E.I. J: eo: Japana Esperanto-Instituto

JEIA US: e: Joint Electronics Information Agency; D: e: nach WK2: Joint Export-Import Agency, Höchst

JEIB D: e: nach WK2: Joint Export-Import Board

JEIDA J: [d: japanische Elektronikindustrie-Entwicklungsvereinigung]

JEK YU: sh: Jugoslovenska Elektrotehnička Komisija

JEL INT: f: Jeunesses européennes libérales, Bruxelles 5 [B, gegr 1952]

J.E.L. E: s: Junta Española de Liberación

J.E.M. e: Jerusalem and the East Mission

JEMC e: Joint Engineering Management Conference; US: e: mil: Junior Enlisted Men's Council

JEMIMA J: e: Japan Electric Measuring Instruments Manufacturers Association

JEN E: s: Junta de Energía Nuclear; P: pt: Junta de Energia Nuclear, Lisboa

JENCA RCA: f: Jeunesse Nationale Centrafricaine

JENER N: NL: e: Joint Establishment for Nuclear Energy Research, Kjeller [N, vgl: JEEP]

JEOCN NATO: e: Joint European Operations Communications Network

JEOL J: e: Japan Electron Optics Company, Ltd., Tokyo

JEPA P: pt: Junta de Exportação da Província de Angola, Luanda

JEPCE NATO: e: Joint Exercise Planning Committee [AFCENT]

JEPM P: pt: Junta de Exportação da Província de Moçambique, Lourenço Marques

JEPS NATO: e: Joint Exercise Planning Staff

JES J: e: Japan Electronic Show Association; Japanese Engineering (Export) Standard

Jes. GB: e: Jesus College, Cambridge

JESA J: e: Japanese Engineering Standards Association

JESC J: e: Japanese Engineering Standards Committee; GB: e: Joint Electronics Standardization Committee; GB: e: mil: Joint Equipment Standardization Committee

Jes.Coll. GB: e: Jesus College [Oxford or Cambridge]

Jes.-O. d: Jesuiten-Orden

JEST US: e: mil: Jungle Environmental Survival Training School [Navy]

JET J: e: Japan-Europa-Trade Co.,Ltd., Tokyo [BRD: 8 München 81] ; US: e: Junior Executives Training, New York

JETEC US: e: Joint Electron Tube Engineering Council

JETRO J: e: Japan Export and Trade Research Organization

JETS US: e: Junior Engineering Technical Society

JEUS D: d: nach WK2: Jugend der Europa-Union im Saarland

J.F. F: f: Jeunesse Française

JF US: e: Jordan Foundation; S: sv: Jordbrukets Forskningsråd; d: Jugendfürsorge

JFA D: d: Junkers Flugzeug- und Motorenwerke, Zweigwerk Aschersleben

JFAP US: e: mil: Joint Frequency Allocation Panel

JFEA J: e: Japan Federation of Employers Associations; D: e: nach WK2: Joint Foreign Exchange Agency [ab 21.1.1948 von JEIA übernommen]

JFES J: e: Japan Federation of Engineering Societies, Tokyo

J.F.F. F: f: Jeunesses Fédéralistes de France

JFF BRD: d: Arbeitszentrum Jugend, Film und Fernsehen eV, 8 München

JFH BRD: d: Jugend- und Familienhilfe Köln eV, 5 Köln-Vingst

J.F.L. L: f: Jeunesses Fédéralistes Luxembourgeoises

JFLU J: e: Japan Federation of Labour Unions

JFM INT: f: Jeunesses Fédéralistes Mondiales, Amsterdam [NL, gegr 1947] s: Juventud Federalista Mundial; BRD: d: Junkers Flugzeug- und Motorenwerke AG, 8 München 8

J.F. of L. J: e: Japan Federation of Labour

JFP US: e: mil: Joint Frequency Panel

JFRO GB: e: Joint Fire Research Organization, Boreham Wood, England; e: Joint Fisheries Research Organization of Northern Rhodesia and Nyassaland, Fort Rosebery

J.F.S. GB: e: Justice for Scotland

J.F.S.R. e: Jewish Fund for Soviet Russia

JFV BRD: d: Jugendfilmverleih, München

JG BRD: d: mil: Jagdgeschwader; DDR: d: mil: Jagd(flieger)geschwader; NL: nl: Jongeren Gemeenschap; B: nl: Jonggezinnenaktie; d: Jugendgericht

J.G.A. GB: e: Jute Goods Association

J.G.A.M. GB: e: Junior Gas Association of Manchester

JGF S: sv: Järnhandlareorganisationens garantiförening

JGIK S: sv: Järnvägsmännens Gymnastik- och Idrottsförening

J.G.O.B. NL: nl: Jongelingen Geheelonthoudersbond

J.G.S. F: f: Jeunes Gardes Socialistes; D: d: Junggermanische Schwesternschaft

J.G.T.C. e: Junior Girls' Training Corps

JGV d: Junggesellenverein

JHAT J: e: Japan Helicopter Air Transport Co.

JHEA RA: s: Junta de Historia Eclesiástica

J.H.F. S: sv: Järnvägsmännens helnykterhetsförbund [gegr 1901]

JHF DK: da: Jydsk Håndbold Forbund

J.H.H. US: e: John Hopkins Hospital

JHM NL: nl: Joodsch Historisch Museum

J.H.O. J: e: Japanese Hydrographic Office

J.H.O.G.B. GB: e: Jewish Health Organization of Great Britain

JHP BlnW: d: Jugendhilfsstelle beim Polizeipräsidium

JHS D: d: nach WK2: Jugendherbergswerk Saarland; US: e: Junior High

School

J.H.S.E. GB: e: Jewish Historical Society of England

JHU/APL US: e: John Hopkins University, Applied Physics Laboratory

JHW d: Jugendhilfswerk

JI S: sv: Journalistinstitutet

JIAS CDN: e: Jewish Immigrant Aid Society

JIB GB: e: mil: Joint Intelligence Bureau

J.I.C. B: f: Jeunesse Indépendante Catholique; F: f: Jeunesse indépendante chrétienne

JIC US: e: Jewelry Industry Council

J.I.C. GB: e: Joint Imperial Conference

JIC US: e: Joint Industrial Conference (Council); GB: e: Joint Industrial Council of Printing and Allied Trades, London W.C. 1; US: e: Joint Industry Committee (Conference); US: e: mil: Joint Intelligence Center; GB: e: Joint Intelligence Committee; Joint Iron Council, London SW 1

JICA US: e: mil: Joint Intelligence Collecting Agency

JICACBI US: e: mil: Joint Intelligence Collecting Agency, China, Burma, India

JICAME US: e: mil: Joint Intelligence Collecting Agency, Middle East

JICANA US: e: mil: Joint Intelligence Collecting Agency, North Africa

JICARC US: e: mil: Joint Intelligence Collecting Agency, Reception Committee

J.I.C.F. B: f: Jeunesse Indépendante Catholique Féminine; F: f: Jeunesse Indépendante Chrétienne Féminine

J.I.C.G.I. e: Joint Industrial Council for the Gas Industry

JICPOA US: e: mil: WK2: Joint Intelligence Center, Pacific Ocean Areas

JICST J: e: Japan Information Center of Science and Technology, Tokyo [gegr 1957]

JICTAR GB: e: Joint Industry Committee for Television Advertising Research

JIDA J: e: Japan Industrial Designers Association

JIDC JA: e: Jamaica Industrial Development Corporation

JI de D INT: s: mil: Junta Interamericana de Defesa, Washington, D.C.

JIE GB: e: Junior Institution of Engineers

JIFA J: e: Japanese Institute of Foreign Affairs

JIG US: e: mil: Joint Intelligence Group

J.I.H.I. e: John Innes Horticultural Institution

JIII J: [d: japanisches Institut für die technische Kontrolle von Teleskopen]

JILA US: e: Joint Institute for Laboratory Astrophysics [gegr 1962]

JIM J: e: Japan Institute of Metals

JIMA J: e: Japan Industrial Management Association

JIMSA J: [d: Studentenaustauschorganisation]

JINR SU: [e: Joint Institute for Nuclear Research, Moscow]

JIOA US: e: mil: Joint Intelligence Objectives Agency

J.I.O.E. GB: e: Junior Institution of Engineers

JIP F: f: Jeunesses Indépendantes et Paysannes de France et de l'Union Française

JIPO JOR: e: Jordan Investment Promotion Office

JIR E: s: Juventudes de Izquierda Republicana

JIRP US: e: Juneau Ice Field Research Project [Alaska]

JIS e: mil: Joint Intelligence Staff

JISC J: e: Japanese Industrial Standards Committee, Tokyo

JITC US: e: Jewelry Industry Tax Committee

JITF J: e: Japan International Trade Fair

JIU P: pt: Junta de Investigações do

Ultramar, Lisboa

J.I.W.C. e: Joint Industrial Whitley Council

J.J.C. d: Jiu-Jitsu-Club

JJF NL: nl: Joodsche Jeugdfederatie

JJJV BRD: d: Judo-Jiu-Jitsu-Vereinigung

J.J.K. d: Jiu-Jitsu-Klub

JJK NL: nl: Joodsche Jeugd Kring

JJP NL: nl: Jong-Java Padvinderij

JJWB D: d: Jungjüdischer Wanderbund

J&K IND: e: University of Jamu and Kashmir

J.K. sv: jockeyklubb

JK BRD: d: Juniorenkreis der deutschen Unternehmerschaft, 53 Bonn

JKB D: d: Jakob-Krause-Bund, Berlin

JKF CS: cs: Jednota Klasických Filologů

J.K.R. PTM: mal: Jabatan Kerja Raya, Kuala Lumpur

J.K.U. S: sv: Jönköpingskretsens kristliga ungdomsförbund

JL J: e: Japan Air Lines [=JAL]

J.L. B: f: Jeunesses Libérales

JLA J: e: Japanese Library Association; US: e: Jewish Librarians Association; YU: sn: Jugoslovanska Ljudska Armada (Armija)

J.L.B. e: Jewish Lads' Brigade

JLC e: mil: Japan Logistical Command; US: e: Jewish Labor Committee; e: mil: Joint Logistics Committee

J.L.E. INT: s: Juventudes Liberales Europeas [f= JEL]

JLFB US: e: mil: Joint Landing Force Board

J.L.N. F: f: Jeunes de la Libération Nationale

JLP JA: e: Jamaica Labour Party [gegr 1944]

JLPC US: e: mil: Joint Logistics Plans Committee

JLPG US: e: mil: Joint Logistics Planning Group

J.L.S. S: sv: Jönköpings läns slakteriförening

JLSC GB: e: mil: Joint Electronic Standardization Committee

JLSGI J: e: Japanese Local Self Government Institute

JM JA: e: Air Jamaica [d: Luftverkehrsgesellschaft] ; D: d: NS: Jungmädel [im BDM] ; d: Justizminister(ium)

JMA GB: e: Joinery Managers' Association

JMAC US: e: mil: Joint Munitions Allocation Committee

JMAU P: pt: Jardim e Museu Agrícola do Ultramar, Lisboa

J.M.C. F: f: Jeunesse Maritime Chrétienn

JMC e: Joint Maritime Commission; US: Joint Meteorological Committee

JMCA US: e: Judges, Marshals and Constables Association

JMCC GB: e: mil: Joint Manœuvre Control Command

JMCPS RC: Jen-min ch'u-pan-she [d: Volksverlag]

JMCY GB: e: Joseph Malins Crusade of Youth

JMD US: e: mil: Japan Medical Depot

JMDBJ = IMDBI

J.M.F. F: f: Jeunesses Musicales de France, Paris

JMF US: e: Jewish Music Forum; The Johnston Mutual Fund, Inc., New York N.Y. 10017

JMG S: sv: Järnmanufakturgrossisternas förening

JMGIU P: pt: Junta das Missões Geográficas e de Investigações do Ultramar, Lisboa

JMI J: [d: Institut für die technische Kontrolle von Industrieanlagen und Metalle

JMK S: sv: Juniorernas magiska klubb

JMMAT US: e: mil: Joint Military Mission for Aid to Turkey

JMNR RCB: f: Jeunesse du Mouvement Nationale Révolutionnaire

JMNS CS: cs: Jednota Mladých Národních Socialistů

JMP P: pt: Juventude Musical Portuguêsa

JMPTC US: e: mil: Joint Military Packaging Training Center

JMRP GB: e: Joint Meteorological Radio

Propagation Sub-Committee
JMS US: e: John Milton Society
JMSAC US: e: Joint Meteorological Satellite Advisory Committee
JMTB e: mil: Joint Military Transportation Board
JMTC US: e: mil: Joint Military Transportation Committee
JMU US: e: James Millikin University
JMUSDC MEX: US: e: mil: Joint Mexico -United States Defense Commission
JMVB e: Joint Merchant Vessels Board
JNA JOR: e: Jordanian News Agency; YU: sh: Jugoslovenska Narodna Armija
JNACC US: e: Joint Nuclear Accident Coordinating Center
JNB YU: sh: Jugoslovenska Narodna Banka; D: d: Jungnationaler Bund; Jungnordischer Bund
JNEMA US: e: Jefferson National Expansion Memorial Association
J.N.F. GB: e: Jewish National Fund
JNFC e: Joint National Frequency Committee
JNK MOR YU: sh: Jugoslovenska Nacionalna Komisijy za Medunarodnu Organizaciju Rada
JNO YU: sh: Jugoslovenski Narodni Odbor
JNOF YU: sh: Jedinstveni Narodnooslobodilački Front; Jugoslovenska Narodnooslobodilačka Fronta; YU: sn: Jugoslovenska Narodnoosvobodilna Fronta
JNPP P: pt: Junta Nacional do Produtos Pecuários
JNR J: e: Japanese National Railways
JNRC INT: e: Joint Nuclear Research Center [Euratom]
JNS S: sv: Järnvägstjänstemännens Nordiska Sammanslutning; Jordbrukareungdomens Nordiska Samorganisation; YU: sh: Jugoslovanska Nacionalna Stranka
JNV CS: cs: Jednotný Národní Výbor
JNW US: e: mil: Joint Committee on New Weapons and Equipment

J.O. F: f: Jeunesse Ouvrière; e: Jewish Orphanage
JO YU: sh: Jugoslovenski Odbor; D: d: Jungdeutscher Orden [= Jungdo]
JOAC E: s: Juventud Obrera de Acción Católica
JOBS US: e: Job Opportunities in the Business Sector [1968]
J.O.C. B: F: f: Jeunesse Ouvrière Chrétienne; INT: f: Jeunesse Ouvrière Chrétienne Internationale
JOC e: Joint Operations Committee; US: e: mil: Juniòr Officers Council; P: pt: Juventude Operária Católica; E: s: Juventud Obrera Católica
J.O.C.F. F: f: Jeunesse Ouvrière Catholique Française; B: f: Jeunesse Ouvrière Chrétienne Féminine
JOCF P: pt: Juventude Operária Católica Feminina
JOCV J: e: Japan Overseas Cooperation Volunteer Service
J.O.D. d: Jüdischer Ordnungsdienst
JÖK S: sv: Journalistöverenskommelsen
Jofa D: d: Johannisthaler Filmatelier, Berlin-Johannisthal
JOFAC s: Juventud Obrera Femininade Acción Católica
Joh. GB: e: St.John's College, Cambridge
Joh.-O. D: d: Johanniter-Orden
JOIDES US: e: Joint Oceanographic Institutions Deep Earth Sampling
JOIN US: e: Jobs or Income – Now [Chicago]
Joint US: = AJDC
JOINTCINCEASTLANT NATO: e: Commander-in-Chief Eastern Atlantic Area, Air Commander-in-Chief Eastern Atlantic Area
JOK NL: nl: Bond van Jonge Oud-Katholieken in Nederland
JOKSO NL: nl: Joodse Kerkgenootschappen en Sociale Organisaties voor Schadevergoedingsaangelegenheden in Nederland

JOKVP NL: nl: Jongerenorganisatie in de Katholieke Volkspartij

JONS E: s: Juntas de Ofensiva Nacional -Sindicalistas; Juventudes Ofensivas Nacional-Sindicalistas

JOPP CS: cs: Jednotná Organisace Podnikového Početnictví

JOS NATO: e: Joint Oil Staff

JOSCO US: e: Joint Overseas Shipping Control Office

JOT US: e: mil: Joint Observer Team [Korea]

JOTC US: e: mil: Jungle Operations Training Center

JoU S: sv: jordbruksutskottet

JOVD NL: nl: Jongerenorganisatie "Vrijheid en Democratie"

J.P. F: f: Jeunesses Patriotes

JP J: e: Jiji Press, Ltd., Tokyo; DDR: d: Junge Pioniere [in der FDJ]; D: d: Jungpioniere

J.P. GB: e: Justice of the peace

JPA GB: e: Joint Palestine Appeal

J.P.B. B: f: Jeunesse Populaire de Belgique

JPB e: Joint Planning Board; Joint Production Board; Joint Purchasing Board

JPC NL: nl: Jeugd-Propagandaclub; e: Joint Planning Committee; Joint Production Committee

J.P.C.A.C. e: Joint Production, Consultative and Advisory Committee

JPD CH: d: Eidgenössisches Justiz- und Polizeidepartement

JPF US: e: Jewish Peace Fellowship

JP FNRJ YU: sh: Javno Pravobranioštvo FNRJ

JPI J: e: Japan Petroleum Institute

J.P.I. s: Juzgado de primera instancia

JPIA J: e: Japan Plastic Industry Association

JPL US: e: Jet Propulsion Laboratory, Pasadena, Calif.

JPO NL: nl: Javaansche Padvinders Organisatie; US: e: Joint Petroleum Office; Joint Project Office

JPPA P: pt: Junta Provincial de Povoamento de Angola

JPPM P: pt: Junta Provincial de Povoamento de Moçambique

JPRS US: e: Joint Publications Research Service, Washington, D.C. [Office of Technical Services]

JPS US: e: Jewish Publication Society of America; GB: e: mil: Joint Planning Staff

JPSC US: e: Joint Production Survey Committee

JPN BRD: d: Junge Presse Niedersachsen

JPWC US: e: Joint Post-War Committee

JQD US: e: mil: Jeffersonville Quartermaster Depot

J.R. F: f: Jeune République; Jeunesses Rurales

JRATA US: e: mil: Joint Research and Test Activity [Vietnam]

JRB US: e: Joint Radio Board; e: mil: Joint Reconnaissance Board; YU: [d: Jugoslawische Flußschiffahrt, Belgrad]

J.R.C. F: f: Jeunesse révolutionnaire communiste; B: f: Jeunesse Rurale Catholique

JRC e: mil: Joint Reconnaissance Center; e: Junior Red Cross

JRCF B: f: Jeunesse Rurale Catholique Féminine

JRDA f: Jeunesse du Rassemblement Démocratique Africain

JRDACI CI: f: Jeunesse du Rassemblement Démocratique Africain de la Côte d'Ivoire

JRDB US: e: mil: Joint Research and Development Board

JRDS YU: sh: Jugoslovenska Republikanska Demokratska Stranka

JREA J: e: Japanese Railway Engineering Association

J.R.E.B. e: Jewish Religion Education Board

JRF S: sv: Jägarnas Riksförbund

J.R.F. F: f: Jeunesse Républicaine de

France
JRF US: e: Julius Rosenwald Fund;
Junior Road Fellowship
JRIF s: Juventud Republicana de Iz-
quierda Federal
JRK A: BRD: Jugend-Rot-Kreuz
JRL GB: e: John Rylands Library
J.R.P. F: f: Jeunesse Rurale Protestante
JRPB e: Joint Radio Propagation Bureau
JRPG US: e: mil: Joint Radar Planning
Group
JRS YU: sh: Jugoslovenska Radnička
Stranka
JRSA J: e: Japan Raw Silk Association
JRSO e: nach WK2: Jewish Restitution
Successor Organization [auch: IRSO]
JRT YU: sh: Jugoslovenska Radiotele-
vizija
JRZ YU: sh: Jugoslovenska Radikalna
Zajednica
JS S: sv: mil: Arméns jägarskola, Kiruna
[gegr 1945]
J.S. e: Japan Society for the Study of
Economic Policy; F: f: Jeunesses Sco-
laires; B: f: Jeunesses Socialistes;
e: Johnson Society; NL: nl: Jeugd-
organisatie "Jonge Strijd"
JS e: mil: Joint Staff; D: d: Junge Schar
[Verband] ; BRD: d: Jungsozialisten
[= Jusos]
JSA J: e: Japanese Standards Associa-
tion, Tokyo; US: e: Jesuit Seismolog-
ical Association
JSAG US: e: mil: Joint Service Advisory
Group
JSASWE GB: e: mil: Joint Services Anti
-Submarine Warfare Establishment
JSB NATO: e: Joint Signal Board; D: d:
Jung-Spartakus-Bund [1924...30]
JSC J: e: Japanese Science Council, Tokyo;
B: f: Jeunes Sociaux Chrétiens
J.S.C. e: Joint Standing Committee; Joint
Stock Company
JSC US: e: mil: Joint Strategic Committee;
Joint Support Command [STRATCOM]

J.S.C.C. GB: e: Joint Synod of the Con-
vocation of Canterbury
J.S.C.C.M.P. GB: e: Joint Services Com-
mittee of Conservative Members of
Parliament
JSCM J: e: Japanese Society for Contem-
porary Music
JSDA J: e: mil: Japanese Self-Defense
Agency
JSDF J: e: mil: Japanese Self-Defense
Forces
JSDIC NATO: e: Joint Services Detailed
Interrogation Center
JSDS YU: sn: Jugoslovanska Socialno
-Demokratska Stranka
J.S.E. B: f: Jeunesses Syndicales des
Employés
JSEE J: e: Japanese Society for Engi-
neering Education
JSF e: Japan Scholarship Foundation
JSG/TCCS US: e: mil: Joint Standardi-
zation Group for Tactical Communica-
tions and Control Systems
JSHS US: e: Junior Science and Humani-
ties Symposium, Washington, D.C.
[1964]
J.S.L. GB: e: Johnson Society of London
JSM D: d: Jugendsache der Mennoniten
[Verband]
JSMA US: e: Joint Sealer Manufacturers
Association
JSME J: e: Japan Society of Mechanical
Engineers, Tokyo
JSO US: e: mil: Joint Service Office
[DOD]
JSOC US: e: Joint Ship Operations Com-
mittee
JSOP US: e: mil: Joint Strategic Objec-
tives Plan
JSOTIA J: [d: japanische Gesellschaft
für die Qualitätskontrolle optischer
Geräte und Gläser]
JSP J: [d: japanische sozialistische Par-
tei]
JSPC US: e: mil: Joint Strategic Plans

Committee

JSPG US: e: mil: Joint Strategic Plans Group

JSPP e: Joint Council of Swaziland Political Parties

JSPS J: e: Japan Society for the Promotion of Science

JSRC US: e: Joint Ship Repair Committee

JSŠ CS: cs: Jedenáctiletá střední škola

JSS NL: nl: Jeugdbond voor Socialistische Studie; d: Jüdische Soziale Selbsthilfe [Polen]

JSSC GB: e: mil: Joint Services Staff College

j.s.s.c. e: mil: Joint services staff course

JSSC US: e: Joint Strategic Survey Committee (Council)

J.S.S.F. J: e: Japanese Society of Scientific Fisheries

JSSL e: mil: Joint Services School of Linguists

JST J: e: Japanese Society of Translators

JSTA J: e: Japan's Science and Technology Agency, Tokyo

JSTI JA: e: Jamaican Sugar Technologists' Institution

J.S.&T.I.C. GB: e: Joint Scientific and Technical Intelligence Committee

J.S.T.U. GB: e: mil: Joint Services Trials Unit

Jsty S: sv: Järnvägsstyrelsen

J.S.U. E: s: Junta Socialista Unida; Juventudes Socialistas Unificadas; Juventud Socialista Universitaria

JSUN E: s: Junta Suprema de Union Nacional [bis 1945]

JSV US: d: e: Jewish Socialist Verband of America

JSWPB US: e: mil: Joint Special Weapons Publication Board

J.T. F: f: Jeunes Travailleurs

JT BRD: d: Deutscher Juristen-Tag

JTA J: e: Japan Tourist Association; US: e: Jewish Telegraph Agency, New York; IL: e: Jewish Telegraphic Agency, Jerusalem

J.T.A. D: d: Jüdische Telegraphen-Agentur GmbH, Berlin-Halensee

JTAC US: e: Joint Technical Advisory Committee

J.T.B. e: Jute Trade Board

JTC e: Jewish Trust Corporation for Germany; US: e: mil: Joint Telecommunications Committee

J.T.C. GB: e: Junior Training Corps

JTF e: mil: Joint Task Force; S: sv: Jordbrukstekniska föreningen [gegr 1947]

JTG e: mil: Joint Task Group; CH: d: Jugend-Theatergemeinde, Zürich; d: Junge Theatergemeinde

JTI S: sv: Jordbrukstekniska institutet, Ultuna; DK: da: Jydsk Teknologisk Institut

JTIC J: e: Japan Trade Information Center

J.T.L.C. GB: e: Joint Technical Language Service, London E.C. 3

JTMA US: e: Joint Traffic Management Agency

JTML US: e: Junior Town Meeting League

JTS S: sv: Jordbrukstekniska föreningens standardiseringskommittén

JTSB NATO e: Joint Target Selection Board

J.T.S.C. D: d: Jüdischer Turn- und Sport-Club 1905, Berlin

JTUAC US: e: Joint Trade Union Advisory Committee

J.U. f: Jeunesse Universelle

JU S: sv: jordbruksutskottet [i riksdagen]; BRD: d: Junge Union [CDU-CSU]; Junge Unternehmer (JU) der Arbeitsgemeinschaft selbständiger Unternehmer eV, 53 Bonn-Bad Godesberg

Ju D: d: Reichsjustizministerium

JUB B: f: Jeunesse Ukrainiennes en Belgique

JUBRIA d: Jubiläums-Briefmarken-Ausstellung

J.U.C. B: f: Jeunesse Universitaire Catholique; F: f: Jeunesse Universitaire Chrétienne

JUC P: pt: Juventude Universitária Católica

JUCSPA GB: e: Joint University Council for Social and Public Administration

JUDCA INT: [d: lateinamerikanische christlich-demokratische Jugend]

JUDE D: e: nach WK2: Committee on Juvenile Delinquency

Jud.Sch. D: d: Judenschule

J.U.F. S: sv: Jordbrukare-Ungdomens Förbund [gegr 1918]

JUFAC E: s: Juventud Universitaria Feminina de Acción Católica

Jufi; Jufiz YU: sh: Jugoslovenska Filatelistička Izložba

JugA d: Jugendamt

JugÄ d: Jugendämter

JugGer. d: Jugendgericht

JugHbge. d: Jugendherberge

JugK d: Jugendkammer

JUGOKOMORA BRD: YU: d: JUGOKOMORA – Jugoslawische Bundeswirtschaftskammer, Vertretung für die BRD, 8 München 2

JUH BRD: d: Johanniter-Unfallhilfe

JUKO d: Deutsch-Schweizerische Jugendkonferenz

JUMAC E: s: Juventud Universitaria Masculina de Acción Católica

JUN S: sv: Jordbrukets upplysningsnämnd

Jungdo D: d: Jungdeutscher Orden

Jung-KKV BRD:.d: Bund der Katholischen Deutschen Kaufmannsjugend

Jungsta D: d: Jungstahlhelm [Verband]

Junk. D: d: Junkers-Flugzeugwerke AG, Dessau (Anhalt)

JUPA pt: Junta da União das Populações de Angola

JUPOSTA BRD: d: Jubiläums-Postwertzeichen-Ausstellung

JUR s: Juventudes de Unión Republicana

Juradat BlnW: d: Juradat GmbH [juri-

stisches Daten- und Forschungszentrum]

Jure C: s: Junta Revolucionaria Cubana

Jurema YU: [d: internationales Symposion über Meßtechnik und Automation in Zagreb]

Jurimü D: d: Jugendring München [um 1920]

Juristinnenbund BRD: d: Juristinnenbund (Vereinigung der Juristinnen, Volkswirtinnen und Betriebswirtinnen) eV, 8 München 22

JUS US: e: Department of Justice

JUSE J: e: Japan Union of Scientists and Engineers

JUSMAG US: e: mil: Joint United States Military Advisory Group; Joint United States Military Aid Group to Greece

JUSMAGG US: e: mil: Joint United States Military Aid Group to Greece

JUSMAP US: e: mil: Joint United States Military Advisory and Planning Group

JUSMAT US: e: mil: Joint United States Military Assistance, Turkey

JUSMG US: e: mil: Joint United States Military Group

Jusos BRD: d: Jungsozialisten [SPD]

JUSPAD SU: YU: [d: jugoslawisch-sowjetische Gesellschaft für Donauschifffahrt]

JUSPAO US: e: Joint United States Public Affairs Office [Vietnam]

JUSSC US: e: mil: Joint United States Strategic Committee

JUSTA SU: YU: Jugoslovenska Sovjet Transport Aviacija, Beograd

Just A. A: d: Staatsamt für Justiz

JustMin; Just.Min. d: Justizminister-(ium)

Just.Sl. CS: cs: Justiční Služba

JUT JA: e: Jamaica Union of Teachers

Juvento TG: f: Mouvement de la Jeunesse Togolaise

JUWTFA US:.e: mil: Joint Unconvential Warfare Task Force, Atlantic

JV NL: nl: Jeugd Vereeniging; Jonge-

lingsverbond; Jongelingsvereeniging
J.V.A. e: Jordan Valley Authority
JVA BRD: d: Justizvollzugsanstalt
JVCC INT: e: Joint Vocabulary Coordination Committee, Geneva [IEC]
JVF NL: nl: Jongeren\Vredes Federatie
JVG NL: nl: Jonge Vrouwen Gilde
JVKA NL: nl: Jeugdverbond voor Katholieke Actie
J.V.L.L. B: nl: Jeugdverbond van de Lage Landen
JVO NL: nl: Jeugdbond voor Onthouding
J.W. D: d: mil: Jugendwehr; d: Jugendwohlfahrt
JWA d: Jugendwohlfahrtsausschuß
JWB US: e: Jewish Welfare Board
J.W.B. e: Joint Wages Board
JWBCA US: e: mil: United States European Command Joint Whole Blood Central Agency
JWCII J: [d: japanisches Institut für die technische Kontrolle von Uhren]
JWD NL: nl: Jeugd-Werklozen-Dienst
JWG e: Joint Working Group
JWGCG US: e: mil: Joint War Games Control Group
JWPC US: e: mil: Joint War Plans Committee
JWPS US: e: mil: Joint War Production Staff [WK2]
J.W.R.V. e: Jewish War Relief Volunteers
JWV US: e: mil: Jewish War Veterans of the United States of America; D: d: Jungwandervogel [Verband]
J.W.V.U.S. US: e: mil: = JWV
JŽ YU: Jugoslovenske Železnice
JZ D: d: Jungdeutsche Zunft
JZS YU: Jugoslovenskt zavod za Standardizaciju, Beograd
J.Z.S. YU: Jugoslavenski Zimskosportski Savez, Ljubljana

K GB: e: mil: King's Regiment [Liverpool]

K. d: Kommissariat; Kommission

K N: no: Kommunistparti; S: sv: Kommunistiska Partiet; D: d: mil: Marinekonstruktionsamt [OKM]; d: Konsulat; d: mil: Korps

K1 BlnW: d: Berliner Ur-Kommune

K '63 BRD: d: Kunststoff-Messe 1963 in Düsseldorf

K.A. S: sv: Kammararkivet

Ka D: d: mil: Kanzlei [Reichskriegsministerium]

KA D: d: Konsularagentie

K.A. D: d: mil: Kraftfahrabteilung; d: Kreisausschuß; D: d: mil: Kriegsakademie; Kriegsamt; S: sv: mil: Krigsarkivet

KA. d: Kriminalabteilung; Kunstakademie

KA S: sv: mil: kustartilleriet

KAA BRD: d: Kosmobiologische Akademie Aalen

KAB NL: nl: Katholieke Arbeidersbeweging; BRD: d: Katholische Arbeiter-Bewegung Westdeutschlands, 5 Köln [seit 1968:] Katholische Arbeitnehmer-Bewegung (KAB) Westdeutschlands; H: hu: Kinevezési és Alkalmazási Bizottság, Budapest; BRD: d: Kommunistischer Arbeiterbund; S: sv: Sveriges Kooperative och Allmännyttiga Bostadsföretag

kabelmetal BRD: d: kabelmetal Kabel- und Metallwerke Gutehoffnungshütte AG, 3 Hannover

KAbnA BRD: d: Bundesbahn-Kohlenabnahmeamt

K.A.C. D: d: Kaiserlicher Automobil-Club

KAC e: Kuwait Airways Corporation

K.A.C.B. B: nl: Koninklijke Automobielclub van België

KACF e: Korean-American Cultural Foundation

KACO BRD: d: Kupfer-Asbest-Co. Gustav Bach, 71 Heilbronn

KAD DDR: d: Kartoffelkäfer-Abwehrdienst

[Kartoffelkäferbekämpfung mit chemischen Pflanzenschutzmitteln]; BRD: d: Komitee Automation der Dokumentation, 6 Ffm [DGD]; DK: da: Kvindelig Arbejderforbund

Ka-de-Ko D: d: Kabarett der Komiker, Berlin

Kadenach D: d: mil: Kameradschaft der Nachrichtentruppe [Waffenring]

Kadeo D: d: Kaufhaus des Ostens GmbH, Berlin

Kadewe; KaDeWe BlnW: d: Kaufhaus des Westens

KADS AFGH: e: Kabul Amateur Dramatic Society

KADU EAK: e: Kenya African Democratic Union [gegr 1960]

KAE GB: e: Keighley Association of Engineers

KÄV BRD: d: Kassenärztliche Vereinigung

KÄVd D: d: Kassenärzteverband

KäVg D: d: Kassenärztliche Vereinigung

K.A.F. S: sv: Kommunalarbetarförbundet; Kreditaffärernas förening

KAF DK: da: Kristelig Akademisk Forening; e: mil: Kuwait Air Force; S: sv: Kvinnliga akademikers förening

Kaff R GB: e: mil: Kaffrarian Rifles

KAFI S: sv: mil: Arméförvaltningens intendenturavdelning

KAFT S: sv: mil: Arméförvaltningens tygavdelning

Kafunka D: d: mil: WK1: Kavallerie-Funkerabteilung

KAG DDR: d: Künstlerische Arbeitsgruppe

KAGIB NL: nl: Katholiek Genootschap voor Internationale Betrekkingen

Kagohl D: d: mil: WK1: Kampfgeschwader der Obersten Heeresleitung

KAH BRD: d: Kraftanlagen AG, 69 Heidelberg

KAI US: e: Korean Affairs Institute

K.A.I. D: d: mil: Inspektion der Küsten-

artillerie und des Minenwesens
KAIF S: sv: mil: Arméintendenturförvaltningen
KAinsp S: sv: mil: Kustartilleriinspektionen, Stockholm
KAJ nl: Katholieke Arbeidersjeugd; d: Katholische Arbeiterjugend; nl: Kristene Arbeidersjeugd
KA.JA.B. CH: d: Katholische Jungarbeiterinnenbewegung
KAJÖ A: d: Katholische Arbeiterjugend Österreichs
K.A.K. DK: da: Københavns Asfaltkompagni; S: sv: kommunistisk arbetarkommun; D: d: mil: Kriegsakademie [auch: K.Ak.] ; S: sv: Kungliga Automobilklubben
KAL BRD: d: Katastrophenabwehrleitung; Südkorea: e: Korean Air Lines
K.A.L.A. D: d: mil: Küstenartillerie-Lehrabteilung
KALP EAK: e: Kenya African Liberal Party
KaMeWa S: sv: AB Karlstads Mekaniska Werkstad
KAMI RI: [e: anti-Communist student union for college students]
Kampnagel BRD: d: Kampnagel AG (vorm. Nagel & Kämp), 2 Hamburg
KAMS S: sv: Kungliga Arbetsmarknadsstyrelsen
K-Amt D: d: mil: NS: Hauptamt Kriegsschiffbau
Kam.Ver. d: mil: Kameradschaftliche Vereinigung
KAN CS: [d: Club der engagierten Parteilosen, liberal] ; S: sv:Kristna Affärsmän och Näringsidkare, Stockholm [gegr 1938]
K.A.N.T. D: d: mil: WK2: Kommandeur Armee-Nachschubtruppen
KANTAFU EAK: e: Kenya African National Traders and Farmers Union
KANU EAK: e: Kenya African National Union [gegr 1960]
KAP PL: pl: Katolicka Agencja Prasowa

[d: Nachrichtenagentur, Warschau] ; D: d: Kommunistische Arbeiterpartei [1920...22]
K.A.P.D. D: d: [entspricht: KAP]
KAPL US: e: Knolls Atomic Power Laboratory, Schenectady
KAPMO GB: e: Kent Apple and Pear Ma‌keting Organization
KAPN NL: nl: Kommunistische Arbeiderspartij Nederland
KAPP EAK: e: Kenya African People's Party
KAPPI RI: [e: anti-Communist student union for high schools]
KAR GB: e: mil: The King's African Rifles [gegr 1904]
KAR-AIR O/Y SF: [d: Luftverkehrsgesellschaft]
KARNA NL: nl: Kweekbedrijf voor Aardappelrassen der Nederlandse Aard‌appelmeelindustrie
KAROF S: sv: mil: Kustartilleriets Reser‌officersförbund
Karol.Inst. S: sv: Karolinska mediko-kirurgiska institutet, Stockholm
Karp.K. D: d: mil: WK1: Karpathenkorp
KartG d: Kartellgericht
KARV D: d: Kartell Akademischer Ruder-Vereine
KARWEI NL: [d: Fachmesse für Do-it -yourself-Artikel, Utrecht 1969]
Ka.S. D: d: Kameradschaft Siemens
KAS BRD: d: mil: Katholische Arbeitsgemeinschaft für Soldatenbetreuung eV GB: e: Kent Archaeological Society; US: e: Kentucky Academy of Science
K.A.S. D: d: Klub alpiner Skiläufer
KAS DK: da: Københavns Amatør-Sejlklub; US: e: Kroeber Anthropological Society
K.A.S. D: d: mil: Küstenartillerieschule
KAS S: sv: mil: Kustartilleriets skjutskola, Stockholm
Kasch D: d: mil: WK1: Kampfeinsitzerschule

KASI RI: [d: Einheitsfront von Akademikern]

KASKA B: nl: Koninklijke Academie voor Schoone Kunsten, Antwerpen

KASKI NL: nl: Katholiek Sociaal-Kerkelijk Instituut

KASL US: e: Kansas Association of School Librarians (Libraries)

Kaspe A: d: Kredit-, Spar- und Einkaufsverband rGmbH, Wien 1

Kass G CH: d: Kassationsgericht

Kass H A: CH: d: Kassationshof

K.A.St. D: d: mil: WK1: Kriegsamtsstelle

Kasta. D: d: mil: Kampfstaffel

KASU EAK: e: Kenya African Study Union

KAT BRD: d: Kommission für arbeitswissenschaftliche Terminologie [Gesellschaft für Arbeitswissenschaft eV]

KatA; Kat.-A. d: Katasteramt

KATAG BRD: d: KATAG AG, Textileinkaufsverband, 48 Bielefeld

KATAK CY: [d: türkische Minderheitspartei]

Katcom GB: e: mil: Korean attached troops, Commonwealth [um 1953]

KATF S: sv: mil: Kungliga Armétygförvaltningen

Kathpress A: d: Katholische Pressezentrale, Wien 1

KATUSA US: e: mil: Korean Augmentation to the U.S. Army [1950]

Kat.V. D: d: Katasterverwaltung

Kat.V.A. D: d: Katastralvermessungsamt

KAU EAK: e: Kenya Africa Union [gegr 1944]; DK: da: Københavns Atlet-Union

Kau.M.St. D: d: WK1: Kautschuk-Meldestelle der Kriegsrohstoffabteilung

K.A.u.S. D: d: mil: Kraftfahr-Ausbildungs- und Sammelstelle

KAussch. D: d: mil: WK1: Kriegsausschuß

K.A.V. B: nl: Katholieke Arbeidersvrouwengilde

KAV BRD: d: Katholischer Akademikerverband, 53 Bonn; BRD: d: Kommunale Arbeitgeberverbände; CS: cs: Krajský Akční Výbor; B: nl: Kristelijke Arbeidersvrouwengilden

KAVA DDR: d: Kabelwerk Vacha

Kav.Div. d: mil: Kavallerie-Division

Kavferna D: d: mil: WK1: Kavallerie-Fernsprechabteilung

KAVG BRD: d: Katholische Arbeitsgemeinschaft für Volksgesundung

KavKS S: sv: mil: Kavalleriets kadettskola, Skövde

KAVNF CS: cs: Krajský Akční Výbor Národní Fronty

Kav.Rgt. d: mil: Kavallerieregiment

Kav.Sch. d: mil: Kavallerieschule

Kav.Sch.D. A: H: d: Kavallerieschützendivision

KAVW NL: nl: Koninklijke Nederlandsche Academie van Wetenschappen

KAW CH: d: Kommission für Atomwissenschaft des Schweizerischen Nationalfonds

KAWAG BRD: d: Kraftwerk Altwürttemberg AG, 714 Ludwigsburg

KAWC EAK: e: Kenya African Workers Congress

KAWU EAK: e: Kenya African Workers Union

KB D: d: Kekulé - Bibliothek, Leverkusen

K.B. GB: e: King's Bench; D: d: Klappholttaler Bund [Jugendverband]

K.-B. D: d: Knappschaftsberufsgenossenschaft, Bochum

K.B. d: Königliche Bibliothek

KB H: hu: Központi Bizottság; DDR: d: Konzessionsbetrieb; d: Kreisbibliothek; D: d: Kronacher Bund der alten Wandervögel; DDR: d: Deutscher Kulturbund [seit 1958 = DKB, gegr 1945 als: Kulturbund zur demokratischen Erneuerung Deutschlands]; Kultureller Beirat für das Verlagswesen [bis 1951]; S: sv: Kungliga Biblioteket, Stockholm; NL: nl: Kweekschool Batavia; D: d: mil: Kyffhäuserbund

KBA BRD: d: Kraftfahrt-Bundesamt, 239 Flensburg

KBAB B: nl: Koninklijke Belgische Atletiekbond

KBAC B: nl: Koninklijke Belgische Automobielclub

KBB D: d: Künstlerbund Bayern

K.B.B.F. B: nl: Koninklijke Belgische Brandweerfederatie

KBBr D: d: Künstlerbund Bremen

KBC BRD: d: Katholisches Besinnungszentrum für Filmschaffende [gegr 1960]

K.B.C. GB: e: King's Bench Court

K.B.D. GB: e: King's Bench Division

KBD. D: d: mil: WK2: Kriegsbetreuungsdienst

KBdBB D: d: Künstlerbund der Bildhauer Bayerns

K.B.D.C. GB: e: King's Bench Divisional Court

KBE BRD: d: Köln-Bonner Eisenbahnen AG, 5 Köln

KbE BRD: d: Krankenkasse bayerischer Erzieher

KBG BRD: d: Kapital-Beteiligungs-Gesellschaft mbH, 6 Ffm [gegr 1969]

KBHagen A: d: Künstlerbund Hagen, Wien

KBK DK: da: Københavns Badminton Klub

K.B.K. S: sv: Kvinnoföreningarnas beredskapskommitté [WK1]

K.B.K.I. RI: [d: demokratische Arbeiterorganisation] ; B: nl: Koninklijk Belgisch Koloniaal Instituut

KBKTSF B: nl: Koninklijke Belgische Katholieke Turn- en Sportfederatie

KBL DDR: d: Kreisbetrieb für Landtechnik

KBL. D: d: mil: WK2: Kriegsbetriebsstofflager

KBM D: d: Künstlerbund Mannheim

K.B.M.J. B: nl: Katholieke Burgers- en Middenstandsjeugd

KBNs D: d: Künstlerbund Niedersachsen, Osnabrück

KBO D: d: Künstlerbund Ostthüringen

K.B.O. S: sv: Kvinnoföreningarnas beredskapsorganisation

KBS d: Kaufmännische Berufsschule;

J: Kokusai Bunka Shinkokai [d: Gesellschaft für internationale kulturelle Verbindungen, gegr 1934]; DK: da: Komiteen for Byggestandardisering; DDR: d: Konstruktionsbüro für Schwemaschinenbau, Magdeburg; US: e: mil Korea Base Section; Südkorea: e: Korean Bureau of Standards, Seoul; S: sv: Kristianstad-Blekinge Slakteriförening; Kungliga Byggnadsstyrelsen Stockholm

KBSch D: d: Künstlerbund Schlesien

K.B.S.I. RI: Kongres Buruh Seluruh Indonesia [d: Arbeitergewerkschaft]

KBSt D: d: Künstlerbund Stettin

KBU DK: da: Københavns Boldspil Unio

KBV BRD: d: Kassenärztliche Bundesvereinigung; d: Kirchenbauverein

KBVB N: nl: Koninklijke Belgische Voet balbond

KBVE B: nl: Koninklijke Belgische Vereniging der Electrotechnici

KBW PL: pl: Korpus Bezpieczeństwa Wewnętrznego

KBWB B: nl: Koninklijke Belgische Wielrijdersbond

KBWP BRD: d: Kernkraftwerk- Baden -Württemberg-Planungsgesellschaft

K.B.Y.C. D: d: Königlich Bayerischer Yacht-Club

KbzdED DDR: d: vgl: KB

K.-C.; KC d: Kajak-Club

K.C. US: e: Kansas Central Railways; D: d: stud: Kartell-Konvent der Verbindungen Deutscher Studenten jüdischen Glaubens; d: Kanu-Club; e: Kennel Club

KC EAK: e: Kenya Coalition

K.C. GB: e: King's College [Cambridge or London] ; US: e: Knights of Colum bus [gegr 1882] ; D: d: stud: Kösener Congreß

KC H: hu: Központi Čimjegyzék, Budapest; PL: pl: Komitet Centralny; BlnW: d: Kurfürstendamm-Center

K.C.A. e: Kikuyu Central Association [gegr 1922]
KCAC US: e: mil: Korean Civil Assistance Command
K Can H CDN: e: mil: King's Canadian Hussars
K.C.C. GB: e: King's College, Cambridge
KCC e: Korean Chamber of Commerce
KCCA e: Korean Chamber of Commerce in America
KCDC EAK: e: Kenya Citizens Democratic Congress
K.C.F. F: f: Kayak-Club de France
K.C.H. GB: e: King's College Hospital, London
KC KPP PL: pl: Komitet Centralny Komunistycznej Partii Polski
KC KPZR PL: pl: Komitet Centralny Komunistycznej Partii Związku Radzieckiego
K.C.L. GB: e: King's College, London
KCNA Nordkorea: e: Korean Central News Agency [d: Nachrichtenagentur]
K.C.N.S. CDN: e: King's College, Nova Scotia
KC PPR PL: pl: Komitet Centralny Polskiej Partii Robotniczej
KC PZPR PL: pl: Komitet Centralny Polskiej Zjednoczonej Partii Robotniczej
KCS US: e: Kansas City Southern Railway Company
K.C.S. GB: e: King's College School
KČSN CS: cs: Královská Česka Společnost Nauk
KCSP PL: pl: Kontrola Cywilna Statków Powietrznych
K.C.S.Ry. US: e: Kansas City Southern Railway Company
K.C.T. US: e: Kansas City Terminal Railway Company
K.Č.T. CS: cs: Klub Československých Turistů
KCT China: Kung-chan-tang [d: kommunistische Partei]

K.C.V.G.G. NL: nl: Katholieke Centrale Vereniging voor Geestelijke Gezondheid
KD S: sv: Kämpande demokratie
K.D. d: mil: Kavallerie-Division
KD PL: pl: Komitet Dzielnicowy; Rußland: [d: Konstitionelle Demokraten, gegr 1905, = Kadetten] ; CH: d: Kreisdirektion
KDA BRD: d: Kampagne für Demokratie und Abrüstung; Katholische Deutsche Akademikerschaft, 5 Köln-Deutz; CS: cs: Klub Demokratických Akademíí
K.d.A. D: d: Kommission des Abgeordnetenhauses [Berlin]
KDA DK: da: Kongelig Dansk Aeroklub
KDAI D: d: Kampfbund deutscher Architekten und Ingenieure
K.D.A.K. DK: da: Kongelig Dansk Automobil Klub, København
KDAP NL: nl: Katholiek-Democratische Arbeiderspartij
KDB D: d: stud: Katholische Deutsche Burschenschaft
K.D.B. NL: nl: Katholiek-Democratische Bond; H: hu: Közületi Döntőbizottság, Budapest
KDB DDR: d: kommunaler Dienstleistungsbetrieb
KDD J: [d: internationale Telefon- und Telegrafengesellschaft]
KdD CS: d: Kreditanstalt der Deutschen
KDE BRD: d: Katholische Deutsche Elternschaft
K.d.F. d: Kammer der Forsten
KdF D: d: NS: Kanzlei des Führers
K.D.F. S: sv: Katarina diskussionsförening [gegr 1890] ; D: d: Katholischer Deutscher Frauenbund
K.d.F.; KdF D: d: NS: NS-Gemeinschaft "Kraft durch Freude"
KDFB BRD: d: Katholischer Deutscher Frauenbund
KDFC Südkorea: e: Korean Development Finance Corporation, Seoul
KDFK DK: da: Københavns Dame Fægte-

klub

KDG GB: e: mil: 1st King's Dragoon Guards

KdgH DDR: d: Kasse der gegenseitigen Hilfe

KDHM CS: cs: Katedra Dialektického a Historického Materialismu

K.d.I. d: Kammer des Innern

KDI NL: nl: Stichting Kwaliteitsdienst voor de Industrie, Rotterdam

KDK H: hu: Közgazdaságtudományi Dokumentációs Központ, Budapest

KDL CGO: f: Société des Chemins de Fer Katanga - Dilolo - Léopoldville

KdoAS BRD: d: mil: Kommando der Amphibischen Streitkräfte

Kdo.d.Flg.F. D: d: mil: WK1: Kommando der Fliegerflotte

Kdo.d.GS.-Sch. BRD: d: Kommando der Grenzschutzschulen [BGS]

KdoDpOrg BRD: d: mil: Kommando Depotorganisation

KdoFlb BRD: d: mil: Kommando Flottenbasis

KdoFlotte BRD: d: mil: Kommando der Flotte

KdoFrwAnBw BRD: d: mil: Kommando der Freiwilligenannahme der Bundeswehr

Kdo.G. D: d: mil: WK2: Kommando der Geleitboote

Kdo GS-Schulen BRD: d: Kommando der Grenzschutzschulen [BGS]

Kdo. L. d: mil: Kommando der Landungsboote

Kdo.L.Sch. D: d: mil: Kommando der Luftschifferschule

KdoM BRD: d: mil: Kommando der Minensuchboote

KdoMAusb BRD: d: mil: Kommando der Marineausbildung

KdoMFlg BRD: d: mil: Kommando der Marineflieger

KdoMFü BRD: d: mil: Kommando des Marineführungsdienstes

KdoMFüSys BRD: d: mil: Kommando Marineführungssysteme

KdoMS BRD: d: mil: Kommando der Minenstreitkräfte

KdoMSan BRD: d: mil: Kommando des Marinesanitätsdienstes

KdoMWa BRD: d: mil: Kommando der Marinewaffen

KdoS BRD: d: mil: Kommando der Schnellboote

Kdoschub. D: d: mil: WK2: Kommando der Schiffe und Boote der Luftwaffe

KdoST BRD: d: mil: Kommando der Schiffstechnik

KdoTroS BRD: d: mil: Kommando der Troßschiffe

KdoTrVsuM BRD: d: mil: Kommando für Truppenversuche der Marine

KdoTV BRD: d: mil: Kommando der Territorialen Verteidigung

Kdo.U. d: mil: Kommando der Unterseeboote

KdoZ BRD: d: mil: Kommando der Zerstörer

KDP NL: nl: Katholiek-Democratische Partij; D: d: Kolonialbund Deutscher Pfadfinder

Kdr.d.Kg. D: d: mil: WK2: Kommandeur der Kriegsgefangenen

Kdr.N. D: d: mil: WK2: Kommandeur der Nachrichtentruppen

Kdr.Pi. D: d: mil: WK2: Kommandeur der Pioniere

KdrSFltl BRD: d: mil: Kommandeur der Schnellbootflottille

KdrUFltl BRD: d: mil: Kommandeur der Ubootflottille

KdrZFltl BRD: d: mil: Kommandeur der Zerstörerflottille

KDS IND: e: Khuzistan Development Service

KDSE BRD: d: stud: Katholische Deutsche Studenteneinigung, 53 Bonn

KdSLw BRD: d: mil: Kommando der Schulen der Luftwaffe

KDSP CS: cs: Kabinet Déjin Státu a Práva

K.D.St.V. D: d: stud: Katholische Deutsche Studentenverbindung

K.D.S.V. BRD: d: Katholische deutsche Schwestern-Vereinigung für Gesundheits- und Wohlfahrtsdienste eV, 5 Köln

KdT DDR: d: Kammer der Technik [gegr 1946]

K.D.T.B. GB: e: Keg and Drum Trade Board

KdtHQ BRD: d: mil: Kommandant Hauptquartier

Kdt.H.Qu. D: d: mil: Kommandant des Hauptquartiers

KdtStQ BRD: d: mil: Kommandant Stabsquartier

Kdt.St.Qu. D: d: mil: Kommandant des Stabsquartiers

KDV BRD: d: Kassendentistische Vereinigung; D: d: Katholischer Deutscher Verband; H: hu:Közlekedési Dokumentációs Vállalat, Budapest; N: no: Kvinnens Demokratiske Verdensforbund; S: sv: Kvinnornas Demokratiska Världsfederation

KDVS DK: da: Kongelige Danske Videnskabernes Selskab

K.d.W.; KdW D: d: Kaufhaus des Westens GmbH, Berlin W 50

KDY DK: da: Kongelig Dansk Yachtklub

KE CS: cs: Katedra Elektroenergetiky

K.E.A. CDN: eo: Kanada Esperanto-Asocio

KEA US: e: Kentucky Education Association

Kea D: d: mil: WK1: Kraftfahr-Ersatzabteilung

KEA. D: d: WK1: Kriegsernährungsamt

K.E.A. C: eo: Kuba Esperanto-Asocio

KEB H: hu: Központi Ellenőrző Bizottság, Budapest

KEBR BRD: d: Kommission für elektronische Bauelemente für Raumfluggeräte

KECO Südkorea: e: Korea Electric Company, Seoul

KEF CS: cs: Kabinet pro Etnografii i Folkloristiku

KEG BRD: d: Katholische Erziehergemeinschaft; D: d: Kaufmännisches Ehrengericht

KEGS GB: e: King Edward VI Grammar School

K.E.H. GB: e: mil: King Edward's Horse [regiment]

K.E.H.L. GB: e: King Edward's Hospital, London

KEI H: hu: Kenőolay Ellenőrző Intézet, Budapest

KEIA Südkorea: e: Korea Electronics Industries Association

Kek. D: d: mil: WK1: Kampfeinsitzerkommando

KEK CY: [d: Arbeiterpartei] ; H: hu: Marx Károly Közgazdasági Egyetem Központi Könyvtára, Budapest

KEL S: sv: Katrineholms Enskilda Läroverk

K.E.L. eo: Kroatia Esperanto-Ligo

KELAG A: d: Kärntner Elektrizitätswerke AG

K.E.L.I. INT: eo: Kristina Esperantista Ligo Internacia [gegr 1911]

KeLiFa S: sv: Kemisk-tekniska och livsmedelsfabrikanters förening, Stockholm [1932...60]

K.E.M. CY: [d: progriechische Anschlußfront, gegr 1959]

KEMA NL: nl: N.V. tot Keuring van Electrotechnische Materialen, Arnhem; BRD: d: Köln-Ehrenfelder Maschinenbau-Anstalt GmbH, 5 Köln

KEMC US: e: mil: Kaiserslautern Equipment Maintenance Center [BRD]

KEMI H: hu: Kereskedelmi Minőségellenőrző Intézet, Budapest

Kem-Tek DK: [d: internationale Messe für chemisch-technische Apparate, Kopenhagen, erstmals 16...22 Aug 1968]

KEOG GB: e: mil: King Edward VII Own Gurkhas

KEOKH H: hu: Külföldieket Ellenőrző Országos Központi Hatóság, Budapest

KEPE GR: [d: Zentrale für Planung und

Wirtschaftsforschung, Athen]

KERM PL: pl: Komitet Ekonomiczny Rady Ministrów [gegr 1945]

KERMI H: hu: Kereskedelmi Minőségellenőrző Intézet, Budapest [= KMI]

K.E.S. US: e: Kansas Engineering Society; eo: Kvakera Esperantista Societo

KES NL: nl: Kwaliteitsbureau voor te Exporteren Schapen

KESC PAK: e: Karachi Electric Supply Corporation

KEST BRD: d: Studiengesellschaft zur Förderung der Kernenergieverwertung in Schiffbau und Schiffahrt eV (Kernenergie-Studiengesellschaft - KEST), 2 Hamburg

KESTAG A: d: Kärntnerische Eisen-und Stahlwerks-Aktiengesellschaft, Wien 4

KET DK: da: Københavns Elektro-Teknikum

KETEA [f: association pour la liberté de l'Afrique, Lesotho]

KEV BRD: d: Katholische Elternvereinigung; D: d: Koks-Einkaufs-Vereinigung, Berlin-Charlottenburg; S: sv: Kolbäcks Elektriska Verkstad AB

K.E.V. D: d: Kommunaler Elektrizitätswerke-Verband Westfalen-Rheinland GmbH, Hagen i.W.; nl: Kongres van het Europese Volk

KEVAG BRD: d: Koblenzer Elektrizitätswerk und Verkehrs-AG, 54 Koblenz

KEZU CH: d: Kehricht- und Schlammverbrennungsanlage Zürcher Unterland, Bülach

KF CS: cs: Kabinet Filosofie; US: e: Kellog Foundation; Kent Foundation; H: hu: Képzőmüvészeti Főiakola, Budapest

K.F. GB: e: King's Fund

KF DK: da: Konservative Folkeparti; S: sv: Kooperativa förbundet; US: e: Kosciuszko Foundation, New York; Kossuth Foundation, New York; Kresge Foundation; N: no: Kristelig folkeparti

KfA DDR: d: Kammer für Außenhandel [gegr 1952]; BRD: d: Kampagne für Abrüstung – Ostermarsch der Atomwaffengegner

K.F.A. B: nl: Katholieke Filmaktie

KFA EAK: Kenya Farmers' Association; BRD: d: Kernforschungsanlage des Landes Nordrhein-Westfalen eV, 517 Jülich; Zentralinstitut für wissenschaftliches Apparatewesen, 51 Aachen; Kreis-Fußball-Ausschuß

K.F.A. D: d: WK1: Kriegsfeuerwerkerei für Artillerie

K.F.B. H: hu: Könyv- és Folyóiratkiadó Bizottsága, Budapest; Községi Földigénylő Bizottság, Budapest

KFB. d: Kreisfeststellungsbehörde

KfBSt BRD: d: Post: Kraftfahrbetriebsstelle

K.F.D. D: d: mil: WK2: Kraftfahrdepot

KfDK D: d: Kampfbund für Deutsche Kultur [später: NS-Kulturgemeinde]

Kfe BRD: d: Bahn: Kraftfahrzeugeinsatzstelle

K.F.F. S: sv: Kooperative föreståndarnas förbund; Kungliga Flygvörvaltningen

KfF N: no: Kunngjøring fra Fyrdirektøren

KFG BRD: d: Bayerische Krankenfürsorge der Gemeinden

K.F.G. D: d: mil: WK2: Küstenfliegergruppe

KfH; **KfHS** d: Kammer für Handelssachen

KFI S: sv: Kungliga Farmaceutiska Institutet

KFIH DDR: d: Komitee zur Förderung des internationalen Handels

KfJ DDR: d: Kreisausschuß für Jugendweihe

KFK BRD: d: Kernforschungszentrum Karlsruhe; Bayerische Krankenfürsorgekasse

KfK BRD: d: Kuratorium für Kulturbauwesen

KFK DK: da: mil: Kvindeligt Flyvekorps

[gegr 1953]

K.F.K. S: sv: Kyrkliga Frivilligkåren, Uppsala

KFKC H: hu: Külföldo Folyóiratok Központi Cimjegyzéke, Budapest

KFKF S: sv: Kommittén för kristen fostran

KfkF BRD: d: Kongreß für kulturelle Freiheit

KFKI H: hu: Központi Fizikai Kutató Intézet, Budapest

KFL B: nl: Katholieke Filmliga; EAK: e: Kenya Federation of Labor

Kfl S: sv: mil: Kustflottan

KFM d: Kaiser-Friedrich-Museum; CH: d: Kommission für militärische Flugzeugbeschaffung

KfmG d: Kaufmannsgericht

KFN PL: pl: Komitet Frontu Narodowego

KFO S: sv: Kooperationens förhandlingsorganisation

KFP EAK: e: Kenya Freedom Party; PL: pl: Komisja Funduszu Posmiertnego

KfR BRD: d: Kommission für Raumfahrttechnik [gegr 1961]

KFS D: d: Verband für Kakao-, Farben-, Seifen- und verwandte Maschinen, Berlin-Lichterfelde W

KfS DDR: d: Koordinierungsstelle für Standardisierung

KFS DDR: d: Kreisfilmstelle; S: sv: mil: Krigsflygskolan, Ljungbyhed; d: Küstenfunkstelle; S: sv: Kungliga Fysiografiska Sällskapet, Lund

Kfst BRD: d: Bahn: Kraftfahrstelle

KFSt d: Küstenfunkstelle

KFUK S: sv: Kristliga föreningen av unga kvinnor; N: no: Kristelig Forening av Unge Kvinner

KFUM N: no: Kristelig Forening av Unge Menn; DK: da: Kristelig Forening for Unge Mænd; S: sv: Kristliga föreningen av unge män

KFuSt d: Küstenfunkstelle

K.F.V. d: Katholischer Fürsorgeverein

KfV A: BRD: d: Kuratorium für Verkehrssicherheit

KFW BRD: d: Katholisches Film-Werk

KfW BRD: d: Kreditanstalt für Wiederaufbau, 6 Ffm; D: d: nach WK2: Kuratorium für Wirtschaftlichkeit [= RKW]

KFZ BRD: d: Kernforschungszentrum, 75 Karlsruhe; Deutsches Krebsforschungszentrum, 69 Heidelberg

KFZK BRD: d: Kernforschungszentrum, 75 Karlsruhe

KfzZulSt BRD: d: mil: Kraftfahrzeugzulassungsstelle

KG CS: cs: Kabinet pro Geomorfologii; d: Kammergericht; D: d: Kampfgemeinschaft für rote Sporteinheit [1930 ...33]; D: d: mil: Kampfgeschwader; Kampfgruppe; DDR: d: Kampfgruppe(n) der Arbeiterklasse; CH: d: Kantonsgericht; d: Karnevalsgesellschaft; CH: d: Kassationsgericht; d: Kaufmannsgericht; DK: da: Københavns Gymnastikforening; PL: pl: Komenda Główna

k.g. PL: pl: komisja gospodarcza

KG PL: pl: Komitet Główny (Gminny); d: Kommanditgesellschaft; Kommissionsgesellschaft; DDR: d: Konsumgenossenschaft; A: d: Kreisgericht; d: Kreisgeschäftsstelle

K.G. D: d: mil: Kreuzergeschwader

KG D: d: mil: Kriegsgericht

K.G. D: d: WK1: Kriegsgetreidegesellschaft m.b.H.

KGaA d: Kommanditgesellschaft auf Aktien

KGB SU: [d: Komitee für Staatssicherheit]

KGC A: d: Kärntner Golf-Club Dellach; BRD: d: Krefelder Golf-Club

KGD DDR: d: Konzert- und Gastspieldirektion Berlin

KGer; K.Ger. d: Kammergericht

K.gew.M. D: d: Kampfbund des gewerblichen Mittelstandes

KGF BRD: d: Kampfgemeinschaft gegen

den Faschismus, Bremen; Kölnische
Gummifäden-Fabrik vormals Ferd.
Kohlstadt & Co., 5 Köln-Deutz; S: sv:
Kristlig gymnasistförening

K.G.F.F. GB: e: King George's Fields
Foundation

K.G.F.S. GB: e: King George's Fund for
Sailors, London

KGG BRD: d: Kreditgarantiegemeinschaft;
Kreditgemeinschaft für das Handwerk

KGG. D: d: WK1: Kriegsgetreidegesellschaft m.b.H.

KGH d: Gerichtshof zur Entscheidung der
Kompetenzkonflikte

K.G.I.L. D: d: mil: WK2: Kraftfahrgerät
-Inspektion der Luftwaffe

K.G.J.T. GB: e: King George's Jubilee
Trust

KGL CH: d: Kunstgesellschaft Luzern

KGM DK: da: mil: Kattegat Marinedistrikt

K.G.M. H: hu: Kohó- és Gépipari Minisz-
ter(ium), Budapest

K.G.N.M.F. GB: e: King George's National Memorial Fund

KGO GB: e: mil: King George's Own
Regiment

K.G.O.B. NL: nl: Kwekelingen Geheel-
ontjoudersbond

K.G.O.H.L. D: d: mil: WK1: Kampfgeschwader der Obersten Heeresleitung

KGPAN PL: pl: Komitet Geograficzny
Polskiej Akademii Nauk

KGps S: sv: Kungliga Generalpoststyrelsen

K.G.R.I.M.S. GB: e: mil: King George's
Royal Indian Military Schools

KGS US: e: Kansas Geological Society;
BRD: d: Kieler Gelehrtenschule

K.-G.-Sch. d: Kunstgewerbeschule

KG-Schule d: Krankengymnastikschule

Kg-Seminar d: Kindergärtnerinnenseminar

KGSt BRD: d: Kommunale Gemeinschafts-
stelle für Verwaltungsvereinfachung

K.G.T. S: sv: Klubben Gamla Tyranner

KGT; K.G.T.S. S: sv: Kungliga General-

tullstyrelsen

KgU BlnW: d: Kampfgruppe gegen Un-
menschlichkeit [gegr 1948]

KGV NL: nl: Katholieke Gezellen Vereeniging; D: d: Katholischer Gesellen-
verein; Katzbachgebirgsverein; DDR
d: Konsumgenossenschaftsverband

Kgw. d: Kunstgewerbeschule

KgwZA D: d: Kunstgewerblerzunft Arch

K.H. d: Kassationshof; GB: e: mil: King
Hussars

KH d: Kirchliche Hochschule; DK: da:
Københavns Håndboldklub (Hockey-
klub); H: hu: Közellátási Hivatal, Budapest; D: d: Kunstgenossenschaft
Hannover

KHB DK: da: Københavns Handelsbank
[gegr 1873]

KHD BRD: d: Katastrophenhilfsdienst;
Klöckner-Humboldt-Deutz AG, 5 Köln
D: d: WK2: Kriegshilfsdienst

KHD-CAB BRD: d: Klöckner-Humboldt
-Deutz Chemie-Anlagenbau GmbH,
5 Köln-Neu-Ehrenfeld

KHF NL: nl: Kinder Herstellings Fonds

KHG CS: cs: Kabinet pro Historickou
Geografii; BlnW: d: Katholische Hoch
schulgemeinde

KhGU SU: [e: Gorkii Kharkov State
University]

K.H.L. NL: [d: Königlich Holländischer
Lloyd, früher: Zuid-Amerika Lijn]

KHLS S: sv: Kungliga Högre Lärarinne-
seminariet

Khm SF: fi: Kansanhuottoministerio

KHM S: [d: Königliches Handelsministe-
rium]

K.H.N. D: d: mil: Kadettenhaus Naum-
burg

KHN PL: pl: Komitet Historii Nauki

KHÖ A: d: stud: Katholische Hochschul-
jugend Österreichs

KHS CS: sk: Knižnica Hudobného Semi-
nára; S: sv: mil: Krigshögskolan, Stock
holm

K.H.S. S: sv: mil: Föreningen Krigshög-
skolan
KHUDOFA NL: nl: e: Kinderherstellings-
uitzending door Old Fellows, Amsterdam
KHVZ CS: cs: Komise pro Hnutí Vyná-
lezců a Zlepšovatelů
K.H.W. D: d: WK2: Kriegshilfswerk
K.I. S: sv: Karolinska mediko-kirurgiska
institutet, Stockholm
KI YU: sn: Kmetijski Inšpektorat; S: sv:
Köpmannainstitutet, Stockholm; INT:
d: Kommunistische Internationale
[1919...43] ; S: sv: Konjunkturinstitutet,
Stockholm; CS: cs:Krajský Inspektorát
KIACS GB: e: mil: Kenya independent
armoured car squadron
Kiag D: d: Kali-Industrie AG, Berlin
KIAG BRD: d: Kohlensäure-Industrie AG,
4 Düsseldorf
KIAZ YU: [d: Ingenieur- und Architekten-
verein, Agram]
KIB S: sv: Karolinska Institutets Bibliotek;
H: hu: Közigazgatási Biróság (Bizottság);
D: d: nach WK2: Kohlenindustriebeirat
[DKBL] ; DDR: d: Konstruktions- und
Ingenieurbüro; BRD: d: Arbeitskreis der
beim Gesamtverband kunststoffverarbei-
tende Industrie registrierten selbständi-
gen Kunststoff-Ingenieure und -Berater,
6 Ffm
KIBA A: d: Wiener Stadthalle - KIBA
Betriebs- und Veranstaltungsgesellschaft
mbH, Wien [KIBA = Kinobetriebsanstalt]
K.I.C. GB: e: Kellog International Corpo-
ration, London
KIC EAK: e: Kenya Indian Congress
Kicks BlnW: d: Internationale Jugend-
messe [2...11 Mai 1969]
KIE H: hu: Keresztény Ifjak Egyesülets
KIF DK: da: København Idrætsforening;
S: sv: Kontrollingeniörernas förening
Kifa S: sv: Kirurgiska Instrument Fabriks AB
Kig/Sodaab BRD: d: Käufer-Interessen
-Gemeinschaft/Selbsthilfe-Organisation
der Arbeiter, Angestellten und Beamten,

3 Hannover
KiHo d: Kirchliche Hochschule
K.I.K. S: sv: Konstnärernas Interesse-
kontor
KIKA D: d: Konföderation der Ingeni-
eur-Konsulenten und Architekten
KILOC NL: nl: Kweekschool, Instituut
vor Lichamelijke Opvoeding Club
K.I.M. EAK: e: Kenya Independence
Movement [gegr 1959] ; d: mil: Kö-
niglich Italienische Marine
KIM DDR: d: Kombinat industrielle Mast;
NL: nl: mil: Koninklijk Instituut voor
de Marine, Den Helder [gegr 1816]
KIMSz H: hu: Kommunista Ifjumunkások
Magyarországi Szövetsége, Budapest
KIN NL: nl: Stichting "Kat in Nood!";
B: nl: Koninklijk Belgisch Instituut
voor Natuurwetenschappen
KIN; KiN; Kin DIN: d: Normenaus-
schuß der Deutschen Kinotechnischen
Gesellschaft, Berlin
KINABU NL: nl: Centrale Commissie
voor Uitzending van Nederlandsche
Kinderen naar Buiten
KINGS GB: e: mil: The King's Regiment
(Liverpool)
KINGS OWN GB: e: mil: The King's
Own Royal Regiment (Lancaster)
KIO EAK: e: Kenya Information Office;
NL: nl: Kunst-Industrieel Onderwijs
KIPA INT: d: Katholische Internationale
Presseagentur, Fribourg [CH, gegr 1917]
Kipho D: d: Kino-und Photo-Ausstellung
[Berlin 1925]
Kip.M. H: hu: Könnyüipari Miniszter-
(ium), Budapest
KIREM BRD: d: KIREM – Kernstrah-
lungs-, Impuls- und Reaktor-Meßtech-
nik GmbH, 6 Ffm 1
KIS CS: cs: Komise pro Industrialisaci
Slovenska; CS: sk: Komisia pre Indu-
strializáciu Slovenska; S: sv: Riksföre-
ningen Konsten i sporten [gegr 1943] ;
CS: cs: Kontrolná Inspekční Skupina;

Kulturní Informační Služba; NL: nl: Kweekschool voor Inlandsche Schepelingen

KISAM DK: da: Kunsttørrings-Industriens Sammenslutning

K.I.S.E.H. GB: e: Kent Incorporated Society for Experiments in Horticulture

KISIF INT: d: Katholisches Internationales Soziologisches Institut für Flüchtlingsfragen

KISz H: hu: Magyar Kommunista Ifjusági Szövetség, Budapest [gegr 1957]

KISzOK H: hu: Kommunista Ifjusági Szövetság Országos Központja, Budapest

KIT NL: nl: Koninklijk Instituut voor de Tropen, Amsterdam; BRD: d: Kuratorium für Isotopentechnik

K.I.U.M.D. nl: Katholieke Internationale Unie voor Maatschappelijk Dienstbetoon

KIVI NL: nl: Koninklijk Instituut van Ingenieurs

KiW PL: pl: Książka i Wiedza [d: Verlag Buch und Wissen]

KIWA NL: nl: Keuringsinstituut voor Waterleidingsartikelen, Rijswijk

KIWI BRD: d: Verlag Kiepenheuer & Witsch, Köln

KJ CS: cs: Katedra Jazyků; D: d: Kreuzfahrer-Jugendschaft [Verband]

KJA BRD: d: Kreisjugendamt; Kreisjugendausschuß [Sport]

KJB NL: nl: De Katholieke Jeugdbeweging; D: d: Kyffhäuser-Jugendbund

KJD D: d: Katholische Jugend Deutschlands; Kommunistische Jugend Deutschlands [1920...25]

KJG BRD: d: Katholische Jungmännergemeinschaft

KJI INT: d: Kommunistische Jugend-Internationale [1919...43]

KJM BRD: d: Katholische Junge Mannschaft

KJMV NL: nl: Bond van Katholieke Jonge Middenstands-Vereenigingen

KJO B: nl: Katholieke Jeugdorganisatie

van België

KJÖ; KJOe A: d: Katholische Jugend Österreichs

KJR A: H: d: mil: Kaiserjägerregiment; NL: nl: Katholieke Jeugdraad voor Nederland

KJS DDR: d: Kinder- und Jugendsportschule

KJSÖ A: d: Katholische Jungschar Österreichs

K.J.V. D: d: stud: Kartell jüdischer Verbindungen

KJV NL: nl: Katholieke Jongemeisjes Vereeniging

KJV; KJVD D: d: Kommunistischer Jugendverband Deutschlands

KJWMD D: d: Katholischer Jugendbund werktätiger Mädchen Deutschlands

KK CS: cs: Kabinet pro Kartografii

K.-K. d: Kajakklub

KK CS: cs: Katedra Knihovnictví

K.K. d: mil: Kavalleriekorps

KK d: Kirchenkanzlei

K.K. H: hu: Közellátási Kormánybiztos, Budapest; PL: pl: Komitet Kuracjuszy D: d: Korporation der Kaufmannschaf D: d: mil: Korpskommando; Kraftwa genkolonne; CS: cs:Krajská Konferen- ce; d: Krankenkasse

KK d: Krankenkasse; Kreiskasse; Kulturkammer

KKB D: d: Karlsruher Künstlerbund; BRD: d: Kundenkreditbank KGaA, 4 Düsseldorf

KKBw BRD: d: mil: Kleiderkasse der Bundeswehr

KKC DK: da: Københavns Kajak Club

KKE GR: [d: kommunistische Partei]

KKF BRD: d: Verband Katholischer Kaufmännischer Berufstätiger Frauen; DDR: d: Deutsches Komitee der Kämp fer für den Frieden [gegr 1949]; PL: pl: Komitet Kultury Fizycznej; S: sv: Kvinnliga kontoristföreningen

K.Kf.K. D: d: Kaiserliches Kraftfahrkorp

KKG DK: da: Københavns Kvindelige Gymnastikforening; BRD: d: Kölnische Karnevalsgesellschaft von 1945; Kunden-Kredit-Genossenschaft des bayerischen Einzelhandels eGmbH, München

KKGH d: Gerichtshof zur Entscheidung der Kompetenzkonflikte

KKH BRD: d: Kaufmännische Krankenkasse Halle, 3 Hannover [gegr 1890] ; S: sv: Kungliga Konsthögskolan; DDR: d: Kreiskulturhaus

K.K.H.G.W. A: d: Kaiserlich-Königliche Heraldische Gesellschaft Adler, Wien

KKI CS: sk: Krajský Kultúrny Inspektorat; H: hu: Kulturkapcsolatok Intézete, Budapest

KKK DDR: d: Kreiskontrollkommission; BRD: d: AG Kühnle, Kopp & Kausch, Frankenthal; US: e: Ku Klux Klan

KKKomm. D: d: Krankenkassenkommission

K.Kl. d: Kanuklub

KKL BRD: d: Jüdischer Nationalfonds Keren Kajemeth Leisrael eV, Berlin -Halensee; DK: da: Københavns Kommunelærerindeforening; N: no: Kommunale Kinematografers Landsforbund

KKM EAK: [e: association of peoples]

K.K.M. H: hu: Kereskedelem- és Közlekedésügyi Miniszter(ium), Budapest; Külkereskedelmi Miniszter(ium), Budapest

KKN BRD: d: Kernkraftwerk Niederaichach GmbH

KKO SF: fi: Korkein Oikeus

K.Kr. BRD: d: Königsteiner Kreis, Vereinigung der Juristen, Volkswirte und Beamten aus der Sowjetischen Besatzungszone

KKS BRD: d: Kernkraftwerk Stadersand; PL: pl: Komisja Kontroli Stronnictwa

K.K.S. eo: Konstanta Kongresa Sekretario

K.K.St.B. A: H: d: Kaiserlich Königliche Staatsbahn

KKU CS: sk: Knižnica Komenského University

K.K.U.V. D: d: Königsberger Künstlerunterstützungsverein

KKV d: Katholischer Kaufmännischer Verein; BRD: d: KKV — Verband der Katholiken in Wirtschaft und Verwaltung eV, 43 Essen; D: d: Kraftkolbenpumpen-Verband, Berlin

KKVI YU: sh: Komisija za Kulturne Veze sa Inostranstvom

KKW BRD: d: Kernkraftwerk Würgassen

KKZVV CS: cs: Krajská Komise pro Zemědělskou Výrobu a Výkup

KL GB: e: mil: King's Liverpool Regiment; d: Kirchenleitung; H: hu: Központi Láboratórium; NL: nl: mil: Koninklijke Landmacht; d: Konsumladen; D: d: NS: Konzentrationslager [= KZ]

KLA Libyen: e: Kingdom of Libya Airways, Bengasi

K.L.A. D: d: mil: Kriegsschiffbau-Lehrabteilung

KLA S: sv: Kungliga Lantbruksakademien

K.L.A.U. D: d: mil: Kriegsschiffbau-Lehrabteilung U-Boote

KLB DDR: d: Kreislichtspielbetrieb

K.L.D.A.N. d: Kaiserlich Leopoldinische Deutsche Akademie der Naturforscher

KLEG CS: sk: Kancelár Legii

KLES NL: nl: Katholieke Limburgse Emigratie Stichting

KLFB CS: cs: Knihovna Lékařské Fakulty, Brno

KLFK CS: sk: Knižnica Lekárskej Fakulty, Košice

KLFOI CS: cs: Knihovna Lékařské Fakulty v Olomouci

KLFP CS: cs: Knihovna Lékařské Fakulty, Praha

KLFPl CS: cs: Knihovna Lékařské Fakulty, Plzeň

K.L.G. GB: e: Kenelm Lee Guinness [spark plugs]

Klgart BlnW: d: Kleingartenamt

KLH S: sv: Kungliga Lantbrukshögskolan

KlHk D: d: Kleinhandelskammer

KLI GB: e: mil: The King's Light In-

fantry (Shropshire Regiment)
KLJ A: d: Katholische Landjugend Österreichs
KLJB BRD: d: Katholische Landjugendbewegung Deutschlands, 4293 Dingden
Klk BRD: d: Bahn: Kleiderkasse [= KlkB]
KLK. D: d: WK1: Kriegslastenkommission
KLK S: sv: Kvinnliga läkares klubb
KlkB BRD: d: Bahn: Kleiderkasse der Deutschen Bundesbahn
Kll BRD: d: Bahn: Kleiderlager
K.L.M. nl: Klub Lange Mensen
KLM BRD: d: Klub der langen Menschen; NL: nl: Koninklijke Luchtvaart Maatschappij, Schiphol [gegr 1919]
KLMA S: sv: Kungliga Lantmäteristyrelsens Arkiv, Stockholm
KLO YU: sn: Krajevni Ljudski Odbor
KLP PL: pl: Krajova Loteria Pieniężna
KLR DDR: d: Kreis-Landwirtschaftsrat; D: d: Kreislehrrat
KLSR S: sv: Kvinnliga legitimerade sjukgymnasters riksförbund
KltrA. d: Kulturamt
KLTV NL: nl: Katholieke Vereniging van Land- en Tuinbouwonderwijzers
KLu NL: nl: mil: Koninklijke Luchtmacht
KLV D: d: WK2: Kinderlandverschickung [der Hitler-Jugend]
KLVHS d: Katholische Landvolkhochschule
K.M.; KM D: d: mil: Kaiserliche Marine
KM H: hu: Közellátási Miniszter(ium), Budapest; Közoktatásügyi Miniszter(ium), Budapest; PL: pl: Komitet Miejski; NL: nl: mil: Koninklijke Marine; D: d: mil: Kriegsmarine; Kriegsministerium; D: d: Kult(us)ministerium
KMA H: hu: Képzőmüvészeti Alap, Budapest; US: e: Incorporated Association of Kinematograph Manufacturers; NL: nl: mil: Koninklijke Militaire Academie, Breda; Südkorea: e: mil: Korean Military Academy, Seoul [gegr 1951]; D: d: mil: Kriegsmarinearsenal; S: sv: Kungliga Musikaliska Akademien

KMAC H: hu: Királyi Magyar Automobil Club, Budapest
KMÄ S: sv: Kontrollanstalten för Mejeriprodukter och Ägg
KMAG US: e: mil: U.S.Military Advisory Group to The Republic of Korea
KMBA BRD: d: mil: Katholisches Militärbischofsamt; B: nl: Koninklijke Maatschappij voor Bouwmeesters van Antwerpen
KMC BRD: d: Kienbaum Management Center; Südkorea: e: mil: Korean Marine Corps
KMD BRD: d: Kampfmittelbeseitigungsdienst
K.M.D.A. B: nl: Koninklijke Maatschappij voor Dierkunde van Antwerpen
KMDG CS: cs: Katedra Matematiky a Deskriptivní Geometrie
Kmdtr. d: mil: Kommandantur
KMEA US: e: Kansas (Kentucky) Music Educators Association
KMF CS: cs: Kabinet Moderní Filologie
KMG NL: nl: Katholieke Meisjesgilde
K.M.G.B. B: nl: Katholieke Meisjesgidsen van België
KMI H: hu: Kereskedelmi Minőségellenőrző Intézet, Budapest; PL: pl: Klub Młodej Inteligencji; B: nl: Koninklijk Meteorologisch Instituut van België
KMJÖ A: d: Katholische Mittelschuljugend Österreichs
KMK BRD: d: Ständige Konferenz der Kultusminister der Länder in der BRD (Kultusministerkonferenz); S: sv: Kungliga motorbåtklubben; BRD: d: Kurhessische Milchversorgung, 35 Kassel; DK:´da: mil: Kvindeligt Marinekorps [gegr 1946]
KML EAK: e: Kenya Muslim League
KMM BRD: d: Krauss-Maffei AG, 8 München
KMMA US: e: Knitting Machine Manufacturers Association
K.M.M.O. NL: nl: Koninklijk Magnetisch

en Meteorologisch Observatorium, Batavia

KMN BRD: d: Kabel- und Metallwerke Neumeyer AG, 85 Nürnberg 2

KMP CS: cs: Kabinet Mezinárodního Práva; H: hu: Kommunisták Magyarországi Pártja, Budapest

KMPP IND: [d: Arbeiter- und Bauernpartei]

KM PZPR PL: pl: Komitet Miejski Polskiej Zjednoczonej Partii Robotniczej

KMR S: sv: Kyrkomusikernas riksförbund

KMS US: e: Kansas Medical Society; CS: cs: Knihovna Matice Slovenské

K.M.S. B: nl: Koninklijke Militaire School

KMT BRD: d: Kölnische Mode- und Textilgroßhandlung GmbH, Köln; Kreis moderner Textilhäuser; China: Kuo Ming Tang (Kuomintang)

KMU DDR: d: Karl-Marx-Universität,Leipzig

K.m.ú. CS: cs: Katastralní měřický úřad

KMUR PL: pl: Komisja Międzyministerialna Upłynnienia Remanentów

KMV D: d: Keramik-Maschinen-Verband, Berlin W 50; BRD: d: Kölner Möbelversand, 5 Köln; CH: d: mil: Kriegsmaterialverwaltung [EMD]

KMW BRD: d: Kraftwerk Mainz-Wiesbaden AG, 65 Mainz; D: d: mil: Kriegsmarinewerft; BRD: d: Kuratorium der Mensch und der Weltraum, 53 Bonn

K.N. H: hu: Közoktatásügyi Népbiztosság, Budapest

KNA BRD: d: Katholische Nachrichtenagentur, 53 Bonn [gegr 1953]; EAK: e: Kenya News Agency; N: no: Kongelig Norsk Automobilklub, Oslo; e: Korean National Airlines

K.N.A.C. NL: nl: Koninklijke Nederlandsche (Nederlandse) Automobiel Club, Den Haag

KNAG NL: nl: Koninklijk Nederlandsch Aardrijkskundig Genootschap

KNAU NL: nl: Koninklijke Nederlandse Athletiek Unie

KNB PKN PL: pl: Komisja Normalizacyjna Budownictwa Polskiego Komitetu Normalizacyjnego

K.N.B.B. NL: nl: Koninklijke Nederlandse Biljartbond

K.N.B.T.B. NL: nl: Koninklijke Nederlandse Boeren- en Tuinders-Bond

KNC e: Kamerun National Congress

K.N.C.B. NL: nl: Koninklijke Nederlandse Cricket Bond

KNChV NL: nl: Koninklijke Nederlandse Chemische Vereniging

KNCU e: Kilimanjaro Native Cooperation Union Ltd.

KNCV NL: nl: = KNChV

KND BRD: d: Kirchlicher Nachrichtendienst, Köln

KNDP e: Kamerun National Democratic Party

K.N.D.S.B. NL: nl: Koninklijke Nederlandse Dames Sportbond

KNE YU: sh: Komisija za Nuklearu Energiju

KNEA US: e: Kentucky Negro Education Association

KNEB H: hu: Központi Népi Ellenőrzési Bizottság, Budapest

KNEP H: hu: Keresztény Nemzeti Egyesülés Pártja, Budapest

KNFU EAK: e: Kenya National Farmers Union

KNGV NL: nl: Koninklijk Nederlands Gymnastiek Verbond

KNH NL: nl: Koninklijke Nederlandsche Hoogovens en Staalfabrieken N.V., IJmuiden

KNIL NL: nl: Koninklijk Nederlandsch -Indisch Leger

KNILM NL: nl: Koninklijk Nederlandsch -Indische Luchtvaart-Maatschappij

KNJBTB NL: nl: Katholieke Nederlandse Jonge Boeren- en Tuindersbond

K.N.J.K. NL: nl: Koninklijke Nederlandse Journalistenkring

KNK BRD: d: Kompakte natriumgekühlte Kernenergieanlage, 7501 Leopoldshafen

KNLC NL: nl: Koninklijk Nederlands Landbouw Comité

KNM CS: cs: Knihovna Národního Musea; N: no: mil: Kongelige Norske Marine; N: no: Kongelig Norsk Motorbatforening; NL: nl: mil: Koninklijke Nederlandse Marine

K.N.M.B. NL: nl: Koninklijke Nederlandse Middenstands Bond

KNMI NL: nl: Koninklijk Nederlands Meteorologisch Instituut

KNMTP NL: nl: Koninklijke Nederlandsche Maatschappij voor Tuinbouw en Plantkunde

KNNV NL: nl: Koninklijk Nederlandse Natuurhistorische Vereeniging

KNO YU: sh: Kotarski Narodni Odbor

KNOJ YU: sh: Korpus Narodne Odbrane Jugoslavije

K.N.O.T. BG: [d: Fachausschuß des Rationalisierungskomitees]

KNOV YU: sn: Korpus Narodnoosvobodilne Vojske

KNP NL: nl: Katholieke Nationale Partij; Katholiek Nederlands Persbureau, Den Haag; EAK: e: Kenya National Party; CS: cs: Komise Národní Pojištění; PL: pl: Kongres Nauki Polskiej; CS: cs: Krajská Nemocenská Pojišt'óvna

KNPCs H: hu: Közoktatásügyi Népbiztosság Propaganda Csoport, Budapest

KNPM CS: cs: Knihovna Náprstkova Musea

KNR PL: pl: Komitet Nauk Rolniczych

KnRV d: Knappschaftliche Rentenversicherung

KNS CS: cs: Komise pro Národní Spotřebu; N: no: Kongelig Norsk Seilforening

K.N.S. B: nl: Koninklijke Nederlandse Schouwburg, Antwerpen

KNS CS: cs: Kumulativní Národní Správa

KNSM NL: nl: Koninklijke Nederlandse Stoomboot Maatschappij

KNSt BRD: d: Kreisnachforschungsstelle [DRK]

KNT H: hu: Keresztény Nöi Tábor, Budapest

K.N.T.B. NL: nl: Koninklijke Nederlandse Toeristenbond

KNTC EAK: e: Kenya National Trading Company

KNTM CS: cs: Knihovna Národního Technického Musea

KNTV NL: nl: Koninklijke Nederlandsche Toonkunstenaarsvereeniging

KNUB NL: nl: Koninklijke Nederlandse Uitgeversbond

KNUST GH: e: Kwame Nkrumah University of Science and Technology

KNUT EAK: e: Kenya National Union of Teachers

KNV CS: cs: Krajský Národní Výbor; CS: sk: Krajský Národný Výbor

K.N.V.B. NL: nl: Koninklijke Nederlandse Voetbalbond

K.N.V.v.L. NL: nl: Koninklijke Nederlandse Vereniging voor Luchtvaart

K.N.W.U. NL: nl: Koninklijke Nederlandse Wieler-Unie

KNZ NL: nl: N.V. Koninklijke Nederlandsche Zoutindustrie, Hengelo [gegr 1918]

K.N.Z.B. NL: nl: Koninklijke Nederlandse Zwembond

KO SF: fi: Kihlakunnan Oikeus; GB: e: mil: King's Own Royal Lancaster Regiment; PL: pl: Komisja Okręgowa; Komitet Okręgowy; D: d: NS: Konzentrationslager Oranienburg; YU: sn: Krajevni Odbor

KOB GB: e: mil: King's Own Scottish Borderers

KO Biuro PL: pl: Kulturalno-Oświatowe Biuro

Kobria BRD: d: Koblenzer Briefmarkenausstellung [1961]

KOC US: e: Kollmorgen Optical Corporation, Northampton, Mass.; e: Kuwait Oil Company

KOD CS: cs: Kurs pro Osvětové Důstojníky

KODA; Koda DK: da: Internationalt Forbund til Beskyttelse af Komponistrettigheder i Danmark

Koeba A: d: Kreditvereinigung für österreichische Beamte und Angestellte r.GmbH, Wien 1

KÖEE H: hu: Külföldi Ösztöndíjasok Egyetemi Előkészítője, Budapest

KÖHV A: d: stud: Katholische Österreichische Hochschulverbindung Mercuria

KÖJAL H: hu: Közegészégügyi és Jarvanyügyi Allomás

KŐTL H: hu: Kőolajbányászati Tudományos Laboratorium, Budapest

KÖY S: sv: Kungliga överstyrelsen för yrkesutbildning

KOFA CH: d: Interessengemeinschaft der schweizerischen Fabrikanten von Kohlepapier, Farbbändern und verwandten Produkten

K. of C. US: e: Knights of Columbus [gegr 1882]

K.of P. US: e: Knights of Pythias

KOFTA S: sv: Kommittén för Teknisk Annonsgranskning

KO&G US: e: Kansas, Oklahoma & Gulf Railway Company

KOG CH: d: mil: Kantonale Offiziersgesellschaft

KOGIS SU: [d: Buchhändlervereinigung der staatlichen Verlage]

KOHHIKI H: hu: Konzerv-, Hus- és Hütőipari Kutató Intézet, Budapest

KOI CS: sk: Krajský Osvetový Inspektorát

KOIP YU: sh: Komisija za Odobravanje Investicionih Programa

Kojastheim D: d: mil: Kommando der Jagdstaffeln im Heimatgebiet

kok SF: fi: kokoomuspuolue

KOK CS: cs: Krajský Odbor Kultury

KOKA D: d: Konversionskasse für deutsche Auslandsschulden, Berlin [gegr 1933]

KOKI H: hu: Kisérleti Orvostudományi Kutató Intézet, Budapest

KoKS BRD: d: Koordinierungsrat Kölner Selbsthilfe [1970]

Kol.A. D: d: mil: Kolonialarmee

KoLa d: NS: Konzentrationslager

Kol.H. D: d: mil: Kolonialheer

K.O.L.I. GB: e: mil: King's Own Light Infantry

Kolk.ú. CS: cs: Kolkovní úřad

KOLLR GB: e: mil: The King's Own Loyal Lancaster Regiment

Kol.Rgt. D: d: mil: Kolonialregiment

KOLUC B: nl: Kongolees Leuvens Universitair Centrum

Koluft D: d: mil: Kommandeur der Luftschiffertruppen [WK1]; Kommandeur der Luftwaffe [WK2]

KOLVO B: nl: Kunstdrukschool Onze -Lieve-Vrouw, Oudstudentenbond

KoM H: hu: Kohászati Miniszter(ium), Budapest

Kom.Adm. D: d: mil: Kommandierender Admiral

Komba D: d: Kommunalbeamten- und Angestellten-Verband; BRD: d: Bund Deutscher Kommunalbeamten und -angestellten (Komba) eV, 53 Bonn -Bad Godesberg

Komdtr. D: d: mil: Kommandantur

KOMEKON d: vgl: Comecon, RGW

Kom.Gen. D: d: mil: Kommandierender General

Kominform INT: d: Kommunistisches Informationsbüro, Bukarest [R, 1947 ...56]

Komintern INT: d: Kommunistische Internationale [1919...43]

Komm.Gen. d: mil: Kommandierender General

KOMO NL: nl: Stichting voor Keuring, Onderzoek en Beoordeling van Materialen en Constructies

Kom.Orient. PL: pl: Komisja Orientalistyczna, Warszawa

KompGH. d: Gerichtshof zur Entscheidung der Kompetenzkonflikte

KOMR GB: e: mil: The King's Own Malta Regiment

Komsomol SU: [d: Leninscher kommunistischer Jugendverband, gegr 1918]

Kom.str. CS: sk: Komunistická Strana

KOMUS YU: sn: Komisija za Učbenike in Skripta

Komut D: d: mil: WK1: Kommandeur der Munitionskolonnen und Trains

KOMZET SU: [d: Ausschuß für die Landbesiedlung der jüdischen Werktätigen, 1939 aufgelöst]

KON PL: pl: Konwent Organizacji Niepodłegiościowych

KONA. D: d: mil: WK2: Kriegsorganisation Nordafrika

Kongro BRD: d: Konditorei-Großeinkaufsgenossenschaft

KONO. D: d: mil: WK2: Kriegsorganisation Naher Osten

KONR [d: Befreiungskomitee der Völker Rußlands]

KonsAbt d: Konsularabteilung

KonsAg d: Konsularagent(ur)

KonsAk d: Konsularakademie

Kons.V. d: Konsularische Vertretung; Konsumverein

KONV CS: sk: Komisia Okresného Národného Výboru

KOP ZA: af: e: Klippfontain Organic Product Corporation; PL: pl: Komenda obrony pogranicznej; Komitet Obrońców Pokoju

KOPI PL: pl: Komisja Oceny Projektów Inwestycyjnych

KORLR GB: e: mil: King's Own Royal Lancaster Regiment

Korm.hat. H: hu: Kormányhatározat

KORO NL: nl: mil: Korps Opleiding Reserve Officieren

KorpsKdo BRD: d: mil: Korpskommando

KORR GB: e: mil: King's Own Royal Regiment

KORSTIC Südkorea: e: Korean Scientific and Technological Information Centre

Korück D: d: mil: Kommandant (Befehlshaber) des rückwärtigen Armeegebietes

KOS CS: sk: Krajské Osvetové Stredisko; PL: pl: Kuratorium Okręgu Szkolnego

KOSB GB: e: mil: The King's Own Scottish Borderers (Edinburgh Regiment)

KOSMETIKA 69 INT: d: Internationale Ausstellung für Kosmetik, Körperpflege und Hygiene mit 71. Deutscher Seifenmesse, 4 Düsseldorf [26...30.9.1969]

Kosomed BlnW: d: Kollektiv sozialistische Medizin [Freie Universität]

KOSTRAD RI: [e: strategic reserve command]

KOT H: hu: Könyvtárak Országos Tanácsa, Budapest

KOT. D: d: mil: WK2: Kriegsorganisation Türkei

KOTI RI: mil: [d: etwa: Oberkommando der Streitkräfte, Djakarta]

KOTRA Südkorea: e: Korea Trade Promotion Corporation, Seoul

KOV CS: cs: Kabinet Odborářské Výchovy

KoV D: d: Kompressorenverband, Berlin

K.O.V.A. D: d: Knappschafts-Oberversicherungsamt

KOVA BRD: d: Kommunalschriftenverlag I. Jehle, München 34

KOW [d: Komitee der vereinigten Wlassowzy]

KOYLI GB: e: The King's Own Yorkshire Light Infantry

K.P. US: e: Knights of Pythias [benevolent society, = K. of P.]

KP H: hu: Központi Bizottság [MSZMP] YU: sh: Komisija za Plate; PL: pl: Komitet Powiatowy; H: hu: Kommunista Párt, Budapest; d: Kommunistische Partei; sh: Komunistička Partija; sn: Komunistična Partija; PI: e: Burea

of Standards of the Philippines, Manila;
CS: sk: Krajská Poradňa;   d: Kriminal-
polizei
K.P.A.   D: d: Kaiserliches Patentamt
KPA   EAK: e: Kalenjin Political Alliance;
US: e: Kansas (Kentucky) Pharmaceu-
tical Association; J: e: Kikuyu Provin-
cial Association; D: d: NS: Kolonial-
politisches Amt der NSDAP [seit 1934];
S: sv: Kommunernas Pensionsanstalt;
d: Kommunistische Partei Albaniens
(Argentiniens) (Australiens); e: mil:
Korean People's Army; US: e: Kraft
Paper Association; BRD: d: Kreisprü-
fungsausschuß;   d: Kriminalpolizeiamt;
S: Kvalitetprovningsanstalt [Svenska
Elverksföreningen]
KPaS   CS: cs: Krajská Poradna a Studovna
KPB   d: Kommunistische Partei Belgiens
(Boliviens) (Brasiliens) (Bulgariens);
d: Kreispolizeibehörde
KP BiH   YU: sh: Komunistička Partija
Bosne i Hercegovine
KP(B)U   d: Kommunistische Partei (Bol-
schewiki) Ukraine
KPBW   D: d: Post: Kraftpostbetriebswerk
KPC   BRD: e: mil: Koblenz Procurement
Center;   d: Kommunistische Partei Cey-
lons (Chinas) (der Tschechoslowakei)
KPČ   d: Kommunistische Partei der Tsche-
choslowakei
KP CG   YU: sh: Komunistička Partija
Crne Gore
KPCh   d: Kommunistische Partei Chiles
(Chinas)
KPD   d: Kommunistische Partei Dänemarks;
D: d: Kommunistische Partei Deutsch-
lands [gegr 1918]; CH: d: Kreispostdirek-
tion; YU: sh: Kulturno-prosvjetno Društvo
KPD/ML   BRD: d: Kommunistische Partei
Deutschlands / Marxisten-Leninisten
[gegr 1968]
KPDR   d: Kommunistische Partei der Domi-
nikanischen Republik
KPdSU   d: Kommunistische Partei der

Sowjetunion [gegr 1903]
KPdSU(B)   d: Kommunistische Partei
der Sowjetunion (Bolschewiki) [1925
...52]
KPdU   d: Kommunistische Partei der
Ukraine
KPdUSA   d: Kommunistische Partei der
Vereinigten Staaten von Amerika
KPE   d: Kommunistische Partei Englands
(Estlands)
K.P.E.V.   D: d: Königlich Preußische Eisen-
bahnverwaltung
KPF   YU: sh: Komisija za Pregled Filmo-
va; d: Kommunistische Partei Finn-
lands (Frankreichs); S: sv: Svenska
järnvägars kontorspersonal- och arbets-
ledarförbund
K.Pf.P.   D: d: mil: Korpspferdepark
KpfTrS   BRD: d: mil: Kampftruppen-
schule
KPG   d: Kommunistische Partei Griechen-
lands (Großbritanniens) (Guadeloupes);
DDR: d: Künstlerische Produktions-
genossenschaft
KPGB   d: Kommunistische Partei Groß-
britanniens
KPGr   d: Kommunistische Partei Grie-
chenlands (Großbritanniens)
KPH   YU: sh: Komunistička Partija Hrvat-
ske; BRD: d: Konferenz der Pädago-
gischen Hochschulen
KPHA   US: e: Kansas Public Health As-
sociation
KPI   d: Kommunistische Partei Indiens
(Indonesiens) (Iraks) (Italiens); D: d:
Kraftpflug-Industrie eV, Berlin
KPJ   d: Kommunistische Partei Japans
(Jordaniens) (Jugoslawiens); YU: sh:
Komunistička Partija Jugoslavije
KPK   d: Kommunistische Partei Kanadas
(Kolumbiens) (Kubas); CS: cs: Krajská
Plánovacia Komisia
KPKK   DDR: d: Kreis-Parteikontrollkom-
mission [SED, 1948...52]
KPL   d: Kommunistische Partei Libanons

(Luxemburgs)

KPLT CS: cs: Krajská Poradna Lidové Tvořivosti

KPM CS: cs: Kancelář Práce a Mzdy; D: d: Königliche Porzellan-Manufaktur [Preußen] ; H: hu: Közlekedés- és Postaügyi Miniszter(ium), Budapest; d: Kommunistische Partei Marokkos (Martiniques) (Mexikos); YU: sh: Komunistička Partija Makedonije; NL: nl: Koninklijke Paketvaart-Maatschappij; BRD: d: Krister Porzellanmanufaktur, Landstuhl (Pfalz)

KPN d: Kommunistische Partei der Niederlande; Kommunistische Partei Nordirlands (Norwegens)

KPO d: Kommunistische Partei Österreichs; D: d: Kommunistische Partei-Opposition; CS: cs: Kulturně Propagační Oddělení; YU: sh:Kulturno-prosvjetni Odbor

KPÖ A: d: Kommunistische Partei Österreichs [gegr 1918]

KPP e: Kamerun People's Party; WAN: e: Kano People's Party; YU: sh: Komisija za Plate u Privredi; CH: d: Kommission für praktische Pharmacie; d: Kommunistische Partei Polens (Portugals); PL: pl: Komunistyczna Partia Polski; e: Korean Pacific Press

KPPR PL: pl: Komunistyczna Partia Polska Robotnicza

KPR CS: sk: Kancelár Prezidenta Republiky

K.P.R. EAK: e: Kenya Police Reserve

KPR d: Kommunistische Partei Rußlands (Bolschewiki); CS: cs: Kulturně Propagační Referát

KPR(B) d: Kommunistische Partei Rußlands (Bolschewiki)

KPRP PL: pl: Komunistyczna Partia Robotnicza Polski

KPS d: Kommunistische Partei des Saarlandes; Kommunistische Partei Schwedens (Spaniens) (Syriens); YU: sh: Komunistička Partija Srbije; YU: sn: Komunistična Partija Slovenije; CS: sk: Krajský Pedagogický Sbor; Krajská

politická škola

KPŠ CS: cs: Kurs Politického Školení

KPSM d: Kommunistische Partei San Marinos

KPSp d: Kommunistische Partei Spaniens

KPSP B: nl: Kring voor Pacifistische Studiën en Propaganda

KP STO YU: sn: Komunistična Partija Svobodnega Tržaškega Ozemlja

KPSU = KPdSU

KPT d: Kommunistische Partei Tunesiens; Kommunistische Partei der Türkei; CH: d: Krankenkasse des Personals des Bundes und der schweizerischen Transportanstalten, Bern

KPTh d: Kommunistische Partei Thailand

KPTI H: hu: Központi Pedagógus Továbbképző Intézet, Budapest

KPTsch d: Kommunistische Partei der Tschechoslowakei

KPU YU: sh: Kazneno-popravne Ustanove; EAK: e: Kenya People's Union; d: Kommunistische Partei Uruguays

KPV CS: cs: Kabinet Pedagogických Věd; BRD: d: Kommunalpolitische Vereinigung [CDU-CSU] ; d: Kommunistische Partei Venezuelas; D: d: Kreiselpumpen-Verband, Berlin

KPVP CS: cs: Komise pro Pomoc při Výstavbě Prahy

KPVS CS: cs: Komise Pomoci Východnímu Slovensku

KPVSS CS: cs: Komise pro Pomoc Velkým Stavbám Socialismu při ČSAV

KPZ BRD: d: Kronprinz AG, 565 Solingen-Ohligs

KPZR pl: Komunistyczna Partia Związku Radzieckiego

KPZU pl: Komunistyczna Partia Zachodniej Ukrainy

KQCPI GB: e: King's and Queen's College of Physicians of Ireland

KR CH: d: Kantonsrat

K.R.; KR. D: d: mil: Kavallerieregiment

K.R. GB: e: mil: The Kenya Regiment;

Kimberley Regiment; King's Regiment

KR S: sv: Konstnärsringen; D: d: nach WK2: Kontrollrat

Kr D: d: mil: Marinearchiv [OKM]; DIN: d: Fachnormenausschuß der Kraftfahrindustrie, Charlottenburg 2 [jetzt: FAKRA]

KR d: Kreisrat; Kreis-Rechtskammer [Sport]; D: d: mil: Kürassier-Regiment

Kr.A. D: d: mil: Kraftfahrabteilung; D: d: Kreisausschuß; d: mil: Kriegsarchiv [A, Preußen]

K.R.A.; KRA. D: d: mil: Kriegsrohstoffabteilung des Preußischen Kriegsministeriums

KrA S: sv: mil: Kungliga Krigsarkivet

Kraftag D: d: Großberliner Kraftdroschken-AG, Berlin N 20

KRAG D: d: Katholische Reichsarbeitsgemeinschaft für Gerichtshilfe, Gefangenen- und Entlassenen-Fürsorge, Düsseldorf

Kr.Ak. D: d: mil: Kriegsakademie

Kr.Arch. D: d: mil: Kriegsarchiv

KRAVAG; Kravag BRD: d: Versicherungsverband des Deutschen Kraftverkehrs V.a.G., 2 Hamburg [gegr 1951]

KRB BRD: d: Kernkraftwerk RWE – Bayernwerk GmbH, Grundremmingen

KRC US: e: Knowledge Research Center

K.R.C.A. GB: e: King's Roll Clerks' Association

KRD BRD: d: Katholische Rundfunkarbeit in Deutschland, 53 Bonn

Kr.-Dir. D: d: Kreisdirektion

KRDÖ D: d: Kampfring der Deutsch-Österreicher

KrDSt. D: d: Kreisdienststelle

Kreda D: d: Kreditverein Deutscher Apotheker, Berlin W 35

Kredita D: d: Kreditanstalt sächsischer Gemeinden, Dresden

Kreish D: d: Kreishauptmannschaft

Kremi D: d: Kreis Mirbt, München [Laienspiel]

Kremödro D: d: Einkaufsgenossenschaft der Krefelder-Mörser Drogisten GmbH, Krefeld

KRF S: sv: Kontorsvaruhandlarnas riksförbund

Krfa.Abt. D: d: mil: Kraftfahrabteilung

Kr.Fl. D: d: mil: Kriegsflotte

KrFU N: no: Kristelig Folkepartis Ungdomsorganisasjon

KrG D: d: Kreisgericht; D: d: mil: Kriegsgericht

K.-R.-G. D: d: Kriegsrohstoffgesellschaft

Kr.-Gen. d: Kreditgenossenschaft

Krger. D: d: Kreisgericht

KrGG d: Kreisgewerbegericht

Krgs. M. D: d: mil: Kriegsmarine

Krgssch. D: d: mil: Kriegsschule

K Rgt GB: e: mil: Kenya Regiment

KRH PL: pl: Komisja Rozbudowy Hutnictwa

Kr.-H. D: d: Kreishauptmannschaft

KrHFürsSt. D: d: Kreishauptfürsorgestelle für Kriegsbeschädigte und -hinterbliebene

K.R.I. GB: e: mil: King's Royal Irish Regiment

KRIH GB: e: mil: King's Royal Irish Hussars

Kripo d: Kriminalpolizei

KrJA D: d: Kreisjugendamt

KrK d: Krankenkasse

Kr.Laz. D: d: mil: Kriegslazarett

KRM PL: pl: Krajowa Rada Ministrów

Kr.M.; Kr.Min.; Krmin. D: d: mil: Kriegsministerium

KRN PL: pl: Krajowa Rada Narodna

KŘNV CS: cs: Komise Řízení Národních Výborů

KRO NL: nl: Katholieke Radio Omroep; BRD: d: Konferenz für Raumordnung; D: e: nach WK2: Kreis Resident Officer [US Zone]

Kröba A: d: Kredit- und Wirtschaftsverband für öffentliche Beamte und Angestellte rGmbH, Wien 1

KRoW PL: pl: Komitet Rozbudowy Otoczenia Wawelu

KRP YU: sh: Komisija za Reviziju Projekata; PL: pl: Krajowa Reprezentacja Polityczna

KrPflS BRD: d: mil: Krankenpflegeschule

Kr.Pr.A. D: d: mil: Kriegspresseamt

KRR GB: e: mil: King's Royal Rifles

KRRC GB: e: mil: The King's Royal Rifle Corps

KŘŘL CS: cs: Kabinet pro Studia Řecká, Římská a Latinská, Praha [ČSAV]

KRS GB: e: Kinematograph Renters' Society; DDR: d: mil: Kontroll- und Reparaturstaffel; D: d: Kraftfahrschule

Kr.Sch. D: d: mil: Kriegsschule

KrSchGer. D: d: Kreisschiedsgericht für Gemeinde- und Bezirksbeamte

KrsK BRD: d: mil: Kreiskommandantur

Krsp; Kr.Sp.; KRSPK d: Kreissparkasse

KRT BRD: d: Kernreaktorteile GmbH, 8752 Großwelzheim

KrV d: Krankenversicherung; Kreisverband

KRV BRD: d: Kunststoffrohr-Verein eV

Kr.V.A. S: sv: mil: Krigsvetenskapsakademien

Kr.Ver. d: mil: Kriegerverein

Kr.-Verb. d: Kreisverband

Kr.-Vers. d: Krankenversicherung; Kreditversicherung; Kriegsversicherung

KRWR i OP PL: pl: Komisja Rządowa Wyznań Religijnych i Oświecenia Publicznego

KS CH: d: Kantonschule; D: d: mil: Kavallerieschule; US: e: Kentucky State College; GB: e: mil: King's Shropshire Light Infantry; GB: e: Kipling Society; pl: Klub Sportowy; CS: cs: Knihovní Stredisko; DK: da: Kφbenhavns Skiklub; YU: sh: Komisija za Standardizaciju

K.S. D: d: mil: Kommando des Südbezirks [Deutsch-Südwestafrika]

KS DIN: d: Kommission Sicherheitstechnik, BlnW; CS: sk: Komunistická Strana; YU: sh: Komunistička Stranka; BRD: d: Kraftfahrerschutz eV; CS: sk: Krajská Správa; D: d: mil: Kriegsschule; S: sv:

mil: Krigsskolan; SU: [d: Normenausschuß] ; d: mil: Küstenschutz; Küstensicherung

KSA US: e: mil: Kaiserslautern Support Activity [BRD] ; B: nl: Katholieke Studenten Aktie Jong-Vlaanderen; d: Katholische Studenten-Aktion; BRL d: Kraftfahrsachverständigenausschuß; d: Kreis-Schiedsrichterausschuß [Sport DDR: d: Kreissportausschuß

KSAK S: sv: Kungliga svenska aeroklubbe

KSAVU CS: sk: Knižnica Slovenskej Akademie Vied a Umeni

KSB BRD: d: Klein, Schanzlin & Becker AG, 6710 Frankenthal; H: hu: Központi Statisztikai Bizottság, Budapest; BRD: d: Kreissportbund

KSC US: e: Kansas State College

K.S.C. GB: e: King's School, Canterbury

KSC D: d: stud: Kösener Senioren-Conver

KSČ CS: cs: Komunistická Strana Československá

KSC d: Kraftsportclub

KSch d: Kinderschule

K.Sch.R. A: H: d: mil: Kaiserschützenregiment

KSČN CS: cs: Královská Společnost Česk Nauk

KSCV; K.S.C.V. D: d: stud: Kösener Senioren-Convents-Verband, 87 Würzburg [gegr 1848]

KSF DK: da: Kφbenhavns Skytteforbund; D: d: Königlich Sächsische Forstakademie; IS: Kristilegt Stúdentafélag

KSFB BRD: d: Kriegssachschadenfeststellungsbehörde

KSG BRD: d: stud: Katholische Studentengemeinschaft; DK: da: Kφbmandsskolens Gymnastikforening; BRD: d: Kohlenscheidungs-Gesellschaft mbH, 7 Stuttgart

KSGÚĆSR CS: cs: = KSÚGČSR

KSH BRD: d: Kernkraftwerk Schleswig-Holstein, 2057 Geesthacht; H: hu: Központi Statisztikai Hivatal, Budapest

KSHS US: e: Kansas State Horticultural Society; S: sv: mil: Kungliga Sjökrigshögskolan

KSIS CS: cs: Krajská Správa Inseminačních Stanic

KSK CS: cs: Klub Socialistické Kultury; Komise Stranická Kontrolny; BRD: d: Kreissparkasse

KSL CS: sk: Krajská Správa Lesov; CS: cs: Krajská Správa Lesů

KSLI GB: e: mil: The King's Shropshire Light Infantry

KSM CS: cs: Katedra Stavební Mechaniky

KSMA e: Keats-Shelley Memorial Association; US: e: Kentucky State Medical Association

KSMW PL: pl: Komitet Studiującej Młodzieży

KSMZO YU: sh: Komisija za Saradnju sa Medunarodnim Zdravstvenim Organizacijama

KSN CS: cs: Kabinet pro Společenské Nauky; S: sv: Kvinnoföreningarnas samarbetskommitté för Nykterhetsfrågor, Stockholm

KSO CS: cs: Krajský Soud Obchadní

KSOS GR: [e: Central Saltana Raisins Co-operative Organization]

KSP EAK: e: Kenya Socialist Party; IND: e: Kerala Socialist Party; YU: sh: Komisija za Proučavnje Stanbene Problematike i Izgradnje; CS: cs: Kulturní Služba Pracujícím

K.Š.P. CS: cs: Kupecká škola pokračovací

KSPE US: e: Kentucky Society of Professional Engineers

KŠPÚ CS: sk: Knižnica Štátneho Pedagogického Ústavu

KS PZPR PL: pl: Komitet Stołeczny Polskiej Zjednoczonej Partii Robotniczej

KSŘŘ CS: cs: Kabinet pro Studia Řecká, Římská a Latinská

KSS CS: cs: Komunistická Strana Slovenska

KSSE [d: vereinigte kurdische Studenten in Europa]

KSSG DDR: d: Kinder-Schwimmsportgemeinschaft

KŠSM CS: sk: Knižnica Štátneho Slovenského Múzea, Bratislava

KSSR RI: [d: nationale Konferenz über revolutionäre Literatur und Kunst, 1964 in Djakarta]

KSSS S: sv: Kungliga Svenska Segelsällskapet

K.S.S.V. B: nl: Katholieke Sociale School voor Vrouwen

KST US: e: Kansas State Teachers' College; CS: cs: Katedra Stojírenské Technologie

KStatA. d: Kaiserliches Statistisches Amt

KSU CS: sk: Knižnica Slovenskej Univerzity, Bratislava; BRD: d: Kölner Studenten-Union, 5 Köln-Lindenthal

KSÚGČSR CS: cs: Knihovna Státního Ústavu Geologického Československé Republiky, Praha

KSV D: d: Kalksandsteinmaschinen-Verband, Berlin; Kieler Segler-Verein; Kölner Segler-Verein; d: Kraftsportverband; Kraftsportverein; Kraftsportvereinigung; d: mil: Küstensicherungsverband; S: sv: Kyrkosångens vänner

KSVB CS: cs: Krajska Správa Veřejné Bezpečnosti

KSW BRD: d: Kammgarnspinnerei Wilhelmshaven AG, 294 Wilhelmshaven

KSZ BRD: d: Katholische Sozialwissenschaftliche Zentralstelle, 405 Mönchengladbach

KSzB H: hu: Kereskedelmi Szakoktatási Bizottság, Budapest

K.Sz.M. H: hu: Kereskedelem- és Szövetkezetügyi Miniszter(ium), Budapest

KSzT H: hu: Kereskedelmi Szakoktatási Tanács, Budapest; Központi Szállitási Tanács, Budapest

K.T. GB: e: Kinsmen's Trust

KT PL: pl: Kontrola Techniczna; d: Kreistag [Sport]

KTA H: hu: Közületek Támogatási Alapja, Budapest

K.T.A. D: d: mil: Korps-Telegrafenabteilung; Krankentransportabteilung

KTA DDR: d: Kraftfahrzeugtechnische Anstalt; Kraftfahrzeugtechnisches Amt; Kreistransportausschuß; CH: d: mil: Kriegstechnische Abteilung, Bern [EMD]

KTAS DK: [d: Kopenhagener Telefon -Aktiengesellschaft]

KTBL BRD: d: Kuratorium für Technik und Bauwesen in der Landwirtschaft, 6 Ffm 1

KTD A: d: mil: Kavallerie-Truppen-Division; CH: d: Kreistelephondirektion

KTDA CS: cs: Katedra Teorie a Dějin Architektury; EAK: e: Kenya Tea Development Authority

KTDU CS: cs: Kabinet pro Teorii a Dějiny Umění

KTEF e: Knights Templar Educational Foundation

Kt G CH: d: Kantonsgericht

KTG BRD: d: Kerntechnische Gesellschaft im Deutschen Atomforum, 6 Ffm [gegr 1969]; Klimatechnische Gesellschaft, 6 Ffm

KTGA EAK: e: Kenya Tea Growers Association

KTH BRD: d: Kleines Theater, 71 Heilbronn; S: sv: Kungliga Tekniska Högskolan, Stockholm [gegr 1827]

K.T.H.B. S: sv: Kungliga Tekniska Högskolans Bibliotek, Stockholm

KTI d: Kriminaltechnisches Institut

KTK H: hu: Központi Technológiai Könyvtar, Budapest; CS: cs: Komise Technických Knihoven

KTL BRD: d: Kuratorium für Technik in der Landwirtschaft eV, 6 Ffm [ab 1968: KTBL]; DDR: d: Kuratorium für Technik in der Landwirtschaft [ab 1946: ZfL]

KTN DDR: d: Kältetechnik Niedersachswerfen

KTP BRD: d: mil: Kraftfahrtechnische Prüfstelle

K.T.R.C. B: nl: Katholiek Televisie- en Radiocentrum

KTS CH: d: Kerntechnische Sektion; CS: cs: Krajský Trestní Soud; CS: sk: Križiacke T'aženie za Slobodu; S: sv: Kvinnliga Teknologernas Sammanslutning

KTTF S: sv: Kvinnliga telefontjänstemannaförbundet

KTTL N: no: Kvinnelige Telegraf- og Tele fonfunksjonærers Landsforening

KTU BRD: d: Kriminaltechnische Untersuchungsstelle

KTV d: Kaufmännischer Turnverein; BR d: mil: Kommando der Territorialen Verteidigung; d: Kreis-Turnverein

KTVTL CS: cs: Katedra Tělesné Výchovy a Tělovýchovného Lékařství

KTVVŠP CS: cs: Katedra Tělesné Výchovy vysoké Školy Pedagogické

KTW DDR: d: Komitee für Touristik und Wandern

KU CS: cs: Karlova Universita; DK: da: Københavns Universitet; CS: cs: Komenského Universita; DK: da: Konservativ Ungdom; S: sv: Konstitutionsutskottet; DDR: d: Konzessionsunternehmen; Konzessionsunternehmung; BlnW: d: Kritische Universität [seit 1967]

Ku d: Kultusministerium

KU: e: Kuwait Airways

KUAP PL: pl: Komisja Usprawnienia Administracji Publicznej

KUD YU: sh: Kulturno-Umjetničko Društvo

Kül.M. H: hu: Külügyminiszter(ium), Budapest

Kür.R. D: d: mil: Kürassier-Regiment

KUF S: sv: Kommunistiska Ungdomförbundet

KÚF CS: cs: Kontrolní Ústav Farmaceutický

KUK CS: cs: Koordinační Ukrajinský Komitét; Krajska Učitelská Knihovna

KUKA BRD: d: Keller & Knappich GmbH

Maschinenfabrik, 89 Augsburg 3

KuKa d: Kulturkammer

K.u.K.YG. A: H: d: Kaiserliches und Königliches Yachtgeschwader, Pola

KUL PL: pl: Katolicki Uniwersytet Lubelski; B: nl: Katholieke Universiteit van Leuven

KultA; KultrA d: Kulturamt

KuM DDR: d: Kulturelle Massenarbeit

KUNC e: Kamerun United National Congress

KÚNZ CS: cs: Krajský Ústav Národního Zdraví

Kuom e: Kuomintang = KMT

KÚOS CS: cs: Krajské Ústředí Osvětových Sborů

KUPM CS: cs: Knihovna Umělecko-Průmyslového Musea

KUR S: sv: Kulturella Ungdomsrörelsen

K.u.RZA. A: d: mil: Kraft- und Radfahrzeugsanstalt

KUS S: sv: Kristliga Ungdomsförbundet i Sydsverige

K.u.St.-K.-V. d: Krankenunterstützungs- und Sterbekassenverein

KUV B: nl: Katholieke Universitaire Vrouwenbeweging; D: d: Künstler-Unterstützungsverein

KuV D: d: Kunststeinmaschinen-Verband

KUVB D: d: Künstlerunterstützungsverein, Berlin

KUVM D: d: Künstlerunterstützungsverein, München

KV d: Kanuverband; CS: cs: Kárný Výbor; BRD: d: stud: Kartellverband der katholischen deutschen Studentenvereine, 463 Bochum [gegr 1865] ; A: d: stud: Kartellverband katholischer nichtfarbentragender Studentenvereine Österreichs; BRD: d: Kassenärztliche Vereinigung; D: d: Katasterverwaltung [Preußen] ; Kellerei-Maschinen-Verband, Berlin; Kirchenvorstand; H: hu: Központi Vezetőség [MDP] ; YU: sh: Komisija za Vodoprivredu; D: d: Konservative Volkspartei; d: Konsumverein; CS: cs: Koordinační Výbor; Krajský

Výbor; d: Krankenunterstützungsverein; Krankenversicherung; Kreisverband; Kreisverein; Kreisvereinigung; Kreisverwaltung; Kreisvorstand; Künstlerverein; Kurzschrift-Verband; D: d: stud: Kyffhäuser-Verband der Vereine Deutscher Studenten

KvA NL: nl: Kantoor van Arbeid

KVA B: nl: Koninklijke Vlaamse Academie voor Wetenschappen, Letteren en Schoone Kunsten van België; DDR: d: Kraftverkehrsamt

K.V.A. D: d: mil: Kriegsverpflegungsanstalt; S: sv: Kungliga Vetenskapsakademien

KVAB BlnW: d: Krankenversicherungsanstalt Berlin

KVAG BRD: d: Kieler Verkehrs-AG

KVAL S: [e: Research Group for Quantitative Linguistics, Stockholm 40]

KV a MV KSČ CS: cs: Krajský Výbor a Městský Výbor Komunistické Strany Československa

KVB BRD: d: Kassenärztliche Vereinigung Bayerns

K.V.B. NL: nl: Katholieke Vrouwenbeweging

KVB CH: d: Kober'sche Verlagsbuchhandlung, Basel; BRD: d: Kölner Verkehrsbetriebe, 5 Köln; Krankenversorgung der Bundesbahnbeamten, 6 Ffm

KVB-AG BRD: d: Kölner Verkehrsbetriebe AG, 5 Köln

KVD BRD: d: Kassenärztliche Vereinigung Deutschlands; Kölnische Verlagsdruckerei GmbH, 5 Köln

KVDA BRD: d: Kraftfahrer-Vereinigung Deutscher Ärzte eV, 2 Hamburg [gegr 1907]

KVDB BRD: d: Kraftfahrer-Vereinigung Deutscher Beamter eV, 8532 Bad Windsheim

KVdR BRD: d: Krankenversicherung der Rentner

KVE S: sv: Kursverksamheten Vår Ekonomi

KVG BRD: d: Kasseler Verkehrs-Gesellschaft AG, 35 Kassel

K.V.G. D: d: WK1: Kleiderverwertungs-Gesellschaft; D: d: konzessionierte Verkehrsgesellschaft [Sachsen] ; Kraftverkehrsgesellschaft

K.V.G.V. B: nl: Katholieke Vereniging voor Gebrekkigen en Verminkten

KVH CS: cs: Krajský Výbor Hornický

KVHA; KVHAA S: sv: Kungliga Vitterhets-, Historie- och Antikvitetsakademien

K.V.H.U. B: nl: Katholieke Vlaamse Hogeschooluitbreiding

K.V.H.V. B: nl: Katholiek Vlaams Hoogstudentenverbond, Leuven

KVIV B: nl: Koninklijke Vlaamse Ingenieursvereeniging

KVJ NL: nl: Katholiek Vrouwelijk Jeugdwerk

KVK CS: cs: Krajská Vodohospodářská Komise; D: d: Künstlerverein, Königsberg

K.V.K. en F. nl: Kamer van Koophandel en Fabrieken

KVKSČ CS: cs: Krajský Výbor Komunistické Strany Československa

KVKSS CS: sk: Krajský Výbor Komunistickej Strany Slovenska

KVL DK: da: Kongelige Veterinær- og Landbohøjskole; D: d: Künstlerinnenverein, Leipzig

KVM D: d: Künstlerverein "Malkasten", Düsseldorf; Künstlerinnenverein, München

KVMD D: d: Künstlerverein "Malkasten", Düsseldorf

KVN BRD: d: Kassenärztliche Vereinigung Niedersachsen; D: d: Künstlerverein, Nürnberg

KVNB CS: cs: Komise Vnitřní Národní Bezpečnosti

KVNT NL: nl: Koninklijke Vereniging "Het Nederlandse Trekpaard"

KVO B: nl: Koninklijke Vlaamse Opera, Antwerpen

KVOM CS: cs: Krajský Výbor Obranců Míru

KVP DDR: d: Kasernierte Volkspolizei; NL: nl: Katholieke Volkspatij; Konservatieve Volkspartij [Nederlandse Antillen] ; B: nl: Kristelijke Volksparti

KVPD DDR: d: Dienststelle der Kasernierten Volkspolizei

K.V.R.O. B: nl: Katholieke Vlaamsche Radio-Omroep

K.V.S. B: nl: Katholiek Vlaams Sekretariaat; Koninklijke Vlaamse Schouwburg, Brussel

KVŠCh CS: cs: Knihovna Vysoké Školy Chemické

KVŠMU CS: cs: Knižnica Vysokej Školy Muzickych Umení

KVŠPLI CS: sk: Knižnica Vysokej Školy Pol'nohospodárskeho a Lesníckeho Inžinierstva, Košice

KVŠT CS: cs: Knihovna Vysokých Škol Technických, Praha; CS: sk: Knižnica Vysokej Školy Technickej, Bratislava

K.V.S.V. B: nl: Katholiek Vlaams Sportverbond

KVŠZ CS: cs: Knihovna Vysoké Školy Zemědělské, Brno

KVÚ CS: cs: Kloknerův Výzkumný Ústav; Krajský Vlastivědný Ústav

KVV CS: vs: Katedra Výtvarné Výchovy; BRD: d: Kölner Versicherungswissenschaftliche Vereinigung eV, 5 Köln

K.V.V.F. B: nl: Katholieke Vlaamse Volkkunstfederatie

KVVS S: sv: Kungliga väg- och vattenbyggnadsstyrelsen

KVW d: Katholisches Volksbildungswerk; D: d: Künstlerverband Wilmersdorf

KVWand D: d: Künstlerverein "Wanderer" München

KVWM NL: nl: Katholieke Vereniging van Werkgevers in de Metaalindustrie, Den Haag

KVZ CH: d: Kredit- und Verwaltungsbank Zug AG [gegr 1933]

K.V.Z.K. B: nl: Katholieke Vereniging voor Zieken en Kranken

K.W. D: d: Katholisches Werkvolk

KW PL: pl: Komitet Warszawski; Komitet Wojewódzki

K+W CH: d: mil: Eidgenössische Konstruktionswerkstätte, Thun

KW BRD: d: Kreditanstalt für Wiederaufbau, 6 Ffm [= KfW]

KWA DDR: d: VEB Kabelwerk, Berlin -Adlershof

K.W.A. D: d: mil: Kaiser-Wilhelm-Akademie für das militärärztliche Bildungswesen

KWA d: Kreiswohnungsamt

K.W.Ak. = K.W.A.

K.W.B. D: d: Kaiser-Wilhelm-Bibliothek, Posen [bis 1918]

KWB BRD: d: Kammer für Wertpapierbereinigung

K.W.B. B: nl: Katholieke Werkliedenbond

KWBA. D: d: WK1: Kriegswollbedarfs-AG

KWC PL: pl: Komitet Walki Cywilnej

KWEA BRD: d: mil: Kreiswehrersatzamt

KWF NL: [d: Königin-Wilhelmina-Fonds für Krebsforschung, gegr 1949]; BRD: d: Kuratorium für Waldarbeit und Forsttechnik, 6079 Buchschlag

K.W.G.; KWG D: d: Kaiser-Wilhelm-Gesellschaft zur Förderung der Wissenschaften, Berlin; Kolping Wandernde Gesellen

KWH DDR: d: Keramische Werke Hermsdorf

KWHW D: d: WK2: Kriegswinterhilfswerk

K.W.I.; KWI D: d: Kaiser-Wilhelm-Institut [1911...45]

KWIE D: d: Kaiser-Wilhelm-Institut für Eisenforschung, Düsseldorf

KWIG D: d: Kaiser-Wilhelm-Institut für Strömungsforschung, Göttingen

KWIM D: d: Kaiser-Wilhelm-Institut für Metallforschung, Stuttgart

KWIU B: nl: mil: Koninklijke Weerkunding Instituut te Ukkel

KWK DDR: d: VEB Kabelwerk, Berlin

-Köpenick; BRD: d: Kälte-Wärme-Klimatechnik GmbH, 7 Stuttgart; D: d: Kolonial-Wirtschaftliches Komitee eV, Berlin; PL: pl: Komitet Walki Konspiracyjnej; BRD: d: Kraftwerk Kassel GmbH, 35 Kassel

KWL BRD: d: Kernkraftwerk Lingen GmbH; Kraftwerk Laufenburg AG, 7887 Laufenburg

KWO DDR: d: VEB Kabelwerk Oberspree, Berlin-Oberschönweide; BRD: d: Kernkraftwerk Obrigheim GmbH

KWP DDR: d: Kittwerk Pirna; PL: pl: Komitet Walki Podziemnej

KWR BRD: d: Kabelwerk Rheydt AG: Kraftübertragungswerke Rheinfelden, 7888 Rheinfelden

KWS BRD: d: Kleinwanzlebener Saatzucht AG vorm. Rabbethge & Giesecke, 3352 Einbeck

KWSH BRD: d: Kernkraftwerk Schleswig -Holstein, Geesthacht

KWU DDR: d: Kommunalwirtschaftsunternehmen [1948...51, dann: VEB(K)]; BRD: d: Kraftwerk-Union AG, Berlin [gegr 1969]

KWV D: d: Katholischer Wandervogel; DDR: d: Kommunale Wohnungsverwaltung

K.W.V. ZA: af: Ko-operatiewe Wijnbouwers Vereniging van Zuid-Afrika Besperkt

K.W.Y.C. D: d: Königlich Württembergischer Yacht-Club

K.Y.C. D: d: Kaiserlicher Yacht-Club

Kyff. Bd. D: d: mil: Kyffhäuserbund

KYMCA EAK: e: Kenya Young Men's Christian Association

Kyodo J: [d: Nachrichtenagentur]

KYP GR: [d: zentraler Nachrichtendienst der Verteidigung]

KZ D: d: NS: Konzentrationslager

KZA CS: cs: Knihovna Zemědelské Akademie

KZAB [d: Koordinationszentrum des antibolschewistischen Kampfes]

KZBG NL: nl: Koninklijk Zoölogisch en
Botanisch Genootschap
KZBV BRD: d: Kassenzahnärztliche Bun-
desvereinigung, 5 Köln
K.Z.K. NL: nl: Koninklijke Zout-Ketjen
N.V., Arnhem
KZM PL: pl: Komunistyczny Związek
Młodzieży
KZMR PL: pl: Komunistyczny Związek
Młodzieży Robotniczej
KZN CS: cs: Kabinet Zdenka Nejedlého
KZO CS: cs: Kabinet Zdravotnické Osvěty;
NL: nl: Koninklijke Zout Organon NV,
Arnhem
KZV d: Kaninchenzuchtverein; BRD: d:
Kassenzahnärztliche Vereinigung
KZVB BRD: d: Kassenzahnärztliche Ver-
einigung Bayern, München
KZVD D: d: Kassenzahnärztliche Ver-
einigung Deutschlands

L GB: e: mil: Lancers; B: f: mil: Lanciers; D: d: mil: Abteilung Landesverteidigung [Wehrmachtamt]; d: Landgericht; d: stud: Landsmannschaft; D: d: mil: Landsturm; d: Landtag; D: d: mil: Landwehr; d: Landwirtschaftsschule; BlnW: d: Langenscheidt KG, Verlagsbuchhandlung, Berlin-Schöneberg; F: f: Librairie Larousse, Paris; d: mil: Lazarett; Lehrregiment; D: d: mil: Leibkompagnie, Leibstandarte [NS]; INT: d: Liberale Fraktion und Nahestehende [Europäisches Parlament]; e: Library; CDN: e: mil: Lincoln and Welland Regiment; DIN: d: Fachnormenausschuß für Luftfahrt, Berlin-Adlershof [D]

9 L GB: e: mil: 9th Queen's Royal Lancers

12 L GB: e: mil: 12th Royal Lancers

16/5 L GB: e: mil: 16th/5th The Queen's Royal Lancers

17/21 L GB: e: mil: 17th/21st Lancers

LA. D: d: mil: Planungsamt [Reichsluftfahrtministerium]

LA e: Labor Administration; d: Landesamt; Landesausschuß; Landratsamt; S: sv: Kungliga Lantbruksakademien; Lantmäteristyrelsens arkiv, Stockholm

L.A. e: Law Association; Legislative Assembly; US: e: Leschetizky Association; GB: e: Library Association of the United Kingdom; e: mil: Light Artillery; f: Ligue Arabe

LA RCH: s: Línea Aérea Nacional de Chile; US: e: Link Aviation, Inc., Binghamton, N.Y.

L.A. GB: e: Liverpool Academy

L&A US: e: Louisiana & Arkansas Railway

LA D: d: Luftamt; DDR: d: mil: Luftarmee; D: d: Verein der Deutschen Antiquariats- und Exportbuchhändler, Leipzig

L.A.A. GB: e: Lancashire Authors' Association

LAA BRD: d: Landesarbeitsamt; Landesausgleichsamt; US: e: League of Advertising Agencies; Lithuanian Alliance of America

L.A.A. GB: e: Liverpool Academy of Arts; London Angling Association; London Architectural Association; London Association of Certified Accountants

LAA US: e: Los Angeles Airways

LAAB F: f: Ligue d'Alsace des Amateurs de Billard

LAÄ d: Landesarbeitsämter

L.A.&A.K. LR: Latvijas automobilu un aero klubs, Riga

L.A.A.M.M. GB: e: London Association in Aid of Moravian Missions

LAA Regt GB: e: mil: Light Anti-Aircraft Regiment

LAB e: Labor Advisory Board; GB: e: Laboratory Animals Bureau

Lab GB: e: Labour Party

LAB S: sv: Landförbundet för arbetslöshetens bekämpande; DK: da: Landsforeningen til Arbejdsløshedens Bekæmpelse; S: sv: Landtmännend Affärsvörmedlingsbyrå AB; BRD: d: Lastenausgleichsbank, 53 Bonn-Bad Godesberg; Lebensabend-Bewegung eV, 35 Kassel [gegr 1958]

L.A.B. e: Legal Advisers' Branch

LAB US: e: Library of American Biography, Boston; Bolivien: s: Lloyd Aéreo Boliviano S.A., Cochabamba

L.A.B. GB: e: Local Appeal Board; London Association for the Blind

LABEX INT: e: International Laboratory Apparatus and Material Exhibition, London

Labi d: Landesbibliothek; BlnW: d: Landesbildstelle

LABOREC B: f: Laboratoire belge de l'industrie électrique nl: Belgisch Laboratorium van de Elektrische Industrie

LABSTAT US: e: United States Bureau of Labor Statistics

L.A.C. GB: e: Lancashire Associated Collieries; Legal Advice Centre

LAC d: Leichtathletikclub; CO: s: Lloyd Aéreo Colombiano

L.A.C. GB: e: Local Advisory Council

LAC US: e: Lockheed Aircraft Corp., Burbank, Calif.

L.A.C. GB: e: London Assembly Centre; London Athletic Club

LACA CDN: US: Life Agency Cashiers Association of the United States and Canada

L.A.C.A. GB: e: London Association of Certified Accountants

LACAP INT: e: Latin American Cooperative Acquisitions Project

LACC US: e: Los Angeles City College

LACFFP INT: e: Latin-American Commission on Forestry and Forest Products

LACH CS: cs: Laboratoř Anorganické Chemie

L.A.C.I. GB: e: London Association of Conference Interpreters

LACMA US: e: Los Angeles County Medical Association

LACOFA f: La Coopération Franco-Africaine

LACP INT: e: Latin American Cooperative Acquisition Project

L.A.C.P. GB: e: London Association of Correctors of the Press

L.A.C.S. GB: e: League Against Cruel Sports

LACSA CR: s: Líneas Aéreas Costarricenses S.A., San José

L.A.C.V.W. B: nl: Landelijk Algemeen Christelijk Verbond van Werkgevers

LAD US: e: Library Administration Division [ACRL]

L.A.D. GB: e: Lord Advocate's Department [Scotland]

LADA GB: e: London Alley Dwelling Authoritiy

LADC US: e: Los Alamos Document Center

LADE RA: s: Líneas Aéreas del Estado, Buenos Aires

LADECO RCH: s: Línea Aérea del Cobre Ltda, Santiago

LADS GB: e: Literary and Debating Society, Malta

LADSIRLAC GB: e: Liverpool and District Scientific Industrial and Research Library Advisory Council

LADWP US: e: Los Angeles Department of Water and Power

L.A.E. GB: e: London Association of Engineers

L.Aé.F. F: f: Ligue Aéronautique de France

L.A.F. GB: e: Legal Aid Fund

LAF S: sv: Livsmedelsbranschens arbetsgivareförbund

L.A.Fam.G. D: d: Landesamt für Familiengüter

LAFC UN: e: Latin-American Forestry Commission [FAO, gegr 1948]

L.A.F.D. GB: e: London Association of Funeral Directors; US: e: Los Angeles Fire Department

LAFTA INT: e: Latin American Free Trade Association [s: ALALC]

LAG BRD: d: Landesarbeitsgemeinschaft zur Verteidigung der demokratischen Rechte und Freiheiten in Bayern [1958 verboten]; BRD: d: Landesarbeitsgericht; e: Laser Advisory Group

LAGE US: e: Los Angeles Grain Exchange

LAgl BlnW: d: Landesausgleichsamt

LAGV-VZ/NRW BRD: d: Landesarbeitsgemeinschaft der Verbraucherverbände − Verbraucher-Zentrale Nordrhein -Westfalen eV, 4 Düsseldorf

LAGW BRD: d: Luftschutzarbeitsgemeinschaft der Spitzenverbände der gewerblichen Wirtschaft, 5 Köln

L.A.H. D: d: mil: WK2: Leibstandarte Adolf Hitler

LaHAL S: sv: Landskrona högre allmänna läroverk

L.A.I. e: Library Association of Ireland; I: i: Linee Aeree Italiane S.p.A.,Roma [gegr 1947]

LAIR US: e: mil: Letterman Army Institute of Research, San Francisco
LAJ L: Letzeburger Arbechterjugend
L.A.J.C. GB: e: London Agreement Joint Committee
LAJS e: Libyan American Joint Service for Agriculture and Natural Resources
LAK BRD: d: Länderausschuß "Technische Kraftfahrzeugüberwachung"
L.A.K. LT: Lietuvos Automobiliu Klubas
LAK BlnW: d: Lohnausgleichskasse
LAKEC LR: Latvijas atbrīvošanas komitejas Eiropos centrs
LAKI H: hu: Lakkipari Kutató Intézet
Lakra BRD: d: Badische Landeskreditanstalt
LAL US: e: Langley Aeronautical Laboratory [NASA]; F: f: Lignes Aériennes Latécoère, Paris
La Leche US: e: La Leche League International [gegr 1950 in Chicago]
LAM CS: cs: Laboratoř Agrometeorologická; DK: da: mil: Langeland Marinedistrikt; e: Latin-American Mission
L.A.M. f: mil: Lignes Aériennes Militaires; GB: e: London Academy of Music
LAMA GB: e: Locomotive and Allied Manufacturers' Association of Great Britain, London; US: e: Los Angeles Maintainability Association
LAMCO Liberia: e: Liberian American -Swedish Minerals Company, Monrovia
L.A.M.D. GB: e: London Association of Master Decorators
L.A.M.D.A. GB: e: London Academy of Music and Dramatic Art [gegr 1861]
L.A.M.I.T. GB: e: Local Authorities Mutual Investment Trust
LAMPF US: e: Los Alamos Meson Physics Facilities
LAMPS GB: e: London Area Mobile Physiotherapy Service
L.A.M.S. GB: e: London Association of Master Stonemasons
LAMS US: e: Los Alamos Scientific Laboratory

LAMSA MEX: s: Líneas Asociadas Mexicanas S.A.
LAN RCH: s: Líneas Aérea Nacional de Chile, Santiago
L.A.N.A. f: Lignes Aériennes Nord-Africaines
LANARK YEO GB: e: mil: The Lanarkshire Yeomanry (TA)
LAND DIN: d: Fachnormenausschuß für landwirtschaftliche Maschinen und Geräte, Berlin [D]
LANDCENT NATO: e: Allied Land Forces Central Europe
LANDENMARK NATO: e: Allied Land Forces Denmark
Landj.K. D: d: Landjägerkorps
Landnorm DIN: d: Fachnormenausschuß Landwirtschaft
LANDNORWAY NATO: e: Allied Land Forces Norway
Landr.-A. d: Landratsamt
LANDSOUTH NATO: e: Allied Land Forces Southern Europe
LANDSOUTHEAST NATO: e: Allied Land Forces Southeastern Europe
Landw. D: d: mil: Landwehr
LandwA d: Landwirtschaftsamt
LandwH d: Landwirtschaftliche Hochschule
Landwk.; LandwK D: d: Landwirtschaftskammer
Landw.Min. D: d: Landwirtschaftsminister(ium)
L.A.N.E. RA: s: Línea Aérea Nor-Este
LANFUS GB: e: mil: The Lancashire Fusiliers
Langnamverein D: d: Verein zur Wahrung der gemeinschaftlichen Interessen in Rheinland und Westfalen
LANICA NIC: s: Líneas Aéreas de Nicaragua S.A., Managua
LANM CS: cs: Literární Archiv Knihovny Národního Musea
LANSA s: Líneas Aéreas Nacionales Consolidadas S.A.

LANTCOM US: e: mil: Atlantic Command
LANTFLT US: e: mil: Atlantic Fleet
LAO BRD: d: mil: Leiter der Annahme-
organisation
L.A.O. e: Licensing Authorities' Office
LAP PY: s: Líneas Aéreas Paraguayas
L.A.P. BR: pt: Línhas Aéreas Paulistas,
Rio de Janeiro
LAP GB: e: London Airport
LAPAG D: d: Landparzellierungs-AG, Berlin
LAPD US: e: Los Angeles Police District;
US: e: mil: Los Angeles Procurement
District
LAPE E: s: Líneas Aéreas Postales Españolas
LAPL US: e: Los Angeles Public Library
Lapo. D: d: Landespolizei
LAPP B: nl: Vereeniging Leuvense Afge-
studeerden in de Psychologie en Paeda-
gogiek
LAPT GB: e: London Association for the
Protection of Trade
LAR. A: d: mil: Leichtes Artillerieregiment
LAR BRD: d: mil: Luftwaffen-Ausbildungs
-Regiment
LARA US: e: Licensed Agencies for Relief
in Asia
LArbA BRD: d: Landesarbeitsamt
LArbG BRD: d: Landesarbeitsgericht
LARC e: Libyan-American Reconstruction
Commission
LArch BlnW: d: Landesarchiv
LARE D: e: nach WK2: Committee on the
Reform of German Law
LAREN I: i: Luigi Amenduni Rappresen-
tanze Estere e Nazionali
LARES R: ro: Liniile Aeriene Romane
Exploatate de Stat, Bucureşti
LARP LR: Latvijas Arodbiedrību Repu-
blikaniskā Padome
L.A.S. GB: e: Land Agents' Society;
e: League of Arab States; GB: e: Legal
Aid Service; Liverpool Architectural
Society; London Ambulance Service;
London Apothecaries' Society; Lord
Advocate of Scotland

LAS US: e: Louisiana Academy of Scienc
Lasag CH: d: Laser AG, Neuenburg
LASCA US: e: Los Angeles State and
County Arboretum
LASCO e: Field Science Cooperation
Office for Latin America
LASECNA INT: f: L'Agence pour la Sé-
curité de la Navigation Aérienne en
Afrique et Madagascar
LASEDECO PI: e: Land Settlement and
Development Corporation
LASH US: e: Legislative Action on Smok
ing and Health
LASIM US: e: Los Angeles Society of
Internal Medicine
LASK A: d: Linzer Athletik-Sportklub
LASKO CH: d: Landesverband Schweizer
scher Kinderfreundeorganisationen
LASL US: e: Los Alamos Scientific Lab-
oratory
L.A.S.O. s: Línea Aérea Sur-Oeste
LASPA BRD: d: Württembergische Lande
sparkasse
LASRA NZ: e: Leather and Shoe Researc
Association
LASSI INT: e: Latin-American Secre-
tariat of the Socialist International
LASt BLnW: d: Lohnausgleichsstelle
La SU US: e: Louisiana State University
LÁSZ H: hu: Legfőbb Állami Számvevő-
szék, Budapest
LAT CS: cs: Laboratoř pro Automati-
zaci a Telemechaniku; NL: nl: Lange
Afstandstippelaars; RA: s: Liga Ar-
gentina contra la Tuberculosis
L.A.T.C.O. CO: s: Líneas Aéreas Trans-
atlanticas Colombianas, Barranquilla
LATI I: i: Linee Aeree Transcontinentale
Italiane
LATN PY: s: Línea Aérea de Transporte
Nacional, Asunción
L.A.U.K. GB: e: Library Association of
the United Kingdom
L.A.U.R.S. F: f: Ligue d'action univer-
sitaire, républicaine et socialiste

LAusglA BRD: d: Landesausgleichsamt

LAussch. A: d: Landesausschuß

L.A.U.W. GB: e: London Association of University Women

LAV D: d: Landesarbeitgeberverband; Landesarmenverband; BRD: d: Landesstelle für Arbeitsvermittlung; Landmaschinen- und Ackerschlepper-Vereinigung, 6 Ffm [VDMA] ; L: Letzeburger Arbechter-Verband; YV: s: Línea Aéropostal Venezolana, Caracas; D: d: Lokomotiv-Ausfuhrverband

La VersA BRD: d: Bahn: Eisenbahn-Versuchsamt für Lager und Lagergießereien

L.A.W. US: e: League of American Wheelmen; League of American Writers

LAW DDR: d: Leipziger Arzneimittelwerk

LAWA BRD: d: Länderarbeitsgemeinschaft Wasser

Laz d: mil: Lazarett

LB D: d: Landbund; d: Landesbibliothek; DDR: d: Landwirtschaftsbank; D: d: Allgemeines Amt [Reichsluftfahrtsministerium] ; d: Leihbibliothek; Leihbücherei; D: d: stud: Leuchtenburgbund; S: sv: AB Linjebuss; Bolivien: s: Lloyd Aéreo Boliviano

L.B.A. F: f: Laboratoire de Biologie Animale

LBA d: Lehrer(innen)-Bildungsanstalt; F: f: Liaison Bibliophilique et Artistique, Paris 15; BRD: d: Luftfahrt-Bundesamt, 33 Braunschweig

LBAB BRD: d: Landesberufsverband Bayern der Architekten und Bauingenieure eV, München

LBB DDR: d: Lotsen-, Bugsier- und Bergungsdienst

L.B.B.B. B: nl: Landsbond der Belgische Brood- en Banketbakkersbazen

L.B.C. B: nl: Landelijke Bediendencentrale; GB: e: London Bankruptcy Court

L.B.C.M. GB: e: London Board of Congregational Ministers

Lbd. D: d: Landbund

L.B.D. GB: e: League of British Dramatists

LBE BRD: d: Gütegemeinschaft Lager- und Betriebseinrichtungen eV, 58 Hagen; Landesverband des Bayerischen Einzelhandels eV, München

LBF BRD: d: Laboratorium für Betriebsfestigkeit, 61 Darmstadt-Eberstadt; S: sv: Landsbygdens Byggnadsförening; Lantbruksförbundets Byggnadsförening, Stockholm

L.B.F.A. GB: e: London Builders Foremen's Association

LBG BRD: d: Landwirtschaftliche Berufsgenossenschaft

LBH DDR: d: Volkseigene Betriebe für Land-, Bau- und Holzbearbeitungsmaschinen

L.B.H. e: Local Board of Health

LBHASA GB: e: London Business Houses Amateur Sports Association

LB Horse GB: e: mil: Lothians and Border Horse

LBI BRD: d: Landesverband der Bayerischen Industrie eV, 8 München; DDR: d: Lehrerbildungsinstitut; US: e: Library Binding Institute, Boston 9, Mass.

LBibl d: Landesbibliothek

L.B.J. US: e: mil: Long Binh Jail [near Saigon, Vietnam]

LBK DDR: d: Landbaukombinat; BRD: d: Landesverein Bayern der Kraftfahrzeugindustrie; Lokalbaukommission; S: sv: Lux Båtklubb

L.B.K.C. GB: e: Ladies' Branch of the Kennel Club

LBL BlnW: d: Landesamt für Besatzungslasten

LBM D: d: Lichtbund Märchenwiese,Berlin

LBNSY US: e: mil: Long Beach Naval Shipyard

L.B.P.C. GB: e: London Building Productivity Committee

L.B.R. B: f: Ligue Belge contre le Rhumatisme

Lbr Svc US: e: mil: Labor Service

LBS BRD: d: Landes-Bausparkasse;

d: Landesbildstelle

L.B.S. GB: e: Life Boat Station; London Botanical Society

L.B.S.C. GB: e: London, Brighton and South Coast Railway [= L.B.S.C.R.]

LBSC US: e: Long Beach State College

LBSch BRD: d: Landwirtschaftliche Berufsschule

L.B.S.C.R. GB: e: = L.B.S.C.

LBTF US: e: mil: Long Beach Test Facility

L.B.T.S. GB: e: London Blood Transfusion Service

L.B.V. F: f: Laboratoire de Biologie Végétale; D: d: Landesbauverwaltung

LBW BRD: d: Landesverband der Badisch -Württembergischen Industrie, 7 Stuttgart

LBZ CS: cs: Laboratoř pro Biologii Rozmnožování Hospodářských Zvířat

LC US: e: Lafayette College

L.C. d: stud: Landsmannschafts-Convent; e: Law Court

LC US: e: Lawrence College

L.C. D: d: Technisches Amt [Reichsluftfahrtministerium]; e: Legal Committee; Legislative Council

LC d: Leichtathletik-Club; US: e: Library of Congress, Washington, D.C. 20540

L.C. e: Licensing Committee; Lions Club; Livestock Commission; Lower Court

L.C.A. F: f: mil: Laboratoire Central de l'Armement, Montrouge

LCA US: e: Lake Central Airlines

L.C.A. US: e: Library Club of America, Inc., Manhattan

LCA GB: e: Liverpool Cotton Association, Ltd., Liverpool 3; US: e: Lutheran Church in America

L.C.A.N. F: f: mil: Laboratoire central de l'artillerie navale

L.C.B. GB: e: Liquor Control Board

L.C.B.T. I: i: mil: Laboratorio chimico batteriologico tossicologico

L.C.C. GB: e: Lancashire Cotton Corporation; NL: nl: Landbouw Crisis Comité

LCC F: f: Le Condensateur Céramique, Montreuil; US: e: Lockheed Corporation of California; NATO: e: Logistic Coordination Center; GB: e: London Chamber of Commerce

L.C.C. GB: e: London City Council; London Communication Committee; London County Council

L.C.C.H. GB: e: London County Council Hospital

L.C.C.O.R.C. GB: e: Lancashire and Cheshire Colliery Owners' Research Committee

LCCR US: e: Leadership Conference on Civil Rights

L.C.C.S. GB: e: London County Council Service

L.C.C.T.F.W.A. GB: e: Legislative Council of the Cotton Textile Factory Workers' Association

L.C.D. GB: e: London College of Divinity; Lord Chamberlain's Department; Lord Chancellor's Department

L.C.D.R. GB: e: London, Chatham and Dover Railway

LCE B: f: Laboratoire Central d'Electricité

L.C.E.T.B. GB: e: Linen and Cotton Embroidery Trade Board

L.C.F.E.U. F: f: Le Conseil Français pour l'Europe Unie

L.C.G.B. GB: e: Locomotive Club of Great Britain; L: [f: Confédération luxembourgoise des syndicats chrétiens]

L.C.G.I.L. I: i: Libera Confederazione Generale Italiana dei Lavoro [gegr 1948]

L.C.H. F: f: mil: Laboratoire Central de l'Habillement

L.C.H.C.A. GB: e: London Cartage and Haulage Contractors' Association

LCHQ NATO: e: Local Command Headquarters

L.C.I.E. F: f: Laboratoire Central des Industries Electriques, Fontenay-aux -Roses (Seine)

LCIGB GB: IRL: e: Locomotive and Carriage Institution of Great Britain and Eire

L.C.L. B: f: Ligue des combattantes loyalistes

L.C.M. CH: f: Laboratoire pour le contrôle des médicaments; e: Lagos Church Missions; GB: e: London City Mission; London College of Music

L.C.M.C. GB: e: London Clinical Manufacturers' Convention

L.C.M.F. GB: e: Lancashire and Cheshire Miners' Federation

L.&C.M.P.S. GB: e: London and Counties Medical Protection Society

LCMS US: e: Lake County Medical Society

L.C.N. US: i: La Cosa Nostra [Mafia]

L.C.O. GB: e: Lee Conservancy Office

L.C.P. f: mil: Laboratoire central de poudres; e: League of Colored Peoples; AUS: e: Liberal and Country Party; GB: e: Liverpool Court of Passage; London College of Printing

LCPC F: f: Laboratoire central des ponts et chaussées

L.C.P.C. GB: e: Lancashire and Cheshire Provincial Council

L.C.P.S. GB: e: London Carthorse Parade Society

LCR S: sv: Lastbilscentralernas Riksförening, u.p.a.

Lcrs GB: e: mil: Lancers

L.C.S. GB: e: London Co-operative Society; Lyon Court, Scotland

L.C.S.C. GB: e: London Child Study Centre

LCSG GB: e: London Construction Safety Group

LCSS GB: e: London Council of Social Service

LCT F: f: Laboratoire Central de Télécommunications, Paris

L.C.T.A. GB: e: London Corn Trade Association

LCTS WAN: e: Lagos City Transport Services

LCTU e: Libyan Confederation of Trade Unions

L.C.T.U. GB: e: London Carmen's Trade

Union

L.C.U. GB: e: Lancashire Congregational Union; London Congregational Union

LCWIO INT: e: Liaison Committee of Women's International Organizations, London [gegr 1925]

L.C.Y. f: Ligue Communiste Yougoslave; e: League of Communists of Yugoslavia

LCZ CH: d: Leichtathletikclub Zürich

LD US: e: Labor Department

L.D. D; d: mil: Landungsdivision; Landwehrdivision

LD D: d: Verwaltungsamt [Reichsluftfahrtministerium]; e: Legal Division

L.D. US: e: Legion of Decency

LD CS: cs: Lidová Demokracie

L.D. GB: e: mil: Light Dragoons; London Division; GB: e: London Docks

LDA e: Lead Development Association

Ldbk d: Landbank

L.D.C. GB: e: Lancashire Dynamo & Crypto Ltd.

LDC e: Liberian Development Corporation

L.D.C.M.W.W. GB: e: London Diocesan Council for Moral Welfare Work

L.D.F. GB: e: London Diocesan Fund

L.D.F.S. GB: e: London District Friendly Society

Ldger.; LdGer. d: Landgericht

L.D.H. f: Ligue des Droits de l'Homme

LDH GB: e: London District Headquarters

LDHM F: f: Ligue des Droits de l'Homme Malade, Sceaux (Seine)

L.D.H.M. GB: e: London Diocesan Home Mission

LDK. D: d: mil: Luftdienstkommando

LDKK DK: da: Landsforeningen Dansk Kunsthaandværk og Kunstindustri

LDM BRD: d: Leistungsgemeinschaft des deutschen Möbelhandels

LDO CS: cs: Literárně Dokumentační Oddělení

L.D.O.S. GB: e: Lord's Day Observance Society

LDP e: Lesotho Democratic Party; Liber-

al-Democratic Party; DDR: d: Liberal
-Demokratische Partei; f: Ligue des Patriotes

LDPC CDN: e: mil: Logistic Data Processing Centre

LDPD DDR: d: Liberal-Demokratische
Partei Deutschlands [gegr 1945]

LdrA; Ldra D: d: Landratsamt

L.D.R.A.C. F: f: mil: Ligue des Droits des
Religieux Anciens Combattants

LDRC US: e: Lumber Dealers Research
Council

L.D.S. US: e: Latter-Day Saints

LDS BRD: d: stud: Liberaler Deutscher
Studentenbund, 53 Bonn; CS: cs: Lidové Demokratické Státy

Ldsb d: Landesbank

LdsKultA d: Landeskulturamt

Lds.Pol. D: d: Landespolizei

Ldst D: d: mil: Landsturm

Ldtg d: Landtag

L.D.U. e: Local Defence Union

L.D.V. GB: e: mil: Local Defence Volunteers [= Home Guards]

Ldw D: d: mil: Landwehr

LDW BRD: d: Lloyd Dynamowerke GmbH,
23 Bremen

Ldw.-Ges. d: Landwirtschaftsgesellschaft

Ldw.-K. d: Landwirtschaftskammer

LDY GB: e: mil: Leicestershire and Derby-
shire Yeomanry

LE CS: cs: Laboratoř pro Elektrotechniku;
D: d: mil: Nachschubamt [Reichsluft-
fahrtministerium] ; RL: e: Lebanese
International Airways

L.E. F: f: mil: Légion Etrangère; F: f:
Ligue de l'Enseignement

LEA P: pt: Laboratório de Engenharia
de Angola, Luanda; GB: e: Labour
Education Authority

L.E.A. eo: Laborista Esperanto-Asocio

LEA BRD: d: Landesentschädigungsamt;
Landesernährungsamt; f: Ligue des
Etats Arabes; GB: e: Local Education
Authority

L.E.A. GB: e: London Employers' Association

LEAA US: e: Law Enforcement Assistan
Administration [Department of Justic

L.E.A.D. F: f: Laboratoire d'Electroniqu
et d'Automatique Dauphinois, Grenob
[gegr 1958]

LEAG CH: d: Aktiengesellschaft für lu-
zernisches Erdöl

LEAP WAN: e: Loan and Educational
Aid Programme; US: e: mil: Logistics
Event and Assessment Program

LEB DDR: d: Landeseigener Betrieb

L.E.B. GB: e: London Electricity Board,
London E.C.2

LEBAG CH: d: Leitungs- und Elektroba
AG, Wettingen

LEBEA D: d: Lebensversicherungsbund
für Beamte und deren Angehörige

L.E.C. e: Local Employment Committee

LEC US: e: Lockheed Electronics Com-
pany, Plainfield, N.J.; GB: e: London
Executive Council of the National
Health Service

LECE INT: i: Lega Europea di Cooperazi
Economica s: Liga Europea de Coope-
ración Económica f: Ligue Européenn
de Coopération Economique, Bruxelles
[B, gegr 1946, e: ELEC]

LED d: Landeseichdirektion; US: e:
Library Education Division

L.E.D. GB: e: London Engine Drivers

L.E.D.A. E: s: Las Ediciónes de Arte,
Barcelona [gegr 1940]

LEDC US: e: League for Emotionally
Disturbed Children

L.E.E. GB: e: London Electrical Enginee

L.E.E.N. NL: eo: Nederlanda Esperanto-
Asocio "La Estonto Estas Nia"

L.E.F. US: e: Lake Erie, Franklin & Cla-
rion Railroad Company

LEF NL: nl: Landbouw Egalisatie Fonds

L.E.F. F: f: Ligue des Enfants de France

LEFA INT: d: Internationale Lebensmit-
tel- und Feinkost-Ausstellung, 2 Hamburg

LEG US: e: Legal Department

LEHG. D: d: Landeserbhofgericht

LEI NL: nl: Landbouw-Economisch Instituut, Den Haag

Leic; Leicesters GB: e: mil: Leicestershire Regiment

LEICESTER YEO GB: e: mil: The Leicester Yeomanry (Prince Albert's Own)

L.E.I.I. E: s: Laboratorio de la Escuela de Ingenieros Industriales

LEINS R GB: e: The Royal Leinster Regiment

LEK D: d: Lichterfelder Ersatzkasse [Krankenkasse]

Leku D: d: Lehr- und Kunstfilm-Gesellschaft, Wiesbaden

LEL GB: e: League of Empire Loyalists

LEM CS: cs: Laboratoř pro Elektronovou Mikroskopii

LEMAR US: e: "Legalize Marijuana"

LEMB CS: cs: Laboratoř pro Elektronovou Mikroskopii v Biologii

LEMEPUL CH: f: Laboratoire d'Essai des Matériaux de l'Ecole Polytechnique de l'Université de Lausanne

LEMIT RA: s: Laboratorio de Ensayo de Materiales e Investigaciónes Tecnológicas

LEMMS P: pt: Laboratório de Ensaios de Materiais e Mecânica do Solo, Lourenço Marques

L.E.M.P. F: f: Laboratoire d'Etudes et de Mesures Photoélectriques

LEN INT: f: Ligue Européenne de Natation

LENTIADE NL: [d: Frühjahrsmesse 1969 in Rotterdam]

LEO CS: cs: Laboratoř Elektronové Optiky

LEP F: f: Laboratoire d'Electronique et de Physique Appliquée, Paris; S: sv: Lotsverkets enskilda pensionskassa

L.E.P.G.T.A. GB: e: London Employers' Plate Glass Trades Association

LEPPU P: pt: Laboratório de Estudos Petrológicos e Paleontológicos do Ultramar, Junta de Investigações do Ultramar, Lisboa

LEPRA GB: e: British Leprosy Relief Association

LEPS f: Laboratoire d'études et de publications scientifiques

LER P: pt: Laboratório de Estudos de Radioisótopos, Junta de Investigações do Ultramar, Lisboa; d: Landesehrenrat; B: nl: Limburgse Ekonomische Raad

L.E.R. GB: e: London Electric Railway

LERC F: f: Laboratoire d'Etudes et de Recherches Chimiques, Paris

LES BRD: d: Fachgemeinschaft Ladeneinrichtungen aus Stahl; DDR: d: Leipziger Eisen- und Stahlwerke

L.E.S. GB: e: Liverpool Engineering Society

LES US: e: Louisiana Engineering Society

L.E.S.A. GB: e: London Electric Supply Association

L.E.S.S. eo: La Esperanto-Spiritista Societo

LET J: [f: Laboratoire électrotechnique de Tokio]

Leta LR: [d: lettisches Nachrichtenbüro, Riga]

LETATA GB: e: Light Edge Tool and Allied Trades Association

LETI F: f: Laboratoire d'électronique et des technologies de l'information, Grenoble; SU: [e: Leningrad Electrotechnical Institute]

LEUSTUKA B: nl: Leuvens Studenten Kabaret

LEVA GR: mil: [e: Greek People Liberation Army]

LEW BRD: d: Lech-Elektrizitätswerke AG, 89 Augsburg; DDR: d: Lokomotivbau - Elektrotechnische Werke, Henningsdorf

L.E.&W.R.R. US: e: Lake Erie & Western Railroad

LEY INT: e: Liberal European Youth, Brussels [gegr 1952]

LF CS: cs: Laboratoř pro Experimentální a Theoretickou Fysiku; S: sv: Länsarkitekternas Förening; US: e: Lakser

Foundation; GB: e: mil: The Lancashire Fusiliers

Lf D: d: Landesfürsorgeamt

LF S: sv: Landsbygdens försäkringsbolag,
Stockholm; Landskommunernas För-
bund, Stockholm

L.F. e: Legion of Frontiersmen

LF CS: cs: Lékařská Fakulta; D: d: Wirt-
schaftsamt [Reichsluftfahrtministerium];
S: sv: Litografiska Föreningen, Stockholm[gegr 1881]; Lotsförbundet

L.F. D: d: mil: WK2: Luftflotte

LfA BRD: d: Bayerische Landesanstalt
für Aufbaufinanzierung, München

LFA BRD: d: Landesfinanzamt; Landesfürsorgeamt

L.F.A. EAK: e: Land Freedom Army;
GB: e: London Floorcoverings Association

L.F.A.C.F. F: f: Ligue Féminine d'Action
Catholique Française

L.F.A.J. F: f: Ligue Française des Auberges
de la Jeunesse

L.F.A.S. D: d: mil: WK2: Luftgau-Flak-
artillerieschule

LFB CH: d: Lehrervereinigung für fort-
schrittliches Bildungswesen, 8001 Zürich

L.F.B. GB: e: London Fire Brigade

L.F.B.M.B. B: nl: Landsbond van Fede-
raties der Beroepsmutualiteiten van België

LFC US: e: Laser Film Corporation, New
York

L.F.C. F: f: mil: Légion Française des Combattants; GB: e: London Fencing Club

LFCh CS: cs: Laboratoř Fysikální Chemie,
Praha [ČSAV]

LFD BRD: d: Landesfilmdienst; d: Lan-
desfinanzdirektion

L.F.D.F. F: f: Ligue Française pour le
Droit des Femmes

L.F.D.H. F: f: Ligue Française pour les
Droits de l'Homme

L.F.E. F: f: Ligue Française de l'Enseignement; GB: e: London Fur Exchange

LFEM CH: f: Laboratoire Fédéral d'Essai

des Matériaux

LFF BRD: d: Land- und Forstwirtschaft
licher Forschungsrat eV; e: Liberian
Frontier Force

LFH BRD: d: Lehrerfortbildungsheim

L.F.H.S.C. GB: e: London Foot Hospital
School of Chiropody

LFinA BRD: d: Landesfinanzamt

LFJ YU: sn: Ljudska Fronta Jugoslavije

LFK BRD: d: Länderfachausschuß Kraft
fahrzeugverkehr; Lehr- und Forschun
institut für industrielle Koordinierung,
205 Hamburg-Bergedorf

LFKU CS: cs: Lékařská Fakulta Komens
kého University

LFKW BRD: d: Lehr- und Forschungs
-Klärwerk, 7 Stuttgart-Büsnau

LFL DK: da:Landøkonomisk Forsøgsla-
boratorium

Lfl.; L.Fl.; LFl d: mil: Luftflotte

LFLRASP US: e: Lifwynn Foundation
for Laboratory Research in Analytical
and Social Psychiatry

LFM BRD: d: Landesfinanzministerium;
DDR: d: Leipziger Frühjahrsmesse;
GB: e: London and South Eastern Fur-
niture Manufacturers' Association;
D: d: Luftfahrtforschungsanstalt Mün-
chen eV [gegr 1943]

L.F.M.A. GB: e: London Flower Manufacturers' Association

L.f.Mr. INT: d: Liga für Menschenrechte

L.F.N. B: f: Ligue des Familles Nom-
breuses; F: f: mil: Ligue Navale Française

LFP CS: cs: Laboratoř pro Fyziologii
a Patofyziologii Přeměny Látek

L.F.P.R.I. GB: e: London Female Preventive and Reformatory Institution

LFR BRD: d: Landesrat für Freiheit und
Recht

LFS BRD: d: Landesfeuerwehrschule

L.F.S. GB: e: London Fire Service

LFS; Lfs S: sv: Kungliga Luftfarts-
styrelsen

‚FSA CH: d: Landesverband Freier Schweizer Arbeiter

‚F.S.C. GB: e: London Fire Salvage Corps

‚F.St. D: d: Landesfilmstelle; D: d: mil: Luftwaffenführungsstab

‚FSU CS: sk: Lekárska Fakulta Slovenskej Univerzity

‚F.T.A. GB: e: London Fur Trade Association

‚F.T.B. GB: e: Lace Finishing Trade Board

‚F.T.F. GB: e: London Furniture Trades Federation

‚FTI SU: [d: Leningrader physikalisch-technisches Institut]

‚ftw D: d: mil: Luftwaffe [= Lw]

LFU BRD: d: Leichtflugzeugtechnik-Union GmbH, 53 Bonn

L.F.U.F. S: sv: Landsföreningen för folknykterhet utan förbud [gegr 1922]

LfV BRD: d: Landesamt für Verfassungsschutz

LFV BRD: d: Landesforstverwaltung; Landesfremdenverkehrsverband; Arbeitsgemeinschaft der Deutschen Landesfürsorgeverbände, 44 Münster; Landesfürsorgeverband

L.F.W. GB: e: Liberal Federation of Wales

LfW INT: d: Liga für Weltregierung

LFW D: d: Luftfahrtforschungsanstalt Wien

LFZ BRD: d: Landwirtschaftliche Fleischzentrale, 3 Hannover

LG A: d: Landesgericht; d: Landesgymnasium; Landgericht; I: i: Lega Giovanile; d: Leichtathletik-Gemeinschaft; A: d: Österreichische Leo-Gesellschaft

L.G. GB: e: St.Francis' Leper Guild; GB: e: mil: The Life Guards; D: d: Lilienthal-Gesellschaft für Luftfahrtforschung; GB: e: London Group [painters and sculptors] ; D: d: mil: Luftgau

LGA BRD: d: Landesgesundheitsamt; Landesgewerbeamt; Liquid Gas Anlagen Union GmbH, 548 Remagen-Rolandseck

L.G.B. GB: e: Local Government Board

L.G.B.C. e: Local Government Boundary Commission

LGC GB: e: Laboratory of the Government Chemist

L.G.C.A. GB: e: Local Government Clerks' Association

L.G.C.O. GB: e: Lord Great Chamberlain's Office

L.G'ds GB: e: mil: The Life Guards

L.G.E. f: Laboratoire Général pour Emballage

L.G.E.B. GB: e: Local Government Examinations Board

LGer A: d: Landesgericht; d: Landgericht

LGF S: sv: Linköpings Gymnastikförening

LGH US: e: mil: Letterman General Hospital

L.G.H.R. D: d: mil: Leibgarde-Husarenregiment

L.G.I.O. GB: e: Local Government Information Office for England and Wales

L.G.I.O.M. GB: e: Lieutenant-Governor of the Isle of Man

LGK BRD: d: Landesgarantiekasse Schleswig-Holstein, Kiel; D: d: mil: Luftgaukommando

LGKdo D: d: mil: Luftgaukommando

L.G.L. D: d: Lilienthal-Gesellschaft für Luftfahrtforschung

L.G.L.P.F.A. GB: e: London and Greater London Playing Fields Association

L.G.O.C. GB: e: London General Omnibus Company

LGP; Lgpa; L.G.P.A. D: d: mil: Luftgaupostamt

L.G's GB: e: mil: The Life Guards

LGS SP: f: Ligue pour la Grande Somalie

L.G.S.A. IRL: e: Leinster Guild of Shop Assistants

LGSt. d: Landesgeschäftsstelle

LGSt BlnW: d: Lohn-und Gehaltsberechnungsstelle

LGTA pt: Liga Geral dos Trabalhadores Angolanos, Léopoldville

L.G.U. e: Ladies' Golf Union

LGU SU: [e: Leningrad State University]

LGV d: Lehrergesangverein
LGW D: d: Luftfahrtgerätewerk Haken-
felde GmbH, Berlin-Spandau
lgz BRD: d: Landesbank und Girozentrale
Rheinland-Pfalz, 65 Mainz
LH CS: cs: Laboratoř Hutnická; d: Land-
wirtschaftliche Hochschule
L.H. F: f: Légion d'Honneur
LH S: sv: Linköpings Högerförbund
L.H.A. e: Local Highway Authority
L.H.A.O. GB: e: mil: The Lord High Admi-
ral's Office
L.H.B.Bekl. D: d: mil: WK2: Hauptstelle
für Beschaffung von Bekleidung und
Ausrüstung der Luftwaffe
L.H.C.C.B.A. GB: e: London and Home
Counties Contract Bridge Association
L.H.C.C.B.C.I. GB: e: London and Home
Counties Conciliation Board of the Cine-
matograph Industry
L.H.C.J.E.A. GB: e: London and Home
Counties Joint Electricity Authority
LHF DK: da: Landbo- og Husmandsfore-
ningernes
LHFürsSt. BRD: d: Landeshauptfürsorge-
stelle für Kriegsbeschädigte und Kriegs-
hinterbliebene
LHG BRD: d: Landwirtschaftliche Haupt-
genossenschaft eGmbH, Koblenz; stud:
Liberale Hochschulgruppe
L.H.H. e: League of the Helping Hand
L.H.I. INT: s: Liga Homeopática Inter-
nacional f: Ligue Homéopathique Inter-
nationale [gegr 1925]
LHK BlnW: d: Landeshauptkasse
LHM DDR: d: Leipziger Herbstmesse
L.H.M.C. GB: e: London Hospital Med-
ical College
LHO S: sv: Labdsbygdens Hemhjälpsor-
ganisation
LHP CS: cs: Lidová Hvězdárna v Praze
LHR S: sv: Lärlingsrådet för hotell och
restauranger
L.H.R. A: d: mil: Landwehrhusarenregiment
L&HR US: e: Lehigh & Hudson River

Railway
LHS CS: cs: Laboratoř Heterocyklickýcl
Sloučenin; NL: nl: Landbouw Hoge-
school; CH: d: stud: Liberale Hochscl
gruppe, Bern; CS: cs: Literárně Histo-
rická Společnost; S: sv: Humanistiska
vetensskapssamfundet i Lund
L.H.T.A. GB: e: London Head Teachers'
Association
LHTM P: pt: Laboratório de Histologia
e Tecnologia de Madeiras, Junta de
Investigações do Ultramar, Lisboa
L.H.T.P.B.I. e: Leather and Hide Trades'
Provident and Benevolent Institution
LHV D: d: Reichsverband landwirtschaft
licher Hausfrauenvereine
L.H.V.P. F: f: Laboratoire d'Hygiène de
la Ville de Paris
L.Hyp.A. A: d: Landeshypothekenanstal
LI NL: nl: Dienst van Landelijke Inkom-
sten; e: Leeward Islands Air Transpor
INT: e: Liberal International (World L
eral Union), London SW 1 d: Liberale Internationale (Liberale Weltunion)
s: La Internacional Liberal (Unión Libe
ral Mundial); INT: f: Light internatio-
nale de la représentation commerciale
LIA US: e: Laser Industry Association;
Lead Industries Association; RL: e:
Lebanese International Airways, Beirut
L.I.A. I: i: Lega Italiana Aeronautica;
e: Liberian International Airways, Rob
erts Field; INT: f: Ligue Internatio-
nale d'Arbitrage; INT: f: Ligue Inter-
nationale des Aviateurs
LIAB S: sv: Lindesbergs Industri AB,
Lindesberg; Lycksele Industri AB
LIAC e: Liberian International Amer-
ican Corporation
LIAP SU: [d: Institut für Luftfahrzeug-
gerätebau, Leningrad]
LIAS NL: nl: Liberale Inter-Academiale
Studiekringen
LIAT e: Leeward Islands Air Transport;
INT: f: Ligue Internationale des Asso-

ciations Touristes

LIB NL: nl: Leyden Internationaal Bureau

LIBA US: e: Long Island Biological Association

LIBANOR; LIBNOR RL: e: Lebanese Standards Institution, Beirut

LIBSA ZA: [d: Befreiungsfront für Südafrika]

LIC S: sv: Lärarnas Inköpscentral; Landstingens Inköpscentral

L.I.C. IND: e: Life Insurance Corporation of India

LIC INT: d: Liga für internationalen Creditschutz eV, 5 Köln e: League International for Creditors f: Ligue internationale pour la protection du crédit; e: Local Intelligence Committee

LICA INT: f: Ligue internationale contre le racisme et l'antisémitisme, Paris 10 s: Liga Internacional contra racismo y antisemitismo

LICCA INT: l: Lige internationalis Catolica contra alcoholismum

LICCD; LICD INT: f: Ligue internationale contre la concurrence déloyale, Paris 8 [gegr 1930] s: Liga Internacional contra la Competencia Desleal

L.I.C.E. F: f: Ligue Indépendante de Coopération Européenne

LICENSINTORG SU: [d: Organisation für internationale Lizenzen, Moskau]

LICRA INT: f: = LICA

LID US: e: League for Industrial Democracy; BRD: d: Lehrinstitut für Dokumentation, 6 Ffm

LIDC GB: e: Lead Industries Development Council

LIDH INT: f: Ligue Internationale des Droits de l'Homme

LIDIA INT: f: Liaison internationale des industries de l'alimentation, Paris 2 [gegr 1952]

LIEN INT: f: Ligue Internationale pour l'Education Nouvelle [gegr 1915]

L.I.F.A. F: f: Ligue d'Île-de-France d'Athlé-

tisme

LIFIDEC B: f: Ligue des femmes pour l'information et la défense du consument

LIFPL INT: f: Ligue Internationale de Femmes pour la Paix et la Liberté, Genève [CH, gegr 1915]

Liftenvereniging NL: nl: Nederlandse Vereniging van Liftnijverheid, Den Haag

L.I.G.E.L. F: f: Librairie Générale de l'Enseignement Libre

Lignum CH: d: Arbeitsgemeinschaft für das Holz

LIGYMM INT: f: Ligue Internationale Gymnastique Moderne d: Internationale Liga für moderne Gymnastik, Graz [A]

LIHG INT: f: Ligue Internationale de Hockey sur Glace [gegr 1908]

LIHS US: e: Long Island Horticultural Society

L.I.I. GB: e: London Insurance Institute

LIKI SU: [d: Kinoingenieurinstitut in Leningrad]

LIKO NL: nl: Liga tegen Imperialisme en Koloniale Overheersching

L.I.L. e: Linguaphone Institute Limited

LIL e: Lunar International Laboratory

LILA INT: s: Liga Internacional de la Librería Antigua f: Ligue internationale de la librairie ancienne, Bruxelles [B, gegr 1947]

LIM BRD: d: Lehrsysteme im Medien-Verbund, 8 München

LIMAS BRD: d: Forschungsgruppe für Linguistik und maschinelle Sprachübersetzung [jetzt: bearbeitung], 53 Bonn

Limex DDR: d: Limex GmbH, Berlin [Gesellschaft für Export von Lizenzen und Patenten]

LIMPL INT: s: Liga Internacional de Mujeres pro Paz y Libertad [f: LIFPL]

LIMRF US: e: Life Insurance Medical Research Fund

Lin GB: e: mil: Lincolnshire Regiment

LIN S: sv: AB Linjeflug [gegr 1957]
LINACO; LINACONGO f: Lignes Natio-
nales Aériennes Congolaises
Linc.Coll. GB: e: Lincoln College, Oxford
Linn. F: f: Société Linnéenne
LINOSCO GB: e: Libraries of North Staf-
fordshire in Co-operation
LINTAS e: Lever International Adver-
tising Service
LIO NL: nl: Laboratorium voor Insekti-
cidenonderzoek
LIP GB: e: London International Press,
Ltd., London E.C. 4
LIPI RI: [e: Indonesian Institute of Sciences]
L.I.P.M. e: Lister Institute of Preventive
Medicine
LIR US: e: Laboratory for Insulation Re-
search [MIT]
LIR. D: d: mil: Landwehrinfanterieregiment
L.I.R. D: d: mil: Lehrinfanterieregiment
LIR GB: e: mil: The London Irish Rifles
(Territorial Army)
LIRA IRL: e: Linen Industry Research
Association
LIRAR F: f: Les Ingénieurs Radio Réunis
LIRC INT: f: Ligue Internationale de la
Représentation Commerciale
LIRI e: Leather Industries Research Institute
L.I.R.R. US: e: Long Island Railroad Com-
pany
LiS S: sv: Liberala studieförbundet, Stock-
holm
LIS F: f: Ligue pour L'Intégration Scolaire
LISA GB: e: Library and Information Science
Abstracts [committee]
LISOD B: nl: Liberaal Syndikaat der Onder-
wijsdiensten
LIT BRD: d: Laboratorium für Isotopen-
technik, 75 Karlsruhe; US: e: Lawrence
Institute of Technology
LITAG A: d: LITAG Literarische Agen-
tur Gredler & Co., Westendorf, Tirol
LITCO RL: e: Lebanese International
Trading Company, Beirut
LITD A: H: d: mil: Landwehrinfanterie

-Truppendivision
LITEF BRD: d: Litton Technische Wer-
ke, 78 Freiburg [gegr 1961]
LiTG BRD: d: Lichttechnische Gesell-
schaft eV
Litkrit INT: [d: Interessengemeinschaft
von Kleinverlagen und Literaturzeit-
schriften sowie deren Autoren aus A,
CH, BRD, gegr 1969 in Göttingen, BR
LITRA CH: f: Ligue Suisse pour l'Organi
sation Rationnelle du Trafic, Bern
LIU US: e: Long Island University
LIV d: Landesinnungsverband
Liv. GB: e: Liverpool University
LIVPL SCOT GB: e: mil: The Liverpool
Scottish (Territorial Army)
LIWENAGEL NL: nl: Vereeniging van
Leraren in Wis- en Natuurkunde aan
Gymnasia en Lycea
LJ D: d: Lutherischer Jugendbund
LJA D: d: Landesjugendamt; d: Lan-
desjugendausschuß; D: d: Verein Leip-
ziger Jahres-Ausstellung
L.J.B.U. GB: e: London Jewish Bakers'
Union
L.J.C. GB: e: London Juvenile Court
L.J.C.B.D.P. GB: e: Local Joint Control
Boards for Dock Pilots
LJP BRD: d: Landesjugendpresse [NRW]
LJR BRD: d: Landesjugendring
L.J.R.T.C. GB: e: London Joint Road
Transport Council
L.J.S. GB: e: London Jews' Society
LjugA D: d: Landesjugendamt
LJustV D: d: Landesjustizverwaltung
LJV BRD: d: Landesjagdverband
LK DDR: d: Länderkammer [1949...58]
BRD: d: Länderkommission [Pferde-
sport]; d: Landeskrankenkasse; d:
mil: Landwehrkavallerie; Landwehr-
korps; d: Landwirtschaftskammer;
D: d: stud: Leipziger Kartell Theolo-
gischer Studentenvereine; D: d: Leuch
tenburgkreis [Jugendverband]; S: sv:
Lidköpings konfektyrindustri;

PL: pl: Liga Kobiet; S: sv: livsmedels-
kommission

.K.A. e: Ladies' Kennel Association

KA BRD: d: Landeskirchenamt; Landes-
kreditausschuß; Landeskriminalamt;
D: d: mil: Luftkriegsakademie [gegr
1935]

KAB S: sv: Luossavaara-Kiirunavaara AB,
Kiruna

Kam. DDR: d: Länderkammer [1949...
58]

KB d: Landeskreditbank; Landeskultur-
behörde

KG DDR: d: Leipziger Kommissions-
und Großbuchhandel, Leipzig C 1

.K.I.S. LR: Latvijas Kara Invalidu Savienība

KJVdSU SU: [d: Leninscher Kommunistischer Jugendverband der Sowjetunion
= Komsomol]

KK DDR: Landeskontrollkommission;
d: Land(es)krankenkasse

.K.K. eo: Loka Kongresa Komitato; D: d:
mil: WK2: Luftkreiskommando

.K.N. S: sv: Landsutskottet för Kristligt
Nykterhetsarbete

.K.N.M.F. GB: e: Lord Kitchener's National Memorial Fund

KP NL: nl: Landelijke Knokploegen;
BRD: d: Landeskriminalpolizei; LR:
Latvijas kommūnistiskā partija; TR: tr:
Liberal Köylü Partisi; LT: Lietuvos Ko-
munistu Partijos

KPA BRD: d: Landeskriminalpolizeiamt

.K.P.R. S: sv: Landsföreningen för kvin-
nans politiska rösträtt

KR D: d: Landeskirchenrat; Landeskul-
turrat; CS: cs: Lidové kurzy ruštiny;
CS: sk: L'udové kurzy ruštiny

.Kr.Ak. D: d: mil: Luftkriegsakademie

KRD SU: [e: Laboratory for the Preservation and Restoration of Documents]

.Krip.A.; L.Kripo.A. D: d: Landeskriminalpolizeiamt

KrK D: d: Landkrankenkasse

L.Kr.Sch.; L.K.S. D: d: mil: Luftkriegs-
schule

LKS PL: pl: Ludowy Klub Sportowy

LKV D: d: Leipziger Künstlerverein

L.L. e: lending library

LL IS: Loftleidir Icelandic Airlines

L.L. GB: e: London Lyceum [ladies' club]

LLA PTM: e: Language and Literary Agency, Kuala Lumpur; LR: Latvijas Lau-
kaimniecības Akadēmija

L.L.A. e: Lend-Lease Administration

L.L.B. e: Local Licensing Bench

LLD DDR: d: mil: Luftlandedivision

LLDiv BRD: d: mil: Luftlandedivision

L.L.E.W. A: d: Lokalbahn Linz — Efer-
ding — Weizenkirchen

L.L.F. GB: e: London Liberal Federation

LLG. D: d: mil: Luftlandegeschwader

LLKJS LR: Latvijas Lenina Kommūnistiskā Jaunatnes Savienība

LLL GB: e: Liberal Liberty League

LLLO US: e: Lend-Lease Liaison Office

LL/LTS BRD: d: mil: Luftlande- und Luft-
transportschule, 8925 Altenstadt

L.L.M. e: Life and Liberty Movement

L.L.P. GB: e: London Labour Party

LLPE US: e: Labor's League for Political
Education

LLS NL: nl: Limburgsch Landbouw Syn-
dicaat

L.&L.S. GB: e: Londonderry and Lough
Swilly [railway]

LLS BRD: d: mil: Luftlandeschule

LLU GB: e: Landing Library Unit, London

LLV BRD: d: Landeslastverteiler

LLZ A: d: Leipnik-Lundenburger Zuckerfabriken AG, Wien 11

L.M. F: f: Laboratoire Municipal

LM CS: cs: Laboratoł Mikrobiologická;
D: d: Landesmusikerschaft

Lm.; LM BRD: d: Landsmannschaft

LM d: Landwirtschaftsminister(ium);
Leipziger Messe; YU: sn: Ljudska Mladina

L.M. GB: e: London Museum

LMA S: sv: Lantmäteristyrelsens arkiv,

Stockholm; LR: Latvijas Mākslas Akadēmija; DDR: d: Leipziger Messeamt

L.M.A. GB: e: Locomotive Manufacturers' Association

L.M.A.A. GB: e: London Master Asphalters' Association

L.M.A.G.B. GB: e: Locomotive Manufacturers' Association of Great Britain

L.M.A.S. GB: e: London and Middlesex Archæological Society

LMB DDR: d: Volkseigene Betriebe des Leichtmaschinenbaus; e: Liquidation and Manpower Board

L.M.B. GB: e: Local Marine Board [Board of Trade]

L.M.B.A. GB: e: London Master Builders' Association

L.M.B.A.T.A. GB: e: Lace Machine Builders and Allied Trades Association

L.M.B.B.I. GB: e: London Master Bakers' Benevolent Institution

L.M.B.C. GB: e: Lady Margaret Boat Club [St.John's College, Cambridge]; Liverpool Marine Biology Committee

LMČ CS: cs: Laboratoř pro Měření Času

L.M.C. e: Labour Management Committee

LMC S: sv: Lantbrukarnas Mjölkcentral, Stockholm; RCH: s: Liga Marítima de Chile

L.M.C. F: f: Ligue Maritime et Coloniale; GB: e: London Musical Club

LMCA GB: e: Lorry Mounted Crane Association

L.M.C.S. GB: e: Leeds Medico-Chirurgical Society

LMD LT: Lietuviu Mokslo Draugija [d: wissenschaftliche Gesellschaft]

L.M.D.C. US: e: Lawyers Military Defense Committee

LME BRD: d: Lehrinstitut für Maschinenbau- und Elektrotechniker, Stuttgart N; S: sv: Telefonaktiebolaget L.M.Ericsson; GB: e: London Metal Exchange

LMEA US: e: Louisiana Music Educators Association

LMED US: e: mil: Light Military Electronics Department [General Electric]

L.M.F. S: sv: Lärarinnornas Missionsförening, Göteborg [gegr 1899]; DK: da: Lærerinnens Misjonsforbund; F: f: Ligue des Mères de Famille; GB: e: London Musical Festival

LMFK S: sv: Kongressen för lärare i matematik, fysik och kemi

LMI SU: [d: Leningrader medizinisches Institut]; US: e: mil: Logistics Management Institute

LMJ YU: sn: Ljudska Mladina Jugoslavije

L.M.K. d: mil: Landesmilitärkommando

LMM D: d: Leipziger Mustermesse

LMO NL: nl: Leraar Middelbaar Onderw

L.M.P. F: f: Laboratoire Municipal de Pa

L.M.P.A. GB: e: London Master Plasterer Association; London Master Printers Association

L.M.P.B. US: e: Labor Management Publ Board

LMPT NATO: e: Logistics and Material Planning Team

L.M.R. GB: e: London Midland Region [railway]

LMRS US: e: Advisory Committee for the Land Mobile Radio Services

LMS CS: cs: Laboratoř Matematických Strojů; S: sv: Riksföreningen för lärare i moderna språk [gegr 1938]; YU: sn: Ljudska Mladina Slovenije, Ljubljana

L.M.S. GB: e: London Malacological Society; London Mathematical Society; London Medical Society; London Me dicity Society; London Microscopical Society; London, Midland and Scottish Railway; London Missionary Soci ety; London Municipal Society

L.M.S.A. GB: e: London Master Stevedor Association

LMSC US: e: Lockheed Missiles & Space Company, Sunnyvale, Calif.

Lmsch. BRD: d: Landsmannschaft

LMSD US: e: Lockheed Missile and Space

Division
.M.S.F. da: Lutherske Menighetssøstres Forening
.M.S.R.; L.M.&S.R. GB: e: London, Midland and Scottish Railway
.MT S: sv: Landsförbundet mot tobaken; F: f: Le Matériel Téléphonique, 92 Boulogne
.M.T.A. GB: e: London Master Typefounders Association
.Mus CH: d: Landesmuseum
.MV D: d: Verband der deutschen Landmaschinenindustrie, Berlin; BRD: d: Fachgruppe Landmaschinen [VDMA]; S: sv: Lidköpings Mekaniska Verkstad
.N.; L/N INT: e: League of Nations
.N. F: f: Libération Nationale; Loterie Nationale
.&N US: e: Louisville & Nashville Railroad Company
.NA D: d: mil: Leitstelle der Nachrichtenaufklärung des Heeres; e: Liberian National Airways; f: Ligue Nationale Aérienne; F: f: Ligue Nationale d'Alsace; US: e: Lithographers National Association
.NČ CS: cs: Laboratoř Vyšší Nervové Činnosti
.N.C.M. f: Laboratoire National de Contrôle des Médicaments
.ND BRD: d: Landesnachforschungsdienst [DRK]
.NE; L&NE US: e: Lehigh & New England Railroad Company
.NEC P: pt: Laboratório Nacional de Engenharia Civil
.. &N. E.R. GB: e: London and North-Eastern Railway
.N.H. F: f: Laboratoire National d'Hydaulique
.N.H.S. GB: e: London Natural History Society
.N.I. I: i: mil: Lega Navale Italiana; I: i: Lega Nazionale Italiana
.N.L. GB: e: mil: Loyal North Lancashire Regiment

L.N.R. F: f: Laboratoire National de Radio-Electricité
Ln.Rgt; L.N.Rgt. D: d: mil: Luftnachrichtenregiment
L.&N.R.R. US: e: = L&N
L.N.S. e: Labour and National Service; Land Nationalization Society; D: d: mil: Luftnachrichtenschule
L.N.S.W.S. GB: e: London and National Society for Women's Service
LNT I: i: Lega Nazionale di Trieste
L.N.T.; Ln.Tr. D: d: mil: Luftnachrichtentruppe
L.N.U. e: League of Nations Union
L.N.W.R.; L.&N.W.R. GB: e: London and North-Western Railway
LO CS: cs: Laboratoř Optiky; NL: nl: Lager Onderwijs; d: Landesorganisation; N: no: Landsorganisasjonen i Norge [d: Gewerkschaftsbund]; S: sv: Landsorganisationen, Stockholm [d: Gewerkschaftsbund]; YU: sn: Ljudski Odbor; PL: pl: Polskie Linie Lotnicze
Lo GB: e: mil: London Regiment
L.O.A. GB: e: London Orchestral Association
L.O.A.S. e: Loyal Order of Ancient Shepherds
LOB NL: nl: Landelijke Organisatie van Bedrijfspluimveehouders; e: Location of Offices Bureau; DDR: d: Lokomotivbau Potsdam-Babelsberg
LOBB NL: nl: Vereniging Landbouwkundig Overleg Bemestings Beleid
LOBE NL: nl: Landelijke Organisatie van Bedrijfseendenhouders
LOBUND US: e: Laboratories of Bacteriology, University of Notre Dame
LoC US: e: Library of Congress
L.O.C. f: Ligue Ouvrière Chrétienne
LOD US: e: Launch Operations Directorate [NASA]
L.O.E. GB: e: League of the Empire
LOF NL: nl: Landelijke Organisatie van Fokkers

L.O.F.C. B: f: Ligue ouvrière des femmes chrétiennes

L.of N. INT: e: League of Nations

LOFTLEIDIR IS: LOFTLEIDIR Icelandic Airlines

LOG N: no: Landbrukets Emballasjeforretning og Gartnernes Felleskjøp

L.O.G. D: d: mil: Landwehroffiziersgemeinschaft

Logair US: e: mil: United States Air Force Logistics Command

LOGEXPO B: f: Logement á l'occasion de l'Exposition universelle et internationale de Bruxelles 1958

Logos E: s: Logos, Información de Prensa, Madrid [d: Nachrichtenagentur]

LogSBw BRD: d: mil: Logistikschule der Bundeswehr, 2 Hamburg

LOK NL: nl: Landelijke Organisatie van Kuikenmesters; H: hu: Levéltárak Országos Központja, Budapest; PL: pl: Liga Obrony Kraju

L.O.M. e: League of Mercy; Loyal Order of Moose

LOMO SU: [d: optisch-mechanische Vereinigung in Leningrad]

LON INT: e: League of Nations

LONA DIN: d: Lokomotiv-Normenausschuß; Fachnormenausschuß Lokomotiven

LOND SCOT GB: e: mil: The London Scottish (Territorial Army)

Lonrho GB: e: London and Rhodesian Mining and Land Company

L.O.O.M. e: Loyal Order of Moose

LOP NL: nl: Landelijke Organisatie van Piepkuikenfokkers

L.O.P. S: sv: Lantbruksorganisationernas Pensionsstiftelse, Stockholm

LOPM DDR: d: Leitende Organe der Partei und der Massenmedien [SED]

L.O.P.M. US: e: Liaison Office for Personnel Management

LOPP PL: pl: Liga Obrony Powietrznej Państwa

L.O.R. e: League of Remembrance

L.o.R.C.S. INT: e: League of Red Cross Societies [= L.R.C.S.]

LORDEX F: f: Société Lorraine de Développement et d'Expansion

LOS NL: nl: Landelijke Organisatie van Pluimveeselecteurs; S: sv: mil: Landstormsofficerssällskap

L.O.S. GB: e: London Orphan School

L.O.S.R. S: sv: mil: Landstormsofficerssällskapens i Sverige Riksförbund

LOT f: mil: Commission logistique organisation Terre - Air - Mer; PL: pl: Polskie Linie Lotnicze, Warszawa

LOTA f: mil: Commission logistique organisation Terre - Air - Mer - Armeme

LOTHIANS GB: e: mil: 1st/2nd Lothian and Border Horse (Territorial Army)

Lott.Ver. d: Lotterieverein

LOV NL: nl: Landelijke Organisatie van Vermeerderaars

LOW NL: nl: Lager Onderwijswet

L.O.W. e: League of Welldoers

LOWA DDR: d: Volkseigene Betriebe de Lokomotiv- und Waggonbaus

LOYALS GB: e: mil: The Loyal Regime (North Lancashire)

L.P. GB: e: Labour Party; d: Landespolizei; Landpolizei; P: pt: Legião Portuguesa; e: Liberal Party; GB: e: Lond Police; D: d: mil: Luftwaffen-Persona amt

LPA F: f: Laboratoire de Physique Appl qué; Laboratoire de Physique de l'At mosphère, Paris; US: e: Labor Press A sociation; d: Landespersonalamt; L despersonalausschuß; Landespolizeia Landespreisamt; Leitpostamt

L.P.A. f: Ligue protectrice des animaux; GB: e: Liverpool Pilots' Association; e: Local Planning Authority

LPAA GB: e: London Poster Advertising Association

LPÄ d: Leitpostämter

L.P.A.-V.S. GB: e: London and Provincia

Anti-Vivisection Society

.P.C. GB: e: Labour Party Conference

PC SF: sv: Lantbruksproducenternas Centralförbund

.P.C. e: Local Productivity Committee; GB: e: London Parochial Charities; London Publicity Club

PC BRD: d: Luftfahrt-Presse-Club eV,6 Ffm

PCC GB: e: London Propaganda Coordinating Committee

.P.C.S. e: League for the Prohibition of Cruel Sports

PD BlnW: d: Landespostdirektion

.P.D.C. GB: e: London Parcels Delivery Company

PE CS: cs: Laboratoř pro Průmyslovou Elektroniku; GB: e: London Press Exchange

.P.E.C. GB: e: Labour Party Education Committee

.P.F. GB: e: Lloyd's Patriotic Fund

.P.F.A. F: f: Ligue Paris Football-Association

.P.F.B.A. GB: e: London and Provincial Fruit Buyers' Association

.P.Form. D: d: Landespolizeiformation

.P.F.S. GB: e: London Playing Fields Society

PG DDR: d: Landwirtschaftliche Produktionsgenossenschaft

PGA e: Ladies Professional Golfers Association

.P.H.A. GB: e: London and Provincial Hairdressers' Association

LPI. D: d: Landespolizeiinspektion

LPI US: e: Louisiana Polytechnic Institute

LPK LR: Latviešu Palīdzības Komiteja; CS: cs: Lékařská Poradní Komise

LPKK DDR: d: Landes-Parteikontrollkommission [SED, 1948...52]

LPL L: f: Ligue Patriotique Luxembourgeoise; US: e: Lunar and Planetary Laboratory, Tuscon, Arizona

L.P.M. PTM: e: Labour Party of Malaya, Kuala Lumpur

L.P.M.A. GB: e: Methodist Local Preachers' Mutual Aid Association

LPN Kamerun: f: Ligue Progressiste des Intérêts Economiques et Sociaux des Populations du Nord Cameroun

LPO CS: cs: Letecký Poradní Orgán

L.P.O. e: Liberal Party Organization;F: f: Ligue française pour la protection des oiseaux; GB: e: London Philharmonic Orchestra

LPÖ A: d: Liberale Partei Österreichs

LPol d: Land(es)polizei

L.P.P. CL: lanka Prajathanthrawadi Pakshaya [d: demokratische Partei]

LPPC CDN: e: Labour Progressive Party of Canada

L.P.P.D. L: Ligue van de Letzeburger Politesche Prisonne'er en Déporte'erten

L.P.P.L. GB: e: Lever's Pacific Plantations Ltd.

L.P.R.S. GB: e: Lancashire Parish Register Society

LPS BRD: d: Landespolizeischule; SF: sv: Lanthushållningssällskapens Centralförbund; I: i: Lavoro e Previdenza Sociale

L.P.S. GB: e: London Philharmonic Society

L.P.T.B. GB: e: London Passenger Transport Board

LPV P: pt: Laboratório de Patologia Veterinária, Lourenço Marques

LPW PL: pl: Laboratorium Przemysłu Węglowego (Wełnianego)

LPZ PL: pl: Liga Przyjaciół Żołnierza

LQFE BR: pt: mil: Laboratório Químico Farmacêutico de Exército

LR S: sv: Läroverkslärarnas Riksförbund [gegr 1912] ; d: Landesregierung; CH: d: Landesring der Unabhängigen; S: sv: Lantbruksförbundets revisionsbyrå AB; Lantmäteriteknikernas riksförening

L.R. GB: e: mil: Leicestershire Regiment; Liaison Regiment; F: f: Ligue de la Republique

LR NL: nl: Schrijvers-Collectief "Links

Richten"

L.R. e: Living Rosary Confraternity; GB: e: Lloyd's Register of Shipping, London; GB: e: mil: The London Regiment; Loyal Regiment

L.R. D: d: mil: Luftwaffen-Rechtsabteilung

LRA US: e: Labor Research Association; e: Lace Research Association; d: Landratsamt; US: e: Lincoln Road Association, Miami Beach

LRAF SU: [e: Long Range Air Force]

L.R.B. D: d: mil: Lehrregiment Brandenburg; GB: e: mil: London Rifle Brigade

L.R.B.A. F: f: Laboratoire de Recherches Balistiques et Aérodynamiques, Vernon

LRB/RANGERS GB: e: mil: London Rifle Brigade/Rangers (Territorial Army)

L.R.C. GB: e: Labour Representation Committee

LRC US: e: Langley Research Center; Lewis Research Center [NASA]

L.R.C. GB: e: London Rowing Club

LRC US: e: Lunar Receiving Center [NASA]

LRCS INT: e: League of Red Cross Societies

LRD GB: e: Labour Research Department, London W.C. 2

L.R.D. GB: e: mil: London Recruiting Depot

LRDG GB: e: mil: WK2: Long-Range Desert Group

LReg d: Landesregierung

L.Reg. D: d: mil: Leibregiment

L.R.F. GB: e: London Regional Federation

LRH BRD: d: Landesrechnungshof

LRI J: e: Labour Research Institute

LRL US: e: Lawrence Radiation Laboratory [University of California]; GB: e: Livermore Research Laboratory; US: e: Lunar Receiving Laboratory, Houston

L.R.M.W. GB: e: Lord Roberts' Memorial Workshops

L.R.N. f: Ligue Républicaine Nationale

LRO NL: nl: Locale Ressorten Ordonnantie

LRO. D: d: mil: WK2: Rohstoffstelle der Luftwaffe

LROC GB: e: Land-Rover Owners' Club

L.Rp. D: d: Liberale Reichspartei

LRPGD US: e: mil: Long Range Proving Ground Division

LRPL US: e: mil: Liquid Rocket Propulsion Laboratory, Dover, N.J.

LRPS GB: e: London Railway Preservation Society

L.R.R. f: Laboratoire Radio-Radar

LRRC GB: e: London Regional Reconstruction Committee

L.R.R.O. e: Land Revenue Record Office

LRS GB: e: Lloyd's Register of Shipping Inc., London E.C. 3

L.&R.Sc.Rgt. GB: e: mil: Lanark and Renfrew Scottish Regiment

L.R.S.L. F: f: Laboratoire de recherches techniques de Saint Louis

LRSM US: e: Laboratory for Research on the Structure of Matter, Philadelphia

L.R.T.L. GB: e: Light Railway Transport League

L.R.W. D: d: mil: Lehr- und Reparaturwerkstatt [Marine]

LRWE GB: e: Long Range Weapons Establishment

LRY US: e: Liberal Religious Youth

LRZ BRD: d: Leibniz-Rechenzentrum, 3 Hannover

LS CS: cs: Laboratoř Strojnická; US: e: mil: Labor Service

L.S. e: Lamb Society; DK: da: Landbrugernes Sammenslutning

LS. D: d: mil: Landesschützen

LS BRD: d: Landsmannschaft Schlesien

L.S. S: sv: Landssekretariatet; e: Law Society; D: d: Leipziger Sezession

LS US: e: Lepidopterists' Society; Leukemia Society; PE: s: Líneas Aéreas Nacionales

L.S. e: Linnaean Society

Ls TR: tr: Lise; Liseler

LS YU: sn: Ljudska Skupščina; S: sv: lokal samorganisation

L.S. GB: e: mil: London Scottish Regiment; GB: e: London Society

L-S. d: Lotsenstation; Lotsenstelle

_S sv: lotsstation
_S SF: mil: Lotta-Svärd
s S: sv: mil: luftbevakningsstation
_.S.; LS d: Luftschutz
_.S. S: sv: Lunds studentkår; Lundsbergs skolas stiftelse; Lyckans soldater, Göteborg
_SA BRD: d: Ländersachverständigenausschuß; d: Landessportausschuß; US: e: Land Settlement Association; Linguistic Society of America, Philadelphia
_SAA US: e: Linen Supply Association of America
_.S.A.C. GB: e: London Sessions Appeal Committee; London Small Arms Company
_SB d: Landessportbund; NL: nl: Liberaal -Socialistische Beweging; BRD: d: Liberaler Schülerbund; S: sv: Linköpings stifts- och landsbibliotek
_.S.B. GB: e: London School Board
_SC US: e: mil: Labor Service Center (Company); Labor Supervision Company; NL: nl: Leidsch Studenten Corps; D: d: Leipziger Sport-Club; Lichtenberger Sport-Club; US: e: Lincoln Sesquicentennial Committee; D: d: Lindauer Segler-Club
_.S.C. GB: e: London Salvage Corps; London Society of Compositors; London Survey Committee
_SC BRD: d: Ludwigshafener Sport-Club
_Sch d: Landesschule
_.Sch.K. D: d: mil: Landesschützenkorps [1919...20]
_SchK D: d: Landesschulkasse [Preußen]
_.Schm. D: d: mil: Lehrschmiede
_.Schupo. D: d: WK2: Luftschutzpolizei
_.S.C.I.A. GB: e: London and Southern Counties Ironmongers' Association
_SCo US: e: mil: Labor Service Company
_SCR INT: f: Ligue des Sociétés de la Croix-Rouge, CH-1211 Genève
_SD BRD: d: stud: Liberaler Studentenbund Deutschlands, 53 Bonn

L.S.D. GB: e: Lightermen, Stevedores and Dockers
LSE US: e: Laser Systems & Electronics, Inc., Tullahoma, Tenn. 37388; e: Laurence, Scott & Electromotors Ltd., Norwich
LSe d: Lehrerseminar
LSE GB: e: London School of Economics and Political Science; London School of English, London W.1; London Stock Exchange
L.S.E.G. e: Livestock Export Group
L.S.F. IRL: e: Local Security Force; S: sv: Luftskyddsförbundet; luftskyddsförening
L.S.F.S. GB: e: Liverpool Seamen's Friend Society
L.S.F.T. GB: e: London School of Foreign Trade, London S.E. 1
LSG BRD: d: Landessozialgericht
L.S.G.C. GB: e: London and Surrey Gliding Club
L.S.H. CDN: e: mil: Lord Strathcona's (Canadian) Horse
LSHA US: e: Louisiana State Horticultural Association
LSHD BRD: d: Luftschutzhilfsdienst
LSHTM GB: e: London School of Hygiene and Tropical Medicine
L.S.I. INT: e: Labour and Socialist International, Brussels [B, gegr 1923]
LS&I US: e: Lake Superior & Ishpeming Railroad
LSI BRD: d: stud: Landesverband der Studentenschaften an Ingenieurschulen
L.S.I. e: Law Society of Ireland
LSI INT: e: Liberal Students International; INT: d: Luzerner Sport-Internationale [gegr 1920]
LSJ GB: e: London School of Journalism, London W.C.1
LSK S: sv: AB Lärarnas Sparköp, Göteborg; d: mil: Landstreitkräfte; D: d: mil: Lotsenkommando- und Seezeichenamt der Kriegsmarine; NL: nl: mil:

Luchtstrijdkrachten; DDR: d: mil: Luftstreitkräfte

L.S.L. GB: e: Linnæan Society of London

LS LRS YU: sn: Ljudska Skupščina Ljudske
Republike Slovenije

LSMB e: Lint and Seed Marketing Board

L.S.M.E. GB: e: London Society of Music
Engravers

LSMI US: e: Lake Superior Mining Institute

LSMS US: e: Louisiana State Medical Society

Lsn S: sv: Lantbruksstyrelsen

LSN LR: Latviešu Studentu Novads

L.S.N. B: f: Ligue sans Nom

LSNR US: e: League of Struggle for Negro
Rights

LSNSW AUS: e: Linnean Society of New
South Wales

L.S.O. e: Labour Supply Organization

LSO BRD: d: Länderfachausschuß für
Straßenbahn- und Obusangelegenheiten

L.S.O. GB: e: London String Orchestra;
London Symphony Orchestra

LSozG BRD: d: Landessozialgericht

LSP BRD: d: Liberal-Soziale Partei [gegr
1967]

L.S.P.C.J. GB: e: London Society for Promoting Christianity amongst the Jews

LSPGA GB: e: London School of Printing
and Graphic Arts

LSPH BRD: d: stud: Landesverband der
Studierenden an Pädagogischen Hochschulen

LSPN CH: f: Ligue Suisse pour la Protection
de la Nature

L.S.Pol. D: d: WK2: Luftschutzpolizei

L.S.R. GB: e: mil: The London Scottish
Regiment (Territorial Army)

L.S.Rgt CDN: e: mil: Lake Superior Regiment

LSRH CH: f: Laboratoire Suisse de Recherches Horlogères

L.S.S. e: Life-Saving Service (Station)

LSS S: sv: Linköpings Segelsällskap

LsS D: d: Luftschutzschule

LSSAH. D: d: NS: Leibstandarte "Adolf

Hitler"

L.S.S.P. CL: Lanka Sama Samaja Party
[gegr 1935]

L.S.S.S.F. S: sv: Lunds svensksocialistisk
studentförening

L.S.S.T.A. GB: e: London Short Sea Tra-
ers' Association

lst S: sv: mil: landstorm(en)

Lst A: d: mil: Landsturm

LST NL: nl: Leidsch Studenten Tooneel

Lst S: sv: Lotsstyrelsen

L.S.T.C. GB: e: London Society of Tie
Cutters

L.S.T.F. GB: e: London and Suburban
Traders' Federation

Lst.HD. A: H: d: mil: Landsturm-Husare
-Division

L.S.T.M. GB: e: Liverpool (London) Sch
of Tropical Medicine

LSTT US: e: mil: Labor Service Transpo
tation Truck ...

L.S.U. e: mil: Labour Service Unit; US:
Louisiana State University

LSUN US: e: mil: Labor Service Unit Na

LSV d: Landessportverband

LSvCo US: e: mil: Labor Service Compar

LSvCtr US: e: mil: Labor Service Center

LSVK CS: cs: Laboratoř pro Studium
Vlastností Kovů

LSvRwyMPCo US: e: mil: Labor Service
Railway Military Police Company

L.S.W.C. GB: e: Liverpool Seamen's Welfare Centre

L.&S.W.R.; L.S.W.R. GB: e: London and
South Western Railway

LŠZ CS: cs: Lidová škola zemědělská

L.S.Z. D: d: WK2: Luftschutzzentrale

L.T. F: f: Laboratoire de Toxicologie

L+T CH: d: mil: Abteilung für Landestop
graphie

LT d: Landtag; S: sv: Lantbruksförbund
Tidskrifts AB; LR: Lauksaimniecîbas
technikums

L.T. GB: e: London Passenger Transport
Board

LTA LR: Latvijas Telegrāfa Agentūra;
e: Lawn Tennis Association; LT: Lietu-
via Tautosakos Archyvas; Lietuvos Tele-
gramu Agentura

L.T.A. GB: e: London Teachers' Association

LTA D: d: Lufttechnische Akademie, Berlin
-Gatow [gegr 1935]

L.T.A.A. AUS: e: Lawn Tennis Association
of Australia

LTAG US: e: mil: Liaison Training and
Advisory Group

LTB NL: nl: Katholieke Land- en Tuin-
bouwbond

L.T.B. e: Laundry Trade Board; GB: e:
London Transport Board, London

L.T.C. e: Land Transfer Committee;
GB: e: Language Tuition Centre, Lon-
don; e: Lawn Tennis Club; GB: e:
London Trades Council

L.T.E.A. e: Licensed Trade Employers'
Association

LFT S: sv: Lantbrukstekniska Förlaget;
US: e: Lithographic Technical Foundation

LTF-QMP P: pt: Laboratório de Técnicas
Físico-Químicas Aplicadas à Mineralogia
e Petrologia, Junta de Investigações do
Ultramar, Lisboa

LTG D: d: Lichttechnische Gesellschaft
[jetzt: LiTG]

L·T·G BRD: d: Lufttechnische Gesellschaft mbH, Stuttgart-Zuffenhausen

LTG BRD: d: mil: Lufttransportgeschwader

LTI US: e: Lowell Textile Institute

LTIB GB: e: Lead Technical Information
Bureau

LTIK BRD: d: Lichttechnisches Institut,
Karlsruhe

L.T.J. F: f: Laboratoire de Toxicologie
Judiciaire

LTJ NL: nl: Land- en Tuinbouw Jongeren

LTK S: sv: Lantbruksförbundets Tidskrifts
AB Korrespondensskola, Stockholm;
BRD: d: mil: Lufttransportkommando

LTKdo BRD: d: mil: Lufttransportkom-

mando

LTM BRD: d: Landesverband der Ton-
künstler und Musiklehrer eV

L.T.M.U. GB: e: London Trousers Makers' Union

LTN PL: pl: Łódzkie Towarzystwo Naukowe

L.T.R.S. e: Low Temperature Research
Station

LTŠ CS: cs: Lesnická Technická Škola

LT&S GB: e: London, Tilbury & South-
end Railway

L.T.S. GB: e: London Topographical
(Typographical) Society

LTSBw BRD: d: mil: Lufttransportschu-
le der Bundeswehr

L.T.Schl. BRD: d: Bayerische Landesanstalt für Tierseuchenbekämpfung.
Schleißheim

L.T.&S.R.; L.T.S.R. GB: e: London,
Tilbury and Southend(-on-Sea) Railway

L.T.T. F: f: Lignes Télégraphiques et Télé-
phoniques, Paris

LTU e: Loughborough University of Technology; BRD: d: Lufttransportunter-
nehmen GmbH & Co. KG, 4 Düsseldorf

LTV US: e: Ling-Temco-Vought, Inc.,
Dallas, Texas

LU S: sv: lagutskottet [riksdagen]; US: e:
Langston University; LR: Latvijas Uni-
versitate; US: e: Lehigh University;
CS: cs: Lidová Universita; INT: f: Ligue
Universelle, Den Haag; US: e: Loyola
University; S: sv: Lunds Universitet

LUA GB: e: Liverpool Underwriters Association

LUAR P: [f: Ligue d'union et d'action
révolutionnaire, Paris]

L.U.B. B: f: Libre Université de Bruxelles

LUB S: sv: Lunds universitetsbibliotek

LUCAF INT: [d: Ausschuß für Frequenz-
zuteilung für Radioastronomie und
Raumwissenschaft]

LUCCO CY: e: Land Utilization Coordination Committee

LUCE I: i: La Unione Cinematografica Educativa

Luck IND: e: Lucknow University

LUF WAN: e: Labour Unity Front; d: Landwirtschaftliche Untersuchungs- und Forschungsanstalt

L.U.F. CH: f: Librairie de l'Université de Fribourg; S: sv: Lunds universitets folkminnesarkiv

LUFA BRD: d: Verband Deutscher landwirtschaftlicher Untersuchungs- und Forschungsanstalten, 61 Darmstadt

LUFORO GB: e: London Unidentified Flying Objects Research Organization

LÚFPT CS: cs: Laktologický Ústav Fakulty Potravinářské Technologie

Luftag BRD: d: Aktiengesellschaft für Luftverkehrsbedarf [gegr 1953]

Luft.Sp.S. D: d: mil: Marineluftsperrschule

L.U.G.I.; Lugi S: sv: Lunds universitets gymnastik- och idrottsförening

LUH BRD: d: Vereinigte Versicherungen für Leben, Unfall und Haftpflicht [Deutsche Angestelltengewerkschaft]

LUHM S: sv: Lunds universitets historiska museum

L.U.I.P.V. INT: f: L'Union internationale contre le péril vénérien

L.U.J.B.M. GB: e: London Union of Journeymen Basket Makers

L.U.J.S. GB: e: London University Journalism Society

LUMF US: e: mil: Lockheed Underwater Missile Facilities, Sunnyvale, Calif.

LUMI I: i: Lega Universitaria Monarchica Italiana

L.U.N. INT: e: League of United Nations

LUNABA CH: d: Luzerner Nationale Briefmarken-Ausstellung [1951]

L.U.O.T.C. GB: e: mil: London University Officers' Training Corps

LUPO 69 CH: d: 1.Luftpostausstellung, Luzern, 26...28 Apr 1969

Luposta BRD: d: Luftpostausstellung, Köln, 1959

L.U.Q. CDN: e: Laval University, Quebec

LUR A: d: mil: Landwehr-Ulanen-Regiment

L.U.R. F: f: Ligue Urbaine et Rurale; GB: e: London Underground Railways

Lurag D: d: Luftverkehrsgesellschaft Ruhrgebiet AG, Essen

L.U.S. e: Land Utilization Society; GB: London Union of Sailmakers

Luschupo. D: d: WK2: Luftschutzpolizei

Lusitania P: pt: Agência Lusitania [d: Nachrichtenagentur]

LuSK. d: mil: Luftstreitkräfte

LuStB d: Landes- und Staatsbibliothek

L.U.T. INT: f: Loge uni des théosophes s: Logia Unida de Teósofos, Bombay [gegr 1909]

LuUB d: Landes- und Universitätsbibliothek

LUV US: e: Let Us Vote [18-year-olds]

Luxair L: [d: Luftverkehrsgesellschaft, gegr 1962]

LV d: Landesverband; Landesverein; A: d: Landesversammlung; A: d: mil: Landesverteidigung; BRD: d: Lebensversicherung; US: e: Lehigh Valley Railroad Company; YV: s: Línea Aeropostal Venezolana

L.V. S: sv: Litteraturvännerna

LV DDR: d: mil: Luftverteidigung des Landes

LV 1871 BRD: d: Lebensversicherung von 1871 aG München, 8 München 33

LVA S: sv: Lackeringsverkstädernas Arbetsgivareförbund; BRD: d: Landesvermessungsamt; Landesversicherungsamt; Landesversicherungsanstalt; Landesversorgungsamt; d: Landesversuchsanstalt; Landesverwaltungsausschuß; CH: d: Landwirtschaftliche Versuchsanstalt; CS: cs: Letecká Vojenská Akademie

L.V.A. D: d: Luftschiff-Versuchsanstalt

LVAB BlnW: d: Landesversicherungsanstalt Berlin [bis Juli 1952: VAB]

VAmt d: Landesversicherungsamt

VAnst d: Landesversicherungsanstalt

V.A.S. GB: e: Land Valuation Assessors of Scotland

VB BRD: d: Landesvermögens- und Bauabteilung; D: d: Landesverwaltung Berlin; Leipziger Verein Barmenia [private Krankenversicherung]; DDR: d: Leipziger Verkehrsbetriebe

V.B. B: f: Ligue Vélocipédique Belge

VB BRD: d: Luftsportverband Bayern

V.B.I. e: Licensed Victuallers' Benevolent Institution

VBS BRD: d: Landesverband der Verleger und Buchhändler Saar

V.C. GB: e: London Visitors Club

Vd d: Landesverband

VD BRD: d: Landesverband der vertriebenen Deutschen; D: d: Literarischer Verein Dom-Gymnasium, Magdeburg

VDiv BRD: d: mil: Luftverteidigungsdivision

V.D.L. GB: e: Licensed Victuallers' Defence League of England and Wales

V.d.Pr.J. D: d: Landesverband der Preußischen Jäger

VersA d: Landesversicherungsamt; Landesversorgungsamt

VersÄ d: Landesversorgungsämter

VersAnst d: Landesversicherungsanstalt

VersG d: Landesversorgungsgericht

VersiA d: Landesversicherungsamt

VersiAnst d: Landesversicherungsanstalt

Vert. D: d: mil: Landesverteidigung

V.F. F: f: mil: Légion Volontaires Français [d: gegen SU, WK2]; F: f: Ligue des Volontaires Français [pendant l'occupation, WK2]

VF INT: sv: Lutherska världsförbundet, Genève [CH]

V.f.F. D: d: Landesvereinigung für Frauenbewegung

VFKI LR: Latvijaś Valsts Fiziskās Kultūras Institūts

VG d: Landesverwaltungsgericht; DDR:

d: Lehr- und Versuchsgut; A: d: Staatlich genehmigte Literarische Verwertungsgesellschaft (LVG), Wien 3; D: d: Luftverkehrsgesellschaft, Berlin-Johannisthal

LVH CS: cs: Laboratoř Vodního Hospodářství; D: d: Lutherisches Verlagshaus, Berlin

LVI LR: Latvijas Valsts Izdevnieciba

LVK CH: d: mil: Landesverteidigungskommission [seit 1891]; d: mil: Luftverteidigungskommando

L.V.Kdo. d: mil: Luftverteidigungskommando

LvKS S: sv: mil: Luftvärnets kadettskola, Linköping

LVL CS: cs: Laboratoř Vysokomolekulárnich Látek; CH: d: Schweizerischer Landesverband für Leibesübungen; D: d: nach WK2: Landesverkehrsleitung

L.V.L. GB: e: Legislative Voters League

LVM CS: cs: Laboratoř Výzkumu Materiálu; A: d: mil: Landesverteidigungsministerium

LVN 131 BRD: d: Landesvereinigung Niedersachsen der 131er, Oldenburg i.O.

LVNČ CS: cs: Laboratoř Vyšší Činnosti

LvOS S: sv: mil: Luftvärnsofficersskola, Stockholm

LVP BRD: d: Liberale Volkspartei, 3056 Rehburg

Lvpt D: d: Landvolkpartei

L.V.R.R. US: e: Lehigh Valley Railroad Company

LVS DDR: d: Landesverwaltung Sachsen

L.V.S. GB: e: London Vegetarian Society

LVSCL CS: cs: Letecká Vyšetřovací Stanice Československého Letectva

LVSČSAC CS: cs: Literárněvědná Společnost při ČSAV

LvSS S: sv: mil: Luftvärnsskutskolan, Stockholm, Väddö

LVU BRD: d: Landesvereinigung Rheinland-Pfälzischer Unternehmerverbände; LR: Latvijas Valsts Universitāte

LVÚ CS: cs: Letecký Výzkumný Ústav

LVuBA BRD: d: Landesvermögens- und Bauabteilung def Oberfinanzdirektion

LVV NL: nl: Ministerie van Landbouw, Visserij en Voedselvoorziening; BRD: d: Landesverkehrsverband

LVZ CH: d: Lebensmittelverein Zürich

Lw d: Landeswohlfahrtsamt

Lw. d: mil: Landwacht; Landwehr; d: Landwirtschaft(sministerium); Landwirtschaftsschule

L.W. GB: e: London Waterguard

Lw BRD: d: mil: Luftwaffe

LWA D: d: nach WK2: Landeswirtschaftsamt; D: d: Landeswohlfahrtsamt; Landwirtschaftsamt [auch: LwA; L.W.A.]

LwA BRD: d: mil: Luftwaffenamt

L.W.A.B. B: f: Ligue Wallonne de l'Agglomération Bruxelloise

LwAusbRgt BRD: d: mil: Luftwaffenausbildungsregiment

LwB d: Landwirtschaftsbehörde

LWB INT: d: Lutherischer Weltbund, Genf [CH]

LWB/RD INT: d: Lutherischer Weltbund – Rundfunkdienst

LWC NL: nl: Landelijk Werklozen Comité; GB: e: London Weather Centre, London W.C.1

L.W.C. GB: e: London Writers Circle

L.W.D. e: Local Work Department; PL: pl: Lotnicze Warsztaty Doświadczalne, Lodz

LWF INT: e: Lutheran World Federation, Geneva [CH]

LwFlaRgt BRD: d: mil: Luftwaffenflugabwehrregiment

Lw.Fü.St.; Lw.Fü.Stb. D: d: mil: Luftwaffen-Führungsstab

LwG d: Landwirtschaftsgericht

LWG NATO: e: Logistic Working Group

LwK; LWK BRD: d: Landwirtschafts-kammer

LWL US: e: mil: Land Warfare Laboratory [Army] ; Limited War Laboratory, Aberdeen, Md.

LwM; LWM d: Landwirtschaftsminister(ium)

LWMEL US: e: Leonard Wood Memorial for the Eradication of Leprosy

L.W.P. GB: e: London Women's Parliament

LwPiRgt BRD: d: mil: Luftwaffenpionier regiment

LwPkRgt BRD: d: mil: Luftwaffenparkregiment

Lw.Pro.Zug D: d: mil: WK2: Luftwaffen-Propagandazug

LWR D: d: mil: Luftwaffenring

LWS NL: nl: Landbouw Winter Scholen; PL: pl: Lubelska Wytwórnia Samolotów Lublin; INT: e: Lutheran World Servic

L.W.T.M.A. GB: e: London Wool Terminal Market Association

Lw.Tr.Rgt. D: d: mil: Luftwaffen-Transport-Regiment

LWU BRD: d: Laboratorium für Werkstoffuntersuchung, 8 München 50

L.&W.V. US: e: Lackawanna and Wyoming Valley Railroad Company

LWV BRD: d: Zweckverband Landeswasserversorgung, 7 Stuttgart; Landeswohfahrtsverband; D: d: nach WK2: Landwirtschaftsversorgungsamt; US: e: League of Women Voters

LwVersRgt BRD: d: mil: Luftwaffenversorgungsregiment

LWVUS US: e: League of Women Voters of the United States

LY IL: EL AL Israel Airlines Ltd., Tel Aviv; GB: e: mil: Prince Albert's Own Leicestershire Yeomanry; Queen's Own Lowland Yeomanry

LYCC GB: e: Lancashire Yorkshire Canary Club

L.&Y.R.; L.Y.R. GB: e: Lancashire and Yorkshire Railway

Lyz. d: Lyzeum

L.Z. F: f: Laboratoire de Zoologie

Lz. D: d: mil: Lazarett

LZ BRD: d: Liga des zwanzigsten Jahrhunderts [gegr 1951 in Heidelberg]

Lz. D: d: mil: Luftzeugamt

L.Z.A. D: d: WK1: Leder-Zuweisungsamt der Kriegsrohstoff-Abteilung; D: d: mil: Luftzeugamt

LZB BRD: d: Landeszentralbank

LZBeh. d: Landeszentralbehörde

LZPO PL: pl: Łódzki Zarząd Przemysłu Odzieżowego

LZS PL: pl: Ludowe Zespoły Sportowe

LZS. D: d: mil: Luftzeugstab

LZT NL: nl: Beurs voor Landbouw Zuivel en Techniek

LZV BRD: d: Verband Deutscher Lesezirkel eV

M. GB: e: Magistrate Court; e: mil: Medical Service

M US: e: Montour Railroad; S: sv: Motormännens riksförbund

3-M BRD: d: 3-M-Puppenfabrik Ma.E.Maar, 8631 Mönchröden

3M Company US: e: Minnesota Mining and Manufacturing Company, St.Paul 6

MA US: e: Magnesium Association

M.A. e: Malayan Airways

MA = MALEV

Ma GB: e: mil: Manchester Regiment

MA D: d: mil: Marineakademie; Marineartillerie; US: e: Maritime Administration; BRD: d: Bahn: Maschinenamt; GB: e: Mathematical Association of Great Britain; D: d: mil: Medizinal-Abteilung; d: Medizinische Akademie; Meldeamt; BRD: d: Messe-Ausschuß des ZVEI, 6 Ffm; US: e: Metric Association

M.A. d: mil: Militär-Akademie

Ma. D: d: Militärarrestanstalt

MA NL: nl: mil: Militaire Academie

M.A. e: mil: Military Academy; e: Mining Association

MA D: d: mil: Ministeramt [Reichswehrministerium]

M.A. F: f: Ministère de l'Agriculture; F: f: mil: Ministère des Armées; s: Ministerio de la Agricultura; R: ro: Ministerul Agriculturii; e: Ministry of Agriculture (, Fisheries and Food); Ministry of Aviation

MA l: Societas Missionarorum Africae; Societas Lugdunensis pro Missionibus ad Africam; PL: pl: Muzeum Archeologiczne

M&A US: e: Missouri & Arkansas Railway Company

MA d: Moralische Aufrüstung [e: MRA]; N: no: Motorførernes Avholdsforbund

M.A. e: mil: Mountain Artillery

MA D: d: Verband des Deutschen Kunst- und Antiquitätenhandels eV, München

Ma; MA.; M.A. D: d: mil: Munitionsanstalt

M.A. F: f: Musée de l'Air; Musée de l'Armée

MA P: pt: Museu de Angola, Luanda

M.A. GB: e: Museums Association; S: sv Kungliga Musikaliska Akademien

MA PL: pl: Muzeum Archeologiczne

MAA DZ: f: Maison de l'Agriculture Algérienne; CDN: e: Manitoba Association of Architects; BRD: d: Mannheimer Abendakademie; GB: e: Manufacturer Agents' Association of Great Britain an Ireland; US: e: Manufacturers Aircraft Association; D: d: mil: Marineartillerie abteilung; US: e: Mathematical Association of America, Ithaca, N.Y. [gegr 191]

M.A.A. D: d: mil: Matrosen-Artillerie-Abteilung; e: Medical Abstainers' Association

M.A.A. US: e: Medieval Academy of America, Massachusetts [gegr 1925]

M.A.A. D: d: Militärische Stelle der Nach richtenabteilung des Auswärtigen Amts Berlin

MAA B: f: Ministère des Affaires Africain Ministère des Affaires Etrangères et du Commerce, Bruxelles; DDR: d: Ministe rium für Auswärtige Angelegenheiten

M.A.A. GB: e: Motor Agents' Association

MAAC GB: e: Mastic Asphalt Advisory Council; NATO: e: Mutual Assistance Advisory Committee

MAACP US: e: mil: Mediterranean-African Airlift Command Post

MAAF e: mil: WK2: Mediterranean Allied Air Forces

MAAG US: e: mil: Military Assistance Advisory Group

M.A.A.G.B. GB: e: Motor Agents' Association of Great Britain

MAAG-J US: e: mil: Military Assistance Advisory Group, Japan

MAAMA US: e: mil: Middletown Air Materiel Area, Middletown, Pa.

M.A.A.M.C. e: Motor Aircraft and Allied Manufacturing Companies

MAAN US: e: Mutual Advertising Agencies Network

MAAR US: e: mil: Mojave Antiaircraft Range [seit 1941]

MAB US: e: Materials Advisory Board

M.A.B. e: Medical Advisory Board; GB: e: Metropolitan Asylums Board; GB: US: e: mil: Munitions Assignment Board

MABA BRD: d: Mannheimer Briefmarken -Ausstellung

M.Abn.I. D: d: mil: Marineabnahmeinspektion

M.Abn.ZK. D: d: mil: Marineabnahmezentralamt (Kriegsschiffbau)

MABV BRD: d: Mittelrheinischer Amateur -Box-Verband

M.A.B.Y.S. e: Metropolitan Association for Befriending Young Servants

MAC US: e: Maintenance Advisory Committee [NSIA]; US: e: mil: Major Air Command; BRD: d: Mannheimer Automobil-Club

M.A.C. F: f: Manufacture Nationale d'Armes de Châtellerault; NZ: e: Massey Agricultural College

MAC NL: nl: mil: Materialen Advies Commissie; US: e: mil: Medical Administrative Corps; Mediterranean Air Command; e: Middle Atlantic Conference; Military and Administrative Committee [China]; US: e: mil: Military Affairs Committee; Military Airlift Command, Scott AFB, Ill. [ab 1 Jan 1966]; UN: e: mil: Military Armistice Commission [Korea]; YV: s: Ministerio de Agricultura y Cría; D: d: Mittelrheinischer Automobil-Club, Köln [gegr 1904]; UN: e: mil: Mixed Armistice Commission

M.A.C. e: Model Airplane Club; B: f: Mouvement d'Action Civile; SN: f: Mouvement Autonome de Casamanoe

MAC pt: Movimento Anti-Colonial; BR: pt: Movimento Anticomunista; P: pt:

Museu Dr. Álvaro de Castro, Lourenço Marques

mac 64 I: [d: Ausstellung chemischer Apparate, Mailand, 26 Nov...4 Dez 1964]

M.A.C.A. e: Mental After-Care Association

MACA US: e: mil: Military Airlift Clearance Authority

MACAF e: mil: WK2: Mediterranean Allied Coastal Air Force

MACAIR US: e: mil: Munitions Assignment Committee Air

MACE US: e: Military and Computer Electronics Corp.

MACEF INT: [d: internationale Ausstellung von Haushaltartikeln, Glas- und Kristallwaren, Keramik, Eisenwaren, Werkzeugen in Mailand]

MACHEVO INT: [d: internationale Fachmesse für die Verfahrensindustrie—Apparate und Maschinen für die chemische und pharmazeutische Industrie, Molkerei-,Nahrungsmittel- und Getränkeindustrie, Luft- und Wasserreinigung, Utrecht]

MACNA Kamerun: f: Mouvement d'Action Nationale

MACOI US: e: mil: Military Assistance Command's Office of Information [South Vietnam]

MACROPLASTIC INT: [d: internationale Kunststoffmesse, Utrecht]

MACTHAI US: e: mil: Military Assistance Command Thailand

MACV US: e: mil: Military Assistance Command Vietnam

M.A.C.V.G. F: f: Ministère des Anciens Combattants et Victimes de la Guerre

M.A.C.Y.G. e: Mabys Association for the Care of Young Girls

MAD D: d: Mädel-Arbeitsdienst; BRD: d: mil: Militärischer Abschirmdienst; US: e: mil: Military Assistance Division [EUCOM]

MADAEC US: e: mil: Military Application Division of the Atomic Energy Commission

MADC US: e: Maritime Administration, Department of Commerce

MADISZ H: hu: Magyar Demokratikus Ifjusági Szövetség, Budapest

MADOME H: [d: Fotoklub]

MADRO PL: pl: Zakłady Budowy i Naprawy Mazyn Drogowych "Madro"

MADU EAT: e: Mombasa African Democratic Union

MADW US: e: mil: Military Air Defense Warning Network

MAE US: e: Maine Association of Engineers; GB: e: Manchester Association of Engineers

M.A.E. IRL: e: Medical Association of Eire; F: f: Ministère des Affaires Etrangères; CGO: f: Mission Anti-Erosive, Bukavu

MAE US: e: Museum of Atomic Energy; PL: pl: Muzeum Archeologiczne i Etnograficzne

MAEA INT: pl: Międzynarodowa Agencja Energii Atomowej

MAECON INT: e: Mid-America Electronics Conference

MAEE GB: e: mil: Marine Aircraft Experimental Establishment

MAEF I: i: Ministero dell'Agricoltura e Foreste

MäKB A: d: Mährischer Künstlerbund, Wien

MAELU US: e: Mutual Atomic Energy Liability Underwriters

MAEM MOC: pt: Missão Antropologica e Etnologica de Moçambique

MAeSz H: hu: Magyar Aero Szövetség, Budapest

M.A.&F.; MAF GB: e: Ministry of Agriculture and Fisheries

MAF S: sv: Motorbranschens Arbetsgivareförbund; DK: da: Motorførernes Afholds Forbund

M.A.F.A. DZ: f: Maison des Agriculteurs Français d'Algérie; GB: e: Manchester Academy of Fine Arts

M.A.F.F. GB: e: Ministry of Agriculture, Fisheries and Food

MÁFI H: hu: Magyar Állami Földtani Intézet, Budapest

MAFIA I: i: Morte alla Francia

MAFISZ H: hu: Magyar Forradalmi Ifjumunkás Szövetség, Budapest

MÁFKI H: hu: Magyar Ásványolaj- és Földgázkisérleti Intézet, Budapest

Mafo BRD: d: Mafo - Institut für Markt-, Meinungs- und Absatzforschung GmbH, 6 Ffm

MAFSI US: e: Manufacturers' Agents for Food Service Industry

MAG US: e: Medical Association of Georgia; BRD: d: Milchabsatz-Genossenschaft; US: e: mil: Military Advisers Group

M.A.G.B. GB: e: Mining Association of Great Britain

Magd. GB: e: Magdalen College, Cambridge Oxford

Maghazet PL: pl: Przedsiębiorstwi Magazynowania Towarów Handlu Zagranicznego

MAGIC US: e: mil: Military Advisory Group in China

MAGU P: pt: Missão de Astronomia e Gravimetria do Ultramar, Junta de Investigações do Ultramar, Lisboa

MAHA PTM: e: Malayan Agri-Horticultural Association

MAHISSA s: Maíces Híbridos y Semillas S.A.

MAI NL: nl: Maatschappelijk Advies- en Inlichtingenbureau van de Nederlandsche Vereeniging ter Behartiging van de Belangen der Jonge Meisjes; S: sv: Malmö Allmänna Idrottsförening

M.A.I. GB: e: Midland Airways Limited

MAI DDR: d: Ministerium für Außen- und Innerdeutschen Handel, Berlin; I: i: Ministero dell'Africa Italiana; R: ro: Ministerul Afacerilor Interne, București; US: e: Museum of the Amer ican Indian

MAiE PL: pl: Muzeum Archeologiczne i Etnograficzne

MAIG J: e: Matsushita Atomic Industrial Group

MAiH PL: pl: Ministerstwo Aprowizacji i Handlu

MAILLEUROP INT: f: Comité des Industries de la Maille de la CEE, Bruxelles

Maintex GB: e: Maintenance Conference and Exhibition, London

MAISAC US: e: mil: Middle Atlantic Inter-Service Athletic Conference

MAJCOM US: e: mil: Major (Air) Command

MAK hu: Magyar Akadémikusok Köre, Praha

M.A.K. S: sv: Malmö Automobilklubb

M.Ak. D: d: mil: Marineakademie; Militärärztliche Akademie

M.Akad. D: d: mil: Marineakademie

M.A.Kdo. D: d: mil: Marineabnahmekommando; Marineabschnittskommando

Maki IL: [d: kommunistische Partei]

MAKK hu: Magyar Akadémikusok Keresztény Köre, Praha

MAKO S: sv: Maskinaktiebolaget Karlebo, Stockholm; Medelålderns arbetskraftsorganisation

MAL PTM: e: Malayan Airways Limited

M.A.L. F: f: Manufacture Nationale d'Armes de Levallois; D: d: mil: Marineausrüstungslager

MALAY GB: e: mil: The Malay Regiment

MALC e: Midwest Academie Librarians Conference

M.A.L.C. CDN: e: Model Aircraft League of Canada

MALERT H: hu: Magyar Légiforgalmi Részvénytársaság, Budapest

MALEV H: hu: Magyar Légiközlekedési Vállalat, Budapest

MALj YU: sn: Mestni Arhiv v Ljubljani

MAllg D: d: mil: Allgemeine Abteilung [OKM]

M.A.L.T. GB: e: mil: Military Administration of Liberated Territory

Malt.-R.-O.; Malt.Rr.O. D: d: Malteserritterorden

MAM BRD: d: Management Akademie München, 8 München

MAMA US: e: mil: Middletown Air Materiel Area

MAMP US: e: mil: Michigan Army Missile Plant

MAN GB: e: mil: Manchester Regiment

Man. GB: e: Victoria University of Manchester

M.A.N. BRD: d: Maschinenfabrik Augsburg-Nürnberg AG; RA: s: Ministerio de Agricultura de la Nación; R: ro: Ministerul Aprarii Naționale, București

MANA US: e: Manufacturers' Agents National Association

Manc. GB: e: Victoria University of Manchester

MANC e: Mozambique African National Congress

MANCH GB: e: mil: The Manchester Regiment

M.A.N.E.X. GB: [d: Marktforschungsfirma]

Manit. CDN: e: University of Manitoba

Manit.Dns CDN: e: mil: Manitoba Dragoons

MANO s: Movimiento de Acción Nacionalista Organizado

MANR WAN: e: Ministry of Agriculture, Northern Region

MANS D: d: mil: Marineartillerienachrichtenschule

Mansf. GB: e: Mansfield College, Oxford

MANTIS GB: e: Manchester Technical and Commercial Information Service

M.A.N.U. e: Mozambique African National Union

MANURHIN F: f: Manufacture de Machines du Haut-Rhin, Mulhouse-Bourtzwiller

MANWD BRD: d: Meteorologisches Amt

für Nordwestdeutschland

MANWEB GB: e: Merseyside and North Wales Electricity Board

M.A.N.Z. e: Montreal, Australia and New Zealand Shipping Co.Ltd.

M.A.Nza. D: d: mil: Marineartillerie-Nebenzeugamt

M.A.O.E. GB: e: Manchester Association of Engineers

MAP MA: f: Maghreb Arabe Presse, Rabat [gegr 1959]

M.A.P. PTM: e: Malaysian Alliance Party, Kuala Lumpur

MAP CS: cs: Masarykova Akademie Práce; F: f: Méditerranée - Atlantique - Pyrénées [d: Hotelkette] ; US: e: mil: Military Aid (Assistance) Program; Military Association of Podiatrists; CS: cs: Ministerstvo Automobilového Průmyslu a Zemědělských Strojů; PL: pl: Ministerstwo Administracji Publicznej

M.A.P. GB: e: WK2: Ministry of Aircraft Production

MAP US: e: Mississippi Action for Progress [poverty program] ; GH: e: Moslem Association Party; B: f: Mouvement d'Action et Propagande

MAPAG US: e: mil: Military Assistance Program Advisory Group

MAPAI IL: [d: sozialdemokratische Partei Israels]

MAPAM IL: [d: sozialistische Arbeiterpartei]

MAPB I: i: Ministero per l'Assistenza Post - Bellica

Mapha d: Mathematisch-physikalischer Arbeitskreis [Universität Berlin]

MAPI US: e: Machinery and Allied Products Institute; J: e: Mitsubishi Atomic Power Industries

MAPONY US: e: Maritime Association of the Port of New York

Mapotel F: f: France-Mapotel [d: Hotelkette]

MAPRC e: mil: Mediterranean Allied Photographic Reconnaissance Comman

MAPS US: e: mil: Military Academy Preparatory School

MAPU RCH: [d: Bewegung der vereinten Volksaktion]

MAQ GB: e: Monmouthshire Associated Quarries

MAR D: d: mil: Marineartillerieregiment; CDN: e: Maritime Central Airways, Limited

M.A.R. D: d: mil: WK1: Matrosen-Artillerie-Regiment; F: f: Mouvement d'Action Rurale

MAR BR: [d: Bewegung der revolutionären Aktion, Rio de Janeiro]

MARA PTM: Majlis Amanah Ra'ayat (Bumiputra), Kuala Lumpur

MARAIRMED NATO: e: Maritime Air Forces Mediterrannean

MarAMA US: e: mil: Marianas Air Materiel Area

MArb. d: Minister(ium) für Arbeit

Marburger Bund BRD: d: Verband der angestellten Ärzte (Marburger Bund) eV

MARCE US: e: mil: Military Assets Redistribution Center, Europe

MARCOGAZ INT: [d: Zusammenschluß der gasfachlichen Organisationen der EWG]

MARCORDISBOF US: e: mil: Marine Corps Disbursing Office

MARDI PTM: e: Malaysian Agricultural Research and Development Institute, Kuala Lumpur

MARG PL: pl: Malarstwo, Architektura, Rzeźba, Grafika [Club] ; IND: e: Modern Architectural Research Group

MarGebSt D: d: mil: Marinegebührnisstelle [OKM]

MarHKzl D: d: mil: Marinehauptkanzlei [OKM]

MarHv D: d: mil: Marinehausverwaltung [OKM]

MaritAdmin US: e: Maritime Administration

MaritCom US: e: Maritime Commission
Mar.K. d: Marianische Kongregation
Mar.-K. D: d: mil: Marine-Korps
Marlag D: d: mil: Marinelager [Kriegs-gefangenenlager für Marineangehörige]
MarMv D: d: mil: Marinematerialienver-waltung [OKM]
MARNAVCOR US: e: mil: Marine Navy Corps
M.A.R.P. I: i: Movimento Autonomie Regionali Padane
MARPAC US: e: mil: Headquarters, Department of the Pacific [USMC]
Marplan GB: [e: market and public opinion research organization] ; BRD: d: Marplan Forschungsgesellschaft für Markt und Verbrauch mbH, 6 Ffm
Mar.Rüst. D: d: mil: Chef der Kriegsmarine-rüstung
MARS H: hu: Magyar Szövegirok Zene-szerzö és Zenemükiadok Szövetsége
MArs BRD: d: mil: Marinearsenal
MARS US: e: mil: Military Affiliate(d) Radio System; GB: e: Modern Architectural Research Society
MARTC US: e: mil: Marine Air Reserve Training Command
MArtS BRD: d: mil: Marineartillerieschule
MArtVsuSt BRD: d: mil: Marineartillerie-versuchsstelle
M.A.R.U. GB: e: mil: Mobile Aircraft Repair Unit
MARVA NL: nl: mil: Marine Vrouwen Afdeling [gegr 1944]
Mar.W. D: d: mil: Marinewerft
Mar.Wehr. D: d: mil: Chef der Kriegsmarine Wehr
MarZahl D: d: mil: Marinezahlstelle [OKM]
M.A.S. GB: e: Manchester Astronomical Society; F: f: Manufacture Nationale d'Armes de Saint-Etienne; D: d: mil: Marineartillerieschule; Marine-Ausrü-stungsstelle; I: i: Marittima Anonima Siciliana, S.p.A. [d: Reederei]
MAS CH: d: Marxistische Aktion der

Schweiz; NL: nl: Marxistische Arbeider-school; US: e: Maryland Academy of Sciences; DDR: d: Maschinenausleih-station [1949...52, dann: MTS] ; US: e: Massachusetts Audubon Society; Michigan Academy of Science; Michigan Audubon Society; NATO: e: Military Agency for Standardization, London
M.A.S. e: Military Antiquarian Society
MAS US: e: Milwaukee Astronomical Society; Mississippi Academy of Science; Missouri Academy of Sciences
M.A.S. e: Model Abattoir Society; I: i: Movimento di Autonomia Socialista; Movimento di Azione Sociale
MASA US: e: Mail Advertising Service Association; BRD: d: Maschinen-Son-derautomatengesellschaft MASA GmbH, 7418 Metzingen; US: e: Medical Association of the State of Alabama
M.A.S.A. e: Mines African Staff Association
MASAF e: mil: WK2: Mediterranean Allied Strategic Air Force
MASC US: e: mil: Middletown Air Service Command
MASCH D: d: Marxistische Arbeiterschule, Berlin [gegr 1926-27]
Maschb.A. D: d: Maschinenbauanstalt
Maschfbr d: Maschinenfabrik
MASCHINOEXPORT BG: [d: Außen-handelsunternehmen der staatlichen Wirtschaftsvereinigung Metallbearbei-tungsmaschinen, Sofia]
MASH US: e: mil: Mobile Army Surgical Hospital
Masjumi RI: [d: indonesischer Moslem-Rat, Partei, gegr 1945]
MASPED H: [d: Gesellschaft für Kühl-transporte]
M.A.St. D: d: mil: Marineausrüstungsstelle
MAST US: e: mil: Military Assistance to Safety and Traffic
MASz H: hu: Magyar Athletikai Szövetség
Maszovlet H: hu: Magyar-Szovjet Légi-

forgalmi Társaság, Budapest

M.A.T. F: f: Manufacture Nationale d'Armes de Tulle

MATA US: e: mil: Military Air Transport Association; Military Assistance Training Advisor; US: e: Motorcycle and Allied Trades Association; INT: e: Museums Association of Tropical Africa

MatABw BRD: d: mil: Materialamt der Bundeswehr, 5205 St Augustin 1

MATAF e: mil: WK2: Mediterranean Allied Tactical Air Force

MatAH BRD: d: mil: Materialamt des Heeres, 5483 Bad Neuenahr

MatALw BRD: d: mil: Materialamt der Luftwaffe, 505 Porz-Wahn

MatAM BRD: d: mil: Materialamt der Marine, 2941 Sengwarden

MATB US: e: mil: Military Air Transport Board

MATCen US: e: mil: Military Air Traffic Center

MATCon US: e: mil: Military Air Traffic Control

MATCU US: e: mil: Marine Air Tactical Control Unit [USMC]

MATE H: hu: Méréstechnikai és Automatizálási Tudományos Egyesület, Budapest

MATERAL INT: [d: internationaler Salon für die Ausrüstung der Nahrungsmittelindustrie, Paris, 9...15 Nov 1970]

Matesa E: s: Maquinaria Textil del Norte de España S.A.

MatHptDp BRD: d: mil: Materialhauptdepot

Math.V. D: d: Mathematischer Verein

MATICO US: e: Mastic Tile Corporation of America, Joliet, Ill.

MATISA CH: f: Matériel Industriel S.A., Lausanne

M.A.T.M.U. GB: e: mil: Mobile Aircraft Torpedo Maintenance Unit

M.A.T.P. F: f: Musée des Arts et Traditions Populaires

Mat.Pr.A. D: d: mil: Materialprüfungsamt

MatPrfStBw BRD: d: mil: Materialprüfungsstelle der Bundeswehr

MATRA F: f: Société Générale de Mécanique Aviation, Traction

Matrez YU: sh: Uprava Materijalnik Rezervi

MatRgt BRD: d: mil: Materialregiment

MATS US: e: mil: Military Air Transport Service [1918...65, dann: MAC]

MATSC US: e: mil: Middletown Air Technical Service Command

MatV BlnW: d: Materialverwaltung

MAU CDN: e: Mount Allison University

M.A.U. F: f: Mouvement d'Action Universitaire

M.Au.Re.B.; Maureb. D: d: mil: Marineausrüstungs- und Reparaturbetrieb

MAusbRgt BRD: d: mil: Marineausbildungsregiment

M.A.V. I: i: Magistrato delle Acque di Venezia

MÁV H: hu: Magyar államvasutak

MaV D: d: Verband der Matrizenbauanstalten für die keramische Industrie, Berlin

MAV CS: cs: Místní Akční Výbor; D: d: Münchener Aquarellistenverein

MAVO NL: nl: Middelbaar algemeen voortgezet onderwijs

MAW DDR: d: Magdeburger Armaturen-Werke; Ministerium für Außenwirtschaf

MAWEV A: d: Verband der Maschinen- und Werkzeughändler, Wien 1

Max.Ges. D: d: Maximilian-Gesellschaft, Berlin [Bibliophilie]

M.A.Y.C. GB: e: Methodist Association of Youth Clubs

MAZ BRD: d: Meldestelle im Anzeigengeschäft von Zeitschriftenverlagen eV; CH: d: Musikakademie Zürich, 8008 Zürich

M.A.Za.; Maza. D: d: mil: Marineartilleriezeugamt

MB d: Magistratsbibliothek; Maschinenbauschule

M.&B. GB: e: May & Baker Ltd., Dagenham

M.B. e: Medical Board; Medical Branch

MB BRD: d: Messerschmitt-Bölkow GmbH, München-Ottobrunn; S: sv: Meteorologiska byrån [SMHI] ; I: i: Ministero del Bilancio; PL: pl: Ministerstwo Bezpieczeństwa (Budownictwa)

M.B. GB: e: Ministry of Blockade

MB S: sv: Monopolutredningsbyrån, Stockholm; BRD: d: Münchener Block; US: e: mil: Munitions Board

MBA D: d: mil: Marinebauamt

M.B.A. GB: e: Marine Biological Association of the United Kingdom

MBA CH: d: Maschinen- und Bahnbedarf AG, 8600 Dübendorf; GB: e: Master Bookbinders' Alliance of London; e: Metropolitan Boxing Alliance; GB: e: Milk Bars Association of Great Britain and Ireland; US: e: Mortgage Bankers Association of America; GB: e: Yacht and Motor Boat Association

MBAA US: e: Master Brewers' Association of America; Mortgage Bankers Association of America

MBAM P: pt: Missão Botânica de Angola e Moçambique, Junta de Investigações do Ultramar, Lisboa

M.B.A.U.K. GB: e: Marine Biological Association of the United Kingdom

MBB BR: pt: Mercedes-Benz do Brasil SA; BRD: d: Messerschmitt-Bölkow-Blohm GmbH [gegr 1969]

MBBA D: d: mil: Marinebaubewirtschaftungsabteilung

M.B.C. GB: e: Metropolitan Borough Council

MBC NATO: e: Military Budget Council; BRD: d: Der Moderne Buch-Club GmbH, 61 Darmstadt

M.B.C. e: Municipal Borough Council

MBC US: e: Mutual Broadcasting Company

MBCA US: e: mil: Munitions Board Cataloging Agency

MBCC GB: e: Migratory Bird Conservation Commission

MBCMC US: e: Milk Bottle Crate Manufacturers Council, Cleveland 15, Ohio

MBD BRD: d: mil: Ministerialbürodirektor [BMVg]

M Bd US: e: mil: Munitions Board

M.Bekl.A. D: d: mil: Marinebekleidungsamt

M.B.F. GB: e: Master Builders' Federation

MBF. D: d: mil: WK2: Militärbefehlshaber

MBF US: e: Milk Bottlers Federation

M.B.F. e: Musicians' Benevolent Fund

MBI S: sv: Malmö Boll- och Idrottssällskap

M.B.I. e: Masonic Benevolent Institution

MBIA US: e: Malting Barley Improvement Association

M.B.I.I. GB: e: Masonic Benevolent Institution (Ireland)

MBiPMB PL: pl: Ministerstwo Budownictwa i Przemysłu Materiałów Budowlanych

MBK H: hu: Magyar Béke-Kongresszus, Budapest; D: d: Mädchenbibelkreis

MBK. D: d: mil: WK2: Marinebefehlshaber Kanalküste

MBK BRD: d: E. Merck AG, Darmstadt, C.F.Boehringer & Söhne GmbH, Mannheim, Knoll AG, Ludwigshafen (Rhein); S: sv: Mora Båtklubb

M.B.L. D: d: mil: Marine-Betriebsstofflager

MBL US: e: Marine Biological Laboratory; BRD: d: mil: Musterprüfstelle der Bundeswehr für Luftfahrtgerät [vorher: Luftwaffengerät] , 8 München 2

M.B.L.E. B: f: Manufacture Belge de Lampes et de Matériel électronique S.A., Bruxelles 7

MBM P: pt: Missão de Biologia Marítima, Junta de Investigações do Ultramar, Lisboa

MBMA US: e: Master Boiler Makers' Association; Metal Building Manufacturers Association, Cleveland 15, Ohio

MBMiO PL: pl: Ministerstwo Budownictwa

Miast i Osiedli

M.B.N. D: d: mil: WK2: Marinebefehlshaber Nord

MBNA Taiwan: e: Min Ben News Agency, Taipeh [gegr 1946]

MBÖ A: d: Monarchistische Bewegung Österreichs

MBP BRD: d: Mathematischer Beratungs- und Programmierungsdienst GmbH, 46 Dortmund [Rechenzentrum Rhein-Ruhr]; PL; pl: Miejska Biblioteka Publiczna; Ministerstwo Bezpieczeństwa Publicznego [1944...54]; Ministerstwo Budownictwa Przemysłowego [1951...56]

M.B.R. BR: pt: Minerações Brasileiras Reunidas

MBS PTM: e: Methodist Boys' School; D: d: Mitteldeutsches Braunkohlen-Syndikat, Leipzig

M.B.S. e: Monumental Brass Society

MBS US: e: Mutual Broadcasting System

MBSA US: e: Modular Building Standards Association

M.B.S.J.C. e: Metropolitan Boroughs Standing Joint Committee

M.B.S.K. D: d: mil: Marine-Bergungs- und Seenotdienstkommando

MBSz H: hu: Magyar Bickózók Szövetseg, Budapest

MBT H: hu: Magyar Béketanács, Budapest; Magyar Bibliophil-Társaság, Budapest

MBTA US: e: Massachusetts Bay Transit (Transportation) Authority

M.B.T.A. e: Metropolitan Board Teachers' Association

M.B.V. D: d: mil: WK2: Marinebaubevollmächtigter

M.B.W. D: d: mil: WK2: Marinebefehlshaber Westküste; GB: e: Metropolitan Board of Works

M.C. GB: e: mil: Maintenance Command [RAF]; F: f: Maison de la Chimie; Maison de la Culture

MC US: e: Manhattan College

M.C. e: Manufacturers' Conference; INT: f: Marché Commun, Bruxelles [B]

MC d: Marianische Congregation; US: e: mil: Marine Corps [= USMC]; US: e: Maritime Commission; Marshall College Marymount College; UN: e: Department of Mass Communication [UNESCO] US: e: mil: Materiel Center (Command) NL: nl: Mathematisch Centrum, Amsterdam; e: Medical College (Committee) (Corporation); e: mil: Medical Corps; US: e: Memorial Commission; e: Mennonite Church; INT: i: Mercato Comun

M.C. US: e: Michigan Central Railroad Company; GB: e: Middlebury College; GB: e: mil: Royal Military College, Sandhurst

MC NATO: e: Military Committee [= MRC

M.C. F: f: Ministère des Colonies; B: f: Ministère du Congo Belge et du Ruanda-Urundi, Bruxelles

MC US: e: Ministry of Commerce; BRD: d: Missionarinnen Christi, 8831 Rebdorf; S: sv: Mjölkcentralen, Stockholm; BRD: d: e: Montan Consulting GmbH, 43 Essen [gegr 1971]

M.C. s: Moto-Club

MC d: Motorclub; Motorklub

M.C. e: Mount Carmel Fraternity

MC US: e: Mundelein College; F: f: Musée Carnavalet; B: f: Musée Royal de l'Afrique Centrale, Tervuren; US: e: Music Corporation of America

M.C.A. PTM: e: Malaysian Chinese Association, Kuala Lumpur; GB: e: Management Consultants Association; Manufactured Copper Association

MCA US: e: Manufacturing Chemists' Association, Inc., Washington 6, D.C.; CDN: e: Maritime Central Airways, Ltd. Charlottetown

M.C.A. e: Master Clothworkers Association

MCA US: e: Material Coordinating Agency; Maternity Center Association; Medical Correctional Association;

Mid-Continent Airlines, Kansas City; US: e: mil: Military Chaplains Association; US: e: Millinery Credit Association; GB: e: Ministry of Civil Aviation; US: e: mil: Movement Control Agency; US: e: Movers Conference of America; Music Corporation of America; Music Critics Association; Musicians Club of America

MCAA US: e: Mason Contractors Association of America

M.C.A.A. F: f: Mouvement contre l'armement atomique

M.C.A.A.A. GB: e: Midland Counties Amateur Athletic Association

MCAB US: e: mil: Marine Corps Air Base

MCAF US: e: mil: Marine Corps Air Facility (Field)

M.C.A.L. GB: e: Master Carvers' Association of London

M.C.A.R.F. GB: e: Mrs. Churchill's Aid to Russia Fund

MCAS US: e: mil: Marine Corps Air Station

MCATS US: e: mil: Marine Corps Aviation Technical School

M.C.B. GB: e: mil: Medical Consultative Board [Admiralty]

MCC BRD: d: Mainzer Carneval-Club

M.C.C. GB: e: Marylebone Cricket Club [gegr 1787] ; Matrimonial Causes Committee; CDN: e: Medical Council of Canada

MCC US: e: Mennonite Central Committee; INT: s: Mercado Común Centroamericano; US: e: Metropolitan Community Church [for homosexuals]

M.C.C. GB: e: Middlesex County Council

MCC e: mil: Military Committee (Chiefs of Staff); NATO: e: Military Complements Committee; US: e: mil: Military Control Center; Military Coordinating Committee; US: e: Mississippi Chemical Corporation

M.C.C. e: Mount Carmel Confraternity; I: i: Movimento Collaborazione Civica

MCCA INT: s: Mercado Común Centroamericano

MCCC US: e: Motor Carrier Claims Commission

MC/CS NATO: e: Military Committee (Chiefs of Staff)

MCCTA GB: e: Manufacturing Confectioners Commercial Travellers Association

MCCTU e: Mongolian Central Council of Trade Unions

MCCUS US: e: Mexican Chamber of Commerce of the United States

M.C.D.A. e: Magna Charta Day Association

M.C.D.M. e: Morden College for Distressed Merchants

MCDN EC: s: Movimiento Cívico Democrático Nacional

MCE B: e: Management Centre Europe, Brussels; US: e: Memphis Cotton Exchange; INT: i: Mercato Comune Europeo; e: mil: Military Corrective Establishment; I: i: Ministero del Commercio con l'Estero; US: e: Montgomery Cotton Exchange

M.C.E.A. e: Map and Chart Engravers' Association

MCEB US: e: mil: Marine Corps Equipment Board; Military Communications-Electronics Board

MCEC US: e: mil: Marine Corps Education Center

MCEGGS AUS: e: Melbourne Church of England Girls' Grammar School

MCES US: e: mil: Marine Corps Exchange System

MCF US: e: Migrant Children's Fund

M.C.F. GB: e: mil: Mine-Clearing Force; F: f: Motocycle-Club de France; Mouvement Communiste Français [gegr 1951] ; e: Movement for Colonial Freedom

MCFA N: [e: Royal Ministry for Consumer and Family Affairs]

M.C.F.I. F: f: Mouvement Communiste Français Indépendant

McG CDN: e: McGill University

MCh. d: Männerchor

M.C.H. IND: e: Mother and Child Health Centre

MCH S: sv: Motorcykelhandlarnas riksförbund

MChAT SU: [d: Moskauer Akademisches Gorki-Künstlertheater]

M.Ch.E. H: hu: Magyar Chemikusok Egyesülete, Budapest

MCHP CS: cs: Ministerstvo Chemického Průmyslu

MCI US: e: mil: Marine Corps Institute

M.C.I. e: Metropolitan Convalescent Institution; f: Ministère du Commerce et de l'Industrie; R: ro: Ministerul Comerţului Interior, Bucureşti; PE: s: Movimiento Cívico Independiente

M.C.I.E. GB: e: Midland Counties Institute of Engineers

MCK INT: pl: Międzynarodowy Czerwony Krzyż

MCL US: e: mil: Marine Corps League; e: Mid-Canada Line [d: Luftverkehrsgesellschaft]

MCLA US: e: mil: Marine Corps League Auxiliary

M.C.L.C. GB: e: The Mayors and City of London Court

MCM f: Marché Commun Maghrebin

McM CDN: e: McMaster University

MCMT; MCM&T US: e: Michigan College of Mining and Technology

M.C.O. e: Methodist Conference Office

3M Co US: e: Minnesota Mining & Manufacturing Company, St. Paul 6

MCO S: sv: Motorbranschens Centralorganisation

M.C.O.D.A. GB: e: Motor Cab Owner Drivers' Association

M.Com. F: f: Ministère du Commerce

MCOMA US: e: Minnesota Creamery Operators' and Managers' Association

MCP e: Malawi Congress Party [gegr 1959]; Malayan Communist Party

M.C.P. GB: e: Metropolitan and City Police; s: Misión Conjunta de Programación

M.C.P.O.F. GB: e: Metropolitan and City Police Orphan Fund

M.C.P.S. GB: e: Mechanical Copyright Protection Society

MC/PS NATO: e: Military Committee in Permanent Session

M.C.R. US: e: mil: Marine Corps Reserve

MCRD US: e: mil: Marine Corps Recruit Depot

M.C.R.O. e: Medical Council and Registration Office

MCROA US: e: mil: Marine Corps Reserve Officers Association

M.C.R.R. US: e: Maine Central Railroad Company; Michigan Central Railroad Company

M.C.S. GB: e: Madras Civil Service; Malayan Civil Service

MCS US: e: Marine Cooks and Stewards; US: e: mil: Marine Corps School (Station)

M.C.S. e: Medico-Chirurgical Society; Merseyside Civic Society; e: mil: Military College of Science

M.C.S.A. GB: e: Malta Civil Service Association; Master Cotton Spinners' Association

MČSA CS: cs: Museum Československé Armády

MCSC US: e: mil: Marine Corps Supply Center

M.C.S.F. e: Master Cotton Spinners' Federation

M.C.S.T. GB: e: Manchester College of Science and Technology; P: pt: Missão Científica de S. Tomé

MCSU NL: nl: Melkcontrôlestation Utrecht

M.C.Sz. H: hu: Magyarországi Cionista Szövetség, Budapest

MCT MOC: pt: Missão de Combate às Tripanosomiases, Lourenço Marques

MCTA e: Mild Coffee Trade Association

M.&C.T.B.F. e: Motor and Cycle Trades' Benevolent Fund

MCTI US: e: Metal Cutting Tool Institute
MCTS e: Moravian College and Theological Seminary
MCTSA US: e: Military Clothing and Textile Supply Agency
MČU CS: cs: Mládež Československých Unitárů
M.C.U. e: Modern Churchmen's Union; GB: e: Motor Cycle Union
MCV BRD: d: Mainzer Carneval-Verein [gegr 1838]
M.C.V.G. F: f: mil: Mutilés, Combattants et Victimes de la Guerre
MCWA NZ: e: Massey College Wool Association
M.C.W.C. GB: e: Maternity and Child Welfare Centre
MCWR CY: e: Ministry of Communications and Works of the Republic of Cyprus
MCZ US: e: Museum of Comparative Zoology [Harvard University]
MD RM: f: Air Madagascar
M.D. GB: e: Manning Department; CH: d: mil: Mannschaftsdepot
MD S: sv: mil: marindistrikt
M.D. D: d: mil: Matrosendivision
MD DDR: d: mil: Mechanisierte Division; e: mil: Medical Department; Meteorological Department
M.D. D: d: mil: WK2: Militärbefehlshaber in Dänemark; e: mil: Military District
MD CS: cs: Ministerstvo Dopravy; GB: e: mil: Ministry of Defence
M.D. e: mil: Mobilization Department (Division); F: f: Musée de la Découverte; P: pt: Museu do Dundo, Dundo
MDA US: e: Marking Device Association; I: i: mil: Ministero della Difesa-Aeronautica
MDAA US: e: Muscular Dystrophy Associations of America
MDAC US: e: McDonnell Douglas Astronautics Company; US: e: mil: Mutual Defense Assistance, General Area of China

MDAGT US: e: mil: Mutual Defense Assistance, Greece and Turkey
MDAIKP US: e: mil: Mutual Defense Assistance, Iran, Republic of Korea, and Philippines
MDA-MP NATO: e: Mutual Defense Assistance - Material Program
MDANAA US: e: mil: Mutual Defense Assistance, North Atlantic Area
MDA-OSP US: e: mil: Mutual Defense Assistance - Offshore Procurement
MDAP US: e: mil: Mutual Defense Assistance Program
MDA-TR US: e: mil: Mutual Defense Assistance - Training Program
M.D.B. e: Mersey Dock Board
MDB BR: pt: Movimento Democrático Brasileiro
MDC MW: e: Malawi Development Corporation; ZA: e: Marine Diamond Corporation; GB: e: Mechanical Development Committee; e: mil: Military District Court; BUR: e: Minerals Development Corporation, Rangoon; GB: e: mil: Mobile Defence Corps
M.D.C. F: f: Mouvement de Défense des Contribuables
M.D.C.F. F: f: Mouvement de démocratie chrétienne en France [gegr 1958]
M.D.D. DY: f: Mouvement Démocratique du Dahomey
M.D.E. I: i: mil: Ministero della Difesa -Esercito
MDF WAN: e: Midwest Democratic Front
MdF DDR: d: Ministerium der Finanzen
MDF e: mil: Mobile Defense (Defence) Force(s)
M.D.F.C.T.A. e: Metropolitan Drinking Fountain and Cattle Trough Association
MDG S: sv: mil: Gotlands marinedistrikt, Visby
M.D.G.M. f: mil: Mission de documentation de géographie militaire
M.D.H.B. e: Mersey Docks and Harbour Board

MDHBA US: e: Medical Dental Hospitals Bureaus of America

MdI DDR: d: Ministerium des Innern

MDI YV: s: Movimiento Democrático Independiente

MDIA CGO: pt: Movimento para a Defesa dos Interesses de Angola, Léopoldville

MDIC e: mil: Multilateral Disarmament Information Centre

MDICAT I: i: mil: Miliza Difesa Contraerea Territoriale

MDIN CGO: f: Mouvement de la Défence des Intérêts Nationaux

MDiv BRD: d: mil: Marinedivision

MDJ BRD: d: Musikalische Deutsche Jugend

MDK PL: pl: Młodzieżowy Dom Kultury; H: hu: Müszaki Dokumentációs Központ, Budapest

MDLC US: e: mil: Material Development and Logistic Command [Army]

M.D.L.N. Sudan: f: Mouvement Démocratique de Libération Nationale

M.D.L.N.-O.R. f: Mouvement Démocratique de Libération Nationale - Ouvriers Révolutionnaires

MDM PL: pl: Marszałkowska Dzielnica Mieszkanowia; CS: cs: Městské Divadlo Mladých; I: i: mil: Ministero della Difesa-Marina

MDN S: sv: mil: Norrlandskustens marindistrikt, Härnösand

M.D.N. F: f: mil: Ministère de la Défense Nationale; I: i: mil: Ministero Difesa Nazionale; GCA: s: Movimiento Democrático Nacionalista

MDNA US: e: Machinery Dealers' National Association; Mobile Homes Dealers National Association

MDNS YU: sn: Ministrstvo za Državne Nabave Slovenije, Ljubljana

MDNSz H: hu: Magyar Diákok Nemzeti Szövetsége, Budapest

MDO S: sv: mil: Ostkustens marindistrikt, Stockholm; PL: pl: Młodzieżowy Dom Oświaty

MDÖ S: sv: mil: Öresunds marindistrikt, Malmö

MDP RM: e: Madagascar-Press f: Madagascar-Presse [d: Nachrichtenagentur]; H: hu: Magyar Dologozók Pártja, Budapest; PE: s: Movimiento Democrático Peruano

MDPA US: e: mil: Mutual Defense Procurement Authority

M.D.R. GB: e: Metropolitan District Railway

MDR D: d: Mitteldeutscher Rundfunk

M.D.R.A. DZ: f: Mouvement démocratique du renouveau algérien

M.D.R.M. RM: f: Mouvement démocratique de la Rénovation Malgache [gegr 1945]

MDS S: sv: mil: Sudkustens marindistrikt, Karlskrona; GB: e: Metropolitan Dairymen's Society; CS: cs: Ministerstvo Dopravy a Spojů; US: e: Minnesota Dermatological Society; Mohawk Data Sciences Corp., Herkimer, N.Y.

MDSO US: e: mil: Medical and Dental Supply Office

MDT PL: pl: Miejski Dom Towarowy

M.D.T.B. GB: e: Milk Distribution Trade Board

M.D.U. GB: e: Medical Defence Union

MDV S: sv: mil: Västkustens marindistrikt, Göteborg

MDv D: d: mil: Marinedruckvorschriftenverwaltung [OKM]

MDV CS: cs: Místný Dozorný Výbor

M.D.V. f: Mouvement Démocratique Voltaique

MDW US: e: mil: Military District of Washington; BRD: d: Möbel Deutscher Werkarbeit

MDX GB: e: mil: Middlesex Regiment

MDZ BRD: d: mil: Militärische Dokumentationszentrale

M.D.z.S. YU: sn: Muzejsko Društvo za Slovenijo, Ljubljana

M.E. F: f: Maison d'Education; Manufacture de l'Etat

Me. D: d: Messerschmitt Flugzeugbau GmbH, Augsburg

ME RL: e: f: Middle East Airlines/Air Liban [= MEA] ; H: hu: Miniszterelnök-(ség), Budapest; d: Minister(ium) für Ernährung; CS: cs: Ministerstvo Energetiky; PL: pl: Ministerstwo Energetyki [1952...57] ; INT: f: Mouvement Européen, Bruxelles 4 [B, gegr 1947] ; H: hu: Müszaki Egyetem

M.E. F: f: Musée d'Ethnographie

ME PL: pl: Muzeum Etnograficzne

MEA US: e: Medical Exhibitors Association; GB: e: Metropolitan Entertainers' Association; T: e: Metropolitan Electricity Authority; RL: e: f: Middle East Airlines/Air Liban, Beirut; d: Mieteinigungsamt; US: e: Minnesota Education Association; Mission of Economic Affairs; Music Editors Association

M.E.A.C. e: Mutual Economic Assistance Council

MEAF e: mil: Mediterranean Expeditionary Allied Forces; Middle East(ern) Air Force(s)

MEAL e: Mission for Economic Affairs in London

MEAS e: mil: Middle East Air Staff

MEAU P: pt: Missão de Estudos Agronómicos do Ultramar, Junta de Investigações do Ultramar, Lisboa

MEAUP P: pt: Missão de Estudos Apícolas no Ultramar Português, Junta de Investigações do Ultramar, Lisboa

M.E.B. e: Medical Examining Board; GB: e: Midlands Electricity Board

MEBA US: e: Marine Engineers Beneficial Association

MEC US: e: Maine Central Railroad; Manufacturing Engineering Council; INT: i: Mercato europeo comune

M.E.C. GB: e: mil: Middle East Command

MEC BR: [e: Ministry of Education and

Culture] ; d: Modelleisenbahnclub

MECAS e: Middle East Center for Arab Studies [near Beirut]

MECCA US: e: mil: Management Enlisted Central Career Administration; GB: e: Missionary and Ecumenical Council of the Church Assembly

M.E.Ch. e: Methodist Episcopal Church

MECHANIK DDR: d: Volkseigene Betriebe der feinmechanischen Industrie

Mechit. d: Mechitaristen-Kongregation

Mechtorg. SU: [d: Hauptverwaltung für Rauchwarenhandel, Handelsministerium]

Mech VersA BRD: d: Bahn: Eisenbahn -Versuchsamt für mechanische Stoffprüfungen

M.E.C.I. f: Société de matériel électrique et de contrôle industriel

M.E.C.M. e: Methodist Episcopal Church Mission

MECNY US: e: Municipal Engineers of the City of New York

MECOM e: mil: Middle East Command; US: e: mil: Mobility Equipment Command, St. Louis, Mo.

MECT US: e: Mellon Educational and Charitable Trust

MED US: e: Medical Department

Med US: e: mil: Army Medical Service

M.E.D. D: d: mil: Militär-Eisenbahn -Direktion

MEDA BRD: d: Messedienst für die Agrar- und Ernährungswirtschaft GmbH, Ffm; CGO: f: Mouvement pour l'Evolution Démocratique de l'Afrique

MEDAC RCA: f: Mouvement d'Evolution Démocratique de l'Afrique Centrale

MEDCAP US: VN: e: Medical Civic Action Programs

MEDCENT NATO: e: Central Mediterranean Area

MEDEA INT: [d: internationale Ausstellung für medizinische Technik und Automation, London, GB, 1969]

MEDEAST NATO: e: Eastern Mediterranean Area

MEDEX 71 INT: d: Internationale Fachmesse und Fachtagungen für Medizinische Elektronik und Bioengineering, Basel [9...13 Mar 1971]

Medgis SU: [d: Verlag des Ministeriums für Gesundheitswesen]

Medgiz SU: [e: State Medical Literature Press]

MEDI DDR: d: VEB Medizintechnik Leipzig, 7035 Leipzig

M.E.D.I.A. US: e: Man's Environments: Display Implications and Applications [symposium 1969 in Arlington, Va.]

Medicaid US: [d: staatliche ärztliche Fürsorge für Unbemittelte]

MEDICO INT: e: Medical International Cooperation

Mediobanca I: i: Mediobanca - Banca di Credito Finanziario S.p.A., Milano

MEDIPLAN BRD: d: MEDIPLAN, Planungsgesellschaft für Krankenhauseinrichtungen mbH, 8 München 2

MEDNOREAST NATO: e: Northeast Mediterranean Area

MEDO e: mil: Middle East Defense Organization

MEDOC NATO: e: Western Mediterranean Area [occidental]

Med.R.C. e: mil: Medical Reserve Corps

MEDSANTRUD SU: [d: Gewerkschaft der Sanitätsangestellten]

Med.Sch. e: mil: Medical School [Navy]

MEDSOUEAST NATO: e: Southeast Mediterranean Area

MEDSUPDEP US: e: mil: Medical Supply Depot

MEE H: hu: Magyar Elektrotechnikai Egyesület, Budapest

MEEC UN: e: Middle East Economic Commission; US: e: Middle East Emergency Committee

MEECO GB: e: Metallurgical Equipment Export Company Ltd.

MEEU P: pt: Missão de Estudos Económicos do Ultramar, Junta de Investigações do Ultramar, Lisboa

MEF e: mil: Mediterranean Expeditionary Force; GB: e: mil: Middle East Forces; US: e: Musicians Emergency Fund; S: sv: Musiketablissementens Förening, Stockholm

MEFA CH: d: Schweizerische Metzgerei -Fachausstellung, Zürich

MEFESz H: hu: Magyar Egyetemisták és Főiskolások Egységes Szövetsége Budapest

MEFHOSZ H: hu: Magyar Egyetemi és Főiskolai Hallgatók Országos Szövetség Budapest

Mefo D: d: Metallforschungs-GmbH

MEFTA INT: e: Metal Industries in the European Free Trade Association

MEG BRD: d: mil: Marine-Elektronik -Planungs-GmbH, 2 Hamburg [gegr 1966]; Max-Eyth- Gesellschaft zur Förderung der Landtechnik

Megu DDR: d: VEB Metallgußwerk

MEHNG P: pt: Missão de Estudos do Habitat Nativo na Guiné, Junta de Investigações do Ultramar, Lisboa

MEHNT P: pt: Missão de Estudos do Habitat Nativo em Timor

MEI US: e: Metals Engineering Institute, American Society for Metals; Middle East Institute

MEKANIK S: [d: technische Fachmesse der mechanischen Werkstattindustrie, Malmö 1970]

MEKK H: hu: Budapesti Müszaki Egyetem Központi Könyvtára

Mekog NL: nl: N.V. Maatschappij tot Exploitatie van Kooksovengassen, IJmuiden

MEL US: e: mil: Marine Engineering Laboratory [Navy]; GB: e: Music Education League

MELF GB: e: mil: Middle East Land Forces; BRD: d: Ministerium für Ernährung, Landwirtschaft und Forste

M.E.L.H. F: f: Maison d'Education de la Légion d'Honneur

MELI SU: [d: Marx-Engels-Lenin-Institut, Moskau]

M.E.L.N. ET: [f: Mouvement Egyptien de Libération Nationale]

MELS-Institut; MELSTI DDR: d: Marx -Engels-Lenin-Stalin-Institut

MEM H: [d: Ausstellungsbüro, Budapest]

M.E.M. INT: eo: Mondpaca Esperantista Movado

MEM BRD: d: Münchener Elektromesse

MEMA S: sv: Mildens Elektriska Motor AB, Sundbyberg; P: pt: Missão para o Estudo da Missionologia Africana, Junta de Investigações do Ultramar, Lisboa; US: e: Motor and Equipment Manufacturers Association

MEMAA P: pt: Missão de Estudos dos Movimentos Associativos em Africa

MEME P: pt: Missão de Estudos das Minorias Étnicas do Ultramar Português, Junta de Investigações do Ultramar, Lisboa

MEMISA NL: nl: Medische Missie-Aktie

MEN ET: e: Middle-East News Agency, Cairo

M.E.N. F: f: Ministère de l'Education Nationale; s: Ministero de Educación Nacional

MENA ET: e: = MEN

MENC US: e: Music Educators' National Conference, Chicago, Ill.

MENCHETA E: [d: Nachrichtenagentur, Madrid]

M.E.N.I. GB: e: Ministry of Education in Northern Ireland; YV: s: Movimiento Electoral Nacional Independiente

MENV CS: cs: Městský Národní Výbor

M.E.O. F: f: Mouvement de l'Enfance Ouvrière

MEOCAM INT: f: Mouvement des Etudiants de l'Organisation Commune Africaine et Malgache

M.E.P. CL: Mahajana Eksath Peramuna; l: Missionarii ad exteras gentes Parisienses; YV: s: Movimiento Electoral del Pueblo

MEPMPU P: pt: Missão de Estudo dos Problemas Migratórios e do Povoamento no Ultramar, Junta de Investigações do Ultramar, Lisboa

MEPOD CS: sk: Mechanizovanie Podohospodárskej Výroby na Slovensku

MEPRA RA: s: Misión de Estudios de Patología Regional Argentina

MEPS US: e: mil: Military Express and Passenger Bus Service [USAREUR]

MEPW WAN: e: Ministry of Economic Planning, Western Region

MER D: d: Mitteleuropäisches Reisebüro [1918...46]

MERC BRD: d: Mannheimer Eis- und Rollsportclub eV, 68 Mannheim

Merc. l: Ordo Beatae Mariae Virginis de Mercede

MERCAST INT: e: Merchant Ship Broadcast

MERCO INT: e: Merchant Ships Reporting

MERDC US: e: mil: U.S.Army Mobility Equipment Research and Development Center, Fort Belvoir, Va.

MERDL US: e: mil: Medical Equipment Research and Development Laboratory, Fort Totten, N.Y.

MERI GH: e: Medical Research Institute, Accra

MERL GB: e: Mechanical Engineering Research Laboratory, Glasgow [DSIR]

MERN P: pt: Missão de Estudo do Rendimento Nacional do Ultramar, Junta de Investigações do Ultramar, Lisboa

MERRA e: Middle East Relief and Rehabilitation Administration

Mert. GB: e: Merton College, Oxford

MERU ZA: e: Mechanical Engineering Research Unit

MES US: e: Mechanical Engineering Society

M.E.S. US: e: South Methodist Episcopal Church; e: mil: Military Engineer Service

MESA US: e: Mechanics Educational

Society of America

MESAN RCA: f: Mouvement pour l'évolution sociale de l'Afrique noire

M.E.S.C. GB: e: mil: Middle East Supply Centre, Cairo

MESCO UN: UNESCO Middle East Centre, Cairo

MESH INT: [d: Firmenkonsortium Engins Matra, Paris, ERNO Raumfahrttechnik GmbH, Bremen, SAAB, Stockholm, Hawker-Siddeley Dynamics, London]

MESPF PTM: e: Malayan Estates Staff Provident Fund

Mesucora INT: f: Exposition Internationale Mesure - Contrôle - Régulation - Automatisme, Paris

MÉSZ H: hu: Magyar Épitőmüvészek Szövetsége, Budapest

Met US: e: Metropolitan Opera, New York [gegr 1883]

met 64 INT: [d: erste europäische metallurgische Ausstellung, Turin, I]

META US: e: mil: U.S. Army Management Engineering Training Agency, Rock Island, Ill.

MetA; Meta. d: Meteorologisches Amt

META US: e: Metropolitan Educational Television Association, Inc., New York; GB: e: Model Engineering Trade Association

Metalexport PL: [d: staatliches Außenhandelsunternehmen, Warschau]

Metalkat CGO: f: Société Métallurgique du Katanga

Met.D.R. GB: e: Metropolitan District Railway, London

METE H: hu: Magyar Elektrotechnikai Egyesület, Budapest

METESCO INT: e: Co-ordinating Committee on mechanical testing of metals [ISO]

METESZ H: hu: Müszaki és Természettudományi Egyesületek Szövetsége, Budapest

METG BRD: d: Mittelrheinische Erdgastransport GmbH

METO INT: e: Middle East Treaty Organization [gegr 1955]

METRA INT: d: internationaler Zusammenschluß von Forschungs- und Beratungsgesellschaften: DIVO, SEMA, SIGMA, SOBEMAP, SOMEA

METRIMPEX H: [d: Außenhandelsunternehmen der staatlichen Wirtschaftsvereinigung "Prüf- und Meßgeräte", Budapest]

Métro F: f: Chemin de fer métropolitain de Paris

METRO US: e: New York Metropolitan Reference and Research Library Agency, Inc.

METRONEX PL: [d: staatliches Außenhandelsunternehmen für Meßgeräte, Warschau]

METU TR: e: Middle East Technical University, Ankara

M.E.U.E. B: f: Mouvement pour les Etats-Unis d'Europe, Wilrijk

M.E.V.A. D: d: mil: Militär-Eisenbahn-Verkehrsamt

MEW D: i: Märkisches Elektrizitäts-Werk AG, Berlin

M.E.W. GB: e: WK2: Ministry of Economic Warfare

MEWA DDR: d: Volkseigene Beriebe der Metallwarenindustrie; US: e: Motor and Equipment Wholesalers Association

MEX PL: pl: Metalexport, Warszawa

MEXE GB: e: mil: Military Engineering Experimental Establishment, Christchurch, Hampshire

Mezentra d: Maschinen-Einkaufszentrale landwirtschaftlicher Genossenschaften

MEZU P: pt: Missão de Estudos Zoológicos do Ultramar, Junta de Investigações do Ultramar, Lisboa

M.F. F: f: Marine Française

MF S: sv: mil: Marinförvaltningen; BRD: e: d: Massey-Ferguson GmbH; S: sv: Medicinska Föreningen

M.F. GB: e: mil: Mediterranean Fleet; F: f: Mères Françaises; D: d: mil:

WK2: Militärbefehlshaber in Frankreich; e: Mineworkers' Federation; F: f: Ministère des Finances

MF d: Ministerium für (der) Finanzen; CS: cs: Ministerstvo Financí; PL: pl: Ministerstwo Finansów

M.F. R: ro: Ministerul Finanţerol, Bucureşti; e: Ministry of Food

MF CS: cs: Mladá Fronta

M.F. F: f: Mouvement Fédéraliste; Mouvements Familiaux

MF H: hu: Müszaki Föiskola

M+F CH: d: mil: Munitionsfabrik

MF CS: cs: Mzdový Fond

MFA BRD: d: Medizinische Forschungsanstalt [Max-Planck-Gesellschaft]

M.F.A. GB: e: Metal Finishing Association; f: mil: Ministère des Forces Armées

MfA DDR: d: Ministerium für Arbeit, Berlin

MFA R: ro: Ministerul Forţelor Armate, Bucureşti

MF&A D: e: nach WK2: Monuments, Fine Arts and Archives [OMGUS]

MFA US: e: Movement for Federation of the American; Museum of Fine Arts

MfAA DDR: d: Ministerium für Auswärtige Angelegenheiten, Berlin [= MAA]

MFAA = MF&A

MFABI GB: e: Metal Fixing Association for Building Insulation

MFAM MOC: pt: Missão de Fotogrametria Aérea de Moçambique, Lourenço Marques

M.F.A.R. F: f: Maison Familiale d'Apprentissage Rural; D: d: mil: Marine-Feldartillerie-Regiment

MfArb. DDR: d: Ministerium für Arbeit, Berlin

MfAuI DDR: d: Ministerium für Außen- und Innerdeutschen Handel, Berlin

MfAusAng. DDR: d: Ministerium für Auswärtige Angelegenheiten, Berlin

M.F.B. GB: e: Metropolitan Fire Brigade [London]

MfB DDR: d: Ministerium für Bauwesen, Berlin

MFBTE GB: e: Midland Federation of Building Trades Employers

MFC IL: e: Maritime Fruit Carriers Company, Haifa; GB: e: mil: Military Forces of the Crown; s: Movimiento Familiar Cristiano

MFD DK: da: Malerforbundet i Danmark; d: Mennonitischer Freiwilligendienst

MfE DDR: d: Ministerium für Eisenbahnwesen

MFE INT: f: Mouvement fédéraliste européen s: Movimiento Federalista Europeo i: Movimento Federalista Europeo

M.Fed. GB: e: Miners' Federation of Great Britain

MfEE DDR: d: Ministerium für Elektrotechnik und Elektronik, Berlin

MfELuF d: Minister(ium) für Ernährung, Landwirtschaft und Forsten

MFF US: e: Mac Fadden Foundation; S: sv: Malmö Fotbollsförening; PL: pl: Międzynarodowy Festiwal Filmowy

MfF DDR: d: Ministerium für Finanzen, Berlin

M.F.F.T.E. F: f: Mouvement fédéraliste français des travailleurs européens

MFG D: d: Märkische Filmgesellschaft; S: sv: Medicinska Föreningen i Göteborg

MfG DDR: d: Ministerium für Gesundheitswesen, Berlin

MFG BRD: d: Modellfluggruppe

MFGA US: e: Master Furriers Guild of America

M.F.G.B. GB: e: Miners' Federation of Great Britain

MfGes. DDR: d: = MfG

MfHF DDR: d: Ministerium für Hoch- und Fachschulwesen, Berlin

MfHuG d: Minister(ium) für Handel und Gewerbe

MfHuK d: Minister(ium) für Heimatvertriebene und Kriegsbeschädigte

MfHV DDR: d: Ministerium für Handel und Versorgung, Berlin

MFI S: sv: Malmö Flygindustri

MfJ DDR: d: Ministerium für Justiz, Berlin

MFK BRD: d: Gesellschaft für Marktforschung für Kaltprofile, 4 Düsseldorf

MfK DDR: d: Ministerium für Kultur, Berlin

MFK d: Modellflugklub; sv: modellflygklubb

M.F.L. GB: e: Midland Forensic Laboratory; Mineworkers' Federation in London

M.f.L. D: d: Ministerium für Landwirtschaft

MfL DDR: d: Ministerium für Leichtindustrie, Berlin

MfLDuF d: Minister(ium) für Landwirtschaft, Domänen und Forsten

MFlgH BRD: d: mil: Marinefliegerhorst

MFlgKdo BRD: d: mil: Marinefliegerkommando

MfLMI DDR: d: Ministerium für Lebensmittelindustrie, Berlin

MfLuF DDR: d: Ministerium für Land- und Forstwirtschaft, Berlin

M.f.L.V. A: d: mil: Ministerium für Landesverteidigung

MfM DDR: d: Ministerium für Maschinenbau, Berlin

M.F.M F: f: Mouvement Français des Mères

MFMA US: e: Maple Flooring Manufacturers Association, Chicago 1, Ill.; Metal Findings Manufacturers Association

MfMaschb. DDR: d: Ministerium für Maschinenbau, Berlin

MFmKdo BRD: d: mil: Marinefernmeldekommando

MFMPK H: hu: Magyar Forradalmi Munkás-Paraszt Kormány, Budapest

MFmS BRD: d: mil: Marinefernmeldeschule

MFNF H: hu: Magyar Függetlenségi Népfront, Budapest

MFNFOT Magyar Függetlenségi Népfront Országos Tanácsa, Budapest

M.F.N.O. GB: e: Midland Federation of Newspaper Owners

MfNV DDR: d: mil: Ministerium für Nationale Verteidigung [seit 1956]

MFO CH: d: Maschinenfabrik Oerlikon, Zürich-Oerlikon; GB: e: mil: Military Forwarding Organization

MFOA CDN: US: e: Municipal Finance Officers Association of the United States and Canada

M.F.Oe. A: d: Mundartfreunde Österreichs, Wien

M.f.ö.A. D: d: Ministerium für öffentliche Arbeiten

M.F.O.M. F: f: Ministère de la France d'Outre-Mer

MFOW US: e: Marine Firemen, Oilers and Wipers Association

MFP H: hu: Magyar Függetlenségi Párt, Budapest; GB: e: mil: Military Foot Police; Ministry of Fuel and Power

MFPA US: e: Massachusetts (Michigan) Forest and Park Association

MfPF DDR: d: Ministerium für das Post- und Fernmeldewesen, Berlin

M.F.P.F. F: f: Mouvement Français pour le Planning Familial

M.F.Pi. D: d: mil: Marine-Festungspionie

MfPuF DDR: d: = MfPF

MFR BRD: d: mil: Militärischer Führungsrat [BMVtdg]

M.F.R. F: f: Mouvement Familial Rural

MFR I: i: Movimento Femminile Repubblicano

M.F.S. D: d: Mädchenfortbildungsschule

MFS US: e: Malleable Founders' Society; d: mil: Marinefernmeldeschule; S: sv: Medicinska Föreningen i Stockholm; US: e: mil: Military Flight Service

MfS DDR: d: Ministerium für Staatssicherheit

MFS YU: sn: Ministerstvo za Finance Slovenije, Ljubljana; l: Missionarii Sancti Francisci Salesii de Annecy

M.F.S. e: Museum of Fisheries and Shipping

MfSAB DDR: d: Ministerium für Schwermaschinen- und Anlagenbau, Berlin

MFSC 1: [d: Comboni-Missionare, 709 Ellwangen]

M.f.s.F. A: d: Ministerium für soziale Fürsorge

MfSI DDR: d: Ministerium für Schwerindustrie, Berlin

MFSM INT: pl: Międzynarodowa Federacja Schronisk Młodziżowych [= e: IYHF]

M.F.S.S. GB: e: Manchester Federation of Scientific Societies

MFSS US: e: mil: U.S. Army Medical Field Service School, Carlisle, Pa.

MFSSC; M.F.SS.C. 1: Missionarii Filii Sanctissimi Cordis

MFTL PL: pl: Międzynarodowy Festiwal Teatrów Ludowych

MFTR H: hu: Magyar Királyi Folyam- és Tengerhajozási Részvénytársaság

MFu GB: e: mil: The Royal Munster Fusiliers

Mf.V. TR: tr: Maarif Vekâleti, Ankara

MfV DDR: d: Ministerium für Verkehrswesen, Berlin; Ministerium für Volksbildung, Berlin; D: d: Ministerium für Volkswohlfahrt

M.F.V. D: d: Mitteldeutscher Funkverband, Leipzig

M.f.V. D: d: Museum für Völkerkunde, Berlin

MfVFuK d: Minister(ium) für Vertriebene, Flüchtlinge und Kriegssachgeschädigte

MFW INT: pl: Międzynarodowy Fundusz Walutowy [= e: IMF]

M.F.W. D: d: Mitteldeutsche Fahrradwerke GmbH, Sangerhausen

M.f.Wi.u.A. D: d: Ministerium für Wirtschaft und Arbeit, Berlin

MfWKuV d: Minister(ium) für Wissenschaft, Kunst und Volksbildung

MfWuA d: Minister(ium) für Wirtschaft und Arbeit

MfWuV d: Ministerium für Wirtschaft und Verkehr

MG d: Mädchengymnasium

M.G. F: f: Marine de Guerre; Marraines

de Guerre; D: d: mil: WK2: Militärbefehlshaber im Generalgouvernement

MG d: mil: Militärgericht; e: mil: Military Government

M.G. f: Ministère de Guerre; s: Ministerio de la Guerra

MG PL: pl: Ministerstwo Górnictwa; I: i: Movimento Giovanile

M.G. F: f: Mutilés de Guerre

M.G.A. IND: e: Madras Geographical Association; GB: e: Midland Gravels Association; US: e: mil: Military Government Association

MGA P: pt: Missão Geográfica de Angola, Junta de Investigações do Ultramar, Nova Lisboa; GB: e: Mushroom Growers Association

MGB CH: d: MIGROS-Genossenschafts-Bund, 8005 Zürich; SU [s: Ministerium für Staatssicherheit [1946...53]

MGC H: hu: Magyar Golf-Club, Budapest; BRD: d: Mittelrheinischer Golf-Club, Bad Ems; Münchener Golf-Club

MGCA US: e: Men's Garden Clubs of America; Mushroom Growers Cooperative Association

MGD BRD: d: mil: Militärgeographische Dokumentation; NL: nl: mil: Militair-Geneeskundige Dienst; NATO: e: Military Geographic Documentation

M.G.E. H: hu: Magyar Geofizikusok Egyesülete, Budapest

MGE US: e: Milwaukee (Minneapolis) Grain Exchange

M.G.E.N. F: f: Mutuelle Générale de l'Education Nationale

MGF I: i: Movimento Giovanile dei Focolari; US: e: Myasthenia Gravis Foundation

MGFA BRD: d: mil: Militärgeschichtliches Forschungsamt, 78 Freiburg

MGFHU P: pt: Missão de Geografia Física e Humana do Ultramar, Junta de Investigações do Ultramar, Lisboa

MGG e: mil: Military Government for

Germany [WK2]

M.G.H. US: e: Massachusetts General Hospital

MGHG P: pt: Missão Geo-Hidrográfica da Guiné

MGI ETH: e: Imperial Ethiopian Mapping and Geographical Institute

M.G.I. B: nl: mil: Militair Geografisch Instituut

MGiE PL: pl: Ministerstwo Górnictwa i Energetyki

M.G.K. NL: nl: Maatschappij voor Gemeentekrediet

MGK SU: [d: Ministerium für Staatskontrolle] ; PL: pl: Ministerstwo Gospodarki Komunalnej

MGKI H: hu: Mezőgazdasági Gépkisérleti Intézet, Budapest

MGM US: e: Metro-Goldwyn-Mayer Picture Corporation; MOC: pt: Missão Geográfica de Moçambique, Junta de Investigações do Ultramar, Lisboa

M.G.M.S. GB: e: Manchester Geological and Mining Society

M.&G.N.; M.&G.N.R. GB: e: Midland and Great Northern Railway ["Muddle and get nowhere"]

MGOTS e: mil: Machine-Gun Officers' Training School

M.Govt e: mil: Military Government

M.G.P.C. e: Medical Group Practice Council

MGS e: mil: Machine Gun School (Section)

M.G.S. GB: e: Manchester Geographical Society; Manchester Grammar School; US: e: Mississippi Geological Society; I: i: Movimento Giovanile Socialista

MGSch e: mil: Machine Gun School

MGST US: e: mil: Military Geography Specialist Team

MGT P: pt: Missão Geográfica de Timor, Junta de Investigações do Ultramar, Lisboa

MGTA D: f: nach WK2: mil: Mission des Grands Travaux Aéronautiques, Baden-Baden

MGU SU: [d: Moskauer staatliche Lomonossow-Universität]

MGV d: Männergesangverein

M.G.W. IRL: e: Midland Great Western [railway]

MGW PL: pl: Ministerstwo Górnictwa Węglowego [1955...57]

M.&G.W.R. IRL: e: = M.G.W.

M.G.W.U. e: Malta General Workers Union Valetta

MGYT H: hu: Magyar Gyógyszertudományi Társaság, Budapest

MH DDR: d: Maschinenfabrik Halle

MH BRD: d: Eisenwerk-Gesellschaft Maximilianshütte mbH, 8458 Sulzbach-Rosenberg Hütte

M.H. e: mil: Military Hospital; s: Ministerio de Hacienda

MH PL: pl: Ministerstwo Hutnictwa

M.H. GB: e: Ministry of Health; nl: More Herbewapening; F: f: Musée de l'Homm Paris

MH S: sv: Musikhögskolan, Stockholm

MHA GB: e: Mansion House Association on Transport; US: e: Marine Historical Association

M.H.A. e: Medical Hospitals Association; Mental Hospitals Association; Methodist Homes for the Aged; GB: e: Ministry of Home Affairs; Mutual Households Association

MHAO US: e: Mental Health Association of Oregon

MHA/OKM D: d: mil: WK2: Marinehelferinnenabteilung beim OKM

MHAP PL: pl: Museum Historyczne Aptekarstwa Polskiego

M.H.A.R.C.T. GB: e: Mansion House Association on Railway and Canal Traffic

MHAST P: pt: Missão Hidrográfica de Angola e S. Tomé

MHBA US: e: Medical Dental Hospital Bureau of America

MHC US: e: Morgan Horse Club; Mount Holyoke College

HCC US: e: Mobile Housing Carriers Conference

HCS US: e: Mental Hygiene Consultation Service

HCV P: pt: Missã Hidrográfica do Arquipélageo de Cabo Verde

HD BRD: d: Malteser-Hilfsdienst; e: Medical and Health Department; DDR: d: Meteorologischer und Hydrologischer Dienst; PL: pl: Miejski Handel Detaliczny; D: d: mil: Munitions-Hauptdepot

&HDA US: e: mil: Medical and Hospital Department, U.S.Army

HDNA US: e: Mobile Homes Dealers National Association

HEA D: d: mil: WK2: Marinehelferinnen-Ersatzabteilung; GB: e: Material Handling Engineers Association

HEDA US: e: Material Handling Equipment Distributors Association

·H·F BRD: d: Mecklenburgische Hagel- und Feuer-Versicherungs-Gesellschaft aG, 3 Hannover [gegr 1797]

HF S: sv: Motorförarnas Helnykterhetsförbund, Stockholm [gegr 1926]

HH CS: cs: Matice Hornicko-Hutnická; BRD: d: Medizinsche Hochschule Hannover

HI US: e: Material Handling Institute

.H.I. GB: e: Ministry of Health Inspectorate

HI J: e: Mitsubishi Heavy Industries Ltd., Tokyo; BRD: d: Mitteldeutsche Hartstein-Industrie AG, Ffm

.H.I.W.U. e: Mental Hospital and Institutional Workers' Union

HJ D: d: NS: Marine-Hitlerjugend

.H.K. D: d: mil: Hochschulkommando der Marine

.H.L.B. GB: e: Ministry of Health, Legal Branch

.H.L.G. GB: e: Ministry of Housing and Local Government

HM PL: pl: Miejski Handel Mięsem;

d: Mill-Hill-Missionare, 44 Münster; MOC: pt: Missão Hidrográfica de Moçambique

MHMA US: e: Mobile Homes Manufacturers Association, Chicago, Ill.

M.H.M.B. GB: e: Ministry of Health, Medical Branch

MHMP CS: cs: Museum Hlavního Města Prahy

M.H.M.S. GB: e: Middlesex Hospital Medical School

MHN RA: s: Museo Histórico Nacional

MHO S: sv: Medicinska högskolornas organisationskommitté; NL: nl: Medisch Hoger Onderwijs

M.H.O.A. GB: e: Mental Hospital Officers' Association

MHP TR: [d: nationale Aktionspartei]

MHPRD CS: cs: Ministerstvo Hutního Průmyslu a Rudných Dolů

MHPRR PL: pl: Muzeum Historii Polskiego Ruchu Rewolucyjnego

MHR CH: f: Musée Historique de la Réformation

MHRA GB: e: Modern Humanities Research Association

MHRI US: e: Mental Health Research Institute [University of Michigan]

MHS US: e: Massachusetts Historical (Horticultural) Society; nl: Meisjes Hogere School; PL: pl: Międzynarodowy Hotel Studencki

M.H.S. e: mil: Military Heraldry (Historical) Society; e: Ministry of Home Security

MHS CS: cs: Mládežnické Hnuti za Svovodu

M.H.S.F. GB: e: Metropolitan Hospital Sunday Fund

MHSM US: e: Mental Hygiene Society of Maryland

M.H.S.S. GB: e: Ministry of Home Security Schools

M.H.T. H: hu: Magyar Hidrológiai Társaság, Budapest

MHT US: e: Manufacturers Hanover Trust, New York, N.Y. 10022

MHuG d: Minister(ium) für Handel und Gewerbe

MHV DK: da; mil: Marinehjemmevaernet

M.H.V.P. F: f: Musée d'Hygiène de la Ville de Paris

MHW PL: pl: Ministerstwo Handlu Wewnętrznego

MHZ PL: pl: Ministerstwo Handlu Zagranicznego

M.I. I: i: mil: Marina Italiana

MI US: e: Mellon Institute of Industrial Research; GB: e: mil: Middlesex Regiment

M.I. GB: e: Midwives' Institute Incorporated; f: Ministère de l'Information (l'Intérieur); s: Ministerio Interior

MI CS: cs: Ministerstvo Informací

M.I. l: Clerici Regulares Ministrantes Infirmes; e: Ministry of Information

M-I US: e: Missouri - Illinois Railroad

M.I. DZ: f: Groupe Musulman Indépendant pour la Défense du Fédéralisme Algérien

M.I.5 GB: e: mil: Military Intelligence Department [War Office]

M.I.6 GB: e: mil: Military Intelligence [Foreign Office]

MIA GB: e: Malleable Ironfounders' Association; US: e: Marble Institute of America, Washington, D.C. 20004; CDN: e: Manitoba Institute of Agrologists; US: e: Mica Industry Association; Millinery Institute of America

M.I.A. R: ro: Ministerul Industriei Alimentare, Bucureşti; US: e: Montgomery Improvement Association

MIAA US: e: Mutual Insurance Advisory Association

MIAG BRD: d: Mühlenbau und Industrie GmbH, 33 Braunschweig

M.I.A.I. RI: Madjelis Islam A'la Indonesia

MIAM DDR: d: Ministerium für Innerdeutschen Handel, Außenhandel und Materialversorgung

MIAMSI INT: f: Mouvement International d'Apostolat des Milieux Sociaux Indépendants

MIAP INT: f: Mouvement International d'Action pour la Paix

MIAPD US: e: mil: Mid-Central Air Procurement District

MIAS INT: [d: Internationaler Sportartikel-Salon, Milano, I]

MIB GB: e: Metal Information Bureau; BRD: d: Münchner Institut für Betriebführung eV, 8 München 14

MIBAU BRD: d: Mitteldeutsche Bau-AG für gemeinnützigen Wohn- und Siedlungsbau, 6 Ffm

M.I.C. PTM: e: Malayan (Malaysian) Indi Congress, Kuala Lumpur; GB: e: Manchester Information Committee; 1: Clerici Clericorum Marianorum Regulares; f: Ministère de l'Industrie et du Commerce; B: f: Mouvement chrétien des indépendants et des cadres

MICE US: e: Mutual Insurance Council of Editors

MICh INT: pl: Międzynarodowy Instytut Chłodnictwa

MichAS US: e: Michigan Audubon Socie

M.I.C.I.A.C. F: f: Mouvement d'Ingénieu et Chefs d'Industrie d'Action Catholiq

MICO IND: e: Motor Industries Co.Ltd., Bangalore

MICOFT US: e: Mutual Insurance Committee on Federal Taxation

MICOM US: e: mil: Missile Command, Redstone (Ala.) Arsenal

Microtecnic 69 INT: d: Zweite Internationale Fachmesse für Präzisionstechnik und dimensionales Messen und Prüfen, Zürich [CH, 30 Jan...4 Feb 1969]

M.I.C.U.M. D: f: nach WK1: Mission Interalliée de Contrôle des Usines et de Mines

MICUMA f: Société des Mines de Cuivre de Mauritanie

ID BRD: d: mil: Militärische Infrastrukturdienststelle; e: mil: Military Intelligence Department (Detachment) (Division)

I.D. GB: e: Mines Inspection Department

ID SU: [d: Ministerium für auswärtige Angelegenheiten] ; RA: s: Movimiento de Integración y Desarrolo

IDA US: e: mil: Major Item Data Agency; GB: e: Midland Industrial Designers' Association

IDEC INT: e: Middle East Industrial Development Projects Corporation [gegr 1958 in Luxemburg]

IDEM INT: f: Marché International du Disque et de l'Edition Musicale, Cannes

IDFC PTM: e: Malayan Industrial Development Finance Co.

idi F: f: Compagnie des chemins de fer du Midi

IEC INT: f: Pax Romana, Mouvement International des Etudiants Catholiques, Fribourg [CH, gegr 1921]

IEG DDR: d: Mineralöle Import und Export GmbH, Berlin W 8

IEL PTM: e: Malaysian Industrial Estates Ltd.

IER US: e: mil: Military Intelligence Enlisted Reserve

IF US: e: Milk Industry Foundation; INT: e: Miners' International Federation, London S.E.1 [gegr 1890] ; INT: f: Mouvement International des Faucons

ifa D: d: Mitteldeutsche Fahrradwerke, Berlin

IFED INT: [d: internationaler Markt des Spiel-, Fernseh- und Dokumentarfilms, 20145 Milano, I]

IFEM I: i: Movimento Italiano per la Federazione Europea e Mondiale

IFERMA f: Société des mines de fer de Mauritanie

IGB GB: e: Millinery Institute of Great Britain

igros CH: d: Migros-Genossenschaftsbund Zürich

M.I.G.S. GB: e: Music Industries Golfing Society

MIH INT: pl: Międzynarodowa Izba Handlowa

M.I.H. f: Mouvement pour l'Indépendance Hongroise [gegr 1943]

MIHAG BRD: d: MIHAG Handelsgesellschaft für Mineralölerzeugnisse mbH, 4 Düsseldorf

MIIA US: e: Mine Inspectors Institute of America

MIIC INT: f: Pax Romana, Mouvement International des Intellectuels Catholiques, Fribourg [CH, gegr 1947]

MIIR US: e: Mellon Institute of Industrial Research

MIJARC INT: f: Mouvement international de la jeunesse agricole et rurale catholique, Louvain [B] s: Movimiento Internacional de la Juventud Agraria y Rural Católica

MIJM INT: f: Mouvement international de Jeunesse Mazdaznan

MIJOC INT: f: Mouvement international de la jeunesse ouvrière chrétienne

MIKI H: hu: Müszeripari Kutató Intézet, Budapest

Mila D: d: Mitteldeutsche Landlichtspiele AG, Magdeburg

Mil.-Ak. d: mil: Militär(technische)-Akademie

MilBGrp BRD: d: mil: Militärische Beratergruppe

Mil.Coll. e: mill: Military College

MILCOM e: mil: Military Committee

MilFR BRD: d: mil: Militärischer Führungsrat [= MFR, BMVtdg]

Mil G CH: d: mil: Militärgericht

Mil.Gef. D: d: mil: Militärgefängnis

MilGeoA BRD: d: mil: Militärgeographisches Amt

MilGeoDSt BRD: d: mil: Militärgeographische Dienststelle

Mil.Ger. D: d: mil: Militärgericht

MILGOV;Mil Govt e: mil: Military Government

MilHydroDSt BRD: d: mil: Militärhydrographische Dienststelle

MILID US: e: mil: Military Intelligence Department (Division)

Mil.Kab. D: d: mil: Militär-Kabinett

Mil Kass G CH: d: mil: Militärkassationsgericht

Milorg N: [d: geheime militärische Widerstandsorganisation, gegr 1940]

MIL P e: mil: Military Police [= MP]

MilR;MilReg d: Militärregierung

MILREP US: e: mil: U.S. Military Representative for Military Assistance in Europe

MILREPS NATO: e: Military Representatives Committee

Mil.San. D: d: mil: Militär-Sanatorium

MILSTAN NATO: e: Military Agency for Standardization, London [= MAS]

MILTAG US: e: mil: Military Technical Assistance Group

Mil.T.Anst. D: d: mil: Militär-Turnanstalt

Mil Trib e: mil: Military Tribunal

MILVA NL: nl: mil: Militaire Vrouwen Afdeling

Mil.Vers.A. D: d: mil: Militär-Versuchsamt

Mil.V.Ger. D: d: mil: Militärversorgungsgericht

MIMA US: e: Magnesia Insulation Manufacturers' Association

M.I.M.E. GB: e: Midland Institute of Mining Engineers

Mimex PL: pl: Centrala Eksportowo-Importowa Wyrobów Przemysłu Mineralnego

MIMM MEX:[e: Mexican Institution of Mining and Metallurgy]

M.I.N. F: f: Marché d'Intérêt National, Rungis [seit 1969]

MINA pt: Movimento para la Independência Nacional de Angola

Min.AA.EE. I: i: Ministero degli Affari Esteri, Roma

Min.AA.EE.-D.G.R.C. I: i: Ministero degli Affari Esteri - Direzione Generale Relazioni Culturali

Min.A.I. I: i: Ministero dell'Africa Italiana Roma

MinArb. D: d: Arbeitsministerium

Min.Bil. I: i: Ministerio del Bilancio, Roma

Mincomes I: i: Ministero del Commercio Estero, Roma

MINCULPOP I: i: Ministero della Cultura Popolare, Roma

Min.d.I. d: Minister(ium) des Innern

Mineis. D: d: [mil:] Eisenbahnministerium

MinErn. D: d: Ministerium für Ernährung und Landwirtschaft

MINEVDET US: e: mil: Mine Warfare Evaluation Detachment, Key West, Fla

M.Inf. D: d: mil: Marine-Infanterie

Min.f.E.L.F. d: Ministerium für Ernährung Landwirtschaft und Forsten

Min.f.HG d: Ministerium für Handel und Gewerbe

MinFin. D: d: Finanzministerium

Min.Fin. I: i: Ministero delle Finanze,Roma

Min.Fin. - Dir.Gen.DD.II.II. I: i: Ministero delle Finanze - Direzione Generale Dogane e Imposte Indirette, Roma

Min.f.U.u.K. d: Ministerium für Unterricht und Kultus

Min.f.V. D: d: Ministerium für Volkswohlfahrt

Min.G.G. I: i: Ministero di Grazia e Giustizia, Roma

MIngK S: sv: mil: Mariningenjörkåren

Min.I.C. I: i: Ministero dell'Industria e del Commercio, Roma

Min.Inf. 1: Ministrantes Infirmes Clerici Regulares

MinInn. D: d: Ministerium des Innern

Min.Int. I: i: Ministero degli Interni, Roma

MINITECH GB: e: Ministry of Technology, London

MinJust. D: d: Justizministerium

MINLANT US: e: mil: Mine Warfare Forces, Atlantic

MINOT LRS YU: sn: Ministrstvo Notranjih Poslov Ljudska Republike Slovenije

MINPAC US: e: mil: Mine Warfare Forces, Pacific

Min.P.I. I: i: Ministero della Pubblica Istruzione, Roma

Min.PiT PL: pl: Ministerstwo Poczt i Telegrafów

MinPost. D: d: Postministerium

Min.PP.TT. I: i: Ministero delle Poste e Telecomunicazioni, Roma

MINSZ H: hu: Magyar Ifjuság Népi Szövetsége, Budapest

M.Int. D: d: mil: Marine-Intendant(ur)

MinTech GB: e: Ministry of Technology, London

MIntK S: sv: mil: Marinintendenturkåren

Min.Trasp. I: i: Ministero dei Trasporti, Roma

Min.v.B.Z. NL: nl: Ministerie van Binnenlandsche (Buitenlandsche) Zaken

Min.v.Def. NL: nl: mil: Ministerie van Defensie

MinVerk. D: d: Verkehrsministerium

Min.v.E.Z. NL: nl: Ministerie van Economische Zaken

Min.v.Fin. NL: nl: Ministerie van Financiën

Min.v.J. NL: nl: Ministerie van Justitie

MinVk. D: d: Verkehrsministerium

Min.v.Kol. NL: nl: Ministerie van Kolonien

Min.v.S.Z. NL: nl: Ministerie van Sociale Zaken

Min.v.W. NL: nl: Ministerie van Waterstaat

Min.Výk. CS: cs: Ministerstvo Výkupu, Praha

MinWehr. D: d: mil: Wehrministerium

MinWirtsch. D: d: Wirtschaftsministerium

MinWiss. D: d: Ministerium für Wissenschaft, Kunst und Volksbildung [Preußen]

MIO CS: cs: Ministerstvo Informací a Osvěty, Praha

MIOT H: hu: Magyar Ifjuság Országos Tanácsa, Budapest

MIP US: e: Manufacturers of Illuminating Products

MiP PL: pl: Miecz i Pług

M.I.P. f: Ministère de l'Instruction Publique

MIP PL: pl: Ministerstwo Informacji i Propagandy; R: ro: Ministerul Învăţămîntului Public, Bucureşti; IND: e: Ministry of Irrigation and Power, New Delhi

MIPEL I: [d: italienische Lederwarenmesse, Mailand] i: Mercato Italiano della Pelletteria

MIPI RI: Madjelis Ilmu Pengetahuan Indonesia, Djakarta

Mipo d: Militärpolizei

MIPO NL: nl: Muziekschool voor Instrumentaal Privaat Onderwijs

MIPROGUERRA I: i: mil: Ministero per la Produzione Bellica

Mipsz H: hu: Magyar Ifjak Pozsonyi Szövetsége

M.I.R. D: d: mil: Marine-Infanterie-Regiment

MIR NL: nl: Mijnindustrieraad; s: Movimiento de Izquierda Revolucionaria; PL: pl: Morski Instytut Rybacki

M.I.R.A. GB: e: The Motor Industry Research Association, Lindley

Mirag D: d: Mitteldeutsche Rundfunk -Aktiengesellschaft

MIRB US: e: Mutual Insurance Rating Bureau

MIRS e: mil: Military Intelligence Research Service

MIS S: sv: mil: Militär Idrotts Stockholmsdistrikt; US: e: mil: Military Intelligence School (Service); Military Interpreter Service

M.I.S. GB: e: Mining Institute of Scotland; I: i: Movimento per la indipendenza della Sicilia [gegr 1943]

M.I.S.C. PTM: e: Malaysian International Shipping Corporation "Berhad"

MISC e: mil: Military Intelligence Service Center

MISLIC GB: e: Mid-Staffordshire Libraries in Co-operation

MISMA US: e: mil: Major Items Supply Management Agency

MISMW PL: pl: Międzynarodowe Igrzyska Sportowe Młodzieży Wiejskiej

MISO I: i: Mostra Internazionale Scambi Occidente

MISR GB: e: Macaulay Institute for Soil Research

MISRAIR ET: [d: Luftverkehrsgesellschaft]

MISSA US: e: mil: Management Information System Support Agency

MISZB H: hu: Magyar Ipari Szabványsitó Bizottság, Budapest

M.I.T. IND: e: Madras Institute of Technology

MIT PTM: e: MARA Institute of Technology, Kuala Lumpur; US: e: Massachusetts Institute of Technology, Cambridge, Mass.; E: s: Ministerio de Información y Turismo, Madrid; PL: pl: Morski Instytut Techniczny

Mita CH: d: Schweizerischer Verband der Mineralwasser- und Tafelgetränke-Industrie

MITAM INT: i: Mercato Internazionale del Tessile e dell'Abbigliamento, Milano

MIT-DIC US: e: Massachusetts Institute of Technology, Division of Industrial Cooperation

MITE H: hu: Mezőgazdasági és Élelmiszer Ipari Tudományos Egyesület, Budapest

MITI J: e: Ministry of International Trade and Industry

MIT-IL US: e: Massachusetts Institute of Technology, Instrumentation Laboratory

MITKhT SU: [e: Lomonosov Moscow Institute of Fine Chemical Technology]

MIT-LIR US: e: Massachusetts Institute of Technology, Laboratory for Insulation Research

MIT-RE US: e: Massachusetts Institute of Technology, Research and Engineering Group

MIT-RLE US: e: Massachusetts Institute of Technology, Research Laboratory of Electronics

Mitropa D: d: Mitteleuropäische Schlafwagen- und Speisewagen-AG

MIV NL: nl: Melk-Inkoop-Vereniging

MIVA B: nl: Maatschappij voor Intercommunaal Vervoer Antwerpen; BRD: d: Missions-Verkehrs-Arbeitsgemeinschaft

MIW NL: nl: Mijnarbeiders-Invalideitsen Ouderdomswet

MIZ BRD: d: mil: Materialinformationszentrum der Marine GmbH, 2940 Wilhelmshaven [gegr 1968]

Mizrahi IL: [d: nationalreligiöse Front]

MJ BRD: d: Marinejugend

M.J. F: f: Ministère de la Justice; GB: e: Ministry of Justice; l: Societas Missionarum Sancti Josephi de Mill Hill

M.J.A. GB: e: Merchant Jewellers' Association

M.J.C. F: f: Maison des Jeunes et de la Culture

MJD BRD: d: Musikalische Jugend Deutschlands

MJGA US: e: Midwest Job Galvanizers Association; D: d: Mittelstelle für Jugendgrenzlandarbeit

M.J.I. s: Ministerio de Justicia y Instrucción

M.J.K. D: d: Marianische Jünglingskongregation

MJK S: sv: Motorjournalisternas klubb

MJÖ; MJOe A: d: Musikalische Jugend Österreichs

MJP f: Mouvement de Jeunesse Panafricain

MJR NL: nl: Moderne Jeugdraad

MJSA US: e: Manufacturing Jewelers

and Silversmiths of America
IJSR CH: f: Mouvement de la Jeunesse Suisse Romande
IJSV D: d: Münchener Journalisten- und Schriftstellerverein
IJSZ H: hu: Magyar Jogász Szövetség, Budapest
IJUPS SN: f: Mouvement des Jeunes de l'Union Progressiste Sénégalaise
IK BRD: d: mil: Marinekameradschaft; INT: pl: Miedzynarodowy Komunistyczna [= Komintern] ; CS: cs: Ministerstvo Kultury; PL; pl: Ministerstwo Kolei (Komunikacji); d: Missionskonferenz; A: d: Mittelschulkongregation; S: sv: motorklubb
IKA US: e: Machine Knife Association; D: d: mil: Marinekommandiertenabteilung [OKM] ; Marinekraftfahrabteilung
1.K.A. D: d: mil: Marine-Küstenartillerie
1.K.A.T.A. GB: e: Machine Knife and Allied Trades Association
IKChZZ INT: pl: Międzynarodowa Konfederacja Chrześcijańskich Związków Zawodowych [e: IFCTU]
IKCK INT: pl: Międzynarodowy Komitet Czerwonego Krzyża [d: IKRK]
I.K.E. H: hu: A Magyar Köztársaság Elnöke
IKE PL: pl: Miejska Kolej Elektryczna
IKEA D: d: mil: Marinekraftfahrersatzabteilung
IKF DDR: d: Maschinenbau-Kombinat Freital
IKFN PL: pl: Miejski Komitet Frontu Narodowego
IKG D: d: Münchener Künstlergenossenschaft
IKhTI SU: [e: Moscow Institute of Chemical Technology]
IKiS PL: pl: Ministerstwo Kultury i Sztuki
IKK S: sv: Metodistkyrkans Kvinnosällskap, Stockholm
IKKF PL: pl: Miejski Komitet Kultury Fizycznej
IKKFiT PL: pl: Miejski Komitet Kultury

Fizycznej i Turystyki
MKKH H: hu: Magyar Külkereskedelmi Hivatal, Budapest
MKKI H: hu: Magyar Külkereskedelmi Igazgatóság, Budapest
MK KPS YU: sn: Mestni Komite Komunistične Partije Slovenije
MKL PL: pl: Miejska Komisja Lokalowa
MK LMS YU: sn: Mladinski Komite Ljudske Mladine Slovenije, Ljubljana
MKLS NL: nl: Middelbare Koloniale Landbouwschool
MKN S: sv: mil: Marinkommando Nord
MKNiK PL: pl: Międzynarodowa Komisja Nadzoru i Kontroli
MKO S: sv: mil: Marinkommando Ost
MKO I INT: pl: Międzynarodowy Komitet Olimpijski
MKOS PL: pl: Miejski Komitet Opieki Społecznej
MKOW PL: pl: Miejski Komitet Odbudowy Warszawy
MKP H: hu: Magyar Kommunista Párt, Budapest; D: d: mil: Marineküstenpolizei; PL: pl: Międzypartyjne Koło Polityczne; Ministerstwo Kontroli Państwowej
MKPG PL: pl: Miejska Komisja Planowania Gospodarczego
MKPN S: sv: Mellankommunala prövningsnämnden
MKR PL: pl: Miejska Komisja Rewizyjna
MKRADC US: e: Middle Kentucky River Area Development Council
M.Kr.Ak. D: d: mil: Marine-Kriegsakademie
MKS BRD: d: Mainkraftwerk Schweinfurt; S: sv: mil: Marinkommando Syd; D: d: mil: Marine-Kriegsschule; PL: pl: Międzyszkolne Koło Sportowe; Międzyszkolny Klub Sportowy; Międzyuczelniany Klub Studencki; Miejski Klub Sportowy; Milicyjny Klub Sportowy; Motorowy Klub Sportowy
MKSz H: hu: Magyar Kerékpáros Szövetség, Budapest

MKT PL: pl: Miejski Klub Tenisowy; US: e: Missouri-Kansas-Texas Railroad Company

MKTiR PL: pl: Międzyzakładowy Klub Techniki i Racjonalizacji

MKU S: sv: Metodistkyrkans Ungdomsförbund; d: Ministerium für Kultus und Unterricht

MKUA PL: pl: Miejski Komitet Urbanistyki i Architektury

MKüDstS BRD: d: mil: Marineküstendienstschule, 2443 Großenbrode

MKV S: sv: mil: Marinkommando Väst

M.K.V. D: d: Mitteleuropäischer Kraftfahrer-Verband eV, Berlin

MKV A: d: stud: Mittelschüler-Kartellverband der katholischen farbentragenden Studentenkorporationen Österreichs

MKVB D: d: Münchener Künstlervereinigung "Der Bund"

MKWZZ INT: pl: Międzynarodowa Konfederacja Wolnych Związków Zawodowych [= ICFTU]

MKZ BRD: d: mil: Materialkontrollzentrum

ML SF: fi: Maalaisliitto

M.L. D: d: mil: Marineleitung

ML BlnW: d: Marxisten-Leninisten; US: e: mil: Materials Laboratory [USAF]; e: Medical Laboratory; PL: pl: Milicja Ludowa

ML PL: pl: Ministerstwo Łączności

ML PL: pl: Ministerstwo Leśnictwa

M.L. CDN: e: Ministry of Labour; F: f: Musée de Louvre; d: Mutterloge

MLA US: e: Maine Library Association; Maine Lobstermen's Association; CDN: e: Manitoba Library Association; D: d: mil: Marinelehrabteilung; US: e: Maritime Law Association of the United States; Maryland Library Association; Massachusetts Library Association; Medical Library Association; Mercantile Library Association; Mich-

igan Library Association; Minnesota (Mississippi) (Missouri) Library Association

M.L.A. GB: e: Modern Languages Association [gegr 1893]

MLA US: e: Modern Languages Association of America, New York; Montana Library Association; Music Library Association

MLAA US: e: Modern Languages Association of America, New York

MLäkK S: sv: mil: Marinläkarkåren

M.L.A.J. f: Mouvement Laïques des Auberges de la Jeunesse

MLAUS US: e: Maritime Law Association of the United States

M.L.B. D: d: mil: Militär-Lehrschmiede Berlin

MLC US: e: Mergenthaler Linotype Company, Brooklyn; e: mil: Military Liaison Committee; AUS: e: Mutual Life and Citizens' Assurance Co.Ltd.

MLCAEC US: e: mil: Military Liaison Committee to the Atomic Energy Commission

M.L.C.R.O. GB: e: Ministry of Labour Claims and Records Office

MLD NL: nl: mil: Militaire Luchtvaartdienst; e: mil: Mixed Liaison Detachment

MLDP CS: cs: Ministerstvo Lesů a Dřevařského Průmyslu

MLDuF D: d: = MfLDuF

MLEA US: e: Metal Lath Export Association

MLEC P: pt: Movimento da Libertação do Enclave de Cabinda [Angola]

MLEU INT: f: Mouvement libéral pour l'Europe unie, Bruxelles [B]

MLF US: e: Medical Liberation Front; S: sv: Modersmålslärarnas Förening

M.L.F. F: f: Mouvement de la Libération Française

MLF e: mil: Mobile Land Force(s); Multilateral Force [1963 geplant]

MLG P: pt: Movimento de Libertação da Guiné

MLGA US: e: Merchant's Ladies Garment Association

MLGC; MLGCV P: pt: Movimento de Libertação da Guiné e Cabo Verde

MLGP pt: Movimento de Libertação da Guiné Português

M.L.I. GB: e: mil: Marine Light Infantry

MLiPD PL: pl: Ministerstwo Leśnictwa i Przemysłu Drzewnego

MLLV BRD: d: Münchener Lehrer- und Lehrerinnen-Verein

M.L.M. PTM: e: Muslim League of Malaya, Kuala Lumpur

MLMA US: e: Metal Lath Manufacturers Association

M.L.M.A. GB: e: Moss Litter Manufacturers Association

M.L.N. f: Mouvement Africain de la Libération Nationale; F: f: Mouvement de la Libération Nationale

MLN GCA: MEX: s: Movimiento de Liberación Nacional

MLNA P: pt: Movimento Nacional de Libertação de Angola

M.L.N.S. GB: e: Ministry of Labour and National Service

MLO YU: sn: Mestni Ljudski Odbor

MLÖ A: d: Marxisten-Leninisten Österreichs

MLP CS: cs: Ministerstvo Lehkého Průmyslu; F: f: Mouvement du Libération du Peuple [gegr 1950]

MLPD BRD: d: Marxistisch-Leninistische Partei Deutschlands

M.LL.PP. I: i: Ministero dei Lavori Pubblici

M.L.P.S. GB: e: Manchester Literary and Philosophical Society

MLPS YU: sn: Ministrstvo za Lokalni Promet Slovenije

MLR D: d: mil: Marine-Lehrregiment

M.L.R. S: sv: Musiklärarnas Riksförbund

ML RPPS PL: pl: Milicja Ludowa Robot-niczej Partii Polskich Socjalistów

M.L.S. GB: e: Medico-Legal Society

MLS NL: nl: Middelbare Landbouwschool

M.L.S. D: d: mil: Militär-Lehrschmiede; GB: e: mil: Military Labour Service; CI: f: Mouvement pour la Libération du Sanwi

MLSA D: d: mil: Marinelandesschützen-abteilung; Z: e: Mines Local Staff Association

M.L.S.A. GB: e: Ministry of Labour Staff Association

M.L.S.D. GB: e: Ministry of Labour Solicitor's Department

MLTA US: e: Modern Languages Teachers Association

MLTS US: e: mil: Military Land Transportation Service

MLÚ CS: cs: Massarykův Lidovýchovný Ústav

MLV B: f: Maison des Langues Vivantes, Bruxelles; NL: nl: Ministerie van Landbouw en Visserij; YV: s: Movimiento Libertario de Venezuela

MLW D: d: mil: Marine-Lehrwerkstatt

M.L.W.S. GB: e: Men's League for Women's Suffrage

MM d: Mädchenmittelschule

M.M. f: Marine Marchande; i: marina mercantile

MM I: i: mil: Marina Militare [d: an Kraftfahrzeugen]; l: Societas de Maryknoll pro Missionibus Externis; BRD: d: Maschinen Miete GmbH, 6 Ffm 18; Matheus Müller, Sektkellerei, 6268 Eltville [gegr 1811]; CS: cs: Matice Moravská; BRD: d: Maybach Mercedes-Benz Motorenbau GmbH, 7990 Friedrichshafen

M.M. e: Mercantile Marine; F: f: Messageries Maritimes; e: mil: Military Mission; F: f: Ministère de la Marine; s: Ministerio de Marina; GB: e: Ministry of Mines (Munitions); Missionary of Maryknoll; f: Mission Militaire;

GB: e: mil: Monmouthshire Regiment
MM H: hu:Müveldödésügyi Miniszter(ium),
Budapest; SF: sv: Muntra Musikanter
[gegr 1878]
M.M. F: f: Musée de la Marine; Musée
Municipal; S: sv: Musikhisoriska Museet
MM D: d: Mustermesse Leipzig
MMA US: e: Maine Medical Association
M.M.A. GB: e: Manchester Mathematics
Association; CDN: e: Manitoba Medi-
cal Association; e: Married Men's As-
sociation
MMA US: e: mil: Materiel Management
Activity; US: e: Merchant Marine Acad-
emy; GB: e: Meter Manufacturers
Association; US: e: Metropolitan Mu-
seum of Art
M.M.A.A.; **MMAA** f: nach WK2: Mission
Militaire pour les Affaires Allemandes
MMB D: d: Märkisches Museum Berlin
M.M.B. GB: e: Milk Marketing Board;
CS: sk: Múzeum Mesta Bratislavy
M.M.C. e: mil: Malaya Military College;
e: Medical Milk Commission; S: sv:
Mellansvenska Mejerisammanslutningar-
nas Centralförening; e: Mixed Medical
Commission; B: f: Mouvement des
Médecins Chrétiens
M.M.D. GB: e: Mercantile Marine De-
partment
M.Mde; **M.Mde.** f: Marine Merchande
MMEA US: e: Maryland (Massachusetts)
(Michigan) (Minnesota) (Mississippi)
(Montana) Music Educators Association
MMEC GB: e: Machinery and Metals Ex-
port Club
MMF S: sv: Mälarens Motorbåtsförbund;
US: e: mil: National Association of Master
Mechanics and Foremen of Naval Shore
Establishments; e: Meals for Millions
Foundation
MMFPA US: e: Man-Made Fiber Producers
Association
MMFPB US: e: Mill Mutual Fire Preven-
tion Bureau

MMG f: Mouvement Mixte Gabonaise;
BRD: d: Münchener Messe- und Aus-
stellungsgesellschaft mbH, 8 München 1
MMH CS: cs: Ministerstvo Místního
Hospodářství
M.M.H.G. F: f: mil: Mutilés Militaires
"Hors Guerre"
M.M.I.Arch. H: hu: Munkásmozgalmi In-
tézet Archivuma, Budapest
M.Mil. f: Marine Militaire
M.M.L.A. F: f: mil: Mission Militaire de
Liaison Administrative
MMM DDR: d: Bewegung Messen der Mei
ster von morgen
M.M.M. F: f: Ministère de la Marine Mar-
chande; I: i: Ministero della Marina
Mercantile
MMM US: e: Minnesota Mining and Man-
ufacturing Company, St. Paul 6 [= 3M
Company] ; Modern Music Masters;
INT: f: Mouvement Mondial des Mères,
Paris[F, gegr 1947] s: Movimiento
Mundial de la Madres
MMMI US: e: Meat Machinery Manufac-
turers' Institute
M.M.M.O.R.F. GB: e: Mercantile Marine
Masters' and Officers' Relief Fund
MMN S: sv: Matematikmaskinnämnden;
B: f: Métallurgie et Mécanique Nuclé-
aires
MMOG US: e: Merchant Marine Officers
Guild
MMP US: e: International Organization
of Masters, Mates and Pilots
M.M.P. GB: e: mil: Military Mounted
Police
MMP US: e: mil: Munich Military Post
[BRD]
MMPA US: e: Magnetic Materials Pro-
ducers Association
MMR NL: nl: mil: Ministerie van Defensie
Materieelraad
M.M.R. S: sv: Motormännens Riksförbun
MMRA CDN: e: Maritime Marshland Re-
habilitation Association

MMRC BRD: US: e: mil: Materiel Management Review Committee

M.M.S. GB: e: Manchester Medical Society

MMS US: e: Massachusetts Medical Society

M.M.S. GB: e:Methodist Missionary Society; f: mil: Mission militaire soviétique; e: Moravian Missionary Society; US: e: Musical Masterpiece Society

M.M.S.A. e: Mercantile Marine Service Society

MMSA US: e: mil: Military Medical Supply Agency; Mining and Metallurgical Society of America, New York 4, N.Y.

MMSW US: e: International Union of Mine, Mill and Smelter Workers

MMT H: hu: Magyar Müvészeti Tanács, Budapest; S: sv: Malmö Mekaniska Tricotfabriks AB

MMUC S: sv: mil: Militärmedicinska undersökningscentralen

MMV TR: tr: Milli Müdafaa Vekâleti, Ankara; D: d: Mischmaschinen-Verband; Mitteleuropäischer Motorwagenverein; BRD: d: e: Leasing Mittelrheinische Maschinenvermietung GmbH, 54 Koblenz

MN NL: nl: Maatschappij van Nijverheid

M.N. F: f: Marine Nationale; Musées Nationaux

MN PL: pl: Muzeum Narodowe

MNA D: d: mil: Marinenachrichtenabteilung; DZ: f: Mouvement national algérien; P: pt: Movimento Nacional de Angola

M.N.A.K. H: [d: Automobilklub]

M.N.A.M. f: Musée Nationale d'Art Moderne

M.N.A.O. GB: e: mil: Mobile Naval Airfield Organization

M.N.A.O.A. GB: e: Merchant Navy and Airline Officers' Association

M.N.Ars. D: d: mil: Marine-Nachrichtenmittelarsenal

M.N.A.S.P. B: f: Mutuelle nationale des agents des services publics

M.N.A.T.P. F: f: Musée nationale des arts et traditions populaires

MNB H: hu: Magyar Nemzeti Bank, Budapest; D: d: mil: Marine-Nachrichtenmittelbetrieb; CS: cs: Ministerstvo Národni Bezpečnosti; GB: e: Moscow Narodny Bank Ltd., London E.C.4 [gegr 1919]

M.N.B. B: f: Mouvement national belge

M.N.B.D.O. GB: e: mil: Mobile Naval Base Defence Organization

MNC S: sv: Metallnormcentralen, Stockholm [gegr 1947]; CGO: f: Mouvement National Congolais [gegr 1958]; US: e: Movement for a New Congress [gegr 1970]

M.N.C.F. GB: e: Merchant Navy Comforts Fund

MNCL CGO: f: Mouvement National Congolais - Lumumba

MNCP e: Mbandzeni National Convention Party

M.N.C.S. GB: e: Merchant Navy Comforts Service

MND D: d: mil: Marinenachrichtendienst

M.N.D. CDN: e: mil: Ministry of National Defence;P: [d: nationaldemokratische Bewegung]

MNDP MW: e: Malawi National Democratic Party

MNDSZ H: hu: Magyar Nők Demokratikus Szövetsége, Budapest; Magyarországi Németek Demokratikus Szövetsége, Budapest

M.N.E. F: f: Mouvement National de l'Epargne

M.N.E.F. F: f: Mutuelle Nationale des Etudiants de France

MNET H: hu: Magyar Népköztársaság Elnöki Tanácsa, Budapest

MNF US: e: Millers' National Federation

MNFF H: hu: Magyar Nemzeti Függetlenségi Front, Budapest

MNG D: d: Medizinisch-Naturwissenschaftliche Gesellschaft, Jena

M.N.H.N. F: f: Muséum National d'Histoire Naturelle

MNHNM MEX: s: Museo Nacional de Historia Natural in México

M.N.I. GB: e: mil: Madras Native Infantry; GB: e: Ministry of National Insurance

M.N.J. F: f: Mouvement National Judiciaire

M.N.J.R. F: f: Mouvement National de la Jeunesse Républicaine

MNK H: hu: Magyar Nemzetgyülés Könyvtára, Budapest

MNL US: e: Medical Nutrition Laboratory; GCA: s: Movimiento Nacional de Liberación

M.N.L.A. e: mil: Malayan National Liberation Army

MNLGE P: pt: Movimento Nacional da Libertação de Guiné Equadorial

M.N.M. F: f: mil: Mutuelle Nationale Militaire

MNME H: hu: Miskolci Nehézipari Müszaki Egyetem

MNMIA US: e: Men's Neckwear Manufacturers Institute of America

MNMT H: hu: Magyar Népköztársaság Minisztertanácsa, Budapest

MNO NL: nl: Middelbaar Nijverheids Onderwijs; YU: sh: Ministarstvo Narodne Odbrane; CS: sk: mil: Ministerstvo Národnej Obrany; CS: cs: mil: Ministerstvo Národní Obrany; YU: Muzej Narodne Osvoboditve LRS, Ljubljana

MNOHSP CS: cs: Ministerstvo Národní Obrany-Hlavní Publikační Správa

M.N.O.P.F. GB: e: Merchant Navy Officers' Pensions Fund

m.n.p. I: i: milizia nazionale portuaria

MNP f: Mouvement National pour la Paix; Bolivien: [e: National Revolutionary Party]

M.N.P.G.D. F: f: Mouvement National des Prisonniers de Guerre et Déportés

MNR RCB: f: Mouvement National Révolutionnaire; B: f: Mouvement National Royaliste; Bolivien: Honduras: s: Movimiento Nacionalista Revolucionario

MNRA Bolivien: s: Movimiento Nacionalista Revolucionario Auténtico

M.N.S. D: d: mil: Marine-Nachrichtenschule (...stelle); B: nl: Middelbare Normaalschool; GB: e: Ministry of National Service; US: e: Minneapolis, Northfield & Southern Railway Company

MNS CS: cs: Mládež Národních Socialistí; I: i: Movimento Nazional-Socialista

M.N.T.B. GB: e: Merchant Navy Training Board

MNTV CS: cs: Místní Národní Tělovýchovný Výbor

MNUC CGO: f: Mouvement National pour l'Unification du Congo

MNUCM I: i: Movimento Nazionale Unione Ceti Medi

M.N.U.G. F: f: Mouvement nationale pour l'union des gauches

MNUT EAT: e: Muslim National Union of Tanganyika

MNV CS: cs: Mad'arský Národní Výbor; DDR: d: mil: Ministerium für Nationale Verteidigung; CS: cs: Místní Národní Výbor

MNza(A) D: d: mil: Marineartillerie-Nebenzeugamt

MNZS YU: sn: Ministrstvo za Notranje Zadeve Slovenije

M.O. GB: e: The Meteorological Office

MO PL: pl: Milicja Obywatelska; CH: d: mil: Militärorganisation; S: sv: mil: Militieombudsman; PL: pl: Ministerstwo Odbudowy (Oświaty); CS: cs: Míst Odbor; GB: e: mil: The Monmouthshir Regiment

M.O.A. e: Ministry of Agriculture

MOA e: Ministry of Aviation; US: e: Music Operators of America

MOAA US: e: Mail Order Association of America

MOACA GB: e: Ministry of Aviation Cataloguing Authority

MOAMA US: e: mil: Mobile Air Materiel

Area, Mobile, Ala.
MOAMA 1968 BRD: d: Motivbriefmarken
-Ausstellung Mannheim [27...28 Apr]
Mob US: e: National Mobilization Com-
mittee to end the war in Viet-Nam,
New York [1967]
MOB CH: d: f: Montreux-Oberland-Bahn;
F: f: Mouvement pour l'organisation
de la Bretagne; H: hu: Müemlékek
Országos Bizottsága, Budapest
MOC E: [d: carlistische Arbeiterbewegung]
M.O.C. B: f: Mouvement Ouvrier Chrétien
MOCOM US: e: mil: Mobility Command,
Warren, Mich. [gegr 1962]
MOCP PY: s: Ministerio de Obras Públicas
y Comunicaciónes
M.O.C.S. e: mil: Mons Officer Cadet School
MOCSz H: hu: Magyar Országos Céllövö
Szövetség, Budapest
MOD US: e: March On Drugs; pl: Mię-
dzynarodowa Organizacja Dziennikarzy;
D: d: mil: Militärökonomiedepartement
[Preußisches Kriegsministerium] ; e: mil:
Ministry of Defence (Defense); GB: e:
Ministry of Overseas Development
MODAG BRD: d: Motorenfabrik Darmstadt
GmbH
MODEF; Modef F: f: Mouvement de défense
des exploitations familiales
MOE: M.o.E. GB: e: Ministry of Educa-
tion
M.O.E.C. CO: [f: Mouvement ouvrier,
étudiant et paysan]
M.O.F.; MOF GB: e: Ministry of Food,
London S.W. 1
M.O.F. F: f: Mouvement Ouvrier Français
M.of A.&F. GB: e: Ministry of Agriculture
and Fisheries
M.O.F.A.P. GB: e: Ministry of Fuel and
Power
M. of Arch. e: Museum of Archaeology
and Ethnology
M. of F. GB: e: Ministry of Food
M. of F.&P. GB: e: Ministry of Fuel and
Power

M. of I. GB: e: Ministry of Information
M. of L.; M. of Lab. e: Ministry of Labour
M. of M. GB: e: Ministry of Munitions
M. of P. GB: e: Ministry of Power
M. of S. GB: e: Ministry of Supply
MOG US: e: Metropolitan Opera Guild
MOGA US: e: Mid-Continent Oil and Gas
Association
MOGA 70 INT: e: 8th International Con-
ference on Microwave and Optical Gen-
eration and Amplification, Amsterdam
[NL, 7...11 Sep]
MOGRAMA BRD: d: Fachausstellung
moderner graphischer Maschinen, Stutt-
gart [21...28 Jun 1970]
MOH BRD: d: mil: Marine-Offizier-Hilfe
eV; US: e: Metropolitan Opera House,
New York [= Met]
M.O.H. e: Ministry of Health
M.O.H.S. e: Medical Officers' Health Service
M.O.I. GB: e: Ministry of Information;
Ministry of the Interior
M.O.I.S. e: Medical Officers' Information
Service
MOiSW PL: pl: Ministerstwo Oświaty i
Szkolnictwa Wyższego
M.O.J.M.R.P. GB: e: Meteorological Office.
Joint Meteorological Propagation Sub-
-Committee
M.O.K. D: d: mil: Marine-Oberkommando
MOK H: hu: Muzeumok Országos Központ-
tja, Budapest
MOKI H: hu: Magyar Országos Közegé-
szségüyi Intézet, Budapest
MOKlk D: d: mil: Marineoffizierkleider-
kasse [OKM]
MOL YU: sn: Mestna Občina Ljubljanska
M.O.L. e: Ministry of Labour
M.O.L.N.S. GB e: Ministry of Labour
and National Service
M.O.M. GB: e: Ministry of Munitions
MOMA US: e: Museum of Modern Art,
New York
MOMS US: e: Mothers for Moral Stability
MOMU P: pt: Missão Organizadora do

Museu do Ultramar, Lisboa

MON PL: pl: mil: Ministerstwo Obrony Narodowej; GB: e: mil: The Monmouth-shire Regiment

MONALIGE f; Mouvement National de Libération de la Guinée Equatorial

MonAmt d: Monopolamt für Branntwein

MONECO f: Mouvement Neutraliste Congolais

MONIMA RM: f: Mouvement National pour l'Indépendance de Madagascar

MONY US: e: Mutual Life Insurance Company of New York, New York 19

Monzame [d: mongolische Nachrichten-agentur]

MO OF YU: sn: Mestni Odbor Osvobodilne Fronte

MOOP SU: [d: Ministerium zum Schutze der öffentlichen Ordnung]

MOP INT: pl: Międzynarodowa Organizacja Pracy

M.O.P. s: Ministerio de Obras Públicas; GB: e: Ministry of Pensions (and Social Insurance); Ministry of Production

Mo-Pac; MoPacRR US: e: Missouri - Pacific Railroad Company

MOPC PY: s: Ministerio de Obras Públicas y Comunicaciónes

MOPI SU: [e: Moscow Regional Pedagogical Institute]

MOPLA pt: Movimento Popular por la Libertação de Angola

MOPR pl: Międzynarodowa Organizacja Pomocy Rewolucjonistom

M.O.P.S. [d: sozialistische Arbeiterpartei in Palästina]

MOPSP CS: cs: Ministerstvo Ochrany Práce a Sociální Péče

MOR d: Oberrealschule für Mädchen

M.O.R. GB: e: Ministry of Reconstruction

M.O.R.C. e: mil: Medical Officers' Reserve Corps

Morflot SU: [d: Vereinigung der internationalen Passagierschiffsreedereien]

MOROCLANT NATO: e: Maritime Forces

Morocco

MOROP INT: d: Modellbahn-Verband Europa, Bern [CH]

MORP PL: pl: Metodyczny Ośrodek Racjonalizacji Produkcji

MORS US: e: mil: Military Operations Research Society; PL: pl: Morska Obsługa Radiowa Statków

M.O.S. GB: e: Managers and Overlookers' Society

MOS BRD: d: mil: Marineortungsschule; B: nl: Middelbare Oefenschool; PL: pl Ministerstwo Opieki Społecznej

MOś PL: pl: Ministerstwo Oświaty

M.O.S.; MOS GB: e: Ministry of Supply

MOS CS: cs: Místní Osvětový Sbor

MOSA pt: Movimento de Solidariedade Africana, Luanda

MOSF; MOSFiz PL: pl: Młodzieżowa Odnaka Sprawności Fizycznej

MOSICP PE: s: Movimiento Sindical Cristiano del Perú

MOSID GB: e: Ministry of Supply Inspection Department

MOSS US: e: Mutually Owned Society for Songwriters

MOSSA Z: e: Mine Officials and Salaried Staff Association

MOSTiW PL: pl: Miejski Ośrodek Sportu, Turystyki i Wypoczynku

MOSVIA NL: nl: Middelbare Opleidings School voor Inlandsche Ambtenaren

MOSZ H: hu: Magyar Orvos Szövetség, Budapest

MOT H: hu: Magyar Országos Tudósitó, Budapest

M.O.T. e: Ministry of Trade; Ministry of Transport

Motag D: d: Versicherungs-Aktiengesellschaft des Deutschen Motorradfahrer-Verbandes, Berlin; BRD: d: Motag Versicherungs-AG, 6 Ffm

MOTOREDE US: e: Movement to Restor Decency

MOTPT e: Ministry of Transport

MOTSz H: hu: Magyar Országos Torna-
szövetség
MOULIAF f: Mouvement de Libération
Africaine
M.O.V. D: d: mil: Marine-Offizier-Verband
MOVEO NL: nl: mil: Meer Ontspanning
voor ernstige Oorlogsslachtoffers
MOVOPC CGO: f: Mouvement de la Voix
du Peuple Congolais
MOVPER US: e: Mystic Order Veiled
Prophets of Enchanted Realm
M.o.W. e: Ministry of Works
M.O.W.B. GB: e: Ministry of Works and
Buildings
M.O.W.T. GB: e: Ministry of War Transport
MOZ BRD: d: Magischer Orts-Zirkel,
Nürnberg
M&P US: e: Maryland & Pennsylvania
Railroad
MP S: sv: Matteuspojkarna, Stockholm
M.P. e: Metropolitan Police
MP NL: nl: Middenstandspartij; d: mil:
Militärpolizei; nl: mil: Militaire Politie;
e: mil: Military Police; Military Post;
TR: [d: Nationalpartei]
M.P. F: f: Ministère Public; YU: sn:
Ministrstvo za Prosveto
MP US: e: Missouri Pacific Railroad;
P: pt: Mocidade Portuguesa, Lisboa
M.P. e: Mounted Police; f: Mouvement
Politique (Populaire); F: f: Municipalité
Parisienne; e: Municipal Police; F: f:
Musée Pédagogique
M.P. 13 F: f: Mouvement populaire du
13 Mai 1958
MPA US: e: Magazine Publishers Asso-
ciation, Inc.; CDN: e: Magazine Pub-
lishers Association of Canada; US: e:
Maine Pharmaceutical Association;
D: d: mil: Marineoffizierpersonalab-
teilung [OKM] ; Marinepersonalamt;
US: e: Maryland Pharmaceutical Asso-
ciation; GB: e: Master Photographers'
Association of Great Britain; BlnW: d:
Staatliche Materialprüfungsanstalt [jetzt:

BAM] ; BRD: d: Staatliche Material-
prüfungsanstalt der TH Darmstadt;
US: e: Mechanical Packing Association;
d: Meisterprüfungsausschuß; S: sv: Me-
kaniska Prövningsanstalten, Stockholm;
US: e: Metal Powder Association, New
York; PL: pl: Miejskie Przedsiębiorstwo
Autobusowe; D: d: Miet- und Pachteini-
gungsamt; Z: e: Mines Police Associa-
tion; US: e: Missouri Pharmaceutical
Association; Mobile Press Association;
Modern Poetry Association; Motion
Picture Association of America; f: Mou-
vement Populaire Africain; US: e:
Music Publishers Association of the
United States of America
MPAA US: e: Motion Picture Association
of America, Hollywood
M.P.A.B.A. e: Malayan People's Anti
-British Army
MPAJ f: Mouvement Panafricaine de la
Jeunesse
M.P.A.J.A. e: Malayan People's Anti
-Japanese Army
M.P.A.J.U. e: Malayan People's Anti
-Japanese Union
MPAM P: pt: Missão de Pedologia de
Angola e Moçambique, Junta de Inves-
tigações do Ultramar, Lisboa
MPATI US: e: Midwest Program on Air-
borne Television Instruction [gegr 1961]
MPB US: e: mil: Military Personnel
Branch; f: Mouvement Progressiste du
Burundi
MPBA US: e: Machine Printers Beneficial
Association
MPBP US: e: Metal Polishers, Buffers,
Platers and Helpers International Union
MPBW GB: e: Ministry of Public Buildings
and Works
MPC US: e: Manpower Policy (Priorities)
Committee;Materials Policy Commission
M.P.C. GB: e: Metropolitan Police College,
Hendon
MPC US: e: mil: Military Personnel

Center; CDN: e: mil: Military Pioneer Corps; US: e: mil: Military Police Corps; PL: pl: Ministerstwo Przemysłu Ciężkiego; BRD: d: Motor-Presse-Club, 8 München; CGO: f: Mouvement Progressive Congolais

M.P.C. F: f: Musée Permanent des Colonies (Ponts-et-Chaussées)

M.P.C.A. Britisch-Guiana: e: Man-Power Citizens' Association

MPCB US: e: Motion Picture Code Board

M.P.Ch. e: Methodist Protestant Church

MPCh PL: pl: Ministerstwo Przemysłu Chemicznego

MPCID US: e: mil: Military Police Criminal Investigation Detachment

MPD US: e: mil: Military Pay (Personel) Division

M.P.D. GB: e: Mines and Petroleum Department

MPD BRD: d: Monarchistische Partei Deutschlands [gegr 1954] ; DOM: s: Movimiento Popular Dominicano

MPDC US: e: mil: Mechanical Properties Data Center, Traverse City, Mich.

M.P. de B.A. s: Museo Provincial de Bellas Artes

MPDFA US: e: Master Photo Dealers and Finishers Association

MPDiP PL: pl: Ministerstwo Przemysłu Drzewnego i Papierniczego

MPDiR; MPDiRz PL: pl: Ministerstwo Przemysłu Drobnego i Rzemiosła

M.P.D.R. F: f: Ministère des Prisonniers, Déportés, Réfugiés

M.P.D.S. GB: e: Metropolitan Police Detective School, Hendon

MPE CS: cs: Ministerstvo Paliv a Energetiky

MPEA US: e: Motion Picture Export Association; Obervolta: f: Mouvement Populaire d'Evolution Africaine

MPEAA US: e: Motion Picture Export Association of America, Inc.

MPEC PL: pl: Miejskie Przedsiębiorstwo Energetyki Cieplnej

MPEHSE CS: cs: Ministerstvo Paliv a Energetiky-Hlavní Správa Elektráren

M.Pen. GB: e: Ministry of Pensions (and Social Insurance)

M.P.F. GB: e: Metropolitan Police Force, London; e: Malaya Police Federation

MPF e: Mexico Pilgrims Foundation; DDR: d: Ministerium für das Post- und Fernmeldewesen; P: pt: Mocidade Portuguêsa Feminia

M.P.F. F: f: Mouvement Populaire des Familles; Mouvement Populaire Français

MPG BRD: d: Max-Planck-Gesellschaft zur Förderung der Wissenschaften

M.P.G. GB: e: Museum of Practical Geology

M.P.G.A. GB: e: Metropolitan Public Gardens Association; Ministry of Pensions General Administration

MPGK PL: pl: Miejskie Przedsiębiorstwo Gospodarki Komunalnej

MPGR PL: pl: Ministerstwo Państwowych Gospodarstw Rolnych

MPHA US: e: Michigan (Minnesota) Public Health Association

MPI BRD: d: Max-Planck-Institut; S: sv: mil: Militärpsykologiska Institutet

MPIA PL: pl: Miejskie Przedsiębiorstwo Imprez Artystycznych; pt: Movimento para a Independendência de Angola

MPIC US: e: Motion Picture Industry Controllers (Council)

M.P.I.C. f: Mouvement pour l'instauration d'un ordre corporatif

MPIF US: e: Metal Powder Industries Federation, New York, N.Y. 10017

MPiH PL: pl: Ministerstwo Przemysłu i Handlu

MPII H: hu: Magyar Párttörténeti Intézet Irattára, Budapest

MPiK PL: pl: Klub Międzynarodowej Prasy i Ksiązki

MPiOS PL: pl: Ministerstwo Pracy i Opieki Społecznej

MPiT PL: pl: Ministerstwo Poczt i Telegrafów

MPL Rhodesien: e: Mashonaland Progressive League; PL: pl: Mazurska Partia Ludowa; Ministerstwo Przemysłu Lekkiego; pl: Mongolska Partia Ludowa

M.P.L. F: f: Mouvement "Paix et Liberté"

MPLA US: e: Mountain Plains Library Association; P: pt: Movimento Popular de Liberação de Angola

MPM PL: pl: Ministerstwo Przemysłu Maszynowego; MA: f: Mouvement Populaire Marocain; I: i: Movimento Popolare Monarchio

MPMA GB: e: Motion Picture Museum Association

MPMB PL: pl: Ministerstwo Przemysłu Materiałów Budowlanych

MPMiM PL: pl: Ministerstwo Przemysłu Mięsnego i Mleczarskiego

MPN U: s: Movimiento Popular Nacional

M.P.N.C. CGO: f: Mouvement pour le Progrès National Congolais

M.P.N.I.; M.P.&N.I. GB: e: Ministry of Pensions and National Insurance

M.P.O. GB: e: Metropolitan Police Office, London

MPO PL: pl: Miejskie Przedsiębiorstwo Oczyszczania; e: mil: Military Permit Office; Military Post Office; CS: cs: Ministerstvo Pošt

MPOS = MPiOS

MPOSiZ PL: pl: Ministerstwo Pracy, Opieki Społecznej i Zdrowia

MPP CS: cs: Ministerstvo Potravinářského Průmyslu; CGO: f: Mouvement pour le Progrès du Peuple

MPPA US: e: Metal Powder Producers Association; Motion Picture Producers Association; Music Publishers Protective Association

MPPD US: e: mil: Military Personnel Procurement Division, TAGO

MPPDA US: e: Motion Picture Producers and Distributors of America

MPPF PTM: e: Malayan Planters Provident Fund

MPPS US: e: mil: Military Personnel Procurement Service; l: Missionares Pretiosissimi Sanguinis

M.PP.TT. I: i: Ministro delle Poste e delle Telecomunicazioni, Roma

MPPV CS: cs: Ministerstvo Potravinářského Průmyslu a Výkupu Zemědělských Výrobků

MPR CS: cs: Ministerstvo Průmyslu

M.P.R. CGO: f: Mouvement populaire de la révolution; F: f: Musée des Plans-Reliefs

MPRB PL: pl: Miejskie Przedsiębiorstwo Remontowo-Budowlane

MPRC US: e: mil: Military Personnel Records Center; US: e: Motion Picture Research Council

MPRD PL: pl: Miejskie Przedsiębiorstwo Robót Drogowych

MPRDO PL: pl: Miejskie Przedsiębiorstwo Remontu Dźwigów Osobowych

MPRF US: e: Motion Picture Relief Fund

MPRiS PL: pl: Ministerstwo Przemysłu Rolnego i Spożywczego

MPRR US: e: Missouri-Pacific Railroad Company

MPRS RI: [d: oberster beratender Volkskongreß]

M.Př.Str. CS: cs: Ministerstvo Přesného Strojírenství

MPRUD PL: pl: Miejskie Przedsiębiorstwo Remontowe Urządzeń Dźwigowych

MPRWK PL: pl: Miejskie Przedsiębiorstwo Robót Wodociągowo-Kanalizacyjnych

M.P.S. e: Medical Protection Society

MPS CS: cs: Ministerstvo Pracovních Sil; PL: pl: Ministerstwo Przemysłu Spożywczego

M.P.S. e: Ministry of Public Security

MPS US: e: Minnesota Pathological Society; SN: f: Mouvement Populaire Sénégalais; BRD: d: Musikproduktion Schwarzwald GmbH, 773 Villingen

M.P.S.A. GB: e: Metropolitan Police Surgeons' Association

MPSA US: e: mil: Military Petroleum Supply Agency

MPSB-PWS NATO: e: Permanent Working Staff, Military Production and Supply Board

MPSC GB: e: mil: Military Provost Staff Corps

MPSCOA US: e: mil: Military Pay Service Center Overseas Areas

MPSiS PL: pl: Ministerstwo Przemysłu Spożywczego i Skupu

MPSP CS: cs: Ministerstvo Práce a Sociální Péče

MP-StK d: Ministerpräsident - Staatskanzlei

MPSz H: hu: Magyar Paraszt Szövetség,Budapest; Magyar Pénzügyi Szindikátus, Budapest

MPT PL: pl: Miejskie Przedsiębiorstwo Taksówkowe; Ministerstwo Poczt i Telegrafów; TG: f: Mouvement Populaire Togolais

MPTA US: e: Mechanical Power Transmission Association; GB: e: Municipal Passenger Transport Association

M.P.T.D. GB: e: Metropolitan Police, Thames Division

MPTEDA US: e: Mechanical Power Transmission Equipment Distributors Association

M.P.T.S. GB: e: Metropolitan Police Training School, Hendon

M.P.T.T. F: f: Ministère des Postes, Télégraphes et Téléphones

MPTUSU e: Malayan Postal and Telecommunications Uniformed Staff Union

MPU GB: e: Medical Practitioners' Union, London WC 1

MPV NL: nl: Moluksch Politiek Verbond

MPVPC CDN: e: Montreal Paint and Varnish Production Club

MPVS NL: nl: Model Politie Vakschool

M.P.W. B: f: Mouvement Populaire Wallon

MPWiK PL: pl: Miejskie Przedsiębiorstwo Wodociągów i Kanalizacji

MQB GB: e: Mining Qualifications Board

MR d: Mädchenrealschule

M.R. GB: e: mil: The Malay Regiment

MR S: sv: Målsmännens riksförbund

M.R. GB: e: mil: Manchester Regiment

MR D: d: mil: Marinerechtsabteilung [OKM]; DDR: d: VEB (VVB) Maschinelles Rechnen

M.R. D: d: mil: WK1: Matrosen-Regiment US: e: McCloud River Railroad Company GB: e: mil: The Duke of Cambridge's Own Middlesex Regiment; GB: e: Midland Railway; GB: e: mil: Midland's Regiment; d: mil: Militärregierung; e: mil: Military Representative; BRD: d: stud: Miltenberger Ring, 6 Ffm

MR d: Ministerrat; PL: pl: Ministerstwo Rolnictwa

M.R. GB: e: Ministry of Reconstruction; S: sv: Motormännens Riksförbund; GB: e: Municipal Reform Party

MR-8 BR: [d: revolutionäre Bewegung des 8.Oktober]

MRA US: e: Manufacturers' Representatives Association; INT: e: Moral Re-Armament

M.R.A.P. F; f: Mouvement contre le racisme, l'antisémitisme et pour la paix, Paris

MRB f: Mouvement Rural du Burundi; US: e: Mutual Reinsurance Bureau

MRBP US: e: Missouri River Basin Project

MRC US: e: Market Research Council; Mathematics Research Center, University of Wisconsin

M.R.C. e: Medical Research Committee (Council); e: mil: Medical Reserve Corps; e: Metals Reserve Company; GB: e: Meteorological Research Committee [Air Ministry]

MRC NATO: e: Military Representatives Committee

M.R.C. e: Miniature Rifle Club

M.R.C.B. B: f: Musée Royal du Congo Belge

M.R.C.I. e: Medical Research Council of Ireland

M.R.C.L. GB: e: Medical Research Council Laboratories

MRE GB: e: mil: Malayan Royal Engineers

MRES e: Missing Research and Enquiry Service

M.R.F. F: f: Mouvement de Résistance Française

MRF US: e: Music Research Foundation

MRFB e: Malayan Rubber Fund Board

MRFV D: d: Mitteldeutscher Rugby-Fuß-ball-Verband, Leipzig

MRG d: Mädchenrealgymnasium

M.R.G. e: Management Research Group; Minorities Research Group; f: Mouvement de la Révolution Gabonaise

MRI US: e: Malt Research Institute; e: Medical Research Institute; US: e: Microwave Research Institute, Brooklyn; Midwest Research Institute; I: i: Movimento Rivoluzionario Italiano

MRIA US: e: Magnetic Recording Industry Association, New York

MRiDP PL: pl: Ministerstwo Rolnictwa i Dóbr Państwowych

MRiRR PL: pl: Ministerstwo Rolnictwa i Reform Rolnych

M.R.J.C. F: f: Mouvement Rural de la Jeunesse Catholique

M.R.J.C.F. F: f: Mouvement Rural de Jeunesse Chrétienne Féminine

MRL e: Medical Research Laboratory

M.R.L. F: f: Ministère de la Reconstruction et du Logement; Mouvement Républicain de la Libération

M.R.L.A. e: Malayan Races' Liberation Army

MRM I: i: Museo del Risorgimento di Milano

MRN PL: pl: Miejska Rada Narodowa; I: i: Movimento Rinascita Nazionale; Honduras: s: Movimiento Reformista

Nacional; Bolivien: s: Movimiento Revolucionario Nacionalista

MRO e: mil: Mandatory Requirements Office; CS: cs: Místní Rada Ostvětová

MRP H: hu: Magyar Radikális Párt, Budapest; INT: e: Mediterranean Regional Program [OECD]; PL: pl: Ministerstwo Robót Publicznych

M.R.P. F: f: Mouvement Républicain Populaire [gegr 1944]; I: i: Movimento di Resistenza Partigiana; YV: s: Movimiento Republicano Progresista

M.R.P.C. CGO: f: Mouvement de Regroupement des Populations Congolaises

MRPGymn. d: Realprogymnasium für Mädchen

MRR PI: e: Manila Railroad; PL: pl: Międzypartyjna Rada Robotnicza; Ministerstwo Reform Rolnych

M.R.R. f: Mouvement Républicain Réformiste

MRRC US: e: mil: Material Requirements Review Committee

M.R.S. GB: e: Market (Medical) Research Society

MRS US: e: mil: Military Railway Service; F: f: Mouvement pour le rattachement de la Sarre à la France

M.R.S.M. RM: f: Mouvement du renouveau social malgache

MRSV US: e: mil: Military Railway Service Veterans ;

MRTA US: e: Marketing Research Trade Association

MRTC US: e: mil: Medical Replacement Training Center

M.R.T.C.B. GB: e: Machine Ruling Trade Conciliation Board

M.R.U. F: f: Ministère de la Reconstruction et de l'Urbanisme

MRUA US: e: Mobile Radio Users' Association

MRV BRD: d: Mainzer Ruder-Verein; D: d: mil: Marine-Regatta-Verein

M.R.V. f: Mouvement du regroupement

voltaïque

MRVP d: Mongolische Revolutionäre Volkspartei

MRwCZ PL: pl: Muzeum Regionalne w Częstochowie

M.S. GB: e: Malone Society; D: d: mil: Marineschule

M.&S. GB: e: Marks & Spencer [retail chain]

MS S: sv: Maskinyrkesskolan, Stockholm; US: e: Massachusetts State College; CS: sk: Matica Slovenská; US: e: Memphis State College; GB: e: Mensa Society, London; US: e: Metallurgical (Meteoritical) Society; Michigan State University; e: mil: Military Staff; NATO: e: Military Status Committee; YU: sh: Ministarstvo Saobraćaja; CS: cs: Ministerstvo Spoju; PL: pl: Ministerstwo Skarbu (Skupu) (Sprawiedeliwości)

M.S. R: ro: Ministerul Sănățatii; e: Ministry of Shipping; Ministry of Supply; l: Missionarii Salettenses e: Missionary of La Salette; GB: e: Missionary Society

MS d: Mittelschule ·

M.S. GB: e: Monitoring Service; I: i: Monopoli di Stato

MS S: sv: Arméns motorskola, Strängnäs; D: d: Münchener Sezession

M.S. F: f: Musée Sociale; YU: Muzejsko Društvo za Slovenijo

MSA US: e: Magazine Shippers Association; PTM: e: Malaysia-Singapore Airlines; GB: e: Manchester Society of Architects

M.S.A. GB: e: Manufacturing Silversmiths Association, London

MSA US: e: Masonic Service Association of the United States

M.S.A. GB: e: Master Silversmiths' Association, Sheffield

MSA S: sv: Mellan-Sveriges Arkitektförening; D: d: mil: nach WK2: Militärisches Sicherheitsamt, Bad Ems

M.S.A. CH: d: mil: Militärsanitätsanstalt; US: e: Mineralogical Society of America; CDN: GB: US: e: Mine Safety Appliances Company; GB: e: Motor Schools Association of Great Britain; f: Mouvement socialiste africain; I: i: Movimenti di Studi per l'Architettura; GB: e: Muncipal School of Art; F: f: Mutualité Sociale Agricole

MSA US: e: mil: Mutual Security Agency; Mycological Society of America

MSA/E US: e: mil: Mutual Security Agency European Office

MŠANO CS: sk: Ministerstvo Školstva a Národnej Osvety

MSAVP CS: cs: Moravsko-Slezská Akademie Věd Přirodních

MSB D: e: mil: nach WK2: Military Security Board; US: e: Montadale Sheep Breeders Association

M.S.B. B: f: Mouvement Social Belge; D: d: Münchener Sängerbund

MSBSS NL: nl: Middelbare Scholieren -Bond voor Sociale Studie

M.S.C. e: Madras Staff Corps

MSC US: e: Manned Spacecraft Center [NASA], Houston, Texas; US: e: mil: Medical Service Corps; UN: e: Mediterranean Sub-Commission [FAO]; CDN: e: Meteorological Service of Canada

M.S.C. GB: e: Metropolitan Special Constabulary

MSC US: e: Michigan State College

MSČ CS: cs: Mikrobiologická Společnost Československá

MSC e: mil: Military Service Committee; Military Staff Committee; NATO: e: Military Status Committee; l: Missionarii Sanctissimi Cordis Jesu; Missionarii Sanctii Caroli Borromei; US: e: Mississippi Central Railway; Mississippi (Montana) State College

MSC; M.-S.-C. d: Motorsportclub

MSCC GB: e: Manchester Ship Canal Company

M.S.C.C. CDN: e: Missionary Society of

the Anglican Church of Canada

M.Sch. D: d: mil: Marineschule; d: Mittel-schule

MSCNY US: e: Medical Society of the County of New York

MSCP US: e: Massachusetts Society of Clinical Psychologists

M.S.C.R. GB: e: Metropolitan Special Constabulary Reserve

MSCW US: e: Mississippi State College for Women

MSD NL: nl: mil: Marine-Stoomvaart-dienst; CS: cs: Masarykův studentský domov

M.S.D. GB: e: Merchant Shipbuilding Department; GB: e: mil: Mine Sweeping Division

MSD DDR: d: mil: Mot.-Schützendivision; S: sv: Motororganisationernas samarbets-delegation

MSDS GB: e: Marconi Space and Defence Systems [d: Firma]

MSE US: e: Midwest Stock Exchange

MSEA US: e: Massachusetts State Engineers' Association; Medical Society Executives Association

M.S.E.B. GB: e: Marine Society for the Equipment of Boys

MSES US: e: Minnesota Surveyors' and Engineers' Society

M.S.E.S.S. GB: e: Manchester School of Economic and Social Studies

MSEUE INT: f: Mouvement Socialiste pour les Etats-Unis de l'Europe, Paris 10 [gegr 1947]

M.S.F. e: mil: Metal and Steel Factory

MSF S: sv: Metodistkyrkans Sångarförbund; e: mil: Mine Sweeping Flotilla; l: Congregatio Missionariorum a Sancta Familia; US: e: mil: Mobile Striking Force

MSF 70 BRD: d: Ausstellung "Motor-Sport - Freizeit 1970", Stuttgart

MSFC US: e: George C. Marshall Space Flight Center [NASA]

MSFS l: Missionarii Sancti Francisci

Salesii de Annecy

MSG BRD: d: mil: Marine-Schiffstechnik Planungs-Gesellschaft mbH, 2 Hamburg 11; BRD: d: Motiv-Sammler-Gilde, 78 Freiburg; Motorsportgemeinschaft

M.S.G.B. GB: e: Muslim Society in Great Britain

M.S.G.C. e: mil: Military Services Grants Committee

MSH CS: cs: Ministerstvo Stavebních Hmot

M/Sh GB: e: Ministry of Shipping

M.S.H. e: Missionaries of the Sacred Heart

M.S.H.C. e: mil: Military Service Hardship Committee

MSHS US: e: Maryland (Minnesota) (Missouri) State Horticultural Society

MSI H: hu: Magyar Szabványügyi Inté-zet, Budapest 9; US: e: Maine Sugar Industries; Maxwell Scientific International Inc.

M.S.I. GB: e: Missions to Seamen Institute

MSI I: i: Movimento Sociale Italiano; US: e: Museum of Science and Industry

MSIA I: i: Movimento Sociale Italiano Autonomo

M.S.I.L.H. R: ro: Ministerul Silviculturii, Industriei Lemnului și Hîrției

MSIRI e: Mauritius Sugar Industry Research Institute

MSIUS US: e: mil: Military Service Institution of the United States

MSJ J: e: Meteorological Society of Japan

MSK S: sv: Malmö Sportklubb; CS: cs: Masarykova Studentská Kolej; Ministerstvo Školství a Kultury; Místní Správní Komise

MSL GB: e: Malacological Society of London; Management Selection Limited, London W 1

M.S.L. GB: e: Medical Society of London

M&SL US: e: Minneapolis & Saint Louis Railway Company

MSL PL: pl: Muzeum Śląskie

MSLCOMD US: e: mil: Missile Command

MSLPT CS: cs: Moravský Soubor Lidových

Písní a Tanců

M.S. & L.R. GB: e: Manchester, Sheffield and Lincolnshire Railway

M.S.M. IND: e: Madras and Southern Mahratta Railway

MSM BRD: d: mil: Marineschule Mürwik; PL: pl: Międzyzakładowa Spółdzielnia Mieszkanowa; Młodzieżowa Spółdzielnia Mieszkaniowa

M.S.M. CGO: f: Mouvement Solidaire Moluba

MSMA US: e: Major Symphony Managers Association

M.S.M.A. GB: e: Master Sign-Makers' Association

MSMA US: e: Minnesota (Missouri) State Medical Association

MSMDA US: e: Mutual Sewing Machine Dealers Association

MSMH US: e: Massachusetts Society for Mental Hygiene

M.S.M.R. IND: e: Madras and Southern Mahratta Railway

MSMS US: e: Michigan State Medical Society

MSNJ US: e: Medical Society of New Jersey

MSNK CS: sk: Matica Slovenská, Národná Knižnica

MŠO CS: cs: Ministerstvo Školství a Národní Osvěty

MSO e: mil: Mixed Service Organization; US: e: mil: Mutual Security Office

MSOCC US: e: Multi Satellite Operational Control Center [NASA]

MS of AIMMPE US: e: Metallurgical Society of the American Institute of Mining, Metallurgical and Petroleum Engineers

MSOS CS: cs: Meziministerský Sbor Obrany Státu

MSOT H: hu: Magyar Sportorvosi Tanács, Budapest

M.S.P. F: f: Ministère de la Santé Publique

MSP CS: cs: Ministerstvo Sociální Péče;

Ministerstvo Spotřebního Průmyslu; Ministerstvo Stavebního Průmyslu

M.S.P. B: f: Mouvement socialiste pour la paix; PE: [e: social progressive movement]

MSP US: e: mil: Mutual Security Program

MSPA US: e: Maine Sardine Packers Association; Massachusetts (Michigan) (Minnesota) State Pharmaceutical Association

MSPE US: e: Massachusetts Society of Professional Engineers

M.S.P.E. CDN: e: McGill School of Physical Education; US: e: Missouri Society of Professional Engineers

MSPGA AUS: e: Melbourne School of Printing and Graphical Arts

M.S.P.P. F: f: Ministère de la Santé Publique et de la Population

M.Sp.S. D: d: mil: Marinesportschule; l: Missionarii a Spiritus Sancto

MSR GB: e: mil: The Malaya Signal Regiment; Mixed Signals Regiment

M.S.R. F: f: Mouvement Social Révolutionnaire; B: f: Mutuelle des Syndicats Réunis

M.S.R.C. GB: e: Medical Students' Representative Council

M.S.R.D. GB: e: Merchant Ship Repairs Department

MSRI US: e: Metal Stamping Research Institute

M.S.S. S: sv: Mälarens Segelsällskap; GB: e: Manchester Statistical Society

MSS US: e: Manufacturers' Standardization Society of the Valve and Fittings Industry, New York; GB: e: MSS [Master Sound System] Recording Company Ltd Colnbrook, Bucks, England; CS: cs: Ministerstvo Státních Statků; l: Missionarii Sancti Spiritus; D: d: NS: Motor-Schutzstaffel

MSSA US: e: mil: Military Subsistence Supply Agency

M.S.S.I.G. GB: e: Manchester Statistical

Society Industrial Group

MSSNY US: e: Medical Society of the State of New York

MSSP US: e: International Association of Marble, Slate and Stone Polishers, Rubbers and Sawyers, Tile and Mosaic and Terrazzo Workers' Helpers; Medical Society of the State of Pennsylvania; CS: sk: Muzeálna Slovenská Spoločnost'

MSSRC INT: e: Mediterranean Social Science Research Council, Beirut

M.S.Ss.T. 1: Missionarii Servi Sanctissimae Trinitatis

M.S.S.V.D. e: Medical Society for the Study of Venereal Diseases

M.S.Sz. H: hu: Magyar Si Szövetség

MST CS: cs: Ministerstvo Strojírenství

M.St. D: d: NS: Motorsturm

MSTA US: e: Manufacturers Surgical Trade Association

M.St.Kdo. D: d: mil: Marinestationskommando

M.&St.L. US: e: Minneapolis & St. Louis Railroad Company

MStpKdo BRD: d: mil: Marinestützpunktkommando

M.St.P.&S.S.M.Ry. US: e: Minneapolis, St. Paul & Sault Ste. Marie Railway

M.St.R. D: d: mil: Marine-Stammregiment

MSTS US: e: mil: Military Sea Transport -(ation) Service

MSTSELM US: e: mil: Military Sea Transport Service, Eastern Atlantic and Mediterranean

MSTSO US: e: mil: Military Sea Transportation Service Office

MSTSOV US: e: mil: Military Sea Transportation Service Office Vietnam

MSTSPACOM US: e: mil: Mediterranean Military Sea Transportation Service Space Assignment Committee

MStV D: d: mil: Marinestandortverwaltung

MSU BRD: d: stud; Marburger Studentenunion; US: e: Michigan (Montana) State

University

M.S.U. B: f: Mouvement Syndical Unifié

MSU BRD: d: stud: Münchener Studentenunion

M.S.U.D. F: f: Mouvement pour un syndicalisme uni et démocratique

M.S.U.L. GB: e: Medical Schools of the University of London

M.Supp. GB: e: Ministry of Supply

M.S.U.S. SN: f: Mouvement Socialiste d'Union Sénégalaise

MSV; M.-S.-V. d: Männerschwimmverein

MSV US: e: Medical Society of Virginia; CS: cs: Ministerstvo Stavebnictví

MŠV CS: cs: Místní Školní Výbor

MSVD US: e: Missile and Space Vehicle Department [General Electric]

MŠVU CS: cs: Ministerstvo Školství věd a Umění

M.S.W. D: d: mil: Marineschule Wesermünde

MSW PL: pl: Ministerstwo Spraw Wewnętrznych; Ministerstwo Szkolnictwa Wyższego

MSWiN PL: pl: Ministerstwo Szkół Wyższych i Nauki

M.&S.W.J.; M.&S.W.J.R. GB: e: Midland & South Western Junction Railway

MSWojsk PL: pl: Ministerstwo Spraw Wojskowych

MSZ CS: cs: Ministerstvo pro Sjednocení Zákonů; PL: pl: Ministerstwo Spraw Zagranicznych

MSzDSz H: hu: Magyarországi Szlovákok Demokratikus Szövetsége, Budapest

MSZH H: hu: Magyar Szabványügyi Hivatal, Budapest 9

MSzI H: hu: Magyar Szabványügyi Intézet, Budapest

MSZMP H: hu: Magyar Szocialista Munkáspárt, Budapest

MSZOSZ H: hu: Mezőgazdasági Szakemberek Országòs Szövetsége, Budapest

MSzP H: hu: Magyarországi Szocialista Párt, Budapest

MSzSz H: hu: Mozgó Szakorvosi Szolgálat

MT H: hu: Magyar Televizio; CS: cs:

Matice Technická; Ministerstvo Techniky

MT; M/T; M.T. GB: e: Ministry of Transport

M.T.A. TR: tr: Maden Tetkik ve Arama Enstitüsü, Ankara [gegr 1935]; H: hu: Magyar Tudományos Akadémia, Budapest; GB: e: Master Tanners' Association; F: f: mil: Bureau des méthodes et techniques d'action

MTA US: e: Metropolitan Transit (Transportation) Authority; GB: e: Mica Trades Association; US: e: Michigan Tuberculosis Association; D: d: mil: Militärtechnische Akademie, Berlin [Preußen]; S: sv: Motala Tekniska Aftonskola

M.T.A. AUS: e: Motor Traders' Association; e: Music Teachers' Association

MTAF US: e: mil: Mediterranean Tactical Air Force

MTAK H: hu: Magyar Tudományos Akadémie Könyvtára, Budapest

Mt.All. CDN: e: Mount Allison University

MTAMTO H: hu: Magyar Tudományos Akadémia Müszaki Tudományok Osztálya, Budapest

MTB e: Malayan Tin Bureau

M.T.B. GB: e: Motor Transport Board

MTBDT NL: nl: Maatschappij tot Bevordering der Toonkunst

MTC e: Maritime Transport Committee

M.T.C. GB: e: mil: Mechanized Transport Corps

MTC US: e: mil: Medical Training Center; NATO: e: Military Transport Committee

M.T.C. AUS: e: Ministry of Trade and Customs; e: mil: Motor Transport Corps

MTC US: e: mil: Mountain Training Center, Saalfelden [A]

MTCA US: e: mil: Military Training Camp Association [gegr 1916]; GB: e: Ministry of Transport and Civil Aviation

MTCC US: e: mil: Military Air Transport Service, Transport Control Center

MTCE INT: f: Mouvement des Travailleurs Chrétiens pour l'Europe

M.T.C.P. GB: e: Ministry of Town and Country Planning

MTD US: e: mil: Material Test Directorate, Aberdeen Proving Ground; e: mil: Military Training Department (Directorate)

MTDE e: mil: Maintenance Technique Development Establishment

MTDiL PL: pl: Ministerstwo Transportu Drogowego i Lotniczego

MTDP NATO: e: Medium Term Defence (Defense) Plan (Program) [1954]

MTE e: mil: Mechanical Training Establishment; H: hu: Mezőgazdasági és Elelmiszeripari Tudományos Egyesület, Budapest

M.T.E. H: hu: Minisztertanács Elnöke

MTEA AUS: e: Metal Trades Employers' Association

MTESZ = METESZ

MTF S: sv: Mälarens Turisttrafikförening; US: e: Men's Tie Foundation; Mississippi Test Facility [NASA]

MTG D: d: Mannheimer Transport-Gesellschaft; BRD: d: mil: Marinetechnik Planungsgesellschaft, 2 Hamburg

MTH H: hu: Munkaerőtartalékok Hivatala, Budapest

MTHS BRD: d: Marktforschungsgemeinschaft an der TH Stuttgart

MTI H: hu: Magyar Távirati Iroda, Budapest [d: Nachrichtenagentur, gegr 1881 f: Marché textile international; US: e: Metal Treating Institute

M.T.I.A. f: mil: Mission technique et industrielle d'armement

MTIC BR: pt: Ministério do Trabalho Indústria e Comércio

MTIN WAN: e: Ministry of Trade and Industry Northern Region

MTIRA GB: e: Machine Tool Industry Research Association

MTIW WAN: e: Ministry of Trade and Industry Western Region

MTK PL: pl: Międzynarodowe Targi Ksi-
ążki
MTKI H: hu: Munkavédelmi Tudományos
Kutató Intézet, Budapest
M.T.L.; M.T.L.D. DZ: f: Mouvement pour
le triomphe des libertés démocratiques
[gegr 1954, später: F.L.N.]
MTMA US: e: mil: Military Traffic Manage-
ment Agency
MTMTS US: e: mil: Military Traffic Manage-
ment and Terminal Service
MTMW INT: pl: Międzynarodowe Towarzy-
stwo Muzyki Współczesnej
MTNA US: e: Music Teachers National
Association, Baldwin, N.Y.
M.T.O. GB: e: Master Tailors' Organization
MTO CS: cs: Mezinárodní Transitní Okruh;
NL: nl: Middelbaar Technisch Onderwijs;
US: e: mil: Military Ticket Office
MTP PL: pl: Międzynarodowe Targi Poz-
nańskie
M.T.P. B: f: Ministère des Travaux Publics
MTP CS: cs: Ministerstvo Těžkého Prů-
myslu
M.T.P. GB: e: Mobile Transport Police;
F: f: Musée des Travaux Publics
M.T.P.T.T. F: f: Ministère des Travaux
Publics, Transport et Tourisme
MTR PL: pl: Małopolskie Towarzystwo
Rolnicze; I: i: Ministero dei Trasporti
M.T.R.D. e: mil: Mechanical Transport
Reserve Depot; GB: e: Ministry of
Transport Roads Division
MTS e: Marine Technical Society; DDR:
d: Maschinen-(und)Traktoren-Station
[1952...59, dann RTS]
M.T.S. GB: e: Merchant Taylors' School;
Merchant Transport Service
MTS NL: nl: Middelbare Technische
School; INT: pl: Międzynarodowy Try-
bunał Sprawiedliwości; e: mil: Military
Traffic Service; CS: cs: Ministerstvo
Težkého Strojírenství
M.T.S. GB: e: Missions to Seamen
MTSH H: hu: Magyar Testnevelési és

Sporthivatal, Budapest
MTSK S: sv: Malmöteknologernas Stock-
holmsklubb
MTS/RTS DDR: d: Maschinen-Traktoren
-Station/Reparatur-Technische Station
M.T.S.S. F: f: Ministère du Travail et de
la Sécurité Sociale
MTST H: hu: Magyar Testnevelési és
Sport Tanács, Budapest
M.T.S.W.D. GB: e: Methodist Temperance
and Social Welfare Department
MTSz H: hu: Magyar Turista Szövetség,
Budapest
MTT H: hu: Magyar Társadalomtudományi
Társulat, Budapest; Magyar Tudomá-
nyos Tanács, Budapest
MTTA GB: e: Machine Tool Trade Asso-
ciation, London SW 1
M.T.T.A. GB: e: Municipal Tramways
and Transport Association
M.T.T.B. GB: e: Made-up Textiles Trade
Board
MTU BRD: d: Motoren- und Turbinen
-Union Friedrichshafen GmbH, 799
Friedrichshafen; Motoren- und Tur-
binen-Union München GmbH, 8 Mün-
chen 50
MTV d: Männerturnverein
MTW DDR: d: Mathias-Thesen-Werft,
Wismar
MTWIU US: e: Marine Transport Workers'
Industrial Union
MU US: e: Marquette University; DDR:
d: Maxhütte, Unterwellenborn; CDN:
e: McGill University; US: e: Mercer
University; DK: da: Metodistkirkens
Ungdomsforbund; US: e: Miami Univer-
sity; = MISRAIR; INT: d: Montan
-Union [= EGKS]; sv: Moralisk upp-
rustining [e: MRA]
M.U. GB: e: Mothers' Union; Motor
Union; Musicians' Union
MU YU: sh: Muzička Akademija
MÚ CS: cs: Mykologický Ústav
M.U.A. e: Malay Union Alliance

M.U.A.J. f: Mouvement Uni des Auberges de la Jeunesse

MUB PL: pl: Miejski Urząd Bezpieczeństwa; S: sv: Monopolutredningsbyrån; CGO: f: Mouvement de l'Unité Basonge

MUBA CH: d: Schweizerische Mustermesse in Basel

MUBEF B: f: Mouvement des universitaires belges d'expression française

MUBP PL: pl: Miejski Urząd Bezpieczeństwa Publicznego

MUC f: Mouvement d'Union Camerounaise

MUCM INT: f: Mouvement universel pour une confédération mondiale

MUCOM US: e: mil: Munitions Command, Dover, N.J.

MÚČSAC CS: cs: Matematický Ústav při ČSAV

MUD BRD: d: Mitfahrer-Union Deutschlands; P: pt: Movimento Unitario Democrático [1945...48] ; I: i: Movimento Unitario Democratico

MUE INT: i: Movimento per l'Unità Europea

MÜAG BRD: d: Mittelschwäbische Überlandzentrale AG, 7927 Giengen

MÜAKI H: hu: Müanyagipari Kutató Intézet, Budapest

Müko BRD: d: Münchner Kommissions -Buchhandlung

Mü.M. H: hu: Munkaügyi Miniszter(ium), Budapest

Müwog BRD: d: Münchener Wohnungsfürsorge GmbH, München

MUFM INT: f: Mouvement universel pour une fédération mondiale, Den Haag[NL]

MuHo d: Musikhochschule

M.U.I.O.O.F. GB: e: Manchester Unity Independent Order of Odd Fellows

MUK;MuK BRD: d: Gesellschaft für Markt- und Kühlhallen, 2 Hamburg

MULO NL: nl: Meer Uitgebreid Lager Onderwijs

MUN CDN: e: Memorial University of Newfoundland

Muna; Mun.Anst. D: d: mil: Munitionsanstalt

MUND BRD: d: Material- und Nachrichtendienst der Arbeitsgemeinschaft Deutscher Lehrerverbände

MUNDIAL PL: pl: Towarzystwo Imporwo-Eksportowe

MUNDO CDN: e: National University Movement for Overseas Development

MunDp BRD: d: mil: Munitionsdepot

Mun.F. D: d: mil: Munitionsfabrik

MUNGE s: Movimiento de Unión Nacional de Guinea Ecuatorial

MUO US: e: Municipal University of Omaha

MUOS S: sv: mil: Marinens underofficersskola, Haninge

M.U.R. F: f: Mouvements Unis de la Résistance

MURA US: e: Midwestern Universities Research Association, Madison, Wisc.

M.U.R.F. F: f: Mouvement Unifié de la Renaissance Française

MUS BRD: d: mil: Marineunteroffizierschule; PL: pl: Miejski Urząd Statystyczny

MUSBA f: Musée des Beaux-Arts; i: Mu seo delle Belle Arti

MÚSz H: hu: Magyar Úszó Szövetség, Budapest

MUSZ H: hu: Magyar Uttörök Szövetség, Budapest

MÚV CS: cs: Mlynářský Ústav Výzkumn

M.U.V. D: d: stud: Münchener Unitas -Verband

M.U.V.S. D: d: mil: Marine-Unteroffiziervorschule

MUW US: e: Municipal University of Wichita

MUWS BRD: d: mil: Marineunterwasserwaffenschule

MUZ NL: nl: Maatschappij ter Uitvoering der Zuiderzeewerken; CS: [e: Institute for international collaboration in agriculture and forestry]

Mv. D: d: mil: Materialverwaltung [Reichs-kriegsministerium]

MV US: e: Midland Valley Railroad

M.V. D: d: mil: Militärverwaltung

MV CS: cs: Ministerstvo Vnitra; d: Mit-gliederversammlung; D: d: Motoren-verband, Berlin W 30; Verband der Mühlenbau-Anstalten, Berlin; BRD: d: Münchener Verein Krankenversicherungs-anstalt aG, München; d: Musikverein

M.V.A. D: d: mil: Marine-Verpflegungsamt; Marineverwaltungsamt

MVA US: e: Missouri Valley Authority

M.V.A.C. I: i: Milizia Volontaria Anticom-munista

M.V.C. GB: e: Motor Volunteer Corps

M.Verm.A. D: d: mil: Marine-Vermessungs-abteilung

MVF S: sv: Mekaniska Verkmästareför-bundet; DDR: d: Ministerium für Ver-arbeitungsmaschinen und Fahrzeugbau, Berlin

MVG D: d: mil: Militärversorgungsgericht

M.V.H. e: Mount Vernon Hospital

MVHA US: e: Mississippi Valley Historical Association

MVI US: e: Merchant Vessel Inspection Division; Metal Ventilator Institute

M.V.i.R. D: d: mil: WK1: Militärverwaltung in Rumänien

MVK D: d: Malerinnenverein, Karlsruhe; BRD: d: Milchverwertungsgenossenschaft Köln; D: d: mil: Minenversuchskomis-sion; CS: cs: Ministerstvo Výkupu

M.V.L. N: no: Mekaniske Verksteders Landsforening

M.V.M. US: e: Massachusetts Volunteer Militia

MvM NL: nl: mil: Ministerie van Marine

MVMS US: e: Mississippi Valley Medical Society

MvO NL: nl: mil: Ministerie van Oorlog

MVO CS: cs: Ministerstvo Vnitřního Obchodu

MvO/HHD NL: nl: mil: Ministerie van Oorlog/ Huishoudelijke Dienst

MVP CS: cs: Ministerstvo Veřejných Prací

MVPCB US: e: Motor Vehicle Pollution Control Board

MVS BRD: d: mil: Marineversorgungs-schule; e: Mennonite Voluntary Serv-ice; CS: cs: Ministerstvo Všeobecného Strojírenství

MVŠ CS: cs: Ministerstvo Vysokých Škol

M.V.S.N. I: i: Milizia Volontaria per la Sicurezza Nazionale

MVst CS: cs: Ministerstvo Výstavby

MVTVS CS: cs: Místní Výbor pro Tělesnou Výchovu a Sport

MVV D: d: Milchversorgungsverband

MVVS CS: cs: Modelářské Výzkumné a Vývojové Středisko

MVZ CH: d: Metzgermeisterverein der Stadt Zürich; CS: cs: Ministerstvo Výživy

MW BRD: d: Mannesmannröhren-Werke AG, 4 Düsseldorf; PL: pl: Marynarka Wojenna

M.W. US: e: Minnesota, Dakota and Western Railway Company

MW DDR: d: VEB Motorenwerk, Karl-Marx-Stadt

MWa D: d: mil: Marinewaffenamt [OKM]

MWa I = Artillerieentwicklungsabtei-lung

MWa II = Waffenbautechnische Abteilung

MWa III = Allgemeine Artillerieabteilung

MWa IV = Gruppe für Unterwasserwaffen

M.W.A. GB: e: Married Women's Associ-ation; Metal Window Association

MWA US: e: Modern Woodmen of Amer-ica; Mystery Writers of America

MWAA US: e: Movers' and Warehousemen's Association of America

M.W.A.B. D: d: mil: Marine-Waffen- und Ausrüstungsbetrieb

MWALw BRD: d: mil: Mobile Werbeaus-stellung der Luftwaffe

M.W.B. D: d: mil: Marine-Waffenbetrieb; GB: e: Metropolitan Water Board, Lon-don; Ministry of Works and Buildings

MWB BRD: d: Motorenwerke Bremerhaven

MWC US: e: Mary Washington College

M.W.C. GB: e: Ministry of War Communications

M.W.D. e: mil: Military Works Department

MWD SU: [d: Innenministerium] ; US: e: mil: Mutual Weapons Development Program [gegr 1954]

M.W.D.D. GB: e: mil: Miscellaneous Weapons Development Department

MWDP US: e: mil: Mutual Weapons Development Program

MWE BRD: d: Gesellschaft der Ärzte für manuelle Wirbelsäulen- und Extremitäten-Therapie eV, 7972 Isny

M-Werft D: d: mil: Marinewerft

M.W.F. GB: e: Medical Women's Federation

MWG US: e: Management Working Group; PL: pl: Międzynarodowa Współpraca Geofizyczna; BRD: d: stud: Münchener Wahlgemeinschaft

MWI US: e: Master Weavers Institute; e: Ministry of War Information

MWIA INT: e: Medical Women's International Association

MWIU US: e: Maritime Workers' Industrial Union

M.W.L. B: f: Mouvement de la Wallonie Libre

MWM BRD: d: Motorenwerke Mannheim AG, 68 Mannheim

MWO INT: d: Meteorologische Weltorganisation [e: WMO]

MWP PL: pl: Muzeum Wojska Polskiego

M.W.R. US: e: Muncie and Western Railroad Company

MWROP PL: pl: Ministerstwo Wyznań Religijnych i Oświecenia Publicznego

M.W.S. e: mil: Military Works Service

MWS Z: e: Mine Workers Society

M.W.S. US: e: Montana, Wyoming and Southern Railroad Company

MWT DDR: d: Ministerium für Wissenschaft und Technik, Berlin

M.W.T. GB: e: Ministry of War Transport

M.W.T.C. GB: e: Ministry of War Time Communications

M.W.T.Co. GB: e: Marconi's Wireless Telegraph Company

MWV D: d: Milchwirtschaftsverband; BRD: d: Mineralölwirtschaftsverband eV, 2 Hamburg 1

MX GB: e: mil: The Middlesex Regiment (Duke of Cambridge's Own)

MYC D: d: Motor-Yacht-Club von Deutschland; Münchener Yacht-Club

M.Y.C.C. M: e: Malta Youth Consultative Council

M.Y.C.v.D. D: d: Motor-Yacht-Club von Deutschland

M.Y.D. e: Methodist Youth Department

MYI US: e: Metallic Yarns Institute

Mys. IND: e: University of Mysore

MYW CDN: e: McLeod, Young, Weir & Company Limited, Toronto [gegr 1921]

M.Z. D: d: mil: Chef des Stabes der Marineleitung, Zentralgruppe [Reichswehrministerium]

MŽ CS: cs: Ministerstvo Železnic

MZ CS: cs: Ministerstvo Zemědělství; PL: pl: Ministerstwo Zdrowia

MŽ PL: pl: Ministerstwo Żeglugi

M.Z.A. E: s: Madrid - Zaragoza - Alicante [d: Eisenbahngesellschaft]

M.Za. D: d: mil: Marinezeugamt

MZA CH: d: Meteorologische Zentralanstalt; CS: cs: Moravský Zemský Archiv

M.Za(A) D: d: mil: Marineartilleriezeugamt

M.Za.(Sp.); M.Za. (Spr) D: d: mil: Marinesperrzeugamt

MZB PL: pl: Mazowieckie Zjednoczenie Budownictwa; BRD: d: Molkerei-Zentrale Bayern

MZBA D: d: mil: Zentrales Beschaffungs- und Ausrüstungsamt der Kriegsmarine für allgemeinen Werft- und Schiffsbedarf

MZBM PL: pl: Miejski Zarząd Budynków Mieszkalnych

MZBMG PL: pl: Mikołowskie Zekłady Budowy Maszyn Górniczych

M.Z.Dv. D: d: mil: Marine-Zentraldruckschriftenverwaltung

MZG PL: pl: Mazowieckie Zakłady Gastronomiczne

MZGebSt D: d: mil: Gebührnisstelle der Zentralgruppe der Marineleitung [Reichswehrministerium]

MZGK PL: pl: Miejskie Zjednoczenie Gospodarki Komunalnej

MZH PL: pl: Miejski Zarząd Handlu

MŻiGW PL: pl: Ministerstwo Żeglugi i Gospodarki Wodnej

MŻiHZ PL: pl: Ministerstwo Żeglugi i Handlu Zagranicznego

MZiOS PL: pl: Ministerstwo Zdrowia i Opieki Społecznej

MZK PL: pl: Miejski Zakłady Komunikacyjne

MZLVH CS: cs: Ministerstvo Zemědělství, Lesního a Vodního Hospodářství

MZM PL: pl: Małopolski Związek Młodzieży; P: pt: Missão Zoológica de Moçambique, Junta de Investigações do Ultramar, Lisboa

MZO PL: pl: Miejskie Zakłady Oczyszczania; CS: cs: Ministerstvo Zahraničního Obchodu; PL: pl: Ministerstwo Ziem Odzyskanych

MZPUK PL: pl: Miejski Zarząd Przedsiębiorstw i Urządzeń Komunalnych

MZPW PL: pl: Mazowieckie Zakłady Przemysłu Wełnianego

MZS BRD: d: Molkereizentrale Südwest eGmbH, 75 Karlsruhe 21

MZST BlnW: d: Mathilde-Zimmer-Stiftung eV, 1 Berlin 15

MZSZ H: hu: Magyar Zenemüvészek Szövetsége, Budapest

MZÚ CS: cs: Moravské Zemské Ústředí Obcí, Měst a Okresů

MZUiM PL: pl: Miejski Zarząd Ulic i Mostów

MZV BRD: d: Mineralöl-Zentralverband eV; CS: cs: Ministerstvo Zahraničních Věcí

N US: e: Department of the Navy;
e: mil: Nursing Service

N.1 D: d: mil: Nachrichtenabteilung 1

N.A. D: d: mil: Nachrichtenabteilung;
Nachrichtenaufklärung; US: e: National Academy; National Airlines; National Archives; e: mil: National Army; US: e: mil: Naval Academy; D: d: mil: Nebelabteilung

NA NL: nl: Nederlands Atoomforum;
BRD: d: Bahn: Bundesbahn-Neubauamt

N.A. US: e: Neurotics Anonymous [gegr 1964]; N: no: Norges Apotekerforening; Norsk avholdsforbund

NAA US: e: National Academy of Arbitrators; e: National Aeronautic(al) Association; US: e: National Arborist Association; National Archery Association of the United States; US: e: mil: National Artillery Association; US: e: National Association of Accountants; National Association of Auctioneers, House Agents, Rating Surveyors and Valuers; National Automobile Association; NL: nl: Nederlandse Aardappel -Associatie

N.A.A. e: "Never Again" Association

NAA US: e: North American Aviation, Inc., Dowmney, Calif.; INT: e: North Atlantic Assembly

N.A.A. e: Northern Architectural Association

NAA BRD: d: Nürnberger Akademie für Absatzwirtschaft, 85 Nürnberg

NAAA US: e: National Auto Auction Association

NAAAP US: e: North American Association of Alcoholism Programs

NAAB US: e: National Architectural Accrediting Board; National Association of Artificial Breeders

NAABC US: e: National Association of American Business Clubs

NAABI US: e: National Association of Alcoholic Beverages Importers

NAABO e: National Association of Approved Basketball Officials

N.A.A.B.P. vgl: NAACP

NAAC GB: e: National Association of Agricultural Contractors, Thornton Heath, Surrey; US: e: North American Aviation Company

NAACC US: e: National Association of American Composers and Conductors; National Association of Angling and Casting Clubs

NAACP US: e: National Association for the Advancement of Colored People

NAACS US: e: National Association of Accredited Commercial Schools

N.A.A.C.T. e: National Association of Assessors and Collectors of Taxes

N.A.A.F. e: mil: Netherlands Army Air Force

NAAFI GB: e: mil: Navy, Army and Air Force Institutes

NAAFW US: e: mil: National Association of Air Forces Women

NAAG NATO: e: NATO Army Armament Group

N.A.A.I. US: e: North American Aviation, Inc.

NAAK NL: nl: Nieuw Amsterdamsch Administratie Kantoor

NAAM US: e: National Association of Automobile Manufacturers

NAAMIC US: e: National Association of Automotive Mutual Insurance Companie

NAAMM US: e: National Association of Architectural Metal Manufacturers, Chicago, Ill. 60601

NAAN US: e: National Advertising Agency Network

N.A.A.N. e: National Association of Assistant Nurses

NAAO US: e: National Association of Amateur Oarsmen; National Association of Assessing Officers

NAAP US: e: National Association of Advertising Publishers

NAAPPB US: e: National Association of Amusement Parks, Pools and Beaches

NAAR GB: e: National Association of Advertising Representatives

NAAS GB: e: National Agricultural Advisory Service, London S.W. 1; US: e: National Association of Art Services; S: sv: Nordiska Sällskapet för Amerikastudier

N.A.A.S. e: North Atlantic Air Service

NAASR US: e: National Association for Armenian Studies and Research

NAAUS US: e: National Archery Association of the United States

N.A.A.W.P. US: e: National Association for the Advancement of White People

NAB US: e: National Alliance of Businessmen; GB: e: National Assistance Board; National Association of Bookmakers, Ltd.; US: e: National Association of Broadcasters, Washington 6, D.C.; J: e: National Association of Commercial Broadcasters; BR: Navegação Aéra Brasileira; US: e: mil: Naval (Navy) Air Base; BRD: d: Neckermann-Anlagen-Beratungs-GmbH, 6 Ffm; BUR: e: News Agency of Burma; DK: da: Nordisk Annonce Bureau, København

NABA CH: d: Nationale Briefmarkenausstellung, Zürich [1934]

NABAC US: e: National Association of Bank Auditors and Comptrollers

NABAG CH: d: Nationale Briefmarkenausstellung St.Gallen

NABBA GB: e: National Amateur Body Building Association

NABBC GB: e: National Association of Brass Band Conductors

NABC US: e: National Association of Basketball Coaches

N.A.B.C. GB: e: National Association of Boys' Clubs

NABC US: e: North American Broadcasting Corporation

NABCA US: e: National Alcoholic Beverages Control Association

NABCM US: e: National Association of Baby Carriage Manufacturers; National Association of Brattice Cloth Manufacturers

NABDC US: e: National Association of Blueprint and Diazotype Coaters

NABE US: e: National Association of Business Economists

NABECOHA B: nl: Nationale Belgische Confederatie van de Handel

NABECOV B: nl: Nationaal Belgisch Comité ter Verdediging van de Christelijke Beschaving

NABECOWO B: nl: Nationaal Belgisch Comité van de Wetenschappelijke Organisatie

NABER US: e: National Association of Business and Education Radio

NABET US: e: National Association of Broadcast Employees and Technicians

NABF US: e: National Amateur Baseball Federation

NABIM US: e: National Association of Band Instrument Manufacturers

Nabisco US: e: National Biscuit Company [in BRD: XOX-Nabisco GmbH, 31 Celle]

N.A.B.M. e: National Association of Biscuit Manufacturers

NABM US: e: National Association of Blouse Manufacturers; GB: e: National Association of British Manufacturers

NABMO NATO: e: NATO BULLPUP Management Office

NABOM US: e: National Association of Building Owners and Managers

NABP US: e: National Association of Boards of Pharmacy

NABPO NATO: e: NATO BULLPUP Production Organization

NABRT US: e: National Association for Better Radio and Television

N.A.B.S. GB: e: National Advertising Benevolent Society, London

N.Abt. D: d: mil: Nachrichtenabteilung

NABT US: e: National Association of

Biology Teachers

NABTE US: e: National Association for Business Teacher Education

NABTTI US: e: National Association of Business Teacher Training Institutions

NABUG US: e: National Association of Broadcast Unions and Guilds, New York

NABW US: e: National Association of Bank Women

N.A.B.W. e: National Association of Blind Workers

NAC US: e: National Achievement Club

N.A.C. e: National Administrative Council; National Advising Commission

NAC US: e: National Advisory Council on International Monetary and Financial Problems; National Aeronautics Council; MW: e: National African Congress of Nyasaland; US: e: National Air Council; NZ: e: National Airways Corporation

N.A.C. US: e: National Americanization Committee; National Archives Council

NAC US: e: National Arts Club; National Association of Chiropodists; National Association of Concessionaires

N.A.C. e: National Association of Coopers; National Atlas Committee; Native Anglican Church [Uganda]

NAC NL: nl: Nederlandse Akkerbouw Centrale; BRD: d: Neuer Deutscher Automobilclub; US: e: New American Cinema; D: d: Niederlausitzer Automobil-Club, Cottbus; BRD: d: Niederrheinischer Automobilclub; D: d: Norddeutscher Automobil-Club, Hamburg; NATO: e: North Atlantic Council; US: e: mil: Northern Area Command [in Ffm, BRD]

NACA US: e: National Acoustical Contractors Association; National Advisory Committee for Aeronautics; National Agricultural Chemical Association; National Air Carrier Association; National Armored Car Association;

e: National Association of Chemists' Assistants; National Association of Cost Accountants; National Athletic and Cycling Association

NACAA US: e: National Association of County Agricultural Agents

NACAF e: mil: Northwest African Coastal Air Force

NACAM e: National Association of Corn and Agricultural Merchants

NACAR ZA: e: National Advisory Committee on Aeronautical Research

NACAS CDN: e: National Advisory Committee on Agricultural Services

NACAW B: nl: Nationaal Comité voor Actie en Waakzaamheid

N.A.C.B.-P.P.O. e: National Association of Coke and By-Product Plant Owners

NACBS US: e: National Association and Council of Business Schools

NACC US: e: National Advisory Cancer Council; National Alliance of Czech Catholics; National Association of Collegiate Commissioners; National Automobile Chamber of Commerce; Norwegian-American Chamber of Commerce

NACCA US: e: National Association of Claimants' Counsel of America

NACCAM US: e: National Coordinating Committee for Aviation Meteorology

N.A.C.C.B.M. e: National Association of Copper Cylinder and Boiler Makers

N.A.C.C.S. e: National Association of Cemetery and Crematorium Superintendents

N.A.C.D. GB: e: National Association for Civil Defence; National Association of Colliery Deputies

NACDEPS NATO: e: North Atlantic Treaty Council Deputies

NACDR US: e: National Association of Collegiate Deans and Registrars

NACDS US: e: National Association of Chain Drug Stores

N.A.C.E. GB: e: National Assembly of the Church of England

NACE US: e: National Association of Corrosion Engineers, Inc.,Houston, Texas; National Association of County Engineers

NACEMO B: nl: Nationaal Centrum voor Metaalonderzoek

NECEPRS US: e: National Advisory Committee on Electronic Products Radiation Standards, Washington, D.C.

N.A.C.F. e: National Art Collections Fund; GB: e: National Association of Church Furnishers

NACFL US: e: National Advisory Committee on Farm Labor

NACGC US: e: National Association of Colored Girls Clubs

NACGG US: e: North American Commercial Gladiolus Growers

NACGM US: e: National Association of Chewing Gum Manufacturers

NACGN US: e: National Association of Colored Graduate Nurses

NachlGer. d: Nachlaßgericht

Nachr.A.; Nachr.Abt. D: d: mil: Nachrichtenabteilung

Nachr.D. D: d: mil: Nachrichtendienst

Nachr.Tr. D: d: mil: Nachrichtentruppe

Nachsch.D.; Nachsch.Dst. D: d: mil: Nachschubdienst

N.A.C.I.C. e: National Association of Clerks to Insurance Committees

NACL US: e: National Association of Clinical Laboratories; J: e: Nippon Aviotronics Co. Ltd.

NACLEO US: e: National Association of Coin Laundry Equipment Operators

NACLSO US: e: National Assembly of Chief Livestock Sanitary Officials

NACM US: e: National Association of Chain Manufacturers; National Association of Clinic Managers

N.A.C.M. e: National Association of Colliery Managers

NACM US: e: National Association of Concert Managers; National Association of Cotton Manufacturers; National Association of Credit Management

NACO VN: e: National Agricultural Credit Office; US: e: National Association of Consumer Organizations

NACOBEB B: nl: Nationaal Comité van de Belgische Expertboekhouders

NACOBROUW NL: nl: Nationaal Comité voor Brouwgerst, Rotterdam

NACOBWEB B: nl: Nationale Confederatie van de Burgerlijke Weerstanders van België

NACODS GB: e: National Association of Colliery Overmen, Deputies and Shotfirers

NACOGGEB B: nl: Nationale Confederatie der Groeperingen der Geteisterden van België

NACom US: e: mil: Northern Area Command [in Ffm, BRD]

NACORCDM US: e: National Advisory Council on Rural Civil and Defense Mobilization

NACOV B: nl: Nationale Confederatie der Oudersverenigingen

NaCoVo NL: nl: Nationaal Comité van Voederbouw

NACOVOR B: nl: Nationaal Comité van de Volksraadpleging

NACOWA B: nl: Nationaal Comité van Waakzaamheid

N.A.C.P.W.D. e: National Association of Creamery Proprietors and Wholesale Dairymen

NACREL ZA: e: National Chemical Research Laboratory, Pretoria

NACS US: e: National Association of Christian Schools; National Association of College Stores; National Association of Convenience Stores, Chicago; National Association of Cosmetology Schools

NACSA US: e: National Association of Casualty and Surety Agents

NACT GB: e: National Association of Cycle Traders

NACTA US: e: National Association of College Teachers of Agriculture

N.A.C.T.U. e: National Affiliation of Carpet Trade Unions

NACW US: e: National Association of College Women

NACWC US: e: National Association of Colored Women's Clubs

NACWPI US: e: National Association of College Wind and Percussion Instructors

Naczpol PL: pl: Naczelny Polski Komitet Wojskowy

NAD US: e: National Academy of Design; National Association of the Deaf

N.A.D. GB: e: mil: Naval Air Division [Admiralty]

NAD e: mil: Naval Ammunition (Armament) Depot

N.A.D. D: d: mil: Neben-Artilleriedepot

NADA US: e: National Automobile Dealers' Association

NADAC US: e: mil: National Damage Assessment Center

NADALT B: nl: Nationale Dienst voor Afzet van Land- en Tuinbouwprodukten

NADASO US: e: National Association of Drug and Allied Sales Organizations

NADC US: e: National Anti-Dumping Council; US: e: mil: Naval Air Development Center [BUWEPS]

NADD US: e: National Association of Distributors and Dealers of Structural Clay Products

N.A.D.E. e: National Association of Dental Examiners

NADE B: nl: Nationale Dienst voor de Emigratie

NADECO GH: e: National Development Corporation

NADEFCOL NATO: e: NATO Defense College

NADEM US: e: National Association of Dairy Equipment Manufacturers

NaDevCen US: e: mil: Naval Air Development Center

N.A.D.F. e: National Association of Dental Faculties

N.A.D.F.S. GB: e: National Association of Drop Forgers and Stampers

NADGECO NATO: e: NATO Air Defense Ground Environment Consortium

NADGEMO NATO: e: NATO Air Defense Ground Environment Management Off

NADI US: e: National Association of Display Industries

NADL US: e: National Association of Dental Laboratories

NADM US: e: National Association of Discount Merchants; National Association of Doll Manufacturers

NADMR US: e: National Association of Drug Manufacturers Representatives

NADO US: e: mil: Navy Accounts Disbursing Office

NADOP US: e: mil: North American Defense Operational Plan

NADPAS e: National Association of Discharged Prisoners' Aid Societies, In

NADPB NATO: e: NATO Defense Production Board

NADRC US: e: National Advisory Dental Research Council

NADR US: e: National Assembly for Democratic Rights

NADREPS NATO: e: National Armament Directors Representatives

NADSA US: e: National Association of Dramatic and Speech Arts

NADSC US: e: National Association of Direct Selling Companies

NADU N: no: Norsk Amatørdanseunion

NADUSM US: e: National Association of Deputy United States Marshals

NAE US: e: National Academy of Engineering; CDN: e: National Aeronautical Establishment, Ottawa; US: e: National Association of Evangelicals; S: sv: Nordisk Angels Export

NAEA US: e: National Art Education Association; Newspaper Advertising Executives Association

NAEB US: e: National Association of Educational Broadcasters, Washington, D.C.; National Association of Educational Buyers; e: North African Economic Board

NAEBM US: e: National Association of Engine and Boat Manufacturers

NAEC CDN: e: National Aeronautical Establishment of Canada, Ottawa; e: National Agricultural Engineering Corporation; US: e: National Association of Electric Companies; National Association of Elevator Contractors; National Association of Engineering Companies; GB: e: National Association of Exhibition Contractors; US: e: National Aviation Education Council

NAECON US: e: National Aerospace Electronics Conference, Dayton [IEEE]

NAED US: e: National Association of Electrical Distributors

NAEF US: e: mil: Naval Air Engineering Facility

NAEGA US: e: North American Export Grain Association

NAEM US: e: National Association of Exhibit Managers

NAEPS US: e: National Academy of Economics and Political Science

NAER US: e: North American Electronic Research Corporation, Los Angeles

N.A.E.R.S.S.A. GB: e: mil: National Association for Employment of Regular Sailors, Soldiers and Airmen

NAES US: e: National Association of Educational Secretaries

NAF NL: nl: Nationaal Arbeidsfront; US: e: National Amputation Foundation; National Arts Foundation; National Association of Foremen of America; e: mil: Naval Aircraft Factory; Naval Air Facility; Naval Assault Force; e: Nether-land - America Foundation; WAN: e: mil: Nigerian Air Force; sv: Nordiska Administrativa Förbundet [gegr 1919]; S: sv: AB Nordiska Armaturfabrikerna, Linköping [gegr 1919]; INT: da: Nordisk Andelsforbund, København [gegr 1918]; N: no: Norge - Amerika Foreningen; Norges Automobil-Forbund; Norsk Arbeidsgiverforening; Norsk Arbeidsmannsforbund; Norske Annonsörers Forening [gegr 1945]; UN: e: North American Forestry Commission [FAO]; e: mil: Norwegian Air Force

Nafa D: d: Norddeutsche Automobilfabrik AG, Hamburg 39

NAFACT US: e: mil: Naval Aircraft Factory

NAFAG NATO: e: NATO Air Force Armaments Group

NAFAS GB: e: National Association of Flower Arangement Societies of Great Britain

NAFBRAT US: e: National Association for Better Radio and Television

NAFC US: e: National Association of Food Chains; US: e: mil: Naval Air Ferry Command; UN: e: North American Forestry Commission [FAO]

NAFCE US: e: National Association of Federal Career Employees

NAFD US: e: National Association of Flour Distributors

N.A.F.D. GB: e: National Association of Funeral Directors

N.A.F.D.U. GB: e: mil: Naval Air Fighting Development Unit

NAFEC US: e: National Aviation Facilities Experimental Center, Atlantic City; NATO: e: NATO Agency for Equipment Codification

NAFEM e: National Association of Farm Equipment Manufacturers

NAFEN GB: e: Near and Far East News Ltd., London [gegr 1948]

NAFFP e: National Association of Frozen

Food Packers (Producers)

NAFGDA US: e: National Auto and Flat Glass Dealers Association

NAFK S: sv: Norrköpings Automobil- och Flygklubb

NAFM US: e: National Association of Fan Manufacturers [jetzt: AMCA]

N.A.F.M. e: National Association of the Feeble-Minded

NAFM US: e: National Association of Furniture Manufacturers

NAFMB US: e: National Association of Frequency Modulation Broadcasters

NAFO GB: e: National Association of Fire Officers

NAFSA US: e: National Association of Foreign Student Advisers; GB: e: National Fire Services Association of Great Britain

NAFSLAC US: e: National Association of Federations of Syrian and Lebanese American Clubs

N.A.F.T.A. e: National Amalgamated Furnishing Trades Association

NAFTA INT: e: North Atlantic Free Trade Association [d: 1968 geplant]

NAFTF US: e: National Association of Finishers of Textile Fabrics

NAFTRAC US: e: National Foreign Trade Council

NAFV US: e: National Association of Federal Veterinarians

NAFWR GB: e: National Association of Furniture Warehousemen and Removers Ltd.

Nag IND: e: Nagpur University

NAG US: e: National Association of Gagwriters; National Association of Gardeners

N.A.G. GB: e: National Association of Goldsmiths; National Association of Groundsmen

NAG CH: d: Nationale Arbeitnehmergemeinschaft; D: d: Nationale Automobil-Gesellschaft AG, Berlin-Oberschöne-weide; US: e: mil: Naval Advisory Group [Army]; D: d: Neckarwerke A Eßlingen; NL: nl: Nederlandsch Aard-rijkskundig Genootschap; NATO: e: New Approach Group; Northern Arm Group; D: d: Büssing Vereinigte Nutz-kraftwagen-AG, Braunschweig

NAGA US: e: Negro Actors Guild of America; BRD: d: Niedersächsische Arbeitsgemeinschaft für Gesamtdeutsc Aufgaben

NAGARD NATO: e: NATO Advisory Group for Aeronautical Research and Development [= AGARD]

NAGC US: e: National Association for Gifted Children

N.A.G.C. e: National Association of Girls Clubs

NAGC US: e: North American Gladiolus Council

NAGCD US: e: National Association of Glass Container Distributors

N.A.G.E.C. GB: e: mil: Naval Air Ground Equipment Committee

NAGEMA DDR: d: VVB Nahrungsmittel Genußmittel- und Verpackungsmaschin

NAGI US: e: National Association of Government Inspectors

N.A.G.L. e: National Anti-Gambling League

N.A.G.M. GB: e: National Association of Glove Manufacturers

NAGM US: e: National Association of Glue Manufacturers

NAGRA DIN: d: Fachnormenausschuß Graphisches Gewerbe [früher: Normen ausschuß für das Graphische Gewerbe]

NAGS US: e: North Atlantic Girl Scouts

NAGTC e: North American Gasoline Tax Conference; National Association of Girls' Training Corps

NAGVG US: e: National Association of Greenhouse Vegetable Growers

NAHA US: e: National Association of Hotel Accountants; e: North American Highway Association; N: US: e: Norwegian-American Historical Association

Nahal IL: [e: fighting pioneering youth]

NAHB US: e: National Association of Home Builders

NAHC US: e: National Advisory Health Council

NAHCSP US: e: National Association of Hospital Central Service Personnel

NAHDDM US: e: National Association of House and Daytime Dress Manufacturers

NAHHVG GB: e: National Association of Hothouse Vegetable Growers

NAHI NL: nl: Nederlands Agronomisch Historisch Instituut

NAHIBS B: nl: Nationaal Hoger Instituut voor Bouwkunst en Stedebouw

NAHM US: e: National Association of Hosiery Manufacturers

NAHRI e: National Animal Husbandry Research Institute

NAHRMP US: e: National Association of Hotel and Restaurant Meat Purveyors

NAHRO US: e: National Association of Housing and Redevelopment Officials

NAHS US: e: National Association of Horological Schools

N.A.H.T. GB: e: National Association of Head Teachers

N.A.H.V.D.E.E. e: National Association of Heating, Ventilating and Domestic Engineering Employers

NAHW US: e: National Association of Hardwood Wholesalers

NAI US: e: National Air Lines Inc.; National Apple Institute

NAIA US: e: National Association of Insurance Agents; National Association of Intercollegiate Athletics

NAIB US: e: National Association of Insurance Brokers

N.A.I.C. e: National Association of Insurance Committees

NAIC US: e: National Association of Insurance Commissioners; National Association of Investment Clubs (Companies)

NAIDA e: National Agricultural and Industrial Development Association

NAIDM US: e: National Association of Insecticide and Disindectant Manufacturers, Inc.

NAIEHS US: e: National Association of Importers and Exporters of Hides and Skins

NAIEM INT: f: Nouvelle Association Internationale d'Essais de Matériaux

NAIG J: e: Nippon Atomic Industry Group Company

NAII US: e: National Association of Ice Industry; National Association of Independent Insurers

NAIIA US: e: National Association of Independent Insurance Adjusters

NAILM US: e: National Association of Institutional Laundry Managers

NAIRE US: e: National Association of Internal Revenue Employees

NAIRO US: e: National Association of Intergroup Relations Officials

NAIS S: sv: Norrköpings Allmänna Idrottssällskap

N.A.I.S.E.O. e: National Association of Inspectors of Schools and Educational Associations

NAITE US: e: National Association of Industrial Teacher Educators

NAITT US: e: National Association of Industrial Teacher Trainers

Naivni 70 YU: [d: Ausstellungen internationaler naiver Kunst in Zagreb und Helbine im Sommer 1970]

NAIW US: e: National Association of Insurance Women

NAIWC GB: e: National Association of Inland Water Carriers

NAJD US: e: National Association of Journalism Directors

NAJJO NL: nl: Nederlandsche Agoedas

Jisrael Jeugd Organisatie

NAK NL: nl: Nederlandse Algemene Keuringsdienst voor Boomkwekerijgewassen; Stichting Nederlandse Algemene Keuringsdienst voor Zaaizaad en Pootgoed van Landbouwgewassen; BRD: d: Neuapostolische Kirche; Neue Augsburger Kattunfabrik AG, 89 Augsburg

N.A.K. CS: d: Nordböhmischer Automobilklub, Reichenberg

NAK N: no: Norsk Aero Klubb

NAKB NL: nl: Nederlandsche Algemeene Keuringsdienst voor Boomkwekerijgewassen

NAKG NL: nl: Nederlandsche Algemeene Keuringsdienst voor Groentezaden

Nakl.ČOS CS: cs: Nakladatelství Československé Obce Sokolské

NAKS NL: nl: Nederlandsche Algemeene Keuringsdienst voor Siergewassen

NAL US: e: National Accelerator Laboratory; IND: e: National Aeronautical Laboratory; US: e: National Agricultural Library, Washington, D.C.; National Airlines, Jacksonville; GH: e: National Alliance of Liberals; US: e: National Astronomical League; The New American Library of World Literature, Inc., New York 22

N.A.L. e: Noise Abatement League

NAL N: no: Den Norske Amerikalinje A/S, Oslo; Norske Arkitekters Landsforbund, Oslo [gegr 1910]; Norske Avisers Landforbund [gegr 1958]; Norske Avisutgivers Landsforbund

NALAM US: e: National Association of Livestock Auction Markets

NALC US: e: National Association of Letter Carriers; National Association of Life Companies; National Association of Litho Clubs; Negro American Labor Council

NALCD H: [e: national agricultural library and centre for documentation]

NALCM US: e: National Association of Lace Curtain Manufacturers

NALCOLANT US: e: mil: Naval Air Logistic Control Office Atlantic

NALCOPACREP US: e: mil: Naval Air Logistic Control Office Pacific Representative

NALF N: no: Norges Arbeidslederforbu␣

NALGM US: e: National Association of Leather Glove Manufacturers

NALGO GB: e: National Association of Local Government Officers, London

NALHI GB: e: National Authority for the Ladies' Handbag Industry

NALI US: e: National Agricultural Limestone Institute

NALLA INT: e: National Long Lines Agency [Europe]

NALLO US: e: National Association of License Law Officials

NALM US: e: National Association of Lift Makers

NALS US: e: National Association of Legal Secretaries; National Association of Lumber Salesmen; e: North American Lily Society

NALSAT GB: e: National Association of Land Settlement Association Tenants

NALSO GB: e: National Association of Labour Student Organizations

NALT US: e: National Association of the Legitimate Theater

NALU US: e: National Association of Life Underwriters

NAM US: e: National Air Museum [Smit␣sonian Institution]; National Association of Manufacturers of the United States of America, New York, N.Y. 10017 [gegr 1895]; NL: nl: N.V.Nederlandse Aardolie Maatschappij

N.A.M. e: North Africa Mission

NAMA US: e: National Automatic Merchandising Association, Chicago 3, Ill.; National Automotive Muffler Association; US: e: mil: Northern Air Materiel Area (Europe)

NAMAC US: e: National Association of Men's Apparel Clubs

NAMAE US: e: mil: Northern Air Materiel Area Europe, Burtonwood

NAMAP US: e: mil: Northern Air Materiel Area, Pacific

NAMARCO PI: e: National Marketing Corporation

NAMATCEN US: e: mil: Naval Air Materiel Center

N.A.M.B. GB: e: National Association of Master Bakers, Confectioners and Caterers

NAMB US: e: National Association of Merchandise Brokers

N.A.M.B.C.C. = N.A.M.B.

NAMBO US: e: National Association of Motor Bus Operators

N.A.M.C. e: National Association of Manufacturers Congresses

NAMC US: e: mil: Naval Air Materiel Center [BUWEPS]

N.A.M.C. GB: e: mil: Naval Air Modification Committee

NAMC = NAMCO

NAMCC US: e: National Association of Mutual Casualty Companies

NAMCO J: e: Nihon Aeroplane Manufacturing Company Ltd., Tokyo

NAMCS US: e: National Association of Marine Cooks and Stewards

NAMD US: e: National Association of Marble (Marine) Dealers; National Association of Market Developers

NAMDB US: e: National Association of Medical-Dental Bureaus

NAME GB: e: National Association of Marine Enginebuilders; CDN: e: National Association of Marine Engineers

N.A.M.E.B. GB: e: mil: Naval Aircraft Maintenance Examination Board

NAMEBA CH: d: Erste Nationale Motiv- und Eisenbahner-Briefmarkenausstellung der Schweiz, Zürich [25...27 Apr 1969]

NAMF US: e: National Association of Metal Finishers

NAMFI NATO: e: NATO Missile Firing Installation

NAMH US: e: National Association for Mental Health

NAMHH US: e: National Association of Methodists Hospitals and Homes

NAMI SU: [d: zentrales Forschungsinstitut für Kraftwagen und Automotoren, Moskau] ; GB: e: National Association of Malleable Ironfounders; S: sv: Nationell Ekonomi [d: Partei, gegr 1958]

NAMIA US: e: National Association of Mutual Insurance Agents

NAMIC US: e: National Association of Mutual Insurance Companies

NAMILCOM NATO: e: North Atlantic Military Committee

NAMILREPCOM NATO: e: North Atlantic Military Representatives Committee

NAMISTESTCEN US: e: mil: Naval Air Missile Test Center

NAML US: e: mil: Naval Aeronautical Materials Laboratory

N.A.M.L. GB: e: mil: Naval Aircraft Materials Laboratory

NAMM US: e: National Association of Margarine Manufacturers; National Association of Mirror Manufacturers; National Association of Music Merchants

NAMMA NATO: e: NATO MRCA [multirole combat aircraft] Development and Production Management Agency, 8 München 86

NAMMC GB: e: Natural Asphalt Mine Owners' and Manufacturers' Council

N.A.M.M.M. e: National Association of Master Monumental Masons

NAMMM US: e: National Association of Musical Merchandise Manufacturers

NAMMO NATO: e: NATO MRCA Development and Production Management Organization [vgl: NAMMA]

NAMMW US: e: National Association of

Musical Merchandise Wholesalers
NAMO US: e: National Association of Marketing Officials; NATO: e: NATO Maintenance Organization

NAMP US: e: National Association of Marble Producers

NAMPBG US: e: National Association of Manufacturers of Pressed and Blown Glassware

NAMPUS US: e: National Association of Master Plumbers of the United States

NAMRU US: e: mil: Naval Medical Research Unit

NAMS US: e: National Associated Marine Suppliers

NAMSA NATO: e: NATO Maintenance and Supply Agency

NAMSB US: e: National Association of Men's Sportswear Buyers; National Association of Mutual Savings Banks

NAMSO NATO: e: NATO Maintenance and Supply Organization

NAMSSA NATO: e: NATO Maintenance Supply Services Agency [= NMSSA]

NAMT US: e: National Association of Music Therapy

NAMTA US: e: National Art Materials Trade Association

NAMTC US: e: mil: Naval Air Missile Test Center

NAMU WAN: e: Northern Amalgamated Merchants' Union

NAMUR BRD: d: Normenarbeitsgemeinschaft für Meß- und Regeltechnik in der chemischen Industrie [VDE, VDI]

NANA US: e: National Advertising Newspaper Association; North American Newspaper Alliance [gegr 1922]

NANBPWC US: e: National Association of Negro Business and Professional Women's Clubs

N.A.N.C. e: Nyasaland African National Congress

NAND US: e: mil: Naval Ammunition and Net Depot

NANE US: e: National Association for Nursery Education

NANFAC US: e: mil: Naval Air Navigatic Facility Advisory Committee

NANM US: e: National Association of Negro Musicians

NANP US: e: National Association of Naturopathic Physicians

NANS US: e: Nevada Academy of Natura Sciences

NANTIS GB: e: Nottingham and Nottinghamshire Technical Information Servic

NANTS US: e: National Association of Naval Technical Supervisors

N.A.O. e: National Accordion Associatio National Arbitration Order; US: e: National Association of Opticians; e: National Association of Outfitters; Nautical Almanach Office

NAO NL: nl: Nederlandse Artiesten Organisatie

NAOA US: e: National Apartment Owner Association

N.A.O.D. e: mil: Naval Air Organization Division

NAOEJ US: e: National Association of Oil Equipment Jobbers

NAOO US: e: National Association of Optometrists and Opticians

N.A.O.P. e: National Association of Operative Plasterers

NAORPG NATO: e: North Atlantic Ocea Regional Planning Group

N.A.O.S.M. e: National Amalgamation of Operative Street Masons

NAOTS US: e: mil: Naval Aviation Ordnance Test Station

NAP US: e: National Association of Parliamentarians (Postmasters) (Publishers) BRD: d: Nationale Arbeiterpartei; e: Niger Agricultural Project; sv: Norska arbetarpartiet; e: North Atlantic Pact

NAPA US: e: National Amateur Press Association; National Association of

Performing Artists; National Association of Purchasing Agents, New York 7, N.Y.; National Automotive Parts Association

NAPB e: National Agricultural Production Board; NL: nl: Nederlandse Aannemers-en Patroonsbond

NAPBL US: e: National Association of Professional Baseball Leagues

NAPBOS NATO: e: North Atlantic Treaty Planning Board on Ocean Shipping

NAPC US: e: National Association of Plumbing Contractors; North American Philips Corp.

N.A.P.E. GB: e: National Association of Port Employers; US: e: National Association of Power Engineers

NAPECW US: e: National Association for Physical Education of College Women

NAPEM US: e: National Association of Public Exposition Managers

NAPET US: e: National Association of Photo Equipment Technicians

NAPF US: e: National Association of Plastic Fabricators

NAPFM US: e: National Association of Packaged Fuel Manufacturers

N.A.P.G.C.M. e: National Association of Plasterers, Granolithic and Cement Workers

NAPH US: e: National Association of the Physically Handicapped

NAPHCC US: e: National Association of Plumbing-Heating-Cooling Contractors

NAPIA US: e: National Association of Public Insurance Adjusters

N.A.P.I.C.M. e: National Association of Perambulator and Invalid Carriage Manufacturers

NAPIM US: e: National Association of Printing Ink Makers

NAPL US: e: National Association of Photo-Lithographers

NAPM GB: e: National Association of Paper Merchants; US: e: National Association of Photographic Manufacturers, Inc.

NAPNE US: e: National Association for Practical Nurse Education

NAPNES US: e: National Association for Practical Nurse Education and Service

NAPNM US: e: National Association of Pipe Nipple Manufacturers

NAPO US: e: mil: Naval Air Priorities Office

NAPOC US: e: United National Association of Post Office Craftsmen

Napola D: d: NS: Nationalpolitische Erziehungsanstalt

NAPOSTA BlnW: d: [Briefmarkenausstellung vom 29 Aug ... 1 Sep 1963]

NAPP US: e: National Association of Play Publishers

NAPPA US: e: National Association of Physical Plant Administrators of Universities and Colleges

NAPPO US: e: National Association of Plant Patent Owners

NAPRE US: e: National Association of Practical Refrigerating Engineers

NAPS US: e: National Association of Postal Supervisors

NAPSAE US: e: National Association of Public School Adult Educators

NAPSG US: e: National Association of Principals of Schools for Girls

N.A.P.T. GB: e: National Association for the Prevention of Tuberculosis

NAPUS US: e: National Association of Postmasters of the United States

N.A.P.V. e: National Association of Prison Visitors

NAR NL: nl: "Na Arbeid Rust" [artiestenvereniging]; e: National Association of Rocketry; B: nl: Nationale Arbeidsraad; N: no: Norske Aviseiers Representantskap; US: e: North American Rockwell; CDN: e: Northern Alberta Railways

NARA GB: e: National Amateur Rowing Association

NARAS US: e: National Academy of Recording Arts and Sciences

NARAW B: nl: Nationale Raad van de Weerstand

NARBA US: e: North American Regional Broadcasting Association

NARBEC US: e: North American Regional Broadcasting Engineering Committee

NARBW US: e: National Association of Railway Business Women

NARC e: National Academy Reviewing Committee; US: e: National Association for Retarded Children

NARCE US: e: National Association for Retired Civil Employees

NARCF US: e: National Association of Retail Clothiers and Furnishers

NARCO US: e: National Aeronautical Corporation, Ambler, Pa.

NARD US: e: National Association of Retail Druggists

NARDA US: e: National Appliance and Radio-Television Dealers Association

NAREB US: e: National Association of Real Estate Boards

N.A.R.F. GB: e: National Association of Retail Furnishers; Nuclear Aircraft Research Facility

NARFRO e: National Radio Frequency Recording Office

NARGUS US: e: National Association of Retail Grocers of the United States

NARHC US: e: National Association of River and Harbor Contractors

NARI ZA: e: Natal Agricultural Research Institute, Pietermaritzburg

NARIC PI: e: National Rice and Corn Corporation

NARICM US: e: National Association of Retail Ice Cream Manufacturers

N.A.R.I.U. GB: e: mil: Naval Air Radio Installation Unit

NARKI B: nl: Nationale Raad van de Kolenindustrie

NARL US: e: mil: Naval Aeronautical Rocket Laboratory

NARM US: e: National Association of Record Merchandisers; National Association of Relay Manufacturers

N.A.R.M.A.T. e: National Association of Radio Manufacturers and Traders

NARMFD US: e: National Association of Retail Meat and Food Dealers

N.A.R.O. e: National Association of Relieving Officers

NARO US: e: North American Regional Office

NAROCTESTSTA US: e: mil: Naval Air Rocket Test Station

NARP US: e: North American Regional Panel

N.A.R.P.A.C. e: National Air Raid Precautions Animals Committee

NARS US: e: National Archives and Records Service of the United States, Washington, D.C. [gegr 1934]

NARSA US: e: National Automotive Radiator Service Association

NARST US: e: National Association for Research in Science Teaching

NARSTI US: e: National Atomic Research Spaceship Testing and Information Bure

NARTB US: e: National Association of Radio and Television Braodcasters, Washington, D.C.

NARTC US: e: North American Regional Test Center

N.A.R.T.M. e: National Association of Roofing Tile Manufacturers

NARTS US: e: mil: Naval Air Rocket Test Station

NARTU e: mil: Naval Air Reserve Training Unit

NARUC US: e: National Association of Railroad and Utilities Commissioners

NARÚS CS: sk: Narodohospodársky Ústav Slovenský

NARW US: e: National Association of Refrigerated Warehouses

NAS NL: nl: Nationaal Arbeidssecretariaa

US: e: National Academy of Sciences

N.A.S. e: National Adoption Society; National Allotment Society

NAS US: e: National Association of Sanitarians; GB: e: National Association of Schoolmasters; e: National Association of Shopfitters; US: e: National Audubon Society; US: e: mil: Naval Air Service; Naval Air Station; US: e: Nebraska Academy of Sciences

N.A.S. US: e: North American Steamship Company, New York; e: Nursing Auxiliary Service

NASA US: e: National Acoustic Suppliers' Association; National Aeronautical Services Association; National Aeronautics and Space Administration; National Appliance Service Association; I: i: Navigazione Aerea S.A., Genova; US: e: North American Securities Administrators; North American Swiss Alliance, Cleveland [gegr 1865]

NASAB US: e: National Association of Shippers Advisory Boards

NASACT US: e: National Association of State Auditors, Comptrollers and Treasurers

NASAF e: mil: Northeast African Strategic Air Force

NASAO US: e: National Association of State Aviation Officials

NASASP US: e: National Association of State Agencies for Surplus Property

NASB US: e: National Association of Small Business

NASBA GB: e: National Automobile Safety Belt Association

NASBO US: e: National Association of State Budget Officers

NASBP US: e: National Association of Surety Bond Producers

NASC US: e: National Aeronautics and Space Council; National Aircraft Standards Committee, Washington, D.C.

N.A.S.C. e: National Association of Spotters' Clubs

NASC US: e: National Association of Student Councils; NATO: e: NATO Supply Center; US: e: mil: Navy Air Systems Command

N.A.S.C. e: Netherlands Advisory Shipping Council; North American Supply Council [CDN, GB, US]

NASCAR US: e: National Association for Stock Car Auto Racing

NAS-CD US: e: National Academy of Sciences - Chemistry Division

NASCD US: e: National Association of Soil Conservation Districts

NASCL US: e: North American Student Cooperative League

NASCO US: e: National Academy of Sciences Committee on Oceanography

NASCOM US: e: National Aeronautics and Space Administrations Communications Network

NASCOSEB B: nl: Nationale Studiecommissie van het Statuut van Expert-Boekhouders

NASCS US: e: National Association of Shoe Chain Stores

N.A.S.D. GB: e: National Amalgamation of Stevedores and Dockers

NASD US: e: National Association of Schools of Design; National Association of Security Dealers; US: e: mil: Naval Air Supply Depot

NASDA US: e: National Association of State Departments of Agriculture

NASDM US: e: National Association of Special Delivery Messengers

NASDSE US: e: National Association of State Directors of Special Education

NASDSSE US: e: National Association of State Directors and Supervisors of Secondary Education

NASDTEC US: e: National Association of State Directors of Teacher Education and Certification

N.A.S.D.U. GB: e: National Amalgamated Stevedores' and Dockers' Union

NASDVE US: e: National Association of State Directors of Vocational Education

N.A.S.E. US: e: National Academy of Stationary Engineers

NASE US: e: National Association of Steel Exporters

N.A.S.F. e: National Amalgamated Society of Foremen

NASFCA US: e: National Automatic Sprinkler and Fire Control Association, New York, N.Y.

NASFM US: e: National Association of Store Fixture Manufacturers

NASKO B: nl: Nationaal Sekretariaat van het Katholiek Onderwijs

NASL US: e: National Association of State Libraries

N.A.S.M. GB: e: National Association for School Magazines

NASM US: e: National Association of Schools of Music; National Association of State Militia

N.A.S.M. e: National Association of Station Masters

NASMBCM US: e: National Association of Sanitary Milk Bottle Closure Manufacturers

NASMD US: e: National Association of Sewing Machine Dealers; National Association of Sheet Metal Distributors, Philadelphia 3, Pa.

NASMI US: e: National Association of Secondary Material Industries

NASMO NATO: e: NATO F-104G Starfighter Production Organization, 54 Koblenz [BRD]

N.A.S.N. e: North Atlantic Steam Navigation Company

NAS-NRC US: e: National Academy of Sciences - National Research Council, Washington, D.C.

N.A.S.O. e: National Association of Symphony Orchestras

NASO e: mil: Naval Aviation Supply Office

NASORRO NL: nl: Nationaal-Socialistische Rijksradio-Omroep [1940...45]

NASPA US: e: National Association of Student Personnel Administrators

NASPM GB: e: National Association of Seed Potato Merchants; US: e: National Association of Slipper and Playshoe Manufacturers

NASPO US: e: National Association of State Purchasing Officials; NATO: e: NATO F-104G Starfighter Production Organization

NASPSM US: e: National Association of Shirt, Pajama and Sportswear Manufacturers

NASR US: e: National Association of Swine Records

NASRC US: e: National Association of State Racing Commissioners

NASS US: e: National Association of Secretaries of State; National Association of Suggestion Systems, Chicago,

N.A.S.S. GB: e: mil: Naval Air Signal School

NASSA US: e: National Aerospace Services Association; National Association of Schools of Social Administration

NASSB US: e: National Association of Supervisors of State Banks

NASSCO PI: e: National Shipyard & Steel Corporation, Manila

NASSDE US: e: National Association of State Supervisors of Distributive Education

NASSHE US: e: National Association of State Supervisors of Home Economics

NASSI NL: nl: Nationale Aktie Steun Spijtoptanten Indonesië

NASSP US: e: National Association of Secondary School Principals

NASSTA US: e: National Association of Secretaries of State Teachers Associations

NASSW US: e: National Association of School Social Workers

NASTBD US: e: National Association of State Textbook Directors

N.A.S.U. GB: e: National Adult School Union

NASU US: e: National Association of State Universities; e: North American Singers Union

NASW US: e: National Association of Science Writers [gegr 1934]; National Association of Social Workers

N.A.S.W.D.U. GB: e: mil: Naval Air/Sea Warfare Development Unit

NAT S: sv: Nämnden för Avkommeundersökning av Tjurar

N.A.T. e: National Arbitration Tribunal; National Association of Theatres

NAT N: no: Norsk Artikkel Tjeneste [d: Nachrichtenagentur]

NATA US: e: National Association of Tax Accountants (Administrators) (Teachers' Agencies); AUS: e: National Association of Testing Authorities of Australia; US: e: National Athletic Training Association; National Automobile Transporters' Association; National Aviation Trades Association; National Aviation Training Association; INT: e: North Atlantic Treaty Alliance

Natak D: d: Nationalpolitische Auslands-Korrespondenz, Berlin-Potsdam

NATAS US: e: National Academy of Television Arts and Sciences

NATAW US: e: National Association of Textile and Apparel Wholesalers

NATB US: e: National Automobile Theft Bureau

Nat.-B. d: Nationalbank

NATB US: e: mil: Naval Air Training Base

NATC US: e: mil: Naval Air Training Command; INT: e: North Atlantic Treaty Council

NATCC US: e: National Air Transport Coordinating Committee

N.A.T.C.G. GB: e: National Association of Training Corps for Girls

NATCOM US: e: National Communications Symposium [IEEE]

NATCS GB: e: National Air Traffic Control Service [gegr 1962]

NAT-CUS NATO: e: North Atlantic Treaty Canada, U.S. Regional Planning Group

NATD US: e: National Association of Tobacco Distributors

N.A.T.E. GB: e: National Association for the Teaching of English; National Association of Theatrical Employees

NATECOM US: e: mil: Naval Airship Training and Experimentation Command

Nateg D: d: Nationale Erdöl-GmbH, Berlin W 50

Nateko INT: d: Interalliierte nautisch-technische Kommission für das Schwarze Meer

NATESA US: e: National Alliance of Television and Electronic Service Associations

NATESTCEN US: e: mil: Naval Air Test Center

N.A.T.G.A. GB: e: National Amateur Tobacco Growers Association

NATI SU: [d: wissenschaftliches Forschungsinstitut für den Kraftverkehr, Moskau]

NATINFORM GB: e: Nationalist Information Bureau, Framlingham, Suffolk

NATIPIJ NL: nl: Nationaal Islamietische Padvinderij

NATIS NATO: e: North Atlantic Treaty Information Service

N.A.T.K.E. GB: e: National Association of Theatrical and Kinematograph Employees

NATL US: e: National Agricultural Transportation League

NATMA US: e: National Association of Teachers of Marketing and Advertising

NATMC US: e: National Advanced Technology Management Conference

NATNAVMEDCEN US: e: mil: National Naval Medical Center

NAT-NE NATO: e: North Atlantic Treaty Northern European Regional Planning Group

NATO US: e: National Association of Taxicab Owners

N.A.T.O. e: National Association of Temperance Officials

NATO US: e: National Association of Travel Organizations; US: e: mil: North African Theater of Operations; NATO: e: North Atlantic Treaty Organization da: Nordatlantiske Traktats Organisation

NATRFD US: e: National Association of Television and Radio Firm Directors

NAT-RPG NATO: e: North Atlantic Treaty Regional Planning Group

NATS US: e: National Association of Teachers of Singing; GB: e: National Association of Training Schools; US: e: mil: Naval Air Transport Service

NAT-SEWM NATO: e: North Atlantic Treaty Southern Europe Western Mediterranean Regional Planning Group

NAT-SG NATO: e: North Atlantic Treaty Standing Group

NATSOPA GB: e: National Society of Operational Printers and Assistants

NATTC US: e: mil: Naval Air Technical Training Command

NATTS US: e: mil: Naval Air Turbine Test Station

NATU PI: e: National Association of Trade Unions; US: e: mil: Naval Aviation Training Unit; NL: nl: Nederlandse Amateur Toneel Unie

N.A.T.U.A.S. e: National Association of Trade Union Approved Societies

Nat.-V. d: Nationalversammlung

NATVAS US: e: National Academy of Television Arts and Sciences

NATWA US: e: National Auto and Truck Wreckers Association

N.A.U.E.F.M. e: National Amalgamated Union of Enginemen, Firemen, Motormen, etc.

NAUI US: e: National Association of Underwater Instructors

N.A.U.L.A.W. e: National Amalgamated Union of Life Assurance Workers

NAUM US: e: National Association of Uniform Manufacturers

N.A.U.S.A. e: National Amalgamated Union of Shop Assistants

Nav; NAV e: mil: Naval Forces; Navy

NAV NL: nl: Nederlandsche Alpen-Vereeniging, Amsterdam; BRD: d: Verband der niedergelassenen Ärzte Deutschlands eV, 5 Köln; D: d: Norddeutsche Ausstellungsvereinigung, Stettin

NAVA US: e: National Audio Visual Association

NAVAC GB: e: National Audio-Visual Aids Centre

NAVADCOM US: e: mil: Naval Administrative Command

NAVAIRLANT US: e: mil: Naval Air Forces, Atlantic

NAVAIRPAC US: e: mil: Naval Air Forces Pacific

NAVANTRACOM US: e: mil: Naval Air Advanced Training Command

NAVBOILAB US: e: mil: Navy Boiler Laboratory

NAVCAG NATO: e: Allied Naval Forces Central Army Group and Bremen Enclave [später: ... and Bremerhaven]

NAVCENFRACO US: e: mil: Navy Central Freight Control Office

NAVCENT NATO: e: Allied Naval Forces Central Europe

NAVCOMP US: e: mil: Comptroller of the Navy

NAVCOSSACT US: e: mil: Naval Command Systems Support Activity

NAVDOCKS US: e: mil: United States Navy Bureau of Yards and Docks

NAVEA B: nl: Nationale Vereniging voor Amateursrechten

NAVED US: e: National Association of

Visual Education Dealers

NAVEKADOS B: nl: Nationaal Verbond van Katholieke Doofstommen

NAVF N: no: Norges Almenvitenskapelige Forskningsråd [gegr 1949]

NavFE US: e: mil: Naval Forces Far East

NAVFORCONAD US: e: mil: Naval Forces Continental Air Defense Command

NAVFOREU US: e: mil: Naval Forces Europe

NAVFORJAP US: e: mil: Naval Forces Japan

NAVFORKOR US: e: mil: Naval Forces Korea

NAVILCO US: e: mil: Navy International Logistics Control Office

Navis S: sv: Navigationssällskapet, Stockholm

NAVITO INT: [d: Internationale Fischerei-Ausstellung, Den Haag, NL]

NAVL US: e: North American Van Lines, Inc., Fort Wayne 1, Indiana

NAVMAR US: e: mil: Naval Forces Marianas

NAVNAW US: e: mil: Naval Forces Northwest African Waters

NAVNON NATO: e: Allied Naval Forces North Norway

NAVNORCENT NATO: e: Allied Naval Forces Northern Area, Central Europe

NAVNORTH NATO: e: Allied Naval Forces Northern Europe

NAVO NATO: nl: Noord-Atlantische Verdrags Organisatie

NAVOBSY US: e: mil: Naval Observatory

NAVOCFORMED NATO: e: Naval On-Call Force Mediterranean

NAVOCS US: e: mil: Naval Officers Candidate School

NAVORD US: e: mil: Bureau of Ordnance [Navy]

NavPhiBase US: e: mil: Naval Amphibious Base

NavPhibTraULant US: e: mil: Naval Amphibious Training Unit Atlantic

NAVPHIL US: e: mil: Naval Forces Philippines

NAVPM US: e: National Association of Vertical Turbine Pump Manufacturers, Los Angeles 13, Calif.

NAVPORCO US: e: mil: Naval Port Control Office

NAVREL US: e: mil: Navy Relief Society

NAVRESLAB US: e: mil: Naval Research Laboratory

NAVROM R: ro: Navigaitsa Maritima si Fluviala Romina, Bucureşti

N.A.V.S. e: National Anti-Vivisection Society

NAVS US: e: National Association of Variety Stores

Nav.S. d: Navigationsschule

NAVSANDA US: e: mil: Bureau of Supplies and Accounts [Navy]

NAVSCAP NATO: e: Allied Naval Forces Scandinavian Approaches

Nav Sch e: Navigation School

Nav.Sch. d: Navigationsschule

NAVSECGRU US: e: mil: Naval Security Group

NAVSECSTA US: e: mil: U.S. Naval Security Station

NAVSHIPSA US: e: mil: U.S.Naval Shipbuilding Scheduling Activity

NAVSHIPYD US: e: mil: Naval Shipyard

NAVSOUTH e: mil: Southern Europe Naval Command

NAVSTA US: e: mil: Naval Staff; Naval Station

NavSupCen US: e: mil: Naval Supply Center

NAVSUPFORANT US: e: mil: Naval Support Forces Antarctia

NAVW NL: nl: Nederlandsche Arbeiders-Vredewacht

NAVWARCOL US: e: mil: Naval War College

NAVWEPS US: e: mil: Bureau of Naval Weapons

NAW US: e: National Association of

Wholesalers; DDR: d: Nationales Auf-
bauwerk [gegr 1952] ; D: d: Nationales
Aufforstungswerk

NAWA US: e: National Apple Week Association; National Association of Women
Artists

NaWAF US: e: mil: Navy with Air Force

NAWAPA CDN: US: North American Water
and Power Alliance

NaWAr US: e: mil: Navy with Army

NAWB US: e: National Association of Wine
Bottlers

NAWC GB: e: National Association of Wom-
en's Clubs; US: e: mil: Naval War College

NAWCAS US: e: National Association of
Women's and Children's Apparel Salesmen

NAWCM US: e: National Association of
Wiping Cloth Manufacturers

N.A.W.C.S. GB: e: National Association of
Women Civil Servants

NAWDC US: e: National Association of
Women Deans and Counselors

NAWDOFF GB: e: National Association
of Wholesale Distributors of Frozen Food

NAWEGEK B: nl: Nationaal Werk voor het
gehandicapte Kind

NAWF US: e: North American Wildlife
Foundation

NAWG US: e: National Association of
Wheat Growers

NAWGA US: e: National American Wholesale Grocers' Association

NAWL US: e: National Association of
Women Lawyers

NAWLA US: e: National American Wholesale Lumber Association

NAWM US: e: National Association of
Wool Manufacturers

NAWMP US: e: National Association of
Waste Material Producers

N.A.W.P. e: National Association of
Women Pharmacists

NAWPM GB: e: National Association of
Wholesale Paint Merchants

NAWTS US: e: National Association of
World Trade Secretaries

NAWU US: e: National Agricultural
Workers Union

NAWWO US: e: National Association of
Woolen and Worsted Overseers

NAXSTA US: e: mil: Naval Air Experimental Station

NAYC GB: e: National Association of
Youth Clubs

NAYFC US: e: National Association of
Young Farmers' Clubs

NAYRU e: North American Yacht Racing
Union

NaZA. D: d: mil: Nachrichtenzeugamt

NAZO NL: nl: Nederlandse Auto Zieken-
vervoer Ondernemingen

NAZPRE [BRD: d: nationale Vertretung
der russischen Emigration]

N.B. D: d: mil: Nachrichtenbetriebsabtei-
lung [Reichswehrministerium]

NB YU: sh: Narodna Banka; e: National
Bank; d: Nationalbibliothek; e: mil:
Naval Base; GB: e: Neath and Brecon
Railway; Netherlands Bank of South
Africa Limited, London E.C. 3

N.B. e: mil: Netherlands Brigade

NB H: hu: Nemzeti Bank, Budapest;
US: hu: Magyar Nemzeti Bizottság,
New York; D: d: nach WK2: Nord-
deutsche Bank, Hamburg

N.B. N: no: Norsk Bladeierforening;
Norsk Bondelag

NB D: d: Nürnberger Bund; BRD: d:
Nordsüd - Nürnberger Bund Großeinkaufsverband eGmbH, 43 Essen

NBA US: e: National Band Association;
National Bar Association; National
Basketball Association; GB: e: Nation-
al Benzole (and Allied Products) Associ-
ation, London S.W. 1; US: e: National
Boat Association; National Boxing
Association of America; GB: e: Nation-
al Brassfoundry Association; US: e:
National Button Association

NbA BRD: d: Bahn: Neubauamt

NBA GB: e: North British Academy;

S: sv: Nya Bokförlags AB, Stockholm

NBAA US: e: National Boxing Association of America; National Business Aircraft Association, Inc.

NBAC CS: d: Nordböhmischer Automobilclub, Reichenberg

NbÄ BRD: d: Bahn: Neubauämter

NBAG BRD: d: Niederrheinische Bergwerks-AG

NBAK CS: d: Nordwestböhmischer Automobilklub, Teplitz-Schönau

NBAPC US: e: National Business Advisory and Planning Council

NBAS NL: nl: Nederlandsche Bond van Abstinent Studeerenden

N.B.B. B: nl: Nationale Bank van België; NL: nl: Nederlandse Biljart Bond; Nederlandse Bioscoopbond; Nederlandse Blinden Bond; Nederlandse Boks Bond

NBBA US: e: Northeastern Bird Banding Association

NBBB US: e: National Better Business Bureau

NBBC GB: e: National Brass Band Club

NBBDA US: e: National Burlap Bag Dealers Association

NBBE GB: e: National Board for Bakery Education

NBBPVI US: e: National Board of Boiler and Pressure Vessel Inspectors, Columbus, Ohio

NBBS NL: nl: Nederlands Bureau voor Buitenlandse Studentenbetrekkingen

N.B.Č. CS: cs: Národni Banka Československá

N.B.C. GB: e: National Association of Boys' Clubs

NBC US: e: National Baseball Congress; National Beef Council; National Beryllia Corporation, North Bergen, N.J.; National Boiler Council; National Book Committee

N.B.C. GB: e: National Book Council

NBC US: e: National Bowling Council; National Broadcasting Corporation, New York, N.Y.; National Bulk Carriers, Inc., New York, N.Y.; NATO: e: National Bureau of Codification

N.B.C. GB: e: mil: Naval Barracks, Chatham

NBC S: sv: Nordens Bondeorganisationers Centralråd

NBCA US: e: National Bituminous Concrete Association

NBCC US: e: National Baby Care Council; National Bidders Control Center; GB: e: National Bituminous Coal Commission; US: e: National Budget and Consultation Committee

NBCL e: National Beauty Culturists League

NBCR US: e: National Bureau of Civic Research

NBCU US: e: National Bureau of Casualty Underwriters

N.B.D. GB: e: mil: Naval Barracks, Devenport

N.B.D.C. GB: e: National Broadcasting Development Committee

N.B.Dns CDN: e: mil: New Brunswick Dragoons

N.B.E. e: National Bank of Egypt; D: d: Niederbarnimer Eisenbahn AG, Berlin

NBEF N: no: Norsk Bladeierforening

NBER US: e: National Bureau of Economic Research

NBF GB: e: National Bedding Federation; N: no: Norsk Bibliotekforening; Norsk Botanisk Forening

NBFA US: e: National Business Form Associates

N.B.F.D. e: National Benevolent Fund for the Deaf

NBFFO US: e: National Board of Fur Farm Organizations

NBFU US: e: National Board of Fire Underwriters, New York, N.Y.

NBG US: e: New Burlington Gallery

NBGQA US: e: National Building Granite Quarries Association

NBHA US: e: National Builders' Hardware Association

NBHCA US: e: National Belgian Hare Club of America

N.B.H.I. B: nl: Nationaal Belgisch Hopinstituut

NBI e: National Bank of India

N.B.I. e: National Benevolent Institution

NBI NL: nl: Nederlands Beheersinstituut; N: no: Norges Byggforskningsinstitutt, Oslo [gegr 1953]

NBIMOD PL: pl: Naukowo-Badawczy Instytut Mechanicznej Obróbki Drewna

NBIW PL: pl: Naukowo-Badawczy Instytut Włókienniczy

N.B.K. BRD: d: Naturistenbund Köln eV; D: d: Neues Brandenburgisches Kreditinstitut (Kur- und Neumärkische Ritterschaftliche Darlehnskasse), Berlin

NBKR S: sv: Nordiska Blåbans- och Blåkorsrådet [gegr 1948]

NBL GB: US: National Basketball League; GB: e: National Book League; CDN: e: New Brunswick Laboratory

N.B.L. N: no: Norske Barnehagelærerinners Landsforbund

NBLP US: e: National Bureau for Lathing and Plastering

NBMDA US: e: National Building Material Distributors' Association

NBME US: e: National Board of Medical Examiners

NBML NL: nl: Noordbrabantse Maatschappij van Landbouw

NBNA US: e: National Bank of North America

NBNI ZA: af: Nasionale Bounavorsningsinstituut

NBO NL: nl: Nederlandsche Vereeniging "Nazorg Buitengewoon Onderwijs"; Neutraal Bijzonder Onderwijs; S: sv: Nordisk Byggnadskooperativ Organisation

NBOEG NL: nl: Nationaal Bureau voor Onderwijs op Economischen Grondslag

NB of S US: e: National Bureau of Standards [= NBS]

NBP PL: pl: Narodowy Bank Polski

N.B.P. GB: e: mil: Naval Barracks, Portsmouth

NBP N: no: Norges Bondelags Pressekont◄

NBPA GB: e: National Butane-Propane Association

NBPI GB: e: National Board for Prices and Incomes

N.B.P.I. e: Newspaper Benevolent and Provident Institution

NBPRP US: e: National Board for the Promotion of Rifle Practice

NBPW US: e: National Brotherhood of Packinghouse Workers

NBR N: no: Norges Byggstandardiseringsrad, Oslo 3; GB: e: North British Railway

N.B.R.C. e: National Birth Rate Commission

NBRI ZA: e: National Building Research Institute, Pretoria

NBRMP US: e: National Board of Review of Motion Pictures

NBRSA US: e: National Bench Rest Shoo◄ ers Association

NBS GB: e: National Bakery School; US: e: National Bookkeepers' Society

N.B.S. NZ: e: National Broadcasting Service; e: National Building Society

NBS US: e: National Bureau of Standards, Washington, D.C. [Department of Commerce]; Netherland Benevolent Society of New York

N.B.S. e: Netherlands Bible Society

NBSA US: e: National Bakery Suppliers' Association

NBSDI US: e: National Brand Soft Drinks Institute

N.B.S.S. GB: e: National Bible Society of Scotland; National British Softball Society

NBT NL: [d: nationales Büro für Tourismus]

NBTA GB: e: National Business Teachers' Association; US: e: National Bus Traffic Association
N.B.T.H. GB: e: North British Trust Hotels
N.B.T.P.I. GB: e: National Book Trade Provident Institution
N.B.T.P.S. GB: e: National Book Trade Provident Society
NBU INT: sv: Nordiska Bankmanaunionen, Stockholm 7; N: no: Norges Bygdeungdomslag
NBV D: d: WK2: Nahverkehrsbevollmächtigter
NBVS NL: nl: Nederlandsche Bond van Vrije Socialisten
NBWAA US: e: National Beer Wholesalers' Association of America
NBWi A: d: Nationalbibliothek Wien
NBYWCA US: e: National Board of the Young Women's Christian Association
N.C. e: National Congress (Council); New Church; GB: e: Newspaper Conference; e: mil: Northern Command
NC US: e: Nuclear Congress; US: e: mil: Nurse Corps
NC⁴ = NCCCC
NCA US: e: National Canners Association, Washington 6, D.C.; National Cashmere (Cheerleaders) (Chiropractic) (Coal) Association
N.C.A. e: National Coat Assembly
NCA US: e: National Coffee Association; US: e: mil: National Command Authorities; US: e: National Commission on Accrediting; National Committee for Aeronautics; National Confectioners' Association; National Constructors' (Costumiers') Association; National Council on Alcoholism; National Cranberry (Creameries) Association
N.C.A. NL: nl: Nationale Commissie tegen het Alcoholisme
NCA US: e: North Central Airlines; North Central Association for Colleges and Secondary Schools; Northern Consolidated Airlines [Alaska]
NCAA US: e: National Collegiate Athletic Association; e: Northern Counties Athletic Association
NCAB US: e: National Collegiate Athletic Bureau; New Council of American Business
N.C.A.C. US: e: National Concerts and Artists Corporation
NCAC US: e: North-Central Association of Colleges; US: e: mil: WK2: Northern Combat Area Command [Burma]
NCACC GB: e: National Civil Aviation Consultative Committee
NCACSS US: e: North Central Association of Colleges and Secondary Schools
N.C.A.D.P. e: National Council for the Abolition of the Death Penalty
N.C.A.E. e: National Council for Agricultural Education
NCAEG US: e: National Confederation of American Ethnic Groups
NCAER IND: e: National Council of Applied Economic Research
NCAI US: e: National Committee on Atomic Information; National Congress of American Indians; National Council of American Importers
N.C.A.I. e: National Council of Associated Ironmasters
NCALL US: e: National Council on Agricultural Life and Labor
NCAR US: e: National Center for Atmosphere Research, Boulder, Colo.
NCARB US: e: National Council of Architectural Registration Boards
NCASF US: e: National Council of American-Soviet Friendship
NCATE US: e: National Council for Accreditation of Teacher Education [gegr 1952]
NCAVAE GB: e: National Committee for Audiovisual Aids in Education
N.C.A.W. e: National Council for Animal Welfare

NCAWE US: e: National Council of Administrative Women in Education

NCB US: e: National Cargo Bureau; National City Bank, New York, N.Y.

N.C.B. GB: e: National Coal Board, London S.W. 1

NCB NATO: e: National Codification Bureau; US: e: National Compliance Board

N.C.B. e: National Conciliation Board

NCB US: e: National Conservation Bureau; NL: nl: Nederlandse Consumenten Bond, 's-Gravenhage; Noordbrabantse Christelijke Boerenbond; DK: da: Nordisk Copyright Bureau, København

NCBA US: e: National Catholic Bandmasters' Association

N.C.B.A. GB: e: National Cattle Breeders' Association

NCBA US: e: National Chinchilla Breeders of America

N.C.B.A. e: Non-County Boroughs Association

NCBC CDN: e: National Cinchilla Breeders of Canada

NCBFCC e: Northern Counties Border Fancy Canary Club

NCBGCW US: e: National Committee on Boys and Girls Club Work

NCBM US: e: National Council on Business Mail

NCBMP GB: e: National Council of Building Material Producers

N.C.B.O. NL: nl: Nederlandse Christelijke Bond van Overheidspersoneel

NCBPE US: e: National Conference of Business Paper Editors

NCBS GB: e: National Council of Business Schools

NCBTB NL: nl: Nederlandse Christelijke Boeren- en Tuindersbond

N.C.B.W.A. e: National Congress of British West Africa

NCC GB: e: National Caravan Council Ltd.;

US: e: National Casting Council

N.C.C. GB: e: National Catering Corporation; National Cavy Club; National Chamber of Commerce

NCC e: National Chemurgic Council; National Christian Council; US: e: National Conference on Citizenship; National Cotton Council, Memphis, Tennessee; National Council of Church

N.C.C. e: National Coursing Club (Committee)

NCC GB: e: The National Computing Centre Ltd., Manchester; NL: nl: Nationaal Crisis Comité; US: e: Navaho Community College, Many Farms, Arizona; e: Netherlands Chamber of Commerce; GB: e: mil: Non-combatant Corps; US: e: North Carolina College, Durham

N.C.C. e: Northern Counties Committee [railway]

NCCA US: e: National Catholic Camping Association; National Concrete Contractors Association; National Cotton Council of America

NCCB US: e: National Council to Combat Blindness

NCCBS US: e: National Citizens Council for Better Schools

NCCC US: e: National Conference of Catholic Charities

NCCCC US: e: mil: Navy Command, Control and Communications Center, San Diego

NCCCCA US: e: National Collegiate Cross Country Coaches Association

NCCCWA US: e: National Cotton Compress and Cotton Warehouse Association

NCCE e: Northern Counties Co-operative Enterprise

NC-CEE NL: nl: Nederlandse Comité voor de CEE

N.C.C.F. US: e: National Committee to Combat Fascism [Black Panther-allied]

NCCF US: e: National Council on Community Foundations

NCCFL US: e: National Catholic Conference on Family Life

NCCHE US: e: National Conference for Cooperation in Health Education

NCCHS US: e: National Council of Chiropractic Hospitals and Sanitariums

NCCI GB: e: National Committee for Commonwealth Immigrants, London W 1; US: e: National Council on Compensation Insurance

NCCIA US: e: North Carolina Crop Improvement Association, Inc.

NCCIJ US: e: National Catholic Conference for Interracial Justice

N.C.C.J. J: e: National Christian Council of Japan

NCCJ US: e: National Conference of Christians and Jews

N.C.C.L. e: National Council for Civil Liberties

N.C.C.M. US: e: National Council of Catholic Men

NCCM DK: da: Nordisk Komite for Konsumentspørgsmal

NCCMT US: e: National Comittee for Careers in Medical Technology

NCCN US: e: National Council of Catholic Nurses

NCCOP GB: e: National Corporation for the Care of Old People

NCCPA US: e: National Cinder Concrete Products Association

NCCPS US: e: National Citizens Commission for the Public Schools

NCCPT US: e: National Congress of Colored Parents and Teachers

NCCR US: e: National Council of Chiropractic Roentgenologists

NCCU CDN: e: National Conference of Canadian Universities

NCCUSL US: e: National Conference of Commissioners on Uniform State Laws

N.C.C.V.D. GB: e: National Council for Combating Venereal Diseases

NCCW US: e: National Council of Catholic Women

NCCWHO US: e: National Citizens' Committee for the World Health Organization

NCCY US: e: National Council of Catholic Youth

NCCYSA US: e: National Conference of Catholics in Youth Serving Agencies

N.C.D. GB: e: mil: Naval Construction Department

N.C.D.A. e: National Council for Democratic Aid

NCDC e: National Civil Defence Corps; US: e: National Communicable Disease Center, Atlanta

NCDH US: e: National Committee Against Discrimination in Housing

N.C.D.L. e: National Canine Defence League

N.C.D.M. e: National Constitution Defence Movement

N.C.D.S. e: National Civil Defence Services

NCE US: e: Newark College of Engineering

NCEA US: e: National Catholic Educational Association; e: North Central Electric Association

NCEB PTM: e: National Commercial Education Board; NATO: e: NATO Communications Electronics Board

NCEC US: e: National Committee for an Effective Congress

N.C.E.C. e: National Conference of Express Carriers; National Council for Equal Citizenship

NCEC US: e: mil: Navy Civil Engineering Corps

NCEFF US: e: National Committee for Education in Family Finance

NCEL US: e: mil: Naval Civil Engineering Laboratory

N.C.E.O. e: National Confederation of Employers' Organizations

NCERT IND: e: National Council for Educational Research and Training

NCET GB: e: National Council for Educational Technology

N.C.E.U. I: i: Nuovo Catasto Edilizio Urbano

NCEW US: e: National Conference of Editorial Writers

NCEY US: e: National Committee on Employment of Youth

NCF US: e: National Cancer Foundation; National Civic Federation; NL: nl: Nederlandsch Centraal Filmarchief; S: sv: Nordiska Civilekonomförbundet; N: no: Norges Cykelforbund

NCFA US: e: National Collection of Fine Arts; National Collegiate Flying Association; National Consumer Finance Association

NCfB N: no: Norsk Centralforening for Boktrykkere

NCFC US: e: National Commercial Finance Conference; National Council of Farm Cooperatives

NCFE US: e: National Committee for a Free Europe

NCFL US: e: National Children's Film Library

NCFP US: e: National Conference on Fluid Power

NCFR US: e: National Conference on Family Relations

NCFRF US: e: National Cystic Fibrosis Research Foundation

NCG US: e: National Council for the Gifted; National Cylinder Gas Company, Chicago 11, Ill.

NCGA US: e: National Committee on Governmental Accounting; National Corn Growers Association; National Cotton Ginners Association

N.C.G.C. e: National Council of Girls' Clubs

NCGE US: e: National Council of Geographic Education

NCGGO B: nl: Nationaal Centrum voor Grasland- en Groenvoederonderzoek

NCGT US: e: National Council of Geography Teachers

NCGW NL: nl: Nederlandsch Comité voor Geschiedkundige Wetenschappen

N.C.H. e: National Children's Home (and Orphanage); GB: e: National Committee on Housing; National Council of House

NCHA US: e: National Campers and Hikers Association; National Capital Housing Authority

N.C.H.O. e: National Children's Home and Orphanage

NCHS US: e: National Committee on Homemaker Service

NCI US: e: National Cancer Institute; National Cheese Institute

NCIC CDN: e: National Cancer Institute of Canada

NCICA US: e: mil: National Counterintelligence Corps Association

NCIESD US: e: National Conference on International Economic and Social Development

NCIH US: e: National Council on Industrial Hydraulics

NCIKB NL: nl: Nederlandsch Centraal Instituut voor de Kennis van het Buitenland

NCIMA US: e: National Cellulose Insulation Manufacturers Association

NCIMC US: e: National Council of Industrial Management Clubs

NCIO J: e: National Council of Industrial Organizations

NCIP US: e: National Council for Industrial Peace

NCIPA GB: e: National Council of Independent Petroleum Associations

NCIS US: e: National Council of Independent Schools

NCIT US: e: National Committee for Insurance Taxation; GB: e: National Council on Inland Transport

NCITD US: e: National Committee on International Trade Documentation

NCJC US: e: National Conference of Judicial Councils

NCJCJ US: e: National Council of Juvenile Court Judges

NCJW US: e: National Council of Jewish Women

NCK J: Nihon Chuo Kyobakai [d: Galopprenngesellschaft]

NCL GB: e: National Central Library, London

N.C.L. Taiwan: e: National Central Library, Taipei; IND: e: National Chemical Laboratory; GB: e: National Chemical Laboratory, Teddington; e: National Church League

NCL US: e: National Consumers' League; GB: e: National Council of Labour

NCLA US: e: National Council of Local Administrators of Vocational Education and Practical Arts

NCLAVPAE US: e: National Council of Local Administrators of Vocational and Practical Arts Education

NCLB NL: nl: Nederlandse Christelijke Landarbeidersbond

NCLC US: e: National Child Labor Committee; GB: e: National Council of Labour Colleges

N.C.L.C. e: mil: Non-Combatant Labour Corps

NCLL US: e: National Conference on Labor Legislation

N.C.L.P. e: Nyasaland Congress Liberation Party

NCLS US: e: National Committee for Liberation of Slovakia

NCLTA US: e: National Cigar Leaf Tobacco Association

N.C.M. GB: e: National College of Music; National Council of Music

NCM NL: nl: Nederlandse Credietverzekering Maatschappij N.V.

NCMA US: e: National Concrete Masonry Association; National Council of Millinery Associations

NCMB WAN: e: Nigerian Cocoa Marketing Board

NCME US: e: National Council on Measurement in Education

NCMEA US: e: National Catholic Music Educators' Association

NCMH US: e: National Committee on Maternal Health; CDN: US: e: National Committee for Mental Hygiene

N.C.M.H. e: National Council for Mental Hygiene

NCMLB US: e: National Council for Mailing List Brokers

NCMO US: e: mil: NAVAIDS [navigational aids] Communications Management Office

NCMP NATO: [d: gemeinsame Militärpolizei]

NCMPA US: e: National Corrugated Metal Pipe Association

N.C.M.U.A. e: National Committee of Monotype Users' Associations

NCMUE US: e: National Council on Measurements used in Education

NCMV B: nl: Nationaal Christelijk Middenstandsverbond

NCN WAN: [d: Nationalkongreß von Nigeria, Partei]

NCNA RC: e: New China News Agency, Peking [gegr 1936]

NCNC e: National Congress of Nigeria and the Cameroons [1944 ... 62]; WAN: e: National Convention of Nigerian Citizens

NCNL ZA: af: Nasionale Chemiese Navorsingslaboratorium

NCNW US: e: National Council of Negro Women

NCOA US: e: National Council on the Aging; US: e: mil: Noncommissioned Officers Association

NCOI GB: e: National Council for the Omnibus Industry

NCONAC US: e: National Council on Naturalization and Citizenship

NCOPA US: e: National Conference of Police Associations [= NCPA]

NCOSTA US: e: National Council of Officers of State Teachers Associations

NCP Libyien: e: National Congress Party; MW: e: National Constitutional Party; PTM: e: National Convention Party, Kuala Lumpur; PI: e: Nationalist Citizens' Party; MW: e: Nyasaland Constitutional Party

NCPA US: e: National Conference of Police Associations [= NCOPA]; National Cottonseed Products Association

NCPAC US: e: National Citizens Political Action Committee

NCPAD US: e: National Council on Psychological Aspects of Disability

NCPC e: National Capital Planning Commission; US: e: National Coal Policy Conference

N.C.P.D. e: National Committee for the Prevention of Destitution

NCPEA US: e: National Conference of Professors of Education Administration

NCPGR B: nl: Nationale Confederatie der Politieke Gevangenen en Rechthebenden

NCPLA US: e: National Council of Patent Law Associations

N.C.P.L.E. e: National Council of Port Labour Employees

NCPMI US: e: National Clay Pipe Manufacturers, Inc.

NCPR US: e: National Congress of Petroleum Retailers

NCPS e: National Committee for Public Safety

NCPT US: e: National Congress of Parents and Teachers

NCPTWA US: e: National Clearing House for Periodical Title Word Abbreviations [USASI]

NCPW US: e: National Council for the Prevention of War

NCPWB US: e: National Certified Pipe Welding Bureau

NCQR GB: e: National Council for Quality and Reliability, London E.C.4

NCR US: e: National Cash Register Co.; National Council of Representatives; NL: nl: Nationale Coöperatieve Raad

N.C.R. US: e: Niagara Central Railroad Company

NCRAA US: e: National Committee of Regional Accrediting Agencies

NCRAC US: e: National Community Relations Advisory Council

NCRC e: National Catholic Resettlement Council; GB: e: National Consumer-Retailer Council; Northern Coke Research Committee

NCRE GB: e: mil: Naval Construction Research Establishment

NCRH US: e: National Center for Radiological Health, Washington, D.C.

NCRL US: e: National Canners' Association Research Laboratory; ZA: e: National Chemical Research Laboratory, Pretoria

NCRP US: e: National Committee on Radiation Protection and Measurement

NCRS US: e: National Camera Repair School

NCRSA US: e: National Commercial Refrigerator Sales Association

NCRT GB: e: National College of Rubber Technology

NCRV NL: nl: Nederlandse Christelijke Radio Vereniging, Hilversum [gegr 1924]

NCS US: e: National Chrysanthemum Society; National Colloid Symposium, American Chemical Society; e: mil: Naval Control of Shipping

N.C.S. GB: e: mil: Naval Canteen Service; NL: nl: Nederlandse Culturele Sportbond; GB: e: New Commonwealth Society

NCS CDN: e: Northwest Communication System; e: Norwegian Confederation of Sport

NCSA US: e: National Civil Service Association; National Confectionery Salesmen's Association; National Crushed Stone Association; National Custom

Service Association; Northern California Soaring Association

NCSAB US: e: National Council of State Agencies for the Blind

NCSBEE US: e: National Council of State Boards of Engineering Examiners

NCSC US: e: National Council on Schoolhouse Construction; North Carolina State College

NCSCEE US: e: National Council of State Consultants in Elementary Education

NCSCT US: e: National Center for School and College Television, Bloomington

NCSE US: e: National Commission on Safety Education; North Carolina Society of Engineers

NCSGC US: e: National Council of State Garden Clubs

NCSI US: e: National Council for Stream Improvement of the Pulp, Paper and Paperboard Industries

NCSL; NC&SL US: e: Nashville, Chattanooga & St. Louis Railway

NCSL US: e: National Civil Service League; National Conference of Standards Laboratories, Sacramento, Calif.

N.C.S.L. WAL: e: National Council of Sierra Leone [gegr 1951]

NCSLA US: e: National Conference of State Liquor Administrators

NCSO US: e: National Council of Salesmen's Organizations; e: mil: Naval Control of Shipping Organization

NCSORG NATO: e: Naval Control of Shipping Organization

NCSP US: e: National Conference on State Parks

NCSR ZA: ę: National Council for Social Research

NCSRA US: e: National Conference of State Retail Associations

NCSS US: e: National Conference on Social Security

N.C.S.S. e: National Council for Social Service

NCSS US: e: National Council for the Social Studies, National Education Association

NCSSBA US: e: National Council of State School Board Associations

NCSSIA US: e: National Council of State Self-Insurers' Associations

NC&StL; N.,C.&St.L.Ry. US: e: Nashville, Chattanooga & St.Louis Railway [Dixie Line, = NCSL]

NCSTSR GB: e: National Conference of Superintendents of Training Schools and Reformatories

NCSV NL: nl: Nederlandse Christelijke Studenten Vereniging

NCSW US: e: National Conference of Social Work; National Conference on Social Welfare

NCSWDI US: e: National Combination Storm Window and Door Institute

N.C.T. GB: e: National Chamber of Trade

NCTA US: e: National Community Television Association

N.C.T.A. GB: e: National Council for Technological Awards

NCTA US: e: North Carolina Tuberculosis Association

NCTC US: e: National Catholic Theater Conference; National Collection of Type Cultures

NCTCA US: e: National Collegiate Track Coaches Association

N.C.T.D. GB: e: National College of Teachers of the Deaf

NCTE US: e: National Council of Teachers of English

NCTEPS US: e: National Commission on Teacher Education and Professional Standards

N.C.T.L. e: National Commercial Temperance League

N.C.T.L.B.P.M. e: National Commercial Temperance League of Business and Professional Men

NCTM US: e: National Council of Teachers of Mathematics

NCTO US: e: mil: Navy Clothing and Textile Supply Office

NCTP US: e: mil: Navy College Training Program

NCTR US: e: National Council on Teacher Retirement

NCTS US: e: National Committee for Traffic Safety; National Council of Technical Schools

NCTSI US: e: National Council of Technical Service Industries

N.C.T.T.F. e: Northern Counties Textile Trades Federation

NCTUN WAN: e: National Council of Trade Unions of Nigeria

NCTW US: e: National Conference of Tuberculosis Workers

N.C.T.W.U. e: National Cigar and Tobacco Workers' Union

N.C.U. e: National Citizens' Union; GB: e: National Cyclists' Union; MW: e: Nyasaland Chiefs Union

NCUMC; N.C.U.M.H.C. GB: e: National Council for the Unmarried Mother and her Child

NCUR US: e: National Committee for Utilities Radio

NCUTAS US: e: National Conference on Uniform Traffic Accident Statistics

NCUTLO US: e: National Committee on Uniform Traffic Laws and Ordinances

NCV NL:nl: Nederlandsche Chemische Vereniging; Nederlandse Christen Vrouwenbond

NCVAE GB: e: National Committee for Visual Aids in Education

NCVP NL: nl: Nederlandsch Christelijk Verbond van Padvinders

NCW e: National Council of Women

N.C.W. GB: e: mil: Naval Communications Workshop and Store

NCWA US: e: National Candy Wholesaler Association; GB: e: National Children Wear Association; e: National Congress of West Africa; WAN: e: Nigerian Citizens Welfare Association

NCWC US: e: National Catholic Welfare Conference [gegr 1919]; National Council of Women Chiropractors

NCWCC US: e: North Central Weed Control Committee

NCWFC US: e: National Council of Women of Free Czechoslovakia

NCWM US: e: National Conference on Weights and Measures, National Bureau of Standards, Washington, D.C. 20230

N.C.W.T.A. e: National Council of Workers' Travel Associations

NCWU US: e: National Catholic Women's Union

NCZ NL: nl: Nationale Coöperatieve Zuivelverkoopscentrale

ND d: Nachrichtendienst; PL: pl: Naczel Dyrekcja; Narodowa Demokracja

N.D. GB: e: National Defence; e: mil: Navy Department

ND D: d: Neudeutschland [katholischer Jugendbund]

NDA PL: pl: Naczelna Dyrekcja Administracyjna; US: e: National Dairy Association; GB: e: National Dairymen's Association; US: e: National Dental Association; National Door Association; Nuclear Development Associates, Inc., White Plains, N.Y.; Nuclear Development Corporation of America

NDAC US: e: National Defense Advisory Commission (Committee); NATO: e: Nuclear Defence Affairs Committee

N.D.A.F. e: National Dental Aid Fund

NDAG US: e: Nonviolent Direct Action Group [Harvard University]

NDALTP B: nl: Nationale Dienst voor Afzet van Land- en Tuinbouwprodukten

N.D.A.N.C. e: Nairobi District African National Congress

NDAP PL: pl: Naczelna Dyrekcja Archiwów Państwowych

NDAW B: nl: Nationale Dienst voor Arbeidsbemiddeling en Werkloosheid

NDB PL: pl: Naczelna Dyrekcjy Bibliotek; US: e: Board of National Delegates; B: nl: Nationale Democratische Beweging; BRD: d: Norddeutsche Bank [seit 1952]; d: Norddeutscher Bund

Nd.Bd. d: Norddeutscher Bund

NDBE D: d: Neue Deutsch-Böhmische Elbeschiffahrts-Gesellschaft, Dresden

NDBI GB: e: National Dairymen's Benevolent Institution

NDC US: e: National Dairy Council

N.D.C. e: mil: National Defence Corps

NDC e: mil: National Defense Council; US: e: National Democratic Club; e: National Development Corporation; NATO: e: NATO Defence College; US: e: New Dramatists' Committee; WAN: e: Niger Delta Congress; e: f: Notre Dame College

NDCA US: e: Nuclear Development Corporation of America

NDCC CDN: e: National Dairy Council of Canada; US: e: mil: National Defense Cadet Corps

NDCO e: mil: Naval Disarmament Control Office

NDCS GB: e: National Deaf Children's Society

N.D.D. GB: e: mil: Net Defence Department

N.D.D.C. e: mil: National Docks Defence Committee

N.d.d.W. D: d: Notgemeinschaft der deutschen Wissenschaft, Berlin C 2

N.D.E. B: nl: Nationale Dienst voor Emigratie

NDEA GB: e: National Display Equipment Association

NDEI US: e: mil: National Defense Education Institute, Boston

NdeM MEX: s: Ferrocarriles Nacionales de México

N.D.F. e: National Democratic Front; ZA: e: National Development Foundation

NDFA US: e: National Dietary Foods Association

NdFtK D: d: Normengruppe der Frankfurter technischen Körperschaften

NDG BRD: d: Neue Deutsche Gewerkschaften [vorher: NDGB]; e: Neutral Democratic Group

NDGB BRD: d: Neuer Deutscher Gewerkschaftsbund [gegr 1969]

NDGS NATO: e: National Defense General Staff

NDGW US: e: Native Daughters of the Golden West

NDHA US: e: National District Heating Association

ND-HSR BRD: d: stud: Bund Neudeutschland - Hochschulring

NDI NL: nl: N.V. Nederlandse Draadindustrie, Blerik; D: d: Normenausschuß der deutschen Industrie [seit 1926: Deutscher Normenausschuß = DNA]

NDIL e: Non-Destructive Inspection Laboratory

NDJ NL: nl: De Nationale Dienst voor de Jeugd

ND-JG BRD: d: Bund Neudeutschland - Jungengemeinschaft

NDL J: e: National Diet Library; BRD: d: Norddeutscher Lloyd, Bremen; US: e: mil: Nuclear Defense Laboratory

N.D.L.C. e: National Dock Labour Corporation

NDLP PL: pl: Naczelna Dyrekcja Lasów Państwowych

NDLS D: d: Neues Deutsches Lichtspiel-syndikat, Berlin

NDMA US: e: National Dress Manufacturers' Association

N.D.M.B. US: e: mil: National Defense Mediation Board

NDMiOZ PL: pl: Naczelna Dyrekcja Muzeów i Ochrony Zabytków

NDO PL: pl: Naczelna Dyrekcja Ogólna

N.D.O. e: National Debt Office; D: d: mil: Nationalverband Deutscher Offiziere [gegr 1918]; GB: e: Northern District Office [Post]

N.D.O.A. GB: e: National Dog Owners' Association

NDOS US: e: mil: National Defense Operations Section [Federal Communications Commission]

NDP e: National Democratic Party; A: BRD: DDR: d: Nationaldemokratische Partei; e: New Democratic Party

NDPC PTM: e: National Development Planning Committee

NDPCh pl: Niemiecka Demokratyczna Partia Chłopska

NDPD DDR: d: Nationaldemokratische Partei Deutschlands [gegr 1948]

NDPIC e: mil: National Defence Public Interest Committee

NDPKC GB: e: National Domestic Poultry Keepers' Council

NDPS GB: e: Post: National Data Processing Service

NDR BRD: d: Norddeutscher Rundfunk, 2 Hamburg [gegr 1956]

NDRC e: mil: National Defence (Defense) Research Committee (Council)

NDRE N: [e: National Defense Research Establishment, Oslo]

NDRF e: mil: National Defense Reserve Fleet

NDS GB: e: National Dahlia Society; BRD: d: Nationaler Deutscher Schülerbund, 635 Bad Nauheim; D: d: Nationalverband Deutscher Schriftsteller

NDSA US: e: National Disposal Service Association

NDSB US: e: Narcotic Drugs Supervisory Body

NDSHS US: e: North Dakota State Horticultural Society

NDSM NL: nl: Nederlandse Droogdok en Scheepsbouw Maatschappij

NDSMA US: e: North Dakota State Medical Association

NDSPE US: e: North Dakota Society of Professional Engineers

NDT PL: pl: Naczelna Dyrekcja Techniczna; P: pt: Núcleo de Documentação, Ministério do Ultramar, Lisboa

NDTA US: e: mil: National Defense Transportation Association

NDTC US: e: National Drug Trade Conference

NDTMA US: e: National Drain Tile Manufacturers' Association

NDU BRD: d: Nationaldemokratische Union

N.D.U. GB: e: National Domestic Union, Edinburgh

NDU BRD: d: Niederdeutsche Union; US: e: Notre Dame University

NDV NL: nl: Nederlandsche Dendrologische Vereeniging

NDW D: d: Notgemeinschaft der Deutschen Wissenschaft

NDWP PL: pl: Naczelne Dowództwo Wojsk Polskiego

NDYL China: e: New Democratic Youth League

NDZ; Ndz D: d: Nachrichtenbüro Deutscher Zeitungsverleger

N.E. e: National Exhibition

NE BRD: d: Neunkircher Eisenwerk AG vorm. Gebrüder Stumm, 668 Neunkirchen (Saar); DIN: e: Normenstelle Elektrotechnik, 6 Ffm; US: e: Northeast Airlines

N.E. GB: e: London and North-Eastern Railway

N.E.A. D: d: mil: Nachrichten-Ersatz
-Abteilung

NEA US: e: National Editorial Association;
e: National Education(al) Association;
IRQ: e: National Electricity Administration; T: e: National Electricity Authority,
Bangkok

N.E.A. GB: e: National Engineers' Association; National Erectors' Association;
ZA: e: Native Education Association
[gegr 1882]; US: Newspaper Enterprise
Association, New York, N.Y.

Nea D: d: Nikotinentziehungsanstalt für
Tabak und Tabakfabrikate GmbH, Charlottenburg 4

NEA US: e: Northeast Airlines, Boston,
Mass.; GB: e: North Eastern Airways,
London; NATO: e: Air Advisory Com-
mittee, Northern European Group

NeA BRD: d: Verband der Notgemeinschaft
ehemaliger Arbeitsdienstangehöriger

N.E.A.C. GB: e: New English Art Club

NEAC US: e: mil: Northeast Air Command

NEACP US: e: mil: National Emergency
Airborne Command Post

N.E.A.C.T. US: e: New England Association of Chemistry Teachers

NEAPD US: e: mil: Northeastern Air
Procurement District

NEATO INT: e: North-East Asia Treaty
Organization

NEAVB GB: e: National Employers' Association of Vehicle Builders, Leeds

NEB e: National Economic Board; PTM:
e: National Electricity Board, Kuala
Lumpur; GB: e: National Employment
Board; NL: nl: Nederlandsch Eiercon-
trôle Bureau

NEBATO NL: [d: Niederländische Bäckerei-Fachausstellung, Amsterdam]

NEBB N: no: Norsk Elektrisk Brown
Boveri, Oslo

Neb.Ma. D: d: mil: Neben-Munitionsanstalt

NEBOS NL: nl: Nederlandse Bond voor
Onderwatersport

NEC US: e: National Economic Council;
National Electronics Conference, Chica-
go, Ill.; e: National Emergency Com-
mittee (Council); US: e: National Ex-
change Club; e: National Executive
Committee; GB: e: National Extension
College [Cambridge]; NL: nl: Neder-
lands Electrotechnisch Comité, Rijs-
wijk; Nederlandse Export Combinatie;
US: e: New England Conservatory of
Music; New England Council; J: e:
Nippon Electric Company Ltd., Tokyo;
NATO: e: Northern European Command

NECA US: e: National Electrical Contractors Association Inc., Washington, D.C.;
Near East College Association; NL: nl:
Nederlands Economisch Cultureel Archief

NECCCRW INT: e: Near East Christian
Council Committee for Refugee Work

NECIES; N.E.C.Inst. GB: e: North-East
Coast Institution of Engineers and Shipbuilders

Neckuna; Neckura BRD: d: Neckermann
Versicherungs AG, 6 Ffm [gegr 1964]

NECPA US: e: mil: National Emergency
Command Post Afloat

NECPP WAN: e: North Eastern Convention People's Party

NECTA GB: e: National Electrical Contractors Trading Association

NED GB: e: National Economic Development Council; B: nl: Nationale Emigratiedienst

N.E.D. GB: e: mil: Naval Equipment
Department (Depot)

NED NL: nl: Nederlandse Emigratiedienst;
BRD: d: Notgemeinschaft Evangelischer
Deutscher; US: e: Nuclear Engineering
Directorate

NEDA US: e: National Electronic Distributors' Association

NEDAL GB: e: National Egg Distributors'
Association, London

NEDC GB: e: National Economic Development Council [gegr 1962, = Neddy]

NEDCO INT: e: Committee for the Study of the Netherlands' Statement Concerning Liaisons and Activities of ISO

NEDCOMP NL: nl: Nederlandse Computer Maatschappij, Amsterdam

Neddy GB: e: = NEDC

NEDELSA NL: nl: Nederlandse Fabrieken van elektrische Schakelapparatuur, Den Haag

NEDEX 69 NL: [d: Ausstellung für Transport und Transportmaterial, Rotterdam, 21 . . . 25 Okt 1969]

N.E.D.L. e: National Equine Defence League

NEDR R: d: Nationale Erneuerungsbewegung der Deutschen in Rumänien, Hermannstadt

NEEA T: e: North East Electricity Authority

NEEB GB: e: North-East Engineering Bureau; US: e: North Eastern Electricity Board; GB: e: North of England Engineering Bureau

NEEC US: e: National Export Expansion Council

NEED US: e: Near East Emergency Donations [gegr 1967]

NEES US: e: mil: Naval Engineering Experimental Station [BUSHIPS]

NEF US: e: Near East Foundation; INT: e: The New Education Fellowship International [gegr 1915]; N: no: Norsk Elektroteknisk Forening

NEFA S: sv: Norrköpings Elektrotekniska Fabriker AB; IND: e: North East Frontier Agency

NEFC UN: e: Near East Forestry Commission [FAO, gegr 1953]

NEFE US: e: New England Fish Exchange

NEFO DK: da: Nordjyllands Electricitetsforsynings Selskap, Nörresundby

NEFPMU P: pt: Núcleo de Estudos de Farmacologia das Plantas Medicinais do Ultramar, Junta de Investigações do Ultramar, Lisboa

NEFSA US: e: National Educational Fiel Service Association

NEFSG CDN: US: e: Northeastern Fores Soils Group

NEFTIC US: e: Northeastern Forest Tree Improvement Conference

NEG NL: nl: Nieuwe Economische Groep

NEGB GB: e: Northeastern Gas Board

NEGRO US: e: National Economic Grow and Reconstructive Organization

NEH US: e: National Endowment on the Humanities

NEHA NL: nl: Vereniging 'Het Nederland Economisch-Historisch Archief'; US: e New England Hospital Association

NEI NL: nl: Nederlands Economisch Instituut; US: e: New England Instrument Company, Natick, Mass.; INT: f: Nouvelles Equipes Internationales, Pari [gegr 1947]

NEIAF e: mil: Netherlands East Indies Air Force

NEIMME GB: e: North of England Institute of Mining and Mechanical Enginee

NEIS GB: e: National Egg Information Service

N.E.K. D: d: mil: Nachrichtenmittelerprobungskommando; NL: nl: Nederlandse Ex-Libris Kring; D: d: Normal-Eichungskommission

NEK N: no: Norsk Elektroteknisk Komité, Oslo

NÉKOSZ H: hu: Népi Kollégiumok Orszá gos Szövetsége

NEL GB: e: National Engineering Laboratory, East Kilbride; US: e: National Epilepsy League; US: e: mil: Naval Electronics Laboratory, San Diego [BUSHIPS]

N.E.L. N: eo: Norvega Esperantista Ligo

NELA US: e: National Electric Light Association, New York, N.Y.; New England Library Association

NELC US: e: mil: Naval Electronics Labo

ratory Center, San Diego, Calif.

NELIA US: e: Nuclear Energy Liability Insurance Association

NELINET US: e: New England Library Information Network

NELM US: e: mil: Naval Elements Atlantic and Mediterranean

NEM N: no: Norges Elektriske Materiellkontroll, Oslo 3

NEMA US: e: National Electric Medical Association; National Electrical Manufacturers Association, New York 17, N.Y.

NEMEC NL: nl: Nederlandse Fabrieken van Elektrische en Elektronische Meeten Regelapparatuur, Den Haag

NEMI US: e: National Elevator Manufacturing Industry, Inc., New York 17, N.Y.

NEMKO N: no: Norges Elektriske Materiellkontroll, Oslo 3

NEMO GB: e: National Egg Marketing Organization

NEMS US: e: National Emergency Medical Service

NEN NATO: e: Naval Advisory Committee, Northern European Group; US: e: New England Nuclear Corporation, Boston, Mass.

NEODTC US: e: Naval Explosive Ordnance Disposal Technical Center

NEOP US: e: New England Order of Protection

NEORMP US: e: Northeastern Ohio Regional Medical Program

NEOS US: e: New England Ophthalmological Society

NEOT US: e: New England Opera Theater, Boston, Mass.

NEPA US: e: Notheastern Pennsylvania Artificial Breeding Cooperative; WAN: e: Northern Element's Progressive Association; US: e: Nuclear Energy for Propulsion of Aircraft Commission

NEPCON US: e: National Electronic Packaging and Production Conference, Chicago, Ill.

NEPG NATO: e: Northern European Planning Group

NEPIA US: e: Nuclear Energy Property Insurance Association

Népmüv. Min. H: hu: Népmüvelési Miniszter(ium), Budapest

NEPP GB: e: National Egg and Poultry Promotion

NEPPCO US: e: Northeastern Poultry Producers Council

NEPU WAN: e: Northern Element's Progressive Union

N.E.R. GB: e: North Eastern Railway, London

NER P: pt: Núcleo de Estudos de Radioisotopos

NERA US: e: National Emergency Relief Administration

NERAG BRD: d: Gewerkschaft Neue Erdölraffinerie, Hannover

NERATU NL: [d: Fachverband Rundfunk-, Fernseh- und Phonogeräte, Den Haag]

NERBA US: e: New England Road Builders' Association

NERC US: e: National Electric Reliability Council; GB: e: National Electronics Research Council, London; National English Rabbit Club; Natural Environment Research Council

NERCO B: nl: Neutrale Repatriëringscommissie

NEREM US: e: Northeast Electronics Research and Engineering Meeting

NERG NL: nl: Nederlands Elektronicaen Radiogenootschap

NEROC US: e: Northeast Radio Observatory Corporation [gegr 1968]

NERPG NATO: e: Northern European Regional Planning Group

NERRA US: e: New England Roentgen Ray Association

NERRS US: e: New England Roentgen Ray Society

N.E.S. IND: e: National Extension Service

NES US: e: mil: Naval Experimenting Station; Nebraska Engineering Society; News Election Service; S: sv: Nordiska Emballage-Sällskapet; Nya Elementarskolan i Stockholm

NESA US: e: National Electric Sign Association

NESC US: e: National Environmental Satellite Center; Nuclear Engineering and Science Conference

Neska BRD: d: "Neska" Niederrheinisches Schiffahrtskontor AG, 5 Köln

NESLA US: e: New England School Libraries Association; New England Shoe and Leather Association

NET US: e: National Educational Television and Radio Center, New York, N.Y.; H: hu: Népköztársaság Elnöki Tanácsa

NETAC GB: e: Nuclear Energy Trade Associations' Conference [gegr 1956]

NETG BRD: d: Nordrheinische Erdgastransport GmbH, 41 Duisburg-Hamborn

N.E.T.h. H: hu: Népköztársaság Elnöki Tanácsának határozata

NETL US: e: National Export Traffic League

NETO nl: Noordelijke Economisch-Technologische Organisatie

NETRC US: e: = NET

NETSO NATO: e: Northern Europe Transshipment Organization

NETT US: e: mil: New Equipment Training Team [Army]

NEU US: e: Northeastern University

NEUCC DK: e: Northern Europe University Computing Centre, Lygnby

N.E.U.M. ZA: e: Non-European Unity Movement

Neuspar BRD: d: Neue Sparcasse von 1864, 2 Hamburg

NEV NL: nl: Nederlandsche Entomologische Vereniging

Nevac NL: nl: Nederlandse Vacuumvereniging

NEVESBU NL: nl: Nederlandse Verenigde Scheepsbouwkundige Bureaus

NEVF N: no: Norske Elektrisitetsverkers Forening

NEVI NL: nl: Nederlands Vlasinstituut

NEVOA NL: nl: Nederlandse Vereniging voor Oppervlakte Activiteit

Nevoge. NL: nl: Nederlandsche Volks-Gemeenschap

NEWA US: e: National Electrical Wholesalers' Association; New England Waterworks Association

NEWAC NATO: e: NATO Electronic Warfare Advisory Committee

NEWAG A: d: Niederösterreichische Elektrizitätswerke AG

NEWCC US: e: Northeastern Weed Control Conference

NEWFPS US: e: New England Wild Flower Preservation Society

NEWLC NATO: e: NATO Electronic Warfare Liaison Committee

NEWO NL: nl: Nederlandse Elektrotechnische Winkeliers Organisatie

NEWWA US: e: New England Waterworks Association

NEZC US: e: New England Zoological Club

NF N: no: Nasjonalforlaget A/S, Oslo; DDR: d: Nationale Front des demokratischen Deutschlands; e: National Foundation; INT: sv: Nationernas förbund [d: Völkerbund, Genf]; S: sv: Nordiska Fjäderfabriken AB, Malmö; Nordiska författarrådet

N.F. GB: e: mil: Royal Northumberland Fusiliers; GB: e: Norwich Festival, GB: e: mil: Nyasaland Force [1916 . .. 17]

NFA US: e: National Farmers' Association; National Federation of Accountants; GB: e: National Federation of Anglers; US: e: National Fertilizer Association; National Food Administration; National Foundry Association; Negro Farmers of America; Northwest Fisheries Association

FAC US: e: National Foundation for Asthmatic Children

F.A.E.A.T. e: National Foremen's Association of the Engineering and Allied Trades

F.A.P.C.V.M. e: National Federation of Associated Paint, Colour, and Varnish Manufacturers

FAS US: e: National Federation of American Shipping

FB US: e: National Federation of the Blind; CDN: e: National Film Board [gegr 1939]; e: National Fire Board; NL: nl: Nederlandsche Fascistische Beweging; J: e: The Nippon Fudosan Bank, Ltd., Tokyo 102

FBA GB: e: National Federation of Beekeepers' Associations

F.B.A. e: National Fire Brigades Association

FBA US: e: National Food Brokers' Association

F.B.A.T. e: National Federation of Bedding and Allied Trades

FBC CDN: e: National Film Board of Canada; US: e: mil: Newfoundland Base Command

FBCa CDN: e: National Film Bureau of Canada

F.B.M. GB: e: National Federation of Branch Managers

FBPM GB: e: National Federation of Builders' and Plumbers' Merchants

FBPWC US: e: National Federation of Business and Professional Women's Clubs

FB-PYP SF: sv: fi: Nordiska Föreningsbanken AB - Pohjoismaiden Yhdyspankki OY, Helsingfors (Helsinki) [gegr 1862]

F.B.T.E. e: National Federation of Building Trades Employers

F.B.T.O. e: National Federation of Building Trades Operatives

FC US: e: National Film Carriers

N.F.C. e: National Fitness Council

NFC US: e: National Food Conference; National Fuel Oil Council

N.F.C. e: mil: Naval Finance Committee

NFCA GB: e: National Federation of Community Associations; US: e: National Fraternity Congress of America

NFCAA US: e: National Fencing Coaches Association of America

NFCC US: e: National Farm Chemurgic Council; National Federation of Citizens Councils; National Foundation for Consumer Credit

NFCCS US: e: National Federation of Catholic College Students

N.F.C.E.B.M. e: National Federation of Colliery Enginemen, Boilermen and Mechanics

NFCG GB: e: National Federation of Consumer Groups

NFCGA GB: e: National Federation of Constructional Glass Associations

NFCGC e: National Federation of Coffee Growers of Columbia

N.F.C.I. e: National Federation of Clay Industries

NFCL US: e: National Federation for Constitutional Liberties

N.F.C.L. e: National Federation of Co-operative Laundries

N.F.C.M.A. e: National Federation of Colliery Mechanics' Associations

N.F.C.M.O. e: National Federation of Cotton Mill Officials

NFCPG US: e: National Federation of Catholic Physicians' Guilds

NFCS GB: e: National Federation of Construction Supervisors

NFCSIT GB: e: National Federation of Cold Storage and Ice Trades

NFCTA GB: e: National Federation of Corn Trade Associations

NFCTC GB: e: National Foundry Craft Training Centre

N.F.C.T.U. GB: e: National Federation

of Catholic Trade Unionists

NFCU US: e: mil: Navy Federal Credit Union

N.F.C.W. e: National Federation of Clerks of Works and Builders Foremen's Associations

N.F.C.W.E. e: National Federation of Colliery Winding Enginemen

NFD e: National Federation of Drapers and Allied Traders Ltd.

N.F.D.A. e: National Federation of Dairymen's Associations

NFDA US: e: National Food Distributors Association

NFDC GB: e: National Federation of Demolition Contractors

N.F.D.C. e: National Federation of Dyers and Cleaners

NFDSP US: e: National Forum on Deafness and Speech Pathology

NFE US: e: National Committee Free Europe, New York, N.Y. [gegr 1949]; GB: e: Non-Ferrous Metals Industry Standards Committee

N.F.E.A. GB: e: National Federated Electrical Association

NFEAC US: e: National Foundation for Education in American Citizenship

N.F.E.R. GB: e: National Foundation for Educational Research

NFETM GB: e: National Federation of Engineers' Tool Manufacturers

NFF US: e: National Football Foundation; GB: e: National Froebel Foundation; N: no: Norges Fotballforbund; Norske Forskningsbibliotekarers Forening; S: sv: Norrmalms Flickläroverks Föreningsnämnd

NFFA CDN: US: e: National Flying Farmers Association; US: e: National Frozen Food Association

NFFAS US: e: National Federation of Financial Analysts Societies

N.F.F.C. GB: e: National Film Finance Corporation

NFFDA US: e: National Frozen Food Distributors Association

NFFE US: e: National Federation of Federal Employees, , Washington, D.C

NFFF GB: e: National Federation of Fish Friers

NFFPT GB: e: National Federation of Fruit and Potato Trades, Ltd.

N.F.F.P.T.A. e: National Federation of Fruit and Potato Trades Associations

N.F.F.Q.O. e: National Federation of Freestone Quarry Owners

NFFS US: e: Non-Ferrous Founders' Society

N.F.F.S.C. US: e: Niagara Frontier Federation of Stamp Clubs

N.F.F.T. e: National Federation of the Furniture Trade

NFFTU GB: e: National Federation of Furniture Trade Unions

N.F.G. e: National Federation of Glassworkers

NFG BRD: d: Nordwestdeutsche Futtersaatbaugesellschaft

NFGC US: e: National Federation of Grain Cooperatives

NFGCA US: e: National Federation of Grandmother Clubs of America

NFGMIC US: e: National Federation of Grange Mutual Insurance Companies

N.F.G.M.S.F.S. e: National Flint Glass Makers' Sick and Friendly Society

N.F.G.R.Q.O. e: National Federation of Granite and Roadstone Quarry Owne

NFHA US: e: National Fox Hunters Association

NFHC US: e: National Foot Health Cou

NFHE US: e: National Farm Home Editors' Association

N.F.H.M.A. e: National Federation of Hosiery Manufacturers' Associations

NFHS GB: e: National Federation of Housing Societies

NFI GB: e: National Federation of Ironmongers; US: e: National Fisheries

Institute; INT: d: Naturfreunde-Internationale

FIA US: e: National Feed Ingredients Association

FIB US: e: National Federation of Independent Business

FIK N: no: Norsk Forening for Industriell Kvalitetskontroll, Oslo

FIP US: e: National Foundation for Infantile Paralysis, New York, N.Y. [gegr 1938]

FIR IND: e: National Federation of Indian Railwaymen; N: no: Norsk Forening for Internasjonal Rett

.F.I.W. e: National Federation of Insurance Workers

FJ d: Naturfreundejugend

FJM US: e: National Federation (Foundation) for Junior Museums

FJMC US: e: National Federation of Jewish Men's Clubs

FL MW: e: National Federation of Labour

.F.L. e: National Federation of Launderers; National Film Library

FL US: e: National Football League; National Forensic League; VN: e: National Front for Liberation

FLA US: e: National Farm Loan Association

FLF US: e: National Family Life Foundation

FLPA US: e: National Football League Players' Association

FLPN US: e: National Federation of Licensed Practical Nurses

FM NL: nl: Nederlandse Filmproductie Maatschappij

FMA GB: e: National Fireplace Makers Association

FMC US: e: National Federation of Music Clubs; National Film Music Council

FMD US: e: National Federation (Foundation) for Muscular Dystrophy

FME US: e: National Fund for Medical Education

NFMLTA US: e: National Federation of Modern Language Teachers Associations

NFMP GB: e: National Federation of Master Painters and Decorators of England and Wales

N.F.M.P.D. e: National Federation of Master Painters and Decorators

N.F.M.P.S. GB: e: National Federation of Master Printers of Scotland

NFMR US: e: National Foundation for Metabolic Research

NFMS e: National Federation of Music Societies

N.F.M.T. e: National Federation of Master Tailors; GB: e: National Federation of Meat Traders

NFN S: sv: Nordiska Farmakopénämnden; DK: da: Nordisk Farmakopénævn

NFND US: e: National Foundation for Neuromuscular Diseases

NFNL ZA: af: Nasionale Fisiese Navorsingslaboratorium

NFO US: e: National Farmers Organization, Corning, Iowa [gegr 1955]; NL: nl: Nederlandse Fruittelersorganisatie

N.F.O.A.P.A. GB: e: National Federation of Old Age Pensioners' Associations

NFOBA US: e: National Fats and Oils Brokers Association

NFOHA GB: e: National Federation of Offlicense Holders Associations of England and Wales

NFPA US: e: National Fire Protection Association, Boston, Mass. 02110; National Flaxseed Processors Association; National Flexible Packaging Association; National Fluid Power Association, Evanston, Ill.

NFPC GB: e: National Federation of Plastering Contractors

N.F.P.D.E. e: National Federation of Plumbers and Domestic Engineers

NFPHC GB: e: National Federation of Permanent Holiday Camps

N.F.P.M. e: National Federation of Produce Merchants

N.F.P.O. e: National Federation of Property Owners

NFPOC US: e: National Federation of Post Office Clerks

NFPR GB: e: National Fund for Research into Poliomyelitis and Other Crippling Diseases

NFPTTE IND: e: National Federation of Post, Telephone and Telegraph Employees

NFPW US: e: National Federation of Press Women

N.F.P.W. GB: e: National Federation of Professional Workers

NFR S: sv: Näringsfrihetsrådet; Statens naturvetenskapliga forskningsråd; R: ro: Navigaţia Fluvială Română

NFRA US: e: National Forest Recreation Association

NFRB GB: e: New Fabian Research Bureau

NFRC GB: e: National Federation of Roofing Contractors

N.F.R.M.T.A. e: National Federation of Retail Meat Traders' Associations

NFRN GB: e: National Federation of Retail Newsagents, Booksellers and Stationers

N.F.R.N.D. e: National Fund for the Redemption of the National Debt

NFRW US: e: National Federation of Republican Women

N.F.S. GB: e: National Fire Service; National Flying Services; e: mil: Naval Flying Station; S: sv: Nordiska Folkhögskolan, Engelsholm

NFS N: no: Norke Filmbyråers Samenslutning

NFSA US: e: National Fertilizer Solutions Association; National Food Service Association

N.F.S.A. e: National Fire Service Association

NFSA US: e: mil: Navy Field Safety Association

NFSAIS US: e: National Federation of Science Abstracting and Indexing Services, Philadelphia, Pa. 19103

NFSC US: e: National Federation of Stamp Clubs

NFSD US: e: National Fraternal Society of the Deaf

NFSE US: e: National Federation of Sa Executives

NFSHSAA US: e: National Federation State High School Athletic Associatio

NFSI US: e: National Foundation for Science and Industry

NFSMA US: e: National Fruit and Syru Manufacturers Associations

N.F.S.M.S.T. e: National Federation of Slate Merchants, Slaters and Tilers

NFS&NC US: e: National Federation of Settlements and Neighborhood Cente

N.F.S.O. e: National Federation of Scri bling Overlookers

N.F.S.P. e: National Federation of Sawmill Proprietors; National Federatio of Sub-Postmasters

NFT US: e: National Federation of Tex tiles; S: sv: Nationalföreningen mot Tuberkulos

NFTA US: e: National Freight Traffic Association

NFTC US: e: National Foreign Trade Council; National Furniture Traffic Conference

N.F.T.M.A. e: National Federation of Textile Managers' Associations

NFTMS GB: e: National Federation of Terrazzomosaic Specialists

N.F.T.U. e: Norwegian Federation of Trade Unions

NFTW US: e: National Federation of Telephone Workers

NFTY US: e: National Federation of Temple Youth

NFU GB: US: e: National Farmers' Unio National Froebel Union; S: sv: Nordiska Försäkringsmannaunionen; Nordisk Farmacevtunion

◄FUDCL GB: e: National Farmers Union Development Company, Ltd.

◄.F.U.S. GB: e: National Farmers' Union of Scotland

◄FV BRD: d: Norddeutscher Fußballverband

◄FVB NL: nl: Nederlandse Federatie van Verenigingen van Bedrijfspluimveehouders

◄.F.V.T. e: National Federation of the Vehicle Trades

◄FW pl: Narodowy Front Wyzwolenia

◄FWA US: e: National Farm Workers Association; National Furniture Warehousemen's Association

◄FWI GB: e: National Federation of Women's Institutes

◄FWO B: nl: Nationale Fonds voor Wetenschappelijk Onderzoek

◄DWRC US: e: National Federation of Women's Republican Clubs

◄.F.W.T. GB: e: National Federation of Women Teachers

◄.F.Y.F. GB: e: National Farm Youth Foundation

◄.F.Y.F.C. GB: e: National Federation of Young Farmers' Clubs

◄FŽ CS: cs: Národní Fronta Žen

◄G CS: cs: Národní Galerie; d: Nationalgalerie

◄.G. e: National Gallery; National Government

◄G US: e: mil: National Guard; NL: nl: Nederlands Gezag; US: e: Newspaper Guild

◄.G. D: d: Nordische Gesellschaft, Lübeck; Novembergruppe [Bildende Kunst]

◄GA CH: d: Nationale Gesellschaft zur Förderung der Industriellen Atomtechnik, Bern; e: National Gallery of Art; US: e: National Gliding Association; GB: e: National Graphical Association; US: e: mil: National Guard Association

◄GAA AUS: e: National Gas Association of Australia; US: e: Natural Gasoline Association of America, Tulsa, Oklahoma

NGAC US: e: mil: National Guard Air Corps

NGAUS US: e: mil: National Guard Association of the United States

NGB US: e: National Garden Bureau; US: e: mil: National Guard Bureau; H: hu: Nemzeti Gondozó Bizottság, Budapest; GB: e: Northern Gas Board

N.G.B.M.S. e: National Glass Bottle Makers' Society

NGC GB: e: National Guild of Co-operators

N.G.C.C. e: National Government Co-ordinating Committee

NGCC D: e: nach WK2: North German Coal Control

NGCDO D: e: nach WK2: North German Coal Distribution Organization

NGCMS US: e: National Guild of Community Music Schools

NGEA US: e: National Gastroenterological Association

NGF US: e: National Genetics Foundation [gegr 1953]; National Golf Foundation; US: e: mil: Naval Gun Factory; S: sv: Nordiska Glastekniska Föreningen, Växjö; N: no: Norsk Geologisk Forening

N.G.F.A.W. e: National Gas Fitters and Allied Workers

NGG BRD: d: Gewerkschaft Nahrung - Genuß - Gaststätten [im DGB]; D: d: Nordische Glaubensgemeinschaft

NGH H: hu: Népgondozó Hivatal

NGI I: i: Navigazione Generale Italiana; N: no: Norges Geotekniske Institutt

NGIMIP SU: [d: nowosibirsker staatliches Institut für Maße und Meßgeräte]

NGISC D: e: nach WK2: North German Iron and Steel Control, Düsseldorf

NGJA D: d: Notgemeinschaft junger Autoren

NGK ZA: af: Nederduitse Gereformeerde Kerk

N.G.L. e: North German Lloyd [d: NDL]

NGMB WAN: e: Nigeria Groundnuts Marketing Board

NGNY US: e: mil: National Guard of New York State

NGO N: no: Norges Geografiske Oppmåling [gegr 1773] ; DDR: d: Nur-gewerkschaftliche Opposition

NGOC D: e: nach WK2: North German Oil Control

NGOMAT EAT: e: Ngomi-Matengo Cooperative Marketing Union

NGORC US: e: National Gas and Oil Resources Committee

NGPA US: e: National Gas Processors Association, Tulsa, Oklahoma

NGPT US: e: National Guild of Piano Teachers

NGRC e: National Government of the Republic of China

N.G.R.C. e: National Greyhound Racing Club

NGRI IND: e: National Geophysical Research Institute

NGRS GB: e: Narrow Gauge Railway Society; National Greyhound Racing Society of Great Britain, Ltd.

NGS GB: e: National Gardens Scheme; US: e: National Genealogical Society; National Geographic Society, Washington, D.C.; CH: [d: Neue sozialistische Linke]

N.G.S. US: e: mil: Naval General Staff; e: mil: Naval Gunnery School

NGSK ZA: af: Nederduitse Gereformeerde Sendingkerk

NGSMA US: e: Natural Gasoline Supply Men's Association

NGTC US: e: National Grain Trade Council; D: e: nach WK2: North German Timber Control

NGTE GB: e: National Gas Turbine Establishment, Whetston

N.G.T.O. S: sv: Nationalgodtemplarorden [gegr 1888]

NGU S: sv: Nordisk Grafikunion; N: no: Norges Geologiske Undersøkelse, Oslo [gegr 1858] ; Norges Godtemplar Ung domsforbund

NGUS US: e: mil: National Guard of the United States

NGV NL: nl: Nederlands Genootschap van Vertalers [gegr 1956]

NGW BRD: d: Niederrheinische Gas- und Wasserwerke GmbH, 41 Duisburg-Ham born; D: d: Notgemeinschaft der Deu schen Wissenschaft

NGWIZACO CGO: pt: Ngwizni a Kongo -Entendimendo do Congo (Associação dos Naturais do Congo Português), Lé poldville

N.G.W.T.P.A. e: National Glass Workers' Trade Protection Association

N.H. e: National Hospital; e: mil: Naval Hospital; US: e: New York,New Have & Hartford Railroad Company; N: no Norges Husmorforbund

NH GB: e: mil: The Northumberland Hu sars (Territorial Army)

NHA GB: e: National Hairdressers' Association; National Hardware Alliance Ltd.; US: e: National Hay Association National Health Assembly; GB: e: National Health Association; Nationa Horse Association of Great Britain; U e: National Housing Administration (Agency); New Homemakers of Ameri

NHAW US: e: North American Heating and Air Conditioning Wholesalers' Association

NHB BRD: d: stud: Nationaldemokratischer Hochschulbund [gegr 1966]

NHBRC GB: e: National House-Builders' Registration Council

NHC GB: e: National Hamster Council; US: e: National Health Council; e: N tional Housing Center; US: e: National Housing Conference

N.H.C. GB: e: National Hunt Committee; e: New Health Club

NHCA US: e: National Hairdressers and

Cosmetologists Association

NHCD US: e: New Hampshire Civil Defense

NHCS NL: nl: Nederlandsch Honing-Contrôlestation

NHDAA US: e: National Home Demonstration Agents Association

NHDC US: e: National House Demonstration Council

N.H.D.H. e: National Hospital for Diseases of the Heart

N.H.D.V.S. e: mil: National Home for Disabled Volunteer Soldiers

NHEC INT: e: Northern Hemisphere Exchange Centre [meteorology]

NHENMA US: e: National Hand Embroidery and Novelty Manufacturers Association

NHF GB: e: National Hairdressers Federation; US: e: National Hemophilia Foundation; e: National Hosiery Federation; US: e: Naval Historical Foundation; H: hu: Nemzeti Harci Front; N: no: Norges Handelsstands Forening; Norsk Historisk Forening

NHFL US: e: National Home Fashions League

NHFRA US: e: National Hay Fever Relief Association

NHG d: Naturhistorische Gesellschaft; NL: nl: Natuur-Historisch Genootschap; CH: d: Neue Helvetische Gesellschaft, Bern

NHH N: no: Norges Handelshøyskole, Bergen [gegr 1939]

NHHRA US: e: National Hereford Hog Record Association

NHHS NL: nl: Nederlandsche Handels-Hoogeschool; US: e: New Hampshire Historical Society

NHI e: National Health Insurance; US: e: National Heart Institute, Bethesda, Md.; NL: nl: Nederlandsch Handels Instituut

N.H.I.J.C. e: National Health Insurance Joint Committee

N.H.I.S. e: National Health Insurance Scheme

N.H.I.S.K. B: nl: Nationaal Hoger Instituut voor Schone Kunsten

NHK CS: cs: Národohspodářská Komise; ZA: af: Nederduitse Hervormde Kerk; J: Nippon Hoso Kyokai, Tokyo [e: broadcasting corporation]

NHKF N: no: Norges Handels- og Kontorfunksjonærers Forbund

NHL CDN: e: National Hockey League

NHLA US: e: National Hardwood Lumber Association, Chicago, Ill.

NHLF N: no: Norges Husmorlagsforbund

NHLPA US: e: National Hockey League Players' Association

N.H.M. CDN: e: National Health Measure; e: National History Museum

NHM NL: nl: Natuurhistorisch Museum

NHMA US: e: National Housewares Manufacturers' Association

NHMEA US: e: New Hampshire Music Educators Association

N.H.M.F. GB: e: National Hosiery Manufacturers' Federation

NHMO NATO: e: NATO Hawk Management Office

N.H.M.R.C. AUS: e: National Health and Medical Research Council

NHMS US: e: New Hampshire Medical Society

NHO US: e: mil: Navy Hydrographic Office

NHPA US: e: National Horseshoe Pitchers' Association of America; New Hampshire Pharmaceutical Association

N.H.P.C. e: National Historical Publications Commission

NHPLO NATO: e: NATO Hawk Production and Logistics Organization

NHPM CS: cs: Národní Hnutí Pracujíčí Mládeže

NHPO NATO: e: NATO Hawk Production Office

NHR NL: nl: Nederlandse Huishoudraad

NHRA US: e: National Hot Rod Association, Los Angeles [d: Automobilclub]

NHRP US: e: National Hurricane Research Project

N.H.R.U. e: National Home Reading Union

N.H.S. GB: e: National Health Service; National Health Society; Natural History Society

NHS US: e: National Honor Society; GR: [e: Ministry of Industry, Direction of Standardization, Athens]; S: sv: Nordiska Handelshögskolestuderande

NHSA US: e: National Horse Shoe Association of America

NHSB US: e: National Highway Safety Bureau

NHSC US: e: National Home Study Council, Washington, D.C.

NHSL US: e: New Hampshire State Library

NHSM US: e: National History Society of Maryland; NL: nl: Nederlandsch Historisch Scheepvaart Museum

NHTPC GB: e: National Housing and Town Planning Council

N.H.U. e: National Homing Union [d: Brieftaubenzüchterverband]

NHUC US: e: National Highway Users Conference

NHV NL: nl: Nederlandsche Handelsreizigers Vereeniging

N.H.W. D: d: Nürnberger Herkules-Werke AG, Nürnberg

NHWRA US: e: National Health and Welfare Retirement Association

N.I. e: National Institute (Insurance); GB: e: mil: Native Infantry; Naval Intelligence

NI H: hu: Népmüvelési Intézet; N: no: Norges Industriforbund; RI: Dana Normalisasi Indonesia, Bandung [vgl: DNI]

NIA PL: pl: Naczelna Izba Aptekarska; US: e: National Ice Association

N.I.A. e: National Indian Association; National Industrial Alliance

NIA US: e: National Insurance Association; National Intelligence Authority; Newspaper Institute of America

NIAA US: e: National Industrial Advertisers Association

N.I.A.A. IND: e: Northern India Automobile Association

NIAA US: e: Nuclear Industries Association of America, Inc.

NIAAA GB: e: Northern Ireland Amateu Athletic Association

N.I.A.B. GB: e: National Institute of Agricultural Botany, Cambridge; S: sv Nordiska Industri Aktie Bolaget, Göte borg

NIAC US: e: National Industry Advisory Committee; NATO: e: NATO Industrial Advisory Conference

NIAD US: e: National Institute for Aller gic and Infectious Diseases

N.I.A.D. e: National Insurance Audit Department

NIADA US: e: National Independent Au tomobile Dealers Association

N.I.A.E. GB: e: National Institute of Agricultural Engineering

NIAE US: e: National Institute for Arch tectural Education

NIAF N: no: Norsk Ingeniör- og Arkitektforening

Niag D: d: Nahrungsmittelindustrie AG, Berlin

NIAG NATO: e: NATO Industrial Adviso ry Group

Niag D: d: Niederrheinische Automobil -GmbH, Moers

NIAK PL: pl: Naczelny Instytut Akcji Katolickiej

NIAL US: e: National Institute of Arts and Letters

NIAM US: e: National Institute of Advertising Management; NL: nl: Nederlandsch Instituut Agrarisch Marktonderzoek

N.I.A.M.P.D. GB: e: Northern Ireland

Association of Master Painters and Decorators

NIAR US: e: National Institute of Atmospheric Research

NIAS NL: nl: Nederlandsch Indische Artsenschool

NIATM INT: e: New International Association for Testing Materials

N.I.B. US: e: National Information Bureau, New York, N.Y.; e: National Institute for the Blind; National Investment Board

NIB US: e: mil: Naval Intelligence Bureau; NL: nl: Nieuwe Internationale Bibliothek; Nieuwe Indische Beweging

NIBA NL: nl: Nederlands Instituut voor Bedrijfsassistentie

NIBCA US: e: National Intercollegiate Boxing Coaches Association

NIBEM NL: nl: National Instituut voor Brouwgerst, Mout en Bier

NIBFBS GB: e: Northern Ireland Budgerigar and Foreign Bird Society

NIBFCC GB: e: Northern Ireland Border Fancy Canary Club

NIBH B: nl: Nationaal Instituut tot Bevordering van de Huisvesting

NIBL US: e: National Industrial Basketball League

NIBS J: e: Nippon Institute for Biological Science

N.I.C. ZA: e: Natal Indian Congress [gegr 1894]

NIC US: e: National Industrial Council (of the National Association of Manufacturers); National Institute of Credit; EAT: e: National Insurance Corporation; US: e: National Interfraternity Conference [gegr 1909]; National Investors Council; US: e: mil: Naval Information Center

N.I.C. e: Non-Intervention Committee

N.I.C.A. e: Netherlands Indies' Civil Administration

NICAP US: e: National Investigations Committee on Aerial Phenomena

NICB US: e: National Industrial Conference Board [gegr 1916]

NICD US: e: National Institute of Cleaning and Dyeing; IND: e: National Institute of Community Development

NICE US: e: National Institute of Ceramic Engineers; Northern Idaho College of Education

NICEIC GB: e: National Inspection Council for Electrical Installation Contracting

NICEM US: e: National Information Center for Educational Media, University of Southern California

NICF GB: e: North of Ireland Cricket and Football Club

NICFC US: e: National Intercollegiate Flying Club

NICHD US: e: National Institute of Child Health Development

NICMA US: e: National Ice Cream Mix Association

NICO US: e: mil: Navy Inventory Control Office

NICS NATO: e: NATO Integrated Communications System

NICTOE US: e: National Institute for Commercial and Trade Organization Executives

N.I.D. e: National Institute for the Deaf; National Institute of Dry Cleaning; e: mil; Naval Intelligence Department (Division)

NID PL: pl: Niedpodległość i Demokracja

NIDA US: e: National Independent Dairies Association; National Industrial Distributors Association, Philadelphia, Pa.; National Institute for Domestic Affairs

NIDB WAN: e: Nigeria Industrial Development Bank

NIDC CDN: e: National Industrial Design Council; IND: e: Nepal Industrial Development Corporation; GB: e: Northern Ireland Development Council

NIDER NL: nl: Nederlands Instituut voor (Informatie,) Documentatie en Registratuur, Den Haag

NIDFA GB: e: National Independent Drama Festivals Association

NIDM US: e: National Institute for Disaster Mobilization

NIDOC ET: e: National Information and Documentation Centre

NIE; Nie PL: pl: Niepodległość [1945]

NIEAF NL: nl: Nederlandse Instrumenten en Elektrische Apparaten Fabriek

Niebag D: d: Niederschlesische Bergbau AG, Waldenburg

Niederberg BRD: d: Niederrheinische Bergwerks-AG, Düsseldorf

N.I.E.F. e: National Impounding Employers' Federation

Niemei D: d: Niederschlesische Maschinen- und Elektrizitäts-Industrie, Hirschberg

NIESR GB: e: National Institute of Economic and Social Research, London [gegr 1938]

NIF N: no: Norges Idrettsforbund; Norges Industriforbund; Norsk Ingeniørforening, Oslo

NIFA US: e: National Intercollegiate Flying Association

NIFB US: e: National Institute of Farm Brokers

N.I.F.E.S. GB: e: National Industrial Fuel Efficiency Service, London

NIFO NL: nl: Nederlandsch-Indische Fascisten-Organisatië

NIFOR IND: e: National Information Office; WAN: e: Nigerian Institute for Oil Palm Research

NIGA GB: e: North of Ireland Grocers Association

NIGFCC GB: e: Northern Ireland Gloster Fancy Canary Club

NIGIS NL: e: Netherlands Indies Government Information Service

NIGP US: e: National Institute of Governmental Purchasing, Washington 6, D.C.

NIH US: e: National Institute of Health, Washington, D.C.

N.I.H. e: National Institute of Houseworkers

NIH GB: e: mil: North Irish Horse (Territorial Army)

NIHA B: nl: Nationaal Instituut van Handel en Ambacht

N.I.H.C. GB: e: Northern Ireland House of Commons

NIHS CH: f: Norme de l'Industrie Horlogère Suisse, CH-2002 Neuchâtel

NII NL: e: Netherlands Industrial Institute, New York, N.Y.; SU: [e: Scientific Research Institute]

N.I.I.K.B. NL: nl: Nederlands Instituut voor Internationale Kulturele Betrekkingen

NIIOMTP SU: [d: wissenschaftliches Forschungsinstitut für Mechanisierung und technische Unterstützung des Bauwese Moskau]

N.I.I.P. GB: e: National Institute of Industrial Psychology, Kingsway

NIIPM SU: [e: Scientific Research Institut of Plastics]

NIITECHIM SU: [d: wissenschaftliches Forschungsinstitut für technisch-ökonomische Fragen der chemischen Industrie]

NIITEPLOPRIBOR SU: [d: wissenschaftliches Forschungsinstitut für Gerätebau der Wärmeenergetik, Ministerium für Gerätebau, Automatisierungsmittel un Steuersysteme, Moskau]

NIJS YU: Nuklearni Inštitut Jošef Stefan, Ljubljana

NIJSI NL: nl: Vereniging de Nederlandse IJzer- en Staalproducerende Industrie, Den Haag

NIK PL: pl: Naczelna Izba Kontroli; Najwyższa Isba Kontroli; H: hu: Nehé pari Központ, Budapest

NIKEX H: [d: ungarisches Außenhandels unternehmen für die Erzeugnisse der Schwerindustrie, Budapest 4]

NIHFI SU: [d: wissenschaftliches Forschungsinstitut für Film und Foto, Moskau]

NIKI NL: nl: Nederlands-Indisch Kankerinstituut

NIL PL: pl: Naczelna Izba Lekarska

NILA US: e: National Industrial Leather Association

N.I.Lab. GB: e: Northern Ireland Labour

NILCA GB: e: National Industrial Launderers and Cleaners Association

NILCI B: nl: Nationaal Instituut voor Landbouwstudie in Belgisch Congo

NILE US: e: National Institute of Labor Education

NILFP US: e: National Institute of Locker and Freezer Provisioners

NILI NL: nl: Nederlandsch Instituut vor Landbouwkundige Ingenieurs

NILOS B: nl: Nationaal Instituut voor Lichamelijke Opvoeding en Sport

NILS NL: nl: Nederlandsch-Indisch Landsyndicaat

Nilu D: d: Luftverkehrs-Aktiengesellschaft Niedersachsen, Hannover

NILW PL: pl: Naukowy Instytut Lekarsko-Weterynaryjny

NIM B: nl: Nationale Inversteringsmaatschappij; ZA: e: National Institute for Metallurgy; H: hu: Nehézipari Miniszter (ium), Budapest

NIMA US: e: National Insulation Manufacturers Association; GB: e: Northern Ireland Ministry of Agriculture

NIMAC US: e: National Interscholastic Music Activities Commission

NIMC US: e: National Institute of Management Counsellors; National Institute of Municipal Clerks

NIMD ET: e: National Institute of Management Development

NIME H: hu: Nehézipari Müszaki Egyetem

NIMH GB: e: National Institute of Medical Herbalists; US: e: National Institute of Mental Health, Bethesda, Md.

N.I.M.H.A. GB: e: Northern Ireland Ministry of Home Affairs

NIMKvt. H: hu: Nehézipari Minisztérium Müszaki Könyvtára, Budapest

NIMLO US: e: National Institute of Municipal Law Officers

NIMM NL: nl: e: Nederlands Instituut voor Motivation en Marketing Research

NIMPA US: e: National Independent Meat Packers Association

N.I.M.R. GB: e: National Institute for Medical Research, Mill Hill, London

N.I.M.S. e: National Industrial Mobile Squad

NIMT NL: nl: Nederlands Instituut van Middelbare en Hogere Technici

N.I.M.U. NZ: e: North Island Motor Union, Wellington

NIN US: e: mil: National Information Network [ASTIA]

NINDB US: e: National Institute of Neurological Diseases and Blindness

NINE I: i: Nucleo Intendenza Nord-Est

NINO BRD: d: Niehues & Dütting, 446 Nordhorn [Bekleidung]

NIO GB: e: National Institute of Oceanography: NATO: e: NATO Information Officers Committee; US: e: Navigational Information Office

NIOC IR: e: National Iranian Oil Company; Liberia: e: National Iron Ore Company [gegr 1961]

NIOG NL: nl: Nederlandsch-Indisch Onderwijzers-Genootschap

NIOGAS A: d: Niederösterreichische Gaswerke

NIOK NL: nl: Nederlandsch-Indisch Onderwijs Kongres

NIOP US: e: National Institute of Oilseed Products

NIP BH: e: National Independence Party; WAN: e: National (Nigerian) Independence Party

NIPA PAK: e: National Institute of Public Administration; US: e: National Institute of Public Affairs

NIPC WAN: e: Nigerian Investment Property Company

NIPH GB: e: National Institute of Poultry Husbandry

Nipho NL: nl: Nederlandsch Instituut voor Practisch Handels-Onderwijs

NIPI NL: nl: Nederlandsch-Indisch Pharmaco-Therapeutisch Instituut

NIPL NL: nl: Nederlands Instituut voor Personeelsleiding

NIPO NL: nl: Nederlands Instituut voor de Publieke Opinienpeiling

NIPR ZA: e: National Institute for Personnel Research, Johannesburg

NIPV NL: nl: Nederlandsch-Indische Padvinders Vereeniging

NIR B: nl: Nationaal Instituut voor Radio-Omroep; R: [f: commission roumaine de normalisation]

NIRA US: e: National Industrial Recovery Administration

NIRB US: e: National Industrial Recovery Board; Nuclear Insurance Rating Bureau

NIRC US: e: National Institute of Rug Cleaning

NIRD GB: e: National Institute for Research in Dairying

NIREB US: e: National Institute of Real Estate Brokers

NIRM US: e: National Individual Rifle Match

NIRNS GB: e: National Institute for Research in Nuclear Science, Harwell

NIRO NL: nl: Nederlandsch-Indisch Instituut voor Rubberonderzoek

NIROM NL: nl: Nederlandsch-Indische Radio-Omroep Maatschappij, Batavia [1934 ... 40]

NIRR ZA: e: National Institute for Road Research, Pretoria

N.I.R.Sig. GB: e: mil: Northern Ireland Royal Corps of Signals

NIS e: National Institute of Science(s)

N.I.S. e: National Insurance Scheme; e: mil: Naval Intelligence Service

NIS US: e: mil: Naval Investigative Service; S: sv: Nordiska Ingenjörs-Samfundet [gegr 1941]; N: no: Norges Industriforbunds Standardiseringskomité

NISA US: e: National Industrial Sand Association; National Industrial Servi Association; National Institute of Su ply Associations

NISBOVA US: e: Northern Indiana Scho Band, Orchestra, and Vocal Associatio

NISBS US: e: National Institute of Socia and Behavioral Science

NISC GB: e: National Industrial Safety Conference, London

NISER WAN: e: Nigerian Institute of So and Economic Research, Ibadan

NISI IND: e: National Institute of Scienc of India

NISRA US: e: National Intercollegiate Squast Rackets' Association

NISS US: e: National Institute of Social Sciences

NIST J: e: National Information System for Science and Technology; PI: e: National Institute of Science and Tech nology; US: e: Northern Illinois State Teachers

NISU NL: nl: Nederlands-Indonesische Suiker Unie

NIT US: e: National Invitational Tournament (Tourney); sv: Naturvännerna internationella turistförening

Nitag D: d: Naphta-Industrie und Tankanlagen-AG, Berlin-Spandau; BRD: d: Niedersächsische Treibstoff-AG, Hamburg

NITBON NL: nl: Nederlands Instituut voor Technisch-Biologisch Onderzoek in de Natuur

NITC US: e: National Instructional Television Center, Bloomington [seit 1968

NITL US: e: National Industrial Traffic League; National Instructional Television Library, New York, N.Y.

NITO N: no: Norges Ingeniør- og Teknikerorganisasjon, Oslo [gegr 1936]

NITPA US: e: National Institutional Teacher Placement Association

NITR ZA: e: National Institute for Telecommunications Research

NIUC US: e: National Independent Union Council

NIUIF SU: [e: scientific institute of fertilizers, insecticides and fungicides]

NIV NL: nl: Nederlands Instituut voor Volksvoeding; Nederlandsch Instituut voor Volksdans en Volksmuziek

NIVA NL: nl: Nederlandsch Instituut van Architecten; Nederlands Instituut van Accountants; N: no: Norsk institutt for vannforskning, Oslo

NIVB ZA: af: Navorsingsinstituut vir die Visserybedryf

NIVE NL: nl: Nederlands Instituut voor Efficiency, Den Haag [gegr 1925]

NIVEE NL: nl: Nederlands Instituut voor Electrowarmte en Electroscheikunde, Arnheim

NIVJO NL: nl: Nederlandsch-Indonesisch Verbond van Jongeren Organisaties

NIVM INT: d: Neuer Internationaler Verband für Materialprüfung [e: NIATM]

NIWKC US: e: National Institute of Wood Kitchen Cabinets

NIWO NL: nl: Nederlandsche Internationale Wegvervoer Organisatie

NIWR ZA: e: National Institute for Water Research

NIWU US: e: National Industrial Workers Union

NIZ CS: cs: Náčelník Intendaněního Zásobování

NIZO US: e: National Industrial Zoning Committee; NL: nl: Nederlands Instituut voor Zuivelonderzoek

Nizo BRD: d: Niezoldi & Krämer, Fabrik für Schmalfilmapparate, München 38

NJ N: no: Norsk Journalistlag [gegr 1946]

NJA US: e: National Jail Association

N.J.A. e: National Jewellers' Association

NJA S: sv: Norrbottens Jörnverks AB; N: no: Norsk Jernbane Avholdsforbund

NJAB GB: e: National Joint Apprenticeship Board for the Building Industry

NJAC GB: US: e: National Joint Advisory Council

NJAS US: e: New Jersey Audubon Society

NJB d: Neue Jugendbewegung

N.J.B.E.M.S. e: National Joint Board of Employers and Members of Staff

N.J.C. e: National Joint Committee (Council); GB: e: National Joint Council for Local Authorities, Administrative, Professional, Technical and Clerical Services; NL: nl: Nederlandse Jeugdherberg Centrale; S: sv: Nordiska Jockeyklubben för sammanhållning mellan svenska och danska höstsports- och avelsföreningar

NJCAA US: e: National Junior College Athletic Association

N.J.C.B.I. e: National Joint Council for the Building Industry

NJCC US: e: National Joint Computer Committee; GB: e: National Joint Consultative Committee of Architects Quantity Surveyors and Builders

N.J.C.D.L. e: National Joint Council for Dock Labour

NJCF US: e: National Juvenile Court Foundation

NJCS US: e: National Jewish Committee on Scouting

NJCW US: e: New Jersey College for Women

NJF S: sv: Nordiska Jordbruksforskares Förening, Stockholm [gegr 1918]; da: Nordiske Jordbrugsforskeres Forening; S: sv: Nordiska Journalistförbundet

NJFF N: no: Norges Jeger- og Fiskerforbund

N.J.G. NL: nl: Nederlandse Jeugdgemeenschap

N.J.H. US: e: National Jewish Hospital, Denver, Colo.

NJHC NL: nl: Nederlandse Jeugdherberg Centrale

NJHSA US: e: New Jersey Health and Sanitary Association

NJI NL: nl: Nederlandsch Jeugdleiders

Instituut

N.J.I.C. GB: e: National Joint Industrial Council

NJJB NL: nl: Nederlandsch Joodsche Jongeren Bond

N.J.K. SF: sv: Nyländska Jaktklubben [gegr 1861]

NJLA US: e: New Jersey Library Association

NJMC US: e: National Jewish Music Council

NJN NL: nl: Nederlandsche Jeugdbond voor Natuurstudie

N.J.O. e: National Juvenile Organization

NJPA US: e: New Jersey Pharmaceutical Association

NJPMB US: e: mil: Navy Jet Propelled Missile Board

NJS NL: nl: Nationale Jeugdstorm in Nederlandsch- Indië; S: sv: Nordiska Järnvägsmannasällskapet

NJSHS US: e: New Jersey State Horticultural Society

NJSPE US: e: New Jersey Society of Professional Engineers

N.J.T.C. e: National Joint Training Committee

NJU S: sv: Nordiska Järnvägsmannaunionen

NJV NL: nl: Nationaal Jongeren Verbond; Nederlandsch Jongelings-Verbond

NJVGA US: e: National Junior Vegetable Growers Association

NJZ US: e: New Jersey Zinc Company

NK PL: pl: Naczelna Komitet; YU: sn: Narodna Knjižnjica, Ljubljana; CS: cs; Národopisný Kabinet; PL: pl: Instytut Wydawniczy "Nasza Księgarnia"; d: Nationalkomitee "Freies Deutschland" [1943 . . . 45] ; S: sv: Navigationsklubben; NL: nl: Nieuwe Koers - Jongerenorganisatie van de Partij van de Arbeid; D: d: Nomenklaturkommission (der Deutschen Anatomischen Gesellschaft); S: sv: Normkommitté

nk 13 BRD: d: Nürnberger Kommune 13

NKA US: e: National Kindergarten Association; NL: nl: Nederlandse Katholieke Arbeidersbeweging

NKAF e: mil: North Korean Air Force

NKAL N: no: Norske Kvinnelige Akademikers Landforbund [gegr 1920]

N.K.B. B: nl: Nationaal Koninklijke Beweging; NL: nl: Nederlandse Kegel Bond Nederlandse Konijnenfokker (Korfbal) (Krachtsport) (Kruideniers) Bond

N.K.B.K. B: nl: Nationale Kas van het Beroepskrediet

NKCA US: e: National Kitchen Cabinet Association

NKD CS: cs: Nejvyšší Kontrolni Dvůr

NKDF US: e: National Kidney Disease Foundation

NKES CH: d: Nationales Komitee für Elitesport

NKF B: nl: Nationaal Krisisfonds; NL: n Nederlandse Kabelfabrieken

N.K.F. D: d: Norddeutsche Kühlerfabrik AG, Berlin-Tempelhof; Norddeutsche Kugellagerfabrik GmbH, Berlin SO 36; S: sv: Nordiska Konstförbundet; DK: da: Nordiske Kunstnerforbund; S: sv: Nordisk Kirurgisk Förening

NKF N: no: Norges Kiøtt of Flesksentral; SU: [d: Volkskommissariat der Finanzen] ; N: no: Norsk Kommunearbeiderforbund; Norsk Komponistforening

NKFD d: Nationalkomitee Freies Deutsc land [1943 . . . 45]

N.K.F.V. N: no: mil: Norske Kvinners Frivillige Verneplikt

N.K.G. D: d: Neue Kinematographische Gesellschaft, München; EAK: e: New Kenya Group [gegr 1959]

NKG J: [e: Japan Institute of Metals]

NKGB SU: [d: Volkskommissariat für Staatssicherheit]

NKI NL: nl: Vereniging de Nederlandse Koeltechnische Industrie, Den Haag; H: hu: Növényvédelmi Kutato Intézet; S: sv: Nordiska Korrespondenzinstitut

Noréns korrespondensinstitut [gegr 1910]

NKIF N: no: Norsk Kommunale Ingeniørveseners Forening

NKII GH: e: Kwame N'Krumah Ideological Institute

N.K.J.K. NL: nl: Nederlandse Katholieke Journalistenkring

N.K.J.V. NL: nl: Nederlandse Katholieke Journalisten Vereniging

NKK CS: cs: Národní Kulturní Komise; H: hu: Népkönyvtári Központ, Budapest; J: [d: japanische Gesellschaft für Klassifikation, Tokio; Stahlwerke und Schiffbaugesellschaft; Luftfahrzeugbauwerke]; BRD: d: Norddeutsche Kundenkreditbank AG; S: sv: Nordiska kulturkommissionen; N: no: Nordiske Kulturkommisjon; S: sv: Norrköpings Kappsimningsklubb

N.K.K.K. B: nl: Nationale Kunstkapperskring

NKL PL: pl: Naczelny Komitet Ludowy [1943 ... 44]; N: no: Norges Kooperative Landsforening [gegr 1906]

N.K.L.F. N: no: Norske Kvinnelige Lægers Forening

NKM S: sv: Nationella komittén för motorbåtssport

NKMB NL: nl: Nederlandse Katholieke Middenstandsbond

NKN PL: pl: Naczelny Komitet Narodowy [1914 ... 17]; N: no: Norske Kvinners Nasjonalråd

NKOA US: e: National Knitted Outerwear Association

NKOJ YU: sh: Nacionalni Komitet Oslobodjenja Jugoslavije

N.K.P. EAK: e: New Kenya Party [gegr 1959]

NKP N: [d: norwegische kommunistische Partei]

NKPA US: e: National Kraut Packers Association; e: mil: North Korean People's Army

NKS NL: nl: Nederlandse Katholieke Sportbond; N: no: Norske Kvinneorganisasjoners Samarbeidsnemnd; Norske Kvinners Sanitetsforening

N.K.S. N: no: Norsk Kjemisk Selskap [gegr 1893]

N.K.S.F. N: no: Norsk Kvinnesaksforening

NKSU S: sv: Nordens konservativa studentunion

NKÚ CS: cs: Nejvyšší Kontrolní Úřad

NKU N: [d: norwegischer kommunistischer Jugendverband]

NKUF N: no: Norges Kristelige Ungdomsforbund

N.K.V. BRD: d: Nationaler Krankenversicherungsverein aG, Stuttgart; NL: nl: Nederlands Katholiek Vakverbond

NKV BRD: d: Verband der niedergelassenen Nichtkassenärzte Deutschlands

NKVD SU: [d: Volkskommissariat für innere Angelegenheiten]

NKVR CS: cs: Národní Komitét pro Vědeckou Radiotechniku

NKW PL: pl: Naczelny Komitet Wykonawczy; Narodowe Komitety Walki; Narodowy Komitet Wyzwolenia

NKWD SU: = NKVD

NKW PSL PL: pl: Naczelny Komitet Wykonawczy Polskiego Stronnictwa Ludowego

NKW SD PL: pl: Neczelny Komitet Wykonawczy Stronnictwa Demokratycznego

NKW SL PL: pl: Naczelny Komitet Wykonawczy Stronnictwa Ludowego

NKW ZSL PL: pl: Naczelny Komitet Wykonawczy Zjednoczonego Stronnictwa Ludowego

NK ZSL PL: pl: Naczelny Komitet Zjednoczonego Stronnictwa Ludowego

NL A: d: Nationale Liga; e: National Laboratory (League); US: e: National League of Professional Baseball Clubs

N.L. e: National Library; GB: e: mil: Native Levies; Navy League

NL DIN BRD: d: Normenstelle Luftfahrt, 7022 Leinfelden 1; GB: e: mil: The

North Lancashire Regiment
N.L. GB: e: North Library [British Museum]
NLA S: sv: Nöringslivets Arkivråd; BRD: d: National-Liberale Aktion [gegr 1970]; US: e: National Lime Association; National Lumbermen's Association; Nebraska Library Association; N: no: Norges Læreravholdslag
NLAA US: e: National Legal Aid Association
NLABS US: e: mil: Natick Laboratories [Army Materiel Command]
NLAPW US: e: National League of American Penwomen
N.L.B. US: e: National Labor Board; e: National League of the Blind; National Library for the Blind
NLB H: hu: Népköztársaság Lefelsö Bírósága, Budapest; DK: da: Nordiske Landes Bokforlag
NLBA GB: e: National League of Band Associations; US: e: National Licensed Beverage Association
NLC US: e: National League Club; National Legislative Conference (Council)
N.L.C. GB: e: National Liberal Club
NLC GH: e: National Liberation Council; GB: e: National Libraries Committee; US: e: National Lutheran Council; Negro Labor Committee
N.L.C. US: e: New Orleans and Lower Coast Railroad Company
NLCIF GB: e: National Light Castings Ironfounders' Federation, London SW 1
N.L.C.N.I. e: National Liberation Committee of Northern Italy
NLCS GB: e: North London Collegiate School for Girls
NLDA US: e: National Livestock Dealers' Association; National Luggage Dealers' Association
NLDP MW: e: National Liberal Democratic Party
NLEA US: e: National Lumber Exporters Association

NLEC US: e: National Lutheran Educational Conference
N.L.F. GB: e: National Liberal Federation; e: National Liberation Front; NL: nl: Nederlandse Landmeetkundige Federatie; N: no: Norges Lærerinneforbund; N: no: mil: Norges Lotteforbund
NLFA US: e: National Livestock Feeders Association
NLfB BRD: d: Niedersächsisches Landesamt für Bodenforschung, 3 Hannover -Buchholz
NLG US: e: National Lawyers' Guild
NLGI US: e: National Lubricating Grease Institute, Kansas City 12, Mo.
N.L.G.O.A. GB: e: National and Local Government Officers Association
N.L.G.S.M.A. e: National Leather Goods and Saddlery Manufacturers' Associatio
N.L.H. N: no: Norges Landsbrukshøyskol
NLHS LAO: Neo-Lao-Hak-Sat [gegr 1957
N.L.I. IRL: e: National Library of Ireland e: National Lifeboat Institution
NLI US: e: National Limestone Institute; NL: nl: Nederlandsch Luchtvaart Instituut
NLISA US: e: National League of Insured Savings Associations
NLJB NL: nl: Nederlandsch Luthersche Jongelings Bond
N.L.J.U. e: New Liberal Jewish Union
NLK BRD: d: Niederrheinische Licht- und Kraftwerke AG, 407 Rheydt
NLL NL: nl: Nationaal Luchtvaart Laboratorium, Amsterdam; GB: e: National Lending Library for Science and Technology, Walton, Boston Spa, Yorkshire
NLM GH: e: National Liberal (Liberation) Movement; US: e: National Library of Medicine, Bethesda, Md.; NL: nl: Nederlands Luchtvaart Maatschappij; S: sv: Norrbottens läns museum, Luleå
NLMA US: e: National Lumber Manufacturers Association

N.L.M.B. GB: e: Natsopa London Machine Branch

NLMC e: National Labor Management Council; US: e: National League of Masonic Clubs

NLN US: e: National League for Nursing

NLNA US: e: National Landscape Nurserymen's Association

N.L.N.D.A. GB: e: Nottingham Lace and Net Dressers' Association

N.L.N.E. e: National League of Nursing Education

NLO GB: e: National Liberal Organization

NLOGF GB: e: National Lubricating Oil and Grease Federation

N.L.P. e: National Labour Party

NLP US: e: National League of Postmasters of the United States

N.L.P. e: National Liberal Party; CR: e: National Liberation Party

NLP D: d: nach WK2: Niedersächsische Landespartei [gegr 1946]; S: sv: Norrbottens läns producentförening

NLPBC US: e: National League of Professional Baseball Clubs

NLPSA US: e: National League to Promote School Attendance

NLPTL US: e: National Lutheran Parent -Teacher League

NLR NL: nl: Nationaal Lucht- en Ruimtevaartlaboratorium, Amsterdam

N.L.R. GB: e: North London Railway

NLRB US: e: National Labor Relations Board [gegr 1953]; e: Newspaper Leases Review Board

N.L.S. D: d: mil: WK2: Nachschubleitstelle

NLS NL: nl: Nationale Luchtvaartschool

N.L.S. GB: e: National Library of Scotland

NLSA US: e: National Liquor Stores Association

NLSB e: National Land Survey Board

NLSC NATO: e: National Logistic Support Command

NLSE US: e: National Livestock Exchange

NLSMB US: e: National Livestock and Meat Board

NLSPA US: e: National Livestock Producers Association

N.L.S.S. e: National Life Saving Society

N.L.S.S.P. CL: Nava Lanka Sama Samaja Party

NLTA US: e: National League of Teachers' Associations

N.L.T.F. e: National Leather Trades Federation; N: no: Norsk Landbruksteknisk Forening

NLTU DK: da: Nordjydsk Lawn Tennis Union

NLU S: sv: Nordisk Lastbil Union

NLUS US: e: mil: Navy League of the United States

NLV BRD: d: Nürnberger Lebensversicherung AG

NLVA BRD: d: Niedersächsisches Landesvermessungsamt

NLVF N: no: Norges Landbruksvitenskapelige Forskningsråd [gegr 1949]

N.L.W. GB: e: National Library of Wales

N.L.W.U. e: National Laundry Workers Union

NLWV US: e: National League of Women Voters [gegr 1920]

N.L.Y.L. GB: e: National League of Young Liberals

NM YU: sh: Narodna Milicija; CS: cs: Národní Museum; YU: sn: Narodni Muzej, Ljubljana

N.M. e: National Museum; e: mil: naval magazine; naval militia

NM H: hu: Nepmüvelési Minisztérium, Budapest; S: sv: Föreningen Nordiska Mässor

N.M. S: sv: Nordiska Museet, Stockholm

NM DIN: BRD: d: Normenstelle Marine, 2 Hamburg 1

N.M.A. D: d: mil: Nachrichtenmittelabteilung

NMA US: e: National Manufacturers Association; National Medical Association; National Microfilm Association, Annapolis, Md.

N.M.A. e: National Motorists Association; non-marine association

NMA US: e: Northwest Mining Association

NMAA US: e: National Machine Accountants' Association; National Metal Awning Association

NMAG D: d: Neue musikalische Arbeitsgemeinschaft

NMAUS US: e: Newsprint Manufacturers Association of the United States

N.M.B. GB: e: National Maritime Board; e: National Mediation Board; e: mil: Naval Meteorological Branch; NL: nl: Nederlandse Meisjes Bond

NMB NL: nl: Nederlandsche Middenstandsbank N.V., Amsterdam

NMBF US: e: National Manufacturers of Beverage Flavors

NMBLA GB: e: North Midland Branch of the Library Association

NMBS B: nl: Nationale Maatschappij der Belgische Spoorwegen [f: SNCB]

N.M.B.S. e: mil: Naval and Military Bible Society

NMC US: e: National Management Council; National Manpower Council; National Marine Consultants, Inc.; e: National Medical Center; e: National Metal Congress (and Exposition); US: e: National Meteorological Center; National Music Camp (Council); US: e: mil: Naval Material Command; Naval Missile Center, Point Mugu, Calif.; NL; nl: Nederlandsche Meisjes Club; US: e: New Mexico College of Agriculture and Mechanic Arts; DK: da: Nordisk Maskinkomité, København

N.M.C. e: Northern Miners' Conference

NMCA US: e: National Meat Canners' Association; US: e: mil: Navy Mothers Clubs of America

NMCB US: e: National Munitions Control Board

NMCC NATO: e: National Military Command Center

NMCO US: e: mil: Navy Material Catalog(ing) Office

N.M.D. e: mil: Naval Manning Department

NMD US: e: mil: Naval Mine Depot

NMDA US: e: National Medical and Dental Association; National Metal Decorators Association

NMDL US: e: mil: Navy Mine Defense Laboratory [BUWEPS]

NMDS US: e: mil: Naval Mine Disposal School

NMDU US: e: Newspaper and Mail Deliverers Union of New York and Vicinity

NME e: mil: National Military Establishment

N.M.E.A. e: Near and Middle East Association

NMEA US: e: Nebraska Music Educators Association

NMEBA US: e: National Marine Engineers Beneficial Association

NMERI ZA: e: National Mechanical Engineering Research Institute

NMF US: e: mil: Naval Missile Facility, Point Arguello, Calif.; N: no: Norges Merkantile Funksjonærforbund; Norsk Matematisk Forening

N.M.F.B.A. e: National Master Farriers' and Blacksmiths' Association

NMFEC US: e: National Medical Foundation for Eye Care

NMFHG US: e: National Master Farm Homemakers' Guild

NMFPO US: e: mil: Naval Missile Facility, Point Arguello, Calif.

NMG US: e: mil: Navy Military Government; NL: nl: Nederlandsch Meisjesgilde

NMGA US: e: mil: National Military Guidance Association

N.M.G.C. e: National Marriage Guidance Council

N.M.G.I. e: Nursery and Market Gardens Industries

NMHF US: e: National Mental Health
Foundation

NMI US: e: National Marconi Institute;
N: no: Norske Meteorologiske Institutt

NMIC US: e: National Meat Industry
Council

NMIS GB: e: Newspaper Mutual Insurance
Society Ltd.

NMK S: sv: Nora Motorklubb; N: no:
Norsk Motorklubb

NMKG D: d: Neue Münchener Künstlergenossenschaft

N.M.K.L. B: nl: Nationale Maatschappij
van het Kleine Landeigendom

N.M.K.N. B: nl: Nationale Maatschappij
voor het Krediet aan de Nijverheid

NML IND: e: National Metallurgical Laboratory, Calcutta; US: e: National Municipal League; National Music League;
N: no: Norske Melkeprodusenters
Landsforbund

NMLCD H: e: National Medical Library
and Center for Medical Documentation

NMLRA US: e: National Muzzle Loading
Rifle Association

N.M.M. GB: e: National Maritime Museum, Greenwich

NMM H: hu: Népjóléti és Munkaügyi Mi-
niszter(ium), Budapest

NMMA US: e: National Macaroni Manufac-
turers Association; NATO: e: NATO
MRCA [Multirole Combat Aircraft]
Management Agency

NMMEA US: e: New Mexico Music Educators Association

NMN PL: pl: Niezależna Młodzież Narodowa

NMND US: e: mil: Naval Magazine and
Net Depot

NMOC GB: e: National Marketing Organization Committee

NMOSU US: e: mil: Naval Mobile Ordnance Service Unit

NMP NL: nl: Nederlandsche Maatschappij tot Bevordering der Pharmacie;

US: e: mil: Nurnberg Military Post [BRD]

NMPATA US: e: National Music Printers
and Allied Trades Association

NMPB US: e: National Millinery Planning
Board

NMPC GB: e: National Milk Publicity
Council

NMPF US: e: National Milk Producers
Federation

NMPO US: e: mil: Navy Motion Picture
Office

N.M.P.P. F: f: Nouvelles Messageries de
la Presse Parisienne, Paris

NMPU S: sv: Nordisk Musikpedagogisk
Union

NMPX US: e: mil: Naval Motion Picture
Exchange

NMR NATO: e: National Military Representatives; US: e: National Museum
of Racing

NMRA US: e: National Model Railroad
Association [gegr 1935]

NMRDE US: e: mil: Nuclear Medical Research Detachment Europe [Landstuhl
Army Medical Center, BRD]

NMRI US: e: Navy Medical Research Institute

NMRL US: e: mil: Naval Medical Research
Laboratory

NMR(S) NATO: e: National Military Representatives (SHAPE)

NMRS US: e: National Mobile Radio
System

NMS US: e: National Malaria Society

N.M.S. e: National Medical Service;
US: e: National Merit Scholarship
Corporation, Evenston, Ill. [gegr 1955];
e: National Missionary Society

NMS US: e: mil: Naval Meteorological
Service; N: no: Norske Meieriers Salgs
Sentral; Norsk Medisinsk Selskap

NMSA US: e: National Metal Spinners
Association; NATO: e: NATO Maintenance Supply Agency

NMSC US: e: National Merit Scholarship

Corporation, Evenston, Ill.

NMSE US: e: mil: Naval Material Support Establishment

NMSS US: e: National Multiple Sclerosis Society

NMSSA NATO: e: NATO Maintenance Supply Services Agency

NMSU US: e: New Mexico State University

NMTA US: e: National Metal Trades Association

NMTAS GB: e: National Milk Testing and Advisory Service

NMTBA US: e: National Machine Tool Builders Association, Cleveland 6, Ohio

NMTF US: e: Naval Mine Test Facility

NMTFA GB: e: National Master Tile Fixers' Association

NMTS US: e: National Milk Testing Service

NMU US: e: National Maritime Union; NL: nl: Nederlandse Melk Unie, Den Haag

N.M.U. S: sv: Nordisk Musiker Union

NMUA US: e: National Maritime Union of America

NMV H: hu: Nemzeti Munkavédelmi Szervezet, Budapest

NMVB B: nl: Nationale Maatschappij van Buurtspoorwegen; NL: nl: Nederlandsche Maatschappij voor Buitenverblijven voor Jongemannen en Jongens

NMVN CS: cs: Náprstkovo Museum Všeobecného Národopisu

N.M.W. GB: e: National Museum of Wales

NMWA US: e: National Mineral Wool Association

NMWIA US: e: National Mineral Wool Insulation Association

NMWS US: e: Naval Mine Warfare School

NMWU WAN: e: Northern Mine Workers Union

N.N. US: e: Nevada Northern Railroad Company; S: sv: Nytta och Nöje [d: Jugendverband]

NNA US: e: National Neckwear Association; US: e: National Notion Association; WAN: e: Nigarian National Alliance

NNAC US: e: National Noise Abatement Council

NNAG NATO: e: NATO Naval Armaments Group

NNB US: e: National Needlecraft Bureau

NNBA NL: nl: Nederlandsch Nationaal Bureau voor Anthropologie

NNBL US: e: National Negro Business League

N.N.C. e: National Negotiations Committee; ZA: e: Native National Congress [gegr 1912]

NNC US: e: mil: Navy Nurses Corps; NL: nl: Noord-Nederlandse Coöperatieve; WAN: e: Northern Nigerian Congress

N.N.C.C. e: mil: National Naval Cadet Corps

NNCI GB: e: National Nursing Council Inc.

NND US: e: mil: Naval Net Depot

NNDP WAN: e: Nigerian National Democratic Party

NNF US: e: National Nephrosis Foundation; INT: e: Northern Nurses Federation, Stockholm; DK: da: Nyt Nordisk Forlag, København

NNFP MA: [d: nationale Volksunion]

NNGA US: e: Northern Nut Growers Association

NNI NL: nl: Nederlands Normalisatie-Instituut, Rijswijk

NNIL WAN: e: Northern Nigeria Investments Ltd.

NNMC US: e: mil: National Naval Medical Center

NNN N: no: Norsk Nærings- og Nytelsesmiddelarbeiderforbund

NNO IND: e: Nagaland Nationalist Organization

NNP NL: nl: Nederlandsche Nieuwsbladpers, Den Haag [gegr 1945]

NNPA US: e: National Newspaper Promotion Association

NNRC Korea: e: Neutral Nations Repa-

triation Commission [1953]
NNRF US: e: National Neurological Research Foundation
NNRI ZA: e: National Nutrition Research Institute, Pretoria
N.N.S. e: National Nautical School
NNS PI: e: National News Service
N.N.S. S: sv: Nedre Norrlands Slakteriförening, Sundsvall
NNSC Korea: e: Neutral Nations Supervisory Commission
NNSF NL: nl: Nationale Nederlandsche Studenten Federatie
NNSS NL: nl: Nederlandsche Nationaal -Socialistische Studenten
NNSY US: e: mil: Norfolk Naval Shipyard, Portsmouth, Va.
NNV NL: nl: Nederlandsche Natuurhistorische Vereeniging
NNVE D: d: Neue Norddeutsche und Vereinigte Elbeschiffahrt-AG, Hamburg
NO S: sv: Näringslivets opinionsnämnd; YU: sh: Narodna Odbrana; Narodni Odbor; Narodnooslobodilački; YU: sn: Narodnoosvobodilni
N.O. S: sv: Neptuniorden
NO NL: nl: Nijverheidsonderwijs
NOA US: e: National Opera Association; National Optical Association; National Orchestral Association [gegr 1930]; National Outboard Association; NATO: e: NATO Oil Authority; US: e: New Obligational Authority; GCA: s: Nueva Organización Anticomunista
NOAA US: e: National Oceanic (Oceanographic) and Atmospheric Administration
NOAB US: e: National Outdoor Advertising Bureau
NOB YU: sh: Narodnooslobodilačka Borba; YU: sn: Narodnoosvobodilna Borba; Narodnoosvobodilni Boj; e: National Oil Board; B: nl: Nationaal Orkest van België; US: e: mil: Naval Operating Base

N.O.B. e: mil: Naval Ordnance Barracks
NOB BR: pt: Estrada de Ferro Noroeste do Brasil
noba BRD: d: Nordbayerische Büroausstellung "noba", Nürnberg
N.O.C. e: National Olympic Committee; PTM: e: National Operations Council
NOC US: e: mil: Naval Oceanographic Office; NL: nl: Nederlands Olympisch Comité; US: e: Nuttall Ornithological Club
NOCMI B: nl: Nationale Onafhankelijke Concentratie van de Middenstand
NOD e: mil: Naval Ordnance Department (Depot)
NODA GB: e: National Operatic and Dramatic Association
NODAC US: e: mil: Naval Ordnance Data Automatic Center
NODC US: e: National Oceanographic Data Center, Washington, D.C.
NODL US: e: National Organization for Decent Literature, Chicago, Ill.
NOEB NATO: e: NATO Oil Executive Board
NOEG A: d: Niederösterreichische Eskomptegesellschaft
NÖSV A: d: Niederösterreichischer Schriftstellerverband
NOF YU: sh: Narodnooslobodilački Front; YU: sn: Narodnoosvobodilna Fronta; US: e: National Osteopathic Foundation; US: e: mil: Naval Operating Facility; S: sv: Nordisk odontologisk förening; INT: e: International NOTAM [Notices to Airmen] Office
NOFA US: e: National Office Furniture Association
NOFM NL: nl: Nederlandse Overzeese Financiërings-Maatschappij
NOFMA US: e: National Oak Flooring Manufacturers Association, Inc., Memphis 3, Tennessee
NOG BRD: d: Nahost-Gemeinschaft [Reedereien]; NL: nl: Nederlandse Onder-

wijzers Genootschap; BRD: d: Neue
Organisationsmaschinen-Gesellschaft
mbH, 7 Stuttgart 1

Noga BRD: d: Nordgau-Ausstellung, Amberg (Oberpfalz)

NOGK NL: nl: Nationaal Overleg voor
Gewestelijke Kultuur

NOGZ YU: sh: Narodni Odbor Grada Zagreba

NOHC US: e: National Open Hearth Steel
Committee

NOHSN US: e: National Organization of
Hospital Schools of Nursing

NOIB NL: nl: Nederlands Opleidingsinstituut
voor het Buitenland, Nijenrode [gegr
1946]

NOIC US: e: National Oceanographic
Instrumentation Center

NOIL GB: e: mil: Naval Ordnance Inspection Laboratory

NOIMA US: e: National Ornamental Iron
Manufacturers Association

NOJ YU: sh: Narodna Omladina Jugoslavije; Narodno Oslobodjenje Jugoslavije

NOJC US: e: National Oil Jobbers Council

NOK d: Nationales Olympisches Komitee;
CH: d: Nordostschweizerische Kraftwerke AG, Baden

NOKZ YU: sh: Narodni Odbor Kotara Zagreba

NOL US: e: mil: Naval Ordnance Laboratory, White Oak, Md.

NOLC US: e: mil: Naval Ordnance Laboratory, Corona, Calif.

NOLIA S: [d: jährliche Großmesse in Piteå]

NOL/WO US: Naval Ordnance Laboratory,
White Oak, Md.

NOMA US: e: National Office Management
Association, Willow Groove, Pa.; National Oil Marketers Association

NOMDA CDN: US: National Office Machine Dealers Association

NOMIC US: e: National Organization for
Mentally Ill Children

NOMTF US: e: mil: Naval Ordnance Missile Test Facility

NONAS PI: e: Negroes Occidental National Agricultural School

NO&NE US: e: New Orleans & Northeastern Railroad

NOO YU: sh: Narodnoosvobodilački Odbor; YU: sn: Narodnoosvobodilni Odbor; US: e: mil: Navy Oceanographic
Office

NOP YU: sh: Narodnooslobodilački Pokret; US: e: mil: Naval Ordnance Plant;
CS: cs: Nový Operativní Plán

NOPAL N: e: Northern Pan-America Line
A/S, Oslo

NOPF US: e: mil: Naval Ordnance Plant,
Forest Park, Ill.

NOPHN US: e: National Organization for
Public Health Nursing

NOPL US: e: mil: Naval Ordnance Plant,
Louisville, Kentucky

NOPP PL: pl: Naczelna Organizacja Polski
Podziemnej

NOPPMB WAN: e: Nigeria Oil Palm Produce Marketing Board

NOR YU: sh: Narodnooslobodilački Rat;
PL: pl: Narodowa Organizacja Radykalna; S: sv: Nordiska Översättarrådet;
US: e: Northrop Aircraft, Inc., Beverly Hills, Calif.

NORAD US: e: mil: North American Air
Defense Command, Colorado Springs

Norag D: d: Norddeutsche Rundfunk-AG

NORASDEFLANT NATO: e: North American Antisubmarine Defense Force Atlantic

NORATOM N: [d: norwegisches Atomforum]

NORBEX GB: [d: internationale Maschinenausstellung, Glasgow]

NORBRALA GB: e: Northern Branch of
the Library Association

NORC US: e: National Opinion Research
Center, Chicago, Ill. [gegr 1941]

NORD US: e: Northern Ordnance, Inc.,
Minneapolis, Minnesota

NORDA BRD: d: Arbeitsgemeinschaft von Hapag und Norddeutscher Lloyd im Nordatlantikdienst

Nordag BRD: d: Norddeutsche Hochseefischerei AG, 285 Bremerhaven

NORDEK INT: [d: geplante Wirtschaftsgemeinschaft DK, N, S, SF]

NORDEL INT: [d: Zusammenschluß für elektrische Stromversorgung DK, N, S, SF]

NORDFORSK INT: sv: Nordiskt samarbetsorgan för de tekniska och naturvetenskapliga forskningsråden, Stockholm [gegr 1959 in Oslo]

NORDITA DK: [sv: Nordiska Institutet för Teoretisk Atomfysik, Köpenhamn, gegr 1957]

NORD-PLAST INT: [d: skandinavische Kunststoffmesse, Kopenhagen]

NORD-PRESS DK: da: Nordisk Press Bureau, København

Nordsüd BRD: d: Nordsüd - Nürnberger Bund Großeinkaufsverband eGmbH, 43 Essen

Nordwolle BRD: d: Norddeutsche Wollkämmerei und Kammgarnspinnerei AG, Bremen

NOREA INT: e: Nordic Radio Evangelic Association

NORECHAN NATO: e: Nore Sub-Area Channel

NORLA WAN: e: Northern Region Literature Agency, Zaria [gegr 1954]

NORLANT NATO: e: Northern Subarea [Atlantic]

NORMCIE NL: nl: mil: Normalisatie Commissie Koninklijke Marine

NOROLO NL: nl: Nederlandsche Ouderraad bij het Openbaar Lager Onderwijs

NORSEACENT NATO: e: North Sea Subarea

NORTHAG NATO: e: Northern Army Group Central Europe

NORTHAMPTONS GB: e: mil: The Northamptonshire Regiment

NORTHANTS YEO GB: e: mil: The Northamptonshire Yeomanry (TerritorialArmy)

Nortraship e: Norwegian Trade and Shipping Mission

NORVEN YV: s: Comisión Venezolana de Normas Industriales

NORWEX N: [d: Briefmarkenausstellung in Oslo 1955]

NOS YU: sh: Narodno Oslobodjenje Jugoslavije; NL: nl: Nationale Opleidingsschool voor Makelaars in Vaste Goederen, Hypotheken en Assurantien; Nederlandse Omroepstichting; US: e: New Orleans Stock Exchange; BRD: d: Nordostbayerischer Saatbauverband GmbH, Marktredwitz

NOSA ZA: e: National Occupational Safety Association; US: e: National Outerwear and Sportswear Association; New Orleans and South American Steamship Company

NOSC US: e: mil: Naval Ordnance System Command

NOSK S: sv: Nordisk Odontologisk Studentkongress

NOSS S: sv: Nordens Organiserade Statstjänstemäns Samråd

NOSV CH: d: Nordostschweizerischer Verband für Schiffahrt Rhein - Bodensee

NOT PL: pl: Naczelna Organizacja Techniczna; SU: mil: [d: wissenschaftliche Organisation der Streitkräfte] ; US: e: mil: Naval Ordnance Test Station, Injokern, China Lake, Calif.; NL: nl: Nederlandse Onderwijs Televisie; H: hu: Népbiróságok Országos Tanácsa, Budapest; e: Netherlands Overseas Trust; S: sv: Nordisk Organisationstjänst [gegr 1958]

N.O.T.B. GB: e: National Ophthalmic Treatment Board

NOTINAC YV: s: Agencia Noticias Nacionales Prensa Venezolana

NOT&M US: e: New Orleans, Texas & Mexico Railway

NOTS US: e: mil: Naval Ordnance Test

Station, China Lake, Calif.

NOTU NL: nl: Nederlandse Organisatie van Tijdschriftenuitgevers

NOV YU: sn: Narodnooslobodilačka Vojska; YU: sh: Narodnooslobodilna Nojska; NL: nl: Nederlandse Onderwijzers Vereeniging; CH: d: Nordostschweizerische Verkehrsvereinigung

NOVA NL: nl: Nederlandse Organisatie van Amateurfilmclubs

NOVIB NL: nl: Nederlandse Organisatie voor Internationale Bijstand

Novocap BR: pt: companhia urbanizadora da Nova Capital do Brasil, Brasilia

NOVOS S: sv: mil: Norrländska officerskårernas vandringsprisförening för orienteringslöping på skidor

NOVS US: e: National Office of Vital Statistics

NOW PL: pl: Narodowa Organizacja Wojskowa; US: e: National Organization of Women [gegr 1966]

Nowea BRD: d: Nordwestdeutsche Ausstellungs-Gesellschaft mbH [jetzt:] Düsseldorfer Messegesellschaft mbH - Nowea, 4 Düsseldorf

Nowosti SU: [d: Nachrichtenagentur, = APN]

NOZEMA NL: nl: Nederlandsche Omroep Zender Maatschappij

NOZWO NL: nl: Nederlandse Organisatie voor Zuiver Wetenschappelijk Onderzoek

NP CS: cs: Národní Pojištění; ZA: af: Nasionale Partij; B: nl: Nationale Partij; e: National(ist) Party; H: hu: Nemzeti Parasztpárt, Budapest; NL: nl: Neutrale Partij; DIN: d: Normenprüfstelle

N.P. N: no: Norsk Presseforbund [gegr 1910] ; US: e: Northern Pacific Railroad

NPA AUS: e: National Packaging Association of Australia; US: e: National Paddleball Association; National Paperboard (Park) (Parking) (Particleboard) Association; GB: e: National Pawnbrokers Association; US: e: National Petroleum (Pharmaceutical) (Pigeon) (Pilots') (Planning) (Preservers) (Proctologic) Association; National Production Authority [gegr 1950] ; National Professional Association of Engineers, Architects and Scientists; Nebraska Pharmaceutical Association

N.P.A. GB: e: Newspaper Proprietors' Association, London [gegr 1941]

NPA WAN: e: Nigerian Ports Authority; N: no: Norske Presters Avholdforening

N.P.A.A.F. CDN: e: mil: Non-Permanent Active Air Force of Canada

NPAC US: e: National Program for Acquisitions and Cataloging; National Project in Agricultural Communications

NPAC BRD: d: Nordbadisch-Pfälzischer Automobil-Club [im AvD]

N.P.A.C.I. GB: e: National Production Advisory Council on Industry

NPACI US: e: National Production Advisory Council for Industry

NPAM CDN: e: mil: Non-Permanent Active Militia

NPAP US: e: National Psychological Association for Psychoanalysis

NPB US: e: National Parks Branch, Department of Resources and Development; National Planning Board; National Plant Board; GB: e: National Provincial Bank of England

N.&P.B. US: e: Norfolk and Portsmouth Belt Line Railroad

N.P.B.A. GB: e: National Pig Breeders Association

NPBEA US: e: National Poultry, Butter and Egg Association

NPBMA US: e: National Paper Box Manufacturers Association

NPBSA US: e: National Paper Box Suppliers Association

NPC US: e: National Panhellenic Conference

N.P.C. e: National Parks Commission

NPC US: e: National Patent Council; e: National Peace Council; US: e: National Peach (Peanut) Council

N.P.C. e: National People's Congress

NPC US: e: National Petroleum Council; National Pharmaceutical Council; National Physicians Committee; National Potato Council; PL: e: National Power Corporation; US: e: National Press Club; National Procurement Center; e: National Production Council; National Productivity Centre; US: e: National Productivity Council; National Publicity Council for Health and Welfare; NATO: e: NATO Parliamentarians' Conference; NATO Pipeline Committee

N.P.C. e: mil: Naval Personnel Committee

NPC S: sv: Nordiska Presscentralen [gegr 1918]; WAN: e: Northern People's Congress

NPCA US: e: National Pest Control Association

NPCh PL: pl: Niezależna Partia Chłopska

NPCHWS US: e: National Publicity Council for Health and Welfare Services

NPCI US: e: National Potato Chip Institute

N.P.C.P. EAK: e: Nairobi People's Convention Party

NPD BRD: d: Nationaldemokratische Partei Deutschlands, 3 Hannover 1 [gegr 1964]

NPDA US: e: National Plywood Distributors Association

NPDAA US: e: National Pharmaceutical Direct Advertising Association

NPEA. D: d: NS: Nationalpolitische Erziehungsanstalt [= Napola]

NPEA US: e: National Printing Equipment Association

NPF CS: cs: Národní Pozemkový Fond; US: e: National Paraplegia Foundation; National Parkinson Foundation

N.P.F. e: National Pearl Federation

NPF US: e: mil: National Powder Factory;

NL: nl: Nederlandse Pluimvee Federatie

N.P.F. e: Newspaper Press Fund; WAN: e: Nigeria Police Force; N: no: Norske Patrioters Forbund; WAN: e: Northern Progressive Front

N.P.F.A. GB: e: National Playing Fields Association; e: National Poultry Farmers' Association

NPFA US: e: National Power Fluid Association

NPFFG US: e: National Plant, Flower and Fruit Guild

NPFFPA US: e: National Prepared Frozen Food Processors Association

NPFI US: e: National Plant Food Institute

NPFO US: e: Nuclear Power Field Office, Fort Belvoir, Va.

NPFS US: e: mil: Naval Pre-Flight School

N.P.G. e: National Portrait Gallery

NPG US: e: mil: Naval Proving Ground, Dahlgreen, Va.; NL: nl: Nederlandsch Padvinders Gilde; NATO: e: Nuclear Planning Group d: Nukleare Planungsgruppe

NPGL GB: e: National Popular Government League

N.P.G.W.A. e: National Plate Glass Workers Association

NPHC e: National Public Housing Conference

N.P.H.T. e: Nuffield Provincial Hospitals Trust

NPI US: e: National Petroleum Institute [gegr 1919]

N.P.I. GB: e: National Provident Institution for Mutual Life Insurance, London E.C. 3 [gegr 1835]

NPI US: e: Neuro-Psychiatric Institute; N: no: Norsk Produktivitetsinstitutt

NPIP US: e: National Poultry Improvement Plant

NPIPF GB: e: Newspaper and Printing Industries Pension Fund

NPIRI US: e: National Printing Ink Research Institute, Bethlehem, Pa.

NPJ N: no: Norsk Presseforbunds Journalistgruppe

NPJPA US: e: National Prune Juice Packers Association

N.P.K. D: d: mil: Nachrichtenmittelprüfungskommission

NPK S: sv: Nordiska privatflygkommittén; BRD: d: Normalprofilbuchkommission [VDEh], 4 Düsseldorf; Nationale Pappelkommission

NPKW PL: pl: Naczelny Polski Komitet Wojskowy

NPL GB: e: National Physical Laboratory, Teddington, Middlessex; ZA: e: National Physical Laboratory, Pretoria

N.P.L. e: National Protestant League

NPL US: e: New York Public Library

N.P.L. US: e: Nonpartisan League [North Dakota]; N: no: Norges pedagogiske landslag [gegr 1924]

NPLO NATO: e: NATO Production and Logistics Organization

NPMA US: e: National Piano Manufacturers Association of America

NPO US: e: mil: Navy Post Office; Navy Purchasing Office; NL: nl: Nederlandse Pluimvee Organisatie

NPOLA US: e: mil: Navy Publishing Office, Los Angeles

NPORI e: National Public Opinion Research Institute

N.P.P. R: [e: National Peasant Party]; JA: e: National People's Party; IRQ: e: National Progressive Party; Z: e: National Progress Party; e: National Prohibition Party

NPP US: e: mil: Naval Propellant Plant, Indian Head, Md.; NL: nl: Nederlandsche Pensioen Partij; H: hu: Nemzeti Paraszpárt, Budapest; GH: e: Northern People's Party [gegr 1954]

NPPA e: National Pickle Packers Association; US: e: National Press Photographers Association; National Probation and Parole Association

NPPC US: e: National Power Policy Committee; Nuclear Power Plant Company, Knutsford

NPPF US: e: National Poultry Producers Federation

NPPO US: e: mil: Navy Publications and Printing Office

NPPPP EAK: e: Northern Province People Progressive Party

NPPSO US: e: Navy Publications and Printing Service Office

NPPTA US: e: National Public Parks Tennis Association

NPPTB GB: e: National Pig Progeny Testing Board

NPR PL: pl: Narodowa Partia Robotnicza [1920 . . . 37]; J: e: National Police Reserve; N: no: Norsk Presseforbunds Redaktørgruppe

NPRCG e: Nuclear Public Relations Contact Group

NPRI US: e: National Psychiatric Reform Institute

NPRL ZA: e: National Physical Research Laboratory

NPRR US: e: Northern Pacific Railroad

NPS US: e: National Park Service; National Philatelic Society; e: National Plumbers' Society

N.P.S. GB: e: National Portrait Society; National Press Service

NPS S: sv: Nordiska Press Syndikatet

NPSB US: e: Newsprint Service Bureau

NPSL US: e: National Professional Soccer League

N.P.T. e: Nine-Power Treaty

NPT US: e: mil: Nonproliferation Treaty [d: nukleare Waffen betreffend, um 1969]

NPTA US: e: National Paper Trade Association of the United States; National Piano Travellers Association; National Postal Transport Association

NPTAUS US: e: National Paper Trade Association of the United States

NPTB PL: pl: Nowohuckie Przedsiębiorstwo Transportowe Budownictwa
NPTFB US: e: National Park Trust Fund Board
N.P.U. GB: e: National Pharmaceutical Union
NPU US: e: National Postal Union; ZA: e: Newspaper Press Union of South Africa
NPV NL: nl: Nederlandsche Padvinders Vereeniging
NPVLA US: e: National Paint, Varnish and Lacquer Association
NPZ CS: cs: Náčelník Proviantního Zásobování
N.Q.B. US: e: National Quotation Bureau
NQBA GB: e: National Quality Bacon Association
N.R. D: d: mil: Nachrichtenregiment
NR S: sv: Näringsfrihetsrådet; YU: sh: Narodna Republika; CS: cs: Národní Rada; A: CH: d: Nationalrat; US: e: mil: Naval Reserve; WAN: e: Nigerian Railway
N.R. GB: e: mil: Nigeria Regiment; S: sv: Nordiska rådet [gegr 1955]
NR S: sv: Nordisk Resebureau, Stockholm; N: no: Norges Rederforbund; Norsk Redaktørforening; Norsk Regnesentral, Oslo
N.R. GB: e: mil: Northamptonshire Regiment
NR N: no: Norsk Rikskringkasting
NRA PL: pl: Naczelna Rada Adwokacka; US: e: National Reclamation Association; National Recovery Administration [gegr 1933]; National Recreation Association; GB: e: National Reform Association; US: e: National Rehabilitation (Renderers) (Restaurants) (Rifle) Association; Negro Radio Association; H: hu: Nemzeti Repülő Alap, Budapest
NRAA US: e: National Railway Appliances Association
N.R.A.B. e: National Railroad Adjustment Board
NRACCO US: e: mil: Navy Regional Air Cargo Central Office
N.R.A.N.C. e: Northern Rhodesia African National Congress
NRAO US: e: National Radio Astronomy Observatory, Green Bank, Va.; US: e: mil: Navy Regional Accounts Office
N.R.A.S. GB: e: Northern Rhodesia Administrative Service
NRB CS: cs: Národní Rada Badatelská; e: National (Natural) Resources Board; GB: e: Natural Rubber Bureau
N.R.C. e: National Radium Commission; National Reconversion Commission; National Recreation Centre
NRC WAL: e: National Reformation Council; US: e: National Republican Club; ET: e: National Research Centre, Cairo; CDN: US: e: National Research Council; PI: e: National Research Council; US: e: National Resources Committee (Council)
N.R.C. ZA: e: Native Representative Council [gegr 1935]; NL: [e: Netherlands Reactor Centre; Netherlands Red Cross]
NRC WAN: e: Nigerian Railway Corp.; GB: e: Northern Railfans' Club
NRCA US: e: National Retail Credit Association; National Roofing Contractors Association; National Resources Council of America
N.R.C.C. US: e: National Republican Congressional Committee; CDN: e: National Research Council of Canada
NRCD GB: e: National Reprographic Centre for Documentation, Hatfield, Herts. [gegr 1967]
NRCI US: e: National Red Cherry Institute
N.R.C.P. e: Northern Rhodesia Commonwealth Party
NRCS e: National Radiation Control Service; GB: e: National Roller Canary Society
N.R.D. e: mil: Naval Recruiting Depart-

ment; Naval Reserves Department

N.R.D.B. e: National Resources Development Board; Natural Rubber Development Board, London

NRDC GB: e: National Research and Development Corporation, London [gegr 1948]

NRDGA US: e: National Retail Dry Goods Association

NRDL US: e: mil: Naval Radiological Defense Laboratory

NRDS US: e: Nuclear Rocket Development Station

NRECA US: e: National Rural Electric Cooperative Association

N.R.F. R: [e: National Regeneration Front]; e: National Relief Fund

NRF BRD: d: Niedersächsischer Rundfunk, 3 Hannover [gegr 1970] N: no: Norges Roforbund; S: sv: Norra Realarnes Förening, Stockholm [gegr 1937]; N: no: Norske Rørleggerbedrifters Landsforening, Oslo; Norsk Radiofabrikantas Forbund

NRFA US: e: National Retail Furniture Association

NRFEA US: e: National Retail Farm Equipment Association

NRFF US: e: National Research Foundation for Fertility

NRFV D: d: Norddeutscher Rugby-Fußball-Verband, Hannover

NRG NL: nl: Nederlands Radiogenootschap

NRGD BRD: d: Niederrheinischer Golf-Club Duisburg

NRH PL: pl: Naczelna Rada Harcerska

NRHA US: e: National Retail Hardware Association, Indianapolis 4, Indiana

NRHC US: e: National Rivers and Harbors Congress

NRHS US: e: National Railway Historical Society

NRIC GB: e: National Reserves Investigation Committee

NRIM J: e: National Research Institute for Metals, Tokyo

NRIMS ZA: e: National Research Institute for Mathematical Sciences

NRITL US: e: Northeastern Regional Instructional Television Library, Cambridge, Massachusetts

NRK INT: sv: Nordiska rotarykongressen; N: no: Norges Røde Kors [gegr 1865]; S: sv: Norra Reals Konstförening, Stockholm; N: no: Norsk Rikskringkasting [gegr 1933]

NRL PL: pl: Naczelna Rada Łowiecka

NRL PL: pl: Naczelna Rada Ludowa; GB: e: National Reference Library; US: e: mil: Naval Research Laboratory, Washington, D.C.; GB: e: Nelson Research Laboratory; N: no: Norske Radiohandleres Landsforbund

NRLB GB: e: Northern Regional Library Bureau

NRLCA US: e: National Rural Letter Carriers Association

NRLDA US: e: National Retail Lumber Dealers Association

NRLP e: Northern Rhodesia Liberal (Liberty) Party

NRLSI GB: e: National Reference Library for Science and Invention, London

N.R.L.T.U.C. e: Native Races Liquor Traffic United Committee

NRM e: National Railways of Mexico

NRMA US: e: National Retail Merchants Association, New York 1, N.Y.

NRMC US: e: National Records Management Council

NRMCA US: e: National Ready-Mixed Concrete Association

NRMCEN US: e: mil: Naval Records Management Center

N.R.M.F. S: sv: Norra Reals Marinförening, Stockholm

NRMS US: e: mil: Naval Reserve Midshipmen's School

NRO CS: cs: Narodní Rada Obchodnictva;

GB: e: Naval Repair Organization
NROS CS: cs: Nejvyšší Rada Obrany Státu
NROTC US: e: Naval Reserve Officers Training Corps
NROW PL: pl: Naczelna Rada Odbudowy Warszawy; Naczelna Rada Organizowania Wystaw
NRP PL: pl: Narodowa Robotnicza Partja; BRD: d: Nationale Reichspartei; NL: nl: Nederlandse Raffinaderij van Petroleumproducten, Haarlem
N.R.P. e: New Rhodesia Party [gegr 1960]
NRPB US: e: National Resources Planning Board
N.R.P.C. e: National Religious Publicity Council
NRPJ YU: sh: Nezavisna Radnička Partija Jugoslavije
NRPRA GB: e: Natural Rubber Producers Research Association
NRR GB: e: mil: The Northern Rhodesia Regiment
NRRB US: e: National Recovery Review Board
NRRS US: e: mil: Naval Radio Research Station
NRS PL: pl: Naczelna Rada Spóĺdzielcza; US: e: National Re-employment Service; National Refugee Service
N.R.S. GB: e: National Rose Society of Great Britain; e: Navy Records Society; News Research Service
N.R.S.C. e: National Railway Shopmen's Council
NRSE YU: sh: Narodna Radikalna Stranka u Egzilu
NRSL US: e: mil: Navy Radio and Sound Laboratory
NRSO US: e: mil: Navy Resale System Office
N.R.T. e: National Radium Trust; GB: e: National Reference Tribunal (coal industry]
NRTA US: e: National Retired Teachers Association

NRTCMA US: e: National Retail Tea and Coffee Merchants Association
N.R.T.F. e: National Road Transport Federation
NRTS US: e: National Reactor Testing Station, Idaho
NRU GR: e: National Radical Union
N.R.U. e: National Reform Union
NRU NL: nl: Nederlandse Radio Unie [gegr 1947]
N.R.U.T.U.C. e: Northern Rhodesia United Trades Union Congress
NRV NL: nl: N.V. Nederlandsche Rijnvaartvereeniging, Rotterdam; Nederlandse Röntgen Vereniging; BRD: d: Norddeutscher Regatta-Verein
NRWC US: e: National Right to Work Committee
N.S. D: d: mil: Nachrichtenschule; S: sv: Namnlösa Sällskapet, Uppsala
NS YU: sh: Narodna Skupština; CS: cs; Národní-Socialistická Strana; Národní Shromáždění; Národní Souručenství
N.S. N: no: Nasjonal Samling; e: National Socialism; National Society
NS d: Nationalsozialismus; US: e: National Steel Corporation; UN: e: Natural Sciences [department of UNESCO]; e: mil: Naval Store Department
N.S. S: sv: Navigationsskolan, Stockholm
NS NL: nl: Nederlandsche Spoorwegen; CS: cs: Nejvyšší Soud; H: hu: Nemzeti Segély, Budapest
N.S. e: Newspaper Society; S: sv: Nordsvenska Köpmanna AB, Östersund; US: e: Norfolk Southern Railroad Company
NS N: no: Norges Skiforbund, Oslo; NL: nl: Normaal Schietschool; S: sv: Norrköpingsortens Slakteriförening; GB: e: mil: The Prince of Wales's North-Staffordshire Regiment; YU: Novosadski sajam [d: Messe]
N.S. e: Numismatic Society; Nursing Service (Staff)

NSA ZA: e: Natal Society of Artists

N.S.A. e: National Salvation Army; GB: e: National Sawmilling Association

NSA US: e: National Secretaries Association; US: e: mil: National Security Agency, Ft. Meade [gegr 1952]; US: e: National Shellfisheries Association; National Sheriffs Association; NATO: e: National Shipping Authority; US: e: National Showmen's (Shuffleboard) Association; National Silo Association, Louisville 7, Ky.; GB: e: National Skating Association; US: e: National Ski Association of America [gegr 1904]; National Slag (Slate) Association; GB: e: National Society of Artists; US: e: National Society of Auctioneers; D: d: Nationalsozialistische Angestelltenschaft; US: e: National Standards Association, Washington, D.C.; National Student Association; US: e: mil: Naval Support Activity; US: e: Neurosurgical Society of America

N.S.A. e: New Society of Artists

NSA N: no: Norges Sosialdemokratiske Arbeiderparti

N.S.A. GB: e: Nursery School Association

NSAA US: e: National Ski Association of America [gegr 1904]; GB: e: National Sulphuric Acid Association; US: e: National Supply Association of America; Norwegian Singers' Association of America

N.S.A.B. e: Nursing Service Advisory Board

NSAC J: e: National Space Activities Council

N.S.A.C.S. e: National Society for the Abolition of Cruel Sports

NSAD US: e: National Society of Art Directors; D: d: Nationalsozialistischer Arbeitsdienst

NSAE US: e: mil: National Security Agency Europe; GB: e: National Society for Art Education

NSÄB = NSDÄB

N.S.A.G. e: National Society for the Advancement of Gastroenterology

N.S.A.G.B. GB: e: Nursery School Association of Great Britain

NSAI e: National Secretaries Association International

N.S.A.M. e: National Society of Art Master

NSAM US: e: mil: Naval School of Aviation Medicine

NSanF US: e: National Sanitation Foundation

NSAP S: sv: Nationalsocialistiska arbetarpartiet

NSAS e: National Smoke Abatement Socie

NSAU S: sv: Nationalsocialistisk Arbetarungdom

NSB NL: nl: Nationaal-Socialistische Beweging; BRD: d: Nationale Sammlungsbewegung

N.S.B. B: nl: mil: Nationale Strijdersbond; GB: e: National Service Board; GB: e: National Society for the Blind; National Softwood Brokers; National Society of Brushmakers

NSB e: National Steel Board; US: e: mil: Naval Submarine Base; NL: nl: Nederlandsche Schildersgezellenbond; H: hu: Nemzeti Sport Bizottság, Budapest; US: e: Newsprint Service Bureau; N: no Norges Statsbaner

NSBA US: e: National Safe Boating Association; National School Boards Association; GB: e: National Sheep Breeders Association; US: e: National Shrimp Breeders Association; GB: e: National Silica Brickmakers Association; US: e: National Sugar Brokers Association

NSBB US: e: National Society for Business Budgeting

NSBC US: e: National Shoe Board Conference

NSBdF D: d: Nationalsozialistischer Bund der Frontsoldaten (Stahlhelm)

NSBdN NL: d: Nationalsozialistische Bewegung der Niederlande

NSBDT D: d: Nationalsozialistischer Bund Deutscher Technik [gegr 1943]

NSBMA US: e: National Small Business Men's Association

N.S.B.M.M. e: National Society of Brass and Metal Mechanics

NSBO D: d: Nationalsozialistische Betriebszellen-Organisation

N.S.B.P. B:nl: Nationaal Syndikaat van de Belgische Politie

NSBY GB: e: mil: North Somerset and Bristol Yeomanry

NSC US: e: National Safety Council; e: National Savings Committee; e: mil: National Security Command; US: e: mil: National Security Council; US: e: National Space Council; e: National Sporting Club; NATO: e: NATO Supply Center; D: d: stud: Naumburger Senioren-Convent; US: e: mil: Naval-Schools Command; Naval Supply Center, Norfolk Navy Yard, Va.

N.S.C. e: Northern States Conference; Nuclear Science Centre

N.S.C.A. e: National Seed Crushers Association

NSCA US: e: National Soccer Coaches Association of America; GB: e: National Society for Clean Air

N.S.C.B.M.W. e: National Society of Coppersmiths, Braziers and Metal Workers

NSCCA US: e: National Society for Crippled Children and Adults

NschSLw BRD: d: mil: Nachschubschule der Luftwaffe

N.S.C.N. e: National Society of Children's Nurseries

NSCO US: e: The National Supply Company Inc., New York 20, N.Y.; e: mil: Naval Security Control Office

N.S.C.R. e: National Society for Cancer Relief

N.S.C.R.S.P.A. GB: e: National Safety Congress of the Royal Society for the Prevention of Accidents

NSČS CS: cs: Národopisná Společnost Československá

NSCS US: e: mil: National Security Council Staff

NSČS CS: cs: Numismatická Společnost Československá

NSCTE US: e: National Society of College Teachers of Education

NSD BRD: d: Nationale Solidarität Deutschlands

NSD GB: e: mil: Naval Stores Department; US: e: mil: Naval Supply Depot

NSDA US: e: National Sprayer and Duster Association; National Surplus Dealers Association

NSDÄB D: d: Nationalsozialistischer Deutscher Ärztebund [gegr 1929]

NSDAP D: d: Nationalsozialistische Deutsche Arbeiterpartei; NL: nl: Nederlandse Sociaal-Democratische Arbeiderspartij

NSDAR US: e: National Society Daughters of the American Revolution

NSDAV D: d: Nationalsozialistischer Deutscher Arbeiter-Verein eV, München

NSDB PI: e: National Science Development Board; D: d: Nationalsozialistischer Deutscher Dozenten-Bund [gegr 1935]

NSDFA US: e: National Steel Door and Frame Association

NSDFB D: d: mil: Nationalsozialistischer Deutscher Frontkämpfer-Bund (Stahlhelm)

NSDJA US: e: Northern Sash and Door Jobbers Association

NSDMB D: d: mil: Nationalsozialistischer Deutscher Marine-Bund [gegr 1935]

NSDoB D: d: = NSDB

NSDP US: e: National Society of Denture Prothetists

NSDR e: mil: National Ships Destination Room

NSDStB D: d: Nationalsozialistischer Deutscher Studentenbund [gegr 1926]

N.S.D.U. e: National Stevedores' and Dockers' Union

NSE US: e: National Sales Executives, New York, N.Y.; e: National Society for Epileptics; e: mil: Naval Store Establishment; GB: e: Nottingham Society of Engineers

N.S.E.A. e: National Sailmakers Employers' Association

N.S.E.C. e: National Service Entertainments Council

NSEC US: e: Nuclear Science and Engineering Corporation, Pittsburgh, Pa.

N.S.E.S. GB: e: National Society of Electrotypers and Stereotypers

NSEVWP CH: d: Nationalsozialistische Eidgenössische Volks- und Wirtschaftspartei

NSF US: e: National Sanitation Foundation [gegr 1945]; National Science Foundation, Washington, D.C.; National Sharecroppers Fund; S: sv: Nationalskautforbundet; D: d: Nationalsozialistische Frauenschaft; GB: e: mil: Naval Stock Fund; NL: nl: Nederlandsche Seintoestellen Fabriek [gegr 1918]; S: sv: Nordens Skogsägareorganisationers Förbund; N: no: Norges Skøyteforbund; Norges Standardiseringsforbund, Oslo 1; Norges Svømmeforbund; Norsk Speiderguttforbund; Norsk Sykepleierforbund; Norsk Syndikalistik Federasjon; e: mil: Nuclear Strategic Forces

N.S.F.A. e: National "Safety First" Association

NSFC GB: e: North Staffordshire Field Club

NSFGA CDN: e: Nova Scotia Fruit Growers Association

NSF-I US: e: National Science Fair-International, Baltimore, Md.

NSFK D: d: Nationalsozialistisches Fliegerkorps

NS FNRJ YU: sh: Narodna Skupština Federativne Narodne Republike Jugoslavije

NSFO sv: Nationalsocialistiska Fackorganisationerna

NSFRC US: e: National Soil and Fertilizer Research Committee

NSFW D: d: Nationalsozialistisches Frauenwerk

NSG B: nl: Nationale Studentengroepering Gent

NSGA US: e: National Sand and Gravel Association; National Sporting Goods Association

NSGB GB: e: Newtonian Society of Great Britain

NSGC US: e: National Swine Growers Council

NSGCI US: e: National Self-Government Committee, Inc.

N.S.G.W. e: National Society of Glass Workers

NSG "KdF" D: d: Nationalsozialistische Gemeinschaft "Kraft durch Freude" [gegr 1933]

NSGPMA GB: e: National Salt Glazed Pipe Manufacturers Association

NSGW US: e: Native Sons of the Golden West

NSH CH: f: Nouvelle Société Helvétique

NSHA US: e: National Steeplechase and Hunt Association; GB: e: National Student Health Association

NS-Hago D: d: Nationalsozialistische Handwerks-, Handels- und Gewerbeorganisation

NSHC INT: e: North Sea Hydrographic Commission [gegr 1962]

N.Sh.Rgt CDN: e: mil: North Shore Regiment

N.S.H.S. B: nl: Nationale Stichting voor Hogere Studiën

NSI US: e: National Shoe Institute; GB: e: National Society of Inventors

NSIA US: e: National Security Industrial Association

NSIC e: Nuclear Safety Information Center

NSID US: e: National Society of Interior

Designers

NSIM e: National Society of Industrial Mediators

NSIME GB: e: North Staffordshire Institute of Mining Engineers

NSIS GB: e: National Softwood Importers' Section, Timber Trade Federation

NSIT f: Nouvelle Société Interafricaine de Transport

N.S.J.V. B: nl: Nationaal-socialistische Jeugd Vlaanderen

NSK D: d: Nationalsozialistische Kulturgemeinde

NSKK D: d: Nationalsozialistisches Kraftfahrkorps

N.S.K.O. B: nl: Nationaal Secretariaat van het Katholiek Onderwijs

NSKOV D: d: Nationalsozialistische Kriegsopferversorgung

N.S.L. GB: e: National Service (Sporting) (Sunday) League; N: no: Norske Sykegymnasters Landsforbund

NSLB D: d: Nationalsozialistischer Lehrerbund

NSLI US: e: mil: National Service Life Insurance

NSLRB US: e: National Steel Labor Relations Board

NSM PL: pl: Nauczycielska Spółdzielnia Mieszkaniowa; GB: e: National Socialist Movement; US: e: National Student Marketing Corporation, Washington, D.C. [gegr 1964] ; NL: nl: Nederlandsch Spoorweg Museum; D: d: Neue Sezession, München

N.S.M. N: no: Norsk Sjøfartsmuseum

NSMA US: e: National Scale Men's Association; National Shoe Manufacturers Association; National Soup Mix Association; Nebraska State Medical Association

N.S.M.C. US: e: National Student Marketing Corporation [vgl: NSM]

NSMHC GB: e: National Society for Mentally Handicapped Children

NSMP GB: e: National Society of Master Patternmakers; US: e: National Society of Mural Painters

NSMPA US: e: National Screw Machine Products Association

NSMR US: e: National Society for Medical Research

NSMSES US: e: mil: Navy Surface Missile Systems Engineering Station

N.S.M.W.T.W. e: National Society of Metal, Wire and Tube Workers

NSNA US: e: National Student Nurses' Association

NSNEW US: e: National Society of New England Women

NSNP [d: Nationalverband der neuen Generation. Russische Emigranten]

NSNRBiH YU: sh: Narodna Skupština Narodne Republike Bosne i Hercegovine

NSNRD YU: sh: Narodne Skupština Narodne Republike Slovenije

N.S.N.-S. e: National Society of Non-Smokers

NSO US: e: National Security Organization

N.S.O. GB: e: National Students' Organization; National Symphony Orchestra; NL: nl: Nederlands Studenten Orkest

NSOEA US: e: National Stationery and Office Equipment Association

NSOG D: d: Nationalsozialistische Opfergemeinschaft

N.S.O.P.A. GB: e: National Society of Operative Printers and Assistants

NSP PL: pl: Narodowe Stronnictwo Pracy; GB: e: National Society of Painters; PL: pl: Nauczycielska Spółdzielnia Pracy; NL: nl: Stichting het Nederlandsch Scheepsbouwkundig Proefstation, Wageningen; S: sv: Nylands Svenska Lantbruksproducentförbund

NSPA US: e: National Scholastic Press Association; National Society of Public Accountants; National Soybean Processors Association

N.S.P.A. e: National Spinsters' Pensions

Association

NSPA US: e: National Standard Parts Association; CDN: e: Nova Scotia Pharmaceutical Association

NSPB US: e: National Security Planning Board; e: National Society for the Prevention of Blindness

NSPC US: e: National Security Planning Commission

NSPCA GB: e: National Society for the Prevention of Cruelty to Animals

NSPCC GB: e: National Society for the Prevention of Cruelty to Children

NSPE GB: e: National Society of Physical Education; US: e: National Society of Professional Engineers, Washington, D.C. 20006

NSPF N: no: Norsk Speiderpikeforbund

NSPFEA US: e: National Spray Painting and Finishing Equipment Association

NSPI US: e: National Swimming Pool Institute

NSPLO NATO: e: NATO Sidewinder Production and Logistics Organization

NSPO US: e: mil: Navy Special Projects Office; NATO: e: NATO Sidewinder Program Office

N.S.P.O.B. B: nl: Nationale Stichting voor het Poolonderzoek van België

NSPP PL: pl: Niezależna Socjalistyczna Partia Pracy; e: Nuclear Safety Pilot Plant

NSPRA US: e: National School Public Relations Association

NSPRI WAN: e: Nigerian Stored Products Research Institute

NSPS US: e: National Ski Patrol System

N.S.P.S.E.P. GB: e: National Society of Painters, Sculptors, Engravers and Potters

N.S.P.V.D. e: National Society for the Prevention of Venereal Diseases

N.S.P.W. e: National Society of Pottery Workers

N.S.P.Y.G. e: National Society for the Protection of Young Girls

NSR PL: pl: Narodowe Stronnictwo Robotników; NL: nl: Nederlandse Studenten Raad; N: no: Norske Studenters Roklubb

N.S.R. CDN: e: mil: North-Shore Regiment; GB: e: Northern Staffordshire Railway

NSRA US: e: National Shoe Retailers Association; National Shorthand Reporters Association; GB: e: National Small Bore Rifle Association

NSRB US: e: mil: National Security Resources Board; D: d: Nationalsozialistischer Rechtswahrerbund

NSRC US: e: National Stereophonic Radio Committee

NSRDA D: d: Nationalsozialistischer Reichsverband der deutschen Arbeitsopfer

NSRDK D: d: Nationalsozialistischer Reichsverband Deutscher Kriegsopfer

NSRDW D: d: Nationalsozialistische Reichsfachschaft Deutscher Werbefachleute

NSRF N: no: Norges Salgs- og Reklameforbund; CDN: e: Nova Scotia Research Foundation

NSRK D: d: Nationalsozialistisches Reiterkorps

NSRL D: d: Nationalsozialistischer Reichsbund für Leibesübungen

NSRMCA US: e: National Star Route Mail Carriers Association

NSRO US: e: National Security Resource Organization

N.S.R.O. NL: nl: Nationaal-socialistische Rijksradio-Omroep

NSRP US: e: National States Rights Party

NSS S: sv: Nathan Söderblom-Sällskapet [gegr 1941]; US: e: National Sculpture Society

N.S.S. e: National Secular Society

NSS US: e: National Serigraph (Snapdragon) Society; GB: e: National Spastics Society; D: d: Nationalsozialistisc

Schwesternschaft; US: e: National Speleological Society [gegr 1929]

N.S.S. e: Nature Study Society; NL: nl: Nederlandse Stichting voor Statistiek; GB: e: New Shakespeare Society; S: sv: Norrköpings segelsällskap; N: no: Norsk Studentsamband

NSSA US: e: National Sanitary Supply Association; National Skeet Shooting Association; National Skirt and Sportswear Association; National Suffolk Sheep Association; North -South Skirmish Association

NSSB D: d: Nationalsozialistischer Schülerbund (Studentenbund)

NSSC US: e: National Society for the Study of Communications; US: e: mil: Naval Ship System Command

N.S.S.C. e: Nelson Steamship Company

NSSCC US: e: National Space Surveillance Control Center

NSSE US: e: National Society for the Study of Education

NSSEA US: e: National School Supply Equipment Association

NSSFNS US: e: National Scholarship Service and Fund for Negro Students

NSSI GB: e: National School Service Institute

NSSO US: e: mil: Navy Ships Store Office

NSSR US: e: New School for Social Research

NSSTC US: e: National Small Shipment Traffic Conference

NSSTE US: e: National Society of Sales Training Executives

N.S.S.U. e: National Sunday School Union

NST S: sv: Nordens Samverkande Tegelindustriföreningar

N.St. GB: e: mil: North Staffordshire Reğiment

NSTA US: e: National Science Teachers Association; National Shoe Travellers Association; S: sv: Norrköpings Stads Tekniska Aftonskola

NSTAFFS GB: e: mil: The North Staffordshire Regiment (The Prince of Wales's)

NSTC US: e: National Screw Thread Commission; National Security Training Commission (Corps); National Shade Tree Conference

N.S.T.C. e: National Society of Tailors' Cutters; CDN: e: Nova Scotia Technical College

NSTIC GB: e: mil: Naval Scientific and Technical Information Centre

NSTP US: e: National Society of Television Producers

NSTU INT: sv: Nordiska studentteaterunionen

NSTV D: d: Nieder-Schlesischer Turn -Verein

NSU US: e: National Seamen's Union; NL: nl: Nederlandsche Scheepvaart Unie [gegr 1969] ; S: sv: Nordiska Skolungdomsförbundet; S: sv: Nordiskt Sommaruniversitet

NSÚ CS: cs: Novinářský Studijní Ústav

NSU BRD: d: [jetzt:] NSU Motorenwerke AG, 7107 Neckarsulm; S: sv: Nusvensk Ungdom

NSUA N: no: Norges Studerande Ungdoms Avholdsforbund

NSUF N: no: Nasjonal Samlings Ungdomsfylking

NSV D: d: Nationalsozialistische Volkswohlfahrt; NL: nl: Nederlands Syndicalistisch Vakverbond; Nieuwe School Vereeniging; D: d: Norddeutscher Ski -Verband, Berlin

N.S.V. EW: Nöukogude Sotsialstlik Vabariik

N.S.V.A.P. B: nl: Nationaal-Socialistische Vlaamse Arbeiderspartij

NSW PL: pl: Najwyższy Sąd Wojskowy; BRD: d: Norddeutsche Seekabelwerke AG, 289 Nordenham

N.S.W.A. e: National Silk Workers' Association

NSWA US: e: National Social Welfare

Assembly

NSWGR AUS: e: New South Wales Government Railways

N.S.W.K.T. e: National Society of Woolcombers and Kindred Trades

NSWMA US: e: National Soft Wheat Millers Association

NSWO NL: nl: Nationaal Socialistische Werknemers Organisatie

NSWPP US: e: National Socialist White Peoples Party

N.S.W.U.T. AUS: e: New South Wales University of Technology

NSY US: e: mil: Naval shipyard

N.S.Y. GB: e: New Scotland Yard

NSY GB: e: mil: The North Somerset Yeomanry (Territorial Army)

NSZ PL: pl: Narodowe Siły Zbrojne

N.T. GB: e: National Trust of Places of Historic Interest or Natural Beauty

NT US: e: National Trust for Historic Preservation

N.T. N: no: Norske Turistforening

NTA PL: pl: Najwyższy Trybunał Administracyjny; US: e: National Tax Association; National Technical Association; National Tuberculosis Association, New York 19, N.Y. [gegr 1904]; NL: nl: Nederlandsch Telegraaf Agentschap, Amsterdam; CDN: e: Newfoundland Teachers Association; S: sv: Nordiska Tidningarnas Arbetsgivarenämnd; WAN: e: Northern Teachers Association; US: e: Northern Textile Association

NTAA US: e: National Travelers Aid Association

NTAC NL: nl: Nederlandse Touring- en Auto Club

NTAST J: e: National Translation Association of Science and Technology

N.T.B. NL: nl: Nederlandse Toonkunstenaarsbond

NTB N: no: Norsk Telegrambyrå, Oslo [gegr 1867]

NTC US: e: National Telemetering Conference; GB: e: National Television Council; US: e: National Theater Conference; National Thrift Committee; EAU: e: National Trading Corporation; US: e: National Travel Club, New York 19, N.Y.; US: e: mil: Naval Training Center (Command); WAN: e: Nigeria Tobacco Company; GB: e: Nuffield Trust Committee

NTCA US: e: National Telephone Cooperative Association

NTCHA GB: e: National Taxi and Car Hire Association

N.T.D. e: mil: Naval Torpedo Depot

NTDA GB: e: National Trade Development Association; National Tyre Distributors Association

NTDC US: e: mil: Naval Training Device Center

NTDF S: sv: Nordiska tidningsdistributionsföretagens förbund [gegr 1948]

NTDMA US: e: National Tool and Die Manufacturers Association

NTDRA US: e: National Tire Dealers and Retreaders Association

NTEF US: e: National Tennis Educational Foundation

NTETA GB: e: National Traction Engine and Tractor Association

NTF S: sv: Nationalföreningen för trafiksäkerhetens främjande, Stockholm

N.T.F. e: National Temperance Federation

NTF US: e: National Turkey Federation; N: no: Norske Tannlegeforening

NTFC US: e: National Television Film Council

NTG BRD: d: Nachrichtentechnische Gesellschaft im VDE, 6 Ffm; Niedersächsische Treuhand GmbH, 3 Hannover

NTGB GB: e: North Thames Gas Board

NTH N: no: Norges Tekniske Høgskole, Trondheim [gegr 1910]

NTHP US: e: National Trust for Historic

Preservation

NTI S: sv: Netzlers Tekniska Institut, Göteborg

NTIST J: e: National Translation Institute for Science and Technology, Tokyo

N.T.L. e: National Temperance League

NTLDO US: e: mil: Navy Terminal Leave Disbursing Office

NTLS US: e: National Truck Leasing System

NTM CS: cs: Národní Technické Museum

NTMA US: e: National Tank Manufacturers Association; National Terrazzo and Mosaic Association

NTN PL: pl: Najwyższy Trybunal Narodowy

NTNF N: no: Norges Teknisk-Naturvitenskapelige Forskningsråd, Oslo [gegr 1946]

NTO S: sv: Nationaltemplarorden

N.T.O. e: National Travel Office

NTP GB: e: National Trade Press; PL: pl: Naukowe Towarzystwo Pedagogiczne; TR: e: New Turkey Party

NTPC US: e: National Temperance and Prohibition Council. US: e: mil: Naval Training Publication Center

NTPG US: e: National Textile Processors Guild

NTPK N: no: Norsk Teknisk Pressekontor

NTRA US: e: National Trailer Rental Association

NTRE GB: e: mil: Naval Tropical Research Establishment, Singapore

NTRL ZA: e: National Telecommunications Research Laboratory

NTRS US: e: Nationwide Trailer Rental System

NTS US: e: National Thespian Society; US: e: mil: Naval Torpedo Station; e: mil: Naval Training Station; Naval Transport Service; r: [d: nationaler Bund des Schaffens, Emigrantenorganisation] ; NL: nl: Nederlandse Televisie Stichting; US: e: mil: Nevada Test Site

NTSB US: e: National Transportation Safety Board

NTSC US: e: National Television System Committee ["never the same color"] ; North Texas State College

NTSNP r: [d: nationaler Bund des Schaffens der neuen Generation, Emigrantenorganisation]

NTT J: e: Nippon Telegraph and Telephone Public Corporation

NTTA US: e: National Tobacco Tax Association

N.T.T.B. NL: nl: Nederlandse Tafeltennis Bond

NTTC US: e: National Tank Truck Carriers; US: e: mil: Navy Technical Training Center

NTTK S: sv: Nordiska Turisttrafikkommittén

NTTPC = NTT

NTTTI US: e: National Truck Tank and Trailer Tank Institute

NTU US: e: mil: Naval Ordnance Test Unit

NTUC US: e: National Trade Union Council for Human Rights; WAN: e: Nigerian Trade Union Congress

NTUF IND: e: National Trades Union Federation [gegr 1930] ; WAN: e: Nigerian Trade Union Federation

N.T.U.W.W.M. e: National Trade Union of Woodworking Machinists

NTV J: e: Nippon Television Network Corporation

N.T.V.B. NL: nl: Nederlandse Tafelvoetbalbond

NTW A: d: Nachrichtentechnische Werke AG, Wien [gegr 1969]

NTWF e: National Transport Workers Federation

N.U. INT: s: Naciónes Unidas

NU RI: [d: Moslem-Liga]

NÚ CS: cs: Národopisný Ústav

NU NL: nl: Nationale Unie; INT: f: Nations Unies; BRD: d: Niederdeutsche Union[Niedersachsen] ; S: sv: Nordisk Ungdom; N: no: Norges Ungdomslag; US: e: Northeastern University

N.U. GB: e: Northern Union [Rugby League Football] ; Norwich University

N.U.A.F. e: National Union of Auxiliary Firemen

N.U.A.H. e: National Union of Allotment Holders

N.U.A.S. e: National Union of Austrian Students

NUAT INT: sv: Nordisk union for alkoholfri trafik [gegr 1934]

NUAW e: National Union of Agricultural Workers

N.U.A.W. e: National Union of Aircraft Workers; National Union of Asphalt Workers

NUBEL B: nl: Nationale Unie van de Bezettingslegers

NUBMO B: nl: Nationale Unie der Belgische Middenstandsorganisaties

N.U.B.O.M.C.W. e: National Union of Blastfurnacemen, Ore Miners, Coke Workers, etc.

NUBS e: National Union of Basutoland Students

N.U.B.S.O. e: National Union of Boot and Shoe Operatives

N.U.C. e: National Union of Clerks

NÚC CS: cs: Nejvyšši Úrad Cenovy

N.U.C.A.W. e: National Union of Clerks and Administrative Workers

N.U.C.B.P.W. e: National Union of Cokemen and By-Product Workers

NUCDA US: e: National Used Car Dealers Association

N.U.C.I.E. National Union of Commercial and Industrial Employees

Nuclex 66 INT: d: Internationale Fachmesse für die kerntechnische Industrie in Basel [CH, Sep 1966]

N.U.C.O. GB: e: National Union of Co-operative Officials; National Union of County Officers

NUCR F: f: Nouvelle Union Corporative des Résineux

NUCS US: e: National Union of Christian Schools

N.U.C.S. e: National Union of Club Stewards

N.U.C.T. e: National Union of Commercial Travellers

N.U.C.U.A. e: National Union of Conservative and Unionist Associations

N.U.D.A.W. e: National Union of Distributive and Allied Workers

N.U.D.B.T.W. e: National Union of Dyers, Bleachers and Textile Workers

NUDO e: National United Democratic Organization [d: Südwestafrika]

NÜ H: hu: Népügyészég, Budapest

NUEA US: e: National University Extension Association

Nüral BRD: d: Aluminiumwerk Nürnberg GmbH, 85 Nürnberg

N.U.E.W.W. e: National Union of Elastic Web Weavers

N.U.F. e: National Union of Firemen; BUR: SP: e: National United Front; I: i: Nucleo Universitario Fascista

Nufcor ZA: e: Nuclear Fuels Corporation of South Africa, Johannesburg

N.U.F.C.T.A. e: National Unitarian and Free Christian Temperance Association

NUFE I: i: Nuova Unione Fabbricanti Elettrodi, Milano

NUFFIC NL: e: Netherlands University Foundation for International Cooperation, Amsterdam

N.U.F.T.O. GB: e: National Union of Furniture Trade Operatives

N.U.F.W. e: National Union of Foundry Workers

N.U.G, e: National Union of Glovers

N.U.G.C.D. e: National Union of Glass Cutters and Decorators

N.U.G.M.W. GB: e: National Union of General and Municipal Workers

NUGS GH: e: National Union of Ghana

Students
N.U.G.S.A.T. e: National Union of Gold, Silver and Allied Trades
N.U.G.W.K.T. e: National Union of Glass Workers and Kindred Trades
N.U.H. N: no: Norske Ungdomsherberger
N.U.I. IRL: e: National University of Ireland
NUIK S: sv: Nordisk Union i Köttbranschen
N.U.J. GB: e: National Union of Journalists
NUJ WAN: e: Nigerian Union of Journalists
NUK YU: sn: Narodna in Univerzitetna Knjižnica, Ljubljana; CS: cs: Národní a Universitní Knihovna, Praha
NUKEM BRD: d: Nuklear-Chemie und -Metallurgie GmbH, 6451 Wolfgang
NÚKÚ CS: cs: Nejvyšší Účetní Kontrolní Úřad
NUL B: nl: Nationale Unie der Leerkrachten; US: e: National Urban League
N.U.L.C.W. e: National Union of Lift and Crane Workers
N.U.L.M.W. e: National Union of Lock and Metal Workers
N.U.L.O.E.A. e: National Union of Labour Organizers and Election Agents
N.U.L.W. e: National Union of Leather Workers
N.U.M. GB: e: National Union of Manufacturers (Mineworkers)
Numak. D: d: mil: WK2: Nachrichten- und Minenauskunftstelle
NUMAS GB: e: National Union of Manufacturers' Advisory Service Ltd., London
N.U.M.C.S. GB: e: National Union of Marine Cooks and Stewards
NUMEC US: e: Nuclear Materials and Equipment Corporation
NumG D: d: Numismatische Gesellschaft
N.U.M.I.M. e: National Union of Musical Instrument Makers
NUMS PTM: e: National Union of Malaysian Students, Kuala Lumpur
N.U.M.W. GB: e: National Union of Mineworkers [= N.U.M.]
N.U.M.W.M.A. e: National Union of Mineral Water Manufacturers Associations
NUNS WAN: e: National Union of Nigerian Students, Ibadan
N.U.O.B.-BSD B: nl: mil: Nationale Unie van de Oudgedienden der Bezettingslegers en de Belgisch Strijdkrachten in Duitsland
N.U.O.H. e: National Union of Operative Heating Workers
NUOS US: e: mil: Naval Underwater Ordnance Station [BUWEPS]
NUP e: National Ukrainian Party; Sudan: e: National Union(ist) Party
N.U.P.A. e: National Union of Pearl Agents
N.U.P.B.P.W. GB: e: National Union of Printing, Bookbinding and Paper Workers
N.U.P.C.M. e: National Union of Packing Case Makers
N.U.P.E. GB: e: National Union of Public Employees
NUPI N: no: Norsk Utenrikspolitisk Institutt, Oslo
N.U.P.I.B. e: National Union of the Professional and Industrial Blind
N.U.P.T. GB: e: National Union of Press Telegraphists
N.U.R. GB: e: National Union of Railwaymen
N-U-R BRD: d: Neckermann und Reisen, 6 Ffm 1
N.U.R.A. GB: e: National Union of Ratepayers Associations
N.U.R.C. GB: e: National Union of Retail Confectioners
NURO B: nl: mil: Nationale Unie van Reserve-Officieren van België
NUROO B: nl: mil: Nationale Unie der Reserve-Onderofficieren van België
N.U.R.T. GB: e: National Union of Retail Tobacconists
N.U.R.W. GB: e: National Union of Railway Workers

N.U.S. GB: e: National Union of Scale-makers; National Union of Seamen; National Union of Students of England, Wales and Northern Ireland

NUS WAN: e: National Union of Students

N.U.S.A. e: National Union of Shop Assistants

NUSAS ZA: e: National Union of South African Students, Capetown

N.U.S.E.C. GB: e: National Union of Societies for Equal Citizenship

NUSG GH: e: National Union of Students of Ghana

N.U.S.G.T.W. e: National Union of Sign, Glass and Ticket Writers

NUSIC NATO: e: Nuclear Strike Information Center

NUSL US: e: mil: Naval Underwater Sound Laboratory

N.U.S.M.O.W. e: National Union of Shale Miners and Oil Workers

N.U.S.M.W.B. e: National Union of Sheet Metal Workers and Braziers

NUSO NL: nl: Nederlandse Unie van Speeltuinorganisaties

NUSS WAL: e: National Union of Students of Sierra Leone

N.U.S.T. e: National Union of School Teachers

N.U.S.U. GB: e: National Union of Students of the Universities and Colleges of England, Wales and Northern Ireland

N.U.T. GB: e: National Union of Teachers

N.U.T.A. EAT: e: National Union of Tanzania

N.U.T.C. e: National United Temperance Council; GB: e: mil: Nottingham University Training Corps (Territorial Army)

N.U.T.G. GB: e: National Union of Townswomen's Guilds

N.U.T.G.W. e: National Union of Tailors and Garment Workers

NUTI B: nl: Nationale Unie van Technische Ingenieurs

N.U.T.N. GB: e: National Union of Trained Nurses

N.U.T.S. GB: e: National Unions of Track Statisticians

NÚTV CS: cs: Národni Ústredni Tělovýchovný Výbor

NUTW EAT: e: National Union of Tanganyika Workers

N.U.T.W. e: National Union of Textile Workers

NUV N: no: Norges Unge Venstre

NUVA NL: nl: Nederlandse Unie van Accountants

N.U.V.B. GB: e: National Union of Vehicle Builders

N.U.V.W. GB: e: National Union Vehicle Workers

NUWC US: e: mil: [d: Forschungsgruppe für unterseeische Kriegführung]

N.U.W.C.M. GB: e: National Unemployed Workers Committee Movement

N.U.W.E. e: National Union of Waterwork Employees

N.U.W.M. GB: e: National Unemployed Workers Movement; RMM: e: National Union of Workers in Mali

N.U.W.S.S. e: National Union of Women's Suffrage Societies

N.U.W.T. GB: e: National Union of Women Teachers

N.U.W.W. GB: e: National Union of Women Workers

NÚZ CS: sk: Najvyšší Úrad Zásobovanie

NV CS: cs: Národní Výbor; d: Nationalversammlung; N: no: Norske Veritas, Oslo

N.V.A. D: d: mil: Nachrichtenmittelversuchsanstalt der Marine

NVA DDR: d: mil: Nationale Volksarmee US: e: National Variety Artists

N.V.A. e: National Vigilance Association; GB: e: National Villa Association

NVA NL: nl: Nederlandsche Vredes Actie Nederlandse Vereniging voor Afvalwater zuivering, Oss; N: no: Norske Viten-

skapsakademi, Oslo [gegr 1857] ; e:
mil: North Vietnamese Army
NVARPT NL: nl: Nederlandse Vereniging
van Artsen voor Revalidatie en Physi-
sche Therapie
NVATA US: e: National Vocational Agri-
cultural Teachers Association
NVA/VM DDR: d: mil: Nationale Volksar-
mee/Volksmarine
NVB CS: cs: Národní Výbor Bezpečnosti
N.V.B. ZA: e: mil: National Volunteer
Brigade
NVB NL: [d: niederländische Vereinigung
der Bibliothekare] ; nl: Nederlandsche
Vrouwenbeweging; Nederlandse Volks-
beweging
N.V.B.D. NL: nl: Nederlandse Vereniging
tot Bescherming van Dieren
N.V.B.F. B: nl: Nationaal Verbond van
Belgische Fiduciairs
NVBF INT: sv: Nordiska Vetenskapliga
Bibliotekarieförbundet, Göteborg 5 [S]
N.V.B.L. B: nl: Nationaal Verbond der
Belgische Landbouwers
NVC NL: nl: Nationale Vredes Centrale;
Nederlands Verpakkingscentrum
N.V.C.D. NL: nl: Nederlandse Vereniging
van Commerciële Directeuren
NVCP NL: nl: Nederlandsch Verkoopkan-
toor voor Chemische Producten N.V.,
Amsterdam
NVDA US: e: National Vitamin Distrib-
utors Association
NVDO NL: nl: Nederlandse Vereniging
voor Doelmatig Onderhoud
NVE D: d: Naturwissenschaftlicher Verein,
Elberfeld; N: no: Norges Vassdrags- og
Elektrisitetsvesen, Oslo
NVEV NL: nl: Nederlandse Vrouwen Elec-
triciteitsvereniging
NVEW NL: nl: Nederlandse Vereniging
van Electrotechnische Werkgevers
NVF US: e: National Vitamin Founda-
tion; NL: nl: Nederlandsch Volks
-Fascisme; Nederlandse Vereniging van

Fruittelers; S: sv: Nordiska Vägtekniska
Förbundet; Nordisk Vanförevårdsföre-
ning
NVFL NL: nl: Nederlands Vereniging van
Fabrikanten van Landbowwerktuigen,
Den Haag
N.V.F.T. NL: nl: Nederlandse Vereniging
voor Fijnmechanische Techniek
N.V.G. NL: nl: Nederlandse Vereniging
van Geluidsjagers
NVG BRD: d: Nordsee-Versorgungs-
schiffahrt GmbH, 2 Hamburg
NVGA US: e: National Vocational Guid-
ance Association
N.V.G.B. B: nl: Nationaal Verbond der
Geteisterden van België
NVGI GB: e: National Voluntary Groups
Institute
N.V.K. D: d: mil: Nachrichtenmittelver-
suchskommando
NVK d: Nationaler Volkskongreß
NVKJMV NL: nl: Nationaal Verbond van
Katholieke Jonge Middenstandsvereni-
gingen in Nederland
N.V.K.M.O. B: nl: Nationaal Verbond
voor Katholiek Middelbaar Onderwijs
N.V.K.T. B: nl: Nationaal Vlaams Kri-
stelijk Toneelverbond
N.V.K.T.O. B: nl: Nationale Vereeniging
Katholiek Technisch Onderwijs
N.V.K.V.V. B: nl: Nationaal Verbond
van Katholieke Verpleegsters Vereni-
gingen
N.V.M. B: nl: Nationaal Verbond van de
Middenstand; NL: nl: Nederlandsche
Vereeniging van Mondartsen
N.V.M.A. GB: e: National Veterinary
Medical Association
NVNI ZA: af: Nasionale Voedingnavor-
singsinstituut
NVNS NL: nl: N.V. Nederlandse Spoor-
wegen
N.V.O.I. B: nl: mil: Nationaal Verbond
van Oorlogsinvaliden
N.V.O.O. N: nl: Nationaal Verbond van

Oorlogsontsnapten

NVP BRD: d: Nationale Volkspartei, 28 Bremen [gegr 1967] ; Niedersächsische Volkspartei

NVPA US: e: National Visual Presentation Association

NVPD BRD: d: Nationale Volkspartei Deutschlands [gegr 1954]

NVPO US: e: Nuclear Vehicle Projects Office [NASA]

N.V.R. GB: e: mil: Naval Volunteer Reserve

NVR NL: nl: Nederlandse Vereniging voor Radiologie; Nederlandse Vereniging voor Ruimtevaart, Delft

NVRSA GB: e: National Vegetable Research Station Association

NVS YU: sn: Narodna Vlada Slovenije

N.V.S. e: National Vegetarian Society; NL: nl: Nederlandse Vereniging van Suikerzieken

NVS CS: cs: Nejvyšší Vojenský Soud; N: no: Det Kongelige Norske Videnskabers Selskab, Trondheim [gegr 1760] ; Norsk Verkstedsindustris Standardiseringssentral, Homansbyen Oslo 3

NVSH NL: nl: Nederlandse Vereniging voor Sexuele Hervorming

N.V.S.M. B: nl: Nationaal Verbond van Socialistische Mutualiteiten

NVst D: d: mil: Nachschub-Verbindungsstelle [Reichskriegsministerium]

NVT NL: [d: niederländische Bühnengenossenschaft]

N.V.T.F.M. B: nl: Nationaal Verbond van Tapijt-, Fluweel- en Meubelstofwevers

N.V.T.I. B: nl: Nationaal Verbond der Technische Ingenieurs

NVV NL: nl: Nederlands Verbond van Vakverenigingen, Den Haag [gegr 1906]

N.V.V.A. B: nl: Nationale Vereniging ter Voorkoming van Arbeidsongevallen

N.V.V.A.O. NL: nl: Nederlandse Vereniging van Vrouwen met Academische Opleiding

NVvJLC NL: nl: Nederlandsche Vereeniging van Jeugd Luchtvaart Clubs

NVVN NL: nl: Nederlandsch Verbond van Nationalisten

N.V.V.N.S. NL: nl: N.V. Vereenigde Nederlandsche Scheepvaartmaatschappij

N.V.V.O.S. B: nl: mil: Nieuw Verbond van Vlaamse Oudstrijders

N.V.v.V. = NVV

NVW NL: nl: NV Nederlands Verkoopkantoor voor Wasserijproducten, IJmuiden

N.&W. US: e: Norfolk & Western Railroad Company

N.W.A. e: Nelson Weavers' Association

NWA US: e: Northwest Airlines; Northwest Orient Airlines

NWAABI US: e: National Women's Association of Allied Beverage Industries

NWAC US: e: National Weather Analysis Center; e: mil: Netherlands Women's Army Corps; US: e: mil: Northwestern Area Command [USAREUR]

NWAHACA US: e: National Warm Air Heating and Air Conditioning Association

NWB US: e: National Wiring Bureau; D: d: nach WK2: Nordwestbank

NWBÁ US: e: National Wooden Box Association

N.W.B.T. B: nl: Nationaal Werk ter Bestrijding van de Tering

NWC US: e: mil: National War College, Washington, D.C.; US: e: National Writers Club; US: e: mil: National Weapons Center, Corona, Calif.[Navy] US: e: Newspaper Women's Club; WAN e: Nigerian Workers Council

NWCA US: e: mil: Navy Wives' Club of America

N.W.C.A.L.D.C.S. GB: e: National Whitley Council for the Administrative and Legal Departments of the Civil Service

NWCC US: e: Northwestern Weed Control Conference

N.W.C.F. e: North-Western Caterers'

Federation

NWCMA GB: e: National Work Clothing Manufacturers Association

NWCTU US: e: National Women's Christian Temperance Union

NWDA US: e: National Wholesale Druggists Association

NWDF BRD: d: Nordwestdeutsches Fernsehen [NWDR]

N.W.D.O. e: North-Western District Office

NWDR BRD: d: Nordwestdeutscher Rundfunk [bis 31 Mar 1956, dann: NWRV]

NWEABI GB: e: North Western Educational Association for the Building Industry

NWEB GB: e: North Western Electricity Board

NWF US: e: National Wildlife Federation; National Women's Forum; BRD: d: Norddeutsche Werbefernsehen GmbH, 2 Hamburg; Nordwestdeutscher Fahrzeugbau; Nord-West-Flug GmbH u. Co., Braunschweig-Flughafen

NWFA US: e: National Wholesale Furniture Association

NWFGA GB: e: National Women's Farm and Garden Association

NWGA e: National Wool Growers Association

NWGB GB: e: North Western Gas Board

N.W.G.E.S. e: National Winding and General Engineers Society

NWI US: e: National Weather Institute

NWIC US: e: National Wheat Improvement Committee

NWIRP US: e: mil: Naval Weapons Industrial Reserve Plant

N.W.K. B: nl: Nationaal Werk van Kinderwelzijn

NWK D: d: Norddeutsche Woll- und Kammgarn-Industrie, Delmenhorst; BRD: d: Nordwestdeutsche Kraftwerke AG, 2 Hamburg

NWKG BRD: d: Nord-West Kavernengesellschaft

NWL US: e: mil: Naval Weapons Labora-

tory, Dahlgren, Va. [BUWEPS]

NWLB US: e: National War Labor Board [gegr 1942]

NWLDYA US: e: National Wholesale Lumber Distributing Yard Association

N.W.L.F. GB: e: North Wales Liberal Federation

N.W.M. e: National War Memorial

NWMA US: e: National Woodwork Manufacturers Association; National Wool and Mohair Association

NWMC US: e: National Wool Marketing Corporation

N.W.M.P. CDN: e: North-West Mounted Police

N.W.N.U. e: North-Western Naturalists Union

NWO BRD: d: Nord-West Ölleitung GmbH, 294 Wilhelmshaven

N.W.O.I. B: nl: mil: Nationaal Werk voor Oorlogsinvaliden

NWOO NATO: e: NATO Wartime Oil Organization

N.W.O.S. B: nl: mil: Nationaal Werk voor Oudstrijders en Oorlogsslachtoffers

NWP US: e: National Women's Party; US: e: mil: Naval Weapons Plant; US: e: Northwestern Pacific Railroad

NWPMA US: e: National Wooden Pallet Manufacturers Association

NWR NL: nl: Nationale Woningraad; Nederlandsche Werkloosheids Raad

NWRA US: e: National Wheel and Rim Association

N.W.R.A. GB: e: North Wales Resorts Association

NWRC US: e: National Water Resources Committee; US: e: mil: Naval Warfare Research Center [Stanford Research Institute]

NWRF US: e: mil: U.S. Navy Weather Research Facility, Norfolk, Va.

NWRLS e: North Western Regional Library System

NWRO US: e: National Welfare Rights

Organization

N&WRR US: e: Norfolk & Western Railroad Company

NWRV BRD: d: Nord- und Westdeutscher Rundfunkverband, 2 Hamburg 13 [seit 1 Apr 1956, vorher: NWDR]

N.W.S. e: National Woolsorters Society

NWSA US: e: National Welding Supply Association; National Winter Sports Association

N.W.S.A. GB: e: National Women's Suffrage Association

NWSA US: e: mil: Naval Weapons Support Activity

NWSB US: e: National Wage Stabilization Board

N.W.S.H.E. e: North-Western Society of Highway Engineers

NWSO US: e: mil: Naval Weapons Services Office

N.W.S.Q.A. GB: e: North Wales Slate Quarries Association

N.W.S.S. US: e: Norfolk and Washington (D.C.) Steamship Company

NWT BRD: d: Deutscher Nationaler Wettbewerb der besten Tonaufnahme

NWTA US: e: National Wool Trade Association

NWTEC GB: e: National Wool Textile Export Corporation

NWTS US: e: mil: Naval Weapons Test Station

NWTUL GB: e: National Women's Trade Union League

N.W.U. e: New Wales Union

NWU WAN: e: Nigerian Women's Union; US: e: Northwestern University [Ill.]

NWV d: Naturwissenschaftlicher Verein; D: d: Neigungswaagen-Verband eV, Berlin-Wilmersdorf

NWW BRD: d: Nordwestdeutscher Wohnungsbauträger GmbH, 33 Braunschweig

NWWA US: e: National Water Well Association

N.W.W.W.A. B: nl: Nationaal Werk voor Weduwen, Wezen en Ascendenten

N.Y.A. US: e: National Youth Administration

NYA US: e: New York Airways; New York Aquarium

N.Y.A.C. US: e: New York Athletic Club

NYAL e: mil: National Yugoslav Army of Liberation

NYAM US: e: New York Academy of Medicine

NYAS US: e: New York Academy of Sciences

N.Y.B. e: New York & Bremen Steamship Company

NYBG US: e: New York Botanical Garden

NYC US: e: New York Central Railroad; WAN: e: Nigerian Youth Congress

N.Y.C. e: Nore Yacht Club

NYCE US: e: New York Cocoa Exchange; New York Commodity Exchange; New York Cotton Exchange

NYCFMA US: e: New York Credit and Financial Management Association

N.Y.C.&H.R.R. US: e: New York Central & Hudson River Railroad

N.Y.C.L.U. US: e: New York Civil Liberties Union

NYCME US: e: New York Clothing Manufacturers Exchange

N.Y.C.R.R. US: e: New York Central Railroad Company

NYCSE US: e: New York Coffee and Sugar Exchange

NYC&SL; N.Y.C.&St.L.R.R. US: e: New York, Chicago & St. Louis Railroad Company

NYDA US: e: New York Diabetes Association

NYF US: e: New York Foundation

NYHA US: e: New York Heart Association

NyHAL S: sv: Nyköpings högre allmänna läroverk

NYHS US: e: New York Historical Society

N.Y.I. US: e: New York Institute of Photography

NYIA US: e: New York International Airport

NYIDA US: e: New York Importers and Distillers Association

NYK J: Nippon Yusen Kaisha [d: Reederei]

N.Y.K.L. N: no: Norges Yrkeskvinners Landsforbund

NYLA US: e: New York Library Association

NYLIC US: e: New York Life Insurance Company, New York 10, N.Y.

NYLS US: e: New York Law School

N.Y.M. WAN: e: Nigerian Youth Movement

NYMA US: e: New York Medical Association

NYMC US: e: New York Medical College

NYME US: e: New York Mercantile Exchange

N.Y.M.S. US: e: New York Mathematical Society [gegr 1858]; New York Medical Society

NYNG US: e: mil: New York National Guard

NYNHH; N.Y.,N.H.&H.R.R. US: e: New York, New Haven & Hartford Railroad Company

NYNS US: e: mil: New York Naval Shipyard

N.Y.O. GB: e: National Youth Orchestra of Great Britain

NYO&W; N.Y.O.&W.Ry. US: e: New York, Ontario & Western Railway

NYPFO US: e: mil: New York Air Force Procurement Field Office

NYPL US: e: New York City Public Library

NYPS US: e: New York Publishing Society

NYPSS US: e: New York Philharmonic Symphony Society

NYRA US: e: New York Racing Association

N.Y.R.B.A. US: e: New York – Rio – Buenos Aires [air line]

NYS US: e: New York School of Writing, New York 17, N.Y.; New York Shipbuilding Corp., Camden, N.J.

N.Y.S.A. US: e: New York Shipping Association

NYSAA US: e: New York State Archaeological Association

NYSAC US: e: New York State Athletic Commission

NYSCC US: e: New York State Crime Commission

NYSDH US: e: New York State Department of Health

NYSE US: e: New York Stock Exchange

NYSEM US: e: New York Society of Electron Microscopists

NYSPA US: e: New York State Pharmaceutical Association; New York State Power Authority

NYSSIM US: e: New York State Society of Industrial Medicine

NYSSMA US: e: New York State School Music Association

NYSSPE US: e: New York State Society of Professional Engineers

NYS&W US: e: New York, Susquehanna & Western Railroad

NYT GB: e: New Yiddish Theatre, London

NYTA US: e: New York Transit Authority

NYTHA US: e: New York Tuberculosis and Health Association

NYTIC US: e: New York Technical Institute, Cincinnati

NYTV US: d: e: New York Turn Verein [gegr 1850]

NYU US: e: New York University

NYUIMS US: e: New York University Institute of Mathematical Sciences

N.Y.W.F. US: e: New York World Fair

N.Y.Y.C. US: e: New York Yacht Club

NYZP US: e: New York Zoological Park

NYZS US: e: New York Zoological Society

N.Z. D: d: mil: Nachrichtenmittelzentrale [Reichswehrministerium]

NZ YU: sn: Narodna Zaščita; CS: sk:

Národné Zhromaždenie; INT: pl: Narody Zjednoczone [e: UN]

N.Z. B: nl: Nationaal Zangfeest; Nationale Zuiveldienst

N.Za.; Nza D: d: mil: Nebenzeugamt

NZAB NZ: e: New Zealand Association of Bacteriologists

NZAEC NZ: e: New Zealand Atomic Energy Committee

N.Z.A.F. NZ: e: mil: New Zealand Air Force

N.Z.A.O.C. NZ: e: mil: New Zealand Army Ordnance Corps

N.Z.A.S. NZ: e: New Zealand Association of Scientists

N.Z.A.S.C. NZ: e: mil: New Zealand Army Service Corps

NZASc = N.Z.A.S.

NZAV nl: Nederlands-Zuidafrikaanse Vereniging

NZBS NZ: e: New Zealand Broadcasting Service

NZCER NZ: e: New Zealand Council for Educational Research

NZCh PL: pl: Narodowy Związek Chłopski

NZDA NZ: e: New Zealand Department of Agriculture; New Zealand Dietetic Association

NZDCS NZ: e: New Zealand Department of Census and Statistics

NZDLS NZ: e: New Zealand Department of Lands and Survey

NZDSIR NZ: e: New Zealand Department of Scientific and Industrial Research

NZE NZ: e: mil: New Zealand Engineers

N.Z.E.A. NZ: eo: Nov-Zelanda Esperanto-Asocio

NZEF NZ: e: mil: New Zealand Expeditionary Force

NZEI NZ: e: New Zealand Electronics Institute

NZES NZ: e: New Zealand Ecological Society

N.Z.E.S.A. NZ: e: New Zealand European Shipping Association

NZFL NZ: e: New Zealand Federation of Labour

NZFMRA NZ: e: New Zealand Fertilizer Manufacturers Research Association

NZFRI NZ: e: New Zealand Forest Research Institute

NZFS NZ: e: New Zealand Forest Service

N.Z.G. ZA: e: National Zoological Gardens of South Africa, Pretoria

NZGA NZ: e: New Zealand Grassland Association

NZGenS NZ: e: New Zealand Genetical Society

NZGR NZ: e: New Zealand Government Railways

N.Z.G.S. NZ: e: New Zealand Geographical Society

NZHP PL: pl: Naczelnictwo Związku Harcerstwo Polskiego

NZIA NZ: e: New Zealand Institute of Architecture

NZIC NZ: e: New Zealand Institute of Chemistry

NZIE NZ: e: New Zealand Institution of Engineers

NZIF NZ: e: New Zealand Institute of Foresters

NZIH NZ: e: New Zealand Institute of Horticulture

NZIIA NZ: e: New Zealand Institute of International Affairs

NZInstW NZ: e: New Zealand Institute of Welding

NZIRE NZ: e: New Zealand Institute of Refrigeration Engineers

NZJCB NZ· e: New Zealand Joint Communications Board

NZK PL: pl: Naczelny Zarząd Kinematografii

NZLA NZ: e: New Zealand Library Association

NZLP PL: pl: Naczelny Zarząd Lasów Państwowych

N.Z.M.C. NZ: e: mil: New Zealand Medical Corps

NZMF NZ: e: mil: New Zealand Military Forces

N.Z.M.N. NZ: e: New Zealand Merchant Navy

NZMS NZ: e: New Zealand Meteorological Service

NZNAC NZ: e: New Zealand National Airways Corporation, Wellington

NZNP NZ: e: New Zealand National Party

N.Z.O. e: New Zionist Organization

NZO PL: pl: Nowotarskie Zakłady Obuwia

NZPA NZ: e: New Zealand Press Association Ltd., Wellington [gegr 1879]

NZPL PL: pl: Nadrodrzańskie Zakłady Przemysłu Lniarskiego

NZPO PL: pl: Nadodrzańskie Zakłady Przemysłu Organicznego

NZPS PL: pl: Nowotarskie Zakłady Przemysłu Skórzanego

NZR PL: pl: Narodowy Związek Robotniczy; NZ: e: mil: New Zealand Rifles

N.Z.R.S.A. NZ: e: mil: New Zealand Returned Services Association

NZSA NZ: e: New Zealand Standards Association, Wellington

NZSAP NZ: e: New Zealand Society of Animal Production

N.Z.S.C. NZ: e: mil: New Zealand Service Corps; NZ: e: New Zealand Shipping Company

NZSCA NZ: e: New Zealand Soil Conservation Association

NZSI NZ: e: New Zealand Standards Institute, Wellington

NZSLO NZ: e: New Zealand Scientific Liaison Office

NZSO NL: nl: Nederlandsche Zionistische Studenten Organisatie

NZSSS NZ: e: New Zealand Society of Soil Science

NZV NL: nl: Nederlands-Zweedse Vereeniging

NZVA NZ: e: New Zealand Veterinary Association

N.Z.V.C. NZ: e: mil: New Zealand Veterinary Corps

NZW BRD: d: Nachforschungszentrale für Wehrmacht-Vermißte, München; PL: pl: Narodowe Zjednoczenie Wojskowe

NZWCC NZ: e: New Zealand Weed Control Conference

O D: d: mil: Oberkommando; D: d: Oberlandesgericht; Oberrealschule; F: f: Observatoire de Paris; e: Office; cs: Okres; e: mil: Operation Section; Ordnance (Department); D: d: Ordnungspolizei; Organisation

O.A. CS: cs: Obchodní akademie; D: d: mil: Oberabschnitt; D: d: Oberamt

OA US: e: Office of Applications [NASA]

O.A. e: mil: Officers' Association

OA GR: e: Olympic Airways, Athens

O.A. e: mil: operational authority; F: f: Ordre des Avocats

OA D: d: Post: Ortsamt; d: Ortsausschuß

O.A. e: Outdoor Association

O.A.A. D: d: mil: Offizier-Anwärter-Abteilung; GB: e: Old Age Administration

OAA CDN: e: Ontario Association of Architects; UN: f: Organisation des Nations Unies pour l'Alimentation et l'Agriculture [e: FAO] s: Organización para la Alimentación y la Agricultura; F: f: Organisation Autonome de l'Artisanat

OAAA US: e: Outdoor Advertising Association of America

OAAPS INT: e: Organization for Afro-Asian Peoples' Solidarity, Cairo [ET]

OAAS CDN: e: Ontario Association of Agricultural Societies

O.A.A.V. F: f: Organisation Autonome de l'Allocation Vieillesse

OAB e: Official Account Bureau

O.AB. D: d: mil: Ortsausbesserungsanstalt

OAB US: e: mil: Overseas Affairs Branch [Army]

O.A.C. CDN: e: Ontario Agricultural College; F: f: mil: Organisation d'Anciens Combattants

OAC US: e: mil: Orleans Area Command; D: d: Ostdeutscher Automobilclub, Königsberg (Pr.); GB: e: Outdoor Advertising Council; US: e: Overseas Automotive Club, New York, N.Y.

OACG D: d: Oberlausitzer Automobilclub, Görlitz

OACI CI: f: Omnium Automobile en Côte d'Ivoire; INT: f: Organisation de l'Aviation Civile Internationale [e: ICAO, Montreal, CDN] s: Organización de Aviación Civil Internacional i: Organizzazione dell'Aviazione Civile Internazionale

OACR US: e: mil: Office of the Admiral Commanding Reserves

OACSFOR US: e: mil: Office of the Assistant Chief of Staff for Force Development [vorher: DCSOPS]

OACSI US: e: mil: Office of the Assistant Chief of Staff for Intelligence [Army]

OACW US: = OCAW

O.A.D. F: f: Office Agricole Départemental

OAD US: e: Office of Area Development; US: e: mil: Officers Assignment Directorate [Army]

OADMS US: e: Office of Automated Data Management Services

OADR US: e: Office of Agricultural Defense Relations

OAE INT: d: Organisation der afrikanischen Einheit [e: OAU]

OAF e: mil: Occupational Air Force; N: no: Oslo Arkitektforening

OaF N: no: Oslo-avisenes Forening

OAF e: mil: Oversea Air Force

OAFIE US: e: mil: Office of Armed Forces Information and Education

OAG d: Oberstes Arbeitsgericht; BRD: d: Ostafrikanische Gemeinschaft; Deutsche Gesellschaft für Natur- und Völkerkunde Ostasiens

OAHS GB: e: Oxford Architectural and Historical Society

OAI US: e: Office Appliance Institute; INT: f: Organisation Artistique Internationale [coiffeurs]

OAIA INT: f: Organisation des Agences d'Information d'Asie

OAIC DZ: f: Office Algérien Interprofessionnel des Céréales

O.A.I.C. F: f: Organisation Autonome de l'Industrie et du Commerce

O.A.I.H.A. GB: e: Office of the Auditor of Indian Home Accounts

OAKV BRD: d: Ostasiatischer Kunstverlag, 5 Köln

O.A.L. e: Order of Ancient Lights

OAL US: e: mil: Ordnance Aerophysics Laboratory

OALP INT: f: Organisation pour la libération de la Palestine

O.A.M. CDN: e: Order of Agricultural Merit, Quebec

OAMCAF INT: f: Office Africain et Malgache du Café

OAMCE INT: f: Organisation africaine et malgache de coopération économique [gegr 1961, seit 1964: UAMCE]

OAMPI INT: f: Office Africain et Malgache de la Propriété Industrielle

OAMS INT: e: Organization of African and Malagasy States

OANA INT: e: Organization of Asian News Agencies, Bombay [IND]

OANDT US: e: mil: Organization and Training [division]

OANS US: e: Overseas American News Service, Washington, D.C.

O.Ant. 1: Ordo Antonianorum

OAOO US: e: Oregon Academy of Ophthalmology and Otolaryngology

OAP US: e: Office of Alien Property, Washington, D.C.

O.A.P.A. GB: e: Old Age Pensioners' Association

OAPC US: e: Office of Alien Property Custodian

OAPE CDN: e: Ontario Association of Professional Engineers

O.A.P.L. F: f: Organisation Autonome des Professions Libérales

OAPROC = OAPC

OAR E: s: Obra Atlética Recreativa; US: e: mil: Office of Aerospace Research

[USAF] ; GB: e: mil: Officers' Appointment and Record Office; US: e: mil: Organized Air Reserve

OARAC US: e: Office of Air Research Automatic Calculator

OART US: e: mil: Oakland Army Terminal; US: e: Office of Advanced Research and Technology [NASA]

OAS US: e: mil: Occupied Areas Section [Military Government] ; US: e: Ohio Academy of Science

O.A.S. F: f: Organisation de l'Armée Secrète

OAS INT: nl: Organisatie van Amerikaanse Staten d: Organisation Amerikanischer Staaten e: Organization of American States, Washington, D.C. [gegr 1890] ; US: e: Organization of Arab Students in the United States of America; GB: e: Oxford(shire) Archaeological Society

OASDI e: Old Age, Survivors and Disability Insurance

OASD(S&L) US: e: mil: Office, Assistant Secretary of Defense (Supply and Logistics)

OASI e: Old Age and Survivors Insurance

OASMS US: e: mil: Ordnance Ammunition Surveillance and Maintenance School [Army]

OAT e: open-air theatre; US: e: Order of Artistic Typists

OATC US: e: Oceanic Air Traffic Center; Overseas Air Traffic Control

OATS US: e: Original Article Tear Sheet [service] ; US: e: mil: Overseas Air Transport Service

OAU INT: e: Organization of African Unity, Addis Ababa [gegr 1963]

OAV CS: cs: Okresní Akční Výbor; D: d: Ortsarmenverband

O.A.W.R. e: Office for Agricultural War Relations

O.a.ž.k. CS: cs: Obchodní a živnostenká komora

OB D: d: nach WK2: Oberrheinische Bank

Ob. d: Oberschule
OB. D: d: Oberste Behörde für Vollblutzucht und Rennen, Berlin
O.B. F: f: Office du Blé; GB: e: Old Bailey; GB: e: mil: Ordnance Board; H: hu: Országos Békebizottság, Budapest
OB ZA: af: Ossewabrandwag; CS: cs: Osvětová Beseda
O.B.A. D: d: mil: Oberbauamt [Marine]; D: d: Oberbergamt; BRD: d: Oberbundesanwalt beim Bundesverwaltungsgericht; D: d: Ortsbildungsausschuß
OBAA GB: e: Oil Burning Apparatus Association
OBAG BRD: d: Oberkasseler-Brauerei AG; Energieversorgung Ostbayern AG, 84 Regensburg
O.B.A.P. B: f: Office Belge pour l'Acroissement de la Productivité
ObArbG BRD: d: Oberstes Arbeitsgericht
O.Barn. 1: Ordo Barnabitarum
O.Bas. 1: Ordo Basilianorum
ObAusschKrSch D: d: WK1: Oberausschuß zur Feststellung von Kriegsschäden
OBB. d: Oberste Baubehörde
Ob.BBeh. BRD: d: Oberste Bundesbehörde
ObBerKomm. D: d: Oberberufungskommission
ObbFA BRD: d: Oberbayerische Forschungsanstalt, Oberammergau
ObBG. BRD: d: Oberstes Bundesgericht
OBC; OBCA US: e: Outboard Boating Club of America, Chicago 1, Ill.
OBCCC US: e: Office of Bituminous Coal Consumers Council
O.B.C.E. B: f: Office Belge du Commerce Extérieur
OBCH GB: e: Overseas Booksellers Clearing House
ObChdSMA D: d: nach WK2: Oberster Chef der Sowjetischen Militäradministration
Ob.DBeh. BRD: d: Oberste Dienstbehörde
Ob.d.H.; ObdH D: d: mil: Oberbefehlshaber des Heeres

Ob.d.K. D: d: mil: WK2: Oberbefehlshaber der Küstenverteidigung
Ob.d.L.; ObdL D: d: mil: Oberbefehlshaber der Luftwaffe
Ob.d.M.; ObdM D: d: mil: Oberbefehlshaber der Kriegsmarine
OBDSt BRD: d: Ortsbaudienststelle [Oberfinanzdirektion]
Ob.d.W.; ObdW D: d: mil: Oberbefehlshaber der Wehrmacht
OBE US: e: Office of Business Economics [Department of Commerce]
Oberbedarf D: d: Oberschlesische Eisenbahnbedarfs-AG
Oberhütten D: d: Verein Oberschlesischer Hüttenwerke
Oberkohle BRD: d: Oberbayerische AG für Kohlenbergbau
Oberkoks D: d: Vereinigte chemische Fabriken und Kokswerke AG
OberldGer; Oberl.Ger. D: d: Oberlandesgericht
Oberost D: d: mil: WK1: Oberbefehlshaber im Osten
OBewAussch D: d: Oberbewertungsausschuß [Finanz]
Ob.Fw.Sch. D: d: mil: Oberfeuerwerkerschule
Ob.Fz.Stb. D: d: mil: WK2: Oberfeldzeugstab
OBG BRD: d: Oberes Bundesgericht; Oberstes Bundesgericht
ObG DDR: d: Oberstes Gericht
OBG BRD: d: Olympia-Baugesellschaft, 8 München [für die Spiele 1972]
OBgAmt D: d: Oberbergamt
ObGerBritZ D: d: nach WK2: Deutscher Oberster Gerichtshof für die britische Zone
ObGerVW D: d: nach WK2: Deutsches Obergericht für das Vereinigte Wirtschaftsgebiet
ObGH A: d: Oberster Gerichtshof
O.B.G.S. GB: e: Official British Government Services

ObGVW D: d: nach WK2: = ObGerVW
OBH D: d: mil: = Ob.d.H.
O.B.I.C. B: f: Office Belge d'Investigations Commerciales
OB i DN PL: pl: Ośrodek Bibliografii i Dokumentacji Naukowej
O.B.I.P. F; f: Office des Biens et Intérêts Privés
OBIS CS: cs: Oborový informacní stredisko
Obj. d: Oberschule für Jungen
OBK D: d: Oberberufungskommission
Ob.Kdo.d.H.Gr. D; d: mil: Oberkommando der Heeresgruppe
OBKE H: hu: Országos Bányászati és Kohászati Egyesület, Budapest
OBKI H: hu: Országos Balneológiai Kutató Intézet, Budapest
Ob.Kom. D: d: mil: Oberkommando
Ob.Kr.Ger. D: d: mil: Oberkriegsgericht
OBL. d: Oberbauleitung; Oberbetriebsleitung
ObLArbG BRD: d: Oberstes Landesarbeitsgericht
ObLG d: Oberstes Landesgericht
OBLI GB: e: mil: The Oxfordshire and Buckinghamshire Light Infantry
Oblit SU: [d: Distriktsbehörde für Literatur und Verlagswesen]
ObLO YU: sn: Občinski Ljudski Odbor; Oblastni Ljudski Odbor
Obl.S. 1: Oblati Salesiani
OBL USZ D: d: nach WK2: Bahn: Oberbetriebsleitung United States Zone
ObM. d: Oberschule für Mädchen
OBMA US: e: Outboard Boat Manufacturers Association, Chicago, Ill.
OBMB DDR: d: Ostdeutscher Bauern- und Mittelstandsbund
O.B.M.E.H. e: Oliver Borthwick Memorial Embankment Home
OBMV 1: Ordo Beatae Mariae Virginis
OBNI H: hu: Országos Bőr- és Nemikórtani Intézet, Budapest
ObNV CS: cs: Obvodní Národní Výbor

OBNYH H: hu: Országos Bünügyi Nyilvántartó Hivatal, Budapest
OBOS N: no: Oslo Bolig- og Sparelag
Ob.Ost D: d: mil: WK1: Oberbefehlshaber im Osten
OBR US: e: Office of Budgets and Reports
OBRA GB: e: Overseas Broadcast Representatives Association
ObREG D: d: nach WK2: Oberstes Rückerstattungsgericht
OBS. D: d: mil: WK2: Oberbefehlshaber Süd
ObS d: Oberschule
Obs. f: observatoire; d: Observatorium; e: observatory
OBS BRD: d: Olympia Bürosysteme GmbH [z.B. 68 Mannheim, P 6, 12–15]
O.B.S. GB: e: Oxford Bibliographical Society
ObSeeA D: d: Oberseeamt
OBSO. D: d: mil: WK2: Oberbefehlshaber Südost
ObstBG. BRD: d: Oberstes Bundesgericht
OBT D: d: Oberste Behörde für Traberzucht und -Rennen
O.B.T.P. F: f: Office du Bâtiment et des Travaux Publics
Ob.Trib. Preußen: d: Obertribunal
OBÚ CS: sk: Obvodný Bánsky Úrad
OBU US: e: Oklahoma Baptist University
OBUW-69 SU: [d: internationale Ausstellung "Schuhe, Leder, Galanteriewaren und ihre Produktionsmittel, Moskau, 24 Sep . . . 8 Okt 1969]
OBV D: d: Oberste Behörde für Vollblutzucht und -Rennen
O.B.V. d: Oberste Bundesverwaltung
OBV CS: cs: Okresní Branný Výbor
OBWK D: d: Oberste Behörde für die Prüfungen von Warm- und Kaltblutpferden
OC US: e: Oberlin College
O.C. e: mil: Observer Corps; US: e: Occidental College; e: Ocean Club; Office of Censorship; F: f: Office des

Changes; Office Colonial; e: mil: operational command; INT: f: Commission de l'opium [d: Völkerbund] ; e: mil: ordnance committee; 1: Ordo Carmelitorum; D: d: Organisation Consul [gegr 1918]

OC INT: f: Organisme de Certification [CEE= Commission internationale de réglementation . . .]

O.C. GB: e: Orphans' Court

OC US: e: mil: Overseas Command

OCA INT: f: Office des Cités Africaines, Bruxelles [B] ; US: e: mil: Office, Comptroller of the Army

O.C.A. GB: e: mil: Old Coldstreamers' Association; Old Comrades' Association

OCA NATO: e: Operational Control Authority; INT: s: Organización de Cooperativas de América, San Juan, Puerto Rico f: Organisation des coopératives d'Amérique e: Organization of the Cooperatives of America; US: e: Osteopathic Cranial Association

OCAA F: f: Office Central des Associations Agricoles du Finistère et des Côtes-du-Nord

OCAC US: e: mil: Office, Chief of Air Corps

OCACHAR B: f: Office central d'approvisionnement des charbonnages belges

OCAD DY: f: Office de Commercialisation des Produits Agricoles du Dahomey

O.C.A.D.O. F: f: Organe Central d'Achat des Denrées d'Ordinaire

OCAFF US: e: mil: Office, Chief of Army Field Forces

O.Cam. 1: Ordo Camaldulensis

OCAM INT: f: Organisation Commune Africaine et Malgache [gegr 1965]

OCAMA US: e: mil: Oklahoma City Air Materiel Area

O.Cap. 1: Ordo Capucinorum

O.Carm. 1: Ordo Carmelitarum

O.Carm.Disc. 1: Ordo Carmelitarum Discalceatorum

O.Cart. 1: Ordo Cartusiensis

O.Carth. 1: Ordo Carthusianorum

OCAS e: mil: Office, Chief of Air Service; INT: e: Organization of Central American States

OCAW US: e: Oil, Chemical and Atomic Workers Union

OCB e: Oil Control Board; US: e: mil: Operations Coordinating Board

O.C.B.A. F: f: Office Central de Bibliographie Agricole

O.C.B.V.M. 1: Ordo Conceptionis Beatae Virginis Mariae

O.C.C. B: f: mil: Post: Office central de comptabilité

OCC US: e: Office of the Comptroller of the Currency [Treasury Department] ; GB: e: mil: Officers' Country Club; US: e: Ohio Circuit Court

O.C.C. 1: Ordo Carmelitarum Calceatorum Ordo Clarissarum Colettarum

OCC DZ: f: Organisation clandestine du continent

O.C.C. B: f: Organisation de Coopération Commerciale

OCCA US: e: mil: Office, Chief of Civil Affairs; GB: e: Oil and Colour Chemists' Association, London EC 2

OCCAJ F: f: Organisation Centrale des Camps et Auberges de la Jeunesse, Paris 8

OCCCA US: e: Office of Civilian Conservation Corps Activities

OCCCRBAR INT: e: Office of the Coordinator of Commercial and Cultural Relations between American Republics

OCCE US: e: mil: Office, Chief of Communications-Electronics

OCCF INT: f: Office Commun des Consommateurs de Ferrailles, Bruxelles [B]

OCCGE INT: f: Organisation de coordination et de coopération dans la lutte contre les grandes endémies

O.C.C.H. B: f: Office Central de Crédit Hypothécaire

O.C.C.L. B: f: Office Central des Contingents et Licenses, Bruxelles

O.C.C.R. F: f: Office Central de Chauffage Rationnel; Office Central de Chimie Rationnelle

OCCS US: e: mil: Office of the Combined Chiefs of Staff

OCCWC US: e: mil: WK2: Office of Chief of Counsel for War Crimes

OCCWS US: e: mil: Office, Chief of Chemical Warfare Service

OCD US: e: Office of Civil Defense; B: f: Office de la coopération au développement, Bruxelles; 1: Ordo Carmelitarum Discalceatorum

O.C.D.E. INT: f: Organisation de Coopération et de Développement Economique [e: OECD]

OCDM US: e: Office of Civil Defense Mobilization

OCDN DY: NIG: f: Organisation Commune Dahomey-Niger des Chemins de Fer et des Transports

OCDO US: e: mil: Office, Chief Disbursing Officer

OCE MA: f: Office Chérifien de Contrôle et d'Exportation, Casablanca; US: e: mil: Office, Chief of Engineers [Army]; CDN: e: Ontario College of Education

OCEA US: e: mil: OMGUS Civilian Employees Association

OCEANEXPO INT: f: Salon International de l'Exploitations des Océans, Bordeaux [9 . . . 14 Mar 1971]

OCEANLANT NATO: e: Ocean Subarea

OCED US: e: mil: Operations, Control and Evaluation Directorate [SATCOM]

O.C.E.E. INT: f: Organisation de Coopération Economique Européenne

O.C.E.F. e: Ordination Candidates Exhibition Fund

OCEFI F: f: Omnium de Construction et de Financement S.A., Paris

OCEM F: f: Omnium des Centres d'Emplois

OCETI INT: f: Organisation Centrale Européenne pour les Transports dans l'Intérieur

OCF US: e: mil: Office, Chief of Finance

O.C.F. B: f: Office central des fournitures

OChR SU: [d: Gesellschaft der Künstler der Revolution, gegr 1922]

OCI US: e: mil: Office, Chief of Information; f: Office de coopération industrielle; US: e: Office of Coordinator of Information

O.C.I. DZ: f: Organisme de coopération industrielle

OCIA US: e: Office of the Coordinator of International Affairs

OCIAA US: e: Office of Coordinator of Inter-American Affairs

OCIBEC B: CGO: f: Office de Commerce et de l'Industrie de la Belgique et du Congo

OCIC INT: f: Office Catholique International du Cinéma, Bruxelles 4 [B]; MA: f: Office Chérifien Interprofessionnel des Céréales; INT: s: Oficina Católica Internacional del Cine

OCINFO US: e: mil: Office of the Chief of Information [Army]

O.Cist. 1: Ordo Cisterciensis

O.Cist.Ref. 1: Ordo Cisterciensum Reformatorum

OCL GB: e: Overseas Containers Ltd.

OCLA f: Organisation commune pour la lutte antiacridienne

OCLAV f: Organisation commune de lutte antiaviaire

OCLL US: e: mil: Office, Chief of Legislative Liaison

O.C.M. B: f: Office central de la matricule; MA: f: Office des Changes Marocaines; F: f: mil: Organisation Civile et Militaire

OCMA GB: e: Oil Companies Materials Association, London W.C.2; NL: nl: Opleidingsschool voor Christelijk Maatschappelijken Arbeid

OCMH US: e: mil: Office, Chief of Millitary History

OCMI INT: f: Organisation Consultative Maritime Intergouvernementale [e: IMCO] s: Organización Consultiva Marítima Intergubernamental

O.C.M.J. F: f: mil: Organisation Civile et Militaire des Jeunes

OCNO US: e: mil: Office, Chief of Naval Operations

OCO US: e: Office of Occupation Costs; US: e: mil: Office, Chief of Ordnance; Office of Civil Operations [Korea]

OC/OASD US: e: mil: Office of Cataloging, Office of the Assistant Secretary of Defense (Supply and Logistics)

O.C.O.B. F: f: Office Central des Œuvres de Bienfaisance (et Services Sociaux)

OCODIS F: f: Office Commercial et de Distribution pour l'Outre-Mer

O.Coel. 1: Ordo Coelestinensis

OCOFE US: e: mil: Office, Chief of Engineers

OCOFF US: e: mil: Office, Chief of Finance

OCOFS US: e: mil: Office, Chief of Staff

OComS US: e: mil: Office of Community Services

O.Conv. 1: Ordo Conventualium

OCORA F: f: Office de Coopération Radiophonique

O.C.O.S. F: f: Ordre des Conseils en Organisation Scientifique

O.C.O.S.S. F: f: Office Central des Œuvres et Services Sociaux

OCOT US: e: mil: Office, Chief of Transportation

OCP MA: f: Office Chérifien des Phosphates; US: e: mil: Office of Civilian Personnel; SYR: f: Office des Céréales Panifiables

OCQM US: e: mil: Office of Chief Quartermaster

O.C.R. f: Office de la Circulation Routière; US: e: WK2: Office for Civilian Requirements, War Production Board; US: e: Office of Civil Rights; 1: Ordo Cister-

ciensium Reformatorum

OCRA B: f: Office Commercial du Ravitaillement et de l'Agriculture; F: f: Office de Coopération Radiophonique; DZ: f: Organisation Clandestine de la Révolution Algérienne; INT: e: Organization for the Collaboration of Railways, Paris

OCRD US: e: mil: Office, Chief of Research and Development [Army]

O.C.R.P.I. F: f: Office Central de Répartition des Produits Industriels

O.C.R.S. f: Organisation commune des régions sahariennes

O.Cruc. 1: Ordo Cruciferorum

O. Crucig. 1: Ordo Crucigerorum

OCS e: mil: Office, Chief of Staff; Office, Chief Surgeon; US: e: Office of Civilian Supply; Office of Contract Settlement; GB: e: mil: Officer Cadet School; US: e mil: Officer Candidate School; INT: f: Organe de contrôle des stupéfiants, Genève [CH] s: Organo de Control de Estupefacientes

OCSA US: e: mil: Office, Chief of Staff, Army

O.C.S.A. e: Operative Cotton Spinners' Amalgamation

OCSI B: f: Office Central de Salaires et Indemnités, Bruxelles

OCSigO US: e: mil: Office, Chief Signal Officer [Army]

O.C.S.O. 1: Ordo Cisterciensis Strictioris Observantiae

OCSPWAR US: e: mil: Office, Chief of Special Warfare

OCSR e: Organization for Comparative Social Research

O.C.S.R.C. GB: e: Office of the Controller of Stamps and Registrar of Companies

OCSS US: e: mil: Office of Chief of Special Services

OCST CH: f: Office Central Suisse du Tourisme

OCSurg US: e: mil: Office, Chief Surgeon
OCT INT: f: Office central des transports internationaux par chemins de fer, Bern [CH] ; TN: f: Office du Commerce de Tunisie; e: mil: Office of the Chief of Transportation; INT: f: Organisation des Communications et du Transit de la Société des Nations
OCTI; OCTIC; OCTICF INT: f: Office central des transports internationaux par chemins de fer, Bern [CH]
OCTRF CDN: e: Ontario Cancer Treatment and Research Foundation
OCU US: e: Oklahoma City University
O.C.U.C. GB: e: Oxford and Cambridge Universities Club
O.D. e: office of distribution; f: office départemental; e: mil: Operations Division
OD NL: nl: Orde Dienst [gegr 1940] ; e: Order of Druids [gegr 1781] ; e: mil: Ordnance Department (Depot); d: Ordnungsdienst
O.D. S: sv: Orphei Drängar [gegr 1853]
ODA CDN: e: Ontario Dental Association
O.D.A.C.V.G.F: f: mil: Office Départemental des Anciens Combattants et Victimes de la Guerre
ODAIR NATO: e: Office Deputy Air
ODAS YU: sn: Osrednji Državni Arhiv Slovenije, Ljubljana
ODB H: hu: Országos Dokumentációs Bizottság, Budapest
ODBA US: e: Oregon Dairy Breeders Association
O.D.C. e: Order of Discalced Carmelites; f: mil: Organe (Organisme) de direction et de contrôle [später: NASMO]
ODC e: mil: Overseas Defence Committee
ODCA INT: s: Organización Demócrata Cristiana de América, Santiago de Chile [gegr 1947]
ODCBA GB: e: Oxford and District Cattle Breeders Association
ODCSOPS US: e: mil: Office of the Deputy Chief of Staff for Military Operations
ODD DDR: d: Organisation Dienst für Deutschland
ODDRE US: e: mil: Office of Director of Defense Research and Engineering
O.D.E. F: f: Office de Documentation Economique
ODEA YU: s: Oficina de Educación de Adultos, Ministerio de Educación
ODECA INT: s: Organización de Estados Centroamericanos [gegr 1951]
O. de M. 1: Ordo de Mercede
O.D.E.M.F. F: f: Office du développement de l'exportation des matériels électriques français, Paris
ODEPLAN RCH: s: Oficina de Planificación Nacional
O.D.F.L. GB: e: Our Dumb Friends' League [d: Tierschutzverein]
O.D.H.W.S. US: e: Office of Defense and Health Welfare Service
ODI US: e: mil: Office, Director of Intelligence; CS: cs: Okresní Dopravní Inspektorát; INT: e: Open Door International for the Economic Emancipation of the Woman Worker, Brussels 5 [B] ; GB: e: Overseas Development Institute
ODIC US: e: mil: Office of Director of Information Control
ODK BRD: d: Obere Donau Kraftwerke AG, 8 München
O.d.K. D: d: mil: Oberkommando der Küstenverteidigung, Hamburg
ODKO PL: pl: Ośrodek Doskolania Kadr Oświatowych
O.D.L. F: f: Office Départemental du Logement; B: nl: Opvoedingsdienst van het Leger
ODM US: e: mil: Office of Defense Mobilization; GB: e: Ministry of Overseas Development
ODMS US: e: mil: Office of the Director for Mutual Security
ODNR INT: [d: Befreiungsbewegung der

Völker Rußlands; Emigranten]
O.D.N.S. e: mil: Operations Division of Naval Staff
O.d.O. ·D: d: mil: Oberbefehlshaber der Ostseestreitkräfte
ODOOS PL: pl: Ośrodek Dokumentacji Obrabiarek i Obróbki Skrawaniem
O.D.P. F: f: Office Départemental des Pensions; Office Départemental du Placement
ODPI US: e: mil: Office of Director of Public Information
O.D.P.N. F: f: Office Départemental des Pupilles de la Nation
O.d.R. BRD: d: mil: Ordensgemeinschaft der Ritterkreuzträger
O.D.S. F: f: Office Départemental de la Seine; GB: e: Office of the Director of Stamping; Ornamental Decorators' Society
ODS BRD: d: stud: Ostpolitischer Deutscher Studentenverband eV, 53 Bonn
ODSAD US: e: mil: Office of Director, Special Activities Division
ODSBA GB: e: Oxford Down Sheep Breeders' Association
ODSLOG US: e: mil: Office of the Deputy Chief of Staff for Logistics
O.D.T. US: e: mil: Office of Defense Transportation
ODUCAL INT: s: Organización de Universidades Católicas de Américas Latina
OE US: e: Office of Education, Department of Health, Education and Welfare
O.E. US: e: Oregon Electric Railway Company
OEA A: d: Obereinigungsamt; US: e: Office of Economic Adjustment (Affairs); e: Officers' Employment Association; US: e: Ohio (Oklahoma) Education Association; GB: e: Orchestral Employers' Association; INT: d: Organisation für die Einheit Afrikas [e: OAU] ; INT: f: Organisation des Etats Américains [e: OAS] ; INT: d: Organisation

Europäischer Aluminiumschmelzhütten, 4 Düsseldorf [BRD] ; INT: pt· Organização dos Estados Americanos s: Organización de los Estados Américanos i: Organizzazione degli Stati Americani; H: hu: Országos Energiagazdálkodási Alap
OÉA H: hu: Országos Épületjavitási Alap
OEA US: e: Overseas Education Association
ÖAAB A: d: Österreichischer Arbeiter- und Angestellten-Bund
ÖABB A: d: Österreichischer Amateur -Billard-Bund, Wien
ÖAC A: d: Österreichischer Automobil -Club, Wien
ÖÄ S: sv: Överståthållarämbetet, Stockholm
ÖÄA S: sv: Överståthållarämbetets Arkiv
ÖAeC A: d: Österreichischer Aero-Club
ÖÄV A: d: Österreichischer Ärzte-Verein
ÖAF A: d: Österreichische Automobilfabrik AG, Wien-Floridsdorf [gegr 1907] S: sv: Östergötlands Andelsslakteriförening
Ö.A.f.W. A: d: Österreichischer Arbeitskreis für Wildtierforschung
ÖAI A: d: Österreichisches Archäologisches Institut
ÖAK A: d: Österreichischer Alpenklub, Wien
ÖAL A: d: Österreichischer Arbeitsring für Lärmbekämpfung, Wien
ÖAM A: d: Österreichisch-Alpine Montangesellschaft, Wien 1
ÖAMTC A: d:.Österreichischer Automobil-, Motorrad- und Touring-Club
ÖAV A: d: Österreichische Arbeitsgemeinschaft für Volksgesundheit, A-1012 Wien 1; Österreichischer Alpenverein
ÖAVK A: d: Österreichischer Arbeitskreis "Verstärkte Kunststoffe", Wien
OEB e: Officers' Employment Board; NL: nl: Ondervakgroep Export van Bloembollen

OeBB; Ö.B.B. CH: d: Oensingen (Önsingen) – Balsthal-Bahn

ÖBB A: d: Österreichischer Bauernbund; Österreichische Bundesbahnen, Wien

ÖBJR A: d: Österreichischer Bundesjugendring

ÖBK A: BRD: d: Österreichisch-Bayerische Kraftwerke AG, Simbach (Inn); S: sv: Östra Reals Bridgeklubb

öBR BRD: d: örtlicher Betriebsrat

ÖBV A: BRD: Österreichisch-Bayerisches Verkehrsbüro, 8 München; A: d: Österreichische Bergsteiger-Vereinigung; Österreichischer Bundesverlag für Unterricht, Wissenschaft und Kunst, Wien 1

OEC US: e: Office of Economic Cooperation

O.E.C. INT: f:Organisation Européenne du Charbon

OECD INT: e: Organization for Economic Cooperation and Development [gegr 1961]

OECE INT: f: Organisation Européenne de Coopération Economique, Paris [gegr 1948] s: Organización Europea de Colaboración Económica i: Organizzazione Europea di Cooperazione Economica

ÖCI A: d: Österreichisches Credit-Institut AG

OE-CMT INT: f: Organisation Européenne de la Confédération Mondiale du Travail i: Organizzazione europea della Confederazione mondiale del Lavoro

OECQ INT: f: Organisation européenne pour le contrôle de la qualité

OeCV; ÖCV A: d: stud: Cartellverband der Katholischen Österreichischen Studentenverbindungen

ÖD BRD: d: Berufsgruppe Öffentlicher Dienst [Deutsche Angestellten-Gewerkschaft]

OED INT: f: mil: Organisation européenne de défense

OEDIP F: f: Office d'Etudes et de Diffusion Pharmaceutiques

ÖDK A: d: Österreichische Draukraftwerke AG, Klagenfurt

OeDTW A: d: Österreichisches Dokumentationszentrum für Technik und Wirtschaft, Wien

OEE H: hu: Országos Erdészeti Egyesület, Budapest

ÖEB S: sv: Östergötlands Enskilda Bank

OEEC INT: e: Organization for European Economic Cooperation, Paris [gegr 1948]

ÖEM A: d: Österreichisches Eisenbahnministerium

ÖEO S: sv: Östergötlands Elevorganisation

OEEPE INT: f: Organisation européenne d'études photogrammétriques expérimentales, Delft [NL, gegr 1953]

OE-ERIC US: e: Office of Education, Educational Resources Information Center

OEF H: hu: Országos Erdészeti Főigazgatóság, Budapest

ÖFB A: d: Österreichische Frauenbewegung; Österreichischer Fußballbund, Wien

Öffa D: BRD: Deutsche Gesellschaft für öffentliche Arbeiten AG [gegr 1930]

Ö.F.G. A: d: Österreichische Friedensgesellschaft, Wien 3 [gegr 1890]

ÖFI DDR: d: Ökonomisches Forschungsinstitut bei der Staatlichen Planungskommission

ÖFT d: Österreichisches Freundschaftstreffen

ÖFVW A: d: Österreichische Fremdenverkehrswerbung

OEG BRD: d: Oberrheinische Eisenbahn-Gesellschaft AG, 68 Mannheim

ÖG A: d: Österreichischer Golf-Verband

ÖGB A: d: Österreichischer Gewerkschaftsbund

ÖGDB A: d: Österreichische Gesellschaft für Dokumentation und Bibliographie, Wien

ÖGEW A: d: Österreichische Gesellschaft für Erdölwissenschaften, Wien 3

ÖGH A: d: Österreichische Gesellschaft für Holzforschung, Wien

ÖGOR A: d: Österreichs betriebswissenschaftliche Gesellschaft für Organisations- und Revisionswesen, Wien 1

OeGRR A: d: Österreichische Gesellschaft für Raumforschung und Raumplanung

OeGV A: d: Österreichische Gesellschaft für Vakuumtechnik

ÖGV A: d: Österreichischer Gebirgsverein

OeGWFT A: d: Österreichische Gesellschaft für Weltraumforschung und Flugkörpertechnik

OÉH H: hu: Országos Épitésügyi Hivatal

OEH GB: e: Oxford Eye Hospital

Ö.H.f.K. A: d: Österreichischer Hauptverband für Körpersport

ÖHV A: BRD: d: Österreichisch-Hanseatisches Verkehrsbüro, 2 Hamburg 36

ÖHW A: d: mil: Österreichische Heimwehr

OEI E: s: Oficína de Educación Iberoamericana, Madrid [gegr 1949]

OEI H: hu: Országos Épitöipari Igazgatóság, Budapest

O.E.I. D: d: Osteuropa-Institut, Breslau

Ö.I.Ä. S: sv: Överintendentsämbetet [gegr 1772]

ÖIAG A: d: Österreichische Industrie-Verwaltungs AG, Wien

ÖIAV A: d: Österreichischer Ingenieur- und Architektenverein

O.E.I.E. F: f: Ouvriers des Etablissements Industriels de l'Etat

ÖIfKf A: d: Österreichisches Institut für Konjunkturforschung, Wien 1

ÖIG A: d: Österreichische Industrie-Verwaltungs-Gesellschaft mbH; Österreichisches Institut für Geschichtsforschung

ÖIS S: sv: Örgryte Idrottssällskap, Göteborg

OEIU US: e: Office Employees International Union

Ö.I.u.A.V. = ÖIAV

ÖIV A: d: Österreichisches Institut für Verpackungswesen

ÖJB A: d: Österreichische Jugendbewegung

ÖJHV A: d: Österreichischer Jugendherbergsverband

ÖJHW A: d: Österreichisches Jugendherbergswerk

ÖJRK A: d: Österreichisches Jugendrotkreuz

ÖJV A: d: Österreichisches Jungvolk

Ø.K. DK: da: A/S Det Østasiatiske Kompagni

Ö.K.B. A: d: Österreichischer Komponistenbund (Künstlerbund)

ÖK-CEE A: d: Österreichisches Komitee der CEE [Commission internationale . . .] Wien

ÖK-IEC A:d: Österreichisches Komitee der IEC [International Electrotech . . .], Wien

ÖKISTA A: d: Österreichisches Komitee für internationalen Studienaustausch

OeKK CH: d: Oeffentliche Krankenkasse

ÖKV A: d: stud: Kartellverband (nichtfarbentragender) Katholischer Studentenvereinigungen in Österreich

Ö.K.V. A: d: Österreichische Kinderdorf-Vereinigung Pro Juventute, Salzburg; Österreichischer Kynologenverband, Wien 1

ÖKW A: d: Österreichisches Kuratorium für Wirtschaftlichkeit, Wien

ÖLA A: d: Österreichische Lehrmittelanstalt, Österreichischer Bundesverlag, Wien

ÖLAG; Oelag A: d: Österreichische Luftverkehrs-AG, Wien

ÖLB DDR: d: Örtliche landwirtschaftliche Betriebe; A: d: Österreichischer Lichtspielerbund

ÖLC S: sv: Östgöta-Lantmännens Centralförening

OELL US: e: Oriental Esoteric Library League

ÖLLC S: sv: Örebro Läns Lantmäns Centralförening

ÖLM S: sv: Östgöta-Lantmännens Maskinaktiebolag, Norrköping

ÖLP: OeLP A: d: Österreichischer Luftfahrt-Pressedienst, Wien 1

ÖLT A: d: Österreichischer Luftschiffertag

ÖLTC A: d: stud: Österreichischer Landsmannschafter- und Turnerschafter-Convent

ÖLV A: d: mil: Österreichische Landesverteidigung

ÖM S: sv: Örebro Missionsförening

OEM US: e: Office for Emergency Management [gegr 1940]

ÖMAG A: d: Österreichische Mineralöl-AG

Oemag A: d: Österreichische Mineralwasser AG, Innsbruck

ÖMF S: sv: Örebro Missionsförenings Förlag

ÖMG A: d: Österreichische Mathematische Gesellschaft; Österreichische Mineralogische Gesellschaft

OEMI US: e: Office Equipment Manufacturers Institute

ÖMV A: d: Österreichische Mineralölverwaltung AG, Wien

ÖNA A: d: Österreichischer Normenausschuß, Wien 1 [jetzt: ON]; S: sv: Övre Norrlands Arkitektförening

ÖNB A: d: Österreichische Nationalbank (Nationalbibliothek)

ÖNIG A: d: Österreichischer Normenausschuß für Industrie und Gewerbe, Wien [später: ÖNA, jetzt: ON]

OEO US: e: Office of Economic Opportunity

ÖOC A: d: Österreichisches Olympisches Komitee

ÖOW A: d: Österreichische Ortswehren

OEP US: e: Office of Emergency Planning

ÖPB A: d: Österreichischer Pfadfinderbund

ÖPD A: d: Österreichischer Pressedienst, Wien

ÖPI A: d: Österreichische Presseinformation; Österreichisches Petroleum-Institut

OEPP INT: f: Organisation européenne et méditerranéenne pour la protection des plantes, Paris [gegr 1951]

ÖPR BRD: d: örtlicher Personalrat

ÖPV A: d: Österreichischer Paddelsport

-Verband, Wien 9

ÖPZ A: d: Österreichisches Produktivitäts-Zentrum, Wien 1

OER INT: f: Organisation Européenne de Radiodiffusion, Bruxelles [B]

ÖRA BRD: d: Öffentliche Rechtsauskunft- und Vergleichsstelle, 2 Hamburg

ÖRCG A: d: Österreichische Renn- und Campagnereiter-Gesellschaft

ÖRF A: d: Österreichischer Rundfunk, Wien; S: sv: Östra Reals Fäktförening

O.E.R.F.S. INT: f: Organisation des états riverains du fleuve Sénégal [gegr 1968]

ÖRHF S: sv: mil: Östra Reals Hemvärnsförening

ÖRIF S: sv: Östra Reals Idrottsförening

ÖRK INT: d: Ökumenischer Rat der Kirchen, Genf [CH]; S: sv: Öregrunds Racerklubb

OERL US: e: mil: Officer Education Research Laboratory

ÖRM S: sv: Östra Reals Marinförening

O.E.R.N. INT: f: Organisation européenne pour la recherche nucléaire

O.E.R.S. INT: f: Organisation européenne de recherches spatiales

O.Er.S.A. 1: Ordo Fratrum Eremitarum Sancti Augustini

ÖRSF S: sv: Östra Reals Skytteförening

ÖRW A: d: Österreichische Rundfunkwerbung, Wien 4

ÖS A: d: Österreichischer Stahlbauverband, Wien 9; Österreichische Sängerschaft

OES US: e: Office of Economic Stabilization

O.E.S. f: Organisation Economique et Sociale

OESA = O.Er.S.A.

ÖSARA S: sv: Östra Sveriges Allmänna Restaurang AB

O.E.S.C. UN: f: Organisation pour l'Education, la Science et la Culture Intellectuelle

ÖSFK S: sv: Östra Södermanlands Flygklubb

Ösig A: d: Österreichische Strangguß -Interessengemeinschaft

ÖSK A: d: mil: Österreichisches Schwarzes Kreuz [Kriegsgräberfürsorge]

OESO INT: nl: Organisatie voor Economische Samenwerking en Ontwikkeling (e: OECD)

OESP 1: Ordo Eremitarum Sancti Pauli

ÖSSW A: d: Österreichische Siemens- und Schuckert-Werke

Ö.St.B. A: d: Österreichische Staatsbahnen

ÖSV; OeSV A: d: Österreichischer Skiverband, Wien

ÖSW A: d: Österreichische Stickstoffwerke AG, Linz

O.E.T. I: i: Organizzazione Editoriale Tipografica, Roma [gegr 1944]

OÉT H: hu: Országos Építésügyi Tanács

ÖTC S: sv: Ömsesidiga Försäkringsbolags Tariffcentral [gegr 1953]; A: d: Österreichischer Touring-Club

Ötex A: d: Erste österreichische Textilfachmesse für Meterware, Dornbirn [1 . . . 3 Jun 1966]

ÖTK A: d: Österreichischer Touristenklub, Wien 1

OETM MEX: s: Oficina Electro-Técnica Mexicana

OÉTTI H: hu: Országos Élelmezés- és Táplálkozástudományi Intézet, Budapest

ÖTTV A: d: Österreichischer Tischtennisverband, Wien

ÖTV BRD: d: Gewerkschaft Öffentliche Dienste, Transport und Verkehr, 7 Stuttgart [gegr 1947]; A: d: Österreichischer Tennis-Verband

ÖVA D: BRD: d: Öffentliche Versicherungsanstalt

OEVA TN: f: Office de l'expérimentation et de la vulgarisation agricoles

Ö.V.B. A: d: Österreichisches Verkehrsbureau

ÖVDI A: d: Österreichischer Verein deutscher Ingenieure, Wien

ÖVE A: d: Elektrotechnischer Verein Österreichs, Wien [= EVÖ]

Ö.V.f.H. A: d: Österreichischer Verband für Handballsport

ÖVG A: d: Österreichische Verkehrswissenschaftliche Gesellschaft

Ö.V.G.W. A: d: Österreichischer Verein von Gas- und Wasserfachmännern, Wien

ÖVP A: d: Österreichische Volkspartei [gegr 1945]

Ö.V.P. S: sv: Östra Värmlands Produktionsförening, Kristinehamn

ÖVSV A: d: Österreichischer Versuchssender-Verband eV, Wien

OEW D: d: Oberschlesische Elektrizitätswerke AG

ÖWB DDR: d: Öffentliche Wissenschaftliche Bibliothek, Berlin

ÖWB; Oe.W.B. A: d: Österreichischer Werkbund

ÖWB A: d: Österreichischer Wirtschaftsbund

ÖWFI SU: [d: östliches wissenschaftliches Forschungsinstitut]

ÖWG A: d: Österreichische Werbegesellschaft KG, Wien 1

ÖWSC A: d: Österreichischer Wintersport -Club

ÖWSGV A: d: Österreichischer Wander-, Sport- und Geselligkeitsverein [gegr 1951]

OEX US: e: Office of the Educational Exchange

ÖZSV A: d: Österreichischer Zivilschutzverband

ÖZV A: d: Österreichischer Ziegel-Verein

O.F. e: Odd Fellows; S: sv: Odontologiska Föreningen, Stockholm; e: Officers' Federation; B: nl: Onafhankelijkheidsfront

OF US: e: Ophthalmological Foundation; Osteopathic Foundation

O.F. YU: sn: Osvobodilna Fronta

OFA CH: d: Orell Füssli-Annoncen AG,

Basel 1; D: d: Ortsfürsorgeausschuß; BRD: d: Offenbacher Frühjahrsausstellung [1968]

O.F.A.C.M. f: mil: Organisation Franco -Anglaise du Capitaine Michel [WK2]

OFADI B: f: Office d'analyse de distribution publicitaire

Ofag BRD: d: Ofenbau-AG, 4 Düsseldorf

OFALAC DZ: f: Office Algérien d'Action Economique et Touristique

OFAR US: e: Office of Foreign Agricultural Relations, Department of Agriculture, Washington, D.C.

OFB H: hu: Országos Földbirtokrendező Bizottság, Budapest

OFBEC F: GB: f: Office Franco-Britannique d'Etudes et de Commerce

OFBT H: hu: Országos Földbirtokrendező Tanács, Budapest

OFBw BRD: d: mil: Ozeanographische Forschungsanstalt der Bundeswehr, 23 Kiel

OFC CDN: GB: e: Office of Fishery Co-ordination; GB: e: Overseas Food Corporation

OFCC US: e: Office of Federal Contract Compliance, Department of Labor, Washington, D.C.

O.F.C.E. F: f: Office Français du Commerce Extérieur

OFCF GB: e: Overseas Farmers Cooperative Federation Ltd.

OFCM US: e: Office of the Federal Coordinator for Meteorological Services and Supporting Research

OFD d: Oberfinanzdirektion; US: e: mil: Office, Fiscal Director; Ordnance Field Depot

OFDI US: e: Office of Foreign Direct Investment, Washington, D.C.

OFE F: f: Office Français d'Edition

O.F.E.A. US: e: Office of Foreign Economic Administration

OFEC US: e: Office of Foreign Economic Coordination

OFEMA F: f: Office Français d'Exportation de Matériel Aéronautique, Paris 16

O.F.F. US: e: Office of Facts and Figures; e: Officers' Families Fund

O.F.F.A. F: f: Office des Fers, Fontes et Aciers

O.F.F.A.F.T.B. e: Ostrich and Fancy Feathers and Artificial Flower Trade Board

OFFBMV.d.MC. l: Ordo Fratrum Beatae Mariae Virginis de Monte Carmelae

Off. Ch. F: f: Office des Changes

OFFI B: nl: Onafhankelijkheidsfront; H: hu: Országos Forditó és Forditáshitelesitő Iroda, Budapest

OFFICOMEX D: f: nach WK2: Office du Commerce Extérieur, Baden-Baden

OFFNAVHIST US: e: mil: Office of Naval History

OFFRO US: e: Office of Foreign Relief and Rehabilitation Operations

Off.-Sch. d: mil: Offizier(s)schule

OFGH d: Oberster Finanzgerichtshof

OFH d: Oberster Finanz(gerichts)hof; H: hu: Országos Földhivatal, Budapest

OFHA US: e: Oil Field Haulers Association

OFI CH: d: Eidgenössisches Oberforstinspektorat; F: f: Office Français d'Information [gegr 1940]

OFIAMT CH: f: Office Fédéral de l'Industrie des Arts et Métiers et du Travail

OFIC F: f: Office Français d'Importation et du Commerce Extérieur

Oficomex = OFFICOMEX

OFILE s: Oficina Liquidadora de Energia Eléctrica

OFINES E: s: Oficina Internacional de Información y Observación del Español, Madrid

OFinK BRD: d: Oberfinanzkasse

OFISARRE D: f: nach WK2: Office Sarrois du Commerce

OFITEC TN: f: Office Tunisien de l'Expansion Commerciale et du Tourisme

OfJ d: Oberschule für Jungen
O.F.K. D: d: mil: Oberfeldkommandantur
OFK d: Oberfinanzkasse
OfL DDR: d: Organisation freiwilliger
Luftschutzhelfer
Oflag D: d: mil: Offizier(s)lager [Kriegs-
gefangene]
OFLC; OFLIC US: e: Office of Foreign
Liquidation Commission
OfM d: Oberschule für Mädchen
O.F.M. 1: Ordo Fratrum Minorum [gegr
1517]
O.F.M.Cap. 1: Ordo Fratrum Minorum
Capucinorum
O.F.M.Conv. 1: Ordo Fratrum Minorum
Conventualium
O.F.M.E. F: f: Organisation Française
du Mouvement Européen
OFMI H: hu: Országos Földméréstani In-
tézet, Budapest
O.F.O.M. F: f: Office de la France d'Outre
-Mer
OFP GB: e: mil: Ordnance Field Park
OFPA US: e: Order of the Founders and
Patriots of America
O.F.R.R. US: e: Office of Foreign Relief
and Rehabilitation
OFRRO US: e: Office of Foreign Relief
and Rehabilitation Operation
O.F.R.S. F: f: Office Français de Re-
cherches Sous-marines
O.F.S. US: e: Office of Field Service;
GB: e: mil: Operational Flying School
OFS e: mil: Ordnance Field Service;
YU: sn: Osvobodilna Fronta Slovenije
OFSC e: Organization and Finance Sub-
committee
OFSIT ZA: e: Orange Free State Invest-
ment Trust, Ltd., Johannesburg
O.F.S.S. e: Operative Flaggers' and Slat-
ers' Society
OFSWFiT PL: pl: Ogólnozwiązkowa Fede-
racja Sportu, Wychowania Fizycznego
i Turystyki
OFT GB: e: Office of Foreign Territories;

H: hu: Országos Földbirtokrendező
Tanács, Budapest; Országos Földmive-
lésügyi Tanács, Budapest
OFTEL F: f: Office Technique des Ele-
veurs
Ofu; OFU D: d: Ofenbau-Union GmbH,
Düsseldorf
O.F.V. D: d: Oberdeutscher Funkverband
eV, Stuttgart
OFV CH: d: Orell Füssli-Verlag, Zürich;
D: d: Ortsfürsorgeverband
OG d: Obergericht; Oberstes Gericht;
DDR: d: Oberstes Gericht, Berlin [seit
1949]; e: Office of Geography
O.G. CH: d: mil: Offiziersgesellschaft
OG d: Ortsgruppe
O.G.A. F: f: Office Général de l'Air, Paris
[gegr 1920]
OGA US: e: Order of Gregg Artists
[d: Stenografenverein]; H: hu: Orszá-
gos Geodéziai Adattár, Budapest
OgAMA US: e: mil: Ogden Air Materiel
Area
OGC US: e: Office of the General Coun-
sel; BRD: d: Osnabrücker Golfclub
O.Gef.G.; O.G.G. d: Oberstes Gefälls-
gericht
O.G.G.A. e: Office of the Grant of Govern-
ment Annuities
OGH d: Oberster Gerichtshof
OGHbrZ; OGHBZ D: d: nach WK2: Ober-
ster Gerichtshof für die Britische Zone
OGIS; OGIZ SU: [d: Vereinigung der
staatlichen Verlage, Moskau]
OGL DDR: d: Ortsgewerkschaftsleitung
OGM US: e: mil: Office of Guided Mis-
siles
O.G.M. GB: e: Oxford Group Movement
OGMA P: pt: Oficinas Gerais de Mate-
rial Aeronáutico, Alverca do Ribatejo
[gegr 1918]
OGP NL: nl: Ondervakgroep in Pootaard-
appelen
OGPU SU: [d: vereinheitlichte staatliche
politische Kontrolle, 1922 . . . 34,

dann NKWD]
O.G.R. e: Office of Government Reports
Ogru d: Ortsgruppe
OGSA DZ: f: Organisation de Gestion et de Sécurité Aéronautique de l'Algérie et du Sahara
O.G.T. f: Organisation Générale du Travail
oGV d: ordentliche Generalversammlung
OGW D: d: NS: Organisation der gewerblichen Wirtschaft [gegr 1934]
OGYE H: hu: Országos Gyógyszerész Egyesület, Budapest
OGYIT H: hu: Országos Gyermek- és Ifjuságvédelmi Tanács, Budapest
OGZ d: Obst- und Gemüsezentrale
O.H. e: Order of Hospitallers; D: d: nach WK1: Organisation Heinz
OHA CDN: e: Ontario Horticultural Association
OHB H: hu: Országos Hondédelmi Bizottmány, Budapest
O.H.C.I. GB: e: Office of the High Commissioner for India
OHE GB: e: Office of Health Economics; e: Office of the Housing Expediter; D: d: Osthavelländische Eisenbahn; BRD: d: Osthannoversche Eisenbahnen AG, 31 Celle
OHF H: hu: Országos Halászati Felügyelőég, Budapest; N: no: Oslo Handelsstands Forening
OHH H: hu: Országos Hadigondozó Hivatal, Budapest
OHI US: e: Occupational Health Institute; Oil-Heat Institute of America
O.H.L. D: d: mil: Oberste Heeresleitung
OHP PL: pl: Ochotnicze Hufce Pracy
OHPL PL: pl: Organizacja Harcerska Polski Ludowej
OHS US: e: Ohio (Oklahoma) Historical Society; NL: nl: Openbare Handelsschool
O.H.S. GB: e: Orphans Homes of Scotland; Oxford High School; Oxford Historical Society

OHSK D: d: Oberharzer Skiklub
O.H.T. GR: f: Office hellénique du tourisme
OHT H: hu: Országos Halgazdasági Tanacs, Budapest; Országos Hitelügyi Tanács, Budapest
OHU CS: cs: Osborné Hornické Učiliště
O.I. B: f: Office d'Identification
OI INT: e: International Federation of Business and Professional Men's Clubs "Optimist International"; H: hu: Orvostovábbképző Intézet, Budapest
OIA GB: e: Office of India Affairs; US: e: Oil Insurance Association; PL: pl: Okręgowa Izba Aptekarska
OIAA e: Office of Inter-American Affairs
OIAC INT: f: Organisation inter-africaine du café, F-92 Neuilly (Seine) s: Organización inter-africana del café; INT: f: Organisation internationale de l'aviation civile [e: ICAO]
OIAM INT: f: Organisation interafricaine et malgache
OIAT GB: e: Osteopathic Institute of Applied Technique
OIB INT: f: Office International de Bibliographie; H: hu: Országos Ifjusági Bizottsága, Budapest
OIBD INT: f: Office International de Bibliographie et de Documentation
OIBT INT: f: Ordre International de Bons Templiers [e: I.O.G.T., gegr 1851]
OIC US: e: Office of Information Control; Office of International Information and Cultural Affairs; INT: f: Office Central des Transports Internationaux par Chemins de Fer, Bern [CH, gegr 1890] US: e: Oil Industry Commission; Oil Information Committee; INT: f: Organisation inter-africaine (inter-américaine) (internationale) du café; INT: f: Organisation internationale catholique; INT: f: Organisation Internationale du Commerce s: Organización Internacional de Comercio
OICA US: e: Office of Information and

Cultural Affairs [gegr 1942]

O.I.C.C. INT: f: Office international du cacao et du chocolat

OICI INT: s: Oficina Internacional Católica de la Infancia, Paris; Organización Interamericana de Coopéración Intermunicipal

O.I.C.M. CH: f: Office Intercantonal de Contrôle des Médicaments

OICMA INT: f: Organisation internationale contre le criquet africain

OICNM INT: f: Organisation intergouvernementale consultative de la navigation maritime [e: IMCO]

OICRF INT: f: Office international du cadastre et régime foncier

OIDA US: e: mil: Ordnance Industrial Data Agency [Army]

OIE US: e: Office of Information and Educational Exchange; INT: f: Office international des épizooties, Paris 17 [gegr 1924]; Organisation Internationale des Employeurs, Genève [CH, e: IOE]

O.I.E.A. INT: f: Office international de l'enseignement agricole

OIEA INT: f: Organisation internationale de l'énergie atomique s: Organismo internacional de energía atómica [Wien, vgl: f: AIEA, e: IAEA]

OIEC INT: f: Office International de l'Enseignement Catholique, Bruxelles [B, gegr 1952] s: Oficio Internacional de Educación Católica [e: CIEO]

OIEP INT: f: Office international d'échange de produits

O.I.E.T.A. INT: f: Office Inter-Etats du Tourisme Africain

OIG e: mil: Office, Inspector-General

O.I.G.W. e: Office of the Inspector-General of Waterguard

OIH H: hu: Országos Idegenforgalmi Hivatal

O.I.H.P. INT: f: Office international d'hygiène publique

OIHR INT: e: Office of International Health Relations

OIIC US: e: Oil Industry Information Committee

O.I.I.C.A. US: e: Office of International Information and Cultural Affairs [= OIC]

OIJ INT: f: Organisation Internationale des Journalistes [Praha, CS, gegr 1946]

OIL US: e: mil: Ordnance Investigation Laboratory

O.I.L. INT: i: Organizzazione Internazionale del Lavoro

OILA e: Office of International Labor Affairs

O.I.M. INT: f: Office international des musées

OIM INT: f: Organisation internationale météorologique [e: IMO]

OIML INT: f: Organisation Internationale de Métrologie Légale, Paris 9

OIMT H: hu: Országos Irodalmi és Müvészeti Tanács, Budapest

OIN INT: f: Organisation Internationale de Normalisation, Genève [CH, gegr 1946, e: ISO]

OINA e: Oyster Institute of North America

O.I.P. B: f: Société Belge d'Optique et d'Instruments de Précision

OIP INT: f: Organisation internationale de la paléobotanique; INT: s: Organización Internacional de Periodistas [= OIJ]

OIPC INT: f: Organisation Internationale de la Police Criminelle, Paris [= INTERPOL] s: Organización Internacional de Policía Criminal; INT: f: Organisation Internationale de Protection Civile, Genève [CH, gegr 1931] s: Organización internacional para la protección civil i: Organizzazione Internazionale per la Protezione Civile [e: ICDO]

OIPEEC INT: f: Organisation Internationale pour l'Etude de l'Endurance des Câbles

OIPM INT: f: mil: Organisation internationale du pentathlon militaire
OIPN INT: f: Office International pour
la Protection de la Nature, Bruxelles [B]
OIR US: e: Office of Industrial Relations;
INT: s: Oficina Interamericana di Radio
[gegr 1937] ; INT: f: Organisation Inter-
nationale de Radiodiffusion [Praha, CS,
gegr 1946] ; UN: f: Organisation Inter-
nationale des Réfugiés [e: IRO]
OIRSA INT: s: Organismo Internacional
de Sanidad Agropecuaria
OIRT INT: f: Organisation internationale
de radiodiffusion et télévision [Praha, CS]
OIS US: e: Office of Industrial Survey;
Office of Investigatory Services; e:
Opium Investigation Service; INT: f:
Organisation internationale de standardisation [e: ISO]
O.I.S. GB: e: Oxford Institute of Statistics
OISB H: hu: Országos Ifjusági Sport Bizott-
ság, Budapest
OISC INT: f: Office international des
scouts catholiques, Paris [F]
OISS INT: s: Organización Iberoamericana
de Seguridad Social, Madrid [E]
OISTT INT: [d: internationale Organisa-
tion der Szenographen und Theater-
techniker, Prag, CS, gegr 1968]
OISTV INT: f: Organisation internatio-
nale pour la science et la technique du
vide
OIT US: e: Office of International Trade,
Department of Commerce, Washington,
D.C.; INT: s: Oficina Internacional de
Trabajo [f: BIT] ; INT: f: Organisation
International du Travail, Genève [CH]
s: Organización Internacional del Tra-
bajo [e: ILO] ; H: hu: Országos Iparok-
tatási Tanács, Budapest; PL: pl: Ośrodek
Informacji Turystycznej
OITA INT: f: Office Inter-Etats du Tourisme
Africaine
OITAF INT: i: Organizzazione Interna-
zionale dei Trasporti a Fune, Roma [I]

OITEB = OITiEB
OITF US: e: Office of International Trade
Fairs; J: e: Osaka International Trade
Fair
OITI H: hu: Országos Idegsebészeti Tudo-
mányos Intézet, Budapest
OITiEB PL: pl: Ośrodek Informacji Tech-
nicznej i Ekonomicznej w Budownictwie
OITiEK PL: pl: Ośrodek Informacji Tech-
nicznej i Ekonomicznej Komunikacji
OITIS Z: e: Overseas Industrial & Trade
Investment Services (Zambia) Ltd.,Kitwe
O.I.u.A.V. D: d: Ostthüringischer Inge-
nieur- und Architektenverein, Weimar
OIUC INT: f: Organisation internationale
des unions de consommateurs
OIV INT: f: Office international de la
vigne et du vin, Paris 8 [gegr 1924]
OIW A: d: Österreichisches Institut für
Wirtschaftsforschung, Wien
OJ d: Oberschule für Jungen [= OfJ]
OJA INT: pl: Organizacja Jedności Afry-
kańskiej
O.J.A.-G. e: Office of the Judge Advocate
-General
O.J.A.M. f: Organisation de la jeunesse
anticolonialiste martiniquaise
OJCS US: e: mil: Office of the Joint
Chiefs of Staff
OJD F: f: Office de Justification de la
Diffusion des Supports de Publicité,
Paris 17
OJHRP CDN: e: Ontario Joint Highway
Research Program
O.J.I. f: Office Juridique International
OJM D: d: Orden junger Menschen
OJR NL: nl: Oecumenische Jeugdraad in
Nederland
OK d: mil: Oberkommando; YU: sn: Ob-
lasni Komitet; CS: [= ČSA. e: air-
lines] ; YU: sh: Okružni Komitet; S: sv:
Sveriges Oljekonsumenters Riksförbund
[gegr 1945] ; Olympiska kommittén;
BRD: d: Organisationskomitee (für
die Olympischen Spiele 1972),

8 München; S: sv: orienteringsklubb;
H: hu: Országgyülés Könyvtára, Buda-
pest; D: d: mil: Ortskommandantur;
D: d: Ortskrankenkasse

O.K. S: sv: Ostasiatiska Kompaniet

OK CS: cs: Osvětová Komise; SF: fi:
Outokumpu Oy, Outokumpu

OKA PL: pl: Okręgowa Komisja Arbitra-
żowa

OKAMA US: e: mil: Okinawa Air Materiel
Area

OKB D: d: Oldenburger Künstlerbund

OKD BRD: d: Osnabrücker Kupfer- und
Drahtwerk AG, 45 Osnabrück

Okdo D: d: mil: Oberkommando

OKDT H: hu: Országos Könyvtárügyi és
Dokumentációs Tanács, Budapest

OKED US: e: mil: Okinawa Engineer
District

OK en W NL: = O.K.&W.

OKET H: hu: Országos Közegészégügyi
Tanács, Budapest

OK FJN PL: pl: Ogólnopolski Komitet
Frontu Jedności Narodu

OKFN PL: pl: Ogólnopolski Komitet
Frontu Narodowego

OKH D: d: mil: Oberkommando des Heeres, Berlin

OKI CS: cs: Okresní Kulturní Inspektorat;
H: hu: Országos Kardiológiai Intézet,
Budapest; Országos Közegészségügyi
Intézet, Budapest

OKISZ H: [d: Verband des Kleingewer-
bes]

OKK CH: d: mil: Oberkriegskommissariat;
D: d: mil: Offizierskleiderkasse; H: hu:
Országos Könyvtári Központ, Budapest;
Országos Köznevelési Tanács, Budapest

OK KPP PL: pl: Okręgowy Komitet Komunistycznej Partii Polski

OK KPS YU: sn: Okrajni Komite Komunistične Partije Slovenije

OKKSČ CS: cs: Okresní Komise Komunistické Strany Československa

OKL D: d: mil: Oberkommando der Luftwaffe, Berlin

O.K.L. PL: pl: Osrodek Konstrukcji Lotniczych, Warszawa

OKM D: d: mil: Oberkommando der
Kriegsmarine, Berlin

OKMZ CS: cs: Osvětová Komise Ministerstva Zemědělství

OKOF NL: nl: Oud-Katholiek Ondersteu-
ningsfonds

OKP PL: pl: Ogólnopolski Komitet Pokoj

OKPIK PL: pl: Ogólnopolski Klub Postę-
powej Inteligencji Katolickiej

OK PP PL: pl: Okręgowa Komenda Policji
Państwowej

OKR PL: pl: Okręgowa Komisja Rewizyjna; Okręgowy Komitet Robotniczy

OKrG; OKrGer. D: d: mil: Oberkriegsgericht

OKS PL: pl: Okręgowy Komitet Studenck

OKT H: hu: Országos Könyvtárügyi Tanác
Budapest; Országos Közoktatási Tanác
Budapest

OKTI H: hu: Országos Korányi Tbc Intéz
Budapest

OKU BRD: d: Oberrheinische Kohlenunio
Bettag, Puton & Co., 68 Mannheim

OKV CS: cs: Odvolací Kárný Výbor

OKW D: d: mil: Oberkommando der Wehr
macht, Berlin; PL: pl: Obwodowa Komisja Wyborcza; Okręgowy Komitet
Wyborczy

O.K.&W. NL: nl: Ministerie van Onderwijs, Kunsten en Wetenschappen

OKWFN PL: pl: Okręgowy Komitet Wybo
czy Frontu Narodowego

OKWV NL: nl: Oud-Katholieke Werklie-
denvereniging

OKZO CS: cs: Okresní Kabinet Zdravotnické Osvěty

OKZZ PL: pl: Okregowa Komisja Zwiazk
Zawodowych

OL d: Oberlyzeum

O.L. D: d: Oberste Luftsportkommission

OL e: Office of Labor; Office of Liaison;
H: hu: Országos Levéltár

O.L. e: Overseas League

OLA US: e: Office of Legal Affairs; Ohio (Oklahoma) Library Association; CDN: e: Ontario Library Association; US: e: Oregon Library Association; Osteopathic Libraries Association

OLAS INT: s: Organización Lation-Americana de la Solidaridad; CGO: f: Organisation Locale des Affaires Sociales, Léopoldville

OLB BRD: d: Oldenburgische Landesbank AG, 29 Oldenburg; H: hu: Országos Létszámbitottság, Budapest

OLC D: e: nach WK2: Office of Land Commissioner [US Zone]

OLCB D: e: nach WK2: Office of the Land Commissioner of Bavaria

OLCH D: e: nach WK2: Office of the Land Commissioner of Hesse

OLCP/EA INT: f: Organisation de lutte contre le criquet pélerin dans l'Est africain, Asmara [ETH]

Old Vic GB: e: Old Victoria Theatre, London

OLERR INT: [d: Organisation europäischer Straßenbauforschungsinstitute]

OLF S: sv: Orkesterledarföreningen

OLG D: d: Oberlandesgericht; D: d: Ostpreußische Landgesellschaft, Königsberg i.Pr.

OLI GB: e: mil: Oxfordshire Light Infantry

O.L.K. D: d: Oberste Luftsportkommission

OLK BRD: d: Offenbach-Lichterfelder Kassen [Krankenkasse]

OLLA US: e: Office of Lend-Lease Administration

OLMA CH: d: Ostschweizerische Land- und Milchwirtschaftliche Ausstellung, St. Gallen [seit 1943, jetzt:] Schweizerische Messe für Land- und Milchwirtschaft

OLO B: nl: Officieel Lager Onderwijs; YU: sn: Okrajni Ljudski Odbor; Okrožni Ljudski Odbor; NL: nl: Openbaar Lager Onderwijs

OLP US: e: Office of Labor Production

O.L.P. f: Organisation de la Libération de Palestine

O&LPWP US: e: mil: Operational and Logistical Procedures Working Party

OLS NL: nl: Openbaare Lagere School

OLSO DZ: [d: Befreiungsorganisation für die besetzte Sahara, gegr 1971]

Ol.Sp. d: Olympische Spiele

O.L.T. 1: Ordo de la Trappe

OLV d: Oberlandesverband; A: d: Oberösterreichischer Landesverlag; DK: da: mil: Orlogsvaerftet

OLWG d: Oberlandwirtschaftsgericht

OLy d: Oberlyzeum

OLYMPIC GR: e: Olympic Airways, Athens

OM d: Oberschule für Mädchen; CS: cs: Obranci Míru

O.M. F: f: Observatoire de Meudon; Office Météorologique

OM H: hu: Oktatásügyi Minisztérium, Budapest; B: NL: nl: Openbaare Ministerie; 1: Ordo Minorum [= O.Min.]

OMA GB: e: Office Management Association of Great Britain; US: e: mil: Office of Military Assistance; Office of the Military Attaché; Office of Mutual Aid; GB: e: Oilskin Manufacturers Association of Great Britain; US: e: Optical Manufacturers Association, New York 36, N.Y.; D: d: Optische-mechanische Anstalt, Berlin

O.M.A. F: f: mil: Organisation Métropolitaine de l'Armée

OMAI INT: f: Organisation Mondiale Agudas Israel [London, gegr 1912]

OMANUT CH: [d: Verein zur Förderung jüdischer Kunst in der Schweiz]·

O.M.B. D: d: Oberste Motor(rad)sportbehörde

OMB US: e: Office of Management and Budget; NL: nl: Openbaare Muziek-

bibliothek; H: hu: Országos Munkabér-
(megállapitó) Bizottság, Budapest
OMBKE H: hu: Országos Magyar Bányás-
záti és Kohászati Egyesület, Budapest
OMC US: e: mil: Office of Munitions
Control; 1: = O.F.M.Cap.; US: e: mil:
Ordnance Missile Command; INT: f:
Organisation Mondiale du Commerce
O.M.C. GB: e: mil: Oxford Military Col-
lege; GB: e: Oxford Mission to Calcutta
O.M.Cap. l: = O.F.M.Cap.
OMCH SU: [d: Verband Moskauer Maler]
OMCI INT: Organisation intergouverne-
mentale consultative de la navigation
maritime [e: IMCO]
O.M.Conv. 1: = O.F.M.Conv.
OMD CS: cs: Ochrana Matek a Dětí
OMEA US: e: Ohio Music Education As-
sociation; Oklahoma Music Educators
Association
OMEH H: hu: Országos Munkaerőgazdál-
kodási Hivatal, Budapest
O.Mel. 1: Ordo Melitensis
OMEP INT: f: Organisation mondiale pour
l'éducation préscolaire [gegr 1948,
e: WOEC]
OMERA F: f: Société d'Optique de Mé-
canique d'Electricité et de Radio, Argen-
teuil (S.-&O.)
OMF US: e: Office of Marketing Facilities
OMFB H: hu: Országos Müszaki Fejlesz-
tési Bizottság, Budapest
OMFP I: i: Officine Meccaniche Ferroviarie
Pistoesi
OMG US: e: mil: Office of Military Govern-
ment
OMGB D: US: e: mil: nach WK2: Office
of Military Government for Bavaria
OMGBS D: US: e: mil: nach WK2: Office
of Military Government for Berlin Sector
OMGBW D: US: e: mil: nach WK2: Office
of Military Government for Baden-Würt-
temberg
OMGE INT: f: Organisation mondiale de
gastro-entérologie; H: hu: Országos

Magyar Gazdasági Egyesület
OMGG(US) D: US: e: mil: nach WK2: Of
fice of Military Government for Germar
United States
OMGH D: US: e: mil: nach WK2: Office
of Military Government for Hesse
OMgK H: hu: Országos Mezőgazdasági
Könyvtár, Budapest
OMGLB D: US: e: mil: nach WK2: Office
of Military Government for Land Breme
OMGStEG; OMGSTEG D: US: e: mil:
nach WK2: Office of Military Govern-
ment for StEG
OMGUS D: US: e: mil: nach WK2: Office
of Military Government (for Germany),
United States
OMGUSZ D: US: e: mil: nach WK2: Of-
fice of Military Government, United
States Zone
OMGWB D: US: mil: nach WK2: Office
of Military Government for Württem-
berg-Baden
OMH H: hu: Országos Mérésügyi Hivatal,
Budapest; Országos Mértékügyi Hiva-
tal, Budapest
O.M.I. 1: Oblati Mariae Immaculatae
OMI INT: f: Organisation Météorologique
Internationale; H: hu: Országos Munka
gészségügyi Intézet, Budapest
O.M.I. I: i: Ottico Meccanica Italiana e
Rilevamenti Aerofotogrammetrici
S.p.A., Roma
OMIKI H: hu: Országos Mezőgazdasági
Ipari Kisérleti Intézet, Budapest
O.Min. 1: Ordo Fratrum Minimorum;
Ordo Minorum
O.Min.Conv. = O.F.M.Conv.
O.Minim. 1: Ordo Fratrum Minimorum
Omira BRD: d: Oberland-Milchverwertung
GmbH, Ravensburg (Württ)
OMK BRD: d: Oberste Motorradsport-Kor
mission, 605 Offenbach (Main); H: hu:
Országos Müszaki Könyvtár, Budapest
OMKDK H: hu: Országos Müszaki Könyv-
tár és Dokumentácios Központ, Budape

O.M.L. B: f: Office médico-légal

OML US: e: mil: Ordnance Missile Laboratories

OMM US: e: Office of Minerals Mobilization; INT: f: Organisation météorologique mondiale s: Organización Meteorológica Mundial i: Organizzazione meteorologica mondiale [e: WMO]

OMMA US: e: Outboard Motor Manufacturers Association, Chicago, Ill.

OMMC US: e: mil: Officer Messenger Mail Center

OMMI H: hu: Országos Mezőgazdasági Minőségvizsgáló Intézet, Budapest

O.M.M.I.A. I: i: Officina Meccanica Misuratori Industriali Affiani, Milano

O.M.N.F. e: Officers' Merchant Navy Federation

OMNIPOL CS: [d: Außenhandelsunternehmen, Prag]

Omnirex F: f: Omnium de Recherches et d'Exploitations Pétrolières

OMO NL: nl: Openbaar Middelbaar Onderwijs

OMP US: e: Office of Management Production

OMPA INT: f: Organisation mondiale pour la protection des aveugles

O.M.P.A. e: Oyster Merchants and Planters' Association

OMPE INT: f: Organisation mondiale des professionnels dans l'enseignement, Washington, D.C.

OMPI INT: [d: Weltorganisation für geistiges Eigentum, Genf]

OMPSA INT: f: Organisation mondiale pour la protection sociale des aveugles, Paris

OMS US: e: Office of Marketing Services; f: mil: Office militaire de sécurité; INT: f: Organisation mondiale de la santé, Genève [CH] s: Organización Mundial de la Salud i: Organizzazione Mondiale della Sanità [e: WHO]

OMSF US: e: Office of Manned Space Flight [NASA]

OMSz H: hu: Országos Mentőszolgálat, Budapest

O.M.T. e: Old Merchant Taylors

OMTA INT: f: Organisation Mondiale du Tourisme et de l'Automobile [e: WTAO]

OMTUR PL: pl: Organizacja Młodzieży Towarzystwa Uniwersytetu Robotniczego

O.M.U.A. e: Office Machinery Users' Association

O.M.V. 1: Oblati Beatae Mariae Virginis

O.M.V.A. MA: f: Office de Mise en Valeur Agricole, Rabat

OMVK CS: cs: Okresní Mimořádná Vyživovací Komise

OMW BRD: d: Oberrheinische Mineralölwerke GmbH, 75 Karlsruhe 21

OMZ BRD: d: OMZ Vereinigte Ost- und Mitteldeutsche Zement-AG, Dortmund

ON A: d: Österreichisches Normungsinstitut, A-1010 Wien 1 [vorher: ÖNA]

O.N. F: f: Office National; B: f: Office de la Navigation

ON NL: nl: Onafhankelijke Nationale Groep

ONA US: e: mil: Office of Naval Adviser; US: e: Overseas National Airways, New York; Overseas News Agency, New York, N.Y.

O.N.A.A. F: f: Office National Anti-Acridien

ONAC B: f: mil: Oeuvre nationale des iens anciens combattants, résistants, prisonniers politiques, déportés et réfractaires

ONACO DZ: f: Office nationale de commercialisation

O.N.A.C.V.G. F: f: mil: Office National des Anciens Combattants et Victimes de la Guerre

ONAF B: F: f: Office National des Allocations Familiales

O.N.A.G. B: f: mil: Oeuvre nationale des anciens combattants et victimes de la guerre

ONAH f: Office National des Hydro-
carbures
ONAP B: f: Oeuvre Nationale d'Aide et
de Protection aux Artistes Belges
ONARES Kamerun: f: Organisation Na-
tionale de la Recherche Scientifique du
Cameroun
ONARMO B: f: Oeuvre nationale d'aide
religieuse et morale aux ouvriers; I: i:
Opera Nazionale per l'Assistenza Reli-
giosa e Morale degli Operai
ONATA US: e: mil: Office of North At-
lantic Treaty Affairs [Department of
Defense]
O.N.A.T.E.R. F: f: Omnium national de
terrassements et de travaux publics
ONB A: d: Österreichische Nationalbi-
bliothek, Wien 1
O.N.B. B: f: Orchestre National de
Belgique
O.N.B.D.T. B: f: Oeuvre nationale belge
de défense contre la tuberculose
O.N.B.I. F: f: Office National des Bre-
vets d'Invention
O.N.B.L.C.C. B: f: Oeuvre Nationale
Belge de Lutte contre le Cancer
O.N.C. F: f: mil: Office National des
Combattants; I: i: mil: Opera nazionale
combattenti
O.N.C.E. F: f: Office National du Com-
merce Extérieur; B: f: Office National
de la Coopération à l'Ecole
O.N.C.E.L. e: Organization Network Com-
mand for Enforcement of Law [d: im
Film]
ONCF MA: f: Office National des Che-
mins de Fer
ONCIC DZ: f: Office National pour le
Commerce et l'Industrie Cinématogra-
phique
O.N.C.L. F: f: Office National des Com-
bustibles Liquides
O.N.C.P.A. RCB: f: Office national de
commercialisation des produits agricoles
ONCSA H: hu: Országos Nép- és Csa-

ládvédelmi Alap, Budapest
O.N.C.V. DZ: f: Office National de Com-
mercialisation des Produits Viti-Vinicole
Alger
OND B: f: Office National du Ducroire,
Bruxelles; PL: pl: Odwód Naczelnego
Dowództwa; I: i: Opera Nazionale Do-
polavoro [gegr 1925]
ONDAH B: f: Office National des Dé-
bouchés Agricoles et Horticoles
ONE B: f: Oeuvre Nationale de l'Enfance
ONEM B: f: Office National de l'Emploi
ONERA F: f: Office National d'Etudes
et de Recherches Aéronautiques [jetzt:]
Office national des études et recherches
aérospatiales, Châtillon-sous-Bagneux
(Seine)
ONF CS: cs: Okresní Národní Front
ONFEP B: nl: Onafhankelijke Nationale
Federatie der Postboden
ONGT f: Office National Gabonaise du
Tourisme
ONH US: e: mil: Office of Naval History
ONI F: f: Office National de l'Immigration
MA: f: Office National d'Irrigation;
US: e: mil: Office of Naval Intelligence;
H: hu: Országos Neveléstudományi
Intézet, Budapest
ONIA F: f: Office National Industriel de
l'Azote, Toulouse
ONIB F: f: Office National Interprofes-
sionnel du Blé
O.N.I.C. F: f: Office national interprofes-
sionnel des céréales; Organisation na-
tionale de l'industrie et du commerce
O.N.I.G. B: f: mil: Oeuvre Nationale des
Invalides de la Guerre
O.N.I.O.P. F: f: Office national pour l'in-
formation et l'orientation pédagogiques
et professionnelles
O.N.I.S.I. I: i: Organizzazione Nazionale
Italiana degli Studenti di Ingegneria
O.N.I.T. B: f: Organisation Nationale
Indépendante des Travailleurs
O.N.L. B: f: Office National du Lait et

de ses Dérivés

O.N.M. F: f: Office National Météorologique; TN: f: Office National des Mines

ONM US: e: mil: Office of Naval Material (Materiel)

O.N.M.G. F: f: mil: Office National des Mutilés de Guerre

O.N.M.I. I: i: Opera nazionale per la maternità e infanzia

ONMP P: pt: Organização Nacional Mocidade Portuguêsa

ONMR MA: [e: office of rural modernization]

O.N.N. F: f: Office National de la Navigation

ONO YU: sh: Okružni Narodni Odbor; Opštinski Narodni Odbor

ONOO YU: sh: Okružni Narodnooslbodilački Odbor

ONOVA B: f: mil: Oeuvre Nationale des Orphelins, Veuves et Ascendants des Victimes de la Guerre

ONP F: f: Office National de Planification; PL: pl: Ośrodek Normowania Pracy

ONPC B: f: Office National de Placement et de Chômage

O.N.P.I. F: f: Office National de la Propriété Industrielle

O.N.P.N. F: f: Office National des Pupilles de la Nation

ONPO B: f: Office National des Pensions pour Ouvriers

ONR PL: pl: Obóz Narodowo-Radykalny; US: e: mil: Office of Naval Research

O.N.R. F: f: Organisation Nationale de Résistance

O.N.R.A. F: f: Office National de la Recherche Aéronautique; DZ: f: Office National de la Réforme Agraire

ONRI NL: nl: Orde van Nederlandse Raadgevende Ingenieurs; s: Organización Nacional de Rehabilitación de Inválidos

O.N.R.S.I. F: f: Office National des Recherches Scientifiques et Industrielles

O.N.R.S.I.I. F: f: Office National des

Recherches Scientifiques et Industrielles et des Inventions

ONS d: Oberste nationale Schiffahrtbehörde; D: d: Oberste Nationale Sportbehörde für die deutsche Kraftfahrt, Berlin; BRD: d: Oberste Nationale Sportkommission für den Automobilsport in Deutschland, 6 Ffm

O.N.S. B: Oeuvre Nationale de Secours

ONS GB: e: Overseas News Service, London; e: Overseas Nursing Service

O.N.S.E.R. F: f: Organisme national de sécurité routière

O.N.S.S. B: f: Oeuvre (Office) National(e) de Sécurité Sociale

O.N.T. F: f: Office National du Tourisme [gegr 1910]; L: f: Office National du Tourisme, Luxembourg; DZ: f: Office National des Transports

ONT H: hu: Országos Népmüvelési Tanács, Budapest

ONTOM F: f: Organisation Nationale du Tourisme Outre-Mer, Paris

Ont.R. CDN: e: mil: Ontario Regiment

ONTV CS: cs: Okresní Národní Tělovýchový Výbor; NL: nl: Stichting Onafhankelijke Nationale Televisie

ONU US: e: Ohio Northern University; INT: f: Organisation des Nations-Unies s: Organización de las Naciones Unidas i: Organizzazione delle Nazioni Unite, New York

ONUC UN: f: Opération des Nations Unies au Congo

ONUDI UN: f: Organisation des Nations Unies pour le Développement Industriel

ONUECC UN: s: Organización de la Naciones Unidas para la Educación, la Ciencia y la Cultura [e: UNESCO]

O.N.U.E.F. F: f: Office National des Universités et Ecoles Françaises

ONUESC UN: f: Organisation des Nations -Unies pour l'Education, la Science et la Culture Intellectuelle [= UNESCO]

ONURC UN: s: Organismo de la Naciones

Unidas para le Reconstrucción de Corea
ONV CS: cs: Obvodní Národní Výbor
ONVOA B: f: Oeuvre Nationale pour les
Veuves, Orphelins et Ascendants
ONT INT: pl: Organizacja Narodów Zjed-
noczonych [e: UN, UNO]
OO YU: sn: Občinski Odbor; CS: cs:
Okresní Odbor; YU: sn: Okrožni Odbor;
YU: sh: Okružni Odbor; NL: nl: Open-
baar Onderwijs
O&O GB: e: Oriental and Occidental
Steamship Company
OO YU: sh: Osnovna Organizacija
OOAA US: e: Olive Oil Association of
America
OOAMA US: e: mil: Ogden Air Materiel
Area, Ogden, Utah
OOC e: Office of Censorship; INT: f:
Organisation des Opérations Commer-
ciales [GATT] ; GB: e: Oxford Ophthal-
mological Congress
OODS CS: sk: Okresná Organizácia Demo-
kratickej Strany
OÖAMTC A: d: Oberösterreichischer Auto-
mobil-, Motorrad- und Touring-Club
OÖVL A: d: Oberösterreichischer Ver-
ein für Luftschiffahrt
OOI CS: cs: Okresní Osvětový Inspektorát;
H: hu: Országos Onkológiai Intézet, Bu-
dapest
OOK CS: cs: Okresní Odbor Kultury;
H: hu: Országos Orvostörténeti Könyv-
tár, Budapest
O.Oliv. 1: Ordo Sancti Beati Montis Oliveti
OOM PL: pl: Okręgowy Ośrodek Meto-
dyczny
OO OF YU: sn: Okrajni Odbor Osvobo-
dilne Fronte
OOP PL: pl: Oddziałowa Organizacja
Partyjna
O.O.P. F: f: Office d'Orientation Profes-
sionnelle
OOP PL: pl: Okręgowa Organizacja Par-
tyjna
OO.PP. I: i: Opere Pubbliche

OOPSRPCO s: Organismo de Obras Púb-
licas y Socorro a los Refugiados de Pa-
lestina en Cercano Oriente
OOR CS: cs: Obvodná Osvětová Rada;
US: e: mil: Office of Ordnance Research
O.O.R. e: Office of the Official Receiver
OOR CS: cs: Okresní Odborová Rada
OOS CS: cs: Okresní Osvětový Sbor
OO SZDL YU: sn: Okrajni Odbor Socia-
listične Zveze Delovnega Ljudstva
O.O.T. F: f: Organisme Officiel du Tourism
O.O.U. e: Office of the Umpire [unem-
ployment insurance]
OOZ PL: pl: Oddziałowa Organizacja
Związkowa
OP BRD: d: Bahn: Oberprüfungsamt für
die höheren technischen Verwaltungs-
beamten
O.P. F: f: Observatoire de Paris; Office
de Placement; Office Professionnel;
e: Old Playgoers [club]
OP D: d: Ordnungspolizei; 1: Ordo Prae-
dicatorum
O&P US: e: Orient & Pacific Lines, San
Francisco
O.P. D: d: Ortspolizei
OPA. BRD: d: Bahn: Oberprüfungsamt
für die höheren technischen Verwal-
tungsbeamten
OPA US: e: Office of Price Administration
[disbanded 1946]
O.P.A. INT: f: Organisation du Pacte
Atlantique [= OTAN] ; Organisation
de la Palestine arabe; DZ: f: Organisa-
tion Politique et Administrative [gegr
1956] ; F: f: Organisme Professionnel
Agricole
OPA INT: pl: Organizacja Państw Amery-
kańskich [e: OAS]
O.P.A. e: Overseas Parliamentary Associ-
ation
O.P.A.C. CGO: f: Office des Produits
Agricoles de Costermansville
OPACI INT: f: Organisation provisoire
de l'aéronautique civile internationale

[e: PICAO, später: e: ICAO]

O.P.A.C.S. e: Office of Price Administration of Commodities and Supplies

O.P.A.E.P. INT: f: Organisation des pays arabes exportateurs de pétrole

O.P.A.K. CGO: f: Office des Produits Agricoles de Kivu

OP and CMIA US: e: Operative Plasterers and Cement Masons International Association

O.P.A.S. CGO: f: Office des Produits Agricoles de Stanleyville

O.P.A.T. TG: f: Office des Produits Agricoles du Togo

OPB. D: d: Ordnungspolizeibehörde; Ortspolizeibehörde

O.P.C. e: Office of Parliamentary Counsel; Office of Petroleum Co-ordination (Co-ordinator); B: f: mil: Office postal centralisateur

OPC US: e: mil: Ordnance Procurement Center

O.P.C. e: Ovamboland People's Congress [gegr 1958]

OPC US: e: Overseas Press Club, New York, N.Y.

OPCMIA = OP and CMIA

O.P.C.W. US: e: Office of Petroleum Coordinator for War

OPD BRD: d: Post: Oberpostdirektion

OpD e: Operations Department (Division)

O.P.D.A. e: Ottoman Public Debt Administration

OpDevFor US: e: mil: Operational Development Force, Atlantic Fleet

OPDL US: e: Office of Production and Defense Lending

OPDn BRD: d: Post: Oberpostdirektionen

OPEC INT: e: Organization of Petroleum Exporting Countries, Wien 4 [A, gegr 1960]

OPED R: ro: Oficiul de Presă, Editura şi Documentare

OPEDA US: e: Organization of Professional Employees of the United States Department of Agriculture

OPEG INT: e: Organization's [OEEC] Petroleum Emergency Group [gegr 1956]

O.P.E.J. f: Oeuvre de protection des enfants juifs

O.P.E.M. F: f: Office National pour la Promotion de l'Exportation; B: f: Organisation pour la Protection des Entreprises Moyennes

OPEMA US: e: Oil Field Production Equipment Manufacturers Association

O.P.E.P. INT: f: Organisation des pays exportateurs de pétrole [e: OPEC]

OPEU US: e: Office and Professional Employees Union

OPF H: hu: Országos Pénzügyi Felügyelőség

OPG D: d: Oberstes Parteigericht [NSDAP]

OPGTM F: f: Office professionnel général de la transformation des métaux

O.P.H. F: f: Office Public de l'Habitation

O.P.H.B.M. F: f: Office Parisien des Habitations à Bon Marché

Ophinab S: sv: Skandinavska Osram-Philips-Neon AB

Ophinag A: d: Österreichische Osram-Philips-Neon-GmbH, Wien 7

OPHO PL: pl: Okręgowe Przedsiębiorstwo Handlu Opałem

O.P.H.S. F: f: Office Public d'Hygiène Sociale

O.P.&I. e: Office of Patents and Inventions

O.P.I. F: f: Office de la Propriété Industrielle; e: Office of Public Information

Opiag A: d: Osteuropäische Petroleum-Industrie AG, Wien 1

OPIC US: e: Overseas Private Investment Corporation [planned 1969]

O.P.I.C.B.A. F: f: Office Professionnel des Industries et Commerces du Bois et de l'Ameublement

OPICND US: e: mil: Office of Petroleum Industry Coordinator for National Defense

OPIF INT: e: Orient Press International

Federation

OPK BRD: d: Post: Oberpostkasse; PL: pl: Organizacja Przysposobienia Kobiet do Obrony Kraju; H: hu: Országos Pedagógiai Könyvtár, Budapest

OPKI H: hu: Onkopatológiai Kutató Intézet, Budapest

OPLA GR: [d: Volkswiderstandsorganisation]

OPLO NATO: f: Organisation de Production et de Logistique de l'OTAN

OPLOH NATO: f: Organisation de Production et de Logistique OTAN du HAWK [e: homing-all-the-way killer d: Boden-Luft-Zielsuchflugkörper]

OPL OK PL: pl: Obrona Przeciwlotnicza Obszaru Kraju

O.P.M. F: f: Observatoire du Parc de Montsouris; Office des Pêches Maritimes

OPM US: e: mil: Office of Procurement and Materiel; Office of Production Management

O.P.M. e: mil: Office, Provost Marshal

OPM CS: cs: Okresní Péče o Mládež; West-Irian: [d: Widerstandsbewegung "Freies Papua"]

OPMA GB: e: Overseas Press and Media Association Ltd.

O.P.M.E. F: f: Office de Protection de la Maternité et de l'Enfance

OPMG US: e: mil: Office of the Provost Marshal General

OPNAV US: e: mil: Office of the Chief of Naval Operations

OPNAVINST US: e: mil: Office of the Chief of Naval Operations Instructions

OPO US: e: mil: Office of the Personnel Officer; Office of Personnel Operations; DDR: d: Ortsparteiorganisation [SED]; PL: pl: Ośrodek Przygotowán Olimpijskich

O.P.O. e: Ovamboland People's Organization [gegr 1958]

O.Poen. 1: Ordo Poenitentiae de Jesu Nazareno

O.P.O.H. NATO: f: [d: Dienststelle für HAWK-Produktion, vgl: OPLOH]

OPol. D: d: Ordnungspolizei

OPolB D: d: Ortspolizeibehörde

OPOSA E: s: Organización de la Patata del Pirineo Occidental

OPP PL: pl: Obrona Powietrzna Państwa

OPR US: e: Office of Public Relations

O.Pr. 1: Ordo Praedicatorum

O.Praem. 1: Ordo Praemonstratensis

O.P.R.D. GB: e: Office of Production Research and Development

OPRIBA; Opriba BRD: d: Ostdeutsche Privatbank, 6 Ffm

OPRS WAN: e: Oil Palm Research Station

OPS PL: pl: Oddział Pracy Socjalistycznej; US: e: Office of Price Stabilization; CS: cs: Okresní Pedagogický Sbor; Okresní Pracovní Středisko; INT: s: Organización Panamericana de la Salud pt: Organização Pan-Americana de Saúde f: Organisation panaméricaine de la santé, Washington, D.C.; PL: pl: Organizacja Polskich Socjalistów

O.P.S.A. F: f: Oeuvre des Petites Sœurs de l'Assomption; GB: e: Old Pharmacy Students' Association of Bristol College od Science and Technology

O.P.S.C. GB: e: Oxford Photographic Survey Committee

OPSI NL: nl: Organisatie van de Progessieve Studerende Jeugd

O.P.St. D: d: Oberprüfstelle für Schund- und Schmutzschriften

OPT PL: pl: Ośrodek Postępu Technicznego

O.P.T. GB: e: Oxford Preservation Trust

Optago D: d: Optische Anstalt Goerz

O.P.T.E.G. A: d: Österreichische Petroleum-Terrain-Exploitations-GmbH, Wien 1

OPTEVFOR US: e: mil: Operational Test and Evaluation Force, Norfolk, Va.

O.P.T.R. F: f: Office Professionnel des Transports Routiers

Opt.S.A. US: e: Optical Society of America

OPUL INT: nl: Organisatie van Petroleum -uitvoerende Landen [e: OPEC]

OPV D: d: Oberprimaner-Verein; BRD: d: Oberweser-Privatschiffer-Vereinigung; CH: d: Ostschweizerischer Presse -Verband

O.P.V.L. D: d: Ostpreußischer Verein für Luftschiffahrt, Königsberg i.Pr.

OPW PL: pl: Obóz Polski Walczącej; INT: [d: Waggon-Pool der Länder des Comecon] ; e: Office of Public Works

O.P.W.C. e: Old People's Welfare Centre

OPWK PL: pl: Organizacja Przysposobienia Kobiet do Obrony Kraju

OPZ d: Oberschule praktischen Zweiges; BRD: d: mil: Offizierbewerberprüfzentrale, 5 Köln

OpZ d: mil: Operationszentrale

O.Q.-M.G.; OQMG e: mil: Office of the Quarter-Master (Quartermaster) General

O.Qu. D: d: mil:Oberquartiermeister

OQuBw BRD: d: mil: Oberquartiermeister der Bundeswehr

OR D: d: Oberrealschule; CS: cs: Obvodní Rada; Odborová Rada

O.R. f: Office à Répartition

OR NL: nl: Dienst van de Opiumregie in Nederlandsch-Indië; 1: Patres Oratorii; US: e: mil: Ordnance Corps; Bureau of Ordnance [Navy] ; YU: sh: Organizacija Rada; US: e: mil: Organized Reserve; CS: cs: Osvětová Rada

ORA D: d: NS: Oberreichsanwalt; F: f: Office des Reinseignements Agricoles; IND: e: Operations Research Association

O.R.A. F: f: WK2: Organisation de la Résistance de l'Armée

O.R.A.F. f: mil: Office de Renseignements et d'Aide aux Familles de Militaires; DZ: f: Organisation de résistance de l'Algérie française

Orag D: d: Ostdeutsche Rundfunk-AG

O.R.A.I.G. B: f: mil: Office de Renseignements et d'Aide aux Invalides de Guerre

ORALIME INT: f: Organisme de Liaison des Industries Métalliques Européennes, Paris

ORAMEI CGO: f: Oeuvre Reine Astrid de la Mère et de l'Enfant Indigènes

ORANA f: Organisme de Recherches sur l'Alimentation et la Nutrition Africaines

O.R.B. B: f: Observatoire Royal de Belgique; e: Official Receiver in Bankruptcy

ORB NL: nl: Opiumregiebond op Java

Orbea BRD: d: Ornithologische Beobachtungsstation Altrhein [bei Mannheim]

O.R.C. e: mil: Officers' Reserve Corps; Operational Requirement Committee; e: Opinion Research Corporation; GB: e: Orange River Colony; US: e: Order of Railway Conductors of America; e: Order of the Red Cross

ORC US: e: mil: Organized Reserve Corps [Army]

O.R.C.A. e: Official Receiver under the Companies' Act

ORCA INT: f: Organisme européen de coordination des recherches sur le fluor et la prophylaxie de la carie dentaire [gegr 1953]

ORCB US: e: Order of Railway Conductors and Brakesmen

ORCEN US: e: mil: Overseas Records Center [Army]

O.R.C.G. F: f: Organe de Recherche des Criminels de Guerre

Orco D: d: Organisation Consul [gegr 1918]

ORCO ISO: e: Organization Committee

ORD e: mil: Officers' Replacement Depot; US: e: Office of Rubber Director

O.R.D. B: nl: Openbare Reinigingsdienst

ORD US: e: mil: Ordnance Corps; Overseas Replacement Depot

OrdA BRD: d: Ordnungsamt

Ord B US: e: mil: Ordnance Board

ORDBA US: e: mil: Frankford Arsenal, Ordnance Corps

ORDBC US: e: mil: Rock Island Arsenal, Ordnance Corps

Ord.Bd. e: mil: Ordnance Board

ORDC; OrdC US: e: mil: Ordnance Corps

ORDDW US: e: mil: Redstone Arsenal, Ordnance Corps

ORDEP US: e: mil: Overseas Replacement Depot

ORDJR US: e: mil: Raritan Arsenal, Ordnance Corps

ORDMC US: e: mil: Ordnance Tank Automotive Center

ORDOK H: hu: Orvostudományi Dokumentációs Központ, Budapest

ORDOW US: e: mil: Rock Island Arsenal, Ordnance Corps

Ord.Pol. D: d: Ordnungspolizei

OrdRC e: mil: Ordnance Reserve Corps

Ord.Sch. e: mil: Ordnance School

OrdTTC US: e: mil: Ordnance Technical Training Center

ORDWD US: e: mil: Rossford Ordnance Depot

ORE INT: f: Office de Recherches et d'Essais de l'UIC, Utrecht [NL, gegr 1950]

O.R.E. B: f: Office de récupération économique

ORE INT: f: Organisation régionale européenne de la CISL, Bruxelles [B] s: Organización Regional Europea de la CIOSL [gegr 1950]

O.R.E.A.M. F: f: Organisation d'Etude d'Aménagement de l'Aire Métropolitaine (du Nord)

OREC B: f: Office de Redressement (Rénovation) Economique

ORechK; ORechnK. D: d: Oberrechnungskammer

ORES INT: [e: European Society for Opinion Surveys and Market Research]

ORF US: e: Occupational Research Foundation; A: d: Österreichischer Rundfunk und Fernsehen; CDN: e: Ontario Research Foundation

ORFI H: hu: Országos Reuma- és Fürdőügyi Intézet, Budapest

ORG D: d: nach WK2: Oberstes Rückerstattungsgericht

Org BRD: d: mil: Gruppe Organisation [BMVtdg] ; BRD: d: Organisation Gehlen

ORG CH: d: Ostschweizerische Radio- und Fernsehgesellschaft, St. Gallen

OrgA D: d: nach WK2: Organisationsausschuß des Parlamentarischen Rats

ORGALIME INT: f: Organisme de liaison des industries métalliques et électriques européennes, Bruxelles [B]

Orgatechnik BRD: d: Ausstellung für Organisation und Technik im Büro und Betrieb, 5 Köln [24 . . . 28 Okt 1971]

Orgéco F: f: Organisation générale des consommateurs, Paris

Orgesch D: d: Organisation Escherich [gegr 1918]

OrgRes BRD: d: mil: Organisation für Betreuung und Weiterbildung der Reservisten der Bundeswehr; US: e: mil: Organized Reserves

ORH BRD: d: Oberrechnungshof; A: d: Oberster Rechnungshof

ORI ZA: e: Oceanographic Research Institute; US: e: Office of Research and Inventions; Operations Research Inc., Silver Spring, Md.; C: s: Organizaciónes Revolucionarias Integradas

ORIA US: e: Oriental Rug Importers Association

ORIEL F: f: Association pour l'orientation des entreprises de la construction électrique, Paris

O.R.I.M. f: Organisation Révolutionnaire Intérieure Macédoine [vgl: IMRO]

ORIN US: e: mil: Orleans Installation, Orleans [= Orléans, F]

O.R.I.N.D. US: e: mil: Office of Research and Inventions, Navy Department

ORINS US: e: Oak Ridge Institute of Nuclear Studies

ORIT INT: f: Organisation régionale interaméricaine des travailleurs de la CISL s: Organización Regional Interamericana de Trabajadores, México, D.F. [gegr 1951]

ORK D: d: Oberrechnungskammer; INT: d: Ökumenischer Rat der Kirchen, Genf [CH] ; CS: cs: Okresní Rolnická Komise; Okresní Rozhodčí Komise

ORKFiSp PL: pl: Okręgowa Rada Kultury Fizycznej i Sportu

ORL US: e: mil: Ordnance Research Laboratory

O.R.L. R: ro: Institutul de Oto-rino-laringologie, Bucureşti

ORLN PL: pl: Ośrodek Rozwojowy Łączników Niskonapięciowych

ORMIG BlnW: d: Organisations-Mittel GmbH, 1 Berlin-Tempelhof

ORMO PL: pl: Ochotnicza Rezerwa Milicji Obywatelskiej [gègr 1946]

ORMOA D: e: nach WK2: Office for Relation with Military and Occupation Authorities

O.R.M.P.D. GB: e: Office of the Receiver for the Metropolitan Police District

ORMUZ PL: [d: Musikorganisation]

ORN PL: pl: Osiedlowa Rada Narodowa

ORNI B: f: Office de régulation de la navigation intérieure

ORNL US: e: Oak Ridge National Laboratory

ORO CS: cs: Okresní Rada Osvětová; NL: nl: Onafhankelijke Radio-Omroep N.V.; US: e: Operations Research Office

ORP DZ: f: Organisation de la résistance populaire

ORPA C: s: Oficina de Regulación de Precios y Abastecimiento

Orpo D: d: Ordnungspolizei

ORR PL: pl: Oddziałowa Rada Robotnicza

ORS PL: pl: Obsługa Ratalnej Sprzedaży; US: e: Office of Rent Stabilization

O.R.S. GB: e: Oxfordshire Record Society

ORSA US: e: Operations Research Society of America; 1: Ordo Recollectorum Sancti Augustini

O.R.S.C. F: f: Office de la Recherche Scientifique Coloniale

ORSch d: Oberrealschule

ORSEC F: f: Organisation de Secours

O.R.S.E.M. F: f: mil: Officiers de Réserve du Service d'Etat-Major [1898]

ORSI H: hu: Országos Röntgen és Sugárfizikai Intézet, Budapest

O.R.S.O.M. F: f: Office de la Recherche Scientifique (et Technique) d'Outre-Mer

ORSORT US: e: Oak Ridge School of Reactor Technology

ORSS f: Organisation technique de mise en valeur des richesses du sous-sol saharien

ORSTOM F: f: Office de la recherche scientifique et technique d'Outre-Mer

ORT PL: pl: Obsługa Ruchu Turystycznego

O.R.T. F: f: Office Régional de Transport; Office Régional du Travail

ORT US: e: Order of Railroad Telegraphers

O.R.T. F: f: Organisation Rationnelle du Travail

ORT e: Organization for Rehabilitation through Training

ORTE H: hu: Országos Református Tanáregyesület, Budapest

O.R.T.F.; ORTF F: f: Office de Radiodiffusion-Télévision Française

ORTHO US: e: American Orthopsychiatric Association

OrthVSt D: d: Orthopädische Versorgungsstelle

ORTN NIG: f: Office de Radio-Télévision du Niger

ORTPA GB: e: Oven-Ready Turkey Producers' Association

O.R.T.R.P. F: f: Office Régional des Transports de la Région Parisienne

OrtsBA D: d: Ortsbildungsausschuß

O.R.T.U. GB: e: mil: Other Ranks Training Unit

ORTUAG US: e: mil: Organized Reserve Training Unit, Vessel Augmentation [USCG]

ORTUPS US: e: mil: Organized Reserve Training Unit, Port Security [USCG]

ORTUR US: e: mil: Organized Reserve Training Unit, Rescue Coordination Center [USCG]

ORU CS: cs: Odborná Rada Učitelská

O.R.U. e: Operational Research Unit

ORUB I: i: Organismo Rappresentativo degli Universitari Bologni

ORUR I: i: Organismo Rappresentativo degli Universitari Romani

ORUS I: i: Organismo Rappresentativo degli Universitari Sabini

Orvir I: i: Organizzazione Viaggi Riedenauer, Roma [d: Reisebüro]

ORW PL: pl: Organizacja Rodzin Wojskowych

ORWN PAN PL: pl: Ośrodek Rozpowszechniania Wydawnictw Naukowych Polskiej Akademii Nauk

ORZ DDR: d: Organisations- und Rechenzentrum

ORZZ PL: pl: Okręgowa Rada Związków Zawodowych

OŠ CS: cs: Obchodní škola

OS 1: Oblati Salesiani; e: mil: Observer School

OŠ CS: cs: Odborná škola

OS PL: pl: Oddział Samoobrony; Oddziały Specjalne; CH: d: mil: Offiziersschule

O.S. d: Olympische Spiele; sv: Olympiska spelen; GB: e: Omnibus Society

OS NL: nl: Openbaare School

O.S. GB: e: Ophthalmological Society of the United Kingdom; e: Optical Society; GB: e: The Ordnance Survey Department; f: Organisation scientifique; Organisation spéciale; Organisation syndicale; DZ: f: Organisme saharien

OS US: e: Organisation Society

O.S. GB: e: Oxford Society

OSA US: e: mil: Office of the Secretary of the Army; US: e: Office of Stabilization Administrator; PL: pl: mil: Oficerska Szkoła Artylerii; CDN: e: Ontario Society of Artists

O.S.A. e: Operative Spinners' Association

OSA US: e: Optical Society of America

O.S.A. 1: Ordo Sancti Augustini; ZA: e: Organic Soil Association

OSA SU: [d: Gesellschaft für moderne Architektur, bis 1932]; US: e: mil: Overseas Supply Agency

OSAF D: d: NS: Oberster SA-Führer [SA =Sturmabteilung der NSDAP]; US: e: mil: Office of the Secretary of the Air Force

OSANY US: e: mil: Overseas Supply Agency New York

OSAPL PL: pl: mil: Oficerska Szkoła Artylerii Przeciwlotniczej

OSARCA GB: e: Old Students' Association of the Royal College of Art

OSB. D: d: Obere Siedlungsbehörde; Oberste Sportbehörde [für Leichtathletik]

OSB US: e: Office of Small Business; e: Opinion Service Branch; 1: Ordo Sancti Benedictini

OSBA US: e: Ohio School Boards Association

Osba D: d: Ostdeutsche Spar- und Bau-AG für Beamte, Angestellte und Arbeiter, Königsberg i.Pr.

OSBA US: e: Outlet and Switch Box Association

O.S.Bas.; O.S.B.M. 1: Ordo Sancti Basilii Magni

O.S.B.M.V. = O.Serv.B.M.V.

OSBPiWS PL: pl: mil: Oficerska Szkoła Broni Pancernej i Wojsk Samochodowych

O.S.B.W. GB: e: Overseas Settlement of British Women

O.S.C. e: Oblate of St.Charles

OSC BlnW: d: Olympischer Sport-Club

O.S.C. GB: e: Ontario Services Club, London; Order of Scottish Clans; GB: e: mil: Ordnance Service Corps; 1: Ordo Sancti Camilli; Ordo Sancti Crucis; e: Overseas Settlements Committee

OSCA I: i: Officini Specializzate per la Costruzione di Automobili, Bologna [gegr 1947]

O.S.Cam. 1: Ordo Sancti Camilli

OSCAS PI: e: Office of Statistical Coordination and Standards

OSCC e: Official Spanish Chamber of Commerce

OSCE INT: f: Office de Statistique de la Communauté Européenne, Bruxelles

OSchG D: d: Oberschiedsgericht

OSchJ d: Oberschule für Jungen

OSchK d: Oberschule für Knaben

OSchM d: Oberschule für Mädchen

O.Sch.P. 1: Ordo Scholarum Piarum

O.Sc.P. e: Office of Scientific Personnel

O.S.Cr. 1: Ordo Sancti Crucis

O.S.C.S.A. GB: e: Ordnance Survey Civil Staff Association

OSD US: e: mil: Office of the Secretary of Defense

O.S.D. GB: e: mil: Ordnance Store Department

OSD US: e: mil: Ordnance Supply Depot

O.S.D. GB: e: The Ordnance Survey Department; 1: Ordo Sancti Dominici

OSD PL: pl: Ośrodek Szkolenisa Dziennikarskiego

O.S.D. e: Overseas Settlement Department

OSD US: e: mil: Overseas Supply Division

OSDAA US: e: mil: Ordnance Supply Demand Analysis Agency, Raritan Arsenal, Metuchen, N.J.

OSD BMC US: e: mil: Office of the Secretary of Defense, Ballistic Missile Center

OSD I&L US: e: mil: Office of the Secretary of Defense, Installations and Logistics

OSdL I: i: Organizzazione Scientifica del Lavoro

OSD SAC US: e: mil: Office of the Secretary of Defense, Scientific Advisory Committee

O.S.E. F: f: Oeuvre de Secours aux Enfants

O.S.E.C. CH: f: Office Suisse d'Expansion Commerciale

OSeeA BRD: d: Oberseeamt

O.S.E.F. F: f: Office Scolaire d'Etudes par le Film

O.Serv.B.M.V. 1: Ordo Servorum Beatae Mariae Virginis

OSEV D: d: Oberschlesischer Spiel- und Eislaufverband

OSF 1: Ordo Sancti Francisci

O.S.F.B. F: f: Organisation Scolaire Franco-Britannique, Paris [gegr 1928]

OSFCW US: e: Office of Solid Fuels Coordinator for War

O.S.Fr. = OSF

O.S.F.S. 1: Oblati Sancti Francisci Salesii

OSG US: e: Office of the Secretary General; US: e: mil: Office of the Surgeon General

OSGG NL: nl: Oud-Studenten in de Geschiedenis van de Gentse Universiteit

OSH H: hu: Országos Sporthivatal, Budapest

O.S.Hier. 1: Ordo Sancti Hieronymi

OSHT US: e: Grand Lodge Order of the Sons of Hermann in Texas

OSI US: e: mil: Office of Special Investigation; Office of Strategic Information

OŠI CS: cs: Okresní Školní Inspektor

OSI H: hu: Országos Sportorvosi Intézet, Budapest; BlnW: d: Otto-Suhr-Institut

OSIGO US: e: mil: Office of the Chief Signal Officer

OSIS US: e: Office of Science (Scientific) Information Service [National Science Foundation]

O.S.J.D.; O.S.J.d.D. 1: Ordo Sancti Joannis de Deo

O.S.J.J.E. GB: e: Order of St. John of Jerusalem in England

OSK D: d: Oberharzer Skiklub, Wernigerode; CS: sk:Okresná Správna Komisia; CS: cs: Okresní Správní Komise; J: Osaka Shosen Kaisha [d: Schiffahrtsgesellschaft]

OSKBW PL: pl: mil: Oficerska Szkoƚa Korpus Bezpieczeństwa Wewętrznego

OSL PL: pl: mil: Oficerska Szkoƚa Lotnicza

O.S.L.R.R. US: e: Oregon Short Line Railroad

OSLw BRD: d: mil: Offizierschule der Luftwaffe

O.S.M. F: f: Office de sécurité mutuelle

OSM PL: pl: Okręgowa Spółdzielnia Mleczarska: 1: Ordo Servorum Mariae

O.S.M. INT: f: Organisation Syndicale Mondiale

OSM NZ: e: Otago School of Mines

OSMW PL: pl: mil: Oficerska Szkoƚa Marynarki Wojennej

OSN US: e: mil: Office of the Secretary of the Navy; CH: f: Office Social Neuchâtelois

O.S.N.C. GB: e: Orient Steam Navigation Company

OSNZ NZ: e: Ornithological Society of New Zealand

OSO SU: mil: [d: Gesellschaft zur Förderung der Verteidigung] ; US: e: mil: Ordnance Supply Office

OSOMPP CS: cs: Okresní Sekce Organizace Masové Práce a Propagandy

OSP PL: pl: Ochotnicza Straż Pożarna; US: e: mil: Office of Surplus Property; PL: pl: mil: Oficerska Szkoƚa Piechoty; SF: fi: Oikeistolehtien Sanomapalvelu, Helsinki; NL: nl: Onafhankelijke Socialistische Partij; 1: Ordo Scholarum Piarum; INT: s: Organización Sanitaria Panamericana, Washington, D.C.; PL: pl: Ośrodek Szkolenia Partyjnego

OSPA INT: f: Organisation Sanitaire Panaméricaine, Washington, D.C.

O.S.P.A.A. INT: f: Organisation de solidarité des peuples afro-asiatiques

OSPAAL INT: s: Organización de la Solidaridad de los Pueblos de Africa, Asia y América Latina, La Habana [gegr 1966]

OSPE US: e: Ohio Society of Professional Engineers

O.S.P.M. e: Original Society of Paper Makers

OSPRD CDN: e: mil: Officers Selection, Promotion, Reclassification and Disposal Board

OSPÚ CS: cs: Orechestrální Sdružení Pražských Účitelů

OSR US: e: mil: Office of Scientific Research [USAF] ; Office of Security Review [DOD] ; US: e: Office of the Special Representative for ECA in Europe, Paris; CH: f: Orchestre de la Suisse Romande, Ansermet; F: f: Organisation pour la Sûreté de la République, Paris; RI: e: Organization for Scientific Research

OSRB GB: e: Overseas Services Resettlement Bureau

OSRD US: e: mil: Office of Scientific Research and Development [USAF]

O.S.S. S: sv: Odontologiska sällskapet, Stockholm

OSS US: e: Office of Space Sciences [NASA] ; US: e: mil: Office of Strategic Services; PL: pl: mil: Oficerska Szkoƚa Amochodowa; R: ro: Oficiul de Stat pentru Standarde, Bucureşti; INT: [d: Organisation für die Zusammenarbeit der sozialistischen Länder im Post- und Fernmeldewesen]

O.S.S. F: f: Organisme de Sécurité Sociale

OSŠ CS: cs: Osmiletá Střední Škola

O.S.S. GB: e: Oxford Shorthand Society

Ossag D: d: Ölwerke Stern und Sonneborn AG, Hamburg

O.S.Salv. 1: Ordo Sanctissimi Salvatoris

O.S.S.B. e: Office of the Secretary of State for Burma

OSSD; OSShD INT: [d: Organisation für die Zusammenarbeit der Eisenbahnen der sozialistischen Länder, gegr 1956]

O.S.S.I. e: Office of the Secretary of State for India

OSSOVIACHIM; OSSOWIACHIM SU: [d: Verband der Gesellschaften zur Förderung der Verteidigung, des Flugwesens und der Chemie]

OSSR US: e: mil: Office of Selective Service Records

O.SS.S.; O.Ss.Salv. 1: Ordo Sanctissimi Salvatoris

O.Ss.T. 1: Ordo Sanctissimae Trinitatis

O.S.S.U. F: f: Office du sport scolaire et universitaire

OST US: e: Office of Science and Technology; 1: Ordo Sanctissimae Trinitatis

O.S.T.A. F: f: Organisation scientifique de travail en agriculture

OSTAG A: d: Österreichische Anzeigen-Gesellschaft Weiss & Co. vormals Weiler & Co., Wien 1

OSTI GB: e: Office for Scientific and Technical Information, London S.E.1; US: e: Office for Scientific and Technical Information [NASA]

OSTIV INT: f: Organisation scientifique et technique internationale du vol à voile

OSTiW PL: pl: Ośrodek Sportu, Turystyki i Wypoczynku

OSTP e: Organization for Scientific and Technical Personnel

OSTROPA D: d: Osteuropäische Postwertzeichenausstellung [1935 in Königsberg i.Pr.]

OSTS e: Official Seed Testing Station

OSTT H: hu: Országos Sport- és Testnevelési Tanács, Budapest

OSU PL: pl: mil: Oficerska Szkoła Uzbrojenia; US: e: Ohio State University; Oklahoma State University

O.S.U. 1: Ordo Sanctae Ursulae

O.S.U.K. GB: e: Ophthalmological So-

ciety of the United Kingdom

OSUS PL: pl: Okręgowy Sąd Ubezpieczeń Społecznych

OŠV CS: cs: Okresní Školní Výbor

OSV d: Olympischer Sportverein

Osvia NL: nl: Opleiding-school voor Inlandsche Ambtenaren van het Binnenlandsch Bestuur in Nederlandsch-Indië

OSVO CS: cs: Oblastní Správa Výchovy a Osvěty

OSW DDR: d: Oberspreewerk, Berlin; US: e: Office of Saline Water [gegr 1952]; US: e: mil: Office of the Secretary of War

OSWChem PL: pl: mil: Oficerska Szkoła Wojsk Chemicznych

OSZH H: [e: national cooperative credit institute]

OSZSZT H: hu: Országos Szénbányászati Szaktanács, Budapest

O.Sz.T. H: hu: Országos Szövetkezeti Tanács, Budapest

OSzVB H: hu: Országos Számviteli Bizottság, Budapest

OT D: d: Obertribunal [Preußen]; PL: pl: Obrona Terytorialna; e: Office of Territories

O.T. F: f: Office des Transports; 1: Ordo Teutonicus; D: d: NS: Organisation Todt

OT H: hu: Országos Tanács; Országos Tervhivatal, Budapest

OTA US: e: Oil Trades Association of New York; INT: f: Organisation mondiale du tourisme et de l'automobile, London SW 1 [gegr 1950] s: Organización Mundial del Turismo y del Automóvil; H: hu: Országos Testnevelési Alap, Budapest

OTAC US: e: mil: Ordnance Tank and Automotive Command, Detroit, Mich.

O.T.A.D. F: f: mil: Omnium des Techniques Auxiliaires de Direction

OTAG US: e: mil: Office of the Adjutant General

OTÁH H: hu: Országos Tervhivatal, Árhivatal, Budapest

OTAN NATO: f: Organisation du traité de l'Atlantique Nord pt: Organização do Tratado do Atlântico Norte s: Organización del Tratado Atlántico Norte [e: NATO]

OTANY US: e: Oil Trades Association of New York

OTASE INT: f: mil: Organisation du traité (pour la défense collective) de l'Asie du Sud-Est

O.T.B. e: Office of Trade Boards

OTB INT: f: Organisation du Traité de Bruxelles [gegr 1948]

OTC US: e: mil: Officers' Training Camp; GB: e: mil: Officers' Training College

O.T.C. GB: e: mil: Officers' Training Corps

OTC US: e: Office of Temporary Controls [gegr 1946]; US: e: mil: Office of the Theater Chaplain; D: f: nach WK2: Office Tripartite de la Circulation

O.T.C. GB: e: mil: Operational Training Centre (Command)

OTC INT: e: Organization for Trade Co-operation [GATT]; AUS: e: Overseas Telecommunication Commission

OTCE US: e: mil: Office of the Theater Chief Engineer

OTCOT US: e: mil: Office of the Theater Chief of Transportation

OTCQM US: e: mil: Office of the Theater Chief Quartermaster

O.T.C.R.P. F: f: Office des Transports en Commun de la Région Parisienne

OTCS US: e: mil: Office of the Theater Chief Surgeon

OTCSigO US: e: mil: Office of the Theater Chief Signal Officer

OTCT US: e: mil: Office of the Theater Chief of Transportation

OTD e: Organization for Technological Development

O.T.D. e: Overseas Trade Department

OTE INT: f: Organisation des transports

européens; GR: [d: staatliche Fernmeldeverwaltung]

OTEF US: e: mil: Overseas Troops Entertainment Fund

OTEM NL: nl: Onafhankelijke Televisie Exploitatie Maatschappij

O.Teut. 1: Ordo Teutonicus

OTF S: sv: Oljeeldningstekniska Föreningen, Stockholm; PL: pl: Opolskie Towarzystwo Fotograficzne

O.T.G.R. F: f: Office Technique du Génie Rural

OTH H: hu: Országos Találmányi Hivatal, Budapest

O.Theat. 1: Ordo Theatinorum

O.T.I. f: Office Technique de l'Imprimerie

OTI H: hu: Országos Társadalombiztositó Intézet, Budapest

OTIG US: e: mil: Office of the Inspector General

OTK PL: pl: Obrona Terytorium Kraju; CS: cs: Oddělení Organizace Technické Kontrolny

O.T.K. S: sv: Oförberedda Talares Klubb

OTK CS: cs: Okresní Technická Kontrola

O.T.K. SF: fi: Osuustukkukauppa

OTKUP YU: [d: staatliche Organisation zur Erfassung der Agrarprodukte]

OTL e: Office of Technical Liaison

OTM US: e: Office of Telecommunications Management, Washington, D.C.

OTMA US: e: Oil Field Tank Manufacturers Association

OTP US: e: Office of Telecommunication Policy, Washington, D.C.; H: hu: Országos Takarékpénztár, Budapest

OTPM US: e: mil: Office of the Theater Provost Marshal

OTPMG US: e: mil: Office of the Provost Marshal General

OTPN PL: pl: Opolskie Towarzystwo Przyjaciol Nauk

OTPO US: e: mil: Overseas Transition Program Office

OTQMG US: e: mil: Office of the Quartermaster General

OTr. D: d: Obertribunal [Preußen]

O.T.R. f: Office des transports routiers

OTR GB: e: mil: Oxford Territorial Regiment

Otraco B: f: Office d'exploitation des transports coloniaux

OTRF US: e: Overseas Teacher Relief Fund

OTrI H: hu: Országos Traumatológiai Intézet, Budapest

O.Trin. 1: Ordo Sanctissimae Trinitatis

O.T.S. e: mil: Officers' Training School

OTS US: e: mil: Officer Training School; US: e: Office of Technical Services, Washington, D.C. [Department of Commerce] ; CR: e: Organization of Tropical Studies; N: no: Oslo Tekniske Skole

OTSB H: hu: Országos Testnevelési és Sportbizottság, Budapest

OTSEA INT: f: mil: Organisation du Traité du Sud-Est Asiatique [e: SEATO]

OTSG US: e: mil: Office of the Surgeon General [Army]

OTSI H: hu: Országos Testnevelés- és Sportegészségügyi Intézet, Budapest

OTSP INT: f: Organisation Tricontinentale de Solidarité de Peuples

O.T.S.U. f: Office du tourisme scolaire et universitaire; I: i: Organizzazioni Tecniche Servizi Urbani

OTT H: hu: Országos Testnevelési Tanács, Budapest

O.T.U. GB: e: mil: Officers' Training Unit [RAF]

OTU US: e: Office of Technology Utilization [NASA]

O.T.U. F: f: Office du Tourisme Universitaire, Paris 5; Omnium Technique d'Etudes Urbaines, Paris 12

OTU US: e: mil: Operational Training Unit

OTUA F: f: Office Technique pour l'Utilisation de l'Acier, Paris 8

OTUS US: e: Office of the Treasurer of the United States; TN: f: Office Tunisien de Standardisation, Tunis

OTV PL: pl: Ośrodek Telewizyjny

OTVT H: hu: Országos Természetvédelmi Tanács, Budapest

OTZ BlnW: d: Oberschule Technischen Zweiges; D: d: NS: Organisation Todt Zentrale

OÚ CS: cs: Obecní Úřad; Obvodný Úřad

OU CS: cs: Odborné Učiliště

OÚ CS: cs: Odúčtovací Ústředna; Osídlovací Úřad

O.U. GB: e: Oxford University

O.U.A. e: Order of United Americans; INT: f: Organisation de l'unité africaine, Addis Abeba [ETH]

OUAC GB: e: Oxford University Athletic Club

OUAFC GB: e: Oxford University Association Football Club

O.U.A.M. US: e: Order of United American Mechanics

OUAS GB: e: mil: Oxford University Air Squadron

OUBC GB: e: Oxford University Boat Club

OUCC GB: e: Oxford University Cricket Club

OÚ-ČSAV CS: cs: Orientální Ústav při ČSAV

OUDS GB: e: Oxford University Dramatic Society

OUFC GB: e: Oxford University Football Club

OUGC GB: e: Oxford University Golf Club

OUHC GB: e: Oxford University Hockey Club

O.U.H.S. GB: e: Oxford University Historical Society

OUK CS: sk: Oblastná Uradovňa Presídl'ovacej Komisie; CS: cs: Okresní Učitelská Knihovna; Okresní Úvěrová Komise

OULC GB: e: Oxford University Lacrosse Club

OULTC GB: e: Oxford University Lawn Tennis Club

O.U.M. GB: e: Oxford Union Mission

OUN cs: Organisace Ukrajinských Nacionalistů nl: Organisatie van Ukraïnische Nationalisten d: Organisation der Ukrainischen Nationalisten pl: Organizacja Ukraińskich Nacjonalistów [gegr 1929]

OÚOP CS: cs: Okrsní Úřad Ochrany Práce

O.U.O.T.C. GB: e: mil: Oxford University Officers' Training Corps

O.U.P. GB: e: Oxford University Press, London

OUPZ CS: cs: Odborné Učiliště Pracovních Záloh

OURA GB: e: Oxford University Rifle Association

OURFC GB: e: Oxford University Rugby Football Club

OURS GB: e: Oxford University Railway Society

OUSAF US: e: mil: Office of the Undersecretary of Air Force

OUSARMA US: e: mil: Office of the United States Army Attache

OUSC GB: e: Oxford University Swimming Club

OUSN US: e: mil: Office of the Undersecretary of the Navy

OUSPZ CS: cs: Odborné Učiliště Státních Pracovních

O.U.S.T.C. GB: e: Oxford University Senior Training Corps

OUSW US: e: mil: Office of the Undersecretary of War

OUT INT: f: Organisation universelle du tourisme

OUTC US: e: mil: Ordnance unit training center

OUTM PL: pl: Okręgowy Urząd Telekomunikacji Międzymiastowej

O.U.U.I. GB: e: Office of the Umpire, Unemployment Insurance

OUYC GB: e: Oxford University Yacht Club

OUZD YU: sn: Okrožni Urad za Zavarovanje Delavcev v Ljubljana

OV CS: cs: Obvodní Výbor; Okresní Výbor

O.-V. D: d: Organisatorenverband eV

OV H: hu: Országos Vezetőség; d: Ortsverband

O.V. D: d: Ostasiatischer Verein zur Wahrnehmung deutscher Interessen in Ostasien, Hamburg

OVA D: d: Oberversicherungsamt

OVAC GB: e: Overseas Visual Aid Centre

OVÄ D: d: Oberversicherungsämter

O.Vall. 1: Congregatio Vallis Umbrosae Ordinis Sancti Benedicti

OVAR B: nl: Oostvlaamse Amateurs-radiëstesisten

OVB NL: nl: Onafhankelijke Verbond van Bedrijfsorganisaties

OVC B: f: Office de vérification de compte

OVEC US: e: Ohio Valley Electric Corp.

OVEF H: hu: Országos Vetőmagfelügyelőség

OVEIP RI: nl: Organisatie Verenigde Exporteurs van Indonesische Producten

OVersA D: d: Oberversicherungsamt

OVerwGer. D: d: Oberverwaltungsgericht

OVET H: hu: Országos Villamosenergia-gazdálkodási Tanács, Budapest

O.V.F. F: f: Office du vocabulaire français

OVF H: hu: Országos Villamosenergia Felügyelet, Budapest; Országos Vizügyi Főigazgató, Budapest; Országos Vizügyi Főigazgatóság, Budapest

OVG BRD: d: Oberverwaltungsgericht

OVH BRD: d: Oberallgäuer Volkshochschule; H: hu: Országos Vizgazdálkodási Hivatal, Budapest

O.V.L. D: d: Oberste Verkehrsleitung

OVM NL: nl: Onderlinge Verzekeringsmaatschappij

OWMR US: e: Office of War Mobilization and Reconversion

OVN INT: d: Organisation der Vereinten Nationen [e: UN]

OVO CS: cs:OdděleníVýchovy a Osvěty

OVOS CS: sk: Okresný Výbor Odbojových

Složiek

OVR BRD: d: Obstbauversuchsring des Alten Landes eV, 2155 Jork; US: e: Office of Vocational Rehabilitation [Health, Education and Welfare Department]

OVRA I: i: Opera Volontaria Repressione Antifascismo

OVSR US: e: Office of Vehicle Systems Research

OVSt BRD: d: Orthopädische Versorgungsstelle; BRD: d: Post: Ortsvermittlungsstelle

OVSz H: hu: Országos Vértranszfuziós Szolgálat, Budapest

OVSZKTI H: hu: Országos Vértransfuziós Szolgálat Központi Tudományos Kutató Intézete, Budapest

OVT B: nl: Opvoedkundige Vereniging der Leraars in het Tekenen, de Kunstgeschiedenis en de Handenarbeid

OVTVS CS: cs: Okresní Výbor pro Tělesnou Výchovu a Sport

OVÚ CS: cs: Ocelářský Výzkumný Ústav

O.V.V.O. NL: nl: Op Volharding Volgt Overwinning, Amsterdam

O.W. e: Office of Works

OW PL: pl: Okręg Wojskowy; B: nl: mil: Oorlogswoekeraar; NL: nl: Openbare Werken; A: d: Ortswehr

OWC US: e: mil: Officers' Wives Club

O.W.C. e: Office of War Cabinet

OWC US: e: mil: Ordnance Weapons Command

O.W.H. e: Organization of Wartime Hospitals

OWI PL: pl: Oddział Wykonawstwa Inwestycyjnego; US: e: mil: Office of War Information

OWIKO A: d: Oberösterreichische Wirtschaftskorrespondenz, Linz (Donau)

OWI-MIS US: e: mil: Office of War Information, Military Intelligence Section

OWI-PWD US: e: mil: Office of War Information, Prisoner of War Division

OWITiE PL: pl: Oddział Wojskowej Informacji Technicznej i Ekonomicznej

OWIU US: e: Oil Workers International Union, Denver 2, Colo.

OWK BRD: d: Odenwaldklub eV

OWKS PL: pl: Okręgowy Wojskowy Klub Sportowy

OWLO NL: nl: Openbaar Westersch Lager Onderwijs in Nederlandsch-Indië

OWM US: e: Office of War Mobilization

OWMR US: e: Office of War Mobilization and Reconversion

OWNA US: e: Optical Wholesalers National Association

OWP PL: pl: Obóz Wielkiej Polski

O.W.P.B. e: Office of Works and Public Buildings

OWPL PL: pl: Organizacja Wsółpracy Przemysłu Łożyskowego

OW PPS PL: pl: Organizacja Wojskowa Polskiej Partii Socjalistycznej

OWRR US: e: Office of Water Resources Research

O.-W.R.R.&N.C. US: e: Oregon – Washington Railroad & Navigation Company

O.W.S. GB: e: Old Water-Colour Society; Old Wellingtonian Society

OWS PL: pl: Ośrodek Wyszkolenia Sportowego

OWT PL: pl: Okręgowe Warsztaty Teletechniczne

OWU US: e: Office of War Utilities; Ohio Wesleyan University

OWW PL: pl: Organizacja Wojskowa "Wilki"

OWZ BlnW: d: Oberschule Wissenschaftlichen Zweiges

OWZE INT: d: Organisation für wirtschaftliche Zusammenarbeit und Entwicklung [e: OECD; f: OCDE]

Oxb.TTC GB: e: Oxbridge Teacher Training College

OXCO DK: da: OXCO Landbrugets Kvaegod Ködsalg, København

OXFAM GB: e: Oxford Committee for Famine Relief

OXF BUCKS GB: e: mil: The Oxfordshire and Buckinghamshire Light Infantry

Oxon GB: e: Oxford University

OXR e: Official and External Relations Commission

O/Y; O.Y.; Oy.; oy. SF: fi: osakeyhtiö [d: Aktiengesellschaft]

OZA PL: pl: Okręgowy Związek Atletyczny; Olsztyński Zarząd Aptek

OZB PL: pl: Opolskie Zjednoczenie Budownictwa

OZBP PL: pl: Ogólnopolski Związek Bratnich Pomocy

OZC NL: nl: Onderwijzers Zendings Commissie

OZD CH: D: d: Oberzolldirektion

OZETO PL: pl: Ośrodek Zastosowań Elektronicznej Techniki Obliczeniowej

OzFStBw BRD: d: mil: Ozeanographische Forschungsstelle der Bundeswehr

OZG PL: pl: Okręgowe Zakłady Gastronomiczne; Okręgowy Związek Gimnastyczny

OZHS CS: cs: Odbytová Základna Hlavní Správy

OŽK CS: cs: Okresní Živnostenská Komise

OZLA PL: pl: Okręgowy Związek Lekkiej Atletyki

OZLP PL: pl: Okręgowy Zarząd Lasów Państwowych

OZM BRD: d: Oberschwäbische Zentralmolkerei, 795 Biberach (Riß)

O.Z.N. ; OZN PL: pl: Obóz Zjednoczenia Narodowego [vgl: OZON]

OZNA YU: sn: Oddelek za Zaščito Naroda; YU: sh: Odjeljenje Zaštite Naroda

OZON PL: pl: Obóz Zjednoczenia Ogólno-Narodowego [vgl: O.Z.N.]

OZOS PL: pl: Olsztyńskie Zakłady Opon Samochodowych

OZPN PL: pl: Okręgowy Związek Piłki Nożnej

OZPR PL: pl: Okręgowy Związek Piłki Ręcznej

OZS CS: cs: Okresní Zdravotní Správa

OZSE PL: pl: Opolskie Zakłady Silników Elektrycznych

OZSI PL: pl: Okręgowy Związek Spółdzielni Inwalidów

P BRD: d: mil: Abteilung Personal [im BMV(td)g] ; US: e: mil: Bureau of Naval Personnel, Washington 25, D.C.

P. GB: e: Police Court; f: Ecole Polytechnique; e: Post Office

PA US: e: mil: Pacific Army; d: Pädagogische Akademie; US: e: Pan-American World Airways [= PANAIR]

PA. d: mil: Panzerarmee; d: Parlamentarischer Ausschuß; D: d: Parteiarchiv der NSDAP, Berlin

P.A. B: f: mil: WK2: Partisans Armés

PA d: Patentamt; 1: Patres Albi; RC: e: Peasant Association; YU: sh: Pedagoška akademija

P.A. e: Pedestrians' Association

PA; P.A.; PA. D: d: mil: Personalamt [OKH]

P&A NATO: e: Personnel and Administration Division, SHAPE

PA e: Petroleum Administration; e: mil: Philippine Army

P.A. s: Policía aduanera

PA. d: Polizeiamt

PA; P-A. d: Postamt

P.A. e: Presbyterian Alliance; Press Association

PA GB: e: The Press Association, Ltd., London [d: Nachrichtenagentur]

P.A. F: f: Direction de la Production Agricole

PA US: e: Proprietary Association

P.A. e: Protestant Alliance

PA BRD: d: Prüfamt für Brenn-, Kraft- und Schmierstoffe, 8 München 13

Pa D: BRD: d: Bahn: Prüfungsamt

PA d: Prüfungsausschuß; I: i: Pubblica Amministrazione; e: Public Administration; GB: e: Publishers Association, London; US: e: Publishers Association; Puppeteers of America

P.A. e: Purchasing Agency (Agent)

PAA US: e: Pan American (World) Airways [= PanAm]

PAA. D: d: mil: Panzerabwehrabteilung

PAA GB: e: Paper Agents' Association; e: Peruvian-American Association

P.A.A. US: e: Photographic Association of America; Potato Association of America

PAA. D: d: mil: WK2: Propaganda-Ausbildungsabteilung

PAAAC e: Pan-American Agricultural Aviation Center

PAAC INT: e: Pan-American Association of Composers

PAAO INT: e: Pan-American Association of Ophthalmology

PAAS PAK: e: Pakistan Association for the Advancement of Science

PAAT s: Programa Ampliado de Asistencia Técnica

PAB BR: pt: Panair do Brasil, S.A.

P.A.B. e: Pensions Awards Branch

PAB US: e: Petroleum Administration Board; Price Adjustment Board; Priorities Allotment Board; YU: sn: Privilegirana Agrarna Banka sh: Privilegovana Agrarna Banka; e: Public Advisory Board

PABEKO CGO: f: Parti de l'Alliance des Bena-Koshi

PAC US: e: mil: Pacific Air Command; Pacific Airmotive Corporation, Burbank, Calif.; ZA: e: Pan-African Congress; INT: e: Pan-American Commission (Conference) (Congress); INT: e: Permanent Agricultural Committee, International Labor Office, Geneva [CH] ; US: e: Political Action Committee [gegr 1943 durch CIO]

P.A.C. D: d: Pommerscher Automobil-Club, Stettin; CS: cs: Posumavský Auto-Club Klatovy; F: f: mil: Prêtres Anciens Combattants, Paris

PAC US: e: mil: Program Advisory Committee [Army]

P.A.C. e: Public Accounts Committee

PAC US: e: Public Affairs Committee

P.A.C. GB: e: Public Assistance Committee

PACAF US: e: mil: Pacific Air Forces
PACB INT: e: Pan-American Coffee Bureau
PACC PI: US: e: Philippine-American
Chamber of Commerce; US: e: mil:
Production Administration Contract
Control
PACCIOS INT: f: Conseil Régional Paci-
fique du Comité International de l'Or-
ganisation Scientifique, Lima [Peru]
PACCS INT: e: Pan-American Cancer Cy-
tology Society
PACDIS INT: e: Pacific Area Communi-
cable Disease Information Service [PI]
PACE PI: e: Philippine Association of
Civil Engineers
PACEX US: e: mil: Pacific Exchange Sys-
tem
PACFLT US: e: mil: Pacific Fleet
PACGO US: e: President's Advisory Com-
mittee on Government Organization
PACH US: e: Public Administration Clear-
ing House
P.A.C.H. GB: e: Publishers' Accounts
Clearing House
PACIOS INT: f: Conseil Pan-Américain
du Conseil International de l'Organi-
sation Scientifique
PACOM US: e: mil: Pacific Command
PACS US: e: Paris American Committee
to Stop War
PACT INT: e: Pan-American Commission
on Tampa; ZA: e: Performing Arts Coun-
cil of the Transvaal
P.A.C.T. F: f: Fédération nationale des
centres de propagande et d'action contre
le taudis
PACUSA US: e: mil: Pacific Air Command,
U.S.Army
P.A.C.Y. F: f: Produits Alimentaires et
Conserves du Landy, St.Denis
PAD BRD: d: Pädagogischer Austausch-
dienst; US: e: mil: Panama Air Depot;
Panama District; GB: e: passive air de-
fence; US: e: Petroleum Administration
for Defense; US: e: mil: Public Affairs
Division
PADE GR: [d: fortschrittliche Agrarunion
PADENA CGO: f: Parti Démocrate Natio-
nal
PADESM RM: f: Parti des Déshérités de
Madagascar
PADF INT: e: Pan-American Development
Foundation, Washington, D.C.
PADL GB: e: Performing and Captive Ani-
mals Defence League
PAE BRD: d: Pädagogische Arbeitsstelle
für Erwachsenenbildung
PÄ D: BRD: d: Postämter
P.A.E. YU: sh: Preduzeće za Automatiza-
ciju i Elektroniku, Beograd
Pä D: BRD: d: Bahn: Prüfungsämter
PAF US: e: mil: Pacific Air Force; e: mil:
Pakistani Air Force; US: e: Performing
Arts Foundation; INT: e: Pan-American
Foundation; e: mil: Portuguese Air
Force
PAFA US: e: Pennsylvania Academy of
Fine Arts
PAFB US: e: mil: Patrick Air Force Base
[Florida]
PAFC PI: US: e: Philippine-American
Financial Commission; US: e: Public
Affairs Field Center
PAFLU PI: e: Philippine Association of
Free Labor Unions
PAFMECA INT: e: Pan-African Freedom
Movement for East and Central Africa
[gegr 1958]
PAFMECSA INT: e: Pan-African Freedom
Movement for East, Central and South-
ern Africa
PAFTU PI: e: Philippine Association of
Free Trade Unions
PAG PL: pl: Państwowy Arbitraż Gospo-
darczy; Polska Agencja Gospodarcza;
UN: e: Protein Advisory Group
P.A.G. e: Public Administration Group
PAGA US: e: Pan-American Grace Air-
ways, Inc. [= PANAGRA]
Pagart PL: pl: Polska Agencja Artystyczna

PAGB GB: e: Poultry (and Egg Producers) Association of Great Britain Ltd.; Proprietary Association of Great Britain

PAGC GB: e: Port Area Grain Committee

PAGED; Paged PL: pl: Polska Agencja Eksportu Drewna [seit 1931]

PAGUAG BRD: d: Pahlsche Gummi- und Asbest-Gesellschaft, 4 Düsseldorf-Rath

P.A.H. INT: nl: Permanent Arbitragehof, Den Haag; D: d: Preußisches Abgeordnetenhaus

PAHMC INT: e: Pan-American Homeopathic Medical Congress

PAHO INT: e: Pan-American Health Organization, Washington, D.C.

PAHRI PAK: e: Pakistan Animal Husbandry Research Institute

PAI PAK: e: Pakistan International Airlines [= PIA]; PA: e: Panama Airways Incorporated; SN: f: Parti africain de l'indépendance; I: i: Polizia Africa Italiana; US: e: Public Affairs Institute

PAIG P: pt: Partido Africano de Independência da Guiné, Conakry

PAIGC; PAIGCV P: pt: Partido Africano de Independência da Guiné e Cabo Cerde

PAIGH INT: e: Pan-American Institute of Geography and History, Mexico 18, D.F.

PAIMEG INT: e: Pan-American Institute of Mining Engineering and Geology

PAINT INT: e: Primera Asociación Internacional de Noticieros y Televisión

PAIS US: e: Public Affairs Information Service

PAJU INT: e: Pan-African Journalists Union

PAK GR: [d: panhellenische Befreiungsbewegung]; PL: pl: Parafialna Akcja Katolicka; BRD: d: Politischer Arbeitskreis

PAKSI PAK: e: Pakistan Standards Institute, Karachi [= PSI]

PAL US: e: Pacific Air Lines; Pan-American League; PI: e: Philippine Air Lines Inc., Manila; US: e: Pioneer Air Lines;

Police Athletic League; PL: pl: Polska Akademia Literatury, Warszawa; Polska Armia Ludowa

P.A.L.I. GB: e: mil: Prince Albert's Light Infantry

PALU CGO: f: Parti Lumumbiste de l'Unité

PAM GR: [d: patriotische antidiktatorische Front] CDN: e: mil: Permanent active militia; YU: sn: Pokrajinski arhiv v Mariboru; PL: pl: Pomorska Akademia Medyczna, Szczecin; BRD: d: Publizistische Arbeitsgemeinschaft für Medizin

PAMA INT: e: Pan-American Medical Association; US: e: mil: Philippines Air Material Area; GB: e: Press Advertisement Managers Association

PAMEE PI: e: Philippine Association of Mechanical and Electrical Engineers

PAMETRADA GB: e: The Parsons and Marine Engineering Turbine Research and Development Association

PAML PL: pl: Polska Akademicka Młodzież Ludowa

PAMO US: e: mil: Port Air Material Office

PAN MEX: s: Partido Acción Nacionalista; US: e: Pennsylvania Association of Notaries; PL: pl: Polska Akademia Nauk, Warszawa [gegr 1951]

PANA HK: e: Pan-Asia Newspaper Alliance, Hongkong [d: Narichtenagentur]

PANAC CGO: f: Parti National Chrétien; e: Plantations Association of Nigeria and the Cameroons

PANACO CGO: f: Parti Nationaliste Congolais

PANAF CGO: f: Parti National Africain

PANAGRA e:= PAGA

PANAIR US: e: = PanAm

PANAJECO CGO: f: Parti National de la Jeunesse Congolaise

PANALI CGO: f: Parti National de la Liberté

PanAm; PAN AM US: e: Pan American

World Airways, Inc., New York, N.Y.
10017
Pananews HK: = PANA
PANARE CGO: f: Parti National de Re-
construction
PANAS PTM: Party Negara Sarawak,
Kuching
PANATRA CGO: f: Parti National du
Travail
Panavia BRD: d: e: ¡Panavia Aircraft GmbH,
8 München
PANJU INT: e: Pan-African Union of
Journalists
PANS US: e: Philadelphia Academy of
Natural Sciences
PANSDOC PAK: e: Pakistan National Sci-
entific and Technical Documentation
Center, Karachi
PAnst D: BRD: d: Postanstalt
PAnwRSt BRD: d: Post: Postanweisungs-
rechenstelle
PANZ NZ: e: Public Accountants' Asso-
ciation of New Zealand
PAO GR: [d: konservative Widerstands-
gruppe]; BRD: d: Politischer Arbeits-
kreis Oberschulen; US: e: mil: Public
Affairs Office [TASCOM]
PAOA INT: e: Pan-American Odontologi-
cal Association, New York [gegr 1935]
PAP C: [d: fortschrittliche Aktionspartei];
PE: s: Partido de Acción Popular; PTM:
e: People's Action Party, Kuala Lumpur;
SGP: e: People's Action Party; BRD: d:
Politische Analysen und Prognosen [So-
ziologen-Gruppe in Köln]; PL: pl: Pols-
ka Agencja Prasowa, Warszawa [d: Nach-
richtenagentur]; Polska Agencja Publi-
cysty [1925 ... 39]; Powiatowe Archi-
wum Państwowe
PAPA PI: e: Philippine Alien Property
Administration
PAPAS PTM: e: mal: Party Peseka Anak
Sarawak, Kuching
PAPBC CDN: e: Pharmaceutical Associa-
tion of the Province of British Columbia

PAPC GB: e: Poster Advertising Planning
Committee
P.A.P.D. e: Plant and Animal Products
Department
PAPPA US: e: Pulp and Paper Prepack-
aging Association
PAR PL: pl: Państwowa Administracja
Rolna; El Salvador: s: Partido Acción
Renovadora; GCA: s: Partido Acción
Revolucionaria; e: Party for African
Reorganization; PL: pl: Polska Agencja
Reklamy; Powszechna Agencja Reklamy
L: e: Preferred American Realty/Secu-
rity Fund S.A., Luxembourg; US: e:
Promotion, Advertising, Research [d:
Komitee der Gasindustrie]; Public Af-
fairs Research Council of Louisiana
PARA GB: e: mil: The Parachute Reg-
iment
PARADA GB: e: Preparatory Academy
for the Royal Academy of Dramatic Art
PARAS RI: Partai Rakjat Sosialis
PARC INT: e: Pan-American Railway Con-
gress
PARCA INT: e: Pan-American Railway
Congress Association
PARDON US: e: Pastors' Anonymous Re-
covery-Directed Order for Newness
PARECO CGO: f: Parti de Regroupement
Congolais
Paribas F: NL: f: Banque de Paris et des
Pays Bas, Paris
Parindra RI: Partai Indonesia Raja
Parki RI: Partai Kebangsaan Indonesia
Parkindo RI: Partai Kristen Indonesia
PARL CDN: e: Prince Albert Radar Lab-
oratory
PARM Mex: s: Partido Auténtico de la
Revolución Mexicana [gegr 1957]
PARMEHUTU RWA: f: Parti du Mouve-
ment de l'Emancipation des Bahutu
PARO e: Palestine Arab Refugee Office
Pa.R.R. US: e: Pennsylvania Railroad
Pars IR: [d: Nachrichtenagentur, gegr
1934]

PARSEPP Neu Guinea: Partai Serikat Pemuda-Papua

PARSI RI: Partai Rakjat Sosialis Indonesia

PART US: e: Pan-American Round Table(s) in the United States of America

PARTAA BRD: d: Partnerschaft mit Asien und Afrika eV, 532 Bad Godesberg

Partindo RI: [d: nationalistische Partei]

Parufamet D: d: e: Paramount - Ufa - Metropolitan-Filmverleih

PAS US: e: Pacific Astronomical Society; PAK: e: Pakistan Academy of Sciences; US: e: Philadelphia Astronautical Society; PL: pl: Pogotowie Akcji Specjalnej; BRD: d: Politischer Arbeitskreis Schulen; e: Pontifical Academy of Sciences; e: Prisoners' Aid Society; BRD: d: Bahn: Prüf- und Ausbildungsanstalt für Schweißtechnik; US: e: Public Administration Service, Chicago

PASA US: e: Pacific American Steamship Association; [e: Palestine Agricultural Settlement Organization]; CGO: f: Parti Socialiste Africain

PASACO US: e: Pacific and Asian Affairs Council

PASB INT: e: Pan-American Sanitary Bureau

PASC US: e: mil: Pacific Air Service Command; e: Palestine Armed Struggle Command [guerillas]; US: e: mil: Panama Area Service Command; INT: e: Pan -American Standardization Conference; Pan-American Standards Commission (Committee)

P.A.S.I. GB: e: Professional Associate Chartered Surveyors' Institution

PASO INT: e: Pan-American Sanitary Organization, Washington, D.C. [gegr 1902]

PASS I: i: Posti di Assistenza Sanitaria nella Regione Siciliana; e: Pure and Applied Science Section

PASSA US: e: Pacific American Steamship Association

PAST; PASTa PL: pl: Polska Akcyjna Spółka Telefoniczna

PASU Rhodesien: e: Panafrican Socialist Union

PASUS US: e: Pan-American Society of the United States

P.A.T. US: e: Parents and Taxpayers, New York

Pat. e: Patent Office

P.A.T. e: Pensions Appeal Tribunal

PAT US: e: People's Assistance Team [in Vietnam]; Political Action Team [in Vietnam]; PL: pl: Polska Agencja Telegraficzna, Warszawa [1918 . . . 45]; T: e: Press Association of Thailand

PATA INT: e: Pacific Area Travel Association, San Francisco, Calif. 94102

PatA. d: Patentamt

PATCO ISO: e: Patent Committee; PI: e: Philippine Aerial Taxi Company; US: e: Professional Air Traffic Controllers Organization

Patexpo '69 US: e: [d: Erfinder- und Hersteller-Messe, Manhattan, Okt 1969]

PATOUMA BRD: d: Partnerschaftsausstellung Toulon - Mannheim [15 . . . 16 Okt 1966 in Mannheim, Briefmarkensammler]

PATRA GB: e: Printing (, Packaging) and Allied Trades Research Association, London

PATWA GB: e: Professional and Technical Workers Alliance

PAU INT: e: Pan-American Union, Washington, D.C.; PL: pl: Polska Akademia Umiejetności

PAUS US: e: Population Association of the United States

PAUSE US: e: Parents Against Universal Sex Education

PAV YU: sh: Pomoć Američke Vlade

PAVE PI: e: Philippine Association for Vocational Education

PAVN e: People's Army of Vietnam

P.A.W. e: Petroleum Administration for

War
PAW PL: pl: Polskie Archiwum Wojenne;
BRD: d: Bahn: Post: Privat-Ausbesse-
rungswerk; NL: nl: Proefstation voor
Akker- en Weidebouw
PAWA INT: e: Pan-American Women's
Association; US: e: Pan American World
Airways [= PanAm]
PAWC INT: e: Pan-African Workers Con-
gress, Brazzaville [RCB]
PAYM INT: e: Pan-African Youth Move-
ment
PAZ YU: sh: Protivavionska Zaštita
PAZZM PL: pl: Polski Akademicki Zwią-
zek Zbliżenia Międzynarodowego "Liga"
P.B. RI: Partai Buruh [d: Arbeiterpartei]
PB nl: Partij Bestuur
p.b. e: penalty bench
P.B. H: hu: Pénzügyi Bizottság; f: Pères
blancs; GB: e: Plymouth Brethren;
e: Political Bureau; H: hu: Politikai
Bizottság
PB. d: Polizeibehörde
PB NATO: e: Working Group on Ports and
Beaches
Pb sv: Pressbyrån
P.B. e: Primitive Baptists
PB US: e: Publications Board, Department
of Commerce, Washington, D.C.
P.B.A. f: Pères Blancs d'Afrique
PBA US: e: Polish Beneficial Association;
Professional Bookmen of America;
Public Buildings Administration
PBAC e: Program Budgeting Advisory
Committee
PBB YU: sh: Privredna Banka Beograd
PBC US: e: Public Broadcasting Corpo-
ration
P.B.C.P. e: Political Bureau of the Com-
munist Party
PBD YU: sh: Pomorsko Brodarsko Društvo
PBE PL: pl: Przedsiębiorstwo Budowni-
ctwa Elektroenergetycznego
PBeaKK BRD: d: Post: Postbeamtenkran-
kenkasse

PBEIST NATO: e: Planning Board for
European Inland Surface Transport
PBGen BRD: d: Post: Postbaugenossen-
schaft
PBI US: e: Paper Bag Institute; RI: Partai
Buruh Indonesia; US: e: Paving Brick
Institute; Plant Breeding Institute;
Plumbing Brass Institute
P.B.I. INT: f: Programme Biologique Inter-
national
PBIM PL: pl: Przedsiębiorstwo Budow-
nictwa Inżynieryjno-Morskiego
PBK US: e: Phi Beta Kappa [d: Studen-
tenvereinigung] ; PL: pl: Polski Biały
Krzyż; A: d: Pressedienst der Bundes-
kammer der gewerblichen Wirtschaft,
Wien 1; S: sv: Pressens bowlingklubb
PBL US: e: Public Broadcast Laboratory
PBLK PL: pl: Przedsiębiorstwo Budowy
Linii Kablowych
PBM NL: nl: Proefstation voor de Neder-
landse Brouw- en Moutindustrie; PL: pl
Przedsiębiorstwo Barów Mlecznych;
Przedsiębiorstwo Budownictwa Miej-
skiego
PBMA US: e: Peanut Butter Manufactur-
ers Association
PBN PL: pl: Państwowe Biuro Notarialne
P.B.N.E. US: e: Philadelphia, Bethlehem
and New England Railroad Company
PBO d: Palästinensische Befreiungsorgani-
sation; NL: nl: Publiekrechtelijke Be-
drijfsorganisatie
PBOS NATO: e: Planning Board Ocean
Shipping
PBP PL: pl: Powiatowa Biblioteka Peda-
gogiczna; Przedsiębiorstwo Budownict-
wa Przemysłowego
PBPW PL: pl: Przedsiębiorstwo Budowlane
Przemysłu Węglowego
PBR PL: pl: Państwowy Bank Rolny
P.B.R. US: e: Patapsco and Back Rivers
Railroad Company
PBR; PBRol PL: pl: Przedsiębiorstwo
Budownictwa Rolnego

PBRU PL: pl: Pracownia Badań Rejonów Uprzemysławianych
PBS e: Plant Breeding Station; US: e: Public Buildings Service
PBSE US: e: Philadelphia-Baltimore Stock Exchange
PBSt DDR: d: Post: Postbezirksstelle
P.B.T. e: President of the Board of Trade
PBT PL: pl: Przedsiebiorstwo Budownictwa Terenowego
P.B.T.B. GB: e: Paper Bag (Box) Trade Board
PBTO GB: PL: pl: Polsko-Brytyjskie Towarzystwo Okrętowe "Polbrit"
PBTRA GB: e: Port of Brixham Trawler Race Association
PBU F: f: d: Progil-Bayer-Ugine, Pont -de-Claix [gegr 1959]
PBV D: d: Preußischer Beamtenverein Hannover
PBW PL: pl: Pedagogiczna Biblioteka Wojewódzka
P-B-W US: e: Philadelphia - Baltimore - Washington Stock Exchange
PBW PL: pl: Przedsiębiorstwo Budownictwa Wodnego
PBZ D: d: Presse-Bild-Zentrale, Berlin
PBZA DDR: d: Post- und Binnenzollamt
P.C. US: e: Pacific Coast Railroad; e: Parish Council; f: Parti Communiste; ro: Partidul Comunist; PE: s: Partido Constitucional [gegr 1885]; i: Partito Comunista; e: mil: Pay Corps; e: Peace Commissioner
P&C BRD: d: Peek & Cloppenburg [Bekleidungshäuser]
P.C. e: Penitentiary Commission; People's Commissariat
PC WAL: e: All People's Congress
P.C. US: e: mil: Pharmacy Corps; e: Philharmonic Choir; PI: e: Philippine Constabulary; e: Pioneer Club; GB: e: mil: Pioneer Corps
PC e: Planning Committee
P.C. e: Playwrights' Club; f: Police Criminelle

PC PL: pl: Politechnika Częstochowska; D: d: Polytechnikum Cöthen; YU: sh: Pravoslavna crkva; UN: e: Preparatory Commission of the United Nations
P.C. GB: e: Prerogative Court of Canterbury; d: Primanerclub; e: Prison Commission; GB: e: Privy Council; e: Probation Committee; Producers' Council; CDN: e: Progressive Conservatives; e: mil: prophylactic center; f: Protection Civile
PCA US: e: Paper Can Association; Parachute Club of America; Paraffined Carton Association
P.C.A. e: Parish Councils Association; DZ: f: Parti Communiste Algérien
PCA CGO: f: Parti Communautaire Africain; pt: Partido Comunista do Angola; US: e: Pennsylvania Central Airlines; UN: e: Permanent Court of Arbitration, Den Haag [NL, f: CPA]
P.C.A. F: f: mil: Pharmacie Centrale de l'Armée; e: Physicians Casualty Association; US: e: Portland Cement Association, Chicago 10, Ill.; Print Council of America; Producers Commission Association; Production Control Agency; Production Credit Association; Progressive Citizens of America; Psychological Corporation of America; Pulp Chemicals Association
PCAC GB: e: Poultry Costings Advisory Council; Professional Classes Aid Council
P.C.B. B: f: Parti Communiste Belge; f: Parti communiste brésilien
PCB Bolivien: s: Partido Comunista de Bolivia
P.C.B. e: Pensions Commutation Board
PCB e: Property Control Branch
P.C.B.F. e: Provident Clerks, Benevolent Fund
PCBS e: Permanent Committee on Biological Standards

PCC US: e: Pacific Coast Conference [football] e: Palestine Conciliation Commission; Panama Canal Company

P.C.C. e: Parks and Cemeteries Committee; Parochial Church Council

PCC C: s: Partido Comunista de Cuba; Rhodesien: e: People's Caretaker Council

P.C.C. GB: e: Prerogative Court of Canterbury

PCC US: e: President's Conference Committee; Price Control Committee; Private Carrier Conference; e: Provincial Congress Committee

PCCA US: e: Power and Communication Contractors Association

PCCC PAK: e: Pakistan Central Cotton Committee

PCCEMRSP INT: e: Permanent Commission for the Conservation and Exploitation of the Marine Resources of the South Pacific

PCCh RCH: [d: chilenische kommunistische Partei]

PCCI US: e: Paper Cup and Container Institute

PCCN CGO: f: Parti Congolais de Conscience Nationale

PCD e: Panama Canal Department; PL: pl: Państwowa Centrale Drzewna "Paged"; US: e: Public Contracts Division [Department of Labor]

PCDG GB: e: Prestressed Concrete Development Group

P.C.E. f: Parti Communiste Egyptien

PCE EC: [d: ecuadorische kommunistische Partei]; E: s: Partido Comunista Español; e: Presbyterian Church of East Africa

PCEA US: e: Pacific Coast Electrical Association; PE: s: Programa Cooperativo de Experimentación Agropecuaria

PCEM INT: e: Parliamentary Council of the European Movement, Brussels 4 [B]

PCES US: e: President's Committee on Economic Security

P.C.F. F: f: Parti Communiste Français, Paris 9 [gegr 1920]

PCF INT: d: Prager Christliche Friedenskonferenz; F: f: Protection Civile Française

PCFA SU: [e: People's Commissariat for Foreign Affairs]

PCFEP US: e: President's Committee on Fair Employment Practice

PCfL SU: [e: People's Commissariat for Labour]

P.C.F.R. F: f: Parti Communiste Française Révisionniste

PCGA US: e: Pacific Coast Gas Association

PCGM US: e: Pacific Coast Garment Manufacturers

PCGN e: Permanent Committee on Geographical Names

PCH PL: pl: Państwowa Centrala Handlowa; Honduras: s: [d: kommunistische Partei]

P.C.H. e: Presbyterian Church House

P.C.I. f: Parti Communiste Internationaliste (Trotskiste); RM: f: Parti du Congrès de l'indépendance; I: i: Partito Comunista Italiano

PCI US: e: Pilot Club International; BRD: d: Polychemie GmbH, 89 Augsburg; US: e: Potato Chip Institute; Prestressed Concrete Institute, Chicago

PCIFC INT: e: Permanent Commission of the International Fisheries Convention

P.C.I.J. INT: e: Permanent Court of International Justice [Völkerbund]

PCIM RM: f: Parti du congrès de l'indépendance

PCIMCO INT: e: Preparatory Committee of the Intergovernmental Maritime Consultative Organization

PCIRO INT: e: Preparatory Commission for the International Refugee Organization [gegr 1946]

PCIZC INT: e: Permanent Committee of International Zoological Congresses

PCJC PAK: e: Pakistan Central Jute

Committee
PCJRI PAK: e: Pakistan Central Jute Research Institute
PCK YU: sh: Podmladak Crvenog Krsta; PL: pl: Polski Czerwony Krzyż
PCKD PL: pl: Polski Centralny Komitet Doradczy
PCL US: e: Pacific Coast League [baseball]; L: f: Parti Communiste Luxembourgeois; J: e: Photo Chemical Laboratories
PCLU GB: e: mil: Pioneer Civil Labour Unit
P.C.M. RM: f: Parti Communiste Malgache; MA: f: Parti Communiste Marocain
PCM MEX: s: [d: kommunistische Partei]; YU: [d: orthodoxe Kirche in Mazedonien]
P.C.M.B. NL: nl: Protestants-Christelijke Mijnwerkersbond
P.C.M.R. e: Privy Council for Medical Research
P.C.M.S. GB: e: Pattern Card Makers' Society
PCN El Salvador: s: Partido de Conciliación Nacional; NIC: s: [d: konservative Partei]
PCNB INT: e: Permanent Central Narcotics Board, Geneva [gegr 1928]
PCNL e: Polish Committee of National Liberation
PCNY US: e: Proofreaders Club of New York
PCO e: Passport Control Office; Port Communications Office; CS: cs: Připraven k Civilní Obraně
P.C.O. e: Privy Council Office; Public Call Office; Public Carriage Office
PCOB INT: e: Permanent Central Opium Board, CH-1211 Genève [gegr 1928]
PCOGA US: e: Pacific Coast Oyster Growers Association
PCOO NL: nl: Stichting voor Protestantsch-Christelijk Onderwijs en Ontwikkeling in het Schependom van Nijmegen

PCP PE: PY: s: [d: kommunistische Partei]
P.C.P. EAK: e: People's Convention Party
PCP US: e: Philadelphia College of Pharmacy and Science; Postgraduate Center for Psychotherapy; CDN: e: Progressive Conservative Party; Malta: e: Progressive Constitutional Party [gegr 1953]
PCPA US: e: Protestant Church-Owned Publishers' Association
PCPEA US: e: Pennsylvania Cooperative Program in Educational Administration
PCPWS ET: e: Permanent Council for Public Welfare Service
P.C.R. R: ro: Partidul Comunist Romîn
P.C.R.C. GB: e: Poor Clergy Relief Corporation
P.C.R.S. GB: e: Poor Clergy Relief Society
P.C.R.V. NL: nl: Protestants-Christelijke Reclasseringsvereniging
PCS L: f: Parti chrétien social; El.Salvador: s: [d: kommunistische Partei]
PCSA US: e: Power Crane and Shovel Association
PCSAS US: e: Policy Committee for Scientific Agricultural Societies
PCSE US: e: Pacific Coast Stock Exchange; President's Committee on Scientists and Engineers
PCSIR PAK: e: Pakistan Council of Scientific and Industrial Research
PCT TN: f: Parti Communiste Tunisien
PCTS US: e: President's Committee for Traffic Safety
P.C.T.T. I: i: Partito Comunista del Territorio Triestino
PCU RCH: s: Partido Conservador Unido; U: s: [d: kommunistische Partei]; US: e: Portuguese Continental Union of the United States of America
P.C.U.M. e: Policy Committee of United Mine Workers
PCUS US: e: Presbyterian Church in the United States; Propeller Club of the United States
PCV YV: s: Partido Comunista Venezolano

PCVM GB: e: Research Association of British Paint, Colour and Varnish Manufacturers

PCW US: e: Pennsylvania College for Women

P.C.W. GB: e: Presbyterian Church of Wales

PCWPC INT: e: Permanent Committee of the World Petroleum Congress

PD DDR: d: mil: Panzerdivision; L: f: Parti démocratique; C: PE: s: Partido Demócrata

P.D. DOM: s: Partido Dominicano; e: Personnel Department (Depot); Petroleum Department; Physics Department

PD YU: sh: Planinarsko Društvo sn: Planinsko Drustvo; NL: nl: Plantenziektenkundige Dienst

P.D. e: Police Department

PD BRD: d: Polizeidirektion; CS: sk: Poverem'ctvo Dopravy a Verejných Prác; YU: sn: Prešernova Družba; F: f: Presse Diplomatique [d: Nachrichtenagentur]

P.D. e: Priorities Division

PDA US: e: Parenteral Drug Association

PdA CH: d: Partei der Arbeit; BRD: d: Partei der Arbeitslosen

PDA pt: Partido Democratico Angolano; GB: e: Photographic Dealers Association; BRD: d: Pressedienst der Deutschen Arbeitgeberverbände

P.D.A.D. GB: e: Probate, Divorce and Admiralty Division

PdAK Nordkorea: [d: Partei der Arbeit Koreas]

PdAS CH: d: Partei der Arbeit der Schweiz

P.d'Az. I: i: Partito d'Azione

PDB BR: pt: [d: sozialdemokratische Partei] ; BRD: d: Polizeigewerkschaft im Deutschen Beamtenbund [gegr 1966]

PDC US: e: Package Designers Council; Burundi: f: Parti démocrate chrétien; Kamerun: f: Parti des démocrates camerounais; CGO: f: Parti démocratique congolais; MA: f: Parti démocratique constitutionnel; CI: f: Parti démocra-

tique de la Côte d'Ivoire; Bolivien: RA: RCH: El Salvador: U: s: Partido Demócrata Cristiano; BR: pt: Partido Democrático Cristão; I: i: Partito Democratico Cristiano

P.D.C. e: Personnel Distribution Center (Centre)

PDC US: e: mil: Petroleum Distribution Command; GB: e: Physical Development Centre; US: e: Prevention of Deterioration Center [gegr 1945]

PDCA US: e: Painting and Decorating Contractors of America

PDCG GCA: s: Partido Democrático Cristiano Guatemalteco

P.D.C.I. CI: f: Parti démocratique de la Côte d'Ivoire

PDCP PI: e: Private Development Corporation of the Philippines, Manila

PDD: PL: pl: Państwowy Dom Dziecka; DY: f: Parti démocratique dahoméen

PDF US: e: Parkinson's Disease Foundation

PdF BRD: d: Partei der Frauen

P.D.F. e: Peabody Donation Fund; People's Democratic Front

P.D.G. f: Parti démocratique guinéen

PDG BRD: d: Patentdokumentationsgruppe in der chemischen Industrie, 6 Ffm

PdgD BRD: d: Partei der guten Deutschen

P.D.G.D. e: mil: Paymaster Director -General's Department

PDH YU: sh: Pedagoško Društvo Hrvatske; Povjesno Društvo Hrvatske

PDI BRD: d: Partei Deutscher Idealisten [gegr 1961] ; MA: f: Parti démocratique de l'Indépendance; I: i: Partito Democratico Italiano

PDiRz PL: pl: Ministerstwo Przemysłu Drobnego i Rzemiosła

PDIUM I: i: Partito Democratico Italiano di Unità Monarchica

PDJTB f: Parti démocratique des jeunes travailleurs du Burundi

PDK PL: pl: Powiatowy Dom Kultury

P.D.L. I: i: Partito Democratico del Lavoro

PDM RM: f: Parti Démocrate Malgache; F: f: Progrès et démocratie moderne [d: Partei]

PDMD PL: pl: Państwowy Dom Małego Dziecka

PDN RCH: s: Partido Democrático Nacional; I: i: Partito della Democrazia Nazionale

P.D.N.S. US: e: mil: Plans Division of Naval Staff

PDO PL: pl: Poznańska Dyrekcja Odbudowy; US: e: mil: Property Disposal Office(r)

PDP PA: s: Partido de Pueblo; e: People's Democratic Party

PDPT TG: f: Parti démocratique des populations togolaises

PDR RI: Partai Demokrasi Rakjat; Burundi: f: Parti démocrate rural; PE: s: Partido Democrático Reformista

P.D.R.C. US: e: Platform Drafting Resolutions Committee

PDS F: f: Parti de la démocratie socialiste; YU: sh: Pedagoško Društvo Srbije; CS: cs: Poddustojnička škola; PL: pl: Polskie Drużyny Strzeleckie

P.D.S.A. GB: e: People's Dispensary for Sick Animals

P.D.S.A.P. GB: e: People's Dispensary for Sick Animals of the Poor

PDT PL: pl: Powszechny Dom Towarowy

P.D.U. DY: f: Parti Dahoméen de l'Unité; Obervolta: f: Parti démocratique unifié

PDUW PL: pl: Polska Dyrekcja Ubezpieczeń Wzajemnych

P.D.V. Obervolta: f: Parti démocratique voltaique

PdVP DDR: d: Präsidium der Volkspolizei

PdW d: Partei der Werktätigen

P.E. US: e: Pacific Electric Railway Company

PE INT: f: Parlement Européen

P.E. F: f: Police Economique

PEA D: d: Pachteinigungsamt; PAK: e: Pakistan Economic Association; S: sv: Pappersemballageindustriens arbetsgivarförbund; US: e: Pennsylvania Electric Association; GB: e: Physical Education Association of Great Britain and Northern Ireland; US: e: Plastic Engineers Association; Potash Export Association; GB: e: Progressive Education Association

P.E.A. D: d: mil: WK2: Propagandaersatzabteilung

PEAB GB: e: Professional Engineers Appointment Bureau

PEACS US: e: Panel on Engineering and Commodity Standards

PEAT UN: f: Programme Elargi de l'Assistance Technique

Pe B CS: cs: Státni Pedagogická Knihovna v Brně

PEB US: e: mil: Physical Evaluation Board [Army]; NL: nl: Politiek-Economische Bond; US: e: mil: Professional Entertainment Branch

PEC US: e: President's Emergency Council; e: Protestant Episcopal Church

PECA US: e: Petroleum Equipment Contractors Association

PECAM Kamerun: f: Société Pêcheries Camerounaises

PEEA GR: [d: politisches Komitee der nationalen Befreiung, 1944 . . . 45]

P.E.F. e: Palestine Exploration Fund

PEF DK: da: Post- og telegrafvæsenets ekstraarbejders fagforening

PEHLA BRD: d: PEHLA [Prüfung elektrischer Hochleistungsapparate] Gesellschaft für elektrische Hochleistungsprüfungen, 6 Ffm

PEI US: e: Petroleum Educational Institute; BRD: d: Philips Elektronik Industrie GmbH, 2 Hamburg; US: e: Porcelain Enamel Institute, Inc.; YU: sh: Pravno-ekonomski Institut

PEK H: hu: Pécsi Tudományegyetem Könyvtára, Pécs; CY: [d: Bauernpartei]

PEKAO PL: [d: Bank in Warschau]
PEL CDN: e: President Electric Limited, Toronto
PEM DDR: d: VVB Plast- und Elastonverarbeitungsmaschinen
Pemex MEX: s: Petróleos Mexicanos [d: staatliche Gesellschaft]
PEN CGO: f: Parti de l'Entente Nationale; INT: e: International Association of Poets, Playwrights, Editors, Essayists and Novelists [gegr 1922 in London]
PENB US: e: Poultry and Egg National Board
Pen.R.R. US: e: Pennsylvania Railroad Company
Pens.-A. D: d: Pensionsanstalt
PEO US: e: International Peace and Educational Organization; US: e: mil: Program Evaluation Office
Pe P CS: cs: Státní Pedagogická Knihovna v Praze
PEP GB: e: Political and Economic Planning; US: e: Political Education Project [Detroit]; Promoting Enduring Peace Association
PEPSU IND: e: Patiala and East Punjab States Union
PEQUA US: e: mil: Production Equipment Agency
PER PL: pl: Przedsiębiorstwo Elektryfikacji Rolnictwa
PERA GB: e: Production Engineering Research Association, Melton Mowbray
PERG US: e: mil: Production Equipment Redistribution Group
PersA d: Personalamt
PERSD e: Personnel Department
PersR BRD: d: Personalrat
PES US: e: Philosophy of Education Society
PESA US: e: Petroleum Equipment Supplies Association
Pesag BRD: d: Paderborner Elektrizitätswerk und Straßenbahn AG, 479 Paderborn

P.E.S.C.G.B. GB: e: Provincial Electric Supply Committee of Great Britain
PEST GB: e: Pressure for Economic and Social Toryism
PETMA GB: e: Portable Electric Tool Manufacturers Association
Petra NL: nl: Permanente Tentoonstellingsraad
PETRANGOL pt: Companhia dos Petróleos de Angola
PETROBRAS BR: pt: Petróleo Brasileiro S.A., Rio de Janeiro
PETROFINA B: f: [= Compagnie financière belge de pétroles, Anvers] PETROFINA S.A., Bruxelles 4
Petrolimpex PL: pl: Państwowe Przedsiębiorstwo Handlu Zagranicznego
Petronor E: s: Petróleos del Norte
Pétropar f: Société de Participations Pétrolières S.A.
PETS US: e: Pacific Electronic Trades Show
PEVE; Peve YV: s: Prensa Venezolana [d: Nachrichtenagentur]
PEXIP F: f: Paris Exposition Internationale Philatélique [18 . . . 26 Jun 1937]
P.F. d: Pädagogische Fakultät; F: f: Partisans Français; e: mil: permanent force(s); US: e: Physicians Forum; GB: e: Punkett Foundation; Police Federation
PF N: no: Polyteknisk Forening; e: mil: Popular Forces; S: sv: Posttjänstemännens förening
P+F CH: d: Pulverfabrik Wimmis
PFA US: e: Papermakers Felt Association; SN: f: Parti fédéraliste africain; US: e: Polish Falcons of America; e: Popular Flying Association; S: sv: Postens filateliavdelning; D: d: Post: Postfuhramt
P.F.A. F: f: Presse Française Associée; e: Professional Footballers Association
P.F.A.A. F: f: mil: Personnel féminin de l'armée de l'Air
P.F.A.C. f: Parti Fédéral de l'Afrique

Central
P.F.A.M. F: f: mil: Personnel féminin de l'armée de Mer
P.F.A.T. F: f: mil: Personnel féminin de l'armée de Terre
P.F.B. GB: e: Petroleum Films Bureau
PFB INT: e: Provisional Frequency Board
PFBCA US: e: Pennsylvania Farm Bureau Cooperative Association
PFC US: e: mil: Panama Ferrying Command; e: Private Flying Corps
PFCA US: e: Plastic Food Containers Association
Pf.D. D: d: mil: Pferdedepot
PFD BRD: d: Private Fachschule für das Dolmetscherwesen, Stuttgart
PFDA US: e: Pure Food and Drug Administration
PFF B: [d: Partei für Freiheit und Fortschritt]
PFI US: e: Pacific Forest Industries; N: no: Papirindustriens Forsknings-Institutt; US: e: Photo Finishing Institute; Pipe Fabrication Institute
PFIA US: e: Police and Firemen's Insurance Association
PFK PL: pl: Państwowa Fabryka Karabinów; S: sv: Pressfotografernas klubb
PFL PL: pl: Pierwsza Fabryka Lokomotyw
PfL D: d: Prüfstelle für Luftfahrzeuge; BRD: d: Prüfstelle für Luftfahrtgerät [vgl: DVL-PfL]
Pf.Laz. D: d: mil: Pferdelazarett
PFLDUQ I: i: Partito del Fronte Liberale Democratico dell'Uomo Qualunque
PFLP e: People's (Popular) Front for the Liberation of Palestine
PFŁT PL: pl: Poznańska Fabryka Łożysk Tocznych
PFM 1: Parvuli Fratres Mariae; PL: pl: Piotrkowska Fabryka Maszyn
PFMA US: e: Pipe Fittings Manufacturers Association; Plumbing Fixture Manufacturers Association
P.F.M.A.A. F: f: mil: Personnel féminin

médical de l'armée de l'Air
PFMŻ PL: pl: Poznańska Fabryka Maszyn Żniwnych
PFN RI: e: Perusahaan Film Negara [d: staatliche Filmgesellschaft]
P.F.P. F: f: Petits Frères des Pauvres
PFPA GB: e: Pitch Fibre Pipe Association of Great Britain, London EC 4
PFRA CDN: e: Prairie Farm Rehabilitation Administration
PFS A: d: Prüfstelle für Funkgerätesicherheit, Wien
PFuhrA BRD: d: Post: Postfuhramt
PFuhrÄ BRD: d: Post: Postfuhrämter
PFV CH: d: Proletarischer Freidenkerverband
PFW PL: pl: Państwowa Fabryka Wagonów, Wrocław; BRD: d: Parteifreie Wählerschaft
PFZ PL: pl: Państwowy Fundusz Ziemi
PFZ PL: pl: Pilska Fabryka Żarówek
PFZ BRD: d: Post: Post- und Fernmeldetechnisches Zentralamt
PFZA PL: pl: Państwowa Fabryka Związków Azotowych
Pfzvb. D: d: Pferdezuchtverband
P.-G. D: d: Paddlergilde
PG D: d: Parteigericht der NSDAP
P.G. e: Philatelic Guild
PG PL: pl: Politechnika Gdańska; DDR: d: Produktionsgenossenschaft; e: Professional Group; D: d: Progymnasium; d: Projektgruppe
P.G. e: Provincial Government
PG US: e: mil: Proving Ground; PL: pl: Przedsiębiorstwo Geologiczne
PGA BRD: d: mil: Personalgutachterausschuß [BMVtdg] ; GB: e: Plate Glass Association; e: Professional Golfers Association (of America); US: e: Professional Group on Audio Frequency
PGAA US: e: Professional Golfers Association of America
PGAC US: e: Professional Group on Automatic Control

PAGH e: Pineapple Growers Association of Hawaii

PGANE US: e: Professional Group on Aeronautical and Navigational Electronics

PGAP US: e: Professional Group on Antennas and Propagation

P.G.B. GB: e: Pilgrims of Great Britain

P.G.b.K.W. A: d: Pensionsgesellschaft bildender Künstler Wiens

PGBTR US: e: Professional Group on Broadcast and Television Receivers

PGBTS US: e: Professional Group on Broadcast Transmission Systems

PGC GB: e: Patent Glazing Conference; US: e: mil: Persian Gulf Command; Proving Ground Command

PGCA I: i: Procuratore Generale della Corte d'Assise

PGCOA US: e: Pennsylvania Grade Crude Oil Association

PGCP US: e: Professional Group on Component Parts

PGCS US: e: Professional Group on Communications Systems

PGCT US: e: Professional Group on Circuit Theory

PGD BRD: d: Papiergroßhandelsgesellschaft Darmstadt GmbH

PGDS YU: sn: Politično in Gospodarsko Društvo za Slovence

P.G.&E. US: e: Pacific Gas & Electric Company, San Francisco, Calif.

P.G.E. US: e: Pacific Great Eastern Railway

PGEA PI: e: Philippine Government Employees Association

PGEC US: e: Professional Group on Electronic Computers

PGECP US: e: Professional Group on Electronic Component Parts

PGED US: e: Professional Group on Electron Devices

PGEM US: e: Professional Group on Engineering Management

PGH D: d: Patentgerichtshof; DDR: d: Produktionsgenossenschaft des Handwerks

PGI US: e: Professional Group on Instrumentation

PGIE US: e: Professional Group on Industrial Electronics

PGIT US: e: Professional Group on Information Theory

P.G.K. D: d: WK2: Polizeigebietskommandantur

PG1 PL: pl: Politechnika Gliwicka

P.G.L. e: Provincial Grand Lodge [Freemasonry]

PGM I: i: mil: Procuratore Generale Militare

P.G.M.A. GB: e: Private Grocers' Merchandising Association

PGME US: e: Professional Group on Medical Electronics

P.G.M.S. GB: e: Pressed Glass Makers' Society of Great Britain

PGMTT US: e: Professional Group on Microwave Theory and Techniques

PGNS US: e: Professional Group on Nuclear Science

P.G.O. e: mil: Paymaster-General's Office

PGPN PL: pl: Przedsiębiorstwo Geofizyki Przemysłu Naftowego

PGPT US: e: Professional Group on Production Techniques

PGR PL: pl: Państwowe Gospodarstwa Rolne; I: i: Procuratore Generale della Republica

PGRO GB: e: Pea Growing Research Organization Ltd.

PGRQC US: e: Professional Group on Reliability and Quality Control

PGRTRC US: e: Professional Group on Radio Telemetry and Remote Control

PGRyb PL: pl: Państwowe Gospodarstwa Rybackie

PGS I: i: Provveditorato Generale dello Stato

PGSCC I: i: Procuratore Generale della Suprema Corte di Cassazione

PGT GCA: s: [de Arbeiterpartei]

P.G.T.S. GB: e: Procurator-General and

Treasury Solicitor
PGUE US: e: Professional Group on Ultrasonics Engineering
PGV NL: nl: Proefstation voor de Groenteteelt in de Volle Grond
PGVC US: e: Professional Group on Vehicular Communications
PGy D: d: Progymnasium
PH d: Pädagogische Hochschule
P.H. e: Pest Hospital; YU: sn: Poštna Hranilnica
PHA US: e: Polomino Horse Association
P.H.A. e: Physicians' Health Association
PHA US: e: Professional Horsemen's Association; Public Housing Administration
PHB BRD: d: Pohlig - Heckel - Bleichert Vereinigte Maschinenfabriken AG, 5 Köln-Zollstock
PHCA GB: e: Pig Health Control Association
PHCAA US: e: Public Health Cancer Association of America
PHCI CI: f: Plantations et Huileries de Côte d'Ivoire
PHCIB US: e: Plumbing - Heating - Cooling Information Bureau
PHD e: Public Health Department
P.H.E.S.F.E.A. e: Pin, Hook and Eye and Snap Fastener Employers' Association
P.H.I. e: Public Health Institute
PHIBLANT US: e: mil: Amphibious Forces, Atlantic
PHIBNAW US: e: mil: Amphibious Forces, North West African Waters
PHIBPAC US: e: mil: Amphibious Forces, Pacific
PhibTraLant US: e: mil: Amphibious Training Command, Atlantic [gegr 1943]
PHILA NSY US: e: mil: Philadelphia Naval Shipyard
PHILASAG PI: e: Philippine Association of Agriculturists
Philatex F: [d: internationale Post- und Briefmarkenausstellung in Paris,

5 ... 21 Jun 1964]
PHILCOA PI: e: Philippine Coconut Administration
PHILCOMAN PI: e: Philippine Council of Management, Manila
PHILCUSA PI: e: Philippine Council for United States Aid
Philluma 1961 BlnW: d: Erste deutsche Zündholzetiketten-Ausstellung, 1 ... 3 Apr 1961]
Phil.Soc. e: Philological (Philosophical) Society
PHILSUGIN PI: e: Philippine Sugar Institute
PHK CH: d: Bahn: Pensions- und Hilfskasse
PHMA US: e: Plastic Housewares Manufacturers' Association
PHN BRD: d: Pädagogische Hochschule Niedersachsen
PHNSY US: e: mil: Pearl Habor Naval Shipyard
Phogeba; Pho-Ge-Ba BRD: d: Photographische Gesellschaft eV Bamberg
Phot.-Inn. D: d: Photographen-Innung
PHOTOKINA; Photokina INT: d: Internationale Photo- und Kino-Ausstellung, 5 Köln
photonorm DIN: d: Fachnormenausschuß Phototechnik, 1 Berlin 30 [BlnW]
PHPC US: e: Post-Hostilities Planning Committee
PHS US: e: Pennsylvania Historical Society
Ph.S. GB: e: The Philosophical Society of England
P.H.S. GB: e: The Postal History Society
PHS US: e: Presbyterian Historical Society; NL: nl: Prins Hendrik School in Nederlandsch-Indië; e: Public Health Service
P.H.S.C. e: Political Honours Scrutiny Committee
PHS of A INT: e: Postal History Society of the Americas

Ph.S. of G.B. GB: e: Pharmaceutical Society of Great Britain

P.H.U. GB: e: mil: Personnel Holding Unit

PHÚ CS: cs: Poštovní Hospodářská Ústředna

PhWJ DDR: d: VEB Pharmazeutisches Werk Johannisthal, Berlin-Johannisthal

PHX BRD: d: Hüttenwerke Phoenix AG, Duisburg-Ruhrort

PHYWE; Phy-We BRD: d: Physikalische Werkstätten AG, Göttingen

PHZ PL: pl: Przedsiębiorstwo Handlu Zagranicznego

PI US: e: Packaging Institute Inc., New York 17; d: Pädagogisches Institut; CR: s: Partido Independente; RM: f: Parti des Indépendants; MS: f: Parti de l'Indépendance; H: hu: Pedagógiai Intézet, Budapest; GB: e: Phonographic Institute; US: e: Photographic Institute; GB: e: Plastics Institute; e: Polytechnic Institute; DDR: d: Polytechnisches Institut; CS: sk: Povereníctvo pre Informácie; US: e: Pratt Institute

PIA PAK: e: Pakistan International Airlines Corporation, Karachi; US: e: Perfumery Importers Association; RI: Persbiro Indonesia Aneta, Djakarta [d: Nachrichtenagentur] ; PI: e: Philippine Institute of Architects: US: e: Pine Institute of America; PL: pl: Polski Instytut Archeologiczny

P.I.A. e: Postal Inspectors' Association

PIA US: e: Printing Industry of America, Inc.; Pumice Institute of America

PIAC PAK: e: Pakistan International Airlines Corporation, Karachi [= PIA] ; GB: e: Petroleum Industry Advisory Committee

PIANC INT: e: Permanent International Association of Navigation Congresses, Brussels 4 [B]

PIAB PL: pl: Przemysłowy Instytut Automatyki i Pomiarów

PIARC INT: e: Permanent International Association of Road Congresses, Paris 16 [F]

PIB GB: e: Petroleum Information Bureau, London W 1; US: e: Polytechnic Institute of Brooklyn; GB: e: Prices and Incomes Board; US: e: Publishers Information Bureau

PIBAC INT: e: Permanent International Bureau of Analytical Chemistry of Human and Animal Food, Paris 7

PIBAL US: e: Polytechnic Institute of Brooklyn Aerodynamics Laboratory

PIBD PL: pl: Państwowy Instytut Biologii Doświadczalnej

PIBSL PL: pl: Państwowy Instytut Badania Sztuki Ludowej

PIC GB: e: Paint Industries Club; e: Petroleum Industry Conference

P.I.C. e: Pianomakers' Industrial Council; pt: Polícia de Investigação Criminal; F: f: Préparation Industrielle des Combustibles [Firma]

PIC US: e: Professional Interfraternity Conference [gegr 1928] ; NATO: US: e: Public Information Committee [in NATO matters]

PICA e: Palestine Jewish Colonization Association

PICAA INT: e: Permanent International Committee of Agricultural Associations

PICAO INT: e: Provisional International Civil Aviation Organization [gegr 1944, seit 1947: ICAO]

PICC INT: e: Provisional International Computation Centre, Rome [I]

PICGC INT: e: Permanent International Committee for Genetic Congresses, Montreal [CDN]

PICIC PAK: e: Pakistan Industrial Credit and Investment Corp.Ltd., Karachi [gegr 1957]

PICIM INT: e: Permanent International Commission on Industrial Medicine

PICM INT: e: Permanent International

Committee of Mothers

PICMME INT: e: Provisional Intergovernmental Committee for the Movement of Migrants from Europe [gegr 1952]

PICO US: e: mil: Project Improvement Control Office

P.I.C.T.B. e: Perambulator and Invalid Carriage Trade Board

PICUTPC INT: e: Permanent and International Committee of Underground Town Planning and Construction, Paris 9

PICV INT: e: Permanent International Commission of Viticulture

PID GCA: s: Partido Institutional Democrático

P.I.D. e: Political Intelligence Department

PID NL: nl: Politieke Inlichtings Dienst in Nederlandsch-Indië

P.I.D. e: Press Intelligence Department

PID US: e: mil: Public Information Division

PIDA GB: e: Pig Industry Development Authority

PIDC PAK: e: Pakistan Industrial Development Corporation

PIDE; Pide P: pt: Policía Internacional e de Defesa do Estado

PIE PL: pl: Przemysłowy Instytut Elektroniki

PIEA US: e: Pencil Industry Export Association; Petroleum Industry Electrotechnical Association

PIEG GB: e: Pianoforte Industries Export Group

PIFC PAK: e: Pakistan Industrial Finance Corporation

PIG PL: pl: Państwowy Instytut Geologiczny; GB: e: Pipeline Industries Guild, London SW 1

PIGM PL: pl: Państwowa Inspekcja Gospodarki Materiałowej

PIGPE PL: pl: Państwowy Inspektorat Gospodarki Paliwowo-Energetycznej

PIH PL: pl: Państwowa Inspekcja Handlowa; Państwowy Instytut Higieny

PIHM PL: pl: Państwowy Instytut Hydro-

logiczno-Meteorologiczny

PIHS PL: pl: Państwowy Instytut Historii Sztuki

PIHPs PL: pl: Państwowy Instytut Higieny Psychicznej

PIHZ PL: pl: Polska Izba Handlu Zagranicznego

PIIA PAK: e: Pakistan Institute of International Affairs

PIIF PAK: e: Pakistan International Industries Fair

PIIP INT: s: Programa Interamericano de Información Popular

PIJR INT: s: Programa Interamericano para la Juventud Rural

PIK PL: pl: Państwowy Instytut Książki YU: sh: Poljoprivredno-Industrijski Kombinat

PIKOPP YU: sh: Preduzeće za Industrijsku Kooperaciju i Preuzimanje Poslova u Zemlji i Inostranstvu

PIL GB: e: Pest Infestation Laboratory; IND: e: Polyolefins Industries Limited, Thana near Bombay [seit 1968]

PIM PL: pl: Państwowa Inspekcja Materiałowa; Państwowy Instytut Matematyczny; Państwowy Instytut Meteorologiczny

PIMA US: e: Paper Industry Management Association

PiMBP PL: pl: Powiatowa i Miejska Biblioteka Publiczna

PIMC US: e: Poultry Industry Manufacturers Council

PIME I: l: Pontificum Institutum Mediolanese pro Missionibus Exteris

PIMR PL: pl: Przemysłowy Instytut Maszyn Rolnczych

PIN PL: pl: Państwowy Instytut Nauczycielski; Polski Instytut Naukowy w Ameryce

PING PL: pl: Państwowy Instytut Naukowo-Gospodarczy

PINGW PL: pl: Państwowy Instytut Naukowy Gospodarstwa Wiejskiego w

Puławach
P.I.O. e: Pensions Issue Office
PIO CS: sk: Povereníctvo Informácie a
Osvety; e: Press Information Office;
US: e: mil: Public Information Office(r)
P.I.O.G. f: Parrainage International des
Orphelins de Guerre
PIOSA IND: e: Pan-Indian Ocean Science
Association
PIP PL: pl: Państwowa Inspekcja Plonów;
Polski Instytut Prasoznawczny; e: Puerto
Rico Independence Party; PL: pl: Przed-
siębiorstwo Instalacji Przemysłowych
PIPR e: Polytechnic Institute of Puerto
Rico
PIPS PL: pl: Państwowy Instytut Peda-
gogiki Specjalnej
PIR US: e: mil: Parachute Infantry Reg-
iment; Bolivien: s: Partido de la
Izquierda Revolucionaria
PIRA GB: e: Printing Industry Research
Association; Prison Industries Reor-
ganization Administration
PiRgt BRD: d: mil: Pionierregiment
PIRI ZA: e: Paint Industries Research
Institute
PIRINC US: e: Petroleum Industry Re-
search, Inc.
PIRRCOM IND: e: Project for the Inten-
sification of Regional Research on Cotton,
Oilseeds and Millets
PIS GB: e: Pan-Islamic Society; PL: pl:
Państwowa Inspekcja Sanitarna; Państ-
wowy Instytut Sztuki; US: e: Postal
Inspection Service
Pi.Sch.; PiSchule d: mil: Pionierschule
PISM PL: pl: Polski Instytut Spraw Mię-
dzynarodowych
PIST PL: pl: Państwowy Instytut Sztuki
Teatralnej
P.I.S.T.M. PTM: mal: Persatuan Islam
Sa-Tanah Melayu, Kuala Lumpur
PISwŁ PL: pl: Polski Instytut Socjolo-
giczny w Łodzi
PIT PL: pl: Państwowy Instytut Teleko-

munikacyjny; Punkt Informacji Tury-
stycznej
P.I.T.A. US: e: Pacific International Trap-
shooting Association
PIU Bolivien: s: Partido Izquierdo Unido
PIW PL: pl: Państwowy Instytut Wydaw-
niczy
P.I.W.C. e: Petroleum Industry War Coun-
cil
PIWR PL: pl: Państwowy Instytut Wy-
dawnictw Rolniczych
P.J. f: Police Judiciaire
PJA PAK: e: Pakistan Jute Association;
DDR: d: mil: Panzerjägerabteilung
PJBD US: e: mil: Permanent Joint Board
on Defense
PJC D: d: Potsdamer Jacht-Club
PJCR NL: nl: Politieke Jongeren Contact
Raad
P.J.F. F: f: Protection de la Jeune Fille
PJGN NL: nl: Plattelands Jongeren Ge-
meenschap in Nederland
P.J.I.C. e: Provincial Joint Industrial
Council
PJMA PAK: d: Pakistan Jute Mills Asso-
ciation
PJS YU: sh: Podmladak Jadranske Straže
PJV D: d: Provinzialjagdverband
P.-K. D: d: Paddelklub
PK PL: pl: Politechnika Krakowska; CS:
sk: Povereníctvo Kultúry; PL: pl: Po-
wiatowy Komitet
PK; P.K.; Pk. D: d: mil: WK2: Propagan-
da-Kompanie
PK BRD: d: Prüfungskammer für Kriegs-
dienstverweigerer; S: sv: Publicistklub-
ben
PKA PL: pl: Państwowa Komisja Arbitra-
żowa
PKB PL: pl: Państwowy Komitet Bezpieczeństwa; Państwowy Korpus Bezpieczeństwa; BRD: d: Pfälzische Kundenkreditbank eGmbH, 67 Ludwigshafen;
DDR: d: Projektierungs- und Konstruktionsbüro

PKC PL: pl: Państwowa Komisja Cen; S: sv: Postverkets Kontorspersonals Centralförbund
PKDZ CS: cs: Posudková Komise Důchodového Zabezpečení
PKE PL: pl: Państwowa Komisja Egzaminacyjna; Państwowa Komisja Etatów; Polski Komitet Elektrotechniczny
PKI RI: Partai Kommunis Indonesia; H: hu: Piackutató Iroda, Budapest; Posta Kisérleti Intézet, Budapest
PKK DDR: d: Pädagogisches Kreiskabinett; PL: pl: Państwowa Komisja Klasyfikacyjna; CS: cs: Pedagogická Knihovna Komenského
PKKB PL: pl: Państwowy Korespondencyjny Kurs Bibliotekarski
PKKF PL: pl: Powiatowy Komitet Kultury Fizycznej
PKKP PL: pl: Polska Krajowa Kasa Pożyczkowa; Powiatowa Komisja Kontroli Partyjnej
PK KPJ YU: sh: Politički Komitet Komunističke Partije Jugoslavije
PKL PL: pl: Państwowa Komisja Lokalowa; Polska Komisja Likwidacyjna; Polskie Koleje Linowe
PKlK BRD: d: Post: Postkleiderkasse
PKM PL: pl: Państwowe Konserwatorium Muzyczne; DDR: d: Projektierungs-, Konstruktions- und Montagebüro
PKN PL: pl: Polska Komitet Normalyzacyjny, Warszawa
PKO PL: pl: Polska Kasa Opieki S.A.; Powszechna Kasa Oszczędności
PKOl PL: pl: Polski Komitet Olimpijski
PKOP PL: pl: Polski Komitet Obrońców Pokoju
PKOS PL: pl: Powiatowy Komitet Opieki Społecznej
PKP PL: pl: Państwowa Komisja Płac; d: philippinische kommunistische Partei; PL: pl: Polityczny Komitet Porozumiewawczy; Polskie Koleje Państwowe; Polski Korpus Posiłkowy

PKPG PL: pl: Państwowa Komisja Planowania Gospodorczego
PKPł PL: pl: Państwowa Komisja Płac
PKPL PL: pl: Polsko-Katolicka Partia Ludowa
PK PPS PL: pl: Powiatowy Komitet Polskiej Partii Socjalistycznej
PKPR PL: pl: Państwowa Komisja Planowania Rolniczego; Polski Komitet Pomocy Repatriantom; Polski Korpus Przysposobienia i Rozmieszczenia
PKPS PL: pl: Polski Komitet Pomocy Społecznej
PKR PL: pl: Powiatowa Komenda Rejonowa; Powiatowa Komisja Rewizyjna
PKRI RI: Partai Katolik Republik Indonesia
PKS PL: pl: Państwowa Komunikacja Samochodowa; NL: nl: Plaatselijke Kader-School; D: pl: Polski Klub Sportowy, Berlin
PKSK YU: sh: Pokrajinski Komitet Saveza Komunista
PK SKOJ YU: sh: Politički Komitet Saveza Komunističke Onladine Jugoslavije
PKSP PL: pl: Powiatowa Komenda Straży Pożarnych
PKT YU: sh: Pamučni Kombinat Titograd; PL: pl: Polski Klub Tańca
P.K.T.F.U.K. GB: e: Printing and Kindred Trades Federation of the United Kingdom
PKTJ PL: pl: Polski Komitet Techniki Jądrowej
PktPA BRD: d: Post: Paketpostamt
PktPÄ BRD: d: Post: Paketpostämter
PKU PL: pl: Powiatowa Komenda Uzupełnień
PKV BRD: d: private Krankenversicherung; Verband der privaten Krankenversicherung eV, 5 Köln
PKW PL: pl: Powiatowy Komitet Wykonawczy
PKWN PL: pl: Polski Komitet Wyzwolenia Narodowego [gegr 1944]
PKZ YU: sh: Pedagoško-Knijiževni Zbor, Zagreb; PL: pl: Pracownie Konserwacji Zabytków; YU: sn: Prosvetno Kul-

turni Zbor
PKZP PL: pl: Pracownicza Kasa Zapomo-
gowo-Pożyczkowa
PKZZ PL: pl: Polskie Klasowe Związki
Zawodowe; Powiatowa Komisja Związ-
ków Zawodowych
PL Bolivien: C: RCH: s: Partido Liberal;
BR: pt: Partido Liberal
P.L. f: Parti Libéral
Pl. d: Planung(sstelle) (sabteilung)
PL PL: pl: Politechnika Łódzka
PL PL: pl: Politechnika Lwowska; C: s:
Prensa Latina [d: Nachrichtenagentur]
P.L. GB: e: Primrose League
PLA US: e: Patent Law Association; Penn-
sylvania Library Association; e: mil:
People's Liberation Army; PI: e: Phil-
ippine Library Association
P.L.A. GB: e: Port of London Authority;
Private Libraries Association
PLA US: e: Public Library Association
[American Library Association] ; Pul-
verized Limestone Association
PLAAF RC: mil: [e: People's Liberation
Army Air Force]
PLACO ISO: e: Planning Committee
PLAF VN: e: [d: Volksbefreiungskräfte]
Plamasta DDR: d: Abteilung für Planung,
Materialversorgung und Statistik [seit
1949]
PLAN F: f: Commissariat général du Plan,
Paris; PL: pl: Polska Ludowa Akcja
Niepodległościowa
PlanA d: Planungsamt
PLANAT NATO: e: North Atlantic Treaty
Regional Planning Group, London [GB]
PLAST 68 INT: [d: internationale Aus-
stellung für Kunststoffe und Kautschuk,
Milano [I] , 5 . . . 13 Okt 1968]
PLASTEC US: e: mil: Plastics Technical
Evaluation Center, Picatinny Arsenal,
Dover, N.J.
PLASTEXPO INT: [d: internationale Aus-
stellung von Kunststoffen und -harzen,
Prag [CS] , 13 . . . 20 Okt 1969]

PLATARUNDI RWA: f: Commerce et
Plantation au Ruanda-Urundi
PLATIN SU: [e: Institute for Study of
Platinum and other precious metals]
PLAV US: e: mil: Polish Legion of Amer-
ican Veterans
Plavole D: d: Planungsstelle für Volks-
schullesebücher der Vereinigung der
Schulbuchverleger
PLB BR: pt: [d: Arbeiterpartei] ; B: f:
Parti Libéral Belge
P.L.B. GB: e: Poor Law Board
PLC US: e: Pacific Logging Congress;
CGO: f: Parti Libéral Congo; I: i: Par-
tito Liberale Corporativo; GB: e: Plastics
Industry Standards Committee
P.L.C. GB: e: Poor Law Commission(er)
PLCA US: e: Pipe-Line Contractors As-
sociation
P.L.C.B.A. GB: e: Port of London Coal
Bunkering Association
P.L.C.W.A. e: Power Loom Carpet Weav-
ers and Textile Workers Association
PLD US: Progressive Land Developers;
e: Public Libraries Division
P&L DIV e: mil: Production and Logis-
tics Division
PLDP CS: sk: Povereníctvo Lesov a Dre-
várskeho Priemyslu
P&LE US: e: Pittsburgh & Lake Erie
Railroad
P.L.F.I.F.L. e: Poetry Lovers' Fellowship
and International Fellowship of Litera-
ture
PLH s: Partido Liberal de Honduras
P.L.H. e: People's League of Health
PLI I: i: Partito Liberale Italiano; US: e:
Practising Law Institute
PLIB US: e: Pacific Lumber Inspection
Bureau
PLI DIV e: mil: Production, Logistics
and Infrastructure Division
PLK CS: cs: Pražký Linguistický Krou-
žek; GB: e: mil: Princess Louise's
South Kensington Regiment

PLL PL: pl: Polskie Linie Lotnicze "Lot"

P.L.M. F: f: Compagnie des Chemins de fer de Paris à Lyon et à la Mediterranée

PLM S: sv: AB Plåtmanufaktur, Malmö; BRD: d: Pommersche Landsmannschaft; D: d: Preußisches Landwirtschaftsministerium

PLMA PL: pl: Pomoc Lekarska dla Młodzieży Akademickiej

PLN CR: s: Partido Liberación Nacional; RI: Perusahaan Listrik Negara, Djakarta

PLO e: Palestine Liberation Organization; PL: pl: Polskie Linie Oceaniczne

P.L.O. e: Principal Librarian's Office

PLOBA CGO: f: Parti de la libre opinion bantue

PLP PL: pl: Państwowe Liceum Pedagogiczne; WAN: e: Parliamentary Labour Party; B: f: Parti de la Liberté et du Progrès; US: e: Progressive Liberal Party; Bahamas: Guiana: e: Progressive Labor Party; CS: sk: Povereníctvo Ľahkého Priemyslu

PLPB US: e: Petroleum Labor Policy Board

PLRA RA: s: Patronato de Leprosos de la República Argentina; GB: e: Photo-Litho Reproducers' Association

P.L.R.C. GB: e: Port of London Registration Committee

PLS MA: f: [d: Partei der Freiheit und des Sozialismus]

P.L.S. e: Provincial Law Society

PLUŅA U: s: Primeras Líneas Uruguayas de Navegación Aérea

PLUVA NL: nl: Stichting voor Onderzoek van Pluimvee en Varkens

PLV D: d: Presse-Landesverband, Berlin; Preußischer Landesmänner-Verein

PLYMCHAN NATO: e: Plymouth Sub-Area Channel

PLZ YU: sn: Protiletalska Zaščita

P.M. PTM: mal: Party Machinda, Kuching

PM US: e: Peabody Museum of Archaeology and Ethnology

P.M. H: hu: Pénzügyminiszter(ium), Budapest

PM US: e: Pere Marquette Railway Company; f: mil: Police Militaire

P.M. F: f: Police Mobile; Police Municipale

PM BRD: r: Portfolio Management, '8 München 33

PM. D: d: Reichspostministerium

P.M. GB: e: Powlesland & Mason Railway

PM CS: sk: Prehrada Mládeže; D: d: NS: Propaganda-Ministerium; GB: CDN: US: e: mil: Provost Marshal

PMA US: e: Pacific Maritime Association; PAK: e: Pakistan Medical Association; PAK: e: mil: Pakistan Military Academy; PL: pl: Państwowe Muzeum Archeologiczne; e: Paper Makers Association; US: e: Peat Moss Association; Pencil Makers Association; e: Permanent Magnet Association; US: e: Pharmaceutical Manufacturers Association; Philadelphia Museum of Art; Philippine Mahagoni Association; PI: e: Philippine Medical Association; US: e: Phonograph Manufacturers Association; GB: e: Pianoforte Manufacturers' Association Ltd.

P.M.A. e: Plane Manufacturers' Association

PMA e: Precision Measurements Association; Production and Marketing Administration

PMAA US: e: Paper Makers Advertising Association

PMAG e: mil: Provisional Military Advisory Group

PMANY US: e: Paper Makers Association of New York

PMASA GB: e: Printers' Medical Aid and Sanatorial Association Ltd.

PMATA GB: e: Paint Manufacture and Allied Trades Association Ltd.

PMAV CS: cs: Pražský Městský Akční Výbor

PMB D: d: Papiermacher-Berufsgenossenschaft; e: Pigs Marketing Board; Potato Marketing Board; Program Manag-

ing Board
P.M.C. e: Permanent Mandates Commission
PMC NATO: e: Military Committee in Permanent Session; e: mil: Physical Medicine Centre
P.M.C. D: d: Polizei-Motor-Club; Preußischer Motorfahrer-Club, Berlin
PMCJA e: Pan-Malayan Council of Joint Action
P.M.D. e: Petroleum and Mines Department
PMDA US: e: Photographic Manufacturers and Distributors Association
PMDG CENTO: e: Permanent Military Deputies Group, Ankara [TR]
P.M.D.R.M.U. e: Paper Mould and Dandy Roll Makers' Union
P.M.E. F: f: Confédération générale des petites et moyennes entreprises
PME PL: pl: Polska Młodzież Esperancka
PMEA US: e: Pennsylvania Music Educators Association; Powder Metallurgy Equipment Association
PMEL US: e: mil: Precision Measurement Equipment Laboratory, Wheelus
PMF e: mil: Panama Military Force
P.M.F. F: f: mil: Personnel Militaire Féminin; F: f: Police Municipale Féminine
Pmf S: sv: Postmästarförening
PMFAA F: f: Personnel militaire féminin de l'armée de l'Air
PMFF YU: sn: Prirodoslovno-Matematično-Filozofska Fakulteta
PMFPAC US: e: mil: POLARIS Missile Facility Pacific
PmGD e: mil: Paymaster-General's Department
PMGD e: mil: Provost Marshal General's Department
PMGO US: e: mil: Office of the Provost Marshal General
PMGS US: e: mil: The Provost Marshal General's School, United States Army
PMH PL: pl: Polska Marynarka Handlowa;

CS: sk: Povereníctvo Miestného Hospodárstva, Bratislava
PMI I: i: Partito Mazziniano Italiano
P.M.I. F: f: Groupement de la Petite et Moyenne Industrie; f: mil: Police Militaire Internationale
PMI US: e: Pressed Metal Institute
P.M.I. f: Protection Maternelle et Infantile
PMIP PTM: e: Pan-Malayan Islamic Party
PMK CS: cs: Pražská Městská Knihovna
PML US: e: Pattern Makers League (of North America); PL: pl: Polski Monopol Loteryjny
PmL BRD: d: mil: Musterprüfstelle für militärisches Luftfahrtgerät [jetzt: MBL]
P.M.L. IND: e: Punjab Muslim League
P.M.L.M. RM: f: Parti Marxiste-Leniniste Malgache
PMLNA US: e: Pattern Makers League of North America
PMM US: e: Professional Music Men, Inc.
PMMA GB: e: Plastic Materials Manufacturers Association
PMMI US: e: Packaging Machinery Manufacturers Institute
P.M.M.S. e: Plainsong and Mediæval Music Society
P.M.M.T.S. e: Printing Machine Managers Trade Society
PMN I: i: [d: nationalmonarchistische Partei]
P.M.N.S. GB: e: mil: Princess Mary's Nursing Service
P.M.O.A. e: Pottery Managers and Officials Association; Printers Managers and Overseers Association
PMOA US: e: Prospectors and Mine Owners Association
P.M.P. f: Parti de Mouvement Populaire; I: i: Partito Monarchico Popolare
PMPC US: e: President's Materials Policy Commission [gegr 1951]
PMPMA US: e: Powder Metallurgy Parts Manufacturers Association
PMR US: e: mil: Pacific Missile Range;

R: ro: Partidul Muncitoresc Romîn, București
P.M.R.A.F.N.S. GB: e: mil: Princess Mary's Royal Air Force Nursing Service
P.M.R.C. e: Prison Medical Reform Council
PMRN PL: pl: Prezydium Miejskiej Rady Narodowej
PMRS US: e: Physical Medicine and Rehabilitation Service
PMS PL: pl: Państwowy Monopol Spirytusowy; Polska Macierz Szkolna; YU: sh: Poljoprivredno-Mašinska Stanica; e: mil: Provost Marshal School
P.M.S.D. f: Parti Mauricien Social-Démocrate
PMSI I: i: Partito del Movimento Sociale Italiano
PMSZ PL: pl: Polska Macierz Szkolna Zagranicą; YU: sh: Prirodnjački Muzej Srpske Zemlje
PMT PL: pl: Polski Monopol Tytoniowy
PMV D: d: Papierverarbeitungsmaschinen-Verband, Leipzig
PMZ PL: pl: Państwowy Monopol Zapałczany
PMZoo PL: pl: Państwowe Muzeum Zoologiczne
PN s: Partido Nacional; PTM: Party Negara; PL: pl: Polska Niepodległość; S: sv: Produktivitetsnämnden
PNA US: e: Pacific Northern Airlines; Paper Napkin Association; Tschad: f: Parti National Africain; E: s: Patronato Nacional Antituberculoso; US: e: Polish National Alliance (of the United States)
P.N.A. e: Provisional National Assembly
PNAUS US: e: Polish National Alliance of the United States
PNB US: e: Philadelphia National Bank; PI: e: Philippine National Bank; IND: e: Punjab National Bank
PNBC US: e: Pacific Northwest Bibliographical Center
PNC I: i: Partito Nazionale Corporativo; e: People's National Congress

P.N.C. e: Prohibition National Committee (Council)
P.N.C.M.H. e: Provisional National Council for Mental Health
PNCP CGO: f: Parti National de la Convention du Peuple
PND DY: f: Parti Nationaliste du Dahomey; I: i: Partito Nazionale Democratico
PNE CDN: e: Pacific National Exhibition
P.N.E.U. GB: e: Parents' National Education Union
PNEUROP INT: f: Comité européen des constructeurs de compresseurs et de l'outillage pneumatique e: European Committee of Manufacturers of Compressed Air Equipment d: Europäisches Komitee der Hersteller von Kompressoren, Vakuumpumpen und Druckluftwerkzeugen, London SW 41 [gegr 1959]
P.N.F. F: f: Parti National Français; I: i: Partito Nazionale Fascista
PNH s: Partido Nacional Hondureno
P.N.H.S.S. e: Purley Natural History and Scientific Society
PNI RI: Partai Nasional Indonesia [gegr 1927]
PNKD PL: pl: Polski Norodowy Komitet Demokratyczny
PNKK PL: pl: Polski Narodowy Kościół Katolicki
PNL NIC: s: Partido Nacional-Liberal
P.N.L. F: f: Parti National Libéral; I: i: Partito Nazionale del Lavoro
PNLA US: e: Pacific Northwest Library Association; Pacific Northwest Loggers Association
PNLC I: i: Partito Nazionale Liberale Corporativo
PNM MEX: s: Partido Nacionalista Mexicana; I: i: Partito Nazionale Monarchico; e: People's National Movement [Trinidad, Tobago]
PNOO YU: sn: Pokrajinski Narodnoosvobodilni Odbor

PNP CGO: f: Parti National de Progrès;
WAL: e: People's National Party
PNPA US: e: Pennsylvania Newspaper Publishers Association
PNPF US: e: Piqua Nuclear Power Facility, Piqua, Ohio
PNR MEX: s: Partido Nacional Revolucionario
PNRC US: e: mil: Potomac Naval River Command
PNRD DOM: s: Partido Nacionalista Revolucionario Democrático
PNS PL: pl: Partia Niezależnych Socjalistów; PI: e: Philippine News Service [d: Nachrichtenagentur]; CS: cs: Prozatimní Národní Shromáždění
PNSA US: e: Pacific Northwestern Ski Association
PNSF I: i: Partito Nazionale Sociale Fusionista
PNSY e: mil: Portsmouth Naval Shipyard
PNT DDR: d: Plan Neue Technik
PNTL PL: pl: Polskie Naukowe Towarzystwo Leśne
PNUD UN: f: Programme des Nations Unies pour le Développement
PNV Overvolta: f: Parti National Voltaïque
P.&N.W. US: e: Prescott & Northwestern Railroad Company
PNYA US: e: Port of New York Authority
PNZ PL: pl: Państwowe Nieruchomości Ziemskie; YU: sh: Poljoprivredni Nakladni Zavod
P.O. F: f: Compagnie de Chemin de fer de Paris à Orléans
PO D: d: Parteiorganisation [NSDAP]; U: s: Partido Obrero; e: Patent Office; Pay Office
P. & O. e: Peninsular & Oriental Steam Navigation Company
PO NL: nl: Persoonlijkheids Onderwijs
P.O. 1: Congregatio Piorum Operariorum
PO CS: cs: Politické Oddělení; D: d: Politische Organisation [NSDAP]; e: Post Office; BRD: d: Praktische Oberschule
POA i: Pontificia Opera Assistenza;
GB: e: Prison Officers Association
PoA BRD: d: Arbeitskreis "Priester ohne Amt", 6 Ffm
P.O.A. GB: e: Purchasing Officers Association
POAA US: e: Property Owners Association of America
POAAPS INT: e: Permanent Organization for Afro-Asian Peoples Solidarity
POAHEDPEARL US: e: mil: Pacific Ocean Areas Headquarters Pearl Harbor
POAU US: e: Protestants and Other Americans United for Separation of Church and State
P.O.B. B: f: Parti Ouvrier Belge; YU: sh: Partizansko Obaveštajni Biro; e: Post Office Board
POBA US: e: Patent Office Board of Appeals
POC NL: nl: Persoonlijkheids Onderwijs Concentratie; Plaatselijke Ongevallen Commissie; e: Post Office Corps
P.O.C.A. e: Post Office Clerks' Association
POCh PL: pl: Polskie Odczynniki Chemiczne, Gliwice
POCM MEX: s: Partido Obrero y Campesino de México [gegr 1940]
PO ČSM CS: sk: Pionierska Organizácia Československého Sväzu Mládeže
P.O.D. e: Post Office Department
POE H: hu: Pécsi Orvostudományi Egyetem
P.Ö A: d: Pfadfinder Österreichs
POED GB: e: Post Office Engineering Department
POEE GB: e: Post Office Electrical Engineers
POEM e: Palm Oil Estates Managers
POERS GB: e: Post Office Engineering Research Station
P.O.E.U. GB: e: Post Office Engineering Union
POH YU: sh: Partizanski Odredi Hrvatske

POIA PL: pl: Państwowa Organizacja Imprez Artystycznych
POIT PL: pl: Powiatowy Ośrodek Informacji Turystycznej
POJ YU: sh: Partizanski Odredi Jugoslavije; CS: sk: Pionyrské Oddily Junáka; NL: nl: Proefstation Oost-Java
POK H: hu: Postai Oktatási Központ
P.O.L. e: Patent Office Library
POL PL: e: Polish Ocean Lines; e: Political Affairs Committee
PolA d: Politischer Ausschuß
POLA PL: pl: Polityczny Ośrodek Lewicy Akademickiej
PolA CH: d: Polizeiabteilung [EJPD]; d: Polizeiamt
POLA US: e: Public Ownership League of America
Pol.-B. D: d: Polizeibehörde
PolBA. D: d: Polizeibauamt; Polizeibezirksamt
Pol.BerSch. D: d: Polizeiberufsschule
Pol.-Dion; Pol.Dir. d: Polizeidirektion
Polfracht PL: pl: Polskie Przedsiębiorstwo Frachtowania
Pol.Gef. D: d: Polizeigefängnis
Polgos PL: pl: Polskie Wydawnictwa Gospodarcze
Poliglob PL: pl: Towarzystwo Importowo-Eksportowe S.A.
Polimex PL: pl: Polskie Towarzystwo Eksportu i Importu Maszyn
Polimport BRD: d: "Polimport" Gesellschaft für die Einfuhr polnischer Kohlen mbH, 2 Hamburg [gegr 1949]
POLIS US: e: mil: Petroleum Intersectional Service
Politbüro d: Politisches Büro
Polko BRD: d: Studiengruppe für politologische Psychologie und Kommunikationsforschung; DA: d: Polnische Kohlen- und Transport-GmbH, Danzig
Pol.P. D: d: politische Partei; Politische Polizei
Pol.Pr.; Pol.Präs. D: d: Polizeipräsidium

Pol.Verw.; Pol.-Vw. D: d: Polizeiverwaltung
Polyt. d: Polytechnikum
POM PL: pl: Państwowy Ośrodek Maszynowy; H: hu: Postaügyi Miniszter(ium), Budapest
POMAS US: e: mil: Procurement Office of Military Automotive Supplies
POME US: e: Protect Our Mountain Environment, Denver, Colo.
Pomet PL: pl: Zakłady Metalurgiczne Poznań
POMFLANT US: e: mil: POLARIS Missile Facility, U.S. Atlantic Fleet
Pomgrad YU: sh: Pomorsko-građevinsko Preduzeće, Split
Pomgrap YU: sh: Poslovno Udruzenje Pomoravskih Građevinskih Preduzeća, Svetozarevo
POMH US: e: National Association of Post Office and Postal Transportation Service Mail Handlers, Watchmen and Messengers
POMV US: e: National Federation of Post Office Motor Vehicle Employees
PON PL: pl: Polska Organizacja Narodowa; Polska Organizacja Niepodległościowa; Polski Ośrodek Naukowy
PONCHO US: e: Patrons of Northwest Culture Organizations [gegr 1963]
PONYA US: e: Port of New York Authority
POOC NL: nl: Permanent Ontwikkelings-Ontspannings-Comité
POOF YU: sn: Pokrajinski Odbor Osvobodilne Fronte
POOFF US: e: Preservation Of Our Feminity and Finances
P.O.O.H.B.I. e: Post Office Orphan Homes Benevolent Institution
POP CH: f: Parti ouvrier populaire; I: i: Partito Operaio Progressista; PL: pl: Podstawowa Organizacja Partyjna
P.O.P.A. e: Property Owners Protection Association

POPAI US: e: Point-of-Purchase Advertising Institute

P.O.P.F. F: f: Parti Ouvrier et Paysan Français

POPP PL: pl: Powiatowy Ośrodek Propagandy Partyjnej

POR Bolivien: s: Partido Obrero Revolucionario

P.O.R.A. SYR: f: Parti ouvrier révolutionnaire arabe

PORO e: Public Opinion Research Office

PORZ Orbis PL: pl: Przedsiębiorstwo Obsługi Ruchu Zagranicznego Orbis

POS US: e: Pacific Orchid Society of Hawaii; YU: sn: Partizanski Odredi Slovenije; PL: pl: Polska Organizacja Skantowa; Polskie Organizacje Studenckie; DDR: d: Polytechnische Oberschule

P.O.S.B. e: Post Office Savings Bank

POŠK YU: sh: Plivački Omladinski Športski Klub, Split

P.O.S.L. L: f: Parti ouvrier socialiste luxembourgeois

P.&O.S.N.Co. = P.&O.

POSP PL: pl: Powszechna Organizacja "Służba Polsce"

POSTI PL: pl: Przedsiębiorstwo Obrotu Spożywczymi Towarami Importowanymi

POSTiW PL: pl: Powiatowy Ośrodek Sportu, Turystyki i Wypoczynku

Pošt.úř.š. CS: cs: Post: Poštovní úřad šekový

POT PL: pl: Punkt Obsługi Turystycznej

POTOR PL: pl: Państwowy Ośrodek Technicznej Obsługi Rolnictwa

P.O.T.S.B. e: Post Office and Trustee Savings Bank

POUM E: s: Partido Obrero Unificada Marxista [gegr 1935]

POUNC GB: e: [d: nationaler Rat der Postbenutzer]

POUP I: i: Partito Operaio Unificato Popolare

P.&O.V. US: e: Pittsburgh & Ohio Valley Railway Company

POVDOP CS: sk: Povereníctvo Dopravy

Po.Vers.Komm. D: d: Postversicherungskommission

POW PL: pl: Polska Organizacja Wojskowa; Pomorski Okręg Wojskowy; US: e: Progressive Order of the West

P.O.W.R.A. e: Prisoners of War Relatives Association

POZ PL: pl: Polska Organizacja Zbrojna

POZLA PL: pl: Poznański Okręgowy Związek Lekkiej Atletyki

POZPP PL: pl: Polska Organizacja Zachowawczej Pracy Państwowej

PP PL: pl: Partia Pracy; AL: [d: Partei der Arbeit]; MEX: s: Partido Popular [gegr 1947]

P.P. f: Parti paysan; CGO: f: Parti du Peuple; I: i: Partido Popolare Italiano

PP NATO: e: Payment and Progress Committee

P.P. F: f: Police Parisienne

PP PL: pl: Policja Państwowa; Politechnika Poznańska; d: Politische Polizei; Polizeipräsidium; CS: sk: Povereníctvo Poľnohospodárstva

P.P. F: f: Préfecture de Police

PP e: Progress(ive) Party

PPA PAK: e: Pakistan Press Association, Karachi [d: Nachrichtenagentur]; US: Paper Pail Association; Paper Plate Association; Parcel Post Association; CGO: f: Parti Populaire Africain; DZ: f: Parti Populaire Algérien; CDN: e: Periodical Press Association of Canada; GB: e: Periodical Proprietors Association; US: e: Periodical Publishers Association; DDR: d: Personalpolitische Abteilung [FDJ]; GB: e: Pianoforte Publicity Association Ltd.; US: e: Poultry Publishers Association; GB: e: Pre-School Playgroups Association; US: e: Produce Packaging Association; GB: e: Produce Packers Association; d: Produktions- und Planungs-Ausschuß;

US: e: Professional Panhellenic Association [gegr 1925] ; Professional Photographers of America; GB: e: Professional Photographers Assiciation of Great Britain and Ireland; US: e: Professional Pilots Association; Public Personnel Association

PP.AA. I: i: Pubbliche Amministrazioni (Assistenze)

P.P.A.G.B.I. GB: e: Professional Photographers Association of Great Britain and Ireland

PPANDO NATO: e: Plans, Policy and Operations Division

PPB PL: pl: Państwowe Przedsiebiorstwo Budowlane

PPBF INT: e: Pan-American Pharmaceutical and Biochemical Federation, New York

PPBI RI: [d: zentraler indonesischer Gewerkschaftsbund]

PPC CGO: f: Parti populaire congolais; RCB: f: Parti progressiste congolais; PTM: e: Penang Port Commission

P.P.C. e: People's Political Council

PPC NATO: e: Petroleum Planning Committee; US: e: Philips Petroleum Co., Idaho Falls, Idaho; d: Ping-Pong-Club

P.P.C. US: e: Price Purchase Commission; GB: e: Printers Pension Corporation; e: Provincial Police Council; GB: e: Publishers Publicity Circle

P.P.Can.L.I.; PPCLI CDN: e: mil: Princess Patricia's Canadian Light Infantry

PPCS NZ: e: Primary Producers Co-operative Society

PPD DY: f: Parti Populaire du Dahomey; Parti Progressiste Dahoméen; NL: nl: Provinciale Planologische Diensten; PL: pl: Przedsiębiorstwo Połowów Dalekomorskich

P.P.D. GB: e: Public Prosecutions Department

PPDA e: Produce Prepackaging Development Association

PPDMG US: e: Popular Priced Dress Manufacturers Group

P.P.E.A. e: Police Pensioners' Employment Association

PP.EE. I: i: Pubblici Esercizi

PPESB US: e: Piping and Process Equipment Standards Board

PPF PL: pl: Państwowe Przedsiębiorstwo Filatelistyczne

P.P.F. F: f: Parti Populaire Français

PPFG GH: e: People's Progressive Front of Ghana

PPG US: e: mil: Personnel Processing Group; US: e: Pittsburgh Plate Glass Company, Pittsburgh, Pa.

PPH PL: pl: Państwowe Przedsiębiorstwo Handlowe

P.P.I. GB: e: Paisley Philosophical Institute; I: i: Partito Popolare Italiano

PPI PI: e: Philippine Press Association [d: Nachrichtenagentur]

PPIE PL: pl: Państwowe Przedsiębiorstwo Imprez Estradowych

PPIP PI: e: Philippine Poultry Improvement Plan

PPIS PL: pl: Państwowe Przedsiębiorstwo Imprez Sportowych

PPiUR PL: pl: Przedsiębiorstwo Połowów i Usług Rybackich

PPK D: d: Parteiamtliche Prüfungskommission zum Schutze des NS-Schrifttums [gegr 1934] ; CGO: f: Parti Progressiste Katangais

PPKM BRD: d: Presse-Pättkes-Klub Münster

P.P.L. CGO: f: Parti Populaire Libéral; e: Phonographic Performance Limited

PPL A: d: Prüfstelle der Physikalischen Laboratorien der Wiener Stadtwerke, Wien

PPLH CS: sk: Poverenictvo Polnohospodárstva a Lesného Hospodárstva

PPLI CDN: e: mil: = PPCLI

P.P.M. f: Parti du peuple mauritanien; I: i: [d: monarchistische Volkspartei,

gegr 1954]
PPMA US: e: Plastic Products Manufacturers Association; Printing Paper Manufacturers Association; Pulp and Paper Machinery Association
P.P.N. f: Parti progressiste national; WAN: f: Parti progressiste nigérien
PPNOO YU: sn: Primorski Pokrajinski Narodnoosvobodilni Odbor
PPO CS: sk: Povereníctvo Priemyslu a Obchodu; GB: e: Privy Purse Office; US: e: mil: Publications and Printing Office
PPOK PL: pl: Premiowa Pożyczka Odbudowy Kraju
PPP CGO: f: Parti du Progrès du Peuple; I: i: Partito Progressista Popolare
P.P.P. PTM: e: People's Progressive Party, Kuala Lumpur; WAG: e: People's Progressive Party; Britisch-Guyana: e: People's Progressive Party [gegr 1950]; PI: [d: fortschrittliche Partei]; PL: pl: Polska Partia Postępowa; F: f: Préfecture de Police de Paris
PPPA US: e: Pulp and Paper Prepackaging Association
PPPEA US: e: Pulp, Paper and Paperboard Export Association of the United States
PPPR CS: sk: Povereníctvo Polnohospodárstva a Pozemkovej Reformy
P.P.P.S. GB: e: People's Press Printing Society; Pit Ponies' Protection Society
PPR PL: pl: Polska Partia Robotnicza; NL: [d: progressive-radikale Partei]
PPRI US: e: Pan-Pacific Research Institution; CDN: e: Pulp and Paper Research Institute of Canada
PPRN PL: pl: Prezydium Powiatowej Rady Narodowej
P.Prüf. D: d: mil: Personalprüfstelle des Heeres
PPS MEX: s: Partido Popular Socialista; RL: f: Parti populaire socialiste (syrien); f: Parti progressiste soudanais; I: i: Partito Popolare Sudtirolese

P.P.S. PTM: mal: Party Pesaka Sarawak, Sibu
PPS PI: e: Philippine Pediatric Society; US: e: Plant Propagators Society; PL: pl: Polska Parti Socjalistyczna
PPSA INT: e: Pan-Pacific Surgical Association, Honolulu
PP.Sch. i: Partito Popolare Schipetaro
PPSEAWA INT: e: Pan-Pacific and Southeast Asia Women's Association
PPSG US: e: Piston and Pin Standardization Group
PP.SS. I: i: Pubblici Servizi
P.P.T. CGO: f: Parti populaire des travailleurs; Tschad: f: Parti progressiste tchadien
P.p.t.t. I: i: Partito popolare tirolese trentino
PP.TT. I: i: [d: Ministerium für das Post- und Fernmeldewesen]
PPU US: e: Pan-Pacific Union; GB e: Peace Pledge Union
PPV D: d: Verband von Pumpen- und Pumpenmaschinenfabriken, Berlin-Charlottenburg
PPZ YU: sh: Papudžijska Peradivačka Zadruga; Poljoprivredna Proizvodačka Zadruga
PQ CDN: f: Parti Québecois
PQAA CDN: e: Province of Quebec Association of Architects
PQD US: e: mil: Philadelphia Quartermaster Depot
P.Q.F. F: f: Plan Quinquennal Français
P.Q.R.P. F: f: Plan Quinquennal pour la Relèvement de la Production
P.R. GB: e: The Parachute Regiment
PR D: d: nach WK2: Parlamentarischer Rat
P.R. PTM: mal: Partai Rakyat, Kuala Lumpur; RCH: U: s: Partido Radical; DOM: s: Partido Reformista; BR: pt: Partido Republicano; PE: s: Partido Restaurador [gegr 1955]; GCA: s: Partido Revolucionario; F: f: Parti radical

PR 1: stud: Pax Romana [d: Vereinigung der Verbände katholischer Studenten] ; BRD: d: Personalrat

P.R. D: d: mil: Pionierregiment; F: f: Police Routière

PR PL: pl: Polskie Radio, Warszawa

Pr. d: Präsidium

P.R. I: i: Presidente della Repubblica; Président de la République

Pr D: d: Presseamt

P.R. GB: e: Pretoria Regiment; YU: sh: Predsednik Republike

PR PL: pl: Prezydium Rządu; I: i: Procura del Re; Procura della Repubblica

P.R. F: f: Procureur de la République

PR e: Public Relations Department (Division)

P.R.A. GB: e: mil: The Parachute Regiment Association

PRA Bolivien: s: Partido Nacional Revolucionario Auténtico

P.R.A. f: Parti radical africain; Parti du rassemblement africaine; Parti de regroupement africain

PRA US: e: Personnel Research Association; D: d: Polizeirechts-Ausschuß [Akademie für Deutsches Recht]

PRA. D: d: Polizeireiterabteilung

PrA(.) Bln: Preisamt

P.R.A. F: f: Comité de la Productivité et de la Recherche appliqué

PrA. D: d: mil: Proviantamt; Prüfungsamt; Prüfungsausschuß

PRA US: e: Psoriasis Research Association; Public Roads Administration

PRAC EAK: e: Pyrethrum Research Advisory Committee

prae-bau BRD: d: "Wie bauen und wohnen wir morgen" [internationale Bauausstellung Dortmund, 15 Jun . . . 30 Sep 1961]

PräsBüro d: Präsidialbüro

Präs.F.L.D. D: d: Präsidium der Finanz-Landesdirektion

Präskzl. d: Präsidialkanzlei

Präs.-R. d: Präsidialrat

PRAGA 1968 CS: [d: Briefmarkenausstellung in Prag, 22 Jun . . . 7 Jul 1968]

Pr.A.Gds GB: e: mil: Prince Alfred's Guards

Pragoinvest CS: [d: Außenhandelsunternehmen, gegr 1968]

Pr.Ak.d.W. D: d: Preußische Akademie der Wissenschaften

PRAKLA BRD: d: PRAKLA Gesellschaft für praktische Lagerstättenforschung GmbH, 3 Hannover 1

PRAS SN: f: Parti de Regroupement Africain Sénégal

PRAW US: e: Personnel Research Activity, Washington, D.C.

PRB B: f: Poudreries Réunies Belge

P.R.B. GB: e: Pre-Raphaelite Brotherhood, London [gegr 1848]

PrB d: Provinzialbibliothek

PRB US: e: Population Reference Bureau

PRC CGO: f: Parti Républicain Congolais; US: e: Petroleum Reserves Corporation; PL: [e: Polish Red Cross] ; GB: e: mil: Polish Resettlement Corps [RAF] ; GB: e: Poultry Research Centre

P.R.C. e: Price Regulation Committee

PRCI CI: f: Parti Républicain de Côte d'Ivoire

PRD El Salvador: s: Partido Radical Democrático; DOM: e: Partido Revolucionario Dominicano; DY: f: Parti Républicain du Dahomey; f: Parti Républicain Démocratique

Pr.D. GB: e: Probate, Divorce, and Admiralty Division

PRD e: Public Relations Department (Division)

PRDC US: e: Power Reactor Development Company, Newport, Michigan

PRDN GCA: s: Partido de Reconciliación Democrática Nacional

PRE INT: f: Fédération européenne des fabricants de produits réfractaires e: European Federation of Refractory Material Producers d: Europäischer Verband der Fabrikanten feuerfesten

Materials, Milano [I]; INT: f: Programme de reconstruction (relèvement) européenne [e: ERP]
PREAG; Preag D: BRD: d: Preußische Elektrizitäts-Aktiengesellschaft, Berlin, Hannover
PREB INT: d: Parlamentarischer Rat der Europäischen Bewegung, Brüssel [B]
PRechnA D: d: Post: Postrechnungsamt
PRELA C: s: Prensa Latine [d: Nachrichtenagentur]
PREMA US: e: Pulp Refining Equipment Manufacturers Association
PREMAG; Premag D: BRD: d: Preßluftwerkzeug- und Maschinenbau GmbH, Berlin [heute:] PREMAG GmbH Preßluftwerkzeug- und Maschinenbau, 6222 Geisenheim
Prepa F: f: Société de Prospection et Exploitation Pétrolières en Alsace
PRESCO INT: e: Preparatory Subcommittee [IEC]
Press BlnW: d: Presseamt des Senats
PRESSA D: d: Presseausstellung Köln 1928
PREST INT: f: Politique de la recherche scientifique et technique [groupe de travail]
Preußenkasse D: d: Preußische Zentralgenossenschaftskasse, Berlin
PREWI US: e: Press-Wireless, Inc., New York
P.R.F. F: f: Parti de la Réconciliation Française
PRF e: Personnel Research Federation; US: e: Petroleum Research Fund; Plywood Research Foundation; Public Relations Foundation
Pr.-G. D: d: Preisgericht; Prisengericht
Prg. d: Progymnasium
PRI US: e: Paint Research Institute; Paleontological Research Institution; MEX: s: Partido Revolucionario Institucional; F: f: Parti Radical Indépendant; I: i: Partito Repubblicano Italiano; US: e: Pineapple Research Institute

[Hawaii]; INT: f: La prévention routière internationale, Paris 9 d: Internationale Verkehrsunfallverhütung e: International Prevention of Road Accidents; RI: [d: Volkspartei]; e: Public Relations Institute
PRIN YV: s: Partido Revolucionario de Integración Nacional
PR/ISC D: e: mil: nach WK2: Public Relations – Information Services Control [British]
P.R.K. D: d: Pommerscher Radioklub eV, Stettin
PRK S: sv: Pressens Korrespondensbyrå
Pr.Kr.Min. D: d: mil: Preußisches Kriegsministerium
P.R.L. f: Parti républicain de la liberté
PRL e: Personnel Research Laboratory
P.R.L. e: Postal Reform League
PRL CDN: e: Prairie Research Laboratory
Pr.L.Kr.V. D: d: mil: Preußischer Landeskriegerverband
PrLM D: d: Preußisches Ministerium für Landwirtschaft, Domänen und Forsten
Pr.Louise's D.Gds CDN: e: mil: Princess Louise's Dragoon Guards
PRM MEX: s: Partido de la Revolución Mexicana; f: Parti de regroupement mauritanien
PrMdI. D: d: Preußisches Ministerium des Innern
PrMfW. D: d: Preußisches Ministerium für Wissenschaft, Kunst und Volksbildung
PRMG US: e: Piston Ring Manufacturers Group
Pr.min.r. CS: cs: Presidium ministerské rady
PrMV. D: d: Preußisches Ministerium für Volkswohlfahrt
PRN -RI: Partai Rakjat Nasional; YV: s: Partido Revolucionario Nacionalista
PRNC CGO: f: Parti de la reconstruction nationale du Congo; US: e: mil: Potomac River Naval Command
PRNM f: Parti de la renaissance natio-

nale mauritannienne

Pro BRD: d: Konsumgenossenschaft "Produktion" eGmbH, 2 Hamburg

PRO GB: e: Public Record Office; e: mil: Public Relations Office

Pro Aqua 69 INT: 1: d: 4. Fachmesse in Basel [CH, 29 Mai . . . 4 Jun 1969, der IAM, Müllforschung]

Pro Art 71 INT: 1: d: [erster Internationaler Markt für aktuelle Kunst, Duisburg, 20 . . . 25 Mai 1971]

Probus US: e: [Professional and Business] Boston [d: Amateur-Musikkapelle von Wissenschaftlern und Geschäftsleuten]

PROCAFE CH: [d: Vereinigung für Kaffeewerbung]

pro domo INT: BRD: l:[d: Bundesausstellung des Deutschen Hausfrauenbundes und 6. Internationaler Frauenkongreß, Köln, 6 . . . 14 Mai 1972]

Prodwi A: d: mil: nach WK1: Produktiv-Werkstätte des Landesverbandes der Kriegsinvaliden und Kriegshinterbliebenen Österreichs rGmbH, Wien 10

PROELECTRON INT: 1: d: Internationale Vereinigung für die Vereinheitlichung der Bezeichnung von Bauelementen, Brüssel [B]

Profintern INT: [d: Rote Gewerkschaftsinternationale [1921 . . . 38, = RGI]

PROFO N: no: Produksjonteknisk Forskningsinstitutt

Profsojus SU: [d: Gewerkschaft]

Pr.of W.O.Rgt CDN: e: mil: Prince of Wales' Own Regiment

prognos CH: d: prognos Europäische Arbeitsgruppe für angewandte Wirtschaftsforschung, Basel [später:] prognos Europäisches Zentrum für angewandte Wirtschaftsforschung AG, CH-4000 Basel

PROHUZA F: f: Centre d'Etudes et d'Information des Problèmes Humains dans les Zones Arides

PROMARCA CH: 1: d: [Schweizer Marken-

artikelverband]

Prombank SU: [d: Handels- und Industriebank, Moskau, 1922 . . . 59]

Promi D: d: NS: Reichsministerium für Volksaufklärung und Propaganda

Promorsa D: d: Promorsa GmbH, Verkaufsgemeinschaft von Weinproduzenten von Mosel, Ruwer und Saar, Trier

PROMOTELEC F: f: [d: Vereinigung der Verbände der Elektroinstallateure und der Verbandsorganisationen, die an elektrischen Erzeugnissen interessiert sind]

PROP PL: pl: Państwowa Rada Ochrony Przyrody; US: e: Portland Regional Opportunities Program

PROPACK INT: [d: 2. internationale Verpackungsausstellung, Brüssel [B] , 7 . . . 13 Jun 1968]

Protectunion INT: e: International Union for the Protection of Literary and Artistic Work

PROTECTUNIONS INT: f: Bureaux Internationaux Réunis pour la Protection de la Propriété Industrielle, Littéraire et Artistique, Bern [CH]

Prov.-A. D: d: Provinzialausschuß

Prov.Anst. D: d: Provinzialanstalt

Prov.Bk. D: d: Provinzialbank

Prov.Ldw. D: d: mil: Provinzial-Landwehr

PROVMAAG US: e: mil: Provisional Military Assistance Advisory Group

Prov.Verw. D: d: Provinzialverwaltung

ProzGer. D: d: Prozeßgericht

Proz BlnW: d: Proletarierinnen-Zentrum

P.R.P. F: f: Parti Républicain Populaire

PRP PL: pl: Polskie Towarzystwo Prehistoryków

P.R.P. e: Production Requirements Plan

Pr.Prov.R. D: d: Preußischer Provinzialrat

PrPrSt D: d: Preisprüfungsstelle

P.R.R. F: f: Parti de la Rénovation Républicaine

PRR US: e: Pennsylvania Railroad Company [= Pa.R.R.]

PRR e: mil: The Puerto Rico Regiment

P.R.R.A. e: Puerto Rico Reconstruction Administration

PRRI US: e: Puerto Rico Rum Institute

PRRM PI: e: Philippine Rural Reconstruction Movement

PRRPA e: Puerto Rico Rum Producers Association

P.R.R.S. F: f: Parti radical et radical-socialiste

PRS US: e: Pacific Rocket Society; e: Paint Research Station

P.R.S. f: Parti du regroupement soudanais, Bamako; Parti républicain socialiste; DZ: f: Parti de la Révolution Socialiste; GB: e: Performing Right Society; Proportional Representation Society; Protestant Reformation Society

PRS D: e: mil: nach WK2: Public Relations Service [British]

PRSA US: e: Public Relations Society of America

Pr.-Sem. d: Priesterseminar

PRSL US: e: Pennsylvania - Reading Seashore Lines [railroad]

P.R.S.R.F. F: f: Parti Républicain et Social de la Réconciliation Française

PRSS SN: f: Parti Républicain Social du Sénégal

PrStD D: d: Provinzialsteuerdirektion

Pr.St.M. D: d: Preußisches Staatsministerium

Pr.St.R. D: d: Preußischer Staatsrat

PRTCA US: e: President's Radio Technical Commission for Aeronautics

PRU J: e: People's Revolutionary Union

PRUCIS PI: e: Philippine Rural Community Improvement Society

PRUD El Salvador: s: Partido Revolucionario de Unificación Democrata

Prüf.Nord. D: d: mil: Dienststelle für Eignungsprüfungen beim Marineoberkommando Nordsee

Prüf.Ost. D: d: mil: Dienststelle für Eignungsprüfungen beim Marineoberkommando Ostsee

PrUM D: d: Preußisches Ministerium für Wissenschaft und Unterricht

PRUPC Kamerun: f: Parti révolutionnaire de l'Union des Populations du Cameroun

PRV D: d: Pommerscher Regattaverein, Stettin

PRWRA e: Puerto Rico Water Resources Authority

PRYC RCH: s: Agencia Noticiosa Prensa, Radio y Cine [d: Nachrichtenagentur]

P.S. GB: e: The Palæontographic Society; US: e: Paleontological Society of America; Palm Society

PS S: sv: mil: Pansartruppskolan, Skövede; US: e: Parapsychological Society

P.S. RI: Partai Sosialis; RA: s: Partido Socialista; f: Parti socialiste; GB: e: Pastel Society; Pathological Society of Great Britain and Ireland

PS CS: cs: Pedagogický Sbor; US: e: Pennsylvania State Teachers College; S: sv: Pensionsstyrelsen

P.S. e: mil: Permanent Staff; personal staff; f: Petites Sœurs des Pauvres

PS. GB: e: Petty Sessions

P.S. GB: e: Pharmaceutical Society of Great Britain; Philantropical Society; Philharmonic Society

PS PI: e: mil: Philippine Scouts

P.S. GB: e: Philological Society, London; e: Philosophical Society; Physical Society; GB: e: mil: Pioneer School; D: d: mil: Pionier-Schule; e: Poetry Society; f: Police sanitaire

PS NL: nl: Polytechnische School; D: d: Präparandenschule

P.S. F: f: Préfecture de la Seine; e: Prehistoric Society; Primary School

P.Š. CS: cs: Průmyslová škola

P.S. I: i: Pubblica Sicurezza; e: Public School

PS CS: cs: Československá Lékařská Společnost J.E. Purkyně

PSA US: e: Pacific Science Association;

Pacific Seedsmen's Association; Pacific Southwest Airlines; RA: s: Partido Socialista Argentino

P.S.A. f: Parti socialiste africain; F: f: Parti socialiste autonome [gegr 1957] ; CGO: f: Parti solidaire africain [gegr 1959]

PSA PI: e: Philippine Standards Association, Manila; US: e: Philippine Sugar Association; Philosophy of Science Association; Photographic Society of America, Philadelphia 3, Pa. [gegr 1937] ; Phycological Society of America; Play Schools Association; Poetry Society of America; PTM: e: Port of Singapore Authority; D: d: Postscheckamt; Postsparkassenamt; US: e: Poultry Science Association; GB: e: Poultry Stock Association Ltd.; CS: sk: Pracovné Sdruženie Architektov

P.S.A. e: Private Schools Association

PSA US: e: Psychological Society of America

PSAA US: e: Pakistan Students Association of America; Polish Singers Alliance of America

PSAB GB: e: Public Schools Appointments Bureau

PSABw BRD: d: mil: Personalstammamt der Bundeswehr [gegr 1963]

PSAC US: e: Preferred Stock Advisory Committee; President's Science Advisory Committee

PSAE PI: e: Philippine Society of Agricultural Engineers

PSÄ BRD: d: Post: Postsparkassenämter

PSAE US: e: National Association of Public School Adult Educators

PSAL GB: e: Public Schools Athletic League

PSAS SN: f: Parti sénégalais d'action socialiste

P.S.B. BR: pt: Partido Socialista Brasileiro; B: f: Parti socialiste belge

psb S: sv: postsparbanken

PSB BRD: d: Projektgesellschaft Schneller Brüter; US: e: Psychological Strategy Board [National Research Council] ; e: Public Safety Branch

PSBA GB: e: Public School Bursars Association

PSC US: e: Pacific Science Council

P.S.C. e: Parliamentary Staff Committee; Bolivien; s: Partido Social Cristiana; B: f: Parti social-chrétien [gegr 1945] ; CGO: f: Parti socialiste congolais

PSC US: e: Pennsylvania State College of Optometry; NL: nl: Peulvruchten Studie Combinatie

P.S.C. GB: e: Philosophical Society of Cambrige; Police Staff College

PSC BRD: d: Politischer Schülerclub [erster Club 1969 in St. Wendel gegr] ; D: e: mil: nach WK2: Postal Subcommittee [Allied Control Authority] ; US: e: Pressed Steel Car Company Inc., Chicago; NATO: e: Principal Subordinate Command; US: e: Public Service Commission

PSCA PAK: SU: e: Pakistan-Soviet Cultural Association; CGO: f: Parti social pour la défense des cultes en Afrique

PSCC INT: e: Power Systems Computation Conference

PSch BRD: d: Post: Postschule

PSch. D: d: Provinzial-Schulkollegium

PSchA BRD: d: Post: Postscheckamt

PSchÄ BRD: d: Post: Postscheckämter

PSchK D: d: Provinzialschulkollegium

PSCJ 1: Presbyteri Sancti Cordis Jesu

PSCLA INT: e: Petroleum Supply Committee for Latin America

PSD Bolivien: s: Partido Social Democrático; BR: pt: Partido Social Democrático; YV: s: Partido Social Democrático; CO: s: Partido Socialista Democrático

P.S.D. RM: f: Parti social-démocrate de Madagascar et des Comores [gegr 1956] ; f: Parti socialiste démocratique; TN: f: Parti socialiste destourien; e: mil: Personnel (Personal) Services Department

(Division)
PSD US: e: mil: Philadelphia Signal Depot
P.S.D. e: Postal Services Department
P.S. d'Az. I: i: Partito Sardo d'Azione
PSDF e: mil: Popular Self Defense Force
PSDI I: i: Partito Socialista Democratico Italiano [gegr 1952]
PSDMC RM: f: = P.S.D.
PSE EC: s: [d: Sozialistenpartei] ; US: e: Philadelphia Stock Exchange
P.S.E. GB: e: Philosophical Society of England
PS&E US: e: Pioneer Service & Engineering Co., Chicago 4
PSEA US: e: Physical Security Equipment Agency; Pleaters, Stitchers and Embroiderers Association
PSEE PI: e: Philippine Society of Electrical Engineers, Inc.
PSEMA Obervolta: f: Parti social d'éducation des masses africaines
PSF PAK: e: Pakistan Seafarers' Federation
P&SF US: e: Panhandle & Santa Fe Railway
P.S.F. F: f: Parti social français; PTM: e: People's Socialist Front, Kuala Lumpur
PSF US: e: Psychiatric Research Fund
PSFC INT: e: Pacific Salmon Fisheries Commission
P.S.F.P. e: Progressive Society of French Polishers
P.S.G. GB: e: Philosophical Society of Glasgow
PSG GB: e: Photoelectric Spectrometry Group, Cambridge
P.S.G.B. GB: e: Pharmaceutical (Philosophical) Society of Great Britain
P.S.G.B.I. GB: e: Pathological Society of Great Britain and Ireland
PSH CS: sk: Povereníctvo Stavebných Hmot
PSHFA GB: e: Public Servants Housing and Finance Association
PSI US: e: Pacific Semiconductors Inc.,

Culver City, Calif.; PAK: e: Pakistan Standards Institution, Karachi; RI: Partai Sosialis Indonesia; I: i: Partito Socialista Italiano
P.S.I. e: Pharmaceutical Society of Ireland
PSI INT: e: Public Services International, London EC 1
PSIA US: e: Paper Stock Institute of America
PSII RI: Partai Sarekat Islam Indonesia
PSIP GB: e: Poultry Stock Improvement Plan
P.S.I.S.C. e: Port Said International Sporting Club
PSIT Tschad: f: Parti Socialiste Indépendant du Tchad
PSIUP I: i: Partito Socialista Italiano di Unità Proletaria
PSK D: d: Provinzialschulkollegium; CS: cs: [Arbeitsgruppe für Klassifikation]
PSKSBw BRD: d: mil: Schule der Bundeswehr für Psychologische Kampfführung
PSL PAK: e: Pakistan Services Limited
P.S.L. e: Personal Service League
PSL PL: pl: Polskie Stronnictwo Ludowe
PSLI I: i: Partito Socialista Lavoratori Italiani
PSL NW PL: pl: Polskie Stronnictwo Ludowe - Nowe Wyzwolenie
PSLVU LR: Pētera Stučkas Latvijas Valsts Universitāte
P.S.M. 1: Pia Societas Missionum e: Pious Society of Missions; e: Protestant Socialist Movement
PSMA US: e: Power Saw Manufacturers Association
PSMS CS: cs: Poradní Sbor pro Mechanisaci Stavebnictví
PSMU CS: cs: Pěvecké Sdružení Moravských Učitelů
P.S.N. GB: e: Pacific Steam Navigation Company, Liverpool [= P.S.N.C.]
PS&N US: e: Pittsburgh, Shawmut & Northern Railroad
P.S.N.C. GB: e: = P.S.N.

P.S.N.I. GB: e: Pharmaceutical Society of Northern Ireland

PSNS US: e: mil: Puget Sound Naval Shipyard, Remerton, Wash.

PŠO CS: sk: Poverenictvo Školstva a Osvety

PSO US: e: mil: Product Support Organization; Provisions Supply Office; Public Safety Office

PSOC e: mil: Principal Staff Officers Committee

P.S.O.P. f: Parti socialiste des ouvriers et paysans

PSP NL: nl: [d: pazifistisch-sozialistische Partei] ; C: s: Partido Socialista Popular; PE: s: Partido Socialista del Peru; BR: pt: Partido Social Progressista; Sudan: f: Parti Soudanais Populaire; ADN: e: People's Socialist Party; PI: e: Philippine Society of Parasitology; PL: pl: Polskie Siły Powietrzne; IND: e: Praja Socialist Party [gegr 1952] ; CS: cs: Právnická škola pracujících; CS: sk: Predsednictvo Sboru Poverenikov; BRD: d: Psychologisches Institut für Personalfragen Limberger & Dilger, 78 Freiburg

PSpA BRD: d: Post: Postsparkassenamt

PSpÄ BRD: d: Post: Postsparkassenämter

PSpDV BRD: d: Post: Postspar- und Darlehnsverein

PSpK DDR: d: Post: Postsparkasse

PSPU CS: cs: Pěvecká Sdružení Pražských Učitelů

P.S.R. S: sv: Pensionerade Statstjänstemäns Riksförbund, Stockholm

P.&S.R. US: e: Petalume & Santa Rosa Railroad Company

P.S.R. F: f: Programme social de relogement

P.S.R.F. F: f: Parti Social de la Réconciliation Française

PSRF US: e: Profit Sharing Research Foundation

PSS US: e: Pacific Sociological Society

P.S.S. e: Pacific Steamship Company

PSS S: sv: Palgrenska Samskolan, Stockholm; I: i: Partito Socialista Sammarinese

P.S.S. GB: e: Portsmouth Signal School; Printing and Stationery Service

PSSA ZA: e: Pharmaceutical Society of South Africa; Photogrammetric (Photographic) Society of South Africa

PSSC INT: e: Physical Science Study Committee [OECD]

P.S.S.C. e: Pious Society of Missionaries of St. Charles

P.S. - S.I.I.S. I: i: Partito Socialista – Sezione Italiano dell'Internazionale Socialista

PSSJ 1: Pia Societas Sancti Josephi

PSSMA US: e: Paper Shipping Sack Manufacturers Association

P.S.S.R.Y.O. e: Philantropic Society and School for the Reformation of Young Offenders

PSSU CS: cs: Pěvecký Sbor Sveromoravských Učitelů

PST BR: pt: Partido Social Trabalhista

PSt D: d: Prüfstelle für Schund- und Schmutzschriften

P.S.T.A. e: Public Service Transport Association

PStB; PStBk. D: d: Preußische Staatsbank

PSTC US: e: Pressure Sensitive Tape Council

P.S.U. e: Pacifist Service Unit; F: f: Parti Socialiste Unifié [gegr 1960]; I: i: Partito Socialista Unitario [gegr 1949]

PSU US: e: Pennsylvania State University

PSUC YV: s: Partido Socialista Unificado de Cataluña

P.S.U.D. f: Parti socialiste unitaire démocratique

P.S.U.L.I. I: i: Partido Socialista Unitario dei Lavoratori Italiani [gegr 1951]

PSV YV: s: Partido Socialista Venezolano; d: Polizeisportverein(igung); d: Post -Sportverein; d: Postwertzeichen-Sammler-Verein; D: d: Potsdamer Segler-Verein

PSVAC GB: e: Public Service Vehicle Advertising Committee

PSVG I: i: Partito Socialista della Venezia Giulia

PSvHS CS: sk: Povereníctvo Stavebníctva, Hlavná Správa

PSVSBw BRD: d: mil: Schule der Bundeswehr für Psychologische Verteidigung

PSVT CS: [d: Arbeitsgruppe zur Erforschung der Klassifizierung]

PŠVU CS: sk: Povereníctvo Školstva, Vied a Umení

PSWA GB: e: Patented Steel Wire Association, Sheffield 10

PSWB GB: e: Patented Steel Wire Bureau

P.S.W.U. e: Pianoforte Supplies Workers Union

PSz H: hu: Pedagógiai Szeminárium; Pedagógus Szakszervezet, Budapest

PSZ PL: pl: Polskie Siły Zbrojne

P.T. I: i: Piccolo Teatro, Milano

PT CS: sk: Pevereníctvo pre Techniku; N: e: Press Telegraph [d: Nachrichtenagentur]

P.T. GB: e: Public Trustee

PTA GB: e: Paper Towel Association; Paper and Twine Association; Parent-Teacher Association [gegr 1897]

P.T.A. SU: d: Petersburger Telegraphen-Agentur [ab 1918: Rosta]

PTA BRD: d: Physikalisch-Technische Anstalt, Braunschweig [gegr 1949]

P.T.A. e: Pianoforte Tuners Association; d: Polnische Telegraphen-Agentur, Berlin SW 68

PTA PL: pl: Polskie Towarzystwo Archeologiczne (Austronautyczne)

P.T.A. e: Printing Trades Alliance

PTA BRD: d: Programmier-technische Arbeitsgemeinschaft; GB: e: Public Transport Association

PTAD US: e: Productivity and Technical Assistance Division

PTAS GB: e: Productivity and Technical Assistance Secretariat [Board of Trade]

PTB BR: pt: Partido Trabalhista Brasileiro; BRD: d: Physikalisch-Technische Bundesanstalt, 1 Berlin 10, 33 Braunschweig; PL: pl: Polskie Towarzystwo Balneologiczne; Polskie Towarzystwo Botaniczn

Ptb S: sv: Presstelegrambolaget [gegr 1919

PTC US: e: Performance Technology Corporation, Waltham, Mass. 02154; Philadelphia Transportation Company

P.T.C. e: Physical Training Centre

PTC US: e: Pipe and Tobacco Council; PL: pl: Polskie Towarzystwo Chemiczne GB: e: mil: Primary Training Centre; US: e: Programming and Training Center

PTCA US: e: Private Truck Council of America

PTCh PL: pl: Polskie Towarzystwo Chemiczne

PTCR US: e: Patent, Trademark and Copyright Research Institute

P.T.D. e: Passenger Transport Department

PTD PL: pl: Polskie Towarzystwo Dermatologiczne

PTE PL: pl: Polskie Towarzystwo Elektryczne; H: hu: Poszony Tornai Egyesület; A: d: Prüfstelle für Funkentstörung, Wien

PTEk PL: pl: Polskie Towarzystwo Ekonomiczne

PTF PAK: e: Pakistan Transport Workers Federation; PL: pl: Polskie Towarzystwo Farmaceutyczne (Filologiczne) (Filozoficzne)

PTFiz PL: pl: Polskie Towarzystwo Fizyczne

PTG US: e: Piano Technicians Guild; US: e mil: POLARIS Task Group; PL: pl: Polskie Towarzystwo Geograficzne (Geologiczne)

PTGANE e: Professional Technical Group on Aerospace and Navigational Electronics

P.T.G.C. e: Passenger Trade Group Committee

PTH PL: pl: Polskie Towarzystwo Historyczne

PTI H: hu: Pedagógiai Tudományos Intézet, Budapest; US: e: Philadelphia Textile Institute; NL: nl: Philips Telecommunicatie Industri; IND: e: Press Trust of India, Bombay [d: Nachrichtenagentur]

PTIDG e: Presentation of Technical Information Discussion Group

PTJ PL: pl: Polskie Towarzystvo Językoznawcze

PTK BRD: d: Prominenten-Tennis-Kreis, München [gegr 1961]

PTL BRD: d: Physikalisch-Technisches Labor Obering. Gg. Müller, 86 Bamberg; Physikalisch-Technische Lehranstalt; PL: pl: Polskie Towarzystwo Lekarskie (Ludoznawcze)

PTM PL: pl: Państwowe Technikum Morskie; Polskie Towarzystwo Matematyczne

PTMA PL: pl: Poznańskie Towarzystwo Miłosników Astronomii

PTMCA GB: e: Pit Tub and Mine Care Manufacturers Association

PTMTS PL: pl: Polskie Towarzystwo Mechaniki Teoretycznej i Stosowanej

PTN BR: pt: Partido Trabalhista Nacional; PL‣pl: Polskie Towarzystwo Neurologiczne

PTO PL: pl: Polskie Towarzystwo Okulistyczne (Orientalistyczne)

P&TO US: e: National Association of Postal and Telegraph Officers

P.T.O. GB: e: Public Trustee Office

P.T.P. TG: f: Parti Togolais du Progrès [gegr 1946]

PTP A: d: Physikalisch-Technische Prüfanstalt für Radiologie und Elektromedizin, Wien [staatlich autorisiert]

PTPA PL: pl: Polskie Towarzystwo Przyjaciół Astronomji

PTPN PL: pl: Poznańskie Towarzystwo Przyjaciół Nauk

PTPONZj PL: pl: Polskie Towarzystwo Przyjaciół Organizacji Narodów Zjednoczonych

PTPreh PL: pl: Polskie Towarzystwo Prehistoryczne

PTR D: d: Physikalisch-Technische Reichsanstalt

PTRD GCA: s: Partido de Trabajadores Republicano Democrático

P.T.&Rec.School e: Physical Training and Recreational School

PTRM PL: pl: Państwowe Technikum Rybołówstwa Morskiego

PTRZ PL: pl: Planowo-Terminowe Remonty Zapobiegawcze

P.T.S. e: Pali Text Society

PTS e: mil: Parachute Training School; GB: e: Philatelic Traders Society Ltd., London

PTŠ CS: sk: Poľnohospodárska-technická škola

P.T.S. GB: e: mil: Portsmouth Torpedo School; GB: e: Printing Technical School; LR: Profesionāli Tehniskā Skola

P.T.S. e: Protestant Truth Society

PTS DDR: d: Prüfdienststelle für technische Schiffsausrüstung, Stralsund

P.T.S.D. GB: e: mil: Physical Training and Sports Department [Admiralty]

PTT F: f: Département de Postes,Télégraphes et Téléphones; CH: d: Eidgenössische Post-, Telegraphen- und Telephonverwaltung, Bern; INT: d: Internationale des Personals der Post-, Telegraphen- und Telephonverwaltungen; NL: nl: Staatsbedrijf der Posterijen, Telegrafie en Telefonie; CS: sk: Poverníctvo pre Poštu a Telegraf

PTTC US: e: mil: Pacific Transportation Terminal Command

PTTI INT: e: Postal, Telegraph and Telephone International, Brussels [B]

PTU GB: e: Plumbing Trades Union, London SW 4

PTW BRD: d: Physikalisch-Technische Werkstätte Prof. Dr.-Ing. W. Heimann

GmbH, 62 Wiesbaden-Dotzheim; PL: pl: Przysposobienie Techniczno-Wojskowe [gegr 1958]

PTWO PI: e: Philippine Transport Workers Organization

PTXI US: e: Philadelphia Textile Institute [= PTI]

PTZ DDR: d: Physikalisch-Technisches Zentralinstitut [DAMG]; PL: pl: Polskie Towarzystwo Zootechniczne; BRD: d: Post: Posttechnisches Zentralamt, 61 Darmstadt

PU CS: cs: Palackého Universita; BRD: d: Papier Union GmbH, 587 Hemer

P.U. F: f: Partisans Unifiés de la Rénovation Française

PÚ CS: cs: Patentní Úřad; Pedagogický Ústav; Prehistorický Ústav

PU I: i: Pretura Unificata; US: e: Princeton University; CDN: e: Purdue University

PUA US: e: Pacific Union Association; GCA: s: Partido Unificación Anticomunista; CGO: f: Parti de l'Unité Africaine

PUAS INT: e: Postal Union of the Americas and Spain, Montevideo [gegr 1911]

PUB CGO: f: Parti de l'Unité Basonge

PUBLICOM R: [d: rumänische Agentur für internationale Werbung, Bukarest]

PUBLIPAC INT: [d: internationale Verpackungs-Biennale, Paris, 14 . . . 23 Okt 1960]

PUBP PL: pl: Powiatowy Urząd Bezpieczeństwa Publicznego

PUC F: f: Paris Université Club [club sportif]; CGO: f: Parti de l'Unité Congolaise; e: Port Utilization Committee; US: e: Production Urgency Committee; e: Public Utilities Commission (Committee)

PÚ-ČSAV CS: cs: Polarografický Ústav při ČSAV

PUD GCA: s: Partido Unión Democrática

P.U.D. US: e: Public Utility District

PUDOC NL: nl: Centrum voor Landbouwpublikaties en Landbouwdocumentatie, Wageningen

PUE INT: d: Philokartisten-Union Europas, 435 Recklinghausen [BRD]

Pü B H: hu: Pénzügyi Bizottság

PUF F: f: Presses Universitaires de France, Paris 6

P.U.F.S.D. e: Public Utilities, Finance and Secretarial Departments

P.U.G.S. F: f: Parti d'Union de la Gauche Socialiste [gegr 1957]

PUK BRD: d: Post: Postunterstützungskasse

PUM CDN: f: Les Presses Universitaires de Montréal

PÚMS CS: cs: Právnický Ústav Ministerstva Spravedlnosti

PUN Honduras: CR: s: Partido Unión Nacional; CGO: f: Parti pour l'Unité Nationale

PUNA CGO: f: Parti de l'Unité Nationale

PUNG f: Parti de l'Unité Nationale de Guinée

PUNGA f: Parti de l'Unité Nationale Gabonaise

PUP GCA: s: Partido de Unión Patriotica; CGO: f: Parti de l'Unité du Peuple; BH: e: People's United Party; INT: e: Public Utilities Panel [EECE]

PUQ I: i: Partito dell'Uomo Qualunque

PUR PL: pl: Państwowy Urząd Repatriacyjny; GCA: s: Partido de Unificación Revolucionaria

PURAQUA INT: [d: amerikanische Ausstellung und internationale Konferenz über Wasserreinigung und Entsalzung, Rom [I], 17 . . . 22 Feb 1969]

PURF F: f: Partisans Unifiés de la Rénovation Française

P.U.R.R. F: f: Partisans Unifiés de la Rénovation Républicaine

PURS C: s: Partido Unido de la Revolución Socialista; Bolivien: s: Partido de la Unión Republicana Socialista

PUS PL: pl: Państwowy Urząd Samochodowy

P.U.S. F: f: Groupe paysan d'Union

sociale; US: e: Pilgrims of the United States

P.U.S.F. IND: e: People's United Socialist Front

PUSR Bolivien: s: Partido Unido Socialista Republicano

PUSRI RI: P.T.Pupuk Sriwidjaja, Palembang

PUT TG: f: Parti d'Union Togolaise; PL: pl: Przedsiębiorstwo Usług Turystycznych; Punkt Usług Transportowych

PÚV CS: cs: Pražský Ústřední Výbor

PUW PL: pl: Państwowy Urząd Wydawniczy; BRD: d: Pforzheimer Uhren-Rohwerke, 753 Pforzheim

PuW D: d: mil: WK1: Prüfanstalt und Werft der Fliegertruppe, Adlershof

PUWF PL: pl: Państwowy Urząd Wychowania Fizycznego

PUWP e: Polish United Workers Party

PUZ PL: pl: Portowy Urząd Zdrówia; Powiatowy Urząd Ziemski

PV d: Parteivorstand

P.-V. d: Pensionsverein

PV d: Personalversammlung; BRD: d: Phenol-Verband, 43 Essen; Photoindustrie-Verband, 6 Ffm; d: Polizeiverwaltung; CS: sk: Povereníctvo Výživy; YU: sh: Predsedništvo Vlade sn: Predsedstvo Vlade; d: Primanerverein; NL: nl: Protestantsche Volkspartij; D: d: Prüfmaschinen-Verband, Berlin-Wilmersdorf

PVA US: e: mil: Paralysed Veterans Association; d: mil: Polnische Volksarmee

PVAP d: Polnische Vereinigte Arbeiterpartei

PVB RI: nl: Padvindersbond; NL: nl: Provinciale Veevoederbureau

P.V.C. e: People's Vigilance Committee; J: e: People's Volunteer Corps

PVC NL: nl: Provinciale Voedselcommissariaat

PvdA NL: nl: Partij van de Arbeid

PVG BRD: d: Presse-Vertriebs-Gesellschaft mbH, Ffm

PVLA e: Paint, Varnish and Lacquer Association

PVMJS D: d: Pensionsverein Münchener Journalisten und Schriftsteller

PVN NL: nl: Padvinders-Vereeniging

PVO NL: nl: Padvinders-Organisatie; BUR: e: People's Volunteer Organization

P.V.O.A. e: Passenger Vehicle Operators' Association

PVP CR: [d: Volksavantgarde]

PVR CS: d: Polytechnischer Verband in der Tschechoslowakischen Republik, Aussig a.E.

PVS NL: nl: Productschap voor Siergewassen

PVT YU: sn: Pomožna Vojaška Tehnika

PVTA PI: e: Philippine Virginia Tobacco Administration

PVU YU: sn: mil: Pehotno Vojno Učilišče sh: Pešadijsko Vojno Učilište

PVV B: nl: Partij voor Vrijheid en Vooruitgang; NL: nl: Proletarische Vrijdenkersvereeniging

PVZ DDR: d: Post: Postvertriebszentrale; CS: sk: Povereníctvo pre Výživu a Zásobovanie

PW PL: pl: Politechnika Warszawska

P&W US: e: Pratt & Whitney [vgl: P&WA]

PW A: d: Pressedienst Wien, Wien 1; NL: nl: Provinciale Waterstaat; US: e: Public Works; NL: nl: Publieke Werken

PWA US: e: Pacific Western Airlines; BRD: d: Papierwerke "Waldhof-Aschaffenburg" AG, 8 München [Fusion 1970]

P&WA US: e: Pratt & Whitney Aircraft

PWA US: e: Public Works Administration

P.W.A.C. e: mil: Polish Women's Auxiliary Air Corps

PWAHD US: e: Public Works Administration Housing Division

PWB BRD: d: Präzisions-Werke GmbH, Bielefeld

P.W.B. e: mil: Psychological Warfare Branch; e: Public Works and Buildings

PWC US: e: mil: Pacific War Council;
e: Peoples World Convention; US: e:
mil: Prisoner of War Cage (Camp)
(Command) (Compound); NL: nl: Provinciale Welstandscommissie; US: e:
Public Works Commissioner

PWCA e: Peoples World Constituent Assembly

P.W.C.A. e: Public Works Contractors
Association

PWCB e: Provincial Water Conservancy
Bureau

P.W.C.B.L.A. GB: e: Public Works Conciliation Board for the London Area

P.W.C.C.C. US: e: Physicians with Crys-
tal Clear Consciences, Detroit [gegr
1953]

PWCen US: e: Public Works Center

P.W.C.L. PL: pl: Państwowa Wytwórnia
Części Lotniczych

P.W.C.O.U. e: Public Works and Constructional Operatives' Union

PWD US: e: mil: Psychological Warfare
Department (Division); e: Public Works
Department

PWE PL: pl: Państwowe Wydawnictwo Ekonomiczne

PWF INT: e: Pansophical World Federation; DDR: d: VEB Pressenwerk Freital, Freital (Sachsen)

PwF DDR: d: Produktionsgenossenschaft
werktätiger Fischer

PWG BRD: d: Päpstliches Werk der Glau-
bensverbreitung, 51 Aachen; e: Par-
liamentarians for World Government;
BRD: d: Parteifreie Wählergemeinschaft;
PL: pl: Polskie Wydawictwa Gospodarcze
"Polgos"

P.W.I. e: Permanent Way Institution

PWIB e: mil: Prisoner of War Information
Bureau

PWIF INT: e: Plantation Workers International Federation, Brussels [B]

PWiT PL: pl: Przedsiębiorstwo Wystaw
i Targów

PWK PL: pl: Powszechna Wystawa Krajowa
Przysposobienie Wojskowe Kobiet do
Obrony Kraju

PWKS PL: pl: Państwowe Wydawnictwa
Książek Szkolnych

PWLB GB: e: Public Works Loans Board

PWLD PL: pl: Państwowe Wydawnictwo
Literatury Dziecięcej

PWM PL: pl: Polskie Wydawnictwo Muzyczne

PWN PL: pl: Państwowe Wydawnictwo
Naukowe

PWNDA e: Provincial Wholesale Newspapers Distributors Association

PWNY US: e: Press-Wireless, Inc., New
York

P.W.O. GB: e: mil: Prince of Wales' Own
West Yorkshire Regiment

PWO US: e: Public Works Office(r)

PWOC US: e: Protestant Women of the
Chapel [d: Frauenverein]

P.-W.P.A. e: Post-War Policy Association

P.-W.P.C. e: Post-War Problems Committee

PWPW PL: pl: Państwowa Wytwórnia Pa-
pierów Wartościowych

PWR e: Police War Reserve

PWr PL: pl: Politechnika Wrocławska

PWRCB US: e: President's War Relief
Control Board

PWRiL PL: pl: Państwowe Wydawnictwo
Rolnicze i Leśne

PWS PL: pl: Państwowa Wytwórnia Samo-
chodów

P.W.S. e: Pattern Weavers' Society

PWS e: mil: Permanent Working Staff;
PL: pl: Podlaska Wytwórnia Samologów

PWSA PL: pl: Państwowa Wyższa Skoła
Aktorska

PWSF PL: pl: Państwowa Wyższa Szkoła
Filmowa

PWSM PL: pl: Państwowa Wyższa Szkoła
Muzyczna

PWSSP PL: pl: Państwowa Wyższa Szkoła
Sztuk Plastycznych

PWST PL: pl: Państwowa Wyższa Szkoła

Teatralna
PWSTiF PL: pl: PWST i Filmowa
PWSZ PL: pl: Państwowe Wydawnictwa Skolenia Zawodowego
PWT PL: pl: Państwowe Wydawnictwa Techniczne; Przedsiębiorstwo Wyciągów Turystycznych
P.W.U. e: Postal Workers Union
P.W.V.;PWV BRD: d: Pfälzerwald-Verein e.V.
P&WV US: e: Pittsburgh & West Virginia Railway
PWV BRD: d: Polizeiwissenschaftliche Vereinigung; D: d: Preßluftwerkzeuge -Verband, Berlin-Charlottenburg; GB: e: mil: Prince of Wales' Volunteers (The South Lancashire Regiment)
P.W.V.S. GB: e: mil: Prince of Wales' Volunteer Service
PWWC e: Post-War World Council
PWWK CH: d: Pensions-, Witwen- und Waisenkasse des Basler Staatspersonals
PWZ PL: pl: Powiatowy Wydział Zdrowia
PX US: e: mil: Post Exchange; Army Exchange; Air Force Exchange
PYA US: e: Parent-Youth Association
PYC D: d: Potsdamer Yacht-Club
PYRESA E: s: Prensa y Radio Española, S.A.
PZ A: d: Peelmooser Zementwerke AG, Wien 4; YU: sh: Pekarska Zadruga; Penzioni Zavod; YU: sn: Pevska Zveza; Pecski Zbor; Planinska Zveza; Pokojninski Zavod; YU: sh: Poljoprivredna Zadruga; PL: pl: Polski Związek Naciarski, Warszawa; CH: f: Ecole Polytechnique de Zurich; YU: sh: Postolarska Zadruga; BRD: d: Produktivitätszentrale; YU: sh: Proizvodačka Zadruga; YU: sn: Prosvetna Zveza
PZA PL: pl: Polski Związek Atletyczny; BRD: d: Post: Postzeitungsamt
Pz.A.A. D: d: mil: Panzeraufklärungsabteilung
PzAbwS BRD: d: mil: Panzerabwehrschule
PZAS PL: pl: Polski Związek Akrobatyki

Sportowej
PZB PL: pl: Polski Związek Bokserski; Poznańskie Zjednoczenie Budownictwa
PZBM PL: pl: Pomorskie Zakłady Budowy Maszyn
Pz.Br. CH: d: mil: Panzerbrigade
PzBrig BRD: d: mil: Panzerbrigade
PZBS PL: pl: Polski Związek Brydża Sportowego
PZBWP PL: pl: Polski Związek Byłych Więźniów Politycznych
PZChZZ PL: pl: Polskie Zjednoczenie Chrześcijańskich Związków Zawodowych
Pz.D. D: d: mil: Panzerdivision
PZD D: d: mil: Pionierzeug(s)depot
P.Z.D. D: d: mil: Pionier-Zwischendepot
PZD CS: sk: Poverenictvo Zdravotnictva; PL: pl: Powiatowy Zarząd Drogowy
PzDiv BRD: d: mil: Panzerdivision
PZE PL: pl: Państwowy Zakład Emerytalny; Polski Związek Esperantystów (Entomologiczny); Poznańskie Zakłady Elektrotechniczne
PZEM NL: nl: N.V.Provinciale Zeeuwse Elektriciteits Maatschappij
PZF PL: pl: Pabianickie Zakłady Farmaceutyczne "Polfa"; YU: sh: Poljoprivredni Zemljišni Fond; PL: pl: Polski Związek Filatelistów; Poznańskie Zakłady Farmaceutyczne "Polfa"
PZFP PL: pl: Państwowe Zakłady Foto -Przeźroczy
PZG PL: pl: Polski Związek Gimnastyczny (Głuchych)
PZGA PL: pl: Polski Związek Gimnastyki Akrobatycznej
PZGLG YU: sn: Poslovna Zveza za Gozdno in Lesno Gospodarstvo
PzGrDiv A: d: mil: Panzergrenadierdivision
PzGrenDiv BRD: d: mil: Panzergrenadierdivision
PZGS PL: pl: Polski Związek Gier Sportowych; Polski Związek Gimnastyki Sportowej
PZH PL: pl: Państwowy Zakład Higieny

PZHDI PL: pl: Polski Związek Hodowców Drobnego Inwentarza

PZHL PL: pl: Polski Związek Hokeja na Lodzie

PZHT PL: pl: PZH na Trawie

PZInż PL: pl: Państwowe Zakłady Inżynierii

PZITS PL: pl: Polskie Zrzeszenie Inżynierów i Techników Sanitarnych

PZJ PL: pl: Polski Związek Jeździecki (Judo)

PZJA YU: sn: mil: Pevski Zbor Jugoslovanske Armade

Pz.K. D: d: mil: Panzerkorps

PZK D: d: Politische Zentralkommission [NSDAP] ; PL: pl: Polskie Związek Kajakowy (Kolarski) (Krótkofalowców)

PZKB PL: pl: Państwowy Zaoczny Kurs Bibliotekarski

PZKO CS: pl: Polski Związek Kulturalno-Oswiatowy

PZKS PL: pl: Poznańskie Zakłady Koncentratów Spożywczych

PZL PL: pl: Państwowe Zakłady Lotnicze

PZŁ PL: pl: Polski Związek Łowiecki (Łuczniczy)

PZL PL: pl: Polski Związek Ludowy

PZŁ PL: pl: Polski Związek Łyżwiarski

PZŁS PL: pl: Polski Związek Łyżwiarstwa Szybkiego

PZLZ PL: pl: Państwowy Zakład Leczniczy dla Zwierząt

PZM PL: pl: Państwowe Zakłady Motorowe, Warszawa; Polski Związek Motocyklowy (Motorowy); Poznańskie Zakłady Metalowe; Puckie Zakłady Mechaniczne

PZN PL: pl: Polski Związek Narciarski, Warszawa; Polski Związek Nauczycielski (Niewidomych); Polskie Zjednoczenie Narodowe

PZNF PL: pl: Poznańskie Zakłady Nawozów Fosforowych

PZNS PL: pl: Poznańskie Zakłady Napraw Samochodowych

PZO PL: pl: Polskie Zakłady Optyczne

PZON PL: [d: staatliches Rüstungswerk]

PZP PL: pl: Polski Związek Pływacki (Powstańczy) (Pszczelarski); INT: pl: Powszechny Związek Pocztowy [e= UPU]

PZPC PL: pl: Polski Związek Podnoszenia Ciężarów

PZPiT PL: pl: Państwowy Zespół Pieśni i Tańca

PZPJ PL: pl: Pabianickie Zakłady Przemysłu Jedwabniczego

PZPR PL: pl: Polska Zjednoczona Partia Robotnicza

Pz.R.; Pz.Rgt. D: d: mil: Panzerregiment

PZRK PL: pl: Przedsiębiorstwo Zmechanizowanych Robót Kolejowych

PZS PL: pl: Państwowa Żegluga Sródlądowa; YU: sn: Planinska Zveza Slovenije; Počitniška Zveza Slovenije; BRD: d: Fachverband Preß-, Zieh- und Stanzteile; PL: pl: Polski Związek Szachowy (Szermierczy)

PZT PL: pl: Polski Związek Turystyczny

PZtgA BRD: d: Post: Postzeitungsamt

PzTrS BRD: d: mil: Panzertruppenschule

PZTS PL: pl: Polski Związek Tenisa Stołowego

PZTT PL: pl: Pabianickie Zakłady Tkanin Technicznych

PZTW PL: pl: Polski Związek Towarzystw Wioślarskich

PZU PL: pl: Państwowy Zakład Ubezpieczeń

PZUW PL: pl: Powszechny Zakład Ubezpieczeń Wzajemnych

PZV D: d: Beamten-Pensions-Zuschuß-Versicherung

PZW PL: pl: Polski Związek Wędkarski (Wolności); Powiatowy Zarząd Weterynarii

PZWL PL: pl: Państwowy Zakład Wydawnictw Lekarskich

PZWS PL: pl: Państwowe Zakłady Wydawnictw Szkolnych

PZZ PL: pl: Polskie Zakłady Zbożowe;

Polski Związek Zachodni (Zapaśniczy)
PZŻ PL: pl: Polski Związek Żeglarski
PZZ YU: sh: Prodavnica Zemljoradničke
Zadruge

Q e: mil: Quartermaster
Q. d: mil: Quartiermeister [= Qu.]
Q CDN: e: Quebec Hydro-Electric Commission, Montreal
Q.A.B. GB: e: Queen Anne's Bounty
Q.A.I.M.N.S. GB: e: mil: Queen Alexandra's Imperial Military Nursing Service [bis 1902]
QAL CDN: e: Quebec Airways, Limited
Q.A.L.A. e: Qualified Associate Land Agents' Society
Q.A.M.F.N.S. GB: e: mil: Queen Alexandra's Military Families Nursing Service
QAMH GB: e: mil: Queen Alexandra's Military Hospital, London-Millbank
QANTAS AUS: e: Queensland and Northern Territory Aerial Service [jetzt:] QANTAS Empire Airways, Sidney, N.S.W. 2000 [= QEA, gegr 1920]
Q.A.O. GB: e: mil: Queen Alexandra's Own
Q.A.P. US: e: Quanah, Acme & Pacific Railway Company
QARANC; Q.A.R.A.N.C. GB: e: mil: Queen Alexandra's Royal Army Nursing Corps
Q.A.R.N.N.S. GB: e: mil: Queen Alexandra's Royal Naval Nursing Service
QB B: f: Qualité belge [Office pour le contrôl de la qualité]
QB; Q.B. GB: e: mil: The Queen's Bays
Q.B. GB: e: The Queen's Bench
QBAA US: e: Quality Brands Associates of America
QBACI US: e: Quality Bakers of America Cooperative, Inc.
Q.B.D. GB: e: Queen's Bench Division
QBPL US: e: Queens Borough Public Library, Jamaica, N.Y.
QC US: e: mil: Quartermaster Corps
Q.C. GB: e: Queen's (Queens') College; Queen's Council
Q.C.B. GB: e: Queen's College of Belfast
Q.C.D. e: Quality Control Division
QCGA AUS: e: Queensland Cane Growers Association

QCGC AUS: e: Queensland Cane Growers Council
QCI US: e: Quota Club International [vgl: QUIFF]
QCPE US: e: Quantum Chemistry Program Exchange [University of Indiana]
QCTAC US: e: Quad-Cities Technical Advisory Council, Inc.
QDG GB: e: mil: Queens's Dragoon Guards
QEA AUS: e: Qantas Empire Airways [vgl: QANTAS]
Q.E.T.C.D. GB: e: Queen Elizabeth's Training College for the Disabled
QF F: f: Qualité France [Association nationale pour la défense de la Qualité France]
Q.F. S: sv: Qvartettsångarförbundet
Q.G. pt: mil: Quartel-General; f: mil: quartier général; i: mil: quartiere generale
Q.G.A. f: mil: quartier général d'armée
Q.G.F.A. NATO: f: Quartier Général des Forces Atlantiques
QICC US: e: mil: Quartermaster Inventory Control Center, Richmond, Va.
Q.I.D.N. GB: e: Queen's Institute of District Nursing
QL GB: e: The Queen's Lancers
Q.L.P. AUS: e: Queensland Labour Party
QM; Q.M. e: mil: Quartermaster (Corps); quarter-master
Qm BRD: d: mil: Quartiermeister
QM AUS: e: Queensland Mines Ltd.
Q.M.A.A.C. GB: e: Queen Mary's Army Auxiliary Corps [1914 . . . 18]
QMC US: e: mil: Quartermaster Corps
Q.M.C. GB: e: Quekett Microscopical Club
QMCA US: e: mil: Quartermaster Catalog Agency
QMC&SO US: e: mil: Quartermaster Cataloging and Standardization Office
QMCTC US: e: mil: Quartermaster Corps Technical Committee
Qm D; QMD e: mil: quartermaster's department

QMDEP US: e: mil: Quartermaster Depot
QMDPC US: e: mil: Quartermaster Data Processing Center
QMEPCC US: e: mil: Quartermaster Equipment and Parts Commodity Center
QMFCIAF US: e: mil: Quartermaster Food and Container Institute for the Armed Forces
QMG e: mil: Quartermaster(-)General
Q.M.G.B. GB: e: mil: Quartermaster -General's Branch
QMGD US: e: mil: Quartermaster General Department
Q.M.G.F. GB: e: mil: Quartermaster-General of the Forces
QMGMC US: e: mil: Quartermaster General of the Marine Corps
QmGO e: mil: Quartermaster-General's Office
Q.M.I. CDN: e: Quebec Metallurgical Industries
Q.M.O.R.C. e: mil: Quartermaster Officers' Reserve Corps
QMPA US: e: mil: Quartermaster Purchasing Agency
QMPCUSA US: e: mil: Quartermaster Petroleum Center, United States Army
QMRECOMD US: e: mil: Quartermaster Research and Engineering Command
QMPRA US: e: mil: Quartermaster Radiation Planning Agency
QMRTC US: e: mil: Quartermaster Replacement Training Center, Fort Lee, Va.
QMS: QMSch US: e: mil: Quartermaster School
Qmstr. D: d: mil: Quartiermeister
QNSL CDN: e: Quebec, North Shore and Labrador Railway
QO US: e: The Quaker Oats Company
Q.O. GB: e: mil: The Queen's Own Regiment
QOCH GB: e: mil: Queen's Own Cameron Highlanders
QOH GB: e: mil: Queen's Own Hussars
Q.O.R. GB: e: mil: Queen's Own Rifles

QORGY GB: e: mil: The Queen's Own Royal Glasgow Yeomanry (Territorial Army)
QORWKR GB: e: mil: The Queen's Own Royal West Kent Regiment
QR AUS: e: Queensland Government Railways; GB: e: mil: Queen's Royal 9th Lancers; Queen's Royal Regiment
QRE US: e: Committee on Quality Reliability Engineering [EIA]
QRF e: mil: Quick Reaction Force
QRICC US: e: mil: Quick Reaction Inventory Control Center, Fort Lee, Va. [später:] Fort Lewis, Wash.
QRIH GB: e: mil: Queen's Royal Irish Hussars
Q.R.R. GB: e: mil: Queen's Royal Regiment; Queen's Royal Rifles
Q.R.V. AUS: e: Qualified Valuer Real Estate Institute of New South Wales
QSA US: e: mil: Quartermaster Service, Army
Q.S.A.C. GB: e: Quarter Sessions Appeals Committee
Q.S.D. e: Quantity Surveyors' Division
Q.S.I.D.C. e: Quarantine Station for Imported Dogs and Cats
QSPP CDN: e: Quebec Society for the Protection of Plants
Qu. D: d: mil: Quartiermeister
QU e: Queen's University
QUANTAS vgl: QANTAS
Q.U.B. GB: e: Queen's University Belfast
QUEENS GB: e: mil: The Queen's (West Surrey) Royal Regiment
QUEST US: e: Queens Educational and Social Team [OEO]
Q.U.I. GB: e: Queen's University of Ireland
QUIFF US: e: Quota International Fellowship Fund
Q.V.C.F. GB: e: Queen Victoria Clergy Fund
QVMM GB: e: Queen Victoria Memorial Museum, Salisbury
QVR GB: e: mil: Queen Victoria's Rifles,

Territorial Army

QVS GB: e: mil: Queen Victoria's School
[d: Kadettenanstalt]

QW GB: e: mil: The Queen's Westminsters
(The King's Royal Rifle Corps), Territorial Army

QZ Z: e: Zambia Airways Corporation,
Lusaka

R D: d: mil: Radfahrer-Bataillon; D: d:
Realschule (für Knaben)
r I: i: mil: reggimento
R d: mil: Regiment; e: mil: regiment;
f: mil: régiment; D: d: mil: reitende
Artillerie-Abteilung; US: e: Rutland
Railroad; Ryan Aeronautical Company
R.A. DZ: f: Radio Alger; e: Ratepayers'
Association; s: Real Academia;
d: Rechtsabteilung
RA BlnW: d: Rechtsamt
R/A. N: no: Rederiaksjeselskap
R.A. GB: e: Referees Association
ra I: i: mil: reggimento artiglieria
R.A. I: i: mil: Regia Aeronautica; F: f:
mil: Régiment d'Artillerie; e: mil: Re-
gular Army
RA US: e: mil: Regular Army
RA. D: d: Reichsamt; Reichsausschuß;
Reiterabteilung [Polizei]
R.A. e: Resettlement Administration
RA S: sv: Riksarkivet, Stockholm
R.A. e: Road Association
RA CS: sk: Robotnicka Akademia
R.A. GB: e: Royal Academy (of Fine Arts)
R&A GB: e: Royal and Ancient Golf Club,
St.Andrews, Scotland
R.A. GB: e: mil: Royal Army; Royal
Arsenal; Royal Artillery
RAA. D: d: mil: Radfahrer-Aufklärungs-
abteilung
R.A.A. e: Railway Assessment Authority;
F: f: mil: Régiment d'artillerie d'Afrique;
Régiment d'artillerie antiaérienne; B: f:
mil: Régiment d'artillerie de l'armée
RAA D: d: Reichsarbeitsamt; Reichsauf-
sichtsamt für die Privatversicherung
R.A.A. D: d: mil: Reiter-Aufklärungsab-
teilung; f: mil: Réserve de l'armée ac-
tive; GB: e: Royal Academy of Arts;
GB: e: mil: Royal Artillery Association
R.A.A.C. F: f: mil: Régiment d'artillerie
antiaérienne coloniale
RAAD NL: nl: Rijks Zuivel-Agrarische
Afvalwaterdienst

R.A.A.D.D. GB: e: Royal Association in
Aid of the Deaf and Dumb
RAAF AUS: e: mil: Royal Australian Air
Force; GB: e: mil: Royal Auxiliary Air
Force
R.A.A.F.M.S. AUS: e: mil: Royal Aus-
tralian Air Force Medical Service
RAAG J: e: Research Association of Ap-
plied Geometry, Tokyo
RAAM GB: e: mil: Royal Alderney Artil-
lery Militia
R.A.A.M.C. AUS: e: mil: Royal Australian
Army Medical Corps
R.A.A.M.S.I. GB: e: Royal Alfred Aged
Merchant Seamen's Institution
RAAOC AUS: e: mil: Royal Australian
Army Ordnance Corps
RAAP SU: [d: Vereinigung proletarischer
Schriftsteller]
RAArbVerm D: d: Reichsamt für Arbeits-
vermittlung und Arbeitslosenversiche-
rung
RAAS GB: e: Racial Adjustment Action
Society; S: sv: Riksförbund mot astma
och andra allergiska sjukdomar; GB: e:
Royal Amateur Art Society
RAASC AUS: e: mil: Royal Australian
Army Service Corps
RAAVAV D: d: = RAArbVerm
RAB US: e: Radio Advertising Bureau;
NL: nl: Rationalisatie van de Arbeids-
techniek in de Bosbouw
R.A.B. F: f: mil: Régiment d'artillerie de
(la) brigade
RAB NL: nl: Rijksarbeidsbureau; GB: e:
mil: Royal Artillery Band
RABA s: Real Academia de Bellas Artes
RABAG D: d: Rheinische Automobilbau
AG, Düsseldorf, Mannheim
R.A.B.D.F. GB: e: Royal Association of
British Dairy Farmers
RABFM GB: e: Research Association of
British Flour Millers
R.A.B.I. GB: e: Royal Agricultural Benev-
olent Institution

R.A.B.L.B. E: s: Real Academia de Buenas Letras de Barcelona

RABMAM GB: e: Research Association of British Motor and Allied Manufacturers

RABPCVM GB: e: Research Association of British Paint, Colour and Varnish Manufacturers

R.A.B.R.M. GB: e: Research Association of British Rubber Manufacturers

RABT S: sv: Rederiaktiebolaget Transatlantic, Göteborg

R.A.C. f: Rassemblement anticommuniste; f: mil: Régiment antichars; Régiment d'artillerie coloniale

RAC US: e: Republic Aviation Corporation; US: e: mil: Research Analysis Corporation, McLean, Va. [gegr 1961]

R.A.C. e: Resettlement Advice Centre

RAC NL: nl: Revolutionair Agitatie Comité

R.A.C. GB: e: mil: Rhine Army College, Göttingen [BRD] ; CDN: e: Royal Academy of Canada; GB: e: Royal Aero Club; Royal Agricultural College

RAC K: e: Royal Air of Cambodge

R.A.C. GB: e: Royal Arch Chapter; GB: e: mil: Royal Armoured Corps; Royal Artillery Charities (Commando) (Corps); GB: e: Royal Automobile Club [gegr 1897]

RAC US: e: Rubber Allocation Committee

RACAOA e: Relief Assistance and Certain Activities in Occupied Areas

R.A.-C.B.; RACB B: f: Royal Automobile -Club de Belgique, Bruxelles

R.A.C.B.D. GB: e: mil: Royal Armoured Corps Base Depot

R.A.C.C. US: e: Regional Agricultural Credit Corporation; GB: e: mil: Royal Army Catering Corps

RACCA US: e: Refrigeration and Air Conditioning Contractors Association

R.A.C.D. GB: e: mil: Royal Armoured Corps Depot; Royal Army Chaplains'

Department; Royal Army Clothing Department (Depot)

R.A.C. d'I. I: i: Reale Automobile-Club d'Italia, Roma

R.A.C.E. E: s: Real Aéreo Club de España

RACES US: e: Radio Amateur Civil Emergency Service

RACF GB: e: mil: Royal Army Clothing Factory; Royal Artillery Charitable Fund

RAChD GB: e: mil: Royal Army Chaplain's Department

RAChemI AUS: e: Royal Australian Chemical Institute [= RACI]

R.A.C.I. I: i: Real Automobile-Club d'Italia, Roma

RACI AUS: e: Royal Australian Chemical Institute, Parkville, Victoria 3052

RACIC US: e: Remote Area Conflict Information Center

R.A.C.M. f: mil: Régiment d'artillerie coloniale de marche

R.A.C.P. f: mil: Régiment d'artillerie de campagne porté; AUS: e: Royal Australasian (Australian) College of Physicians

R.A.C.S. AUS: e: Royal Australasian (Australian) College of Surgeons

RACSA C: s: Radio Aeronáutica de Cuba S.A.

RACTC GB: e: mil: Royal Armoured Corps Training Centre

R.A.C.U. GB: e: mil: Royal Armoured Car Unit

RACV AUS: e: Royal Automobile Club of Victoria, Melbourne

R.A.D. f: mil: Régiment d'artillerie divisionnaire

RAD US: e: mil: Regional Accountable Depot; D: d: NS: Reichsarbeitsdienst

R.A.D. GB: e: Royal Academy of Dancing

R.A.D.A. GB: e: Royal Academy of Dramatic Art, London [gegr 1904 .

RadarS S: sv: mil: Arméns Radarskola, Göteborg [gegr 1952]

RADC US: e: mil: Rome Air Development

Center, Rome, N.Y.; GB: e: mil: Royal Army Dental Corps

RADECO CGO: f: Rassemblement Démocratique Congolais

RADER RWA: f: Rassemblement Démocratique Ruandais [gegr 1959]

RAD-Gr. D: d: NS: Reichsarbeitsdienstgruppe

RadI D: d: Reichsamt des Innern

RADIC US: e: mil: Research and Development Information Center

Rad.Ind. F: f: Radicaux Indépendants

Radiopress J: [d: Nachrichtenagentur]

R.A.Dks. GB: e: Royal Albert Docks

RADL D: d: NS: Reichsarbeitsdienstleitung

RADLCEN US: e: mil: Radiological Center

RADm D: d: NS: Reichsarbeitsdienst, männlich

RADOR R: ro: Societatea Rador, Bucureşti [d: Nachrichtenagentur]

Rad.Soc. F: f: Radicaux socialistes

RADw D: d: NS: Reichsarbeitsdienst, weiblich

RADwJ D: d: NS: Reichsarbeitsdienst für die weibliche Jugend

RAE RA: s: Radiodifusión Argentina al Exterior, Buenos Aires

R.A.E. E: s: Real Academia Española

RAE GB: e: mil: Royal Aircraft Establishment, Bedford [gegr 1918]; AUS: e: mil: Royal Australian Engineers

R.Ae.C. GB: e: Royal Aero Club

RAEC GB: e: mil: Royal Army Educational Corps

RAEHIST E: s: Real Academia Española de la Historia

R.Ae.S. GB: e: Royal Aeronautical Society

R.A.F. F: f: Rassemblement pour l'Algérie Française [gegr 1959]; F: f: mil: Régiment d'artillerie de forteresse

RAF S: sv: Rörledningsfirmornas Arbetsgivareförbund, Stockholm

R.A.F. GB: e: mil: Royal Aircraft Factory

RAF; R.A.F. GB: e: mil: Royal Air Force

RAfA D: d: = RAArbVerm; Reichs-

anstalt für Arbeitsvermittlung und Arbeitslosenversicherung

RAFA GB: e: mil: Royal Air Force Association

RAfAA D: d: Reichsanstalt für Arbeitsvermittlung und Arbeitslosenversicherung

R.A.F.A.C.S. GB: e: mil: Royal Air Force Airfield Construction Service

RAfAF e: mil: Royal Afghanistan Air Force

RAFAMET PL: pl: Raciborska Fabryka Wyrobów Metalowych

RAFASC GB: e: mil: Royal Air Force Association Stamp Club

RAFB US: e: mil: Ramey Air Force Base

R.A.F.B.F. GB: e: mil: Royal Air Force Benevolent Fund

RAFBU GB: e: mil: Royal Air Force Balloon Unit

R.A.F.C. GB: e: mil: Rear Air Freight Centre [Royal Air Force]; Royal Air Force Club; Royal Air Force College

R.A.F.C.C. GB: e: mil: Royal Air Force Coastal Command

R.A.F.C.F. GB: e: mil: Royal Air Force Comforts Fund

RAFD US: e: mil: Rome Air Force Depot

RAFECO CGO: f: Rassemblement Fédéral Congolais

Rafena DDR: d: VEB Rafena-Werke, Radeberg (Sachsen) [Fernsehgeräte]

RAFEOER GB: e: mil: Royal Air Force Ex-Officers Emergency Reserve

R.A.F.E.S. GB: e: mil: Royal Air Force Educational Service

R.A.F.F.C. GB: e: mil: Royal Air Force Ferry Command; Royal Air Force Fighter Command; Royal Air Force Flying College

RAFHOS; R.A.F.Hosp. GB: e: mil: Royal Air Force Hospital

R.A.F.I. GB: IRQ: e: mil: Royal Air Force in Iraq

R.A.F.I.A.M.; RAFIAM GB: e: mil: Royal Air Force Institute of Aviation Medicine

RAFMF GB: e: mil: Royal Air Force Memory Fund

R.A.F.M.S. GB: e: mil: Royal Air Force Medical Service

R.A.F.N.S. GB: e: mil: Royal Air Force Nursing Service

RAFO GB: e: mil: Reserve of Air Force Officers

RA.f.P. D: d: Reichsanstalt für Polizeisport

RAfP D: d: Reichsaufsichtsamt für die Privatversicherung

R.A.F.P. GB: e: mil: Royal Air Force Police

R.A.F.R. GB: e: mil: Royal Air Force Regiment; Royal Air Force Reserve

R.A.F.R.O. GB: e: mil: Royal Air Force Reserve of Officers

R.A.F.S.A. GB: e: mil: Royal Air Force Sailing Association

R.A.F.S.A.A. GB: e: mil: Royal Air Force Small Arms Association

R.A.F.S.C. GB: e: mil: Royal Air Force Staff College

R.A.F.S.P. GB: e: mil: Royal Air Force Service Police

RAFSWA GB: e: mil: Royal Air Force Ski and Winter Sports Association

R.A.F.T.C. GB: e: mil: Royal Air Force Transport Command

R.A.F.V.R. GB: e: mil: Royal Air Force Volunteer Reserve

RAG D: d: Reichsarbeitsgemeinschaft der Berufe im sozialen und ärztlichen Dienst; Reichsarbeitsgemeinschaft zugelassener Verkaufsstellen der Reichszeugmeisterei [NSDAP] ; Reichsarbeitsgericht; BRD: d: mil: Reservistenarbeitsgemeinschaft; BRD: d: Revierarbeitsgemeinschaft für kulturelle Bergmannsbetreuung [gegr 1949] ; A: d: Rohöl-Gewinnungs-AG; BRD: d: Ruhrkohle AG, 43 Essen [gegr 1970]

RAGB GB: e: Refractories Association of Great Britain

R.A.G.C. GB: e: Royal and Acient Golf Club, St.Andrews, Scotland

RAGD; R.a.G.D. D: d: Reichsverband ambulanter Gewerbetreibender Deutschlands

RagL D: d: Reichsbund akademisch gebildeter Landwirte [gegr 1919 in Magdeburg, ab 1933 RDL]

RAG/RO BRD: d: mil: Reservisten-Arbeitsgemeinschaft für Reserveoffiziere

R.A.H. GB: e: Royal Albert Hall

RA-HA CH: d: Schweizerische Ausstellung für rationelles Haushalten

R.A.H.S. AUS: e: Royal Australian Historical Society

R.A.H.S.I. IND: e: Royal Agricultural and Horticultural Society of India

RAI I: i: Radio Audizioni Italiane; Radio Televisione Italiana; Reale Accademia d'Italia; D: d: Reichsamt des Innern; Reichsverband der Automobilindustrie; NL: nl: Nederlandsche Vereeniging de Rijwiel- en Automobiel-Industri

R.A.I. GB: e: Royal Albert Institution; Royal Anthropological Institute of Great Britain and Ireland; Royal Archaeological Institute; GB: e: mil: Royal Artillery Institute

RAIA AUS: e: Royal Australian Institute of Architects

RAIC CDN: e: Royal Architectural Institute of Canada, Toronto

RAIF AUS: e: mil: Royal Australian Imperial Force

Raiffeis D: d: Deutsche Raiffeisenbank AG, Berlin

Raiff-K D: d: Raiffeisenkasse

R.A.I.G.B.&I. GB: e: Royal Archaeological Institute of Great Britain and Ireland

Raildoc INT: e: Institute for World Railroad Documentation, Amsterdam [NL]

RAI-TV I: i: Radiotelevisione Italiana

RAIV BRD: d: Ruhrländischer Architekten- und Ingenieur-Verein eV, 43 Essen

RAJ D: d: Reichsarbeitsgemeinschaft für alkoholfreie Jugenderziehung

RAK BRD: d: Rechtsanwaltskammer

Rak. D: d: Reichsabwicklungskommissar(iat)
RAK D: d: Reichsausschuß für Ärzte und Krankenkassen; Reichsausschuß der Kraftverkehrswirtschaft
R.A.K. D: d: mil: Reserve-Armeekorps
RakS(H) BRD: d: mil: Raketenschule des Heeres
RakSLw BRD: d: mil: Raketenschule der Luftwaffe
R.A.L. f: mil: Régiment d'artillerie lourde
RAL D: d: Reichsanstalt (Reichsausschuß) für Leibesübungen; Reichsausschuß für Lieferbedingungen [gegr 1925, seit 1951:] Ausschuß für Lieferbedingungen und Gütesicherung beim DNA [BRD; DIN]
RåL S: sv: Riksförbundet Rättvisa åt Landsorten
R.A.L. GB: e: Royal Academy of Literature
R.A.L.Ap. f: mil: Régiment d'artillerie légère aéroporté
R.A.L.D. f: mil: Régiment d'artillerie lourde divisionnaire
R.A.L.P. f: mil: Régiment d'artillerie légère parachutiste
RALV. D: d: Reichsamt für das Landvolk
R.A.L.V.F. f: mil: Régiment d'artillerie lourde sur voie ferrée
RAM INT: f: Réarmement Moral [e: MRA]
R.A.M. f: mil: Régiment d'artillerie de montagne; Régiment d'automitrailleuses
RAM. D: d: Reichsarbeitsminister(ium); Reichsaußenminister(ium); Reichsverband der Automechaniker eV, Berlin -Charlottenburg
RAM US: e: Revolutionary Action Movement [gegr 1965]
R.A.M. GB: e: Royal Academy of Music; GB: e: mil: Royal Artillery Museum
R.A.Ma. F: f: mil: Régiment d'artillerie de Marine
RAMAC e: Radio Marine Associated Companies
RAMaß. D: d: Reichsanstalt für Maß und Gewicht [gegr 1918]
RAMC GB: e: mil: Royal Army Medical College, London-Millbank; Royal Army Medical Corps
RAMCD GB: e: mil: Royal Army Medical Corps Depot, Aldershot
R.A.M.D. GB: e: Royal Academy of Medicine, Dublin
R.A.M.E. AUS: e: mil: Royal Australian Mechanical Engineers
RAMF AUS: e: mil: Royal Australian Military (Militia) Forces
RAMin. D: d: Reichsarbeitsministerium
RAMNAC e: Radio Aids to Marine Navigation Application Committee
RAMO US: e: mil: Rear Airfield Maintenance Organization
RAMR GB: e: mil: Royal Artillery Marine Regiment
R.A.M.S. GB: e: mil: Royal Army Medical Service
RAMSA MEX: s: Radio Aeronáutica Mexicana S.A.
RAmt D: d: Reichsamt
R.A.N. f: Régie du Chemin de Fer Abidjan - Niger; AUS: e: mil: Royal Australian Navy
RANA CGO: f: Rassemblement National Congolais
R.A.N.A. e: Rhodesia and Nyasaland Airways Ltd.
R.A.N.C. AUS: e: mil: Royal Australian Naval College
RAND US: e: mil: Research and Development Corporation
R.A.N.R. AUS: e: mil: Royal Australian Naval Reserve
RANSA YV: s: Rutas Aéreas Nacionales S.A., Carácas
RAnst D: d: = RAArbVerm
R.A.N.V.R. AUS: e: mil: Royal Australian Naval Volunteer Reserve
R.A.O. GB: e: Royal Albert Orphanage; Royal Almonry Office
R.A.O.B. GB: e: Royal Antediluvian Order of Buffalos
RAOC GB: e: mil: Royal Army Ordnance

Corps

R.A.O.D. GB: e: mil: Royal Army Ordnance Depot

RAÖ S: sv: Riksarkivets Östermalmsavdelning, Stockholm

RAOTA GB: e: Radio Amateur Old Timers' Association

RAOU AUS: e: Royal Australasian Ornithologists Union

R.A.P. I: i: Raggruppamento Antipartigiano; F: f: Régie Autonome des Pétroles; Renseignement-Action-Protection [Deuxième Bureau]

RAP PL: pl: Robotnicza Agencja Prasowa; R: [d: rumänische Arbeiterpartei]

Rapag A: d: Reklame-, Plakatierungs- und Ankündigungs-Unternehmen rGmbH, Wien 1

R.A.P.C. GB: e: mil: Royal Army Pay (Police) Corps

RAPCh SU: [d: russischer Verband proletarischer Künstler]

R.A.P.C.M.O. GB: e: mil: Registry of the Admiralty and Prize Courts and Marshal's Office

RAPELU CGO: f: Rassemblement des Peuples Luba

RAPM SU: [d: russische Vereinigung proletarischer Musiker]

RAPP SU: [d: russischer Verband proletarischer Schriftsteller]

RAPR GB: e: mil: Rhine Army Public Relations

RAPRA GB: e: Rubber and Plastics Research Association of Great Britain

RAPS F: f: Groupe Républicain d'Action Paysanne et Sociale

RAPSA PE: s: Rutas Aéreas de Perú S.A.

RAPV D: d: Reichsaufsichtsamt für Privatversicherung

RAR e: mil: Regular Army Reserve

r.A.R. D: d: mil: reitendes Artillerie-Regiment

RAR GB: e: mil: The Rhodesian African Rifles; Royal Army Reserve; AUS: e: mil: Royal Australian Regiment (Rifles)

RArbG(.) ; **RArbGer.** D: d: Reichsarbeitsgericht

RArbM D: d: Reichsarbeitsminister

RArbVerw. D: d: Reichsarbeitsverwaltung

R.Arch.I.C. CDN: e: Royal Architectural Institute of Canada

R.A.R.D.E. GB: e: mil: Royal Armament Research and Development Establishment

R.A.R.O. GB: e: mil: Regular Army Reserve of Officers

R.Art.; R.Arty GB: e: mil: Royal Artillery

RAS e: Railway Air Services Ltd.

R.A.S. f: mil: Régiment d'artillerie de siège; e: Research Advisory Service; Resettlement Advice Service

RAS BRD: d: Baugesellschaft Rhein-Agger-Sieg

R.A.S. I: i: Riunione Adriatica di Sicurtà; GB: e: Royal Academy of Science; Royal Aeronautical Society, London [gegr 1886]; Royal African Society; Royal Agricultural Society of England, London [gegr 1838]; Royal Albert School; Royal Asiatic Society, London [gegr 1823]; Royal Astronomic Society, London [gegr 1820]

R.A.S.B. IND: e: Royal Asiatic Society of Bengal

RASC US: e: mil: Rome Air Service Command; GB: e: mil: Royal Army Service Corps; Royal Artillery Saddle Club; CDN: e: Royal Astronomical Society of Canada; AUS: e: mil: Royal Australian Staff Corps

RASCC US: e: mil: Rear Area Security Control Center

RASC/EFI GB: e: mil: Royal Army Service Corps/Expeditionary Force Institute

R.A.S.E. GB: e: Royal Agricultural Society of England, London [gegr 1838]

RASG D: [d: russischer akademischer Verein in Deutschland]

R.A.S.K. EAK: GB: e: Royal Agricultural Society of Kenya

RAS(NZ) NZ: e: Royal Astronomical Society of New Zealand

RASO e: mil: Rear Airfield Supply Organization

RASOFC GB: e: Royal Agricultural Society of the Commonwealth

RaSpo BRD: d: Rasensportverein

R.A.T. F: f: mil: Réserve de l'Armée Territoriale

RATA BRD: d: Vereinigung für raketentechnische Ausbildung, Bonn

Ratau SU: [d: ukrainische Nachrichtenagentur]

R.A.T.C. GB: e: mil: Royal Artillery Training Centre

RATCC US: e: Radar Air Traffic Control Center

Rateb D: d: Reichsarbeitsgemeinschaft technischer Beamtenverbände eV

RATEKO S: sv: Radiobranschens tekniska och kommersiella organisation

RATEKSA DK: da: Radiobranchens Tekniske og Kommercielle Sammenslutning, København

RATEM A: d: Arbeitsgemeinschaft RATEM, Institut für wissenschaftliche Berichterstattung über Elektronentechnik

RATI S: sv: Rationaliseringstekniska institutet

R.A.T.P. F: f: Régie Autonome des Transports Parisiens

RATSC US: e: mil: Rome Air Technical Service Command

RAUS US: e: mil: Regular Army of the United States

RAusglA D: d: Reichsausgleichsamt

R.Aux.A.F. GB: e: mil: Royal Auxiliary Air Force

RAV. D: d: Reichsarbeitsverwaltung

Rav. D: d: Reichsarchiv

RAV D: d: Reichsverband kommunaler und anderer öffentlicher Arbeitgeberverbände Deutschlands eV; Reichs-

verband der Beamten und Angestellten der öffentlichen Arbeitsvermittlung und Arbeitslosenfürsorge; Reichsverband der Anzeigenvertreter; NL: nl: Rotterdamsche Assistenten Vereeniging

Ravag A: d: Österreichische Radioverkehr AG, Wien; D: d: Rauchwarenversteigerungs-AG, Leipzig

RAVC GB: e: mil: Royal Army Veterinary Corps

RAVEC NL: nl: Rijkscommissie van Advies voor Exportcreditgarantia

RAVH D: d: Reichsamt "Volkstum und Heimat" der NSG "KdF"

RAVS GB: e: mil: Royal Army Veterinary School

RAW D: d: nach WK2: Rationalisierungsausschuß der deutschen Wirtschaft [vgl: RKW]; DDR: d: mil: Regiments-Artilleriewerkstatt; D: DDR: d: Reichsbahn-Ausbesserungswerk

R.a.W. D: d: Ruderclub am Wannsee

RAWAG D: d: Rauchwaren-Versteigerungs-AG, Leipzig

RAWPI e: mil: Recovery of Allied Prisoners of War and Internees

RAWR. D: d: Reichs-Arbeits- und Wirtschaftsrat

R.A.Y.C. GB: e: Royal Albert Yacht Club

Raz. D: d: Reichsarchiv-Zweigstelle

RB YU: sh: Radio Beograd; BRD: d: Radio Bremen [gegr 1945]; d: Ratsbibliothek

R.B. e: Refugee Board

Rb D: d: Reichsbank

RB D: d: Reichsbanner [Verband]; BRD: d: Reichsblock [Partei, gegr 1953]

R.-B.; RB D: d: Reichsbund

R.B. D: d: mil: Reiterbrigade

RB US: e: Renegotiation Board; D: d: Rentenbank

rb S: sv: AB Reportagebild, Stockholm

RB GB: e: mil: The Rifle Brigade (Prince Consort's Own)

R.B. S: sv: Riksbanken

RB DK: da: Ritzaus Bureau [d: Nach-
richtenagentur]
RBA D: d: Reichsbahnamt
Rba DDR: d: Reichsbahnbetriebsamt
RBA D: d: Reichsbauamt; Reichsbund
der Beamten und Angestellten; GB: e:
Retail Book, Stationery and Allied
Trades Employers Association; Road
Bitumen Association
R.B.A. e: Roads Beautifying Association
RBA US: e: Roadside Business Association;
GB: e: Royal British Architects
R.B.A. GB: e: Royal Society of British
Artists
RBahnA D: d: Reichsbahnamt
RBAI GB: e: Royal Belfast Academical
Institution
R.B.A.S. GB: e: Royal Blind Asylum and
School
RBauD DDR: d: Reichsbahnbaudirektion
RBBC US: e: Ringling Brothers Barnum
and Bailey Circus
RBBV D: d: Reichsbetriebsgemeinschaft
Banken und Versicherungen
R.B.C. GB: e: Royal British Colonial Soci-
ety of Artists
R.B.C.B. GB: e: Racecourse Betting Control
Board
RBD: Rbd DDR: d: Reichsbahndirektion
RBDir. D: d: Reichsbahndirektion
RbDMÖ A: d: Reichsbund Deutscher Mund-
artdichter Österreichs
RBEC US: e: Roller Bearing Engineering
Committee, New York, N.Y. 10017
RB.e.K. D: d: mil: Reichsbund ehemaliger
Kadetten
R BERKS GB: e: mil: The Royal Berkshire
Regiment (Princess Charlotte of Wales's)
R.B.F.M. F: f: Régiment blindé de fusiliers
marins
RBG BRD: d: Reaktor-Brennelemente
GmbH, 6451 Wolfgang; D: d: Reichs-
betriebsgemeinschaft
R.Bg. D: d: mil: Reiterbrigade
R.B.G. GB: e: The Royal Botanic Gardens

RBGD D: d: nach WK2: Reichsbahn-Gene-
raldirektion [Britische Zone]
R.B.G.E. GB: e: Royal Botanic Gardens,
Edinburgh
Rbh D: d: Reichsbahnhauptkasse
RBI DDR: d: Radio Berlin International
[gegr 1955]
R.B.I. e: Railway Benevolent Institution
RBI D: d: Reichsverband der Batterie
-Industrie
Rbk(.) D: d: Reichsbank
RBK D: d: Reichsbund der Körperbehin-
derten eV, Berlin; Reichskammer der
bildenden Künste; D: d: mil: Reichs-
verband der Baltikumkämpfer, Grenz-
schutz- und Freikorpskämpfer; S: sv:
Riksförbundet för bildande konst
RBKA D: d: Deutsche Rentenbank-Kredit-
anstalt
Rbkw DDR: d: Reichsbahnkraftwerk
R.B.L.E. B: eo: Rega Belga Ligo Esperan-
tista
RBLV. D: d: Reichsbund für das Landvolk
R.B.M.D. GB: e: Registrar of Births, Mar-
riages and Deaths
Rbn D: d: Reichsbanknebenstelle
R.B.N.A. GB: e: Royal British Nurses As-
sociation
RbNst = Rbn
R.B.O.S. GB: e: Royal British Orphan
Schools
R.B.P. B: f: Raffinerie Belge de Pétroles
RBPCA US: e: Rare Breeds Poultry Club
of America
R.B.P.S. GB: e: Royal Blind Pension Society
R.B.R. e: Registrar of Bank Returns
RbRV D: d: Reichsbank-Ruder-Verein
Rbs D: d: Reichsbankstelle
R.B.S. GB: e: Royal Botanic Society,
London; Royal Society of British
Sculptors
R.B.S.A. GB: e: Royal Birmingham So-
ciety of Artists
RBT DDR: d: Radio-Berlin-Tanzorchester;
D: d: Reichsbetriebsgemeinschaft Textil;

BRD: d: Rundfunk-Betriebstechnik GmbH, 85 Nürnberg
R.B.T.T.B. e: Retail Bespoke Tailoring Trade Board
RBV.; R.B.V. D: d: Reichsbahnvertretung
RBV BRD: d: Rheinischer Braunkohlen-brikett-Verkauf, 5 Köln
Rb.V.u.H. D: d: Reichsbund Volkstum und Heimat
RBW DDR: d: Reichsbahn-Werbung
RBWK D: d: NS: Reichsberufswettkampf
RBZ. D: d: Reichsbahnzentrale
R.C. e: Racing Club
RC US: e: Radcliffe College; d: Radfahrer -Club; GB: e: Radio Components Standardization Committee [= RCSC]
R.C. e: Rationing Committee
RC d: Raucher-Club; e: mil: Reception Center (Centre); NL: nl: Rechter Commissaris
R.C. e: Reconstruction Committee; e: mil: Recruiting Centre; e: Red Cross; I: i: Regia Camera; Regia Consulta; f: mil: Régiment de cavalerie (chasse) (chasseurs) (colonial); I: i: Regio Cesareo; e: Regional Commissioner
RC d: Reitclub; BRD: d: Republikanischer Club
R.C. e: Rescue Committee; Research Committee (Council); e: mil: Reserve Corps
RC NL: nl: Rijksconsulentschap
R.C. l: Fraternitas Rosaceae Crucis; GB: e: Royal College
RC d: Ruderclub
RCA US: e: Radio Corporation of America, Princeton, N.J. [gegr 1919]; Railway Clerks Association
R.C.A. US: e: Reformed Church of America; F: f: Régie Commerciale des Alcools; F: f: mil: Régiment de chasseurs d'Afrique (alpine)
RCA GB: e: Reinforced Concrete Association, London SW 1; CDN: e: Research Council of Alberta
R.C.A. f: mil: réserve de corps d'armée

RCA PI: e: Rice and Corn Administration; US: e: Rodeo Cowboys Association
R.C.A. GB: e: Royal Cambrian Academy (of Art); CDN: e: Royal Canadian Academy
RCA CDN: e: mil: Royal Canadian Army (Artillery); GB: e: Royal College of Art; Royal Commission on Awards; Royal Company of Archers
RCAA US: e: Railway Car Appliance Association; Rocket City Astronomical Association; CDN: e: Royal Canadian Academy of Arts
RCAC US: e: Radio Corporation of America Communications, Inc.; CDN: e: mil: Royal Canadian Army Cadets
R.C.A.F. e: Red Cross Agricultural Fund
RCAF CDN: e: mil: Royal Canadian Air Force
RCAG BRD: d: Reichhold Chemie Aktiengesellschaft, 2 Hamburg
R.Cam.A. GB: e: Royal Cambrian Academy
RCAMC CDN: e: mil: Royal Canadian Army Medical Corps
RCAPC CDN: e: mil: Royal Canadian Army Pay Corps
RCAS GB: e: Royal Central Asian Society
RCASC CDN: e: mil: Royal Canadian Army Service Corps
RCAVC CDN: e: mil: Royal Canadian Army Veterinary Corps
RCB BRD: d: Rallye-Club, Bodensee, 775 Konstanz
R.C.B. e: Regular Commission Board; Representative Church Body [Ireland]; Rubber Control Board
RCBWF GB: e: Research Council of the British Whiting Federation
RCC US: e: Rag Chewer Club [radio amateurs]; Red Cross Club (Commission)
R.C.C. F: f: mil: Régiment de chars de combat; GB: e: Representative Church Council [Scotland]; ET: e: Revolution (ary) Command Council [1952]; e: Roman Catholic Church; GB: e: Royal

Caledonian Curlingclub, Edinburgh; Royal Canoe Club; Royal College of Chemistry; Rural Community Council

RCCC US: e: Regular Common Carrier Conference

R.C.C.C. GB: e: Royal Caledonian Curling Club [gegr 1838]

R.C.C.F. e: Russian Clergy and Church Aid Fund

R.C.C. of S.; RCCS CDN: e: mil: Royal Canadian Corps of Signals

RCD CDN: e: mil: Royal Canadian Dragoons

RCDC GB: e: Royal Civil Defence Corps

RCDMB US: e: mil: Regional Civil Defense Mobilization Board

RCDS BRD: d: stud: Ring Christlich-Demokratischer Studenten, 53 Bonn; GB: e: Royal College of Dental Surgeons

R.C.E. e: mil: Railway Construction Engineers; e: Regional Committee for Education

RCE CDN: e: mil: Royal Canadian Engineers

RCECA US: e: Railway Car Export Corporation of America

RCEEA GB: e: Radio Communication and Electronic Engineering Association

RCEI pt: Repartição Central de Estatistica Informação

RCEME CDN: e: mil: Royal Canadian Electrical and Mechanical Engineers

R.C.F. F: f: e: Racing Club de France

R.C.F.O.D.S. GB: e: mil: Royal Cambridge Fund for Old and Disabled Soldiers

R.C.F.S. F: f: Recette Centrale des Finances de la Seine

R.C.G. F: f: mil: Régiment colonial du génie

RCG US: e: mil: Regular Coast Guard

RCGS CDN: e: Royal Canadian Geographical Society

R.C.H. GB: e: Railway Clearing House; Royal Cancer Hospital

RCHA CDN: e: mil: Royal Canadian Horse Artillery

RCHM GB: e: Royal Commission on Historical Manuscripts

RChOB PL: pl: Robotniczo-Chłopska Organizacja Bojowa

R.C.H.S. GB: e: Railway and Canal Historical Society

Rchsfst. D: d: Reichsfilmstelle

R.C.H.S.W. GB: e: mil: Royal Cambridge Home for Soldiers' Widows

RCI BRD: d: Reichhold Chemie Aktiengesellschaft, 2 Hamburg [= RCAG]; US: e: Reichhold Chemicals, Inc., White Plains, N.Y.; GB: e: Research & Control Instruments Ltd., London; CDN: e: Royal Canadian Institute

R.C.I. GB: e: Royal Colonial Institute

RCIA US: e: Retail Clerks International Association; Retail Credit Institute of America

R.C.J. GB: e: Royal Courts of Justice

RCK PL: pl: Rada Czytelnictwa i Książki; e: Revolutionary Committee of the Kuomintang

R.C.L. GB: e: Railway Conversion League

RCL BRD: d: Rhein-Container-Linie, 41 Duisburg-Ruhrort [gegr 1969]; Rhodesien: e: Rhodesia Constitutional League

RCM RM: f: Rassemblement Chrétien de Madagascar; e: mil: Regimental Court Martial; INT: s: República de los Ciudadanos del Mundo f: République des Citoyens du Monde, London

R.C.M. GB: e: Royal College of Mines; Royal College of Music [gegr 1883]

RCMA NL: nl: Rubber Cultuur Maatschappij Amsterdam

RCMD US: e: Rice Council for Market Development

RCMF US: e: Radio Component Manufacturers Federation

RCMP CDN: e: Royal Canadian Mounted Police

RCN NL: nl: Reactor Centrum Nederland, Den Haag [gegr 1955]; CDN: e: mil:

Royal Canadian Navy; GB: e: Royal College of Needlework (Nursing)

R.C.N.C. GB: e: mil: Royal Corps of Naval Constructors

RCNCOA US: e: mil: Reserve Component Noncommissioned Officer Academy

RCNR CDN: e: mil: Royal Canadian Naval Reserve

R.C.N.V.R. CDN: e: mil: Royal Canadian Naval Volunteer Reserve

R.C.O. e: Regional Capacity Office; GB: e: Royal College of Organists

RCOC CDN: e: mil: Royal Canadian Ordnance Corps

R.C.O.G. GB: e: Royal College of Obstetricians and Gynecologists

R.C.O.S. GB: e: mil: Royal Corps of Signals

R.C.P. F: f: mil: Régiment de chasseurs parachutistes; Rhodesien: e: Rhodesian Citizens Party; F: f: Rotary-Club de Paris; GB: e: Royal College of Physicians, London; Royal College of Preceptors; e: Russian Communist Party

RCPA GB: e: Research Council of Problems of Alcohol; PI: e: Rice and Corn Production Administration; US: e: Rural Cooperative Power Association

RCP(C); RCPCan CDN: e: Royal College of Physicians of Canada

R.C.P.E. GB: e: Royal College of Physicians of Edinburgh

RCPI IND: e: Revolutionary Communist Party of India; e: Royal College of Physicians of Ireland

R.C.P.K. CGO: f: mil: Régiment de chasseurs parachutistes katangais

RCPK LR: Rīgas Centrālais Paukošanās Klubs

RCPP GB: e: Roman Catholic People's Party

R.C.P.S. GB: e: Royal Cornwall Polytechnic Society

RCPSC CDN: e: Royal College of Physicians and Surgeons of Canada

RCR CS: sk: Riaditeľstvo pre Cestovný Ruch; CDN: e: mil: The Royal Canadian Regiment

R.C.R. CDN: e: mil: Royal Canadian Rifles

RCRC US: e: Reinforced Concrete Research Council

RCRDC GB: e: Radio Components Research and Development Committee

RCRF CH: 1: Rei Cretariae Romanae Fautores

R.C.S. e: Red Cross Society; GB: e: Royal Caledonian School; Royal Choral Society; Royal College of Science; Royal College of Surgeons; Royal Commonwealth Society; GB: e: mil: Royal Corps of Signals

RCSB US: e: Red Cedar Shingle Bureau

RCSC GB: e: Radio Components Standardization Committee, London WC 1

R.C.S.C. CDN: e: mil: Royal Canadian Sea Cadets

RCSC CDN: e: mil: Royal Canadian Signal Corps

R.C.Sc. GB: e: Royal College of Science

RCS(C); RCSCan CDN: e: Royal College of Surgeons of Canada

R.C.S.C.M. GB: e: Royal Commission on Safety in Coal Mines

R.C.S.E.; RCSEd GB: e: Royal College of Surgeons of Edinburgh

RCS(Eng); R.C.S.(Eng.) GB: e: Royal College of Surgeons of England

R.C.S.I. e: Royal College of Surgeons in Ireland

RC Sigs S GB: e: mil: Royal Corps of Signals School, Catterick

R.C.S.J.W.O. GB: e: Red Cross and St. John War Organization

RCSR CDN: e: mil: Royal Canadian Signals Regiment

R.C.S.T. GB: e: Royal College of Science and Technology, Glasgow [gegr 1796]

RCT CDN: e: Royal Conservatory of Music of Toronto; GB: e: mil: Royal Corps of Transport

R.C.T.C. I: i: mil: Regio corpo truppe

coloniali

RCTS GB: e: Railway Correspondence and Travel Society

RCV I: i: Reale Commissione Vinciana

R.C.V.S. GB: e: Royal College of Veterinary Surgeons, London

R.C.W.F. e: Red Cross War Fund

R.D. D: d: Reichsdruckerei; D: d: mil: Rekrutendepot

RD US: e: mil: Replacement Depot

R.D. F: f: Républicains Démocrates; e: Research Department

R&D; RD e: Research and Development

R.D. D: d: mil: Reservedivision

RD S: sv: Riksdagen; Riksdriftbyrån

R.D. e: Roads Department; GB: e: mil: Royal Dockyard; Royal Dragoons

RD DDR: d: mil: Rückwärtige Dienste

R.D.A. F: f: Rassemblement Démocratique Africain; DZ: f: Rassemblement Démocratique Algérien; f: Rassemblement démocratique afar

RDA D: d: Reichsbund Deutscher Angestellten-Berufsverbände; Reichsverband der Automobilindustrie eV [auch: RdA], Berlin; Reichsverband Deutscher Artistik; Reichsverband der deutschen Adventjugend; BRD: d: Reisering Deutscher Autobus-Unternehmungen

R.D.A. GB: e: mil: Research and Development Air; Royal Docks Association

RDABV D: d: Reichsbund Deutscher Angestellten-Berufsverbände

RDAF BRD: d: stud: Ring der Akademischen Freischaren; e: mil: Royal Danish Air Force

RDAO D: d: Reichsverband Deutscher Augenoptiker eV

R.d.B. DDR: d: Rat des Bezirks

RdB D: d: Reichsverband des Büromaschinen- und Organisationsmittel-Handels

RDB D: d: Reichsbund der deutschen Beamten [gegr 1933]; Reichsverband Deutscher Baumeister, Ffm; US: e: Research and Development Board; BRD: d: Ring

Deutscher Bergingenieure eV, 43 Essen

RdbK. D: d: Reichskammer der bildenden Künste

RDC D: d: Reichsverband der Chirurgie-Mechanik, Berlin; GB: e: mil: Reorganization and Disbandment Centre; GB: e: Research and Documentation Centre, Wembley, Middlesex; BRD: e: Royal Dark Club, 851 Fürth [Förderung der Pelzmode]; GB: e: mil: Royal Defence Corps; US: e: Rubber Development Corporation; D: d: stud: Rüdesheimer Deputierten-Convent

R.D.C. e: Rural District Council

R.D.C.A. GB: e: Rural District Councils Association

RDC TDA GB: e: Research and Development Committee of the Timber Development Association

R.D.D. DY: f: Rassemblement démocratique dahoméen

RDD. D: d: Reichsbund Deutscher Diplomvolkswirte, Berlin; Reichsverband des Deutschen Dachdeckerhandwerks; Reichsverband Deutscher Dentisten

R.d.D.G.u.Ü. D: d: Reichsverband des Deutschen Groß- und Überseehandels eV

R.d.d.I. D: d: Reichsverband der deutschen Industrie

R.d.d.J. D: d: Reichsausschuß der deutschen Jugendverbände

R.D.D.L. D: d: Reichsbund Deutscher Diplomlandwirte

R.d.d.l.G. D: d: Reichsverband der deutschen landwirtschaftlichen Genossenschaften - Raiffeisen eV

RDDS D: d: stud: Reichsbund Deutscher Demokratischer Studenten

RDDZ; RDDZV D: d: Reichsverband der Deutschen Zeitungsverleger

RDE D: d: Reichsverband Deutscher Erfinder eV, Mannheim

R. de G. F: f: Républicains de Gauche

RDemobA. D: d: mil: Reichsdemobilmachungsamt

RderVolksb. d: Rat der Volksbeauftragten
R.D.F. F: f: Radiodiffusion Française;
ZA: af: Reddingsdaadfonds; D: d:
\ Reichsbund Deutsche Familie
RdF D: d: Reichsminister der Finanzen
RDF D: d: Reichsverband der deutschen
Fischhändler
R.d.F. D: d: Reichsverband der Verkehrs-
flughäfen
RDF D: d: Reichsverband Deutscher Funk-
händler eV, Berlin; Reichsverband Deut-
scher Auto-Ferntransport-Unternehmen
eV
RdF BRD: d: Komitee "Rettet die Frei-
heit" [gegr 1959 in Bad Godesberg]
RDF S: sv: Riksföreningen Deltidsanställda
Folksbibliotekarier [gegr 1952]
R.D.F. GB: e: mil: Royal Dublin Fusiliers
RDG US: e: Reading Company [railroad]
R.d.G. D: d: Reichsverband der Garagen-
besitzer eV
RDG D: d: Reichsverband des Deutschen
Groß- und Überseehandels; Reichsver-
band Deutscher Gurkenkonservenfabri-
kanten eV
RDGÜ D: d: Reichsverband des Deutschen
Groß- und Überseehandels
RDGW D: d: Reichsverband deutscher
Gebirgs- und Wandervereine, Ffm
RDH D: d: Reichsdienststrafhof; Reichs-
disziplinarhof; Reichsfachgruppe Deut-
sches Hundewesen; Reichsgemeinschaft
Deutscher Hausfrauen eV; Reichsver-
band des Deutschen Handels; Reichs-
verband Deutscher Hausfrauen; Reichs-
verband Deutscher Heimstätten; Reichs-
verband für das Deutsche Hundewesen;
Reichsverband Deutscher Hundezüchter
RDHdw. D: d: Reichsstand des deutschen
Handwerks
RDHG D: d: Reichsverband Deutscher
Handelsvertreter und Geschäftsreisender
RdI D: d: Reichsminister(ium) des Innern
RDI D: d: Reichsstand (Reichsverband)
der Deutschen Industrie

RDisH.; RDiszH D: d: Reichsdisziplinarhof
RDiszK D: d: Reichsdisziplinarkammer
RDJ D: d: Reichsausschuß der deutschen
Jugendverbände
RdJ D: d: Reichsminister(ium) der Justiz
RDJA f: Rassemblement démocratique de
la jeunesse angolaise
RDJH D: d: Reichsverband Deutscher Ju-
gendherbergen
R.d.K. DDR: d: Rat des Kreises
RDK. D: d: Reichsbund der Kinderreichen
RdK D: d: mil: Reichsbund der Kriegs-
beschädigten; Reichsbund der Kriegs-
und Zivilbeschädigten, Sozialrentner
und Hinterbliebenen
RDK D: d: Reichsdisziplinarkammer;
Reichsgewerkschaft Deutscher Kommu-
nalbeamter
RdK D: d: Reichsverband der Kinderreichen; Reichsverband der Kraftfahr-
zeugbesitzer eV; Reichsverband des
Kraftfahrzeughandwerks, -handels und
-gewerbes eV
RDK BRD: d: Rheinhafen-Dampfkraft-
werk, 75 Karlsruhe; Rikadenki Electron-
ics GmbH, 78 Freiburg-St.Georgen
R.d.kd.J.Ö. A: d: Reichsbund der katho-
lisch-deutschen Jugend Österreichs
RDL D: d: Reichsbund Deutscher Diplom-
landwirte
R.d.L.; RdL. D: d: Reichsminister der
Luftfahrt
RDL D: d: Reichsverband Deutscher Leih-
büchereien; Reichsverband der Deut-
schen Luftfahrtindustrie
RDLI D: d: Reichsverband der Deutschen
Luftfahrtindustrie
R.D.L.I. GB: e: mil: Royal Durban Light
Infantry
RdL. u. Ob.d.L. D: d: mil: Reichsminister
der Luftfahrt und Oberbefehlshaber der
Luftwaffe
RDM D: d: Reichsverband Deutscher Mak-
ler für Immobilien, Hypotheken und
Finanzierungen eV, Berlin; Reichsver-

band des Mechanikergewerbes eV; BRD:
d: Ring Deutscher Makler für Immobilien,
Hypotheken und Finanzierungen eV,
6 Ffm

RDMB D: d: Reichsverband Deutscher Mineral-Brunnen

RDMI US: e: Roof Drainage Manufacturers Institute, Cleveland 15, Ohio

RDN GB: e: mil: Research and Development Naval

RDN e: mil: Royal Danish Navy

R.Dns GB: e: mil: Royal Dragoons

RDO D: d: mil: Reichsbund Deutscher Offiziere; Reichsverband Deutscher Offiziere [gegr 1934] ; D: d: Reichsverband Deutscher Orchester, Weimar; BRD: d: Rhein-Donau-Ölleitung GmbH, 75 Karlsruhe

R.D.P. F: f: mil: Régiment de Dragons Portés

RDP D: d: Reichsschaft Deutscher Pfadfinder; Reichsverband der Deutschen Presse; Südkorea: [d: republikanische demokratische Partei]

R.D.P.K. D: d: Reichsverband Deutscher Privater Krankenkassen

R.D.P.T. f: Rassemblement démocratique des populations tahitiennes

RDR PL: pl: Rada Delegatów Rabotniczych

R.D.R. F: f: Rassemblement démocratique révolutionnaire

Rdr D: d: Reichsdruckerei

RDR D: d: Reichsverband Deutscher Rundfunkteilnehmer

RDRI D: d: Reichsverband der Deutschen Rundfunkindustrie eV

RDRS CH: d: Radio- und Fernsehgesellschaften der deutschen und der rätoromanischen Schweiz

RDS DK: da: mil: [d: Radarschule] ; D: d: Reichsbund für Deutsche Seegeltung; BRD: d: mil: Reichsverband der Soldaten eV; D: d: Reichsverband des Deutschen Sprechmaschinen- und Schallplattenhandels eV, Berlin; Reichsverband

Deutscher Sauerkrautfabrikanten eV; Reichsverband Deutscher Schriftsteller; Reichsverband Deutscher Spezialgeschäfte in Porzellan, Glas, Haus- und Küchengeräten eV; Reichsverband Deutscher Sportangler eV

R.D.S. GB: e: Religious Drama Society of Great Britain; Research Defence Society; F: f: Résistance démocratique et socialiste

RDS BRD: d: Ring Deutscher Siedler eV 5628 Heiligenhaus [gegr 1948]

R.D.S. GB: e: Royal Drawing Society; Royal Dublin Society for Promoting Natural Knowledge

RDS e: Royal Dutch Shell

RDSD D: d: Reichsverband der Standesbeamten Deutschlands

RDStH D: d: Reichsdienststrafhof

RDT. D: d: Reichsbund Deutscher Technik

RdT BRD: d: Ring der Tonbandfreunde

RDV D: d: Reichsbahnzentrale für den Deutschen Reiseverkehr [gegr 1928] ; D: d: Reichsdevisenverwaltung; Reichsverband Deutscher Volkswirte; Reichsverband Deutscher Volks- und Betriebswirte

R.D.V.V. S: sv: Riksorganisationen de vanföras väl

RDW D: d: Reichsfachschaft deutscher Werbefachleute

R.D.Y.; R.D.Yd. GB: e: mil: Royal Dockyard

R.d.Z. D: d: Reichsbund der Zivildienstberechtigten

R.D.Z. CS: d: Reichsverband Deutscher Zahnärzte

RDZV D: d: Reichsverband der Deutschen Zeitungsverleger

RE INT: pl: Rada Europejska; IRL: Radio Eireann Telefis Eireann

R.E. I: i: mil: Regio Esercito

R.&E.; R&E e: Research and Experimental Department

R.E.; RE GB: e: mil: Royal Engineers

R.E. GB: e: Royal Society of Painter Etchers and Engravers

REA US: e: Railway Express Agency; BRD: d: Rationalisierungsgemeinschaft Elektrizitätsanwendung, 6 Ffm [RKW]; D: d: Reichseisenbahnamt; D: d: Reichsentschädigungsamt; Reichsverband der Elektrizitätsabnehmer eV, Berlin; US: e: Religious Education Association; Rubber Export Association; Rural Electrification Administration

R.E.A.F. ET: e: mil: Royal Egyptian Air Force

R.E.A.L. BR: pt: Redes Estaduais Aereas, Ltds., São Paulo

REB US: e: Real Estate Board

ReB D: d: Ring ehemaliger Bergschüler

REB GB: e: mil: Royal Engineers Board

REBAG BRD: d: Rheinische Blattmetall AG, 4048 Grevenbroich

REBerG D: d: nach WK2: Rückerstattungsberufungsgericht

REC GB: e: Railway Enthusiasts Club

R.E.C. e: Railway Executive Committee; F: f: Régiment étranger de cavalerie

RECGA US: e: Research and Engineering Council of the Graphic Arts Industry

RECMF GB: e: Radio and Electronics Component Manufacturers Federation, London SW 1

RECO CGO: f: Regroupement congolais

RED US: e: Railroad Employees Department [AFL-CIO]

R.E.D. e: Research and Experimental Department

RED US: e: mil: Rhine Engineer Depot, Kaiserslautern [BRD]

REDERIATOM N: [d: Atomforschungsgruppe der Reeder, gegr 1958]

REDP PL: pl: Rada Ekonomiczna Dróg Publicznych; Rejon Eksploatacji Dróg Publicznych

REE INT: f: Comité européen de la Reconstruction économique européenne

REEA GB: e: Radio and Electronics Engineering Association

REEF INT: e: Refugee European Emergency Fund [gegr 1952]; F: f: Répertoire des Ensembles et Eléments Fabriqués du Bâtiments, Paris 16

REF S: sv: Riksnämnden för ekonomisk försvarsberedskap

R.E.F. GB: e: mil: Royal Engineer Force

REFA D: d: Reichsausschuß für Arbeitszeitermittlung [1924 ... 36]; Reichsausschuß für Arbeitsstudien [ab 1936]; BRD: d: Verband für Arbeitsstudien - REFA - eV, 61 Darmstadt [seit 1951]

REFC GB: e: mil: Royal Engineers Flying Club

REFCD US: e: Research and Education Foundation for Chest Diseases

Refico US: e: Reconstruction Finance Corporation

Refis S: sv: Rörledningsentreprenörernas Förening i Stockholm

REFRIBEL B: [d: Gesellschaft für Kühltransporte]

R.E.F.S. GB: e: Royal English Forestry Society

Reg. d: mil: Regiment; e: mil: regiment

rég. f: mil: régiment

reg. pt: mil: regimento; s: mil: regimiento

REG D: d: Reichsverband des Elektrogroßhandels

RegAF US: e: mil: Regular Air Force

RegB d: Regierungsbibliothek

Reg.Bd. e: Regional Board

RegGer. d: Registergericht

RegHK d: Regierungshauptkasse

REGIFERCAM Kamerun: f: Régie des Chemins de Fer du Cameroun

RegKdF D: d: Bayerische Regierungskammer der Finanzen

RegKdI D: d: Bayerische Regierungskammer des Innern

Reg.Kzl. D: d: Regierungskanzlei

Rego D: d: Reichslieferungsgenossenschaft des Deutschen Schneidergewerbes eGmbH

Reg.P. GB: e: Regent's Park College, Oxford

Reg.-Rat CH: d: Regierungsrat [Regierung eines Kantons]

Regt. d: mil: Regiment

regt.; regt; REGT; Regt e: mil: regiment

Régt. f: mil: régiment

REHG D: d: Reichserbhofgericht

REHVA INT: e: Representatives of European Heating and Ventilating Associations

REI INT: d: Rat der Europäischen Industrieverbände, Paris 16 [e: CEIF]

R.E.I. F: f: mil: Régiment étranger d'infanterie

REI D: d: Reichsverband der elektrotechnischen Industrie

REIC US: e: Radiation Effects Information Center, Columbus, Ohio; INT: e: Regional Electric Integration Commission, Rio de Janeiro [BR, for Latin America]; US: e: Republic Electronic Industries Corporation, Melville, N.Y.

Reifag BRD: d: Reifag Reifen-Spezialbetriebe Gablenz-Schurig GmbH, 61 Darmstadt, 75 Karlsruhe

Reikuba D: d: Reichsverband der kurzschriftkundigen Beamten und Angestellten, Berlin NW 40

Rein BlnW: d: Stadtreinigung

Reipha D: d: Reichsfachschaft der pharmazeutischen Industrie eV

REisenbA D: d: Reichseisenbahnamt

REJ D: d: Reichsverband der Evangelischen Jungmännerbünde

Reka CH: d: Schweizer Reisekasse

Reklame 70 CH: d: Internationale Messe für die Werbung, Zürich [3 . . . 7 Mai 1969]

Rekofei D: d: Reichsverband Deutscher Kaufleute des Kolonialwaren-, Feinkost- und Lebensmitteleinzelhandels

ReKrgf. D: d: mil: nach WK1: Reichsvereinigung ehemaliger Kriegsgefangener

reku BRD: d: Renneroder Kunststoffwerk GmbH, 5439 Rennerod

R.E.K.Y. GB: e: mil: Royal East Kent Yeomanry

REL US: e: Radio Engineering Laboratory, Dynamics Corporation of America, Long Island City, New York 11101

R.E.L. f: Rassemblement européen pour la liberté

REL S: sv: Riksförbundet för elektrifieringen på landsbygden, Stockholm

RELLA NATO: e: Regional Long Lines Agency [Europe]

Relma D: d: Reichsverband der Elektromaschinenfabriken, Apparatebau- und Reparaturwerke eV, Düsseldorf

Relufind. D: d: Reichsverband der Deutschen Luftfahrtindustrie [= RDL.]

REM. D: d: Reichsernährungsminister(ium); Reichsminister(ium) für Ernährung und Landwirtschaft

REM NL: nl: Reklame Exploitatie Maatschappij; BRD: d: Rheinische Elektromaschinen-Fabrik GmbH, 415 Krefeld [gegr 1901]

REMA US: e: Radio Electrical Manufacturers Association [später: RETMA]

Rema D: d: Braunschweiger Rechenmaschinenfabrik GmbH, Braunschweig

REMA US: e: Refrigeration Equipment Manufacturers Association

Rema BRD: d: Reichmann & Sohn Elektromaschinenfabrik, 7912 Weißenhorn

Rem.A. D: d: mil: Remonteamt; Remonteämter

REMA BRD: d: Rentner-Einkauf-Genossenschaft, 68 Mannheim

Rema D: d: Rheinische Maschinenfabrik AG, Neuß

REMAFER f: Société de Construction et de Réparation de Matériel Ferroviaire

REMC GB: e: Radio Electronics Measurement Committee

REME GB: e: mil: Corps of Royal Electrical and Mechanical Engineers

REMP INT: e: Research Group for European Migration Problems, Den Haag

[gegr 1952]
REMSA US: e: Railway Electrical and Mechanical Supply Association
RENAICAM Kamerun: f: Renaissance Camerounaise
RENFE E: s: Red Nacional de los Ferrocarriles Españoles , Madrid
R.Eng. GB: e: mil: Royal Engineers
Rentb.; Rentbk D: d: Rentenbank
RENTCON BRD: d: e: RENTCON Rent-a -Container Container Vermietdienst von Carl Tiedemann, 2 Hamburg 11
R.Ent.S. GB: e: Royal Entomological Society of London
REntschA D: d: Reichsentschädigungsamt
R.E.P. F: f: mil: Régiment étranger parachutiste
REPAL DZ: [d: staatliche Erdölgesellschaft]
Rep.Bk. CH: d: Bank für Internationalen Zahlungsausgleich, Basel
REPESA E: s: Refinería de Petróleos de Escombreras S.A.
Repfrance F: f: Compagnie Française pour le Financement de la Recherche et de l'Exploitation du Pétrole
Rep.-K.; Rep.-Ko.; Repko D: d: nach WK1: Reparationskommission
REPLEX INT: [d: 5. internationale Ausstellung für verstärkte Kunststoffe, London, 1 . . . 5 Jun 1970]
repro 63 BRD: d: Reprographie 1963 [Fachausstellung in Köln 14 . . . 19 Okt]
REPS GB: e: mil: Royal Engineers Postal Service
Req. F: f: Chambre de Requêtes
R.E.R. F: f: Réseau Express Régional, Paris
RER LR: Rīgas Elektromašīnu Rūpnīca
RErbhG D: d: Reichserbhofgericht
R.E.R.O. GB: e: mil: Royal Engineers Reserve of Officers
RES DDR: d: Reichsbahnentwicklungsstelle
R.E.S. e: River Emergency Service; GB: e: Rothamsted Experimental Station; GB: e: Royal Economic Society; Royal

Empire Society; Royal Entomological Society of London; Royal Ethnological Society
RESA US: e: Scientific Research Society of America
Res.A. D: d: mil: Reserve-Armee
R.E.&S.C. GB: e: mil: Royal Engineers and Signals Corps
Res.K. D: d: mil: Reservekorps
R.E.S.L. GB: e: Royal Entomological Society of London
Res.Ldw. D: d: WK1: Reserve-Landwehr
RESMA US: e: Railway Electric Supply Manufacturers Association
RESO S: sv: Folkrörelsernas Rese- och Semesterorganisation, Stockholm [gegr 1937]
R.E.S.R. GB: e: mil: Royal Engineers Special Reserve
R.Et.C. F: f: mil: Régiment étranger de cavalerie
R.Et.I. F: f: mil: Régiment étranger d'infanterie
RETMA US: e: Radio-Electronics-Television Manufacturers Association, Washington 5, D.C. [jetzt: EIA]
Rett BlnW: d: Rettungsamt
Reuter GB: e: Reuter's Telegram Company Ltd., London [d: Nachrichtenagentur]
REV D: d: Reichseinheitsverband des Deutschen Gaststättengewerbes; Reichsverband der Elektrizitätsversorgung, Berlin
RevG; RevGer. D: d: Revisionsgericht
Revico D: d: Revisionsverband des Reichsverbandes deutscher Kolonialwaren- und Lebensmittel-Händler, Berlin
REVIMA F: f: Société pour la Révision et l'Entretien du Matériel Aéronautique
REW BRD: d: Rheinische Elektrizitätswerke
Rewa D: d: mil: Reichswehrwirtschaftsausschuß
REWA GB: e: Refrigeration Equipment

Wholesalers Association

Rewe BRD: d: Rheinisch-Westfälische Einkaufs-Genossenschaft der Lebensmittelhändler

REWS GB: e: mil: Royal Engineers Works Services

Rezag BRD: d: Rheinische Ziehglas AG

R.F. N: no: Radikale Folkeparti

RF F: f: Radiodiffusion Française

R.F. F: f: Ralliement Français; Réconciliation Française [parti]; Régie Française; f: mil: Régiment de forteresse; e: mil: regular forces; reserve force

R/F US: e: mil: Reserve Forces

R.F. F: f: Résistance Française

RF Rhodesien: e: Rhodesian Front; S: sv: Riksförbund; Riksidrottsförbundet [gegr 1903] ; US: e: Rockefeller Foundation; GB: e: mil: The Royal Fusiliers

RFA e: Radio Free Asia; D: d: Regierungsforstamt

RfA D: d: Reichsanstalt für Arbeitsvermittlung und Arbeitslosenversicherung

R.F.A. D: d: Reichsforstamt

RfA D: d: Reichsversicherungsanstalt für Angestellte

R.F.A. S: sv: Riksförsäkringsanstalten; GB: e: mil: Royal Field Artillery

RFAC GB: e: Royal Fine Art Commission, London

R.F.A.C.S. GB: e: Royal Fine Art Commission for Scotland

RfAuA; R.f.AVAV D: d: Reichsanstalt für Arbeitsvermittlung und Arbeitslosenversicherung

RFB e: mil: Regimental Funds Board

RfB D: d: Reichsausschuß für Betriebswirtschaft

RFB NL: nl: Roode Frontstrijders Bond; D: d: Roter Frontkämpferbund [gegr 1924]

RFC US: e: Reconstruction Finance Corporation, Washington, D.C.; d: Reit- und Fahr-Club

R.F.C. GB: e: mil: Royal Flying Corps; e: Rugby Football Club

RFCMC US: e: Reconstruction Finance Corporation Mortgage Company

R.F.D. F: f: Rassemblement des Forces Démocratiques [gegr 1959]

RfD D: d: Reichsfachschaft für das Dolmetscherwesen in der Deutschen Rechtsfront, Berlin

RFDI D: d: Reichs-Fachverbandsgruppe Druckluft-Industrie, Berlin

RFDS AUS: e: Royal Flying Doctor Service

R.f.d.Ukr. D: d: WK2: Reichskommissar für die Ukraine

RFE BRD: e: Radio Free Europe d: Radio Freies Europa, 8 München 22 [gegr 1951] ; D: d: Reichsfachschaft der elektrotechnischen Industrie

RFEA GB: e: mil: Regular Forces Employment Association [gegr 1885]

R.F.F. S: sv: Röda Front-Förbundet

RFFU BRD: d: Rundfunk-Fernseh-Film-Union, 54 Koblenz

RfG D: d: Reformgymnasium; Reichsforschungsgesellschaft für Wirtschaftlichkeit im Bau- und Wohnungswesen [bis 1931] ; Reichsstelle für Getreide, Futtermittel und sonstige landwirtschaftliche Erzeugnisse

RFGB CH: d: Radio- und Fernsehgenossenschaft Basel

RFH D: d: Reichsfinanzhof; GB: e: Royal Festival Hall, London

RFI YU: sh: Republički Finansijski Inspektorat

RFinH D: d: Reichsfinanzhof

R.F.I.V. I: i: Regia Federazione Italiana della Vela

RFK D: d: Reichsfilmkammer; S: sv: Riksförbundet för Kortdistansskytte; D: d: Rotfrontkämpferbund

RFL US: e: Radio Frequency Laboratories Inc., Boonton, N.J.

R.Fl.; R.-Fl. D: d: mil: Räumbootflotille

RfL; R.f.L. D: d: Reichsakademie für Leibesübungen [gegr 1936]
RfL. D: d: Reichsamt für Landesaufnahme; Reichsbund für Leibesübungen
RFL GB: e: Rugby Football League
RFlSt. D: d: WK1: Reichsfleischstelle
R.F.M. F: f: mil: Régiment de fusiliers marine
RFM D: d: Reichsminister(ium) der Finanzen
RFME E: s: Real Federación Motociclista Española
RFN BR: pt: Rede Ferroviária de Nordeste
R.F.O. S: sv: Röda Fackoppositionen; GB: e: Royal Female Orphanage
RF&OOA US: e: Railway Fuel and Operating Officers Association
RfP D: d: Reichsausschuß für Polizeisport
RFP; RF&P US: e: Richmond, Fredericksburg & Potomac Railroad
RFP GB: e: Royal Faculty of Procurators in Glągsow
RFPOS˙ PL: pl: Rada Federalna Polskich Organizacji Studenckich
RFPS GB: e: Royal Faculty of Physicians and Surgeons
R.F.P.S.G. GB: e: Royal Faculty of Physicians and Surgeons of Glasgow
RFR(.) D: d: WK2: Reichsforschungsrat
R.F.R. GB: e: mil: Royal Fleet Reserve
R.F.S. GB: e: Registrar of Friendly Societies
RFS. D: d: NS: Reichsführerschule
R.F.S. e: mil: Reserve Flying School
RFS S: sv: Riksförbundet för sockersjuka; A: d: stud: Ring freiheitlicher Studenten; NL: nl: Roode Frontstrijders; GB: e: Royal Forestry Society of England and Wales
Rf.Sch. D: d: NS: Reichsführerschule
RFSEW GB: e: Royal Forestry Society of England and Wales
RFSSuChdDtPol. D: d: NS: Reichsführer SS und Chef der Deutschen Polizei
RFSU S: sv: Riksförbundet för sexuell upplysning [gegr 1933]
RFT DDR: d: Volkseigene Betriebe für Radio- und Fernmeldetechnik
R.F.T. F: f: Régie Française des Tabacs
RFT D: d: Reichsverband für Frauenturnen; Reit- und Fahrturnier
RFTEA US: e: Railway Fuel and Traveling Engineers Association
R.F.T.F. e: Retail Fruit Trade Federation
RFTN D: d: Reichsführung der Technischen Nothilfe, Berlin-Steglitz
RFTS e: mil: Reserve Flying Training School
R.f.U. D: d: Reichsausführungsbehörde für Unfallversicherung
RfU D: d: Reichsstelle für den Unterrichtsfilm [gegr 1934]
R.F.U. GB: e: Rugby Football Union
RFU BRD: d: Rundfunk- und Fernseh-Union, 54 Koblenz [später: RFFU]
R.F.U.B. S: sv: Riksförbundet för utvecklingsstörda barn
RFV D: d: Reichsfinanzverwaltung; Reichsforstverband, Verband der höheren Forstverwaltungsbeamten des Deutschen Reiches
Rfv S: sv: Riksförsäkringsverket
RfW D: d: Reichsstelle für Wetterdienst
RfWT D: d: Reichsfachschaft für Wirtschaftstreuhänder
RFZ CH: d: Radio- und Fernsehgenossenschaft in Zürich; DDR: d: Rundfunk- und Fernsehtechnisches Zentralamt, Berlin
RFZA D: d: Reichsfinanzzeugamt
RG PL: pl: Rada Główna (Gospodarcza); BRD: d: Rationalisierungsgemeinschaft
Rg.; RG d: Realgymnasium
RG CS: cs: Reálné gymnasium
R.G. f: mil: Régiment de gendarmerie; Régiment du génie
Rg. s: mil: Regimiento
RG D: d: Reichsgericht; d: Renngemeinschaft
R.G. F: f: Renseignements Généraux

[Sûreté Nationale] ; f: mil: réserve générale

RG D: d: Ringgemeinschaft [Pfadfinderbund] ; d: Rudergesellschaft

RGA D: d: Reichsgesundheitsamt; Rhodesien: e: Responsible Government Association; US: e: Ring Guild of America; GB: e: mil: Royal Garrison Artillery; Royal Guernsey Artillery; GB: e: Rubber Growers Association

RGAHS GB: e: Royal Guernsey Agricultural and Horticultural Society

RGB CH: d: Radio- und Fernsehgenossenschaft Bern

RGBau BRD: d: Rationalisierungsgemeinschaft Bauwesen, 6 Ffm [im RKW]

RGC BRD: d: Regensburger Goggo-Club 1954

RGCO e: Regional Government Coordinating Office

R.G.D. D: d: mil: WK2: Regiment Großdeutschland

RGD NL: nl: Rijksgebouwendienst

RGDATA e: Retail Grocery, Dairy and Allied Trades Association

RGDH D: d: Reichsgemeinschaft deutscher Hausfrauen eV

RgDPTschl D: d: Reichsgewerkschaft der deutschen Presse in der Tschechoslowakei

RGE INT: d: Rat der Gemeinden Europas, Paris 17 [e: CEM, gegr 1951]

RGer D: d: Reichsgericht

RGesA D: d: Reichsgesundheitsamt

RGesR D: d: Reichsgesundheitsrat

R.G.F. I: i: Regia Guardia di Finanze; GB: e: mil: Royal Gun Factory

R.G.G. D: d: mil: WK2: Regiment General Göring; GB: e: mil: Royal Grenadier Guards

RGGrSZ D: d: Reichsgericht, Großer Senat in Zivilsachen

RGGS.; RGGSSt. D: d: Reichsgericht, Großer Senat in Strafsachen

RGGSZ = RGGrSZ

RGH BRD: d: Rationalisierungsgemeinschaft des Handels, 5 Köln [im RKW] ; GB: e: mil: The Royal Gloucestershire Hussars

RGI D: d: Reichsverband der Gießerei-Maschinen-Industrie

R.G.I. INT: d: Rote Gewerkschaftsinternationale [gegr 1920]

RGIVE BRD: d: Rationalisierungsgemeinschaft Industrieller Vertrieb und Einkauf, 6 Ffm [im RKW]

R.G.K. S: sv: Riksgäldskontoret

RGKn A: d: Realgymnasium für Knaben

RGM A: d: Realgymnasium für Mädchen; GB: e: mil: Royal Guernsey Militia

RGN PL: pl: Rada Gospodarki Narodowej

RG NOT PL: pl: Rada Główna Naczelnej Organizacji Technicznej

RGO PL: pl: Rada Główna Opiekuńcza; DDR: d: VVB Regelungstechnik, Gerätebau und Optik; D: d: Revolutionäre (Rote) Gewerkschaftsopposition; GB: e: Royal Greenwich Observatory

RGP Rhodesien: e: Responsible Government Party

R.G.P.D. e: Rating of Government Property Department

RGPH PL: pl: Rada Główna Przyjaciół Harcerstwa

R.G.R. F: f: Rassemblement des Gauches Républicaines [gegr 1955]

R.G.S. GB: e: Royal Geographical Society [gegr 1830]

RGSA AUS: e: Royal Geographical Society of Australasia

RGSNiSW PL: pl: Rada Główna do Spraw Nauki i Szkolnictwa Wyższego [gegr 1947]

RGSt. D: d: WK1: Reichsgetreidestelle

RGsuA D: e: Reichsgesundheitsamt

RGTF GB: e: Royal General Theatrical Fund

R.G.U.F.S. e: Railway Guards' Universal Friendly Society

RGV D: d: Radio-Großhändler-Verband;

BRD: d: Rationalisierungsgemeinschaft Verpackung, Berlin [im RKW] ; D: d: Riesengebirgsverein

RGVZ.; RGVZS. D: d: Reichsgericht, Vereinigte Zivilsenate

RGW INT: d: Rat für gegenseitige Wirtschaftshilfe (der sozialistischen Länder), Moskau [e: Comecon] ; BRD: d: Reitergruppe Wiesbaden

RGy d: Realgymnasium

RG ZLZS PL: pl: Rada Główna Zrzeszenia Ludowych Zespołów Sportowych

RGZM BRD: d: Römisch-Germanisches Zentralmuseum, 65 Mainz [gegr 1852]

RH D: d: Rechnungshof des Deutschen Reichs; BlnW: d: Rechnungshof; D: d: mil: Reichsheer; GB: e: The Royal Highland Regiment (Black Watch)

R.H.A. GB: e: Road Haulage Association; Royal Hibernian Academy of Painting, Sculpture and Architecture; GB: e: mil: Royal Horse Artillery

R.H.A.A. GB: e: Royal Hibernian Academy of Arts

RHAF e: mil: Royal Hellenic Air Force

RHamps GB: e: mil: The Royal Hampshire Regiment

Rh.A.R. GB: e: mil: Rhodesian African Rifles

R.H.A.S.I. GB: e: Royal Horticultural and Arboricultural Society of Ireland

R.H.B. e: Regional Hospital Board

R.h.B. D: d: Reichsbund der höheren Beamten

Rh.B. CH: d: Rhätische Bahn

RHB BRD: d: Rhein-Haardt-Bahn-Gesellschaft mbH, 68 Mannheim

RHBS NL: nl: Rijks Hoogere Burgerschool

R.H.C. GB: e: Royal Hospital, Chelsea

R.H.C.A. e: Residential Hotels and Caterers Association

RHD D: d: Rote Hilfe Deutschlands [gegr 1924]

Rheag D: d: Rheinische Elektrizitäts-AG, Mannheim

RHEIMA BRD: d: Rheinische Maschinenbau- und Handelsgesellschaft mbH, 4 Düsseldorf

Rheina D: d: Rheinische Nachrichtenagentur

Rheinboden BRD: d: Rheinisch-Westfälische Boden-Credit-Bank in Köln, 5 Köln

Rheinbraun BRD: d: Rheinische Aktiengesellschaft für Braunkohlenbergbau und Brikettfabrikation, 5 Köln [später:] Rheinische Braunkohlenwerke AG, 5 Köln

Rheineisen BRD: d: "Rheineisen" Eisengroßhandlung GmbH, 4 Düsseldorf

Rheinelektra BRD: d: Rheinelektra Aktiengesellschaft, 68 Mannheim [gegr 1897 als: Rheinische Schuckert-Gesellschaft für elektrische Industrie, 1917 . . . 66: Rheinische Elektrizitäts-Aktiengesellschaft]

RHEINERZ BRD: d: Rheinischer Erz- und Metallhandel GmbH, 5 Köln

RHEINMETALL BRD: d: RHEINMETALL GmbH, Düsseldorf 1

Rheinrohr BRD: d: Rheinische Röhrenwerke AG, 433 Mülheim

Rheinstahl BRD: d: Rheinische Stahlwerke AG, 43 Essen

Rheinstroh BRD: d: Rheinische Stroh-Zellstoff AG, 6521 Rheindürkheim

Rheintextil BRD: d: "Rheintextil" Rheinische Einkaufsvermittlungs- und Beratungsgesellschaft für Textilgeschäfte, 5 Köln

Rhein-Textil D: d: Rheinische Textilfabrik AG, Elberfeld

Rheinwestkalk BRD: d: Rheinisch-Westfälische Kalkwerke AG, 5601 Dornap

RHEL GB: e: Rutherford High Energy Laboratory, Chilton

RHEMAG BRD: d: Rhein-Mainische A.G. für Siedlungs- und Wohnungsbau, 6 Ffm

Rhemag D: d: Rhenania-Motorenfabrik AG, Berlin

RHENA BRD: d: RHENA Mineralölhandelsgesellschaft, 5 Köln

RHENAG BRD: d: Rheinische Energie-Aktiengesellschaft, 5 Köln

RHF. D: d: Reichsstelle für Hochfrequenzforschung

R.H.F. GB: e: Roll of Honour Fund; GB: e: mil: Royal Highland Fusiliers

Rh.F.W.U. BRD: d: Rheinische Friedrich-Wilhelm-Universität, 53 Bonn

R.H.G. GB: e: mil: Royal Horse Guards (The Blues)

RHH GB: e: Royal Herbert Hospital, Woolwich

RHIB US: e: Rain and Hail Insurance Bureau

RHK D: d: Reichshauptkasse

RHKDF GB: e: mil: Royal Hong Kong Defence Force

RHLI GB: e: mil: Robert Hamilton Light Infantry

RHMS GB: e: mil: Royal Hibernian Military School

RHN D: d: Reichshochbaunormung, Berlin

R.H.R. GB: e: mil: Royal Highland Regiment

RHS D: d: Ring Hannoverscher Schriftsteller

R.H.S. GB: e: Royal Historical Society [gegr 1868]; Royal Horticultural Society [gegr 1804]; Royal Hospital School; Royal Humane Society

RHSI US: e: Rubber Heel and Sole Institute

RHSV CDN: e: Royal Historical Society of Victoria

RHTB D: d: Reichsbund der höheren technischen Beamten

RHU GB: e: mil: Regimental (Reinforcement) Holding Unit

RHV CS: cs: Rada Hospodářská Všestátní

RHw. D: d: Reichsverband des deutschen Handwerks

R.I. e: mil: Regimental Institute; f: mil: Régiment d'infanterie

RI D: d: mil: Remonte-Inspektion

R.I. F: f: Républicains Indépendants

RI US: e: Chicago, Rock Island & Pacific

Railway; INT: e: Rotary International, Illinois [US, gegr 1905]

R.I. GB: e: Royal Institute of Painters in Water Colours, London [gegr 1831]; Royal Institution

R.I.A. F: f: mil: Régiment d'infanterie alpine; Régiment interarmes; US: e: Research Institute of America

RIA US: e: mil: Rock Island Arsenal

R.I.A. GB: e: Royal Irish Academy, Dublin [gegr 1786] Roads Improvement Association

RIAA US: e: Record Industry Association of America, New York 22, N.Y.

R.I.A.C. INT: f: mil: Rassemblement International des Anciens Combattants; GB: e: Royal Irish Automobile Club, Dublin

RIAF e: mil: Royal Indian Air Force; Royal Iraqi Air Force

R.I.A.I. GB: e: Royal Institution of Architects in Ireland

R.I.A.M. RM: f: mil: Régiment interarmes malgache; GB: e: Royal Irish Academy of Music

R.I.A.O.-M. F: f: mil: Régiment interarmes d'outre-mer

RIAS BlnW: e: Radio in the American Sector d: Rundfunk im amerikanischen Sektor [gegr 1946]; US: e: Research Institute for Advanced Studies, Martin Co., Baltimore, Md.

R.I.A.S. GB: e: Royal Incorporation of Architects and Surveyors

R.I.A.S.C. GB: IND: e: mil: Royal Indian Army Service Corps

R.I.B. e: Railway Information Bureau

RIB BRD: d: Recheninstitut für das Bauwesen, 7 Stuttgart; NL: nl: Rijks Inkoopbureau

R.I.B. e: Rural Industries Bureau

R.I.B.A. GB: e: Royal Institute of British Architects

R.I.Bg. D: d: mil: Reserve-Infanterie-Brigade

R.I.B.I. GB: IRL: e: Rotary International in Great Britain and Ireland
R.I.Br. = R.I.Bg.
RIC GB: e: Radio Industry Council, London WC 1
R.I.C. e: Refugees Industries Committee; F: f: mil: Régiment d'infanterie coloniale
RIC INT: f: [règlement internationale pour l'emploi réciproqie des convois] Union Internationale des Voitures et des Fourgons, Bern [CH]
R.I.C. GB: e: Royal Institute of Chemistry; Royal Irish Constabulary
RICA GB: e: Research Institute of Consumer Affairs
RICASIP US: e: Research Information Center and Advisory Service on Information Processing, Washington, D.C.
R.I.C.M. F: f: mil: Régiment d'infanterie coloniale de Maroc
RICM INT: f: Registre International des Citoyens du Monde, Paris [gegr 1949] s: Registro Internacional de los Ciudados del Mundo, Paris [e: IRWC]
RICOB PI: e: Rice and Corn Board
RICS GB: e: Royal Institute of Chartered Surveyors, London
RID NL: nl: Reactor Institute Delft
R.I.D. D: d: mil: Reserve-Infanterie-Division
RIDA PTM: e: Rural and Industrial Development Authority [gegr 1950]
R.I.D.G. GB: e: mil: Royal Inniskilling Dragoon Guards
R.I.E.C. GB: IND: e: Royal Indian Engineering College
R.I.E.L.S.A. E: s: Riegos y Elevaciónes de Aguas, S.A., Madrid
RIF S: sv: Realläroverkets idrottsförening, Stockholm
R.I.F. F: f: mil: Régiment d'infanterie de forteresse
RIF D: d: Reichsstelle für industrielle Fette und Waschmittel
R.I.F. F: f: Résistance Intérieure Française; GB: e: mil: Royal Inniskilling Fusiliers;

Royal Irish Fusiliers
Rifo S: sv: Sällskapet Riksdagsmän och Forskare [gegr 1959]
R.I.F.T. F: f: mil: Régiment d'Infanterie des Forces du Territoire
RIG A: d: Reaktor-Interessengemeinschaft; D: d: Reichsinteressengemeinschaft der deutschen Geflügelwirtschaft; BRD: d: Rosenthal-Isolatoren GmbH, 8672 Selb
R.I.G. GB: e: Royal Institute Galleries
R.I.G.B. GB: e: Royal Institute of Great Britain
RIGC INT: [f: Conférence intergouvernementale au sujet des réfugiés] [Völkerbund]
RIGO BRD: d: Ring-Organisation der deutschen Damenfriseur- und Perückenmacher-Gehilfen-Vereine, Ffm
RIH BRD: d: Ruhr-Intrans-Hubstapler GmbH, 433 Mülheim
R.I.H.S. US: e: Rhode Island Historical Society
R.I.I.A. GB: e: Royal Institute of International Affairs, London [gegr 1920]
RIK S: sv: Redbergslids Idrottsklubb
RIKO CH: d: Ringerkommission
R.I.L. NL: e: Royal Interocean Lines, Amsterdam
RILEM INT: f: Réunion Internationale des Laboratoires d'Essais et de Recherches sur les Matériaux et les Constructions, Paris [F, gegr 1947]
RILO US: e: mil: Research and Industrial Liaison Office [gegr 1968]
RILU INT: e: Red International of Labour Unions
R.I.M. F: f: mil: Régiment d'infanterie marocain; Régiment d'infanterie motorisé
RIM D: d: Reichsminister(ium) des Innern
R.I.M. GB: IND: e: mil: Royal Indian Marines
RIMa. F: f: mil: Régiment d'infanterie de Marine
RIMAS DK: da: Ringsted Jernstøberi &

Maskinfabrik A/S, Ringsted

RIMEA US: e: Rhode Island Music Educators Association

R.I.Méca F: f: mil: Régiment d'infanterie mécanisé

RI-MI I: i: Ricerche Minerarie S.p.A., Torino

RIN CDN: f: Rassemblement pour l'Indépendence Nationale, Quebec; S: sv: Riksidrottsnämnden

R.I.N. GB: IND: e: mil: Royal Indian Navy

R.I.N.A. GB: e: Royal Institution of Naval Architects

R INNISKS GB: e: mil: Royal Inniskilling Fusiliers

R.I.N.V.R. GB: IND: e: mil: Royal Indian Navy Volunteer Reserve

R.I.O. GB: e: Royal Infant Orphanage

R.I.O.P. GB: e: Royal Institute of Oil Painters

RIP NL: nl: Rijksinstituut voor Pluimveetelt

R.I.P.H. GB: e: Royal Institute of Public Health

R.I.P.H.H. GB: e: Royal Institute of Public Health and Hygiene

R.I.P.M. f: mil: Régiment d'infanterie partiellement mécanisé (motorisé)

RIPSA F: f: Représentations Internationales de Publicité S.A., Paris 8

RIPTO NL: nl: Rijks-Instituut voor Pharmaco-Therapeutisch Onderzoek

R.I.P.W.C. GB: e: Royal Institute of Painters in Water Colours

R.I.R. F: f: mil: Régiment d'infanterie de réserve; D: d: mil: Reserve-Infanterie-Regiment

Rir. GB: e: mil: Royal Irish Rifles

RIRB PTM: e: Rubber Industry Replanting Board

R IR F GB: e: mil: The Royal Irish Fusiliers (Princess Victoria's)

R.Ir.R. GB: e: mil: Royal Irish Rifles

R.I.S. F: f: mil: Régiment d'infanterie de sécurité

RISCOM Rhodesien: e: Rhodesian Iron and Steel Commission [gegr 1942]

Riso CH: d: "Riso", Schweizerische Propagandastelle für die Förderung des Reiskonsums, Bern

RISPA e: Research Institute of the Sumatra Planters Association, Medan [gegr 1916]

RISPE US: e: Rhode Island Society of Professional Engineers

RISRR US: e: Rhode Island Southern Railroad

RiStaKri D: d: Vereinigung der Berliner Richter, Staatsanwälte und Kriminalisten

R.I.S.W. GB: e: Royal Institution of South Wales

RIT US: e: Radio Network for Inter-American Telecommunications

R.I.T. B: f: Recherche et Industrie Thérapeutique; F: f: mil: Régiment d'infanterie territoriale; US: e: Rochester Institute of Technology, Rochester, N.Y.

RITA US: e: mil: Resistance in the Army (Resist inside the Army)

RITS GB: e: mil: Regimental Instructor Training School

R.I.T.S. f: mil: Régiment d'infanterie type spécial

Ritzau; Ritz.B.; Ritz.Bur. DK: da: Ritzaus Bureau, København [d: Nachrichtenagentur, gegr 1866]

RIV BRD: d: Rasierklingenindustrie-Verband; INT: [i: Regolamento Internazionale Veicoli d: Internationaler Güterwagenverband e: International Wagon Union, gegr 1921]; NL: nl: Rijks-Instituut voor de Volksgezondheid

RIVI S: sv: Riksförbundet för vilohem, Stockholm

RIWA NL: nl: Rijncommissie Waterleidingsbedrijven

RIZA NL: nl: Rijks-Institúut inzake Zuivering van Afvalwater en Verontreiniging van Openbare Wateren

RJ CH: f: Rassemblement Jurassien

R.J. NL: nl: mil: Regiment Jagers

RJA D: d: Reichsjustizamt

R.J.A. GB: e: mil: Royal Jersey Artillery

RJäM D: d: Reichsjägermeister

RJAF e: mil: Royal Jordanian Air Force

RJB D: d: Reichsjagdbund; NL: nl: Revolutionnaire Jeugdbond

R.J.C.B.I. GB: e: Regional Joint Committee for the Building Industry

R.J.F. F: f: Rassemblement de la jeunesse française

R.j.F.; R.J.F. D: d: mil: Reichsbund jüdischer Frontsoldaten

RJF(.) D: d: NS: Reichsjugendführung

RJLB D: d: Reichsjunglandbund

R.J.L.I. GB: e: mil: Royal Jersey Light Infantry

Rjm.; RJM. D: d: Reichsjägermeister

RJM D: d: Reichsminister(ium) der Justiz

R.J.M. GB: e: mil: Royal Jersey Militia

RJN PL: pl: Rada (Rząd) Jedności Narodowej

RJP D: d: Reichsjustizprüfungsamt

RJS D: d: Reichsjugendsekretariat

RJV D: d: Reichsausschuß der Jüdischen Jugendverbände

RK D: d: Radierverein, Karlsruhe; S: sv: Radikala Klubben, Uppsala; LR: Rajona Komiteja; D: d: Reichskammer

Rk.; RK D: d: Reichskanzlei

RK D: d: Reichskasse; Reichskuratorium für Jugendertüchtigung; CH: d: Rekurskammer

R.K. D: d: mil: Reservekorps

RK BRD: d: mil: Reservistenkameradschaft; D: d: Restitutionskammer

R.K. S: sv: Riksgäldskontoret; Röda Korset; D: d: stud: Roter Kreis [Kösener Seniorenconvent] ; d: Rotes Kreuz

RK BRD: d: Rudolph Karstadt AG, 2 Hamburg; D: d: stud: Rüdesheimer Kartell

RKA S: sv: Ränte- och Kapitalförsäkringsanstalten, Stockholm; D: d: Reichskolonialamt; Reichskriegsanwaltschaft; Reichskriegsschädenamt; Reichsverband

der katholischen Auslanddeutschen; Rentenbankkreditanstalt

RKAG BRD: d: Ruhrkohle AG [= RAG]

RKaliR. D: d: Reichskalirat [1919]

RKAP NL: nl: Roomsch-Katholieke Arbeiderspartij in Nederland

RK.a.W. D: d: Ruderklub am Wannsee

RKB BRD: d: Rad- und Kraftfahrerbund; D: d: Reichskolonialbund; Reichskraftwagenbetriebsverband [gegr 1935] ; D: d: nach WK2: Rheinische Kreditbank

RKbK D: d: Reichskammer der bildenden Künste

RKBLO NL: nl: Roomsch-Katholiek Buitengewoon Lager Onderwijs

RKC NL: nl: Rotterdamsche Kustvaart Centrale N.V.

RKD D: d: Reichsbund der Kinderreichen Deutschlands

RKD. D: d: Reichskriminaldirektion

RKDB BRD: d: stud: Ring katholischer deutscher Burschenschaften, 53 Bonn [gegr 1924]

RKdbK D: d: = RKbK

R.K.E.F.B. S: sv: Rikskommissionen för ekonomisk försvarsberedskap

RKFDV D: d: NS: Reichskommissar für die Festigung des deutschen Volkstums

RKfPr. D: d: NS: Reichskommissar für die Preisbildung

R.K.G. S: sv: Realläroverkets kristliga gymnasieförening, Stockholm

RKG D: d: Reichskreditgesellschaft AG, Berlin [gegr 1924] ; D: d: mil: Reichskriegsgericht; BRD: d: Rheinische Kraftwagen-Gesellschaft mbH, 53 Bonn -Bad Godesberg; PL: pl: Robotniczy Komitet Gospodarczy

RKI D: d: Reichsverband der Kraftfahrzeugteile- und -zubehör-Industrie

RKIE H: hu: Református Keresztyén Ifjusági Egyesület, Budapest

RKJ BRD: d: Revolutionär-Kommunistische Jugend

RKJB NL: nl: Rooms-Katholieke Jonge

Boerenstand

RKK D: d: WK2: Reichskommissariat für Kaukasien; D: d: Reichskreditkasse; Reichskulturkammer

RKKF S: sv: Resande Köpmäns Kristliga Förening [gegr 1919]

RKKohle D: d: WK1: Reichskommissar für die Kohleverteilung [1917]

R.K.M.; RKM. D: d: mil: Reichskriegsminister(ium)

RKM. A: d: mil: Reichskriegsministerium

RKMuObdW D: d: mil: Reichskriegsminister und Oberbefehlshaber der Wehrmacht

RKnV D: d: Reichsknappschaftsverein

RKO US: e: Radio Keith Orpheum Corp. [gegr 1928]; BRD: d: Rheinisches Kammerorchester

RKolA D: d: Reichskolonialamt

RKP; R&KP GB: e: Routledge & Kegan Paul Ltd., London E.C. 4

RKPA D: d: Reichskriminalpolizeiamt

RKPD D: d: Revolutionäre Kommunistische Partei Deutschlands [gegr 1918]

RKPf D: d: Reichskommissar für Pferdesport und Pferdezucht

R.Kr.M. D: d: Reichskriegsministerium

RKS. D: d: Reichskommissar für die Seeschiffahrt

RKS D: d: Reichskraftsprit-Gesellschaft, Berlin; Reichskultursenat; NL: nl: Rijkskweekschool voor Onderwijzers; PL: pl: Robotniczy Klub Sportowy

RKSH NL: nl: Roomsch-Katholieke Sociale Hoogeschool

RKSP NL: nl: Roomsch-Katholieke Staatspartij

RKSt. D: d: WK1: Reichskartoffelstelle [1915]

RKSV NL: nl: Roomsch-Katholieke Studenten Vereeniging "Sanctus Thomas Aquinas"

RKSW D: d: Reichskommissar für das Siedlungswesen

RKT S: sv: Racerbåtklubben Torpederna; D: d: Reichsbund der Kraftverkehrs-

technik; Reichskammer der Technik; D: d: mil: Reichskriegertag 1934

RKTL D: d: Reichskuratorium für Technik in der Landwirtschaft [gegr 1927]

RKU. D: d: WK2: Reichskommissariat Ukraine

RKU S: sv: Riksförbundet Kyrklig Ungdom; PL: pl: Rejonowa Komenda Uzupełnień

R.Ku.Ka. D: d: Reichskulturkammer

R.K.V. D: d: Radiatoren- und Kesselfabrikanten-Vereinigung

RKV D: d: Reichsbahnkrankenversorgung; Reichskohlenverband; Rentner-Kranken versicherung; BRD: d: Rheinischer Kunsthändler-Verband eV, 5 Köln; NL: nl: Roomsch-Katholieke Verkenners; D: d: stud: Rudelsburger Kartell-Verband (Deutsche Sängerschaft)

RKVP NL: nl: Roomsch-Katholieke Volkspartij

RKW BRD: d: Rationalisierungskuratorium der Deutschen Wirtschaft (RKW) eV, 6 Ffm; D: d: Reichsbahnkraftwerk; Reichskuratorium für Wirtschaftlichkeit [gegr 1921]

RL US: e: Radio Liberty, München [BRD, seit 1953]; YU: sh: Radio Ljubljana

R.L.; RL. D: d: Reichsleitung [NSDAP]

RL S: sv: Rörfirmornas Landsförbund, Norrköping; GB: e: mil: Royal Laboratory; e: Rugby League

R.L.A. f: Rassemblement de la libération africaine

RLA. D: d: Reichsluftamt [gegr 1918]

RLAD. D: d: Reichsluftaufsichtsdienst

RLB INT: e: Reciprocal Licensing Body [CEE]; e: Regional Library Bureau; D: d: Reichslandbund; Reichsluftschutzbund; BRD: d: Rheinische Linoleumwerke Bedburg Richard Holtkott, 5152 Bedburg

RLC NL: nl: Rijkslandbouwconsulentschap

R.L.D.P.A.S. GB: e: Royal London Discharged Prisoners' Aid Society

RLE US: e: Research Laboratory of Electronics [MIT, gegr 1946]

RLEA US: e: Railway Labor Executives Association

R LEICESTERS GB: e: mil: The Royal Leicestershire Regiment

RLF S: sv: Radikala Landsföreningen; US: e: Religion and Labor Foundation; S: sv: Riksförbundet Landsbygdens Folk, Stockholm

R.L.F. GB: e: Royal Literary Fund

R.L.F.C. GB: e: Rugby League Football Club

R.L.H. S: sv: Riksförbundet Lin och Hampa [gegr 1942]

R LINCOLNS GB: e: mil: The Royal Lincolnshire Regiment

RLK CS: cs: Rada Lidových Komisařů

RLL N: no: Radio-Leverandørenes Landsforbund, Oslo

RLM D: d: Reichsluftfahrtministerium

R.L.M.u.Ob.d.L. D: d: mil: Reichsluftfahrtminister und Oberbefehlshaber der Luftwaffe

R.L.O. GB: e: Returned Letter Office

RLP PL: pl: Rejon Lasów Państwowych

RLPS NL: nl: Rijkslandbouwproefstation

R.L.S. e: Reich Labour Service [D: d: = RAD]

RLS NL: nl: Rijksluchtvaartschool, Eelde

R.L.S.C. e: Robert Louis Stevenson Club

R.L.S.F. S: sv: Riksluftskyddsförbundet

R.L.S.S. GB: e: Royal Life Saving Society

RLU CS: sk: Rozhlasová Ludová Univerzita

R.L.U.H. GB: e: Royal Liverpool United Hospitals

RLV NL: nl: Rijks Leeraren Vereeniging

RLVD NL: nl: Rijkslandbouwvoorlichtingsdienst

RLWS NL: nl: Rijkslandbouwwinterscholen

ŘLZ CS: cs: Ředitelství Lesních Závodů

RM D: d: Radierverein, München

R.M. I: i: mil: Regia Marina; F: f: mil: Régiment de matériel

RM.; R.M. D: d: mil: Reichsmarine

RM. D: d: Reichsmusikerschaft

R.M. F: f: Républicains modérés; GB: e: Resident Magistrate [Ireland] ; I: i: Rete Mediterranea

RM BRD: d: Rhein-Main-Bank AG [gegr 1952]

R.M. S: sv: Riksmuseum; GB: e: Royal Mail; GB: e: mil: Royal Marines; GB: e: Royal Mint

R.M.A. e: Radio Manufacturers Association; NL: nl: mil: Regiment Motorartillerie

RMA D: d: Reichsbahnmaschinenamt; D: d: mil: Reichsmarineamt; D: d: Reichsausschuß zur Förderung des Milchverbrauchs eV, Berlin

Rm.A. D: d: mil: Remonteamt

R.M.A. GB: e: mil: Royal Malta Artillery; Royal Marine Artillery; Royal Marine Asylum; Royal Military Academy, Woolwich; Royal Military Asylum

RMA US: e: Rubber Manufacturers Association, Washington, D.C.

RMAB GB: e: mil: Royal Military Academy Band

RMAF PTM: e: mil: Royal Malayan Air Force; e: mil: Royal Moroccan Air Force

RMAFVR PTM: e: mil: Royal Malaysian Air Force Voluntary Reserve

RMAI IND: e: Radio Manufacturers Association of India

RMAM GB: e: mil: Royal Military Academy Museum, Sandhurst

R.Mar.A.; RMarA D: d: mil: Reichsmarineamt

R.Mar.A.; R.Mar.Arty GB: e: mil: Royal Marines Artillery

RMAS GB: e: mil: Royal Military Aacdemy, Sandhurst

R.M.A.S.A. GB: e: Royal Mint Artificer Staff Association

RMB GB: e: mil: Royal Marine Brigade

R.M.B.F. GB: e: mil: Royal Military (Medical) Benevolent Fund

RMB-Schule D: d: Reichs-Modellbau-Schule [DLV]

R.M.C. GB: e: Radio Modification Committee; MC: f: Radio Monte-Carlo, Monaco

RMC GB: e: Ready Mixed Concrete Limited

R.M.C. F: f: mil: Régiment mixte colonial; GB: e: mil: Royal Marine Commandos; Royal Marine Corps; Royal Military College, Sandhurst

RMCE E: s: Real Moto Club de España

R.M.C.M. GB: e: Royal Manchester College of Music

R.M.C.S. GB: e: mil: Royal Military College of Science

R.M.D. D: d: mil: Reichsmarinedienststelle

RMD A: d: Österreichischer Kanal- und Schiffahrtsverein Rhein-Main-Donau; BRD: d: Rhein-Main-Donau AG, 8 München; US: e: mil: Rhine Medical Depot [near Kaiserslautern, BRD]

RMdA D: d: Reichsminister(ium) des Auswärtigen

RMdF D: d: Reichsminister der Finanzen

RMdI D: d: Reichsminister(ium) des Innern

RMdJ D: d: Reichsminister(ium) der Justiz

RMdL D: d: Reichsminister(ium) der Luftfahrt

RMdLuObdL D: d: mil: = R.L.M.u.Ob.d.L.

RME F: f: Recherches sur les Machines Électroniques, Issy-les-Moulineux

R.Met.S. GB: e: Royal Meteorological Society, London [gegr 1850]

R.M.F. Rhodesien: e: Rhodesian Mining Federation; GB: e: mil: Royal Munster Fusiliers

RMfdbO. D: d: WK2: Reichsminister für die besetzten Ostgebiete

RMfE; RMfEuL D: d: Reichsminister(ium) für Ernährung und Landwirtschaft [seit 1920]

RMfkirchlAngel. D: d: Reichsminister(ium) für kirchliche Angelegenheiten

R.M.F.U. GB: e: mil: Royal Marine Fortress Unit

RMFVR GB: e: mil: Royal Marine Forces Voluntary Reserve

RM.f.V.u.P. D: d: Reichsminister(ium) für Volksaufklärung und Propaganda

RMfWEuV; RMfWEV. D: d: Reichsminister(ium) für Wissenschaft, Erziehung und Volksbildung

RMG. D: d: mil: Reichsmilitärgericht

R.M.H. GB: e: Royal Masonic Hospital

R.M.I. D: d: Reichsbund der deutschen Metallwaren-Industrie

RMI D: d: = RMdI; LR: Rigas Medicinas Institūts

R.M.I.B. GB: e: Royal Masonic Institution for Boys

R.M.I.C. F: f: mil: Régiment de mitrailleurs d'infanterie coloniale

R.M.I.G. GB: e: Royal Masonic Institution for Girls

RMin.d.I. D: d: = RMdI

RMin.f.d.bes.Geb. D: d: Reichsministerium für die besetzten Gebiete

RMin.f.E. D: d: = RMfE

RMJ D: d: = RMdJ

RMK D: d: Reichsmusikkammer

R.M.L.E. F: f: mil: Régiment de marche de la Légion Etrangère

R.M.L.I. GB: e: mil: Royal Marine Light Infantry

RMLuObdL D: d: mil: = R.L.M.u.Ob.d.L.

R.M.M. 1: Religiosi Missionarii de Mariannhill

RMMP GB: e: mil: Royal Mounted Military Police

R.M.M.S. GB: e: mil: Royal Marine Military School

RMN PTM: e: mil: Royal Malayan (Malaysian) Navy

R.M.N.S. GB: e: Royal Merchant Navy

School
RMO US: e: Raw Materials Operation, Washington, D.C. [AEC] ; D: d: WK2; = RMfdbO.
R.M.O. GB: e: mil: Royal Marine Office
R.M.O.A. GB: e: Royal Mint Operatives' Association
R MON GB: e: mil: Royal Monmouthshire Regiment
RMonA; RMonAmt D: d: Reichsmonopolamt für Branntwein
RMonV D: d: Reichsmonopolverwaltung für Branntwein
R.M.P. F: f: Recette Municipale de Paris
RMP US: e: mil: Rhine Military Post [BRD] ; S: sv: Riksföreningen mot Reumatism, Stockholm
R.M.P. GB: e: mil: Royal Marine Police; Royal Military Police
R.M.P.A. GB: e: Royal Medico-Psychological Association
R.M.P.C. GB: e: mil: Royal Military Police Corps
RM PRL PL: pl: Rada Ministrów Polskiej Rzeczypospolitej Ludowej
RMR BRD: d: Rhein-Main-Rohrleitungstransportgesellschaft mbH, 5039 Godorf [gegr 1965]
R.M.R. CDN: e: mil: Royal Montreal Regiment
RMRE GB: e: mil: Royal Monmouthshire Royal Engineers Supplementary Reserve
RMS S: sv: mil: Arméns radar- och luftvärnsmekanikerskola, Göteborg; NL: nl: Rijksmiddelbare School
R.M.S. GB: e: Royal Mail Service; US: e: Railway Mail Service; GB: e: Royal Meteorological Society, London; Royal Microscopical Society; Royal Society of Miniature Painters
R.M.S.A.S. GB: e: mil: Royal Marine Small Arms School
R.M.S.M. F: f: mil: Régiment de marche des spahis marocains; GB: e: mil: Royal Military School of Music

R.M.S.P. GB: e: Royal Mail Steam Packet Company
R.M.T. F: f: mil: Régiment de marche du Tchad
RMT S: sv: Riksförbundet mot tobaken, Stockholm
R.M.T.S.A. GB: e: Royal Mint Temporary Staff Association
RMV D: d: Röstmaschinen-Verband, Bocholt
R.M.V.E. F: f: mil: Régiment de marche des volontaires étrangers
RMVP D: d: = RM.f.V.u.P.
RMW D: d: RMW-Motorrad-Werke GmbH, Neheim (Ruhr)
RMWP PL: pl: Rada Młodzieżowa Wojska Polskiego
RMZ. D: d: NS: Reichsmusikzug
RN NL: nl: Radio Nederland Wereldomroep, Hilversum
RN. D: d: NS: Reichsnährstand
R.N. GB: e: mil: Royal Navy
R.N.A. GB: e: mil: Royal Naval Association
RNAC BRD: d: Rhein-Neckar Automobil -Club, 68 Mannheim
R.N.A.F. GB: e: mil: Royal Naval Air Force
RNAF e: mil: Royal Netherlands (Norwegian) Air Force
R.N.A.H. GB: e: mil: Royal Naval Auxiliary Hospital
R.N.A.S. GB: e: mil: Royal Naval Air Service (Station)
RNASOCA GB: e: mil: Royal Naval Air Service Old Comrades' Association
R.N.A.T.E. GB: e: mil: Royal Naval Air Training Establishment
R.N.A.V. GB: e: mil: Royal Naval Artillery Volunteers
R.N.A.Y. GB: e: mil: Royal Naval Aircraft Yard
ŘNB CS: cs: Ředitelství Národní Bezpečnosti
R.N.B. GB: e: mil: Royal Naval Barracks

RNbA D: d: Reichsbahn-Neubauamt
R.N.B.S. GB: e: mil: Royal Naval Benevolent Society
R.N.B.T. GB: e: Royal Naval Benevolent Trust
R.N.C. US: e: Republican National Committee; GB: e: mil: Royal Naval College; e: Royal Niger Company
R.N.C.B. GB: e: mil: Royal Naval College of the Blind
R.N.C.C. CDN: e: mil: Royal Naval College of Canada
R.N.C.F. GB: e: mil: Royal Naval Cordite Factory
RND NL: nl: Rijksnijverheidsdienst, Den Haag [gegr 1910]; GB: e: mil: Royal Naval Division
RNE E: s: Radio Nacional de España, Madrid
R.N.E.C. GB: e: mil: Royal Naval Engineering College
R.N.E.I.A.F. NL: e: mil: Royal Netherlands East Indies Air Force
R.N.E.I.N. NL: e: mil: Royal Netherlands East Indies Navy
RNethN e: mil: Royal Netherlands Navy
R.N.F. S: sv: Realläroverkets naturvetenskapliga förening, Stockholm [gegr 1895]; GB: e: mil: Royal Naval Fund; The Royal Northumberland Fusiliers
R.N.F.C. GB: e: mil: Royal Navy Film Corporation; Royal Navy Flying Club
RNG D: d: Reichsverband des deutschen Nahrungsmittel-Großhandels eV, Berlin
RNH PL: pl: Rada Naczelna Harcerstwa; GB: e: mil: Royal Naval Hospital
R.N.H.D. GB: e: Royal Naval Hydrographic Department
RNI BRD: d: Radio Nordsee International [Privatsender ab 24 Jan 1970]
R.N.L.B.I. GB: e: Royal National Lifeboat Institution, London S.W.1
R.N.L.R.S. GB: e: mil: Royal Naval Lay Readers' Society
R.N.M. RM: f: Rassemblement national malgache [gegr 1958]
R.N.M.C. GB: e: mil: Royal Navy Medical Corps
R.N.M.D.S.F. GB: e: Royal National Mission to Deep-Sea Fishermen
R.N.M.O.H. GB: e: mil: Royal Naval and Marine Orphan Home
RNMS GB: e: mil: Royal Naval Medical Service
RNN S: sv: Radionavigeringsnämnden; e: mil: Royal Netherlands Navy
R.N.N.A.S. e: mil: Royal Netherlands Naval Air Service
R.N.N.S. GB: e: mil: Royal Naval Nursing Service
RNoAF e: mil: Royal Norwegian Air Force
RNOCA GB: e: mil: Royal Naval Old Comrades' Association
R NORFOLK GB: e: mil: The Royal Norfolk Regiment
RNorN e: mil: Royal Norwegian Navy
R.N.P. F: f: WK2: Rassemblement national populaire
R.N.P.F.N. GB: e: Royal National Pension Fund for Nurses
RN PKPS PL: pl: Rada Naczelna Polskiego Komitetu Pomocy Społecznej
RNPS GB: e: mil: Royal Naval Patrol Service
RNR GB: e: mil: Royal Naval Reserve
R.N.R.A.C. GB: e: mil: Royal Naval Reserve Advisory Committee
R.N.R.M.C.H. GB: e: mil: Royal Naval and Royal Marine Children's Home
R.N.R.S. GB: e: mil: Royal Naval Reserve of Skippers
R.N.S. GB: e: Railway Nationalization Society
RNS NL: nl: Rijksnormaalschool
R.N.S. GB: e: Royal Numismatic Society
R.N.S.A. GB: e: mil: Royal Naval Sailing Association
R.N.S.C. GB: e: mil: Royal Naval Staff College
R.N.S.R. GB: e: mil: Royal Naval Spe-

cial Reserve; CDN: e: mil: Royal Nova Scotia Regiment

RNSS GB: e: mil: Royal Naval Scientific Service

RNSt. D: d: NS: Reichsnährstand

RNSW BRD: d: Rheinstahl Nordseewerke GmbH, 297 Emden

R.N.T.F. GB: e: mil: Royal Naval Torpedo Factory

R.N.T.S. GB: e: mil: Royal Naval Temperance Society

R.N.U.R. F: f: Régie Nationale des Usines Renault; Regroupement national pour l'unité de la République [gegr 1960]

R.N.V. GB: e: mil: Royal Naval Volunteers

R.N.V.R. GB: e: mil: Royal Naval Volunteer Reserve

R.N.V.S.R. GB: e: mil: Royal Naval Volunteer Supplementary Reserve

R.N.W.A.R. GB: e: mil: Royal Naval Wireless Auxiliary Reserve

R.N.W.C. GB: e: mil: Royal Naval War College

R.N.W.L. GB: e: mil: Royal Naval War Libraries

R.N.W.M.P. e: Royal Northwest Mounted Police

RNY US: e: Radio New York Worldwide, New York, N.Y.; GB: e: mil: Royal Navy

R.N.Z.A. NZ: e: mil: Royal New Zealand Army

RNZA NZ: e: mil: Royal New Zealand Artillery

RNZAC NZ: e: mil: Royal New Zealand Armoured Corps

RNZAF NZ: e: mil: Royal New Zealand Air Force

R.N.Z.A.M.C. NZ: e: mil: Royal New Zealand Army Medical Corps

RNZASC NZ: e: mil: Royal New Zealand Army Service Corps

RNZEME NZ: e: mil: Royal New Zealand Electrical and Mechanical Engineers

RN ZHP PL: pl: Rada Naczelna Związku Hacerstwa Polskiego

R.N.Z.N. NZ: e: mil: Royal New Zealand Navy

RN ZSP PL: pl: Rada Naczelna Zrzeszenia Studentów Polskich

R.O. PL: pl: Rada Obrony (Okręgowa); NL: nl: Rechterlijke Organisatie; GB: e: Reedham Orphanage; Royal Observatory

ROA US: e: mil: Reserve Officers Association [Army]; S: sv: Riksorganisationen av Artistarbetsgivare; [d: mil: WK2: Russische Befreiungsarmee − Wlassow −]

ROAK PL: pl: Ruch Oporu Armii Krajowej

ROAL US: e: mil: Reserve Officers Association Ladies

ROB D: d: mil: Reichsoffiziersbund

ROBECO NL: nl: Rotterdamsch Beleggungs consortium N.V., Rotterdam

R.Ob.SeeA. D: d: Reichsoberseeamt

ROC GB: e: mil: Royal Observer Corps

R.O.C.C. GB: e: mil: Royal Observer Corps Club

R.O.D. GB: e: mil: Royal Ordnance Department

RöffO. D: d: Reichskommissar für öffentliche Ordnung

R.O.F. GB: e: mil: Royal Ordnance Factory

R.of O. GB: e: mil: Reserve of Officers

R.O.F.W. GB: e: mil: Royal Ordnance Factories Worktakers' Association

R.O.G. GB: e: Royal Observatory, Greenwich

Roges D: d: Rohstoffhandels-GmbH

Rohag D: d: [Rohproduktenhandelsgesellschaft] Reichsverband für Knochenverwertung Rohag GmbH, Berlin

ROHG D: d: Reichsoberhandelsgericht

ROI PL: pl: Resortowy Ośrodek Informacji;I: i: Ricerche Occidentali Idrocarburi

R.O.I. GB: e: Royal Institute of Oil Painters (. . . of Painters in Oils), London [gegr 1883]

ROIE PL: pl: Resortowy Ośrodek Informacji Ekonomicznej

ROIT PL: pl: Regionalny Ośrodek Informacji Turystycznej

ROKA e: mil: Republic of Korea Army

ROKN e: mil: Republic of Korea Navy

ROL. D: d: Reichsorganisationsleitung [NSDAP]

Rolimpex PL: pl: Centrala Handlu Zagranicznego

RON PL: pl: Rada Obrony Narodu

RONDD [d: russische nationale Volks- und Reichsbewegung in der Emigration]

RONP PL: pl: Resortowy Ośrodek Normowania Pracy

R.O.O. GB: e: mil: Reserve of Officers

R.O.P. PL: pl: Rada Obrony Państwa

ROP PL: pl: Referat Ochrony Przemysłowej

ROPL PL: pl: Rejon Obrony Przeciwlotniczej

R.O.R.C. GB: e: Royal Ocean Racing Club

RO/RO US: e: mil: U.S.Army Transportation Trailer Service Roll-On/Roll-Off

ROS PL: pl: Regionalne Ognisko Studenckie

RoS S: sv: Reso och Studier

R.O.S. GB: e: Royal Order of Scotland

R.O.S.A.U.K. GB: e: Railway Officers' and Servants' Association of the United Kingdom

R.O.S.C. GB: e: mil: Reserve of Officers' Sanitary Corps

ROSIS S: sv: mil: Reservofficerssällskapet i Stockholm

Ro.S.P.A. GB: e: Royal Society for the Prevention of Accidents

ROSTA SU: [d: Nachrichtenagentur]

ROTC US: e: mil: Reserve Officers Training Corps

Rotkol d: Rotes Kollektiv Proletarische Erziehung

Rotzan BlnW: d: Rote Zelle Anglistik [Freie Universität]

Rotzbau BlnW: d: Rote Zelle Bauwesen

Rotzeg BlnW: d: Rote Zelle Germanistik

ROTZEPH BlnW: d: Rote Zelle der Pädagogischen Hochschule

Rotzeps BlnW: d: Rote Zelle Psychologie

Rotzhis BlnW: d: Rote Zelle Historiker

Rotzjur BlnW: d: Rote Zelle Jura

Rotzmath BlnW: d: Rote Zelle Mathematik

Rotzmed BlnW: d: Rote Zelle Medizin

Rotzök BlnW: d: Rote Zelle Ökonomie

Rotzphys BlnW: d: Rote Zelle Physik

Rotzrom BlnW: d: Rote Zelle Romanistik

Rotzlav BlnW: d: Rote Zelle Slawistik

Rotzsoz BlnW: d: Rote Zelle Soziologie

ROW BRD: d: Rheinische Olefinwerke GmbH, 5047 Wesseling

ROWS [d: mil: Verband russischer Krieger]

ROYALS GB: e: mil: 1st The Royal Dragoons

RP GB: e: mil: Regimental Police

R.P. f: mil: Régiment de Pionniers

Rp.; RP D: d: Reichspartei

RP D: d: Reichspfadfinder; Reichspost; Reichsverband der deutschen Presse

R.P. F: f: Républicains Populaires

RP BRD: d: Republikanische Partei

R.P. GB: e: Royal Society of Portrait Painters, London [gegr 1891]

RPA D: d: Rassenpolitisches Amt der NSDAP [gegr 1933]

R.P.A. GB: e: Rationalist Press Association

RPA. D: d: Reichspatentamt; Reichspostamt; Reichspropagandaamt

RPatA; R.Pat.A. D: d: Reichspatentamt

RPAW D: d: Renten- und Pensionsanstalt für deutsche bildende Künstler, Weimar

RPB B: f: mil: Réformés pour Blessures

RPC US: e: mil: Recruiting Publicity Center [Army]; d: Reit- und Poloclub

R.P.C. e: Republican Party Conference

RPC NL: nl: Rijkspluimveeteeltconsulentschap; GB: e: mil: Royal Pioneer Corps

R.P.Ch. e: Reformed Presbyterian Church

RPD S: sv: Rätts- och Polisdirektionen

R.P.D. GB: e: Recorder Programme Department [BBC]

RPD D: d: Reichspostdirektion; BRD: d: Republikanische Partei Deutschlands
R.P.D. GB: e: Royal Parks Division
RPdG D: d: Reichsausschuß zur Pflege des Gesellschaftstanzes
RPDn D: d: Reichspostdirektionen
R.P.E. GB: e: Royal Society of Painter -Etchers and Engravers
R.P.E.U. GB: e: Royal Parks Employees' Union
R.P.F. IND: e: Raos Press Features [d: Nachrichtenagentur] ; F: f: Rassemblement du Peuple Français [gegr 1947]
RPF D: d: Forschungsamt der Deutschen Reichspost
R.P.F.C. GB: e: Royal Patriotic Fund Corporation
R.P.F.S.F. GB: e: Royal Provident Fund for Sea Fishermen
Rpg d: Realprogymnasium
R.P.G. GB: e: Royal Parks and Gardens
R.P.G.M.A. GB: e: Rubber-Proofed Garment Maker's Association
RPI S: sv: Religionspedagogiska Institutet [gegr 1953] ; US: e: Rensselaer Polytechnic Institute, Troy, N.Y.
R.P.I. F: f: Républicains Populaires Indépendants
RPI LR: Rigas Politechnikais Institūts
RPIO US: e: mil: Registered Publication Issuing Office
RPJ BRD: d: Ring Politischer Jugend
RPK CH: d: Rechnungsprüfungskommission; D: d: Reichspressekammer
RPL CDN: e: Radio Physics Laboratory; LAO: [e: Laotian People's Rally, gegr 1958]
RPL. D: d: NS: Reichspropagandaleitung
RPM D: d: Reichspostministerium; PL: pl: Rejonowe Przedsiębiorstwo Melioracyjne
RPMIO US: e: mil: Registered Publication Mobile Issuing Office
R.P.N.C. e: Republican Party National Convention
R.P.O. e: Railroad (Railway) Post Office

RPoA D: d: Reichspostamt
RPoM; RPostMin. E d: Reichspostministerium
RPPA D: d: Reichspresse- und Propagandaamt
RP PH PL: pl: Rada Powiatowa Przyjaciół Hacerstwa
RPPS PL: pl: Robotnicza Partia Polskich Socjalistów
R.P.R.C. e: Regional Price Regulation Committee
RPrK D: d: Reichspressekammer
RPropM D: d: = RM.f.V.u.P.
RPS CS: cs: Referát Pracovních Sil; CH: DDR: e: Roundup Press Service, Zürich [Organ des SSD der DDR]
R.P.S. GB: e: Royal Philatelic (Philharmonic) (Philosophical) (Photographic) Society
R.P.S.E. GB: e: Royal Physical Society of Edinburgh
R.P.S.F. F: f: Rassemblement du Peuple Socialiste Français
RPSV S: sv: Riksförbundet psykiskt sjukas vänner
RPT D: d: NS: Reichsparteitag
RPTC GB: e: mil: Royal Physical Training Corps
RPVZ NL: nl: Rijksproefstation voor Zaadcontrôle
R.P.W.A.C. US: e: Republican Post-War Advisory Council
R.P.W.P.A. US: e: Republican Post-War Policy Association
RPŻ PL: pl: Rada Pomocy Żydom
RPZ PL: pl: Rada Przyjaciół Zrzeszenia; D: d: Reichspostzentralamt [seit 1928, vorher: TRA]
R.R. US: e: Raritan River Railraod Company; F: f: Rassemblement Républicain; NL: nl: Regentschapsraad in Nederlandsch-Indië; D: d: mil: Reiter -Regiment
RR S: sv: Rektorernas Riksförening
RR CS: cs: Revírní Ŕeditelství
RR Rhodesien: e: Rhodesia Railways;

GB: e: mil: The Rhodesia Regiment;
GB: e: Rhymney Railway; S: sv: Riks-
registraturet; Rörledingsfirmornas Riksorganisation, Stockholm; GB: e: Rolls
-Royce Ltd., Derby, England

RRA US: e: Retraining and Re-employment Administration; GB: e: mil: The
Royal Regiment of Artillery

R.R.A. e: Rural Reconstruction Association

RRAF GB: e: mil: Royal Rhodesian Air
Force

R.R.A.T. e: Road and Rail Appeal Tribunal

RRAussch. D: d: Ausschuß der Kammer
der Reichsräte

RRB e: Radio Research Board; US: e:
Railroad Retirement Board; BRD: d:
Rhein-Ruhr Bank AG; e: Rubber
Reserve Board

RRC US: e: Rocket Research Corp.

R.R.C. GB: e: Royal Red Cross

RRC CDN: e: mil: The Royal Regiment
of Canada; US: e: Rubber Reserve
Company

RRCC US: e: mil: Ramstein Recovery
Control Center [BRD]

RR.CC. I: i: Reali Carabinieri

RR&D D: e: nach WK2: Reparations Re-
moval and Demolition [ACA]

RRDE GB: e: Radar Research and Development Establishment

RRE GB: e: Royal Radar Establishment,
Malvern

R.-Reg. D: d: Räteregierung

RReg D: d: Reichsregierung

RRFO D: e: nach WK2: Rhine River Field
Organization

RRG CS: cs: Reformní reálné gymnasium

R.Rg. D: d: Reichsregierung

RRG D: d: Reichs-Rundfunkgesellschaft
mbH [gegr 1925] ; Rhön-Rositten-Ge-
sellschaft, Ffm

R.R.G.C. e: Red Rose Guild of Craftsmen

RR.GG. I: i: Raggruppamenti Giovanili

R.Rgt. D: d: mil: Reiter-Regiment

RRGy d: Reformrealgymnasium

RRH D: d: Rechnungshof des Deutschen
Reiches

RRI RI: Radio Republik Indonesia, Djakarta [gegr 1945]

R.R.I. F: f: mil: Régiment régional d'infanterie

RRI US: e: Rocket Research Institute;
MEX: [e: party of revolutionary insti-
tutions]

RRIM PTM: e: Rubber Research Institute
of Malaya

RRiŻ PL: pl: Rada Robotnicza i Żołnierska

RRK D: d: Reichs-Rundfunkkammer [bis
1938]

RRL J: e: Radio Research Laboratory,
Tokyo; GB: e: Road Research Laboratory, Harmondsworth

R.R.O. GB: e: Radio Research Organization

RRO S: sv: Raggarnas Riksorganisation

R.R.P. IND: Ram Rajya Parishad [d: Par-
tei] ; Rhodesien: e: Rhodesia Reformed
Party [gegr 1960]

RRP NL: nl: N.V. Rotterdam-Rijn Pijp-
leiding, Den Haag

RRPA D: e: nach WK2: Ruhr Regional
Planning Authority

RRPGy d: Reformrealprogymnasium

RR.PP. I: i: Regie Poste

R.R.P.W.P.A. US: e: Regional Republican
Post-War Policy Association

RRR NL: nl: Rotterdam-Rijn-Rijleiding

R.R.R.S. F: f: Parti Républicain Radical
et Radical-Socialiste, Paris 1

RRS US: e: Radiation Research Society

R.R.S. F: f: Parti Radical et Radical-Socialiste

RRSA ZA: e: Radio Republic of South
Africa, Johannesburg

RRSt BRD: d: Post: Rentenrechnungsstelle

RRSTRAF US: e: mil: Ready Reserve
Strategic Army Forces

RRT US: e: Brotherhood of Railroad
Trainmen; NATO: e: Working Group
on Railroad Transport

R.R.T. e: Railway Rates Tribunal

R.R.U.P.B.F. e: Reformatory and Refuge Union Provident and Benevolent Fund

RRZB PL: pl: Rolniczy Rejonowy Zakɫad Badawczy

RRZD PL: pl: Rejonowy Rolniczy Zakɫad Doświadczalny

R.S. F: f: Parti Radical et Radical-Socialiste; Radicaux Socialistes

RS S: sv: Radio Sverige, Stockholm; NL: nl: Rapport Staatscommissie

R.S. e: Ray Society; e: mil: Recruiting Service; F: f: mil: Régiment de Spahis

RS D: d: NS: Reichsschrifttumsstelle; CH: d: mil: Rekrutenschule; A: d: Revolutionäre Sozialisten [Partei]; D: d: Rheinische Sezession; S: sv: mil: Arméns kör- och ridskola; NL: nl: Rijschool

R&S BRD: d: Rohde & Schwarz, 8 München 9

RS S: sv: Rosenlundska Sällskapet, Stockholm [gegr 1902]

R.S. e: Rosicrucian Society; GB: e: mil: The Royal Scotts [gegr 1633]; Royal Corps of Signals; GB: e: Royal Society, London [gegr 1662]; GB: e: mil: Royal Sussex Regiment; e: Rural Society; Russian Society

RSA GB: e: Radical Students Alliance; Railway Signal Association

R.S.A. F: f: mil: Régiment de Spahis Algériens

RSA D: d: NS: Reichsschulungsamt; US: e: Retail Shoe Association, Miami Beach

R.S.A. GB: e: Royal Scottish Academy; GB: e: mil: Royal Signals Association; GB: e: Royal Society of Antiquarians (Antiquaries); Royal Society of Arts

RSAAF GB: e: mil: Royal South African Air Force

RSAF e: mil: Royal Saudi Air Force; Royal Siamese Air Force

R.S.A.F. GB: e: mil: Royal Small Arms Factory, Enfield

RSAF e: mil: Royal Swedish Air Force

R.S.A.I. e: Royal Society of Antiquaries of Ireland, Dublin [gegr 1849]

R.San.I. GB: e: Royal Sanitary Institute, London [gegr 1876]

RSAO S: sv: Riksförbundet Sveriges Amatörorkestrar, Stockholm [gegr 1944]

RSAP NL: nl: Revolutionnair Socialistische Arbeiderspartij

R.S.A.S. GB: e: Royal Sanitary Association of Scotland; Royal Surgical Aid Society

RSB D: d: nach WK2: Reichsbahn-Schlafwagen- und Speisewagenbetrieb [Britische Zone]; D: d: Reichsschleppbetrieb; Reichssender Berlin; NL: nl: Rotterdamsche Studenten Bond

R.S.B.A. GB: e: Royal Society of British Artists

RSBS BRD: d: Rettungsdienst-Stiftung Björn Steiger eV, 7057 Winnenden

R.S.B.S. GB: e: Royal Society of British Sculptors

R.S.B.U. S: sv: Riksförbundet för svenskhetens bevarande i utlandet

RSČ CS: cs: Rada Svobodného Československa

R.S.C. GB: e: Railways Staff Conference; e: Raise the Standard Campaign; Road Safety Committee

RSC NL: nl: Rotterdamsch Studentencorps

RSc GB: e: mil: The Royal Scots

RSC GB: e: Royal Shakespeare Company, London

R.S.C. CDN: e: Royal Society of Canada, Ottawa [gegr 1882]

RSC D: d: stud: Rudolstädter Senioren-Convent

R.S.C.C. e: Raw Silk Classification Committee

RSch; R.-Sch. d: Realschule

RSchA D: d: Reichsschatzamt; Reichsschiedsamt für Ärzte und Krankenkassen

RSchatzM D: d: Reichsschatzminister(ium)

RSchG D: d: Reichsschiedsgericht

RSchK D: d: NS: Reichsschrifttumskammer

RSCI US: e: mil: Redstone Scientific Information Center, Redstone Arsenal, Ala.

R.S.C.L. B: f: Rassemblement Social-Chrétien de la Liberté

RSČSL CS: cs: Rodopisná Společnost Československá

RSD D: d: Reichsverband der beeidigten und öffentlich bestellten Sachverständigen Deutschlands eV

R.S.D. GB: e: Royal Society of Dublin

RSDAP d: Russische Sozialdemokratische Arbeiterpartei

R.S.D.D.C. GB: e: Royal School for Deaf and Dumb Children

R.S.d.F. D: d: Redakteur- und Schriftstellerverband der Fachpresse

R.S.D.H. GB: e: mil: Royal Soldiers' Daughters' Home

R.S.D.L.P. e: Russian Social Democratic Labor Party

R.S.D.O.A. GB: e: mil: Royal School for Daughters of Officers of the Army

RSDRP = R.S.D.L.P.; RSDAP

RSDS GB: e: mil: Royal Soldiers' Daughters School, Hampstead

RSE BRD: d: Rhein-Sieg Eisenbahn, 53 Bonn

R.S.E. GB: e: Royal Society, Edinburgh

R.S.E.A. GB: e: Royal Society for the Encouragement of the Arts

RSES US: e: Refrigeration Service Engineers Society

RSF BRD: d: Radikale Soziale Freiheitspartei [gegr 1949]; S: sv: Riksförbundet för Sveriges Försvar, Stockholm

R.S.F. GB: e: mil: Royal Scots Fusiliers

R.S.F.A. e: Railway Supervisors and Foremen's Association

R.-Sfl.-Schule D: d: Reichssegelflugschule

RSFPP US: e: mil: Retired Serviceman's Family Protection Plan

R.S.F.S. GB: e: Royal Scottish Forestry Section

RSG D: d: Reichsverband der Samen-Kommissions-Großhändler; GB: e: Richard S. Gothard & Co. Ltd., International Technical Booksellers, Henley, Oxon.; NL: nl: Rotterdamsch Studenten Gezelschap

R.S.G.B. GB: e: Radio Society of Great Britain

R.S.G.S. GB: e: Royal Scottish Geographical Society

RSHA D: d: NS: Reichssicherheitshauptamt

R.S.H.N. E: s: Real Sociedad de Historia Natural, Madrid

RSI CH: [d: Radio der italienischen Schweiz, Radio Monte Ceneri]; US: e: mil: Research Studies Institute; NL: nl: Rijks Serologisch Instituut

R.S.I. GB: e: Royal Sanitary Institute; GB: e: mil: Royal Signals Institution

R.S.I.B. GB: e: Royal School for the Indigent Blind

RSIC US: e: Radio Shielding Information Center, Oak Ridge

R.Sig.; R.Signals; R.Sigs.; R SIGS GB: e: mil: Royal Corps of Signals

RSK PL: pl: Rada Szkolna Krajowa; BRD: d: Reaktor-Sicherheitskommission für das Kernforschungszentrum, 75 Karlsruhe; D: d: Reichsschrifttumskammer; Reichssiedlungskommission; Ring- und Stemmklub

RSKO PL: pl: Robotniczy Sportowy Komitet Okręgowy

ŘSL CS: cs: Ředitelství Státnich Lesů

RSL AUS: e: mil: Returned Soldiers League

R.S.L. GB: e: Royal Society, London; Royal Society of Literature

RSLtg D: d: Reichssendeleitung

R.S.M. F: f: mil: Régiment de spahis marocains

RSM D: d: Reichsschatzmeister [NSDAP];

PL: pl: Robotnicza Spółdzielnie Mieszkaniowa

R.S.M. GB: e: Royal School of Mines, London; Royal Society of Medicine, London [gegr 1805]; Royal Scottish Museum

R.S.M.G.B. GB: e: Royal Society of Musicians of Great Britain

RSN e: mil: Royal Siamese Navy

R.S.N.A. GB: e: Royal School of Naval Architecture; Royal Society of Northern Antiquaries

R.S.N.M.O.D. GB: e: mil: Royal School for Naval and Marine Officers' Daughters

RSNSF D: d: NS: Reichsschule der Nationalsozialistischen Frauenschaft

R.S.N.T. GB: e: Railway Staff National Tribunal

R.S.N.Z. NZ: e: Royal Society of New Zealand

RSO BlnW: d: Radio-Symphonie-Orchester

R.S.O. e: Railway Sorting Office; Railway Station Office; Railway Sub-Office

RSO PL: pl: Rejonowa Spółdzielnia Ogrodnicza

R.S.O.D. GB: e: mil: Royal School for Officers' Daughters, Bath

R.S.O.G.S.H. GB: e: Royal Sailors' Orphan Girls' School and Home

RSP INT: pt: Repartição Sanitaria Panamericana, Washington, D.C. [gegr 1902]; IND: e: Revolutionary Socialist Party; S: sv: Riksförbundet Sveriges Polismän [gegr 1954]; PL: pl: Rolnicza Spółdzielnia Produkcyjna; Rzemieślnicza Spółdzielnia Pracy

R.S.P.A. GB: e: Royal Society for the Prevention of Accidents

R.S.P.B. GB: e: Royal Society for the Protection of Birds

R.S.P.C.A. GB: e: Royal Society for the Prevention of Cruelty to Animals

R.S.P.C.C. GB: e: Royal Society for the Prevention of Cruelty to Children

R.S.P.E.E. GB: e: Royal Society of Painter-Etchers and Engravers

R.S.P.F. GB: e: Royal Seamen's Pension Fund

RSpK D: d: Reichssparkommissar

R.S.P.P. GB: e: Royal Society of Portrait Painters

R.S.P.W.; R.S.P.W.C. GB: e: Royal Society of Painters in Water Colours

R.S.R.; R.S.Regt GB: e: mil: Royal Sussex Regiment

RSS IND: Rashtriya Swayamsevak Sangh [d: militante Hinduorganisation]; D: d: Reichsschrifttumsstelle [gegr 1934]

R.S.S. GB: e: Royal Statistical Society; Royal Stuart Society

R.S.S.A. GB: e: Royal Scottish Society of Arts; Royal Society of South Africa

R.S.S.A.I.L.A. AUS: e: mil: Returned Sailors, Soldiers and Airmen's Imperial League of Australia

R.S.S.P.C.A. GB: e: Royal School Society for the Prevention of Cruelty to Animals

R.S.S.P.C.C. GB: e: Royal Scottish Society for the Prevention of Cruelty to Children

RSSR CDN: e: mil: The Royal South-Saskatchewan Regiment

RSSt. D: d: NS: Reichsschrifttumsstelle

R.S.T. e: Rhodesian Selection Trust Exploration Ltd.

RST D: S: sv: Riksföreningen Sverige – Tyskland

R.S.T. GB: e: Royal Society of Tasmania; Royal Society of Teachers

RStAusw D: d: Reichsstelle für Auswanderungswesen

RStGH. D: d: Staatsgerichtshof für das Deutsche Reich

R.S.T.M.H. GB: e: Royal School of Tropical Medicine and Hygiene

RStNachl D: d: Reichsstelle für Nachlässe und Nachforschungen im Ausland

RStT D: d: Reichsstädtetag

RStW D: d: NS: stud: Reichsstudentenwerk

R.S.U. GB: e: Ragged School Union
RSUF D: d: Reichsstelle für den Unterrichtsfilm
R SUSSEX GB: e: mil: The Royal Sussex Regiment
RSV BRD: d: Rasensportverein; Reitersportverein; NL: nl: Religieus Socialistisch Verbond
R.S.V.D.C. AUS: e: mil: Returned Soldiers' Volunteer Defence Corps
RSW D: d: Reichsschwimmwoche; PL: pl: Rolnicza Spółdzielnia' Wytwórcza
R.S.W.S. GB: e: Royal Scottish Water -Colour Society
R.Sx GB: e: mil: The Royal Sussex Regiment
R.S.Y.C. GB: e: Royal Southampton Yacht Club
R.T. F: f: mil: Régie de Transport; GB: e: mil: Regimental Transport; F: f: mil: Régiment territorial; Régiment de tirailleurs; Régiment des transmissions
RT D: d: Reichstag
RT; R.T.; r.t. hu: részvénytársaság [d: Aktiengesellschaft]
R.T. GB: e: Reuter's Trust
RT N: no: Riksteatret, Oslo
RTA DZ: f: Radiodiffusion-Télévision Algérienne, Alger
R.T.A.; r.t.a. F: f: mil: Régiment des tirailleurs algériens
RTA D: d: Reichsgemeinschaft der technisch-wissenschaftlichen Arbeit; Rhodesien: e: Rhodesian Tobacco Association; e: mil: Royal Thai Army
R.T.A.F. e: mil: Royal Thai Air Force
RTB B: f: Radiodiffusion-Télévision Belge, Bruxelles; S: sv: Redovisningstekniska Byrån, Göteborg; D: d: mil:Reichstreubund ehemaliger Berufssoldaten im Soldatenbund, Berlin
R.T.B. GB: e: Road Transport Board
Rtbk D: d: Rentenbank
RTC F: f: R.T.C. La Radiotechnique-Compelec, Paris 11; NATO: e: Radio Transmitting Center; GB: e: mil: Railway Training Centre, Longmoor; Railway Transport Corps; Recruit Training Centre
r.t.c. F: f: mil: régiment de tirailleurs coloniaux
RTC US: e: mil: Replacement Training Center; Reserve Training Corps; NL: nl: Rijkstuinbouwconsulentschap; GB: e: mil: Royal Tank Corps
RTCA US: e: Radio Technical Commission for Aeronautics
R.T.C.B. B: f: Royal Touring Club de Belgique
r.t.c.m. F: f: mil: régiment de tirailleurs coloniaux marocains
RTCMA e: Rubber and Thermoplastic Cable Manufacturers Association
RTCP NATO: e: Radio Telecommunications (Transmissions) Control Panel [EMCC]
RTD US: e: mil: Research and Technology Division, Bolling AFB, Washington, D.C.
R.T.E. D: d: WK2: Reichsbeauftragter für technische Erzeugnisse
RTE IRL: [d: Rundfunk und Fernsehen]
RTF F: f: Radiodiffusion-Télévision Française, Paris [gegr 1939]
R.T.F. F: f: Rassemblement travailliste français
RTg.; Rtg. D: d: Reichstag
RTG D: d: Reichstreuhandgesellschaft; Reichsverband der Tabakwaren-Großhändler; BRD: d: Revisions- und Treuhandgesellschaft mbH, 8 München 22; Rheinische Telefon Gesellschaft und Apparatebau Ernst Springorum KG, 46 Dortmund
RThK D: d: Reichstheaterkammer
R.Th.Y.C. GB: e: Royal Thames Yacht Club
RTI CI: f: Radiotélévision Ivoirienne, Abidjan
R.T.I. F: f: mil: Régiment de tirailleurs indigènes
RTI INT: e: Round Table International,

London [gegr 1927] ; BRD: d: Rund-
funktechnisches Institut GmbH, Nürnberg
RTK D: d: Reichstheaterkammer
R TKS GB: e: Royal Tank Regiment (Ter-
ritorial Army)
RTL L: f: Radiotélévision de Luxembourg
RTM MA: f: Radiodiffusion-Télévision
Marocain, Rabat
R.T.M. F: f: Régiment de tirailleurs maro-
cains
RTM I: i: Ricerche di Tecnologia Mec-
canica [Institut]
RTMA US: e: Radio-Television Manufac-
turers Association, Washington, D.C.
RTMC e: mil: Royal Thai Marine Corps
RTMF NZ: e: Radio and Television Man-
ufacturers Federation of New Zealand
RTN PL: pl: Radomskie Towarzystwo
Naukowe; e: mil: Royal Thai Navy
RTNDA US: e: Radio-Television News
Directors Association
R.T.N.M.F. GB: e: Rope, Twine and Net
Manufacturers' Federation
R.T.N.T.B. GB: e: Rope, Twine and Net
Trade Board
RTO BlnW: d: RIAS-Tanzorchester
R.T.O. e: Road Transport Organization
RTP P: pt: Radiotelevisão Portuguêsa
RTPB e: Radio Technical Planning Board
RTPD PL: pl: Robotnicze Towarzystwo
Przyjaciół Dzieci
RTPN PL: pl: Rzeszowskie Towarzystwo
Przyjaciół Nauk
RTR; R.T.R. GB: e: mil: Royal Tank Reg-
iment
RTRA GB: e: Radio and Television Retail-
ers' Association
RTS F: f: Radio-Télévision Scolaire
R.T.S. F: f: mil: Régiment de tirailleurs
sénégalais; GB: e: Religious Tract Society
RTS PL: pl: Robotnicze Towarzystwo
Sportowe "Widzew"
R.T.S. GB: e: Royal Toxophilite Society
RTSD US: e: Resources and Technical
Services Division [American Library

Association]
RTT N: no: Radet for teknisk terminolo-
gie, Oslo; S: sv: Föreningen Rationell
Textilvätt; B: f: Régie des Télégraphes
et Téléphones, Bruxelles
R.T.T. F: f: mil: Régiment de tirailleurs
tunisiens
RTT PL: pl: Robotnicze Towarzystwo
Turystyczne
RTTA US: e: Radio-Television Training
Association, New York 3, N.Y.
RTUO BRD: d: Rundfunk-Tanz- und
-Unterhaltungsorchester [NDR]
RTV d: Reichstelegraphenverwaltung
R.T.V. BRD: d: Reise-Tümmler-Verein;
Rhodesien: e: Rhodesian Television Ltd.
RTVE E: [d: Rundfunk und Fernsehen]
RTVS GB: e: Radio-Television Society
R.T.Y.C. GB: e: Royal Thames Yacht
Club
RTZ D: d: nach WK2: Rhein-Transport
-Zentrale; GB: e: Rio Tinto-Zinc Cor-
poration Ltd., London S.W. 1
RTZV BRD: d: Reisetaubenzüchter-Verein
RU PL: pl: Rada Uczelniana
R.U. DK: da: Radikal Ungdoms Landsfor-
bund
RÚ CS: cs: Státni Radiologický Ústav
R.U. I: i: Rappresentanza Universitaria
RU NL: nl: Rijksuniversiteit
R.U. GB: e: Rugby Union
R.U.A.S. GB: e: Royal Ulster Agricul-
tural Society
R.U.C. GB: e: Rhodes University College;
Royal Ulster Constabulary
RUD d: Republikanische Union Deutsch-
lands; BRD: d: RUD-Kettenfabrik Rie-
ger & Dietz, 7084 Unterkochen [gegr
1875]
RüA; RüAmt d: mil: Rüstungsamt
Rü.In. D: d: mil: Rüstungsinspektion
RuFC BRD: d: Reit- und Fahr-Club
R.U.F.C. GB: e: Rugby Union Football
Club
RuFV BRD: d: Reit- und Fahrverein

RÚH CS: cs: Státní Výzkumný Ústav Rybářský a Hydrologický
RUHR N BRD: d: Ruhr-Stickstoff AG, 463 Bochum
R.U.I. GB: e: Royal University of Ireland
RUK D: d: WK2: Reichsminister für Rüstungs- und Kriegsproduktion
R.U.K.B.A. GB: e: Royal United Kingdom Beneficent Association
RUL PL: pl: Rejonowy Urząd Likwidacyjny
R.U.N.A.; Runa I: i: Reale Unione Nazionale Aeronautica
R.Univ. I: i: Regia Università
RÚNV CS: cs: Rada Ústředního Národního Výboru
R.U.P. F: f: Rassemblement Universel pour la Paix, Paris [gegr 1936]
RUP e: Revolutionary Ukrainian Party
RuPrAM D: d: Reichs- und Preußisches Arbeitsministerium
RuPrJM D: d: Reichs- und Preußisches Justizministerium
RuPrLFM D: d: Reichsforstmeister und Preußischer Landesforstmeister
RuPrMdI D: d: Reichs- und Preußisches Ministerium des Innern
RuPrMfdkirchlA D: d: Reichs- und Preußisches Ministerium für die kirchlichen Angelegenheiten
RuPrMfEuL D: d: Reichs- und Preußisches Ministerium für Ernährung und Landwirtschaft
RuPrMfWEuV D: d: Reichs- und Preußisches Ministerium für Wissenschaft, Erziehung und Volksbildung
RuPrWiM D: d: Reichs- und Preußisches Wirtschaftsministerium
RUR GB: e: mil: The Royal Ulster Rifles
RUschla D: d: Reichs-Untersuchungs- und Schlichtungsausschuß der NSDAP
RuSHA. D: d: NS: Rasse- und Siedlungshauptamt
R.U.S.I. GB: e: mil: Royal United Service Institution

RUT PL: pl: Rejonowy Urząd Telekomunikycyjny
RUTT PL: pl: Rejonoqy Urząd Telefoniczno-Telegraficzny
Ruwo D: d: Reichsunfallverhütungswoche
RU ZSP PL: pl: Rada Uczelniana Zrzeszenia Studentów Polskich
RV d: Radfahrverein; DK: da: Det radikale venstre [d: Partei]; BRD: d: Rationalisierungsverband des Steinkohlenbergbaus; d: Regatta-Verein
R.V. D: d: Reichsverband für Prüfung des Warmblutpferdes
RV BRD: d: Reisetaubenzüchter-Verein; Reiterverein; Rentenversicherung; S: sv: Riksidrottsförbundets Vänner [gegr 1916]; d: Rodelverein
R.V. D: d: Roheisen-Verband; Rohrleitungs-Verband, Berlin-Charlottenburg
RV d: Ruderverein
RVA NL: nl: Raad van Arbeid
R.V.A. NL: nl: mil: regiment veldartillerie
RVA US: e: mil: Regular Veterans Association; D: d: Reichsbahnverkehrsamt; Reichsverband des Versicherungsaußendienstes eV, Berlin; Reichsversicherungsamt; Reichsversicherungsanstalt
R.V.A. nl: Rijksdienst voor Arbeidsvoorziening
RVA D: d: nach WK2: Ruhr Valley Authority
RVAAng D: d: Reichsversicherungsanstalt für Angestellte
RVaG D: d: Reichsverband ambulanter Gewerbetreibender
RVAZ NL: nl: Regeringsgemachtigde voor Algemeene Zaken in Nederlandsch-Indië
RVB NL: nl: Raad van Beheer; D: d: Reichsverkehrsgruppe Binnenschiffahrt
RVB BlnW: d: Rollsport-Verband Berlin
Rv.b.K. D: d: Reichsverband bildender Künstler Deutschlands, Berlin
ŘVC CS: cs: Ředitelství Vodních Cest
RVC NL: nl: Revolutionnaire Vrijdenkers Club

R.V.C. GB: e: mil: Rifle Volunteer Corps; GB: e: Royal Veterinary College

R.V.C.I. GB: e: Royal Veterinary College of Ireland

RVD NL: nl: Regeringsvoortlichtingsdienst; D: d: Reichsverkehrsdirektion

RVDB D: d: Reichsverband Deutsche Bühne

RVDI D: d: Reichsverband der Deutschen Industrie

RVdZD. D: d: Reichsverband der Zahnärzte Deutschlands

RVE D: d: Reichsverband Deutscher Essigfabrikanten, Berlin

R.Verk.Min. D: d: Reichsverkehrsministerium

R.Verm.V. D: d: Reichsvermögensverwaltung

RVersA D: d: Reichsversicherungsamt

RVersG D: d: Reichsversorgungsgericht

RVerwA. D: d: Reichsverwaltungsamt

RVerwG D: d: Reichsverwaltungsgericht

RVG D: d: Reichsverband der Deutschen Versicherungs-Generalagenten eV, Berlin; Reichsversorgungsgericht; Reichsverwaltungsgericht

RVGW D: d: Reichsverband des Deutschen Gas- und Wasserfachs

RVH D: d: Reichsbund Volkstum und Heimat; GB: e: Royal Victoria Hospital, Netley

RVHM D: d: Reichsverband des Handels mit Metallhalbfabrikaten

RVI NL: nl: Raad van Nederlandsch-Indië

RVJ NL: nl: Raad van Justitie [Nederlandsch-Indië]

RVK. D: d: WK2: Reichsverteidigungskommissar

RVkM D: d: Reichsverkehrsminister(ium)

ŘVL CS: cs: Ředitelství Vojenských Lesů

RVM D: d: Reichsverkehrsminister(ium)

RVNAF e: mil: Republic of Vietnam Armed Forces

R.V.O. D: d: Reichsvereinigung der Ortskrankenkassen

RVOG ETH: e: Radio Voice of the Gospel, Addis Ababa

RVP D: d: nach WK2: Rheinische Volkspartei [Britische Zone]; NL: nl: Rijksvoorlichtingsdienst voor die Pluimveeteelt

RVS NL: nl: Raad van State; N.V. Rotterdamse Verzekering-Societeiten

RVSV D: d: stud: Rotenburger Verband schwarzer schlagender Verbindungen; NL: nl: Rotterdamsche Vrouwelijke Studenten Vereeniging

RVU NL: nl: Radio Volksuniversiteit

RVV D: d: Reichsbund der Deutschen Versicherungsvertreter eV., Berlin

RVW D: d: Ruderverein Wannsee, Berlin

R.V.Y.S.O.A. GB: e: Royal Victualling Yard Subordinate Officers' Association

RVZI NL: nl: Rijksfonds voor Verzekering tegen Ziekte en Invaliditeit

RW PL: pl: Rada Wydziałowa; D: d: Radierverein, Weimar

R.W. NL: nl: mil: regiment wielrijders

RW D: d: mil: Reichswehr

R.W. GB: e: mil: Royal Warwickshire Regiment

R.W.A. D: d: Reichsstelle für Wirtschaftsausbau

RWA D: d: Reichswirtschaftsamt

R.W.A. GB: e: Royal West of England Academy

RWAC D: d: Rheinisch-Westfälischer Automobilclub, Düsseldorf

RWAFF GB: e: mil: Royal West African Frontier Force

RWAG BRD: d: Rheinisch-Westfälische Auslandsgesellschaft, 46 Dortmund

RWandA D: d: Reichswanderungsamt

R.War.R.; R WARWICK GB: e: mil: The Royal Warwickshire Regiment

R.W.B. GB: e: Railway Wages Board

RWB D: d: Rheinische Werkstätten für Bühnenkunst, Bad Godesberg; D: d: nach WK2: Rheinisch-Westfälische Bank AG, Düsseldorf [gegr 1952]

R.W.B.R.A. GB: e: Railway Wagon Builders' and Repairers' Association

R.W.B.T.T.B. GB: e: Ready-Made and Wholesale Bespoke Tailoring Trade Board

RWC INT: e: Regional Warning Center Europe, 61 Darmstadt [BRD. Funkwellen] ; e: Regional Welfare Committee; GB: e: mil: Royal War College

RWD D: d: Reichswetterdienst

RWE BRD: d: Rheinisch-Westfälisches Elektrizitätswerk AG, 43 Essen

RWehrM; RWeM D: d: mil: Reichswehrminister(ium)

RWEVO BRD: d: Rheinisch-Westfälische Elektrizitäts-Versorgungs-GmbH, 45 Osnabrück

RWF NL: nl: Rijkswoningfonds; GB: e: mil: The Royal Welch Fusiliers

RWG US: e: Radio Writers Guild; D: d: Reichswirtschaftsgericht [gegr 1920]

RWHH BRD: d: Rat der wissenschaftlichen Hilfskräfte der hessischen Hochschulen

RWI BRD: d: Rheinisch-Westfälische Immobilien-Anlagegesellschaft & Co., 4 Düsseldorf; Rheinisch-Westfälisches Institut für Wirtschaftsforschung; Rheinisch-Westfälische Isolatoren-Werke GmbH, 52 Siegburg; NL: nl: Rijkswerkinrichting

RWiEPP PL: pl: Rada Wzornictwa i Estetyki Produkcji Przemysłowej

RWiG D: d: Reichswirtschaftsgericht

R WILTS YEO GB: e: The Royal Wiltshire Yeomanry (Prince of Wales Own)

RWiM D: d: Reichswirtschaftsminister(ium)

RWiR D: d: Reichswirtschaftsrat

RWJV BRD: d: Rheinisch-Westfälischer Journalisten-Verband

R.W.K. D: d: Reichswirtschaftskammer; Reichswohnungskommissar

RWK GB: e: mil: The Queen's Own Royal West Kent Regiment

RWKS D: d: Rheinisch-Westfälisches Kohlensyndikat, 43 Essen

Rw.M.; RWM D: d: mil: Reichswehrminister(ium)

RWM D: d: Reichswirtschaftsminister(ium)

RWMA US: e: Resistance Welder Manufacturers' Association, Philadelphia 3, Pa.

RWMin.; RwMin. D: d: mil: Reichswehrministerium

RwMinHLtg. D: d: mil: Reichswehrministerium, Heeresleitung

RWOW PL: pl: Rybnicko-Wodzisławski Okręg Węglowy

RWP PL: pl: Radomska Wytwórnia Papierosów; e: Rumanian Workers Party

RWPG INT: pl: Rada Wzajemnej Pomocy Gospodarczej [e: Comecon]

RWPH BRD: d: stud: Ring Wehrpolitischer Hochschulgruppen [gegr 1962]

RWR D: d: Reichswirtschaftsrat; BRD: d: Rhein-Wupper-Ruhr-Anzeigenring

R.W.Regt. GB: e: mil: Royal Warwickshire Regiment

RWS D: d: Reichswasserschutz; Rheinisch-Westfälische Sprengstoff-AG, Nürnberg

R.W.S. GB: e: Royal Society of Painters in Water-Colours, London [gegr 1804] GB: e: mil: Royal West Sussex Regiment

RWSch D: d: Reichswasserschutz

RWSR GB: e: mil: The Royal West Surrey Regiment

R.W.S.S.N.C. GB: e: Railway Workshop Supervisory Staff National Council

RWTH BRD: d: Rheinisch-Westfälische Technische Hochschule, 51 Aachen

RWTÜV BRD: d: Rheinisch-Westfälischer Technischer Überwachungs-Verein eV, 43 Essen

R.W.U. e: Railway Workers Union

RWU D: d: Reichsanstalt für Film und Bild in Wissenschaft und Unterricht, Berlin

RWV D: d: Reichswasserstraßenverwaltung

R.Y.A. GB: e: Royal Yachting Associ-

ation
RYC D: d: Rostocker Yacht-Club
R.Y.C. de B. B: f: Royal Yacht-Club de
Belgique, Anvers
R.Y.C.I. I: i: Regio Yacht Club Italiano
RYM US: e: Revolutionary Youth Move-
ment
Ry R; Ry Regt e: mil: Railway Regiment
R.Y.S. GB: e: Royal Yacht Squadron
[gegr 1812]
RZ d: Rechenzentrum
R.Z. F: f: mil: Régiment de Zouaves;
PL: pl: Rejonowy Zakład
RZA D: d: Reichsbahnzentralamt für
Bau- und Betriebstechnik; PL: pl:
Rzeszowski Zarząd Aptek
RZB PL: pl: Rzeszowskie Zjednoczenie
Budownictwa
RZBw BRD: d: mil: Rechenzentrum der
Bundeswehr
R.Z. de A. NL: nl: Roei en Zeilvereeniging
"de Amstel"
RZE D: d: Reichsbahnzentralamt für
Einkauf
R.Z.G. PL: pl: Rjonowy Zakład Gospo-
darcza
RZM D: d: Reichsbahnzentralamt für
Maschinenbau; Reichszeugmeisterei
[NSDAP] ; PL: pl: Rewolucyjny Związek
Młodzieży
RZS NL: nl: Rijkszuivelschool
R.Z.S.I. GB: e: Royal Zoological Society
of Ireland
RZSt. D: d: WK1: Reichszuckerstelle
RZW NL: nl: Rijkszuivelconsulentschap
R.Z.Ż. PL: pl: mil: Rejonowy Zakład
Żywonościowy

In der Reihe „Handbuch der technischen Dokumentation und Bibliographie" sind folgende Bände erschienen:
In the series of „Handbook of Technical Documentation and Bibliography" you may find the following volumes:

Verlag Dokumentation · München-Pullach und Berlin

JUL 24 1971